LINUX® Network Toolkit

LINUX®
Network Toolkit

Paul G. Sery

IDG Books Worldwide, Inc.
An International Data Group Company

Foster City, CA ◆ Chicago, IL ◆ Indianapolis, IN ◆ New York, NY ◆ Southlake, TX

LINUX® Network Toolkit

Published by
IDG Books Worldwide, Inc.
An International Data Group Company
919 E. Hillsdale Blvd., Suite 400
Foster City, CA 94404
www.idgbooks.com (IDG Books Worldwide Web site)

Library of Congress Catalog Card Number: 97-075020

ISBN: 0-7645-3146-8

Printed in the United States of America

10 9 8 7 6 5 4 3 2 1

1B/QZ/QU/ZY/FC

Distributed in the United States by IDG Books Worldwide, Inc.

Distributed by Macmillan Canada for Canada; by Transworld Publishers Limited in the United Kingdom; by IDG Norge Books for Norway; by IDG Sweden Books for Sweden; by Woodslane Pty. Ltd. for Australia; by Woodslane Enterprises Ltd. for New Zealand; by Addison Wesley Longman Singapore Pte Ltd. for Singapore, Malaysia, Thailand, and Indonesia; by Distribuidora Norma S.A.-Colombia for Colombia; by Intersoft for South Africa; by International Thomson Publishing for Germany, Austria, and Switzerland; by Toppan Company Ltd. for Japan; by Distribuidora Cuspide for Argentina; by Livraria Cultura for Brazil; by Ediciencia S.A. for Ecuador; by Addison-Wesley Publishing Company for Korea; by Ediciones ZETA S.C.R. Ltda. for Peru; by WS Computer Publishing Corporation, Inc., for the Philippines; by Unalis Corporation for Taiwan; by Contemporanea de Ediciones for Venezuela; by Computer Book & Magazine Store for Puerto Rico; by Express Computer Distributors for the Caribbean and West Indies. Authorized Sales Agent: Anthony Rudkin Associates for the Middle East and North Africa.

For general information on IDG Books Worldwide's books in the U.S., please call our Consumer Customer Service department at 800-762-2974. For reseller information, including discounts and premium sales, please call our Reseller Customer Service department at 800-434-3422.

For information on where to purchase IDG Books Worldwide's books outside the U.S., please contact our International Sales department at 650-655-3200 or fax 650-655-3297.

For information on foreign language translations, please contact our Foreign & Subsidiary Rights department at 650-655-3021 or fax 650-655-3281.

For sales inquiries and special prices for bulk quantities, please contact our Sales department at 650-655-3200 or write to the address above.

For information on using IDG Books Worldwide's books in the classroom or for ordering examination copies, please contact our Educational Sales department at 800-434-2086 or fax 817-251-8174.

For press review copies, author interviews, or other publicity information, please contact our Public Relations department at 650-655-3000 or fax 650-655-3299.

For authorization to photocopy items for corporate, personal, or educational use, please contact Copyright Clearance Center, 222 Rosewood Drive, Danvers, MA 01923, or fax 978-750-4470.

ABOUT IDG BOOKS WORLDWIDE

Welcome to the world of IDG Books Worldwide.

IDG Books Worldwide, Inc., is a subsidiary of International Data Group, the world's largest publisher of computer-related information and the leading global provider of information services on information technology. IDG was founded more than 25 years ago and now employs more than 8,500 people worldwide. IDG publishes more than 275 computer publications in over 75 countries (see listing below). More than 60 million people read one or more IDG publications each month.

Launched in 1990, IDG Books Worldwide is today the #1 publisher of best-selling computer books in the United States. We are proud to have received eight awards from the Computer Press Association in recognition of editorial excellence and three from *Computer Currents'* First Annual Readers' Choice Awards. Our best-selling *...For Dummies®* series has more than 30 million copies in print with translations in 30 languages. IDG Books Worldwide, through a joint venture with IDG's Hi-Tech Beijing, became the first U.S. publisher to publish a computer book in the People's Republic of China. In record time, IDG Books Worldwide has become the first choice for millions of readers around the world who want to learn how to better manage their businesses.

Our mission is simple: Every one of our books is designed to bring extra value and skill-building instructions to the reader. Our books are written by experts who understand and care about our readers. The knowledge base of our editorial staff comes from years of experience in publishing, education, and journalism — experience we use to produce books for the '90s. In short, we care about books, so we attract the best people. We devote special attention to details such as audience, interior design, use of icons, and illustrations. And because we use an efficient process of authoring, editing, and desktop publishing our books electronically, we can spend more time ensuring superior content and spend less time on the technicalities of making books.

You can count on our commitment to deliver high-quality books at competitive prices on topics you want to read about. At IDG Books Worldwide, we continue in the IDG tradition of delivering quality for more than 25 years. You'll find no better book on a subject than one from IDG Books Worldwide.

John Kilcullen
CEO
IDG Books Worldwide, Inc.

Steven Berkowitz
President and Publisher
IDG Books Worldwide, Inc.

Eighth Annual Computer Press Awards ≥1992

Ninth Annual Computer Press Awards ≥1993

Tenth Annual Computer Press Awards ≥1994

Eleventh Annual Computer Press Awards ≥1995

IDG Books Worldwide, Inc., is a subsidiary of International Data Group, the world's largest publisher of computer-related information and the leading global provider of information services on information technology. International Data Group publishes over 275 computer publications in over 75 countries. Sixty million people read one or more International Data Group publications each month. International Data Group's publications include: **ARGENTINA:** Buyer's Guide, Computerworld Argentina, PC World Argentina; **AUSTRALIA:** Australian Macworld, Australian PC World, Australian Reseller News, Computerworld, IT Casebook, Network World, Publish, Webmaster; **AUSTRIA:** Computerwelt Osterreich, Networks Austria, PC Tip Austria; **BANGLADESH:** PC World Bangladesh; **BELARUS:** PC World Belarus; **BELGIUM:** Data News; **BRAZIL:** Annuário de Informática, Computerworld, Connections, Macworld, PC Player, PC World, Publish, Reseller News, Supergamepower; **BULGARIA:** Computerworld Bulgaria, Network World Bulgaria, PC & MacWorld Bulgaria; **CANADA:** CIO Canada, Client/Server World, ComputerWorld Canada, InfoWorld Canada, NetworkWorld Canada, WebWorld; **CHILE:** Computerworld Chile, PC World Chile; **COLOMBIA:** Computerworld Colombia, PC World Colombia; **COSTA RICA:** PC World Centro America; **THE CZECH AND SLOVAK REPUBLICS:** Computerworld Czechoslovakia, Macworld Czech Republic, PC World Czechoslovakia; **DENMARK:** Communications World Danmark, Computerworld Danmark, Macworld Danmark, PC World Danmark, Techworld Denmark; **DOMINICAN REPUBLIC:** PC World Republica Dominicana; **ECUADOR:** PC World Ecuador; **EGYPT:** Computerworld Middle East, PC World Middle East; **EL SALVADOR:** PC World Centro America; **FINLAND:** MikroPC, Tietoverkko, Tietoviikko; **FRANCE:** Distributique, Hebdo, Info PC, Le Monde Informatique, Macworld, Reseaux & Telecoms, WebMaster France; **GERMANY:** Computer Partner, Computerwoche, Computerwoche Extra, Computerwoche FOCUS, Global Online, Macwelt, PC Welt; **GREECE:** Amiga Computing, GamePro Greece, Multimedia World; **GUATEMALA:** PC World Centro America; **HONDURAS:** PC World Centro America; **HONG KONG:** Computerworld Hong Kong, PC World Hong Kong, Publish in Asia; **HUNGARY:** ABCD CD-ROM, Computerworld Szamitastechnika, Internetto online Magazine, PC World Hungary, PC-X Magazin Hungary; **ICELAND:** Tolvuheimur PC World Island; **INDIA:** Information Communications World, Information Systems Computerworld, PC World India, Publish in Asia; **INDONESIA:** InfoKomputer PC World, Komputek Computerworld, Publish in Asia; **IRELAND:** ComputerScope, PC Live!; **ISRAEL:** Macworld Israel, People & Computers/Computerworld; **ITALY:** Computerworld Italia, Macworld Italia, Networking Italia, PC World Italia; **JAPAN:** DTP World, Macworld Japan, Nikkei Personal Computing, OS/2 World Japan, SunWorld Japan, Windows NT World, Windows World Japan; **KENYA:** PC World East African; **KOREA:** Hi-Tech Information, Macworld Korea, PC World Korea; **MACEDONIA:** PC World Macedonia; **MALAYSIA:** Computerworld Malaysia, PC World Malaysia, Publish in Asia; **MALTA:** PC World Malta; **MEXICO:** Computerworld Mexico, PC World Mexico; **MYANMAR:** PC World Myanmar; **NETHERLANDS:** Computer! Totaal, LAN Internetworking Magazine, LAN World Buyers Guide, Macworld Netherlands, Net, WebWereld; **NEW ZEALAND:** Absolute Beginners Guide and Plain & Simple Series, Computer Buyer, Computer Industry Directory, Computerworld New Zealand, MTB, Network World, PC World New Zealand; **NICARAGUA:** PC World Centro America; **NORWAY:** Computerworld Norge, CW Rapport, Datamagasinet, Financial Rapport, Kursguide Norge, Macworld Norge, Multimediaworld Norge, PC World Ekspress Norge, PC World Nettverk, PC World Norge, PC World ProduktGuide Norge; **PAKISTAN:** Computerworld Pakistan; **PANAMA:** PC World Panama; **PEOPLE'S REPUBLIC OF CHINA:** China Computer Users, China Computerworld, China InfoWorld, China Telecom World Weekly, Computer & Communication, Electronic Design China, Electronics Today, Electronics Weekly, Game Software, PC World China, Popular Computer Week, Software Weekly, Software World, Telecom World; **PERU:** Computerworld Peru, PC World Profesional Peru, PC World SoHo Peru; **PHILIPPINES:** Click!, Computerworld Philippines, PC World Philippines, Publish in Asia; **POLAND:** Computerworld Poland, Computerworld Special Report Poland, Cyber, Macworld Poland, NetworkWorld Poland, PC World Komputer; **PORTUGAL:** Cerebro/PC World, Computerworld/Correio Informático, Dealer World Portugal, Mac*In/PC*In Portugal, Multimedia World; **PUERTO RICO:** PC World Puerto Rico; **ROMANIA:** Computerworld Romania, PC World Romania, Telecom Romania; **RUSSIA:** Computerworld Russia, Mir PK, Publish, Seti; **SINGAPORE:** Computerworld Singapore, PC World Singapore, Publish in Asia; **SLOVENIA:** Monitor; **SOUTH AFRICA:** Computing SA, Network World SA, Software World SA; **SPAIN:** Communicaciones World España, Computerworld España, Dealer World España, Macworld España, PC World España; **SRI LANKA:** Infolink PC World; **SWEDEN:** CAP&Design, Computer Sweden, Corporate Computing Sweden, Internetworld Sweden, it.branschen, Macworld Sweden, MaxiData Sweden, MikroDatorn, Nätverk & Kommunikation, PC World Sweden, PCaktiv, Windows World Sweden; **SWITZERLAND:** Computerworld Schweiz, Macworld Schweiz, PCtip; **TAIWAN:** Computerworld Taiwan, Macworld Taiwan, NEW ViSiON/Publish, PC World Taiwan, Windows World Taiwan; **THAILAND:** Publish in Asia, Thai Computerworld; **TURKEY:** Computerworld Turkiye, Macworld Turkiye, Network World Turkiye, PC World Turkiye; **UKRAINE:** Computerworld Kiev, Multimedia World Ukraine, PC World Ukraine; **UNITED KINGDOM:** Acorn User UK, Amiga Action UK, Amiga Computing UK, Apple Talk UK, Computing, Macworld, Parents and Computers UK, PC Advisor, PC Home, PSX Pro, The WEB; **UNITED STATES:** Cable in the Classroom, CIO Magazine, Computerworld, DOS World, Federal Computer Week, GamePro Magazine, InfoWorld, I-Way, Macworld, Network World, PC Games, PC World, Publish, Video Event, THE WEB Magazine, and WebMaster; online webzines: JavaWorld, NetscapeWorld, and SunWorld Online; **URUGUAY:** InfoWorld Uruguay; **VENEZUELA:** Computerworld Venezuela, PC World Venezuela; and **VIETNAM:** PC World Vietnam.   3/24/97

Credits

ACQUISITIONS EDITOR
Anne Hamilton

DEVELOPMENT EDITORS
John Pont
Matthew E. Lusher

TECHNICAL EDITOR
Phil Hughes

COPY EDITORS
Judy J. Brunetti
Michael D. Welch

PRODUCTION COORDINATOR
Ritchie Durdin

BOOK DESIGNER
Jim Donohue

GRAPHICS AND PRODUCTION
SPECIALISTS
Linda Marousek
Hector Mendoza
Elsie Yim

QUALITY CONTROL SPECIALISTS
Mick Arellano
Mark Schumann

ILLUSTRATOR
Milton Lau III

PROOFREADER
Christine Sabooni

INDEXER
Liz Cunningham

About the Author

Paul Sery is a systems administrator working for Productive Data Systems, Inc. in support of Sandia National Laboratories in Albuquerque, New Mexico. He has a Bachelor of Science degree in electrical engineering from the University of New Mexico. Paul and his wife Lidia enjoy riding their tandem bike together in the Rio Grande valley as well as traveling in Mexico.

To my aunt, Jean L. Dragner, 1929–1997

Preface

This book helps you design, install, and manage a Linux-based network. You can use the Linux computer (or computers) to serve a network of Microsoft Windows computers. (You can also use Macintosh or proprietary UNIX workstations, but my instructions are not oriented to those platforms.) You can also use the Linux computers as workstations themselves. I also show you how to safely connect computers or a network to the Internet.

I target my instructions to the person with some Microsoft Windows 95 experience. No Linux or UNIX experience is required, although it is helpful. This book is intended as a tutorial and not as a reference. If you don't have any Linux or UNIX experience, I recommend you use one of the several good Linux reference books available to supplement my descriptions. (I list several helpful Linux references in Chapter 3.)

Terms and Definitions

I should define some terms, to avoid confusion. The term *Linux* can mean two things. First, it refers to the core operating system or kernel: the program – such as DOS – that runs the computer. However, it also describes the entire system, including the Linux kernel, the file system, and all the libraries, programs, and shell scripts and macros that start everything running when you power up the computer. Basically, the term *Linux* refers to everything you configure your computer with off the install CD – such as this book's CD. But you are really talking about the distribution (for example, Red Hat, Debian, Slackware, or Yggdrasil distributions). Generally, I distinguish between the two by referring to the kernel as *Linux* and the distribution as either *the Linux distribution* or *Red Hat*.

Samba enables the Linux systems to "talk" to the SMB protocol that Microsoft Windows understands. Think of Samba as the glue that holds everything together in a Linux network. Basically, Windows expects certain things to happen in certain ways and at certain times on the network in order to see things such as files and printers on other computers. (I describe the mechanics of Samba in more detail later in the book.) Until now, manufacturers such as Novell, Sun Microsystems, Intergraphics, and Microsoft have provided the software to do this – at a price. Now, with Linux and Samba, you don't need them.

When I refer to the *DOS disk*, I am referring to a FAT formatted disk. This is the traditional method. Other newer methods exist, such as VFAT for Windows 95 and NTFS for Windows NT. I refer to the newer formats by name.

How This Book Is Organized

This book is organized to help you construct your computer network quickly and efficiently. You may read it from cover-to-cover, or focus on those parts that interest you or meet your needs. I present information in this book in the same way I try to learn a new system: Read a brief description, try a simple example, read more of the details, try a more complex example, and so on. I offer relatively brief instructions on how to set up software that is described elsewhere – for example, Microsoft Windows 95 and Linux itself. Many good books cover those topics, and I want to concentrate on the overall construction of a network.

Here's a quick overview of the book's structure:

◆ The **Introduction** describes a bit of my own history as a systems and network administrator. It also introduces the Linux operating system and the client-server model, which is the basis for the networks I describe in this book.

◆ In **Part I**, I present a simple example of a client-server network that you can quickly set up. In this most simple client-server configuration, one computer acts as a file and print server to another computer. Part I also introduces the concept of troubleshooting. You solve an example problem by using the Microsoft Troubleshooter, and I introduce the basic tools for troubleshooting Linux and Samba.

◆ **Part II** goes into some detail about how Linux and Samba work. I describe the concept and the organization of Linux and Samba, as well as the history of Linux, UNIX, Samba, and the Free Software Foundation. I also offer some suggestions for finding and using Linux-related resources.

◆ The chapters in **Part III** offer guidance for using the tools that help you to construct a "real-world" client-server network. I describe the details of Samba and show you how to use it. I offer guidance for configuring Linux using both the Red Hat Package Manager (RPM) system and the old tar file system, and I explain how you can safely connect your LAN to the Internet.

◆ **Part IV** introduces the essential issues of systems administration: managing computers, networks, people, and security. And to help you put it all together, I show you how to construct an office network complete with a firewall.

◆ The **Appendixes** include an inventory of the CD-ROM that comes with this book, as well as a quick guide to the vi text editor, copies of the General Purpose License (GPL) and other licenses that make all Linux, Samba, and the Free Software Movement possible. I also include a sample of the Request For Proposal (RFC) that describes how Internet protocols are constructed.

Conventions Used in This Book

To help you distinguish the various types of commands (Linux, DOS, and so on) that appear throughout the book, I use a few simple typographic conventions:

♦ For DOS commands, (for example, **DIR**) and their parameters (for example, **FDISK /MBR**) that I want you to type, I use bold, uppercase letters.

♦ For Linux commands (for example, **ifconfig**) and their parameters (for example, **ifconfig eth0**) that I want you to type, I use bold, lowercase letters.

♦ When I use Linux filenames, commands, command parameters, and Windows 95 icon names, and such, within a body of text, I italicize them for emphasis.

♦ The first time I introduce a Linux application or utility program as a command, I use the full pathname. I do this to give you some familiarity with the location of the various files.

♦ For Windows 95, I use italics to denote elements of the interface.

In the margins throughout the book, I use icons to flag specific types of information:

 The Note icon highlights useful information to keep in mind as you work.

 The Tip icon highlights information that can save you time and effort.

 A Caution icon points out something that may cause you problems.

Acknowledgments

I want to thank my wife, Lidia, for her patience, support, and good advice, which enabled me to write this book. Without her, I would not have even thought of engaging in this project, much less been able to finish it.

Anne Hamilton put this entire project together. She recognized a niche that needed to be addressed, and her vision helped to fill it.

I owe much to my editors, John Pont, Matt Lusher, Judy J. Brunetti, and Michael D. Welch. Their experience, feedback, and hard work kept me on track and produced a much better product.

Special thanks go to Phil Hughes who helped me in many technical areas. Thanks also to Frank Filingeri for all his technical help.

I also appreciate the opportunity that my former employer, Patrick J. Roache, gave me in using new technologies such as Linux to construct the computer systems and networks for his company.

Finally, I want to thank Milton Lau III for creating the artwork for this book.

Contents at a Glance

Contents

Part III   A Significant Client-Server Network

Introduction

BEFORE YOU START the installation and administration tasks presented in this book, I want to introduce you to the power of Linux and Samba. Linux is a UNIX clone that was designed to perform the same functions as UNIX. It was written from scratch, however, and does not share any copyrights with UNIX. Therefore, it does not require a licensing fee and is distributed at no cost. Samba was designed to provide file and print sharing to Microsoft Windows–based computers. It too is distributed at no cost.

Linux is an operating system that can act as a platform for most, if not all, of your computing needs. It can work as a file and print server for your Windows-based computers. It can also act as the platform for your personal workstation. You can get Linux off the Internet for free or purchase it preloaded on a CD-ROM for just a few dollars. It is a powerful system that is readily learned and used.

Samba is a suite of several programs that run under Linux. It speaks the same network language or protocol (NetBIOS) as Microsoft Windows (Windows 95, Windows NT, Windows-for-Workgroups). Because Samba can communicate with Windows, your Windows-based computers can access the resources that Linux provides without any additional software. For almost no cost, you can configure a powerful network based on the Linux-Samba combination.

Computers Inherit the Earth – Sort Of

In the beginning of time – way back in the late 1970s – PCs were expensive oddities. Cumbersome and slow, they had little use beyond simple word processing and games. Sophisticated applications such as databases quickly became available, PCs proliferated in the workplace, and prices started dropping rapidly.

Today, the notion of PCs becoming more powerful while dropping in price is considered a law of the same level as Adam Smith's law of supply and demand. Adam Smith who? Moore's Law (formulated by the cofounder of Intel, who predicted that the power of microprocessors would double every 18 months while the price would be cut in half during the same interval) rules my life. The fact that a Pentium costing $1,000 today outperforms a million-dollar mainframe of the recent past is almost a yawn.

After PCs had been around for a while, someone figured how to interconnect them into networks of networks. The genius of interconnecting the world's networks – as the Internet – has further changed the world. Now, PCs are used by all sorts of people in ever expanding and creative ways.

But while computer prices have plunged and internetworking has skyrocketed, the middle ground of plain-vanilla networks has remained, at best, moderately expensive. Compared to the cost of a standalone computer or Internet access, the cost of a simple network remains relatively high. The complexity of setting up and administering even a simple network typically pushes this cost well beyond the sum of the prices of the individual components.

Budget-minded businesses and individuals who need to have a small to moderate number of computers work together in a network have not prospered in the same way as individuals or large organizations have. The big shops can afford proprietary systems that offer economies of scale, and individuals just need a modem to get to the Internet. Those who are in-between need to struggle with the cost and complexity of Windows NT, Novell NetWare, or proprietary UNIX to have a small network.

Well, the balance of computing power has shifted with the invention of two amazing products. Linux is a UNIX clone developed by Linus Torvalds and a number of individuals. Samba was designed by Andrew Tridgell and others to add file and print sharing under Linux to Microsoft Windows–based computers. Together, Linux and Samba provide the framework for creating and managing powerful, robust networks. You no longer need to purchase Windows NT or Novell NetWare for your computers to work together, because the folks who developed Linux and Samba have offered their work to anyone who wants to use it. Amazing. It is all free!

Although I provide in-depth coverage of these products, they are, in and of themselves, merely interesting devices. The other piece of the puzzle is the amorphous profession of systems administration. After you get your Linux-Samba network going, you have to manage it effectively. In addition to helping you set up your Linux-Samba network, I lay out a framework for mastering systems administration so that you can create and manage an inexpensive, professional system.

The Client-Server Model

The first step to setting up and managing a network with Linux and Samba is understanding the client-server model. This model forms the basis for the networks that I help you to build in this book. Figure I-1 shows the client-server model, which defines the way that computers and computer software interact with each other. Simply put, a service is provided to a client. In practical terms, one or more server computers provide their resources to one or more client computers. In this way, resources and work are economized.

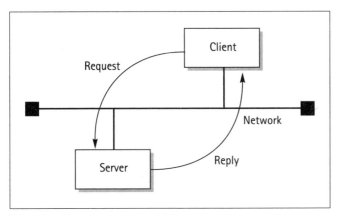

Figure I-1: The client-server model

How does this model help you to economize your resources and work? A quick look at the alternative brings the benefits of the client-server model into focus. In a small business, you may have several PCs. Each PC has its own resources, such as disk drives and CD-ROMs, and maybe a few have printers. When you back up your disks, you may use floppies, a dedicated tape drive, or a portable Zip drive. To print, you use any of several printers. Figure I-2 shows such a system.

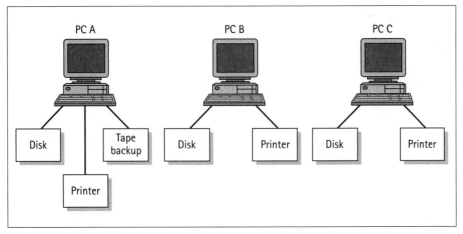

Figure I-2: A diagram of an amorphous system

As you can see, this configuration suffers from a lot of nasty duplication of resources, to say nothing of confusion. For example, did I back up the right computer last night? With a simple client-server network, however, one printer, one tape drive, and one fairly large disk can reasonably serve quite a few PCs. Figure I-3 shows this new client-server configuration. It helps minimize wasted money and time. Why make a backup of each machine when you can do one backup and go home early? Hey, that's the sign of a good systems administrator — okay, a great administrator.

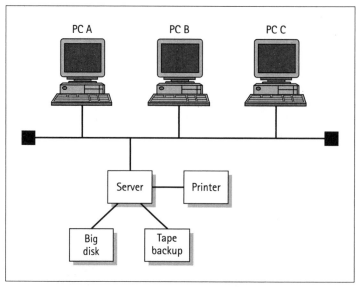

Figure I-3: A diagram of the reconfigured, client-server system

Keep in mind, however, that a client-server network does more than simply share computer hardware. It also helps to distribute your human resources. As more people work on a project, modifications of each other's work and files become disproportionately more difficult. Just two people working on the same spreadsheet can become intolerable as each user modifies individual copies that differ only slightly from one another. Add an entire department, and the work becomes very inefficient. On the other hand, if that spreadsheet exists in only one place and can be written to by only one user at a time, then work can continue. That is what the client-server model does for you.

You may be thinking, "Well, I know all that, but the technology is expensive and worst of all is difficult to use, and I just want to run my business. I'll need a systems administrator and expensive consulting, too." Well, that may be true for other networking tools, but not for Linux and Samba. With these powerful tools, you can easily set up and administer your own client-server network. In this book,

I show you how to work with Linux and Samba to set up and run both simple and not-so-simple networks. I also offer guidance for handling the role of systems administrator – a role that Linux and Samba greatly simplify.

The History of a Dummy

A bit of retrospection is in order to show you the process that I hope you can avoid. My sordid history should scare you straight.

Ten years ago, I started a job as a scientific programmer. As the business grew from a couple of scientists and engineers – world-class ones, actually – I found myself increasingly in the role of managing the computers and their interaction. But we had very few capital equipment dollars and could not afford a Novell network or even a poor cousin. I hate to admit it, but we basically had a manually operated, serial network. Later I used a network of switch boxes to connect all our serial lines! Talk about advanced technology.

Well, beat me over the head with a stick long enough and I'll get smart. What was my solution? We ended up with a terminal-based, multiuser version of WordPerfect for VMS on a MicroVAX II. For those of you who don't know what that means, just think of the phrase *slow and cumbersome*. We did have an i386 SCO XENIX box running. I made several aborted attempts to get a terminal-based word processing system running on it. Needless to say, it didn't work well enough, either.

I did have the luck of inheriting a monochrome Sun SLC, which was slow even by 1990 standards. But it did run SunOS UNIX, and it had an Ethernet port. I eventually hooked it to another workstation and was amazed when they were able to communicate.

The Sun eventually became the company file and print server, based on the Network File System (NFS). It was a vast improvement over our switched network, but was still shaky. Maintenance was difficult and expensive, and we were tied into a proprietary system. I kept it going on a shoestring while ever more demands were placed on it. It worked, but I never felt comfortable. I wished for a better way to run our system.

Well, I hope you are still reading and not thinking too badly of me. I wish that IDG Books had offered a *Systems Administration For Dummies* book back then. I started looking for a solution. As I discuss in more depth later in this book, very few classes or books dealt with the subject of systems (or network) administration – at least that I could find.

In part, I faced quite a dilemma. How do you maintain, upgrade, and manage such a system unless you know how to maintain, upgrade, and manage such a system? SunOS and Solaris weren't terribly difficult to manage if you knew what you were doing. I knew some of the basics (performing backups, editing users, doing NFS exports), but I was concerned about what I did not know. I was always afraid that something bad would happen and some consultant would come in to clean up the mess and ask me how I could not know that the sky is blue.

The more administration I did, the more I realized how much I didn't know. Taken individually, each task or system is not very complicated – but systems administration involves so many tasks and systems, and they all interact. I was trying to solve a big puzzle, and I didn't know how many pieces it had.

I gradually learned the trade in fits and spurts. In 1992, I took a very useful Networks course at the University of New Mexico. I had started the same course in 1985, only to drop it when we spent the first three weeks writing statistical equations for packet collisions or whatever. I was more than a little surprised and very happy when I came out of this course knowing that I had a good overview of networks and was finally in possession of some specific information.

In 1994, I ran across this interesting UNIX clone called Linux. I eventually realized that I had seen an advertisement for it distributed on a CD-ROM, so that summer I purchased it. At first, I pulled out my hair trying to get it installed. Then I found it really worked.

In 1995, I found this interesting thing called Samba. At first glance, it looked like an NFS clone. I pulled it off the Net and was stunned when it compiled, installed, and worked immediately. I must not have believed my own eyes, because I promptly forgot about Samba and went on with my eternal NFS struggles.

In 1996, our Sun finally died. I had it in mind that when that occurred I would be able to substitute Linux and Samba for our Sun-NFS setup. In just a handful of hours, I got a Pentium PC running Linux-Samba to provide the same basic function as the Sun-NFS had provided. Within a couple of days, I had our network working exactly as it had before. The dividend was that we eliminated the expensive, third-party software that had been required for our PCs to work with NFS.

Who Can Use This Book?

My systems administration history is important, not because it is unusual, but because it is very typical. In businesses of any size that use computers and networks, people often inherit network and computer administration responsibilities even though they don't have much (or any) background in this field. In this book, I show you how to create inexpensive, powerful networks of computers and manage them effectively. Those of you who are fortunate to receive the proper training in systems administration can still find useful information in this book. But my primary desire is to provide a basic tool especially for those folks who don't have access to many resources.

If you are an experienced user of UNIX, you should be familiar with the general concepts and recognize the workings of Linux. You should be able to skip many sections where I give detailed instructions for installation or administration tasks. The Linux operating system is based on the Berkeley standard. Like all flavors of UNIX, it has evolved to a hybrid of System V and Berkeley.

About Linux and Samba

Linux, Samba, and a number of other related tools bring unprecedented power to your desktop. Linux enables you to do the same things as UNIX does in the workstation world. If you don't use UNIX regularly, your eyes are just about to glaze over, or worse, you're shaking in terror. But it's not that bad. Linux – an operating system that works just like UNIX – can be easy to install and use, and it is inexpensive. Just remind yourself how many hundreds of dollars a five-user Windows NT server or Novell license costs. And, as I said before, Linux is FREE! This book's companion CD-ROM contains everything you need.

For those readers who are frequent users of computers but without much knowledge of their mechanics, I put a reasonable boundary around the tasks that you have to learn and I show you how to do them. I provide detailed instructions that should minimize the in-depth knowledge you need to possess. Figure I-4 shows the basic administration functions that you need to address.

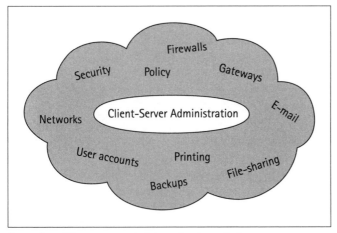

Figure I-4: Client–server administration boundaries

After you have set up the basic system – primarily Linux and Samba – it will be reasonable, if not straightforward, to run your business or home office with this incredibly powerful operating system. This book will help you on your way. Let's get started!

Part I

The Simple Client–Server Network

IN THIS PART:

Part I covers Linux installation on a PC. You then learn how to create a simple Client-Server Network by connecting a Windows 95 computer to the Linux server using Samba. Troubleshooting network problems by using the fault-tree method is also introduced.

Chapter 1

Setting Up a
Simple Network

IN THIS CHAPTER

- ◆ Deciding whether your PC meets the hardware requirements for your anticipated workload
- ◆ Deciding how to partition or repartition your disk
- ◆ Deciding how to install Linux
- ◆ Configuring Linux
- ◆ Configuring Windows 95
- ◆ Configuring Samba
- ◆ Wiring your network
- ◆ Getting Windows 95 to work with Samba

THIS CHAPTER SHOWS you how to produce a full-fledged client-server network based on Linux, Samba, and Windows 95. The network is a simple one of two computers – one server and one client – but it is still a complete system. Figure 1-1 shows the topology (diagram) of the system. Think of this configuration as your basic building block. The more complex examples that I introduce later in the book simply add onto this system.

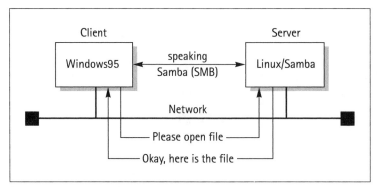

Figure 1-1: A simple client-server network

The server runs the Linux operating system and the Samba file/printer sharing system. The client runs Windows 95. In this chapter, I detail the installation and configuration of these particular systems. Subsequent chapters and the appendixes address clients that run other Microsoft Windows versions.

I assume you are an experienced user of computers – that is, I expect you are familiar with such basic concepts as directory structures and the difference between software operating systems and applications. It helps if you have installed and configured your own computer at least once; the more times the better. The relatively simple process of setting up Microsoft Windows helps to prepare you for the unfamiliar task of installing Linux and Samba. The process of answering installation questions and making decisions about the particulars of any operating system and application is basically the same no matter what system you use. I concentrate on providing detailed instructions in this chapter so that even with no such experience you should be able to get this simple example running. After you set up the simple client-server network in this chapter, I show you how to evolve your network to a more complex, "real-world" system. I introduce Linux/UNIX concepts and facilities along the way, as needed.

In this chapter, I give detailed instructions for two Linux installation methods. The first method allows you to modify your PC without eliminating your DOS or Windows operating system. However, please realize that these methods have associated risks. Specifically, you may accidentally erase your valuable data. My instructions are detailed and tested, but you may have an unusual configuration or simply make a mistake. So please keep in mind that the devil is in the details and please, please back up anything that you do not want to lose!

I include lots of screen shots throughout this chapter. Even though you are an experienced computer user, I want to provide many visual references because you are required to do many configurations, and the process can get confusing. Plus, you are going to perform several possibly destructive procedures, so the more detail the better.

TIP I highly recommend that you consider using an old hard disk for your initial Linux installation. This option increases your freedom to experiment without the fear of significant damage to your valuable data. I have found usable 300MB disks for $40! You can feel free to experiment on such a disk. If you are serious about creating a real-world server, having an experimental disk allows you to try many different configurations.

Installing Linux

Installing Linux is not much more difficult than installing Windows 95. You must make more choices along the way, but I explain these choices to make them as simple as possible to understand. Linux may seem mysterious at first, simply because you aren't familiar with it. Just keep in mind that it puts its pants on one leg at a time and the questions it asks are simple, if you take them one at a time. The CD-ROM that comes with this book contains the Red Hat Linux distribution and makes the process even simpler.

Installing Red Hat Linux from a CD-ROM involves the following steps:

1. Optionally repartitioning an existing disk to free up room for Linux

2. Starting the Red Hat installation process

3. Making choices about how to format the disk

4. Choosing the various software options (called *packages*) that Red Hat makes available to you

5. Answering the system configuration questions that Red Hat asks you about your network, time zone, mouse type, and so on

Choosing a PC

You must choose a PC on which to install Linux. You don't need a Pentium PC to run Linux or Samba. Until you start serving more than a handful of clients, a 486 machine will do nicely. Table 1-1 shows my recommendations for the load that various PC configurations can handle. Note that these suggestions are based on my own experience. You could easily break them down depending on your specific environment. This information is intended only to give you a starting point. Your mileage may vary.

TABLE 1-1 PC REQUIREMENTS FOR VARIOUS PROCESSING LOADS

Processor	RAM	Number of Clients	Type of Load
386	8MB	1	Experiment with Linux/Samba; firewall
386 with DMA and SCSI disks	16MB	1–8	Word processing, user data storage; firewall
486	8MB	1–4	Word processing, user data storage; firewall
486 with DMA and SCSI disks	16MB	1–10	Word processing, user data storage; firewall
Pentium with DMA and SCSI disks	16MB+	10–20	Word processing, spreadsheets, databases, and user data storage
Pentium with DMA and SCSI disks	16MB+	20+	Word processing, spreadsheets, databases, and user data storage
Pentium Pro with DMA and SCSI disks	32MB+	20–40+	Word processing, spreadsheets, databases, and user data storage

Of course, you probably will choose the handiest PC available to you. No matter; almost any PC will do for a start. Later, if you are serious about running your network off of Linux, you can fret over absolute speed and power.

No matter which processor you have, your most cost-effective upgrade is always to add memory. I would rather have a 486 PC with 32MB of memory than a Pentium with only 8MB. Even with 16MB, I still prefer the 486 to a Pentium with only 8MB. I am writing this book in Microsoft Word on my Windows 95 client: a 486 with 24MB. The technical writing process requires me to switch back and forth between many tasks. Having a fast processor doesn't help you if it must wait for something to load from a mechanical disk. The 486 is just fine except when I play with graphics (but that is only a small percentage of time).

To get adequate results from a PC that relies on the server for high-end graphics or very large databases, you need at least a Pentium and lots of memory. You must also pay close attention to the system's I/O throughput. When you start pushing a lot of data through a PC, I/O plays a major factor. Pay close attention to the bus type – using a PCI bus is a good bet – and the type of network adapter. A 3Com 3C509 is significantly faster than an NE2000, for example.

I have been inheriting or paying a few bucks for 486 motherboards here and there. For a tiny investment, I now have a network of three computers running – and a motherboard waiting for a monitor switch-box. The monitors are by far the costliest part of my network. Don't scoff, a 486 does just fine for word processing and such. With a Linux-Samba network, you can even work off a floppy drive in some cases.

Note: Recompiling Linux can take an hour or longer on a 486, depending on how much memory it has. On a Pentium, the process can take less than ten minutes if you have 16MB of RAM or more.

Choosing a Linux Distribution

With several distributions currently available, choosing a Linux distribution can be difficult. The various distributions reflect differing philosophies as to what Linux should do and how it should operate. This diversity is one of the healthiest aspects of Linux today. In 1992, Linux was available only on the Internet. Today, at least a half-dozen distributions and resellers are vying for a growing market. It's a fascinating juxtaposition of free software and the free market feeding each other.

I have used both Red Hat and Slackware extensively. I currently use the Red Hat distribution and include it with this book. I have installed Caldera for clients and briefly used Yggdrasil when I first experimented with Linux. I have purchased Slackware from several vendors.

In the following sections, I offer my (generally anecdotal) experience and opinions about the various Linux distributions. You may end up running a business with Linux, so the choices you make now are very important for determining your general course. Even though I believe that Red Hat is the best choice for this book, your needs differ from mine, and I want to help you make an educated choice.

Slackware

Slackware takes a generally straightforward and linear approach to both installation and configuration. It doesn't try to do too much for you. The setup process uses a simple menu system that you can't easily break. It is divided into disk sets – reflecting the days when the distribution came on floppies – from which you choose the components that you want to install. Simple, linear startup scripts – the *rc* scripts – handle everything from mounting your disk drives to initializing your network interface. These scripts are stored in a single directory and are quite readable.

A *script* is a file that contains Linux commands that you could execute manually from your shell prompt. The commands are run sequentially, dependent on conditional and loop constructs such as If...Then and Do...While. A script also can use variables. Input can be received from either the command line or other files.

Scripts are similar to DOS batch files but are more powerful. The default Linux script language is the Bourne Again Shell (bash). After you install Linux, you can view the structure and syntax of bash by looking at its manual page, referred to as a *man page* (/usr/bin/man bash).

Listing 1-1 shows a fragment of the shell script rc.inet1. This segment turns on the Ethernet card and attaches an IP address to it (note that lines beginning with the pound character (#) are comments).

Listing 1-1: Slackware /etc/rc.d/rc.inet1 shell script fragment

```
# Edit for your setup.
IPADDR="192.168.1.254"  # REPLACE with YOUR IP address!
NETMASK="255.255.255.0"  # REPLACE with YOUR netmask!
NETWORK="192.168.1.0"  # REPLACE with YOUR network address!
BROADCAST="192.168.1.255"  # REPLACE with YOUR broadcast address, if you
#GATEWAY="192.168.1.254"  # REPLACE with YOUR gateway address!
# Uncomment ONLY ONE of the three lines below. If one doesn't work, try again.
# /sbin/ifconfig eth0 ${IPADDR} netmask ${NETMASK} broadcast ${BROADCAST}
# /sbin/ifconfig eth0 ${IPADDR} broadcast ${BROADCAST}\ netmask ${NETMASK}
/sbin/ifconfig eth0 ${IPADDR} netmask ${NETMASK}
# Uncomment these to set up your IP routing table.
# route local traffic over ethernet
#/sbin/route add -host ${GATEWAY} gw ${IPADDR} metric 1
#/sbin/route add -net default gw ${GATEWAY} metric 1
/sbin/route add -net 192.168.1.0
```

You simply set the variables to your own network parameters and uncomment the appropriate command lines (for instance, I have uncommented the route line at the end of Listing 1-1 so that my machine can communicate with my personal network), and then you are ready to go. You may need to experiment a little to get it right – for instance, choosing between the three ifconfig commands – but it is not difficult to see what is being done. Setups like this one make me feel confident that I should be able to modify them appropriately. It is very easy to understand and edit.

Unfortunately, Slackware does not provide any comprehensive upgrade mechanism. If you need to update your system, you basically must reinstall the entire system or significant subsystems. The lack of an easy upgrade mechanism is a serious limitation, especially in a production environment where you must be able to perform upgrades with as little impact on your running system as possible.

For instance, if you want to upgrade a system such as Samba, the Slackware system blindly writes over the current files you already have in place. Problems occur because configuration files get erased (unless you remember to manually save and restore them), and if the updated version rearranges the location of any files, you end up with files scattered around your disk. This process is confusing and forces you to have to keep track of each package that you use.

You also have to know more of what you are doing from the start or else have a PC on which you can experiment. Slackware's Xfree86 X Window setup scripts are okay if you have equipment that the scripts recognize; if not, be prepared for a lot of testing.

Caldera

When Caldera got started, they bundled Netscape in their distribution. It was a serious attempt to target application users with a popular product that ran under Linux — a consumer-oriented approach. The market for common functions such as Web browsers, word processors, and the like is huge and Caldera is addressing it. Currently, they have three levels of their OpenLinux product line: Lite, Base, and Standard. Their highlights are as follows:

♦ **Lite** version 1.1 is freely available and can be downloaded from their Web site; you can also obtain a CD-ROM for U.S. $7.99. It includes the Linux 2.0 kernel, the X Window system, installation tools, a 90-day evaluation copy of the Caldera Desktop, and the typical Linux utilities.

♦ **Base** version 1.1 provides Netscape Navigator, an easy-to-use Metro X X-server, the Caldera Desktop, and installation tools including a bootable floppy disk. They also include an office productivity suite with word processor, spreadsheet, and graphics presentation. The Java Development Kit from Sun Microsystems, Inc. is also included. It costs U.S. $59.

♦ **Standard** version 1.1 includes everything in the Base system and adds Netscape Gold and WWW services such as Netscape's FastTrack commercial Web server. It also includes NetWare connectivity software. It costs U.S. $399.

Caldera WordPerfect 6.0 and Motif bundle can be purchased separately. It is a native Linux version of Corel's WordPerfect for UNIX.

Caldera uses the Red Hat Package Management (RPM) system for installing, deinstalling, and updating system, utility, and application software. The RPM system is discussed in detail throughout this book. Caldera also uses a configuration management system called LISA, which eases the administration of the Linux installation.

I was able to use Caldera briefly in late 1995. I liked the consumer approach with Netscape bundled into the system. With this approach, Caldera has expanded their line extensively, including both application and server functions. If their word processor evolves to match those in the Microsoft world, then Linux will be able to serve the general computer user community to a much greater extent than it is today.

Debian

The Debian distribution is produced by a nonprofit organization – Software in the Public Interest – that currently has some 200 volunteer developers. They use the Internet, of course, to produce their software. And they release everything that they produce to the public.

If you view their URL – `http://www.debian.com` – you'll notice that one of their selling points is their presence on a recent space shuttle flight. Debian Linux is used to control an experiment in the Microgravity Science Lab. This is a good example of the maturity and acceptance of Linux.

I have not used Debian, but it has a high-quality reputation. It uses its own package manager that many knowledgeable Linux users and developers consider being superior to RPM.

Yggdrasil

Yggdrasil is the oldest CD-ROM-based distribution. (I purchased their CD-ROM in 1994 and it got me started.) They pioneered the method and currently ship a very stable, if slightly dated, Linux kernel. Yggdrasil has a very good X Window–based installation and configuration system.

Red Hat 5.0

Red Hat takes an active, value-added approach to Linux installation and administration. This distribution has a full-featured installation and update process based on the Red Hat Package Manager (RPM) system. They put a great deal into RPM. For instance, RPM backs up your current setup so you can return to it if necessary. RPM can also retain your configuration files so that when you update a package, you do not lose your setup. If you are running a professional system or just value your sanity, these capabilities are essential.

Red Hat includes a graphical system management window called the *Control Panel*. It is similar to management tools you find in high-end workstations such as Silicon Graphics. It provides a Graphical User Interface (GUI) for management of user and group configuration, file system management, printer configuration, network configuration, time and date, and kernel modules.

Red Hat has a simple, straightforward, graphical installation and upgrade system. It is also linear – you start at the top and flow down to the finish. It has clear, reasonably detailed directions and a simple help system. The CD-ROM is also significantly cleaner than the last Red Hat release. Gone are the numerous files that mostly cluttered up the *root* directory. I don't know if they are still resident deep within the bowels of the CD-ROM, but you don't have to bother with them anymore.

I personally prefer managing a system the old-fashioned way — that is, from a shell command line (for example, the DOS prompt, C : \). I like that method, not because of a masochistic streak, but because it forces me to understand the details of a system, and thus helps to keep my skills sharp. The Control Panel offers an alternative to the command line, for the times when you want to do an administrative task quickly or when you don't remember exactly how to do something.

When I first experimented with Red Hat, I was a little put off by its startup scripts. (A Linux startup script is similar to the DOS AUTOEXEC.BAT and Windows *.INI files, but more powerful.) They do not use as simple a system as Slackware's — in which all the scripts reside in one directory and start at the top and fall out the bottom. However, after I tracked everything down, they were not bad. Separate scripts typically handle specific startup tasks. For example, the rc.inet1 script in the Slackware distribution (refer to Listing 1-1) configures every network interface on the PC. Red Hat divides *rc.inet1* into several scripts, with each script performing a specific function.

For the cost of a little extra complexity, Red Hat does more things than the other distributions. The Red Hat script fragment in Listing 1-2 performs the same function as the Slackware script in Listing 1-1.

Listing 1-2: Red Hat /etc/sysconfig/network-cripts/ifcfg-eth0

```
DEVICE=eth0
IPADDR=192.168.1.254
NETMASK=255.255.255.0
NETWORK=192.168.1.0
BROADCAST=192.168.1.255
ONBOOT=yes
```

With a single menu selection, Red Hat comes out of the box configured to run Samba! It also seems to be one of the top distributions in terms of market presence. Because of those qualities and its overall professionalism, I have chosen to use it for this book.

When I got version 4.1 (since upgraded to 4.2 and now 5.0), I knew Red Hat had an advanced update mechanism, but I was surprised and impressed by the overall level of sophistication. Its installation has evolved nicely and, of course, it configures and starts Samba by default. The addition of *Disk Druid*, *Control Panel*, and *Metro-X*, which is a commercial configuration system for X Window, as well as the tightness of the 300-page manual, impresses me. In just three years, Red Hat has reached a level of professionalism that rivals the big-time workstation manufacturers.

Other Distributions

Many companies offer Linux distributions. Several companies package Slackware, and one company – InfoMagic – sells a six-CD set that includes Red Hat, Slackware, and Debian. It also includes a complete SunSite mirror (copy of the file system on CD-ROM). Note that some companies resell the distribution and others, such as Red Hat, create their own distribution and sell it. Table 1-2 lists some of these companies.

TABLE 1-2 COMPANIES THAT OFFER LINUX DISTRIBUTIONS

Distributor	Link	Phone
Caldera, Inc.	http://www.caldera.com	800-850-7779
Craftwork Solutions, Inc.	http://www.craftwork.com	408-985-1878
Debian[1]	http://www.debian.org	None
DOSLINUX[1,2]	http://ftp.sunsite.unc.edu/ pub/Linux/distributions/ doslinux	None
InfoMagic, Inc.	http://www.infomagic.com	800-800-6613
Linux System Labs (LSL)	http://www.lsl.com	248-399-5354 (fax)
Pacific HiTech	http://www.pht.com	801-261-1024
Red Hat Software, Inc.	http://www.redhat.com	888-733-4281
S.u.S.E.	http://www.suse.com	888-875-4689
Trans-Ameritech	http://www.zoom.com/tae	408-727-3883
Walnut Creek CD-ROM[3]	http://www.cdrom.com	800-786-9907
WorkGroup Solutions, Inc.	http://ftp.wgs.com/pub2/wgs	303-699-2793
Yggdrasil Computing, Inc.	http://www.yggdrasil.com	800-261-6630

[1] *Noncommercial*
[2] *Runs under DOS*
[3] *Official distributor of Slackware*

More organizations are entering the fray all the time.

TIP

Here are some World Wide Web sites with information and reviews about these distributions:

```
ftp://sunsite.unc.edu/pub/Linux/distributions
http://www.ecr.mu.oz.au/%7Enamoorth/Dist_howto.html
http://www.linuxjournal.com/distable.html
```

Although I like the simplicity of Slackware, I have chosen to use Red Hat for this book. It is probably the most popular distribution now, which is important for longevity. It offers so much in terms of upgrade help, systems configuration, and general professionalism that I have recently switched over to it in both my personal and professional use. I believe it is the best package for the type of system I want to show you how to build. In particular, it does some things that will assist you in setting up your first system. Overall, I think it offers the best value.

Deciding How to Partition Your Disk

After you pick a PC and a distribution, you must decide how you want to install Linux on the hard disk. You have the following choices:

◆ Load Linux onto an existing DOS (FAT) file system and run it on that limited system.

◆ Shrink an existing DOS file system with the *FIPS* program (described in the upcoming section titled "Method 1: Multiple Partitions")and then install the Linux file system – ext2 – on the freed-up space. This approach creates multiple partitions on a single disk and allows you to run either Windows or Linux when you start the PC.

◆ Format the entire disk for Linux and run only Linux. You create a single partition by using the entire disk, and you devote it to Linux. You cannot run any other operating system.

TIP

Caldera offers a bootable CD-ROM. This CD-ROM is useful for demonstration purposes as it does not require any modification to your existing system.

Table 1-3 summarizes your choices.

TABLE 1-3 DISK OPTIONS FOR LINUX

Method	Advantages	Disadvantages
Single partition (FDISK)	Maximizes resource	Destroys existing data; requires dedicated disk
Multiple partitions (FIPS)	Retain existing data	Less space for Linux
UMSDOS	Requires no disk repartition	Inefficient; DOS limitations
CD-ROM/Live	Requires no disk repartition; good for demonstrations	Slow; cannot write to disk

Note: Red Hat no longer supports the *UMSDOS* and *CD-ROM/Live* options.

The simplest method is to start Linux from DOS. With this method, a Linux file system — called UMSDOS — is installed on top of the DOS file system. It inherits all the limitations of the DOS file system (FAT). I don't recommend this method because it is of limited use for creating a full-blown network. (Some distributions other than Red Hat also make this method available.)

No single method is best for all situations. In this chapter, however, I concentrate on using what is called a Linux *boot/root* floppy. This is a floppy disk that contains the basic Linux operating system, a number of modules to communicate with your hardware (disks, network adapters, and so on), and a minimal number of system and application programs. With it, you can start – boot – Linux and then mount the CD-ROM from which you can install a complete Linux system. This method works under more circumstances than the other methods, but requires a little more up-front work.

Of course, if you format an entire disk, you have use of the entire disk. This approach makes sense when you are ready to run your Linux box as a server or if you want to experiment on an unneeded disk. If you only want to experiment with Linux, use the multiple-partition method at first, as it is the least disruptive to your current setup.

Making Room for Linux

Before you can install Linux, you must make room for it. In this section, I outline the following two methods to do that:

- Creating multiple partitions on one hard disk to have access to multiple operating systems (DOS and Linux, for instance)

- Leaving the existing single partition in place, in anticipation of using the entire disk for Linux

If you choose to use multiple partitions, you can use a DOS program called *FIPS* to shrink your current partition in order to make room for a Linux partition (in addition to your current operating system). If you decide to use a single partition, you do not have to do anything to your current partition until you are prompted to do so during the Red Hat installation process. The following lists describe the steps involved for both methods.

With the multiple-partition method, you start the installation process by completing the following steps:

1. Shrink the current partition with FIPS.EXE (this step makes room for both DOS/Windows and Linux on the same disk).

2. Create a boot/root floppy by copying a special file with the DOS program RAWRITE.EXE.

3. Boot the computer with the boot/root floppy.

4. Install and configure Linux via the Red Hat installation process that comes on the boot/root floppy. Adding the Linux partitions – in addition to the DOS partition – is part of the process.

With the single-partition (destructive) method, you begin the installation process by completing the following steps:

1. Create a boot/root floppy disk by copying a special file with the DOS program RAWRITE.EXE.

2. Boot the computer with the boot/root floppy.

3. Install and configure Linux via the Red Hat installation process that comes on the boot/root floppy. Partitioning the entire disk for Linux is part of the process.

Method 1: Multiple Partitions

You can repartition your disk without destroying the current OS (for instance, DOS or Windows 95) and data. FIPS (the *First Nondestructive Interactive Partition Splitting* program) is a DOS-based program, written by Arno Schaefer, that can shrink your DOS partition down by as much as all the free space you have. You have the choice of any amount to that level or less. Any or all of the unused space can be freed up for one or more Linux partitions.

To prepare your disk, run *ScanDisk* and have it scan the surface of your disk for any damaged areas that it could possibly repair. You should also defragment the disk with *Disk Defragmenter*, which reorganizes the disk so that all the unused parts are combined into one contiguous area. This reorganization can increase the usable space on your disk. You can run both programs from Windows 95:

1. Click the Windows 95 *Start* button.

2. Choose *Programs→Accessories→System Tools*.

3. You can select both utilities from the *System Tools* submenu. From the *System Tools* submenu, choose the *ScanDisk* utility.

4. In the *ScanDisk-Ms-dos_6* dialog box, click the *Thorough* button, click the *Automatically Fix Errors* button, and then click the *Start* button. *ScanDisk* performs a check of your disk. (Be prepared for a long wait. *ScanDisk* must check every cluster on your disk as the last part of its check.) If *ScanDisk* encounters any problems, it prompts you with the action to take.

5. After *ScanDisk* has finished, repeat Steps 1 and 2, and from the *System Tools* submenu, choose the *Disk Defragmenter*.

6. When the *Select Drive* dialog box appears, select the appropriate drive and then click *OK*.

7. In the *Disk Defragmenter* dialog box that appears, click *Start*.

You can also run these programs from DOS.

 Read the documentation that comes with FIPS. You can find detailed instructions for using FIPS on the Red Hat CD-ROM in the first level directory DOSUTILS. The CD-ROM contains more documentation in \DOSUTILS\FIPS-DOCS. Several plain-text files can help you understand the process and the caveats of FIPS: README, FIPS, a FAQ, and other useful documents.

FIPS can't run in a multitasking environment, so complete the following steps to shut down Windows and boot in MS-DOS mode:

1. Click the *Start* button (lower left-hand corner of your screen).

2. Click the *Shut Down* button.

3. Click the *Restart the computer in MS-DOS mode?* button.

4. Click *Yes.*

After your computer restarts in MS-DOS mode, you can run FIPS. FIPS.EXE is stored on the CD-ROM in the DOSUTILS directory. To run FIPS, follow these steps:

1. Change to the \DOSUTILS directory and start FIPS. Assuming the CD-ROM drive is drive D, you start FIPS from the prompt by entering the following commands:

   ```
   CD D:\DOSUTILS
   FIPS
   ```

2. After you enter the command to start FIPS, you see the copyright and disclaimer screen shown in Figure 1-2. After you read it, press any key.

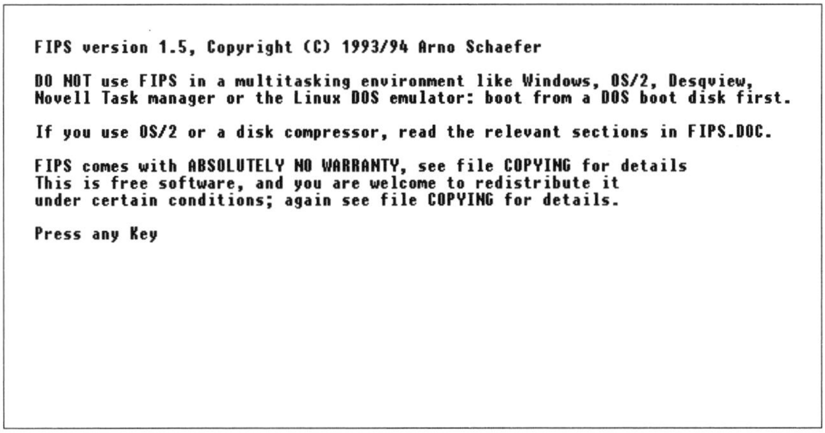

```
FIPS version 1.5, Copyright (C) 1993/94 Arno Schaefer

DO NOT use FIPS in a multitasking environment like Windows, OS/2, Desqview,
Novell Task manager or the Linux DOS emulator: boot from a DOS boot disk first.

If you use OS/2 or a disk compressor, read the relevant sections in FIPS.DOC.

FIPS comes with ABSOLUTELY NO WARRANTY, see file COPYING for details
This is free software, and you are welcome to redistribute it
under certain conditions; again see file COPYING for details.

Press any Key
```

Figure 1-2: The initial FIPS screen

Note: When FIPS prompts you to enter a character (for example, *y*, *n*, *c*, *r*), it does not require you to press *Enter* after the single character. When you press a valid key, FIPS accepts it and moves to the next step in its process.

3. If you are running under Windows 95 or another multitasking system, FIPS displays the warning shown in Figure 1-3. Press *N* to exit FIPS and restart the computer under DOS. Otherwise, proceed at your own risk.

```
FIPS version 1.5, Copyright (C) 1993/94 Arno Schaefer

DO NOT use FIPS in a multitasking environment like Windows, OS/2, Desqview,
Novell Task manager or the Linux DOS emulator: boot from a DOS boot disk first.

If you use OS/2 or a disk compressor, read the relevant sections in FIPS.DOC.

FIPS comes with ABSOLUTELY NO WARRANTY, see file COPYING for details
This is free software, and you are welcome to redistribute it
under certain conditions; again see file COPYING for details.

Press any Key

WARNING: FIPS has detected that it is running under MS-Windows version 4.0
FIPS should not be used under a multitasking OS. If possible, boot from a DOS
disk and then run FIPS. Read FIPS.DOC for more information.

Do you want to proceed (y/n)? _
```

Figure 1-3: FIPS multitasking warning screen

4. As shown in Figure 1-4, FIPS displays your present partition table. It displays the size of your disk and other information such as the number of cylinders. Press any key to continue.

```
This is free software, and you are welcome to redistribute it
under certain conditions; again see file COPYING for details.

Press any Key

WARNING: FIPS has detected that it is running under MS-Windows version 4.0
FIPS should not be used under a multitasking OS. If possible, boot from a DOS
disk and then run FIPS. Read FIPS.DOC for more information.

Do you want to proceed (y/n)? y

Partition table:

       |        |      Start       |      |      End        | Start |Number of|
Part.|bootable|Head Cyl. Sector|System|Head Cyl. Sector| Sector |Sectors  |  MB
-----+--------+------------------+------+-----------------+--------+---------+----
1    |  yes   |  1    0     1|  06h| 15 1023      63|     63| 1032129| 503
2    |  no    |  0    0     0|  00h|  0    0       0|      0|       0|   0
3    |  no    |  0    0     0|  00h|  0    0       0|      0|       0|   0
4    |  no    |  0    0     0|  00h|  0    0       0|      0|       0|   0

Checking root sector ... OK

Press any Key
_
```

Figure 1-4: FIPS partition table

5. FIPS calculates and displays a summary of your disk parameters. It asks you if you wish to save a copy of your root and boot sector to a floppy. Load an unused, DOS-formatted and bootable floppy, and then press *Y*.

6. FIPS then asks whether you have a floppy in drive A. Insert the floppy, press *Y*, and then FIPS saves the information about your current boot sector setup on the floppy. Figure 1-5 shows the entire process. I implore you; I beseech you to make a backup!

```
Bytes per sector: 512
Sectors per cluster: 16
Reserved sectors: 1
Number of FATs: 2
Number of rootdirectory entries: 512
Number of sectors (short): 0
Media descriptor byte: F8h
Sectors per FAT: 252
Sectors per track: 63
Drive heads: 16
Hidden sectors: 63
Number of sectors (long): 1032129
Physical drive number: 80h
Signature: 29h

Checking boot sector ... OK
Checking FAT ... OK
Searching for free space ... OK

Do you want to make a backup copy of your root and boot sector before
proceeding (y/n)? y
Do you have a bootable floppy disk in drive A: as described in the
documentation (y/n)? y
_
```

Figure 1–5: FIPS saves your current partition information to a floppy

TIP

If you encounter problems later or simply want to return to your previous DOS setup, run the program **RESTORRB.EXE** (located in D:\DOSUTILS) to restore the old boot sector to your disk. Then you can run **FDISK**, to see that the old partition is reinstalled.

7. The next screen, shown in Figure 1-6, is a miniature partition table showing the current partition size in megabytes, the starting cylinder of the potential new partition, and the potential partition size. You alter the current and potential partitions with the left-arrow, right-arrow, up-arrow, and down-arrow keys. Each time you press the arrow key, the partition changes in increments of several hundred kilobytes. The up- and left-arrow keys increase the size of the new partition while decreasing the size

of the old partition by the same amount. The down- and right-arrow keys do exactly the opposite.

```
Sectors per FAT: 252
Sectors per track: 63
Drive heads: 16
Hidden sectors: 63
Number of sectors (long): 1032129
Physical drive number: 80h
Signature: 29h

Checking boot sector ... OK
Checking FAT ... OK
Searching for free space ... OK

Do you want to make a backup copy of your root and boot sector before
proceeding (y/n)? y
Do you have a bootable floppy disk in drive A: as described in the
documentation (y/n)? y

Writing file a:\rootboot.002

Enter start cylinder for new partition (823 - 1023):

Use the cursor keys to choose the cylinder, <enter> to continue

Old partition        Cylinder        New Partition
_ 405.1 MB             823               98.9 MB
```

Figure 1-6: The FIPS miniature partition table preceded by the disk parameters

8. Experiment with the possible configurations. You can install Red Hat Linux on as little as 50MB for experimental purposes. A usable system requires as little as 100–150MB, but if possible, set up your system with at least 200MB – that is, enough space to install the basic file system, a fair number of utilities, and some data.

   If you have a modern disk – 1.0GB or larger – try starting with 500MB. With that much space, you can comfortably load most everything you may want initially, including the X Window system. Obviously, the less space you have for Linux, the less you'll have to use for a file server. If you know for sure that you want to construct a file server that will store many megabytes or gigabytes of files, use the largest disk you can afford now. But if you are merely curious or want to use Linux as a home system, you can start with a relatively small space.

9. When you're ready to take the plunge, press *Enter*. FIPS displays the screen shown in Figure 1-7 and prompts you to press *c* to continue or *r* to reedit the partition. Make your choice, or exit completely by pressing *Ctrl+C* to go back to the DOS prompt.

```
Enter start cylinder for new partition (823 - 1023):

Use the cursor keys to choose the cylinder, <enter> to continue

Old partition       Cylinder      New Partition
   405.1 MB           823            98.9 MB

First Cluster: 51813
Last Cluster: 64475

Testing if empty ... OK

New partition table:

      !        !    Start     !      !     End      ! Start !Number of!
Part.!bootable!Head Cyl. Sector!System!Head Cyl. Sector! Sector !Sectors  ! MB
-----+--------+---------------+------+---------------+--------+---------+----
1    !   yes  !  1    0    1 ! 06h! 15  822   63!     63! 829521! 405
2    !   no   !  0   823   1 ! 06h! 15 1023   63! 829584! 202608!  98
3    !   no   !  0    0    0 ! 00h!  0    0    0!      0!      0!   0
4    !   no   !  0    0    0 ! 00h!  0    0    0!      0!      0!   0

Checking root sector ... OK

Do you want to continue or reedit the partition table (c/r)? _
```

Figure 1-7: Continue or reedit the miniature partition table?

10. FIPS recalculates the disk partition values and displays them, as shown in Figure 1-8. FIPS then asks if you are ready to write the new partition scheme to disk. Press *y* or *n*, and FIPS returns you to the DOS prompt.

```
Checking root sector ... OK

Do you want to continue or reedit the partition table (c/r)? c

New boot sector:

Bytes per sector: 512
Sectors per cluster: 16
Reserved sectors: 1
Number of FATs: 2
Number of rootdirectory entries: 512
Number of sectors (short): 0
Media descriptor byte: F8h
Sectors per FAT: 252
Sectors per track: 63
Drive heads: 16
Hidden sectors: 63
Number of sectors (long): 829521
Physical drive number: 80h
Signature: 29h

Checking boot sector ... OK

Ready to write new partition scheme to disk
Do you want to proceed (y/n)?
```

Figure 1-8: Are you ready to write the new partition to disk?

You can look at the new partition with FDISK if you wish. The next step is to create a boot/root floppy, which is used to install Linux. Go to the section: "Making a Boot/Root Floppy Disk" for instructions on creating such a disk.

If you reboot your computer at this point, the system may not recognize your CD-ROM with its current configuration. The system recognizes the partition you just created as drive D, which was probably the designation for your CD-ROM. In some cases, where you have two disk drives installed, the system may simply recognize the CD-ROM as drive E, which could cause problems.

You can delete that new partition with FDISK and eliminate the problem — doing so will not affect your Linux installation. However, FIPS labels the new partition as Red. The version of FDISK that I use with Windows 95 does not permit the use of lowercase letters when specifying the label during the delete process. Consequently, you have to live with the problem until you delete the new partition during the Linux installation process.

Note: Before you proceed, you should create a boot/root floppy, just as you have to do in the single-partition method. Just as you should make an emergency Windows 95 startup disk, you should have a boot/root floppy for emergencies. I provide instructions for creating a boot/root floppy just a bit later in this chapter.

Method 2: Single Partition (Destructive)

The single-partition method is straightforward and conceptually simple. Whatever partition(s) you have are completely written over. Using the single-partition method destroys all the data on your disk. For this discussion, I assume that you have only one partition, which is typical of DOS and Windows installations.

If you choose to use your entire disk for Linux, you need not do anything else at this point. The Red Hat installation process includes the process for repartitioning the disk. I describe the repartitioning process in Steps 9 through 22 in the section titled "Installing Red Hat Linux," later in this chapter.

I use the single partition (destructive) method for my examples in this book.

Making a Boot/Root Floppy Disk

Red Hat Linux purchases include both a CD-ROM and a boot/root floppy disk. The boot/root disk allows you to start your computer with a minimal Linux system and then install the complete system. However, this book does not include a boot/root floppy, and you need to create one in order to install Linux. The floppy disk contains a basic Linux kernel and file system. The file system provides a foundation from which the kernel can operate; it is essential to Linux's operation.

 TIP The boot/root floppy can also be used later on to restore a corrupted Linux partition. (If your system becomes corrupted and cannot be started, you can always boot from the floppy.) The boot/root floppy can also be used to update an older Red Hat distribution.

On the Red Hat CD-ROM, the directory D:\IMAGES contains a number of files that are images of a Linux kernel and file system. A program called RAWRITE, which you find in D:\DOSUTILS, transfers your kernel and basic file system image – containing the most essential system and application programs – byte-for-byte onto the floppy disk. When that disk is inserted into your floppy drive and you reboot your computer, Linux takes control and copies the file system into your system memory (RAM disk), and the Red Hat installation program starts. Then, you can install a complete Linux system.

Here are the steps for creating a boot/root floppy:

1. Insert a floppy into drive A. It must be a new floppy or one whose contents are disposable because all data on it will be irretrievably lost. Enter the following commands:

```
D:\
CD \IMAGES
\DOSUTILS\RAWRITE
```

2. RAWRITE prompts you for the file you want to install and the location to install it. Enter **BOOT.IMG** – for a bootable image – and A: for the floppy disk. RAWRITE puts the image onto the disk and returns to the DOS prompt.

3. Repeat the process in Step 2 to create a supplemental disk. The supplemental disk allows you to boot a basic Linux system completely from floppies and is useful for troubleshooting. Run RAWRITE again, using **SUPP.IMG** as the input file.

4. Reboot the PC with the boot floppy inserted. The first prompt you see is *boot:*, along with some text describing your options. Simply press any key, unless you need to enter special parameters. You see the word *linux* displayed and then several lines of dots. This is the Linux kernel being loaded into memory. Then you see a screen full of information similar to the example in Listing 1-3.

Listing 1-3: Information from a typical Linux startup screen

```
Console: 16 point font, 400 scans
Console: colour VGA+ 80x25, 1 virtual console (max 63)
pci_init: no BIOS32 detected
Calibrating delay loop.. ok - 33.18 BogoMIPS
Memory: 6848k/8448k available (736k kernel code, 384k reserved, 480k data)
This processor honours the WP bit even when in supervisor mode. Good.
Swansea University Computer Society NET3.035 for Linux 2.0
NET3: Unix domain sockets 0.13 for Linux NET3.035.
Swansea University Computer Society TCP/IP for NET3.034
IP Protocols: IGMP, ICMP, UDP, TCP
VFS: Diskquotas version dquot_5.6.0 initialized
Checking 386/387 coupling... Ok, fpu using exception 16 error reporting.
Checking 'hlt' instruction... Ok.
Linux version 2.0.31 (root@porky.redhat.com) (gcc version 2.7.2.3) #1 Sun Nov 97
Starting kswapd v 1.4.2.2
Serial driver version 4.13 with no serial options enabled
tty00 at 0x03f8 (irq = 4) is a 16450
tty01 at 0x02f8 (irq = 3) is a 16450
Real Time Clock Driver v1.07
Ramdisk driver initialized : 16 ramdisks of 4096K size
hda: WDC AC21600H, 1549MB w/128kB Cache, CHS=3148/16/63
ide0 at 0x1f0-0x1f7,0x3f6 on irq 14
Floppy drive(s): fd0 is 1.44M
FDC 0 is an 8272A
md driver 0.35 MAX_MD_DEV=4, MAX_REAL=8
scsi : 0 hosts.
scsi : detected total.
Partition check:
 hda: hda1 hda2 hda3 hda4
VFS: Mounted root (ext2 filesystem) readonly.
Adding Swap: 24188k swap-space (priority -1)
sysctl: ip forwarding off
Swansea University Computer Society IPX 0.34 for NET3.035
IPX Portions Copyright (c) 1995 Caldera, Inc.
Appletalk 0.17 for Linux NET3.035
eth0: 3c509 at 0x330 tag 1, BNC port, address  00 a0 24 2f 30 69, IRQ 10.
3c509.c:1.12 6/4/97 becker@cesdis.gsfc.nasa.gov
eth0: Setting Rx mode to 1 addresses.
```

Installing Red Hat Linux

After you complete either the single- or the multiple-partition method (which I describe in previous sections of this chapter) and have created a boot/root floppy you can use the Red Hat installation program to install Linux. Insert the boot/root floppy disk into the floppy drive and reboot the computer (press the *Ctrl+Alt+Del* keys all at once). The following instructions detail the Red Hat installation process.

You have another way to start the Red Hat installation process. If you are running from DOS or Windows and have your Red Hat CD-ROM recognized as drive *D:*, then you can start the installation process by entering the following commands for a DOS prompt window:

```
D:
CD \DOSUTILS
AUTOBOOT.BAT
```

The batch file AUTOBOOT.BAT loads the Linux kernel into memory and turns control over to the Red Hat installation program. (This is the same program that the boot/root floppy installation method uses — the method for getting the Linux kernel booted is the only difference.)

Red Hat uses a menu-based installation system. For each step in the installation process, you see a different window. Most windows offer a submenu for selecting specific items, such as the type of CD-ROM drive. In other cases, however, you choose an option by selecting an on-screen button. You use the arrow keys to select submenu options. You toggle the buttons on and off by pressing the spacebar. You can also select a highlighted button by pressing *Enter*. The *Tab* key and the *Alt+Tab* key combination shift control from one place to another in the menu window. The *F12* key shifts control to the next window, saving whatever selections you have already made (use with caution).

The CD-ROM includes many useful documents that elaborate on the Linux installation process. The top-level directory on the CD-ROM contains a couple of particularly helpful documents: INSTALL.TXT and LINUX.TXT. These documents describe the installation and general Linux stuff very well.

If you do not have a CD-ROM drive, you can still install Linux. You can obtain floppy disk distributions from various vendors. If your PC is connected via the network to a computer that has a CD-ROM drive, you can mount the CD-ROM with NFS or even Samba, and install from there. You can also get Linux via anonymous FTP from the multitude of SunSite mirrors around the world (for example, `ftp.cc.gatech.edu/pub/linux`). The Red Hat Web page (`http://www.redhat.com`) provides instructions for using the alternative installation methods.

Within the submenus, use the arrow keys to choose specific items, such as the network adapter model. Press *Tab* and *Alt+Tab* to move between a submenu and the command buttons such as *OK* and *Cancel*.

Unfortunately, the Red Hat installation system lacks an abort mechanism. After you start the installation, the system offers no way to exit gracefully. In some parts of the process you can go back a step; but, to restart the installation you must reboot your computer.

Linux makes use of a facility called a *virtual terminal*. A virtual terminal allows you to make your single computer screen work like several separate terminals. By pressing *Alt+F1* through *Alt+F5*, you can switch between different screens, each independent of the others. Red Hat takes advantage of this facility by providing different information about your installation process. Table 1-4 describes the function of each virtual terminal.

TABLE 1-4 VIRTUAL TERMINAL FUNCTIONS

Key Combination	Displays
Alt+F1	Installation progress
Alt+F2	The shell prompt
Alt+F3	Installation log
Alt+F4	System log
Alt+F5	Program output

Here are the steps for completing the Red Hat Linux installation process (I have included the name of the menu window that my instructions refer to in bold text at the beginning of each step):

1. If you have not rebooted your computer with the Linux boot/root floppy, then do so now.

2. **Welcome to Red Hat Linux!** You get an initial installation screen that gives you several methods to create your Linux system. The *Kickstart* method, for instance, lets you use a script to make custom systems and would be very useful if in the future you plan to sell custom Linux servers. However, for our purposes we will use the *General* method, so simply press the *Enter* key. Note, if you do not choose anything, the installation will default to the *General* method after about 30 seconds.

3. **Color Choices.** As shown in Figure 1-9, the first window in the Red Hat installation process asks whether you have a color screen. Press *Tab* and *Alt+Tab* to highlight the correct response – *Yes* or *No* – and then press *Enter*.

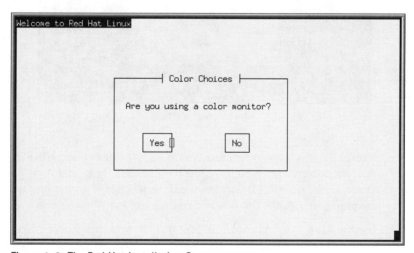

Figure 1-9: The Red Hat Installation Startup screen

4. **Red Hat Linux.** The installation program displays the *Welcome to Red Hat Linux!* screen. Select the *OK* button to continue.

5. **Keyboard Type.** You are asked to select your keyboard type from an international list. Select the one that matches your keyboard and press *Enter* to select the *OK* button.

6. **Installation Method.** As shown in Figure 1-10, the installation program asks you to identify the media from which you plan to install Red Hat Linux. Use the arrow keys to highlight the correct media – Local CD-ROM, NFS image, hard drive, or FTP image – and press *Tab* and then *Enter* to select the *OK* button. I select *Local CD-ROM.*

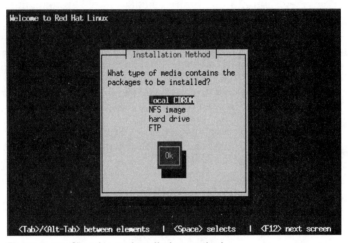

Figure 1-10: Choosing an installation method

7. **Note.** The next screen reminds you to insert your Red Hat CD-ROM. Select the *OK* button when you have inserted the disk. Note that if you do not have an IDE/ATAPI CD-ROM you will be prompted for the type and manufacturer of the CD-ROM drive that you have.

8. **Installation Path.** As shown in Figure 1-11, you can choose from two types of installations: *Install* or *Upgrade.* Select *Install* and press *Enter.*

9. **SCSI Configuration.** If you are using SCSI drives, the next window allows you to specify the type of SCSI drive. If you do not have a SCSI, select *No.*

Figure 1–11: Install or Upgrade?

10. **Disk Setup.** You are given two choices for partitioning your disk as shown in Figure 1-12. Red Hat 5.0 introduces the graphical *Disk Druid* partitioning utility. You also can use the traditional *fdisk* method. (If you do so, then please select the *fdisk* option and follow the instructions in the sidebar "Partitioning Your Disk with fdisk.") The following steps describe the use of *Disk Druid*. Select *Disk Druid*.

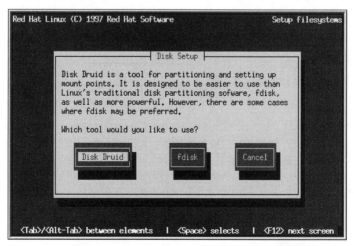

Figure 1–12: Choosing the Disk Druid disk partitioning utility

11. **Current Disk Partitions.** The *Disk Druid* screen is displayed as shown in Figure 1-13. The number of partitions that are displayed depends on how your disk is already configured.

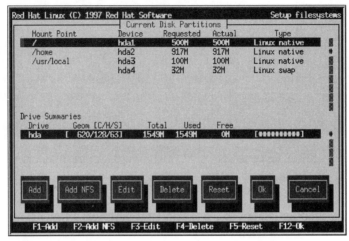

Figure 1-13: Disk Druid displays your current partitions.

12. In this example I will assume that you will use your entire disk for Linux. This requires that you delete any existing partitions. (If you retain your existing DOS/Windows partition(s), then you will not do anything to them.) To delete a partition, use your Up/Down cursor keys to highlight the appropriate partition and then use the *Tab* key to move to the menu at the bottom of the screen and select *Del*. Press *Enter* and you are prompted if you really want to delete the partition. If you do, select *Yes* and press *Enter*.

13. Repeat Step 11 for each existing partition you want to delete.

14. Now you need to add one or more *Linux Native* partitions as well as a *Linux Swap* partition to be used for storing information that does not fit into memory; this is because Linux uses a *Demand-Page Virtual* memory system described in more detail in Chapter 3. Select the *Add* option and you get an *Edit New Partition* screen shown in Figure 1-14.

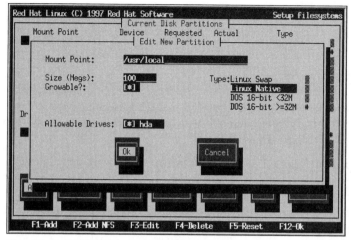

Figure 1–14: Editing a new partition with Disk Druid

15. In general I prefer to use three partitions for my Linux systems: *root* (/), */home* and */usr/local*. The Root file system is used to store the standard Linux programs, libraries, and so forth. The */home* is used for the user's data. The */usr/local* is used to store application programs, libraries, and configuration files that are specific to a single machine. For instance, I store my copy of Netscape in */usr/local*. This enables me to completely reinstall a Linux system without removing or modifying my personal data or third-party software.

    For the Root partition enter a single slash (/) for the mount point and whatever size is appropriate for your system. Select *OK*.

16. Repeat Step 14 for */home* and */usr/local* using the size appropriate to your system.

17. Add your swap partition by selecting *Add*. At the *Edit New Partition* menu do not choose a mount point but instead select the size of your swap partition and *Linux Swap* in the *Type* submenu. Note that a general rule of thumb is to select a swap space at least as large as the amount of memory on your system. Thus, if you have 16MB then you'll want to use that as your swap size. (For my 8MB system, however, I use 16MB swap space.)

18. When you are satisfied, select *OK* to put your configured partitions into effect. Note that if you become confused, you can select *Reset* to restore your original partitions. You can also select *Cancel* to void any selections.

The following steps will be slightly different if you use the *fdisk* method here. You will be prompted, for example, to specify which partition will be the *Root* partition.

19. **Active Swap Space.** The *Active Swap Space* menu is displayed on your screen. The swap space partition is displayed with an asterisk next to it. Select *OK*. Red Hat formats the swap space partition. If you select the *Check for bad blocks during format* option it will do a more thorough format and also take more time.

20. **Format Partitions.** The *Format Partitions* menu is displayed on your screen. Red Hat wants to know which partition to format. If you followed my three-partition example in Steps 11 through 18, you will need to press the spacebar for each partition in order to format it. The spacebar toggles an asterisk (*) on and off — the asterisk indicates that the partition will be formatted. If you also select the *Check for bad blocks during format* option, a more thorough format will be done and take more time. Select *OK*.

21. Red Hat displays the *Root partition* submenu, which lets you specify whether to format the Root partition. To toggle the *Format* button, press the spacebar. *Tab* to the next submenu, which asks if you want to check for bad blocks. This extra step takes a long time but is worthwhile if this is your first time through the installation process. Press the spacebar to toggle this option. Select *OK*.

22. **Components to Install.** The *Choose components to install* menu appears. Red Hat needs to know which Linux components to install. It preselects several of the generally useful packages listed as follows. I want to keep this introductory chapter as simple as possible and also leave you with a useful installation so I will leave the default selections as is but add the *SMB (Samba) connectivity* component.

    X Window System

    X multimedia support

    Mail/WWW/News Tools

    File Managers

    Console Multimedia

    Networked Workstation

    Dialup Workstation

    SMB (Samba) Connectivity

    DNS Name Server

To keep it simple, install the entire contents of the Red Hat distribution. If you have a large disk, you can install everything by choosing the *Everything* option. (Please note that my instructions in this chapter and subsequent chapters are based on installing only the packages I mention in the following steps. In subsequent chapters, you use the Red Hat Package Manager, or RPM, installer to add packages as needed.)

23. **Install Log.** Red Hat informs you that a complete log of your installation is kept in */tmp/install.log* and that you may want to keep it for future reference. Select *OK* and press *Enter*.

Red Hat makes (formats) the appropriate file systems on the selected partitions and starts installing the selected components to disk. This process can take a long time if you have a slow machine – in particular, a slow CD-ROM or hard drive. Red Hat displays two progress bar graphs: one for each component and one for the total installation. A time-to-go estimate and a running total of subsystems installed versus those-to-go are also shown. These times are calculated on an ongoing basis and change as the installation process runs.

Installing Red Hat Components

Throughout this book I have you add extra functionality by adding Red Hat software components. If you wish to skip my manual instructions and include everything that I discuss here, then add the components identified in the following list now.

- ◆ Printer Support
- ◆ Print Server
- ◆ Network Management Workstation
- ◆ C Development
- ◆ Perl
- ◆ Development Libraries
- ◆ Extra Documentation

Partitioning Your Disk with fdisk

The following steps describe how to partition your disk with the fdisk program. This is the second option in Step 10 in the instructions for installing Red Hat Linux.

1. After you select the *fdisk* option, the screen that is displayed shows you your existing disk or disks. You are given the choices: *Done*, *Edit*, and *Cancel*. To start, select *Edit* and follow Steps 2 through 14.

   The following steps are somewhat involved. You need to partition part or all of your disk for Linux to use. If you used the multiple-partition method that I described earlier in this chapter, you will use that new space for the Linux partition. Otherwise, simply delete the old partition(s) and use the entire disk (minus the swap area).

2. The screen goes blank except for two lines at the bottom. Red Hat has started the Linux version of *fdisk*. This is not the DOS FDISK that you used earlier, but the function is the same — Linux *fdisk* has more capabilities, however.

3. It is helpful to see how the disk is partitioned at this point. At the last line, enter p and then press *Enter*. The current partition is displayed.

   Notice that *fdisk* gives the sector numbers on which each partition starts and ends.

4. This step, and Step 5, are used to delete existing partitions and are optional. Note that even if you are using the single-partition method, you still need to delete whatever partition(s) currently exist. From the *fdisk* prompt, enter d. You are prompted to enter a partition number. Because you have already decided to use the entire disk (in this example), simply enter the number of an existing partition.

5. Repeat Step 4 for each of the existing partitions. Don't worry too much about completing these two steps. The deletions — or any changes — *don't take effect* until you use the w, for write, command. You can simply enter q, for quit, at any time and no changes — no damage — will be made to your disk.

6. Now you need to add one or more partitions. Enter n, for new, at the prompt, and the Linux *fdisk* asks if you want a primary or an extended partition. Enter p for a primary and then 1 if you are using the entire disk for Linux, or 2 if you are using multiple partitions and already have a DOS partition as the first partition. Then press *Enter*.

7. This next part can be tricky. You need to decide where to start and end the new partition. You are asked for the starting sector, which is easy because the Linux *fdisk* suggests the next available sector. Enter the default number that you are given and press *Enter*.

8. You can choose the ending sector by entering its absolute number, or the size of the partition in bytes (+), megabytes (+ M), or kilobytes (+ K). Remember to leave yourself at least 8MB of swap space.

9. Display the information about the new partition, as in Step 3, and check it to see if the size turned out as you expected.

10. If the size of any of the partitions did not turn out the way you wanted them, you can easily remake them. Return to the main *fdisk* menu by pressing the *Esc* key. Print out the new partitions as in Step 2 or 9. If one or more partitions are not the correct size, press *d* to delete a partition, as described in Steps 4 and 5. Repeat that process for any or all of the partitions. Next, repeat Steps 6 through 9 as many times as necessary to create one or more new partitions.

    Please make note that until you tell *fdisk* to write all these changes to the disk, they are not made permanent.

11. You should see that the second partition is of type Linux, but you must change the one you want to be a swap partition to the swap type. From the *fdisk* prompt, enter t and then press *Enter* to change the partition ID (you can get a list of all the types by entering L (82 = Linux swap).

12. To change the file system type of, say, the third partition to the swap type, enter 3 to specify the third partition and then enter 82 to change it to the swap type. Press *Enter*.

13. You must save all the changes that you just made. To write the new partition to disk, enter w and then press *Enter*. If you want to quit without changing anything, enter q and then press *Enter*.

14. Control is returned to the Red Hat installation system. From the *Partition Disks* window, select *Done*.

Configuring Linux for General Operation

After the Red Hat packages have been installed, you are asked for some basic configuration information. In the following procedure, I describe the information you are prompted to enter, and I offer guidance for completing this portion of the Linux installation and configuration process:

1. **Probing Result.** Red Hat probes for the port that your mouse is on. If it locates it, proceed to Step 2. If not, you will be presented with the *Pick Your Serial Port* menu of the four possible serial ports to use for your mouse. Select the appropriate one. I have my mouse connected to the first serial port, */dev/cua0* (which is COM1 under DOS).

2. **Configure Mouse.** I select *Microsoft compatible (serial)*. I choose not to use the *Emulate Three Buttons* option even though I have a two-button mouse because I get confused by that option. You may want to use that option, however.

3. **Choose a Card.** The installation script runs the *Xconfigurator* program that lets you pick your video adapter and monitor from a large list of manufacturer's models. Once you choose your card, the XFree86 server that works with that card is installed.

4. **Monitor Setup.** The second screen shows the available monitors. If your monitor appears on the list then you simply select it and go to the next step. If it is not on the list, then I generally choose the *Custom* option at the top of the screen and go to another window that explains the basics of choosing the monitor parameters.

   The next screen lets you choose from among ten generic monitor configurations. These configurations include the horizontal and vertical resolutions as well as the horizontal sync rate. This information is contained in the manual that comes with your monitor. As the instructions point out, it is very important that you not pick a horizontal sync range that is greater than your monitor can handle. This is because a monitor can be damaged if you choose too high a value.

   If you are in doubt, choose a conservative setting. The first choice, Standard VGA, 640×480 at 60Hz, is generally a safe one. My monitor can only handle 800×600 at 60Hz and is the lowest value that I find useful with the X Window system. I recommend that you be careful and search through that pile under your desk for your manual.

5. **Screen Configuration.** The next step is to probe or not probe your video card. If you successfully probe your video card, then it returns the exact values you can use. After those values are returned, you can let the system use them as the default or enter your own values. I generally use the return values as they are returned.

   If you choose to probe, then you are asked if it is okay to begin. Once probing has finished, acquired information is displayed. You can either select it as the default or enter new values yourself. I select to use the defaults.

6. **Network Configuration.** Red Hat has a straightforward network configuration procedure. Choose Yes.

7. **Load Module.** You must tell Linux what type of network adapter module to load. You get a list of the supported Ethernet adapters. I select *3c509*, which is the first menu option.

   Note: The menu in Step 5 makes the first hint of the powerful Linux feature of modules. Loading a module is a way of adding a new component to the kernel without recompiling it. Thus, Linux loads an Ethernet module when it boots (modules can be loaded and unloaded at any time while Linux is running, too) and you can access your network! If you are familiar with Linux distributions from the recent past, you may recall that you had to choose between dozens of precompiled kernels to find one that matched your system. That was bulky. Now, the kernel simply loads the precompiled driver as a module – only a few kilobytes for the Ethernet. This is another great Linux feature.

8. **Module Options.** Red Hat wants to know if you need to specify any options, such as the interrupt number or I/O address (that is, 10, 11, or 0x300), for the Ethernet adapter. Because I have the well-known 3Com 3c509, I choose to let Red Hat determine my setting. I select *Autoprobe*.

9. **Configure TCP/IP.** You need to configure TCP/IP. If you don't already have a legal IP address, see the following Tip for information on public IP addresses. I use *public address*, so from Table 1-5 (later in this chapter), I choose the class C address of 192.168.1.254. (You cannot use the numbers 0 or 255 because 0 is the network address and 255 is the broadcast address. I use *254* here to distinguish the Linux box as a server.) Remember to include the dots between each octet (for example, 192.162) when entering the number. Enter the IP address, and Red Hat automatically guesses that 255.255.255.0 is a reasonable net mask.

Red Hat chooses the last available address in your class C subnet, 254, for your default gateway. This is a reasonable choice in general. However in this case I leave it blank because it will interfere with the PPP connection to the Internet – via the phone system – that I configure in Chapters 8, 10, and 11. If you intend to use a phone connection to connect your Linux computer and/or network to the Internet, then leave this field blank. If, however, you need to connect to another LAN or the Internet through permanent connection, then you enter the address of your gateway here.

The last field is for your *Primary nameserver*. This is the address of the computer that converts an Internet name to a numeric IP address. For example, *bart.paunchy.com* translates to 192.168.1.254 within your network. On your own LAN it is reasonable to use your Linux box as your name server. Thus, if you include all your local network addresses in the */etc/hosts* table, then your other computers can ask your Linux box for the actual addresses of any computer on your LAN by name and you do not have to store individual tables on each computer. Enter **192.168.1.254** for this field.

After you have entered all the values, select *OK*. Figure 1-15 shows my TCP/IP values.

Figure 1-15: My TCP/IP network values

Setting Network Parameters for Red Hat

Red Hat wants to start by getting the network information. Even if you do not have a network running yet, it is best to set your parameters now. One of the most important parts of your network is the network address and your host(s) address(es). If your PC is part of an established TCP/IP network, consult your systems administrator for what is called an *IP address*. It must be unique in the whole world so as not to bring the entire Internet crashing down. Well, that will not happen but you can wreak havoc for whoever's IP (internet protocol) address you borrow, so its uniqueness is essential. If you do not have access to an IP address, don't worry. The smart people who designed the internet protocols (notice the lowercase *i*) set aside some addresses for you to use as long as you do not use them outside your LAN. If you do not try to access the Internet — the WWW, e-mail, and so on — then the IP address spaces shown in Table 1-5 are legal. Chapter 8 discusses IP masquerading — that is, how to mask these addresses, or any IP, from the rest of the Internet — so don't worry about choosing this type of address now.

I recommend using a class C address space. It can handle as many as 254 hosts, which should be enough. I prefer to assign my server the highest address in the subnet, so I give it the address 192.168.1.254. This convention makes it easy to remember which machine is the server.

TABLE 1-5 GENERAL-PURPOSE IP ADDRESSES

Network Class	Start Address	Last Address	Subnet Mask
A	10.0.0.0	10.255.255.255	255.0.0.0
B	172.16.0.0	172.31.255.255	255.255.0.0
C	192.168.1.0	192.168.255.255	255.255.255.0

Internet Addresses and the Internic

The internet protocols are an impressive work (remember that the lowercase *i* refers to the protocols that make the Internet possible). It encompasses a huge number of disparate requirements and seamlessly glues the entire world together. Your TCP/IP Local Area Network (LAN) contains nearly all the elements that enable it to scale up to network the entire world.

If you intend to advertise or use your network name out on the Internet, you must register it with the Internic via an Internet Service Provider (ISP). See http://ds.internic.net and the Requests for Comment (RFC) rfc2050 for more information.

Internic is getting stingier with IP addresses. All class C address spaces are distributed from ISPs and they must prove they are using more than 50 percent of their space. Therefore, you must now have at least 128 hosts to qualify for your own class C address space.

A new system under development will correct much of this problem. It is the Internet Protocol version 6, IPv6, and makes use of 128-bit long IP addresses instead of the current 32 bits. It is compatible with the current protocol but allows for considerably more growth. One engineer estimated that it would be possible to allocate several addresses to every square meter on the earth.

TIP

If you do not have a network adapter, you can proceed with this installation and install one later. However, you can't create a client-server network unless you configure one based on a serial interface.

10. **Configure Network.** Red Hat wants you to select a domain and host name for your network. Unless you already have one, have some fun and pick a name for your network. Anything will do because your network is private. (In Chapter 8 I describe how your local addresses are translated into entirely new – and valid – Internet addresses. Here, I choose the name of the top dog in all of Albuquerque, *paunchy.com.*)

TIP In Internet parlance, *com* refers to a commercial venture, *edu* to an educational institution, *gov* for the feds, and *org* for noncommercial organizations. Codes such as *au* for Australia refer to countries. Because your network isn't visible to the Internet, you do not have to worry about being legal — yet. Pick a name that you like.

If you already have an Internet Service Provider (ISP), then now is a good time to enter your secondary and tertiary name server; you can leave them blank if you do not have one. A name server converts an alphanumeric name into numeric IP address. Select *OK*. I show the result of my installation in Figure 1-16.

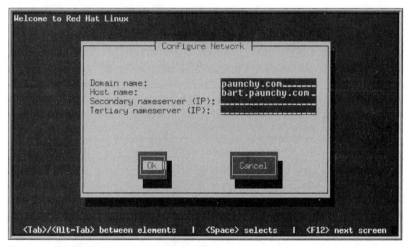

Figure 1-16: Setting your host and domain name

11. **Configure Time Zone.** Red Hat wants to know your time zone. I skip *Hardware clock set to GMT* and page down to the *US/Mountain* time zone. Select *OK* and press *Enter*.

12. **Configure Services.** You are shown a list of services that start automatically when you start up Linux (reboot your computer). The selected services correspond to *symbolic links* (essentially pointers) in the */etc/rc.d/rc0.d* through the */etc/rc.d/rc6.d* directories that point to the startup scripts in */etc/rc.d/init.d* scripts. Links and startup scripts are discussed in more detail in Chapter 3.

13. **Set Up Your Printer.** Red Hat gives you the option to set up Linux printing. It is a straightforward process. If you have the typical printer connected to the Linux box's parallel port, then select *Local* printer and accept the defaults. When asked to choose a manufacturer, select the appropriate one from the given list of printers. I select a *Local* printer; my queue and spool directory are *lp* and */var/spool/lpd/lp*. My local printer device is */dev/lp1* (the standard LPT1 in DOS), and finally I select *HP LaserJet 4/5/6* series and specify the printer capabilities. To put all this into effect, select *Done*. I give more instructions in the section "Configuring the Print Server" in Chapter 10.

Using these settings, I can print from my Windows 95 computer using Samba. Instructions are given for setting up such a computer later in this chapter and in Chapter 6.

14. **Root Password.** You need to give the *root* login a password. The root user is also referred to as the Super User and has the privilege to do anything. Always use caution when working as the root user. Enter the same password on each line. Be careful because your keystrokes are not echoed.

Passwords are the foundation of all security. The *Root* password is the most important one you will assign, because you can do anything as *Root*; so take care. I suggest you consider my method described in the following warning.

Generating Passwords

I discuss the issue of passwords in depth in Chapter 9 but for now I suggest that you use the following method: Pick two unrelated words and concatenate them with a special character such as the dollar sign ($). Thus, you could look out the window and see a car pass by while the sun is shining, and construct the password sunny$car. Linux still only treats the first eight characters as significant, but the password sunny$car is effective.

This method, I think, strikes a good compromise between maximum and minimum protection. The maximum would require randomly generated letters, which are generally impractical to remember and, in my opinion, relax security because you will probably keep your password in written form and end up leaving it around to be found, thus compromising security. The minimum, such as a simple word, is open to being cracked by automated programs. The fact that you use actual words probably increases the mathematical odds of cracking it, but my philosophy is that something has to be practical to be truly effective.

Red Hat 5.0 comes with Programmable Authentication Modules (PAM) already installed. As configured, they force the password setting program — */usr/bin/passwd* — to check your choices. For instance, it does not allow you to pick a password related to your login or that can be found in a dictionary. It is a very helpful feature.

15. **Lilo Installation.** You need to specify how Linux is to be loaded. The Linux Loader (LILO) determines where the PC will start when it is booted. Red Hat gives you two options: *Master Boot Record* and *First sector of boot partition.* In most cases, choose *Master Boot Record.*

16. **Lilo Installation.** In some cases you need to pass hardware configuration information to Linux for it to boot properly. You can pass that information to Linux on this line (for example, mcd=0x300, which is the I/O address for one of my Mitsumi CD-ROM drives). In this case, I leave it blank because I'm working off an ATAPI CD-ROM drive, which does not require any extra configuration information. Select *OK.*

17. **Bootable Partitions.** If you have one or more non-Linux partitions, you will be given a chance to specify one to be booted automatically. For instance, if you used FIPS to install Linux along with DOS or Windows, you will be given a chance to have the DOS partition be the default operating system.

18. **Done.** Red Hat gives some basic instructions. Select *OK* and your computer will reboot. Make sure that you remove the boot/root floppy.

19. I have encountered a problem that requires some post-installation work to fix. The Red Hat installation scripts leave the */etc/hosts* table incomplete and this prevents several network-based systems, such as Samba, from being started correctly. When your computer reboots, it presents you with the *Linux Loader* (LILO) prompt. You have five seconds to enter your choice or it will default to your newly installed Linux system. To edit the */etc/hosts* file, however, you need to enter **linux 1** at this prompt. This starts up Linux in the *Single User* mode without any networking or multiple users capability. By doing this, you can edit the hosts table. Otherwise, your system might hang up or take a very long time to boot.

TIP   At the LILO prompt you can first press the *Tab* key to display a list of the bootable operating systems. If you have saved your DOS partition, you will see both dos and linux.

20. You will be prompted to log in while Linux boots to *Single User* mode. Do not log in because Linux will eventually settle into the *root* user prompt. When it does, edit the */etc/hosts* file so it looks like Listing 1-4. Note that I have added the name of the Windows computer *maggie* in anticipation of using it to connect via Samba. I describe the vi editor in Appendix A.

Listing 1-4: The /etc/hosts table

```
127.0.0.0              localhost      localhost.localdomain
192.168.1.254          bart           bart.paunchy.com
192.168.1.2            maggie         maggie.paunchy.com
```

21. Samba wants a *lock* file in */var/locks/samba* for its internal bookkeeping, so create one by entering the following command verbatim (observing case and syntax):

    ```
    /bin/touch /var/lock/samba/STATUS..LCK
    ```

    In this case, *touch* creates an empty file *STATUS..LCK* in the */var/lock/samba* directory. This filename must be in uppercase, because *smbd* looks for that lock file when it starts.

22. You also need to create a mount directory for a CD-ROM drive:

    ```
    /bin/mkdir /mnt/cdrom
    ```

23. Reboot your computer again by entering the **reboot** or **init 6** command. It should start all the networking systems correctly.

The system reboots. Instead of starting Windows 95 automatically, it displays a screen with the LILO prompt (as mentioned earlier, you have five seconds to make your choice or the system defaults to Windows – unless you have changed the default). Enter either name. If you choose *linux*, a couple of dot lines are rapidly written as the program that loads the kernel is loaded into memory. Next, two or three pages of dense text is displayed, as shown in Listing 1-5. It is the same information shown in Listing 1-3. However, if you look closely you'll notice that three disk partitions now exist – hda1, hda2, and hda3 – as opposed to just the one in Listing 1-3. This difference simply indicates that you have added partitions since then.

Listing 1-57: Information displayed upon startup of Linux

```
Console: 16 point font, 400 scans
Console: colour VGA+ 80x25, 1 virtual console (max 63)
pci_init: no BIOS32 detected
Calibrating delay loop.. ok - 33.18 BogoMIPS
Memory: 6848k/8448k available (736k kernel code, 384k reserved, 480k data)
This processor honours the WP bit even when in supervisor mode. Good.
Swansea University Computer Society NET3.035 for Linux 2.0
NET3: Unix domain sockets 0.13 for Linux NET3.035.
Swansea University Computer Society TCP/IP for NET3.034
IP Protocols: IGMP, ICMP, UDP, TCP
VFS: Diskquotas version dquot_5.6.0 initialized
Checking 386/387 coupling... Ok, fpu using exception 16 error reporting.
Checking 'hlt' instruction... Ok.
```

```
Linux version 2.0.31 (root@porky.redhat.com) (gcc version 2.7.2.3) #1 Sun Nov 97
Starting kswapd v 1.4.2.2
Serial driver version 4.13 with no serial options enabled
tty00 at 0x03f8 (irq = 4) is a 16450
tty01 at 0x02f8 (irq = 3) is a 16450
Real Time Clock Driver v1.07
Ramdisk driver initialized : 16 ramdisks of 4096K size
hda: WDC AC21600H, 1549MB w/128kB Cache, CHS=3148/16/63
ide0 at 0x1f0-0x1f7,0x3f6 on irq 14
Floppy drive(s): fd0 is 1.44M
FDC 0 is an 8272A
md driver 0.35 MAX_MD_DEV=4, MAX_REAL=8
scsi : 0 hosts.
scsi : detected total.
Partition check:
 hda: hda1 hda2 hda3 hda4
VFS: Mounted root (ext2 filesystem) readonly.
Adding Swap: 24188k swap-space (priority -1)
sysctl: ip forwarding off
Swansea University Computer Society IPX 0.34 for NET3.035
IPX Portions Copyright (c) 1995 Caldera, Inc.
Appletalk 0.17 for Linux NET3.035
eth0: 3c509 at 0x330 tag 1, BNC port, address  00 a0 24 2f 30 69, IRQ 10.
3c509.c:1.12 6/4/97 becker@cesdis.gsfc.nasa.gov
eth0: Setting Rx mode to 1 addresses.
```

In general, this startup screen provides the system with information about every-thing from the Ethernet adapter interrupt number to the disks being mounted. It looks dense now, but you'll eventually understand it. It is very informative.

Configuring Windows 95 for Network Operations

Your Samba network uses the TCP/IP protocol. TCP/IP is really a number of indi-vidual protocols that when put together allow two computers, or twenty, or the entire world's computers to connect and work together. It is truly amazing that it scales so well. For now, however, your concern is to get just two computers to work together. After that you can do anything.

I assume you have a PC already running Windows 95. If you don't have Windows 95 installed, don't worry – its installation is a relatively simple process. Follow Microsoft's instructions and in most circumstances you will be okay. If not, many good books can help you set up Windows 95.

My Windows 95 network instructions are for configuring the network from scratch. If you do not have a network interface card installed or have not configured your network settings yet – other than a modem connection – you need to use the following instructions exactly. If you already have your network working, look through my instructions for those steps that you need to complete. For instance, if you have NetWare or NetBEUI working, you need to install TCP/IP but not the network adapter. I also explain how to optionally remove your network configuration if you wish to start from that point.

Here are the steps you must complete to configure Windows 95 for network operations:

1. You want to have your Windows 95 CD-ROM accessible for this process, so go ahead and mount it in your CD-ROM drive.

2. Double-click the *My Computer* icon (it's usually located in the upper-left corner of your screen), to open the *My Computer* window shown in Figure 1-17. It is usually located in the upper-left corner of your screen.

Figure 1-17: The My Computer window

3. Note the Windows 95 resources displayed in the *My Computer* window. Double-click the *Control Panel* icon, to open the *Control Panel* window shown in Figure 1-18.

Figure 1-18: The Control Panel window

4. In the *Control Panel* window, double-click the *Network* icon. As shown in Figure 1-19, Windows 95 opens the *Network* dialog box, which shows the essential networking components that Windows 95 must have installed to work with the Linux and Samba server:

   ■ *Client for Microsoft Networks* allows your computer to work as a network client with a network server(s). This mechanism is necessary to work with Samba.

   ■ *3Com Etherlink* is the network interface that I use on my computer.

   ■ *TCP/IP* is the protocol your PC uses to communicate with your LAN and the Internet.

   ■ *File and print* sharing button for Microsoft Network (optional) allows other Microsoft Network clients to share your files and printers. This is of little interest to us because we will use Samba to share files and printers.

5. Items such as IPX and NetBEUI are optional because they do not interfere with the network you are setting up.

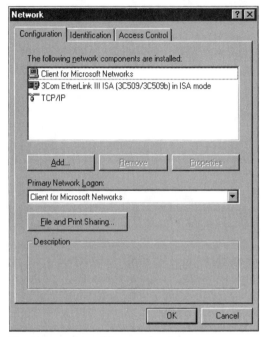

Figure 1-19: Essential network components

6. OPTIONAL: Eliminate your current network configuration.

I prefer to start with a clean slate and reinstall the network components to end up where I started. I do not recommend using this approach yourself, unless you are confident in your Windows 95 savvy.

If you choose to eliminate your network temporarily (even though I do not recommend it), start with the *Network* dialog box shown in Figure 1-20. Click the *Network Adapter* item (on my machine, it is a 3Com EtherLink III) and the *Add*, *Remove*, and *Properties* buttons become active. Click *Remove* and then click *OK*. Windows 95 displays the *System Settings Change* dialog box shown in Figure 1-20. To make the new configuration active, you must reboot the PC. Click *Yes* to restart Windows 95, or click *No* and reboot manually later. I click *Yes* and wait for my computer to restart.

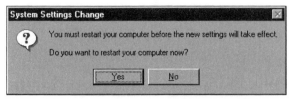

Figure 1-20: The System Settings Change dialog box

After you reboot your computer and Windows 95 reactivates, the *Network Neighborhood* icon is not displayed. Your computer no longer has any network access. To reinstall it and access the Linux box, double-click the *My Computer* icon and then the *Control Panel* icon and finally the *Network* icon just like before. The *Network* dialog box should be blank – with no components displayed.

7. Click the *Add* button to open the *Select Network Component Type* dialog box shown in Figure 1-21.

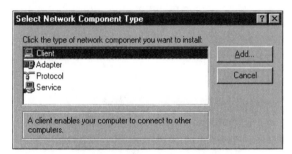

Figure 1-21: The Select Network Component Type dialog box

8. Select the *Client* option and then click the *Add* button, which becomes active after you select *Client*. The resulting *Select Network Client* dialog box, shown in Figure 1-22, gives you several choices. Select the *Microsoft* option in the *Manufacturers* list and the *Client for Microsoft Networks* under the *Network Clients* dialog box. Click *OK*.

Note: You must select the *Client* option before any of the others.

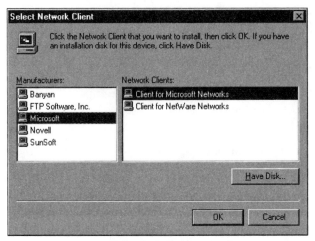

Figure 1–22: The Select Network Client dialog box

9. Windows 95 opens the *Select Device* dialog box shown in Figure 1-23. It gives you two lists for selecting the manufacturer and then the model of your adapter. As you can see, I select *3Com* as the manufacturer and *3Com EtherLink III ISA (3C509/3C509b)* as the adapter. Find and select the appropriate ones for your system and then click *OK*.

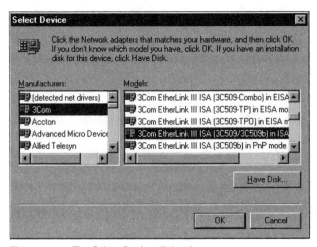

Figure 1–23: The Select Device dialog box

10. You are returned to the *Network* dialog box. As shown in Figure 1-24, four components should be listed.

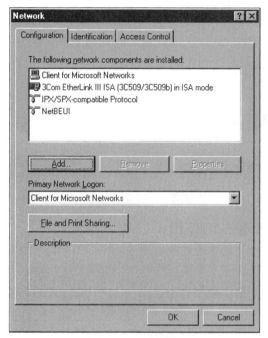

Figure 1-24: The Network dialog box displaying various components

11. Next you need to add the TCP/IP protocol, so click the *Add* button again. In the *Select Network Component Type* dialog box, select the *Protocol* component and finally click *Add*. In the dialog box that's displayed, select *Microsoft* in the *Manufacturers* list and *TCP/IP* in the *Network Protocols* list, as shown in Figure 1-25. Click *OK*.

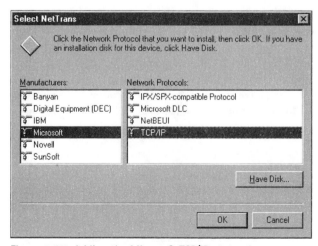

Figure 1-25: Adding the Microsoft TCP/IP protocol

12. Back at the *Network* dialog box again, you should see the screen shown in Figure 1-26. Two of the protocols, IPX and NetBEUI, are superfluous to your needs. They are optional protocols, and I prefer to select and then remove each in order. I do this to keep things simple for myself, but you may require them for your existing network so do what is best for your needs.

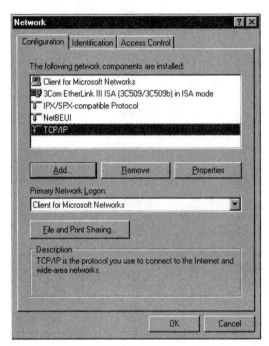

Figure 1-26: The Network dialog box displaying the installed network components

13. Now you need to configure the *Client for Microsoft Networks Properties*. Select *Client for Microsoft Networks* and then click the *Properties* button. The dialog box shown in Figure 1-27 appears. Make sure that the Log on to Windows NT domain check box is set and the Windows NT domain is WORKGROUP. The *Logon and restore network connections* check box should be set. Click *OK* and you return to the *Network* dialog box.

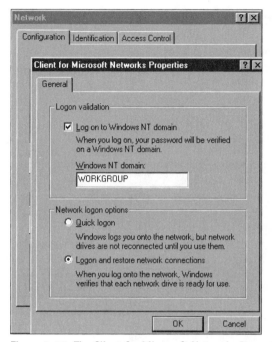

Figure 1–27: The Client for Microsoft Networks Properties dialog box

14. Next you need to configure the TCP/IP properties. Select the *TCP/IP* protocol and then click the *Properties* button.

The *TCP/IP Properties* dialog box appears. Each of the six property types is important, but to get your simple client-server network running, just set your *IP Address* option. Click the *IP Address* tab. Set the *Specify an IP address* radio button, and enter an address and a subnet address. I enter the values as shown in Figure 1-28 (192.168.1.2 and 255.255.255.0). Don't worry about the extra spaces in the text fields; this is just the way the numbers are displayed here. Click *OK* and you return to the *Network* dialog box.

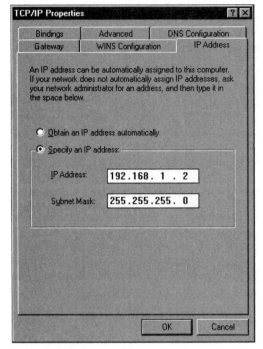

Figure 1-28: The TCP/IP Properties dialog box

You can also configure your computer to make use of the optional name service (DNS) provided by the Linux box. Recall that you were prompted to enter the Primary Nameserver during the network configuration in the Configuring TCP/IP step in the section "Configuring Linux for General Operation." To do so, click the *DNS* tab, enter the IP address for the name server – 192.168.1.254 – and the name of the network, which is *paunchy.com.*

Note: The dialog box shown in Figure 1-28 lists my IP address and subnet mask. Recall from my discussion of IP addresses that the TCP/IP protocol allows for unregistered addresses as long as they don't appear out on the Internet. You are not currently connected, so this address is a good choice. As you can see, I am using the class C address space. My Linux server is 192.168.1.254 and I have chosen 192.168.1.2 for my Windows 95 client. This is a class C address, so the standard subnet mask is 255.255.255.0, which masks out the first three octets (255) for local communications.

TIP   By typing a period (.), you move to the next IP or subnet octet (for example, *168*).

15. Back at the *Network* dialog box again, click the *Identification* tab (at the very top, middle of the window) and you see the dialog box shown in Figure 1-29. Enter the name that you want to identify your PC as on the network. Initially, you want to set your Workgroup name to WORKGROUP, because that is Samba's default.

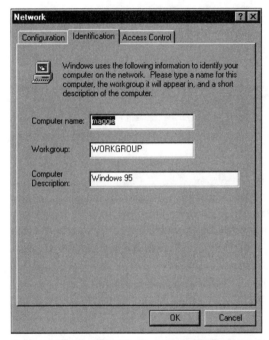

Figure 1-29: The Identification tab in the Network dialog box

16. In the *Network* dialog box, click the *Access Control* tab. Make sure the *User-level access control* radio button is activated and the *Obtain list of users and groups from* box is set to WORKGROUP, as shown in Figure 1-30. Click *OK*.

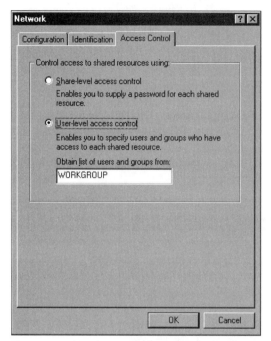

Figure 1-30: The Access Control tab in the Network dialog box

17. Windows 95 displays the *System Settings Change* window, shown previously in Figure 1-20. You must reboot your computer for the new, Samba-ready, configuration to work. After you reboot, you need to do a minimal configuration of Samba — create a lock file — on the Linux box to be able to access its files and printers.

18. Reboot your computer by clicking the *Start* button and then the *Shut Down* menu item. A *Shut Down Windows* dialog box appears. Click the *Restart* button and then click *Yes*. It may take a while to finish, so be patient.

Fixing an Unresponsive Network with the Windows 95 Registry

After reconfiguring an existing Windows 95 network configuration, I can't always browse my Linux server, even after I reinstall the network adapter, client, and protocol. The problem, as far as I can tell, is that Windows 95 loses track of what is installed. It shows the proper items installed in the *Network* window but gets confused somewhere along the line.

Windows 95 uses a system called the *Registry* to keep track of all hardware and software and configuration parameters. I use REGEDIT.EXE, which Microsoft supplies, to edit the Registry as shown in Figure 1-31 by double-clicking the keys shown. Remove the key HKEY_LOCAL_MACHINE\System\CurrentControlSet\Services\VxD\MSTCP by clicking it and using the *Edit* menu to delete it. Reenter all the components in the *Network* window as described in the following steps. This process removes the erroneous information that Windows 95 has about its network settings. After redoing the network setup and rebooting the PC, everything should work. I am not a Windows 95 expert, but this looks like a bug.

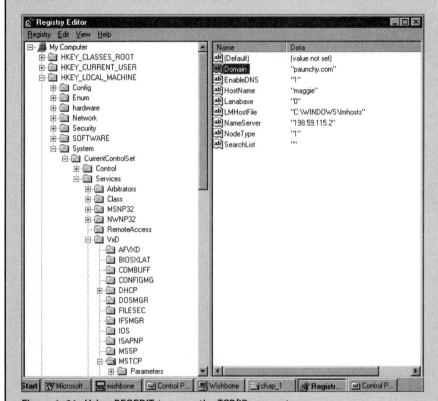

Figure 1-31: Using REGEDIT to erase the TCP/IP parameters

To redo the network setup, follow Steps 7 through 18 in the section titled "Configuring Windows 95 for Network Operations" earlier in this chapter.

Note: I understand that third-party software is available to correct Registry problems. I haven't used them but I *have* heard and read good reviews about both Norton Utility's WinDoctor and Helix Software's Nuts & Bolts being able to fix problems with the Registry.

Checking That Samba Is Running

The Red Hat installation process has installed the Samba suite of programs for you. It has also started the two Samba daemons, *smbd* and *nmbd*. It has also installed a simple configuration file, */etc/smb.conf*. It should be exporting the home directories of the Linux users to your network. However, the instructions in this chapter have only installed one user – root – on the Linux box (see Step 14 in the section "Configuring Linux for General Operation").

Note: A *daemon* is a process that runs in the background to service their requests on a continual basis.

The heart of Samba consists of two programs – *smbd* and *nmbd* – that listen for SMB requests from clients and respond with SMB services. *Smbd* handles file and print requests, and *nmbd* handles browsing. In the recent past, they could also be run on an as-needed basis where a program that runs all the time, *inetd*, launched them when they were called for. However, now *smbd* is only run as a daemon while *nmbd* can still be launched by *inetd* but will then work as a daemon. I guess it is still reasonable to run it from inetd in case the daemons stop, in which case it will be restarted the next time a request comes.

TIP You can get more Samba information as well as updates from the Samba Web site at the following address:

```
http://lake.canberra.edu.au/pub/samba/samba.html
```

This site also lists numerous *mirrors* (computers that make frequent copies of the central site's files) that you should try to make use of to lessen the burden on Canberra's server.

The configuration file that is in place will not do anything useful for you, but you can see a bit about how Samba works. I describe how to modify the configuration file in Chapter 6.

All the commands that I describe in the following paragraphs are given with absolute pathnames, except where otherwise noted. The shell prompt is assumed and not otherwise noted.

If you have a LAN running and have already connected your Windows 95 and Linux-Samba box on it, you can go directly to the Network Neighborhood and start browsing. In that case, the lock file will be created automatically.

Enter the following command to see the resources that Samba exports:

```
/usr/bin/smbstatus
```

TIP You can restart the daemons manually. However, you must do this as Root, the all-powerful user. After you log on, use the **su -** command to become root. Then enter the following commands:

```
/etc/rc.d/init.d/smb stop

/etc/rc.d/init.d/smb start
```

Verify that the two Samba daemons are running by entering the following command:

```
/bin/ps -x | /bin/grep mbd
```

This command returns the following information on the Samba daemon processes:

```
[root@bart /]# !ps

ps -x |grep mbd

  749  ?   S    0:00 smbd -D

  758  ?   S    0:00 nmbd -D

  763  p0  R    0:00 grep mbd
```

Note that the *grep* process used to filter out the text that you want to view sometimes catches itself because it includes the text you are looking for.

If you have already browsed the server, the public share is displayed. Otherwise, you see just the header with the version number. However, this utility is very useful because it shows what services (printers and files) clients are accessing.

Red Hat supplies a Samba configuration file that comes with the RPM package. It is located at */etc/smb.conf*. The *smbd* daemon reads this file when it starts. This default configuration lets you mount the home directory of the Linux user that matches the name of your Windows 95 computer as found in the Network configuration described in the section titled "Configuring Windows 95 for Network Operations." This capability is important because if your Windows 95 TCP/IP computer name matches a user name, you will automatically be able to browse and use the Samba service without having to modify the *smb.conf* file.

If you want to customize *smb.conf*, check out Appendix A, and then follow these instructions:

1. Save the *smb.conf* file to *smb.conf.orig* by entering the following command:

   ```
   cp /etc/smb.conf /etc/smb.conf.orig
   ```

2. Inspect the manual page, referred to as a *man page*, by entering the following command:

```
/usr/bin/man smb.conf
```

Pay close attention to the examples.

3. Open *smb.conf* with vi:

```
/bin/vi /etc/smb.conf
```

You can experiment on your own; see Chapter 6 for more information on *smb.conf*.

4. Samba must reread the *smb.conf* file. Run the Samba startup and stop scripts by entering the following commands:

```
/etc/rc.d/init.d/smb stop
/etc/rc.d/init.d/smb start
```

Installing the Network Wiring

For this great network to work, you must wire it together. Two primary types of wire exist: twisted-pair and Thinnet. Twisted-pair is telephone wire. Several different categories of this wire exist, the best being Category 5. Thinnet is coaxial cable such as that used for cable TV, although Thinnet has 50-ohm impedance versus 75 ohm for cable TV.

 The process of wiring your business or home for a network can be dangerous. It is best to hire a licensed electrician or other professional. But if you decide to do it, please follow all related building codes and common sense.

Twisted-pair is also referred to as 10baseT — 10 means 10 megabits per second, and T refers to twisted-pair. To work, it requires either an active or passive hub or concentrator. It offers the advantage that individual hosts can be connected and disconnected independent of each other. The wiring can be conveniently connected to phone jacks. The disadvantage is that it costs extra to purchase and maintain the hub. The price of passive hubs has fallen below $100 so it is no longer very expensive to use this technology.

It is possible to connect two 10baseT adapters directly without an active hub, but it requires a special cross-over cable. I suggest you look at the newsgroups *comp.os.linux.network* or *comp.os.linux.answers* for instructions. The newsgroup *comp.os.linux.answers* contains scores of HOWTOs on most subjects concerning the operation of Linux. Check it out.

Thinnet is also referred to as 10base2. Its main advantage is that it's a passive system and requires no active circuitry to work; it simply connects to each Ethernet transceiver on the bus. Its main disadvantage is that it's a wave guide or transmission line and must be properly terminated to work. That means that each end of the cable must have a 50-ohm terminator attached to it, and a proper BNC tee connector must be used at each Ethernet adapter. If it is not terminated or the cable is broken (either by disconnecting it or breaking it), the entire network will not work.

I use Thinnet on my network at home. I have also used it professionally. In many ways, it is cumbersome, but Thinnet's passive (does not need electronic hubs), inexpensive nature makes it ideal for learning about your client-server network. This is the system I am using for this book.

Using coaxial cables (that is, cable TV–type wiring) can present special problems. It is possible to conduct dangerous currents across these types of cables if your building's grounding is not connected to a central ground. This situation occurs when one power circuit is grounded at one location and another circuit is grounded elsewhere. Note that by spanning the two locations with a Thinnet (10base2) coaxial cable, you have a conductor that bypasses the building grounds. If the Thinnet cable touches an open electrical circuit, or a short circuit occurs in one of the connected computers, or the building's grounds are at different potentials, disaster can occur to your computer equipment and you! Be careful and forewarned.

It Works!

Hang on. You are in the homestretch now! You only need to authenticate your Windows 95 computer with the Linux/Samba server, and you will have access to its disk over the network.

The Red Hat Samba configuration specifies *user* security. To access a Samba resource, a Linux user name must match a Samba share name. I have not had you configure any regular Linux users that you could match up with yet. However, the Red Hat installation has configured the user *root* by default. Therefore, you need to log off your Windows 95 system and then log on again as the user *root* and enter the same password as you set on your Linux box. After you log on to your Windows 95 box as *root*, you will appear to the Linux box as *root*, too. If this seems to be dangerous do not worry because you will only be able to access the home directory of *root – /root*. This is just like any other user home directory except that it is owned by *root*.

1. Log out of Windows 95 by clicking the *Start* button at the lower-left corner of the Desktop. Choose *Close all programs and log on as another user* and then select *Yes*. Your system closes all open programs and prompts you for your user name and password.

2. The first dialog box asks you to log in as a Windows 95 user. It defaults to the last user name that was logged on. Press *Shift+Tab* to go to the user name box and enter the name **root**. *Tab* down to the password and enter the same one that you used in the Red Hat Linux configuration for *root*.

3. If you have never logged on as *Root* before, Windows 95 will prompt you for the password that you just entered twice. This step confirms that you got it right. Reenter the password in both boxes. The system then creates the user ID Root, which you can use in the future.

TIP   The Windows 95 user name is important for Samba only if Samba is using *share* security. This is the default but has been replaced by *user* security in the Red Hat configuration. You can specify it by modifying */etc/smb.conf* from *security = user* to *security = share*. Frankly, it's a much more confusing setting because Samba uses four to five steps to authenticate a share request — the sequence is described in the man page *smb.conf* in the section titled "Note About Username/Password Validation." The user security default is much simpler. If your user name/password combination matches a Linux user name/password pair, you will gain access to any Samba share that belongs to the Linux user name. In the long run, this is the method to follow.

4. The question in the next dialog box looks ominous but isn't. The system thinks that it must find a domain server, but that is unnecessary in most situations and certainly for this example. Simply click the *OK* button.

When your computer has restarted, use the following steps to view your new Linux-Samba server.

5. Double-click the *Network Neighborhood* icon (generally in the upper-left corner of your screen) to open the *Network Neighborhood* window shown in Figure 1-32.

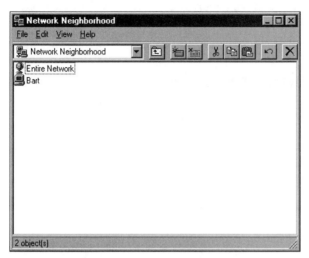

Figure 1–32: The Network Neighborhood window

6. Double-click the icon for your Linux-Samba server. In my case, it is the *Bart* icon. The password that I entered for Windows 95 matches the one for Root on the Samba server, and I am given access to the Samba share that provides access to the home directory of Root as shown in Figure 1-33!

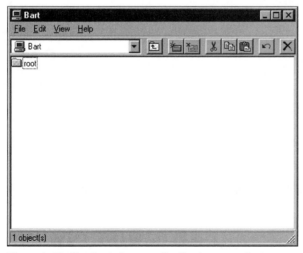

Figure 1–33: The Root share on the Samba server Bart

7. Finally, if you double-click the *Root* icon you will see the contents of that directory. Because it has just recently been created, the only files are "dot" configuration files. (They are files whose names have a period as the first character. The default of the *ls* command is to not display files like that — you need to specify the *-a* option to do so. Because they are not displayed by default, the convention is to use them as configuration files.) Figure 1-34 shows the contents of the *root* directory.

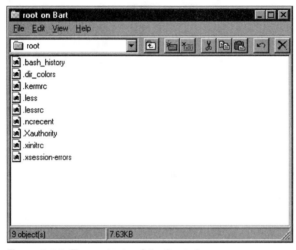

Figure 1-34: The contents of the Root share

If it didn't work, don't worry. It's probably a simple problem. Check out Chapter 2 for help with troubleshooting.

Red Hat Linux is already running the Samba daemons. If you have your Windows box set up with TCP/IP and a Microsoft Network client, you should be able to browse your new Linux-Samba server. Go to the Network Neighborhood and see if you can do it.

If your Samba server does not appear in your Network Neighborhood, you can sometimes find it with Microsoft Explorer. The following steps describe that method:

1. Click the Windows 95 *Start* button. It is generally located in the lower-left corner of your screen.

2. Open the *Find* menu.

3. Open the *Computer* menu.

4. Enter the name of your Samba server in the *Find: Computer* dialog box. Click the *Find Now* button. If the Windows 95 Explorer finds your server, it displays an icon representing the server. You can double-click the icon and access the server's resources as if you had accessed it through the Network Neighborhood.

Summary

This chapter covered the following topics:

◆ Taking care of the preparation and the considerations necessary for constructing a client-server network.

◆ Choosing from the various Linux distributions. I use Red Hat Linux because of its mature installation and upgrade system, its helpful configuration process (which runs Samba as a default), and its perceived future commercial viability.

◆ Preparing your hard disk for installation by using two alternative methods. One method uses the entire disk, erasing all data; the other method shrinks your current partition and allows Linux to reside with MS-DOS, or other operating systems.

◆ Installing Linux and Samba. I provide detailed instructions to help the novice as well as experienced users through the entire process.

◆ Reconfiguring Windows 95 for Samba. I provide detailed instructions to help the novice as well as experienced users through the entire process.

◆ Wiring your computers together. Thinnet coaxial cables are used because of their low cost and simplicity.

◆ Browsing the Samba resources from the Network Neighborhood. This capability gives you a way of seeing what is available and then connecting to it.

◆ Using the Microsoft Explorer as another method for finding and attaching to Samba shares.

Chapter 2

Troubleshooting

IN THIS CHAPTER

- ◆ Understanding the philosophy of troubleshooting
- ◆ Solving an example problem by using the Microsoft Troubleshooter
- ◆ Examining the Microsoft Troubleshooter fault tree
- ◆ Diagnosing the client-server network using Paul's Troubleshooter

FIXING PROBLEMS WITH computers and networks is the one constant of systems administration. The primary job of a systems administrator is to minimize problems by designing and managing the network properly and anticipating problems. That is why you install a tape backup drive on a server and use it regularly to back up your data. Because you can't predict everything, however, you must learn how to deal with problems as they occur.

Troubleshooting is more an art than a science. The more intimately you know your system, the easier it is to deal with problems. Some people can see a problem and its solution better than others can. Unfortunately, you can't teach talent. However, the art of systems administration also includes some fairly simple science. You must deal with any problem that arises in a systematic fashion. You need to identify the problem and then systematically eliminate each possible cause until you solve the problem.

Chapter 1 guides you through the process of creating a simple client-server network. However, that simple network has tens of thousands of code lines within its simple exterior. The network has many subsystems — disks, memory, interface cards, and so on — as well as all those interacting protocols (for example, *udp*, *tcp*, *icmp*, *ip*). Many things need to work together in precisely the right way, and just one bad subsystem can prevent that simple system from working. If something goes wrong and the network doesn't work, how do you fix it? The best way is to identify exactly what is causing the problem. The best way to do that is to eliminate each possible problem, one by one. This chapter describes some simple methods for solving problems this way.

Troubleshooting with the Fault Tree

As I have already stated, the better you know your system, the greater the likelihood that you can fix it. If you don't try to solve problems, you won't fully understand your system; if you don't fully understand your system, you won't be able to fix your network. So, make a point to learn your system – and systems in general – by solving problems. You learn by struggling to get the simple things to work; then you struggle with the more complex problems. I have set up dozens of networks in my career, but I encountered some problems that I had never seen before while I was writing the example in Chapter 1. By solving those problems, I gained additional insights about my own system, and now I can solve problems just a little bit better than before. You never stop learning.

The formal model that I use for understanding troubleshooting is the *fault tree*. In a fault tree, the trunk represents the problem, and each branch represents a potential cause of the problem. This conceptual model simplifies the process of finding the solution. What if the client in Chapter 1 can't communicate with the server? If you are new to networks, this may seem like an impossible problem. However, the answer soon becomes apparent if you break down the problem into distinct parts.

How do you break down the problem? First, look at Figure 2-1, which shows a tree of the possible answers to the problem. The first branch on the left involves problems with the physical connection: Do you have a network adapter? Is the Thinnet cable connected properly? Do you have a break in the cable? The second branch deals with the network interface with Windows 95: Have you installed the network interface to the adapter or Microsoft Client for Networks or the TCP/IP protocol? The third branch follows the thread of the network interface on the Linux box.

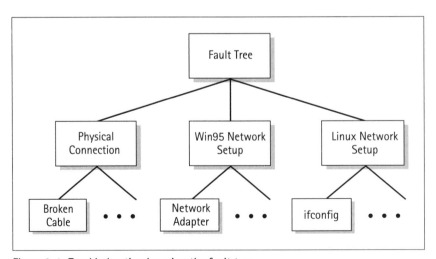

Figure 2-1: Troubleshooting by using the fault tree

Each subbranch deals with the specifics of the more general problem. For example, if the problem relates to the physical connection, you can trace the problem to one of several causes: no adapter, a misconfigured adapter, a break in the wire, a faulty connector, or no connector at all. Or if the problem involves the network configuration, you know that it can be only one of several things. By using the fault tree, you can break down any problem into simpler ones and eventually into a binary one.

Your goal in troubleshooting problems with your network is first to identify the problem and then pick a plan of attack.

Solving a Sample Problem

Microsoft provides a helpful, interactive fault tree analyzer called the Network Troubleshooter. You access this informative tool via the Help system:

1. Click the Windows 95 *Start* button and then choose *Help* from the resulting menu. As shown in Figure 2-2, Windows 95 displays the *Help Topics: Windows Help* window.

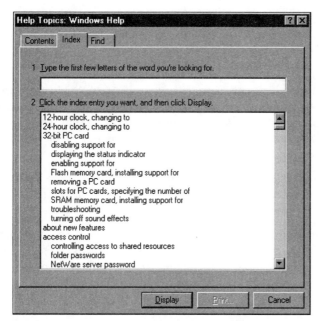

Figure 2-2: The Help Topics: Windows Help window

2. Click the *Contents* tab and then double-click the *Troubleshooter* icon. (*Note:* As you can see, Windows 95 also has a number of different troubleshooters that can come in handy.)

3. Windows 95 opens the *Network Troubleshooter* window, shown in Figure 2-3.

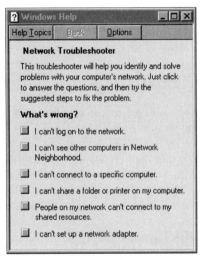

Figure 2-3: The Network Troubleshooter

For this example, I assume that you have configured Windows 95 and mistakenly failed to install the network client. For instance, perhaps you have not configured a *Client for Microsoft Networks*. Thus, you can't get the *Network Neighborhood* window, because Windows 95 has no way to access the network.

4. In the Network Troubleshooter, click the button labeled *I can't see other computers in Network Neighborhood.* The Network Troubleshooter responds by opening the window shown in Figure 2-4.

5. Click the button next to the explanation that comes closest to describing your problem: *I can't see any computers on the network.* (In some cases, you have to make the best of the options that are available to you, even if they don't fit perfectly.)

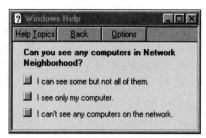

Figure 2-4: The Network Troubleshooter asks questions
to help you track down the cause of the problem.

The Troubleshooter opens another window, shown in Figure 2-5, to ask if
you see the *Entire Network* icon in Network Neighborhood.

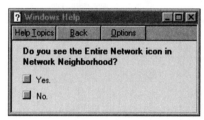

Figure 2-5: No Network Neighborhood window

6. Again, use your best judgment and answer *No*.

   Figure 2-6 shows the Troubleshooter's reply. This window gives you the
   probable explanation — you do not have the network software installed —
   and offers three paths that you can take.

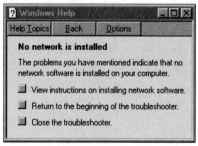

Figure 2-6: The Network Troubleshooter
identifies the problem.

7. Click the button for the option labeled *View instructions on installing the network software*, and the Troubleshooter opens another help window, shown in Figure 2-7. This window details a four-step process for correcting the problem. It also gives a two-part explanation as to why your system isn't working. It also gives a shortcut to the *Network* window.

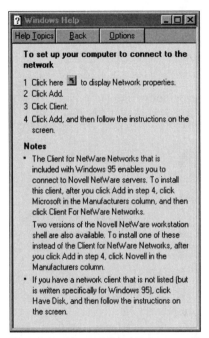

Figure 2–7: Network Troubleshooter tells you how to solve the problem.

8. Click the shortcut button, and the Network Troubleshooter opens the *Network* dialog box shown in Figure 2-8. The Troubleshooter was correct; you have no Microsoft Client or other Client installed. If this were a real problem, you would fix it by clicking the *Add* button and then proceeding to install the Microsoft Client for Microsoft Networks (described in Chapter 1).

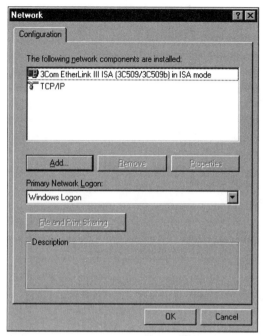

Figure 2-8: The Network Troubleshooter takes you straight to the dialog box you use for solving the problem.

That was a good example of troubleshooting. You often encounter relatively simple problems such as leaving out an essential software component. The path to the answer was complicated by the real-world problem of having to add the incomplete questions that the Troubleshooter asks. Nothing's perfect but every tool helps.

For relatively inexperienced systems administrators, little problems like that can seem impossible to fix. But if you follow the Troubleshooter's logic, problem solving becomes less mysterious. There is nothing mysterious or even outstanding about it. However, it is a good tool for your portfolio and it demonstrates the fault tree method. As you become more experienced, that kind of thinking becomes second-nature, and you will be able to solve more complex problems.

Microsoft's Network Troubleshooter

In this section, I examine the Troubleshooter in more detail. As you may have guessed, I like it both as a problem-solving tool and as a teaching aid. Further examination is helpful to your education in the art and science of systems administration.

The first menu in the Network Troubleshooter offers a synopsis of all the primary problems that you can have with Windows 95 networking. Figure 2-9 shows the menu again.

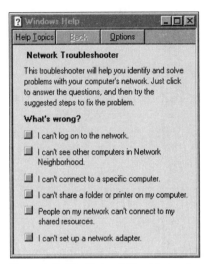

Figure 2-9: The Network Troubleshooter, again

The first menu helps you identify what you can't do — that is, the problem. To work toward a solution for that problem, the Troubleshooter queries you further to traverse a fault tree and solve the problem. The pseudocode in Listing 2-1 shows all the branches in the Troubleshooter's fault tree.

Listing 2-1: Pseudocode for the Microsoft Troubleshooter (TS) fault tree

```
I can't log on to the network.
    If you are using the Client for Microsoft Networks
        If no domain server could validate your password
            Go to Network properties and make sure Log On To
                Windows NT  Domain is checked.
            If you can log on now. Close the
                Troubleshooter, then
                Your problem is solved.
            If not, then
                TS failed. (See Note for further
                    suggestions.)
        If a duplicate computer name exists on the network,
            then
            Go to Network properties, select the
                Identification tab, and enter a different
```

name.
If you forgot your password, then
    Have your administrator give you a new one.
If a different problem occurred, then
    TS failed. (See Note for further suggestions.)
If you are using Novell NetWare, then
    If you see the message "Server name is not valid or
        server is not available,"
    then
        Go to Network properties and open the properties
            for Client for NetWare Networks. Make sure
            the correct preferred server is listed.
            Consult with your administrator if
            necessary.
    No domain server could validate your password.
    If the network processed a login script when it
        shouldn't have,
    then
        Go to Network properties and open the properties
            for Client for NetWare Networks. Make sure
            the correct preferred server is listed.
            Consult with your administrator if
            necessary.

    If the network did NOT process a login script when
        it should have,
    then
        Go to Network properties and open the properties
            for Client for NetWare Networks. Make sure
            the Enable Logon Script Processing is
            checked. Consult with your administrator if
            necessary.
        If that fixed the problem, then
            Exit TS
        Else,
            TS failed. (See Note for further
            suggestions.)
    If you forgot your password, then
        Have your administrator give you a new one.
    If a different problem occurred, then
        TS failed. (See Note for further suggestions.)

If you are using a different network, then
    TS failed. (See Note for further suggestions.)

```
If you don't know, then
    Go to Network properties and list the clients.
    If you are using the Client for Microsoft Networks,
        then
        If no domain server could validate my password,
            then
            Go to Network properties and make sure that
                Log On to Windows NT Domain is checked.
            If that solved the problem, then
                    Exit TS.
            Else,
                    TS failed. (See Note for further
                    suggestions.)
        If a duplicate computer name exists on the
            network,
            then
            Go to Network properties, click the
                Identification tab, and enter a
                different name for your computer.
        If you forgot your password, then
Have your administrator give you a new
                    one.
        If a different problem occurred, then
                    TS failed. (See Note for further
                    suggestions.)
    If you are using the Client for NetWare Networks,
        then
        If you see the message "Server name is not valid
            or server is not available",
            then
            Go to Network properties and open the
                properties for Client for NetWare
                Networks. Make sure the correct
                preferred server is listed. Consult with
                your administrator if necessary.
        No domain server could validate your password.
        If the network processed a login script when it
            shouldn't have,
            then
            Go to Network properties and open the
                properties for Client for NetWare
                Networks. Make sure the correct
                preferred server is listed. Consult with
                your administrator if necessary.
```

If the network did NOT process a login script
when it should have,
then
Go to Network properties and open the
properties for Client for NetWare
Networks. Make sure the Enable Logon
Script Processing is checked. Consult
with your administrator if necessary.
If that fixed the problem, then
Exit TS
Else,
TS failed. (See Note for further
suggestions.)
If you forgot your password, then
Have your administrator give you a new one.
If a different problem occurred, then
TS failed. (See Note for further
suggestions.)
If you are using a different network, then
TS failed. (See Note for further
suggestions.)

I can't see other computers in Network Neighborhood.
If you can see some but not all of them, then
Go to Network properties, click the Identification
tab, and specify a different workgroup.
If the problem is solved, then
Exit TS
Else,
TS failed.
(See Note for further suggestions.)
If you see only my computer, then
Go to Network properties, click the Identification
tab, and specify a different workgroup.
If the problem is solved, then
Exit TS
Else,
TS failed.
(See Note for further suggestions.)
If you still can't find it, then
TS failed. (See Note for further suggestions.)
If you can't see any computers on the network.
If you cannot see the Entire Network icon, then
The network is not installed.

```
                    See my instructions in Chapter 1 or
                    view the instructions listed in the TS.
            Else,
                    Double-click the Entire Network icon.
    If you can see other computers on the network, then
                Go to Network properties, click
                the Identification tab, and
                select a new workgroup name.
        If the problem is solved, then
            Exit TS.
        Else,
            TS failed (See Note for further suggestions.)
        Else,
            If you can not see other computers
            on the network, then
                    Check the physical cable connections
                    and devices.
        If the problem is solved, then
                Exit TS.
        Else,
                Go to Network properties and see if
                the correct client is installed.
            If NOT, then
                Click Add, Client, and Add again. Follow
                the instructions.
            Else,
                Go to Network properties and see if
                the correct protocol is installed.
            If NOT, then
                    Click Add, Protocol, and Add
                    again. Follow the instructions.
            Else,
                    Select Network properties and make
                    sure the correct network adapter is
                    installed.
                    If NOT, then
                        Select Network properties
                        and make sure that Log
                        On To Windows NT Domain
                        is checked.
                    If the problem is solved, then
                        Exit TS.
                    Else
                        TS failed. (See Note for
```

```
                                further suggestions.)
                        Else,
                                The problem is solved. Exit TS.
        Else,
            Troubleshooter failed.
            If not, the network software is not installed.
                TS points to a solution.
                    Restart the Troubleshooter.
                Close the Troubleshooter.
```

I can't connect to a specific computer.

```
    If you can't find the computer on the network, then
        Use the Find Computer functions to find it.
        If you find it, then
            Open it.
            If you can view its resources, then
                You may not have permission to access it.
            Else, if you can NOT view its resources, then
                It may not have any available.
        Else, if you don't find it, then
            It may have a problem; contact your
            administrator.
    If you find the computer on the network, but you can't
        view the shared resources, then
            The computer may not currently have any shared
            resources available. Contact your administrator.
    If you can view the shared resources, but you can't
        connect to them, then
            You may not have permission to use its
            resources. Contact your administrator.
    Else, if a different problem occurred, then
        TS failed. (See Note for further suggestions.)
```

You can't share a folder or printer on my computer.

```
    If the File and Print Sharing button is available in
        Network properties, then
        If both boxes are not checked, then
            Check (activate) them.
            If you can share your files, then
                Your problem is solved, exit TS.
            Else, if you are still having problems, then
                TS failed.
    Else, if it is not available, then
        Either your network does not support file sharing,
```

or it is not enabled for that feature (ask your
administrator for help).

People on my network can't connect to my shared resources.
    If other clients on the network can see you in the
    Network Neighborhood, then
        If they see the correct shares, then
            Sharing is enabled on your computer (see Network
            properties).
            If File & Print Sharing button is
            available then,
                Turn it on.
                If it does not work, then
                    TS failed.
            If File & Print Sharing button not available,
                then
                    Either your network does not support file
                    sharing or your Network Administrator has
                    not enabled it.
    Else, if other network clients can NOT see you in the
    Network Neighborhood, then
        If the correct client is NOT listed in Network
            properties, then
                Go to Network properties and add the
                client.
        If the correct client is listed, then
            If the correct protocol is NOT listed, then
                Go to Network properties and add the
                protocol.
        Else, if the correct protocol is listed, then
            In the Network properties window, select the
            network adapter, then its properties, and
            finally its Bindings tab. Make sure the
            correct protocol button is checked.

I can't set up a network adapter.
    If you've set up new hardware on your computer recently,
        then
            If your Device Manager reported any conflicts,
                then
                    Start the Hardware Conflict
                    Troubleshooter (see Help: Find) and
                    restart the Network Troubleshooter
                    afterwards.

```
Else, if it did not, then
    Check the network cable.
    If the computers are available on the network,
        then
            Your problem is solved; exit
            Troubleshooter.
    Else, if they are not available, then
        Go to Network properties.
        If you are NOT using the correct client,
            then
                Go to Network properties and install
                the correct client.
            If problems persist, then
                Start Network Troubleshooter again.
        If you are using the correct client, then
            If you are NOT using the correct
            protocol, then
                Go to Network properties and install
                the correct protocol.
                    If the problem persists, then
                        Start Network Troubleshooter
                        again.
            If you are using the correct protocol,
                then
                    Go to Network properties and
                    make sure the adapter recognizes
                    that protocol.
            If the problem persists, then
                Check Network properties and
                make sure that Log On To Windows
                NT Domain is checked.
                    If the problem persists,
                    then
                        TS failed.
```

Note: If the TS fails, consider the following possible causes for the problems with your network:

◆ A duplicate computer name exists on the network.

◆ You forgot your network password.

◆ A problem unknown by the Troubleshooter occurred – it could have nothing to do with the network.

The Troubleshooter contains a lot of information. Much of it is repetitive, of course, but if you follow the logical structure, you can see how it thinks. The logic is general and can be adapted for solving almost any technical problem.

The Troubleshooter can't solve every problem. But even in those cases, it still serves its purpose. Sometimes, it is useful to know what you don't know. In those cases, it narrows down the areas that you must search and frees up your resources to look elsewhere.

The original Windows 95 network configuration seems to have a bug. (I have been informed that the version released in late 1996 may fix this problem.) While I was preparing the first two chapters in this book, I went through the process of configuring my network many times. Sometimes, I inexplicably could not access either the Samba services or the general network; other times, neither could be accessed. I performed the setup exactly the same and had everything in order. I was perplexed and discouraged.

I finally started looking through the Windows 95 Registry, which keeps all the configuration information on every aspect of the machine. Theoretically, the Network manager that you have been using should update everything in the Registry. I used REGEDIT.EXE to fix the problem. I started by removing the register *key* (shown in Figure 2-10) that stores some of the information about Windows 95 in the network (the TCP/IP settings) setup:

```
HKEY_LOCAL_MACHINES\System\CurrentControlSet\Services\VxD\MSTCP
```

Then, I reentered all the components in the network window (described in Chapter 1). After rebooting the PC, everything worked. Apparently, Windows 95 can get confused after two or more network reconfigurations.

I started by removing the register *key* (shown in Figure 2-10) that stores some of the information about Windows 95 in the TCP/IP setup:

```
HKEY_LOCAL_MACHINES\System\CurrentControlSet\ServicesVxD\MSTCP
```

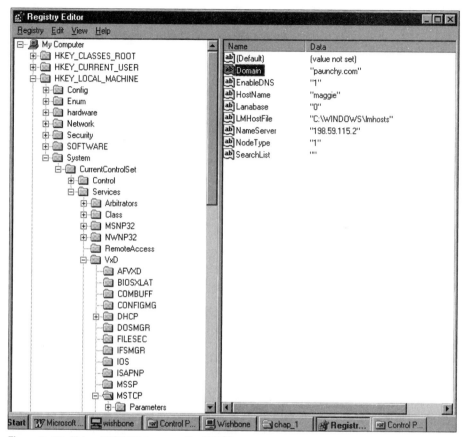

Figure 2-10: Using REGEDIT to erase the TCP/IP parameters

Tools of the Trade

When you need to solve a problem, you must use the tools you have at your dis-
posal – tools such as the Network Troubleshooter. An auto mechanic who figures
out that you have a bad spark plug is of no use without a socket wrench and an
extra plug. In the following sections, I discuss some of the other tools you can use
to solve problems with your network.

Diagnosing the Linux Box: Paul's Troubleshooter

Your Linux box is the foundation of your network. It must be set up correctly for anything to run. If you carefully followed the installation instructions that I provided in Chapter 1, your network should be up and running like a champ. If it isn't running, or if you have some unusual setup, you can check for several different causes. The following sections describe several steps you can take. Think of the guidelines I offer in these sections as Paul's Troubleshooter.

If the network on your Linux computer is not working, use the following sections as a simple fault tree that you can follow to troubleshoot your network. I divide this Troubleshooter into two major areas: Linux networking and Samba. The Troubleshooter is not comprehensive, but it does cover some of the typical problems that I have encountered.

CHECKING LINUX NETWORKING

You can take several steps to check your network for problems. The following sections identify common problem areas to check. Over time, you'll find that these areas account for most of the problems you see.

IS THE POWER TURNED ON?   First, verify that you have turned on the power. Sounds simple, but hey, sometimes the simplest things go wrong. This is the problem I am best able to solve.

HAS YOUR NETWORK CABLE BEEN COMPROMISED?   Thinnet is topologically a bus structure. In other words, each computer that is on a Thinnet cable is connected electrically to all the other computers in the network. Each computer sees all the network traffic on that cable. If any part of that bus is compromised, all traffic ceases. For example, if you disconnect the terminator at either end of the cable, all communication ends. The best way to troubleshoot that type of problem is to start at one end and work your way down the line. Try to get just two computers connected, then three, and eventually you'll find the fault.

Determining whether your network cable has been compromised requires addressing the following issues:

◆ Make sure the Bayonet Nut Connector (BNC) connectors are securely attached if you are using Thinnet cables.

◆ Look at the interface between the coaxial cable and the BNC connector to make sure they are in good physical contact. Sometimes, the cable can pull out a little bit so the little pin in the center of the cable does not reach the other end of the BNC connector.

◆ Look at the cable itself and make sure it hasn't been cut or crushed.

- If you have an ohmmeter, test the continuity of both the center conductor and the outer shield conductor. Make sure the cable is not attached to anything.

- Make sure that the center conductor is not touching (which would be a short-circuit) the shield (the thin, braided metal wires immediately under the outer insulation).

- Make sure that each end of the cable has a 50ohm terminator attached to it. A Thinnet cable must be terminated or else it will not work, just as it will not work if the cable is broken. The reason for this is the radio frequency (RF) signal reflects from the unterminated end and interferes with the incoming signals.

If you have a cable that you know is good, try substituting it. The idea is to eliminate as many segments that you are unsure about as possible. If you have just two computers in close proximity and you suspect a problem with the cable you are using, all you can do is try another cable. If the computers are far apart and rely on several segments or a long cable, try moving them close together and using one short segment. If you have three or more computers, try getting just two of them working together. Then try adding another one. Proceed until you find the faulty segment.

IS YOUR NETWORK ADAPTER CONFIGURED CORRECTLY?   When I list commands or programs to execute in the following paragraphs, I show the absolute pathname. Red Hat sets up the path for most of these commands in the root environment in much the same way that DOS uses the PATH= environmental variable. By giving the entire path, however, I ensure that my examples will work no matter how you set up your environment, and I also give you a peek into the Linux file system.

Rather than give generic parameters, I use my own values (such as my IP address) in the commands that I describe in the following paragraphs. I also italicize the parameters. Use your own values where appropriate.

Sometimes a startup script is misconfigured and the startup screen goes by but you don't see an error message. Login as *root* and, from the shell prompt, enter the following command:

```
/sbin/ifconfig
```

You see a listing of two different interfaces, as shown in Listing 2-2, or three interfaces if you have PPP configured. (See Chapter 8 for information on how to use PPP to establish network connections to the Internet.) The program *ifconfig* tells the Linux kernel that you have a network adapter and gives it an IP address and network mask. This is the first step in connecting your Linux box to your network.

Listing 2-2: Network interfaces listed

```
lo        Link encap:Local Loopback
          inet addr:127.0.0.1  Bcast:127.255.255.255  Mask:255.0.0.0
          UP BROADCAST LOOPBACK RUNNING  MTU:3584  Metric:1
          RX packets:217 errors:0 dropped:0 overruns:0
          TX packets:217 errors:0 dropped:0 overruns:0

eth0      Link encap:Ethernet  HWaddr 00:A0:24:2F:30:69
          inet addr:192.168.1.254  Bcast:192.168.1.255  Mask:255.255.255.0
          UP BROADCAST RUNNING MULTICAST  MTU:1500  Metric:1
          RX packets:730 errors:0 dropped:0 overruns:0
          TX packets:556 errors:0 dropped:0 overruns:0
          Interrupt:10 Base address:0x330
```

If you do not see the line containing lo, which is the loopback interface, or eth0, which is your network adapter, then your physical network connections have not been set up correctly. The loopback interface is not a physical device; it is used for the network software's internal workings. It must be present for the network adapter to be configured.

If the loopback interface is not present, enter the following command:

```
ifconfig lo 127.0.0.1
```

If the network adapter – generally an Ethernet card – is not present, enter the following command:

```
ifconfig eth0 192.168.1.254
```

Because this is a class C network address, *ifconfig* automatically defaults to the 255.255.255.0 netmask.

If you have an unusual netmask – which you shouldn't – enter the following command:

```
ifconfig eth0 192.168.1.254 netmask 255.255.255.252
```

Enter **/sbin/ifconfig** and you should see your network adapter displayed correctly. If it is not, examine the manual page on *ifconfig*. Display this manual page by entering the following command and then pressing *Enter*:

```
man ifconfig
```

You can page through the document by pressing *Enter* to go line by line, the spacebar to go forward a page at a time, *Ctrl+B* to page backward, or *Q* to quit. It shows a great deal of information on what and how *ifconfig* works.

If you are still having problems, look inside the Linux kernel and see which devices it has. Enter the command to change to a special directory where process information is located (it is called *proc* for short):

```
cd /proc/net
/bin/cat dev
```

You should see a line with your network adapter listed. If you don't, then Linux does not know that it exists.

If your network device is listed, you may have an interrupt or address conflict. Look at the list of interrupts and then the *I/O* addresses of all the devices that the kernel knows about by entering the following commands:

```
cat /proc/interrupts
cat /proc/ioports
```

The I/O address is either the actual location in memory or the port address where the device – such as the network adapter – is accessed by the microprocessor (that is, your Pentium or 486 chip). The interrupt is a way that the microprocessor is stopped – or interrupted – from whatever it is doing to process information that has arrived at the device that is sending the interrupt. Thus, when I stop to save this text, my Windows 95 computer sends this new information to my Linux server. The Ethernet adapter sends packets containing this text and the Ethernet adapter on the Linux side collects a bunch of packets and then sends an interrupt to the processor. Linux picks up on what is happening and directs the information to Samba, which takes care of saving the data in the correct file. See Chapters 6 and 7 for details of that process.

Listing 2-3 shows my Linux system's interrupts. An interrupt is a signal that a computer device, such as a disk or a mouse, uses to tell the microprocessor that it needs to be serviced. (An interrupt is often referred to as an IRQ.)

Listing 2-3: My Linux interrupts

```
 0:      406446    timer
 1:           2    keyboard
 2:           0    cascade
 4:          20 +  serial
 8:           1 +  rtc
10:         897     3c509
13:           1    math error
14:       23150 +  ide0
```

Listing 2-4 shows the Linux box's input/output (I/O) addresses. An I/O address is a location in the computer's memory that the microprocessor uses to communicate with a device like a mouse.

Listing 2-4: My Linux I/O addresses

```
0000-001f : dma1
0020-003f : pic1
0040-005f : timer
0060-006f : keyboard
0070-007f : rtc
0080-009f : dma page reg
00a0-00bf : pic2
00c0-00df : dma2
00f0-00ff : npu
01f0-01f7 : ide0
02f8-02ff : serial(auto)
0330-033f : 3c509
03c0-03df : vga+
03f0-03f5 : floppy
03f6-03f6 : ide0
03f7-03f7 : floppy DIR
03f8-03ff : serial(auto)
```

Look for your network adapter. In my case, it is the 3C509. No conflicts exist, or I would not be writing this page because my server would not work. If a conflict exists, you have to reconfigure the adapter. In my case, I run a DOS program called *3C509.EXE* and set the adapter's parameters in its EEPROM. Older adapters may have jumpers or little switches called DIP switches to set. If you think you have to do this, remember to write down the other device's interrupts and *I/O* addresses so you don't end up conflicting with something else.

You also may be using a kernel that does not have networking installed. (This is unlikely in the newer versions of Red Hat because the daemon *kerneld* will automatically load networking (and other) modules on demand. However, it is still informative to go ahead and look at these files to gain an understanding of how Linux works.) From the */proc/net* directory, display the networking devices by entering the following commands:

```
cd /proc/net
cat dev
```

Listing 2-5 shows that the kernel is configured for loopback, SLIP, PPP, IP tunneling, a dummy interface, and most importantly, an Ethernet (eth0). Ignoring the other interfaces for now, the Ethernet is what you want to see. If you don't see it, you may have an unsupported network adapter or a defective or misconfigured one. Red Hat installs, by default, the daemon *kerneld* that automatically loads modules as they are needed. You can look back at the results of your boot process by using the *dmesg* command. Look for a message that says `delaying eth0 configuration`. That most likely means that Linux was not able to load the network adapter module or the adapter is not working.

Listing 2-5: Linux kernel network configuration

```
Inter-|   Receive                       |  Transmit
face  |packets errs drop fifo frame|packets errs drop  fifo colls carrier
lo:       116    0    0    0    0      116    0    0     0    0     0
eth0:   16292   19   19   23   19     7245    0    0     0   54     0
```

Sometimes, a network adapter will only work if you compile its driver directly into the kernel. This is the case for me when I use two 3Com 3C509 adapters for my gateway in Chapter 10. For information on building a kernel from source, see Chapter 7.

IS YOUR NETWORK ROUTING CONFIGURED CORRECTLY?   This is also an easy thing to get confused. You do not need to set up routing outside your LAN yet, but Linux needs to know where to send packets on its own network. Look at your routing by entering the following command:

```
/sbin/netstat -r -n
```

You should see a listing like the one shown in Listing 2-6. The *destination* is the location – IP address – that you want to send packets to; for instance, the address 192.168.1.0 refers to my local network. The *gateway* is the address (computer or router) where the packets need to be sent so they can find their way to their destination. In the case where the destination is the local network, then the 0.0.0.0 means "no gateway." The *genmask* is used to separate the parts of the IP address that are used for the network address from the host number (more on that in Chapter 10). The flags are used to indicate things like *U* for up and *G* for gateway. The metric is used as a measure of how far a packet has to travel to its destination (a number greater than 32 is considered to be infinite). The next two flags – *Ref* and *Use* – are not important for this discussion. Finally the *Iface* is self-explanatory.

Listing 2-6: Routing table displayed

```
Kernel IP routing table
Destination     Gateway       Genmask         Flags     MSS Window  irtt Iface
192.168.1.0     0.0.0.0       255.255.255.0   U        1500 0          0 eth0
127.0.0.0       0.0.0.0       255.0.0.0       U        3584 0          0 lo
```

You must have a route to the loopback interface (also referred to as *lo*), which is the 127.0.0.0 address.

If you are missing either or both parameters, you must set them. To set the loop-back device – which must be set for the network adapter to work – enter the following command:

```
/sbin/route add -net 127.0.0.0
```

To set the route for the network adapter and your local network, enter the following command:

```
route add -net 192.168.1.0
```

This route is assigned automatically to your network adapter. However, if you wish to assign it explicitly, enter the command as follows:

```
route add -net 192.168.1.0 dev eth0
```

Run **netstat -r -n** to see your routing table. You should have entries for the loopback and the Ethernet, as shown in Listing 2-6.

If you do not see a route to your network interface, try repeating the preceding steps. You may have to delete a route. To delete a route, enter the following command:

```
route del 192.168.1.0
```

If the network adapter is configured correctly and the routing is correct, check the network. The best way to do this is to ping the loopback interface first and then the other computer. Enter the following command – which sends a very simple message to the IP address and waits for a reply – let it run for a few seconds (one ping occurs per second), and stop it by pressing *Ctrl+C*:

```
/bin/ping 127.0.0.1
```

You should see a response like the one shown in Listing 2-7.

Listing 2-7: Ping the loopback interface

```
PING 127.0.0.1 (127.0.0.1): 56 data bytes
64 bytes from 127.0.0.1: icmp_seq=0 ttl=64 time=2.0 ms
64 bytes from 127.0.0.1: icmp_seq=1 ttl=64 time=1.2 ms
64 bytes from 127.0.0.1: icmp_seq=2 ttl=64 time=1.1 ms
64 bytes from 127.0.0.1: icmp_seq=3 ttl=64 time=1.1 ms
64 bytes from 127.0.0.1: icmp_seq=4 ttl=64 time=1.1 ms
64 bytes from 127.0.0.1: icmp_seq=5 ttl=64 time=4.6 ms

--- 127.0.0.1 ping statistics ---
6 packets transmitted, 6 packets received, 0% packet loss
round-trip min/avg/max = 1.1/1.8/4.6 ms
```

Each line shows the number of bytes returned from the loopback interface, the sequence, and the round-trip time. The last lines are the summary, which shows if any packets did not make the trip. This is a working system, but if you don't see any returned packet, something is wrong with your setup and you should review the steps outlined in the preceding paragraphs.

Next, try to *ping* the Windows 95 computer. Enter the following command, let it run for 10–15 seconds, and stop it by pressing *Ctrl+C*:

```
ping 192.168.1.2
```

You should see a response like the one shown in Listing 2-8:

Listing 2-8: Ping the Windows 95 PC

```
PING 192.168.1.2 (192.168.1.2): 56 data bytes
64 bytes from 192.168.1.2: icmp_seq=0 ttl=32 time=3.1 ms
64 bytes from 192.168.1.2: icmp_seq=1 ttl=32 time=2.3 ms
64 bytes from 192.168.1.2: icmp_seq=2 ttl=32 time=2.5 ms
64 bytes from 192.168.1.2: icmp_seq=3 ttl=32 time=2.4 ms
64 bytes from 192.168.1.2: icmp_seq=4 ttl=32 time=2.3 ms

--- 192.168.1.2 ping statistics ---
5 packets transmitted, 5 packets received, 0% packet loss
round-trip min/avg/max = 2.3/2.5/3.1 ms
```

If you get a continuous stream of returned packets and the packet loss is zero or very near zero, your network is working. If not, the problem may be in the Linux computer or the Windows 95 machine. Review the troubleshooting steps described in this chapter. Note that the ICMP is taking about 1 full millisecond (ms) longer to travel to my Windows 95 box than to the loopback device. That is because the loopback is completely internal to the Linux box.

TIP

If you can't locate the problem and you are using a PPP connection to an Internet service provider (ISP), establish a PPP connection and try to ping the computer where you have your account. It is considered a security breach to continuously ping someone else's computer — and at least bad manners — so don't leave it running. Also, the ISP's firewall may not allow the Internet Control Message Protocol (ICMP) packets that ping uses. ICMP packets are the simplest type of packet defined in the Internet protocol. They are used for doing simple things such as a ping.

CHECKING SAMBA'S SERVICES

If your basic networking is working but you can't access the Samba resources, the next likely culprit is Samba. The Samba suite of programs includes several tools that can help you troubleshoot problems that occur. The following tests address a much wider range of problems than should occur if you have not modified the *smb.conf* file that Red Hat installed for you. In this section, I describe several methods for troubleshooting some of the problems you might encounter.

The Samba configuration file, */etc/smb.conf*, is quite complex. It contains dozens of variables and they can interact in hundreds, if not thousands, of ways. Although I've kept the examples simple so far in this book, to get a useful client-server system going, you have to experiment. To facilitate that experimentation and to help you troubleshoot problems, Samba provides a useful suite of test programs.

Start by making sure the daemons are running. From the command line, enter the following command:

```
ps -x | grep mnb
```

As shown in Listing 2-9, you should see a line for *smbd* and one for *nmbd*. (Note that the *grep* command filters out all the output from *ps* except for those lines that contain the string *mnb.*

Listing 2-9: Looking for the smbd and nmbd daemons

```
[root@bart /]# ps -x |grep mbd
  227  ?   S    0:00 smbd -D
  236  ?   S    0:00 nmbd -D
  360  ?   S    0:06 smbd -D
  742  p0  S    0:00 grep mbd
```

If the daemons are not running, start them by entering the following commands from root's command line:

```
/etc/rc.d/init.d/smb start
```

Repeat the *ps* command, as shown in the previous paragraphs, to make sure they ran. If they didn't, enter the following command to make sure the files exist and are executable:

```
/bin/ls -l /sbin/smbd /sbin/nmbd
```

The second, third, and fourth characters in the resulting output should be *r*, *w*, and *x*, respectively, and the owner should be *root*. If not, enter the following commands:

```
/bin/chmod 750 /usr/sbin/smbd /usr/sbin/nmbd
/bin/chown root /usr/sbin/smbd /usr/sbin/nmbd
```

Try running the daemons again. If they still don't work, they are probably corrupted and you have to reinstall them. See Chapter 7 for instructions on reinstalling a Red Hat Package, and then try reinstalling the Samba package again.

 The following tests follow the outline described in the document /usr/doc/samba-1.9.17p4/DIAGNOSIS.TXT.

If those processes are running, test the configuration by entering the following command:

```
/usr/bin/testparm | /bin/more
```

Several pages of Samba information are displayed. Listing 2-10 shows the first and last pages of the lengthy listing. The output reports any errors that occur, but sometimes you have to look closely to see through all the information that *testparm* displays.

Listing 2-10: First and last parts of output from testparm

```
Load smb config files from /etc/smb.conf
Processing section "[homes]"
Processing section "[printers]"
Loaded services file OK.
Press enter to see a dump of your service definitions
Global parameters:
  debuglevel: 2
  syslog: 1
  syslog only: No
  protocol: 5
  security: 1
  printing: 0
  max disk size: 0
  lpq cache time: 10
  announce as: 1
  encrypt passwords: No
  getwd cache: Yes

  (...lines deleted...)

  dos filetimes: No
```

```
Service parameters [homes]:
 comment: Home Directories
 browseable: No
 read only: No
 create mask: 0750

Service parameters [printers]:
 comment: All Printers
 browseable: No
 path: /var/spool/samba
 create mask: 0700
 print ok: Yes

Service parameters [lp]:
 comment:
 path: /var/spool/samba
 read only: No
 create mask: 0700
 print ok: Yes
 share modes: No
 printer: lp

Service parameters [IPC$]:
 comment: IPC Service (Samba 1.9.17p4)
 path: /tmp
 status: No
 guest ok: Yes
```

CHECKING THE SMBD SETUP

The next test involves running a program that looks to see what shares Samba is exporting. As you may have guessed, my Linux server is named *bart*. I use that name in my examples. Enter the following command (enter the *root* password when prompted):

```
/usr/bin/smbclient -L bart
```

As shown in Listing 2-11, this command returns the basic information about what services *bart* is serving. This test is useful for detecting errors in your password setup or mistakes of that nature.

Listing 2-11: The output of smbclient

```
Added interface ip=192.168.1.254 bcast=192.168.1.255 nmask=255.255.255.0
Unknown socket option TCP_NODELAY
Server time is Mon Dec 29 10:02:05 1997
Timezone is UTC-7.0
Password:
Domain=[WORKGROUP] OS=[Unix] Server=[Samba 1.9.17p4]
security=user

Server=[BART] User=[root] Workgroup=[WORKGROUP] Domain=[WORKGROUP]

Sharename      Type      Comment
---------      ----      -------
IPC$           IPC       IPC Service (Samba 1.9.17p4)
lp             Printer
root           Disk      Home Directories

This machine has a browse list:

Server            Comment
---------         -------
BART              Samba 1.9.17p4
```

Listing 2-12 presents an outline of what you should look for, depending on the output of *smbclient*.

Listing 2-12: If-then logic for smbclient

```
If you see the message "Bad Password", then
    Check your smb.conf for incorrect:
        Hosts allow, Hosts deny, or Valid users
    Then run testparam again and look specifically for these
    problems.

If you see the message "connection refused", then
    The smbd daemon is probably not running. Check it again.

If you see the message "session request failed" then
    If it says "your server software is being unfriendly",
    then
        You may have an invalid entry (or entries) in
        smb.conf,
            Or, smbd is not running,
            Or another service may be running on port 139.
```

```
You can check the first two as described previously;
You can check the last one by running the following
command:
```

```
netstat -a
```

```
And looking for anything using port 139.
```

CHECKING THE NMBD SETUP

You can check the status of the *nmbd* process by entering the following command:

```
/usr/bin/nmblookup -B bart
```

where *bart* is my Windows 95 client. You should get that PC's IP address back. If you do not, check the PC setup.

To do a general search of every PC on your network, enter the following command:

```
nmblookup -d 2 "*"
```

You should see a response from every client on the network, as shown in Listing 2-13.

Listing 2-13: Search for the Windows 95 PC on your network

```
Added interface ip=192.168.1.254 bcast=192.168.1.255 nmask=255.255.255.0
Sending queries to 192.168.1.255
Got a positive name query response from 192.168.1.2 (192.168.1.2)
Got a positive name query response from 192.168.1.254 (192.168.1.254)
192.168.1.254 *
```

You can check your passwords more precisely by entering the following command:

```
smbclient //bart/root -U root
```

(I use the username *root* here because that is the only user that has been installed — in Chapter 1. I discuss adding users in Chapter 7. The root service is used because it is the only service that I can guarantee to be available at this point.)

After you enter the password for *root*, you get the information displayed in Listing 2-14. The last line includes the *smb:* \> prompt, which indicates that your setup is correct. At the prompt, enter ? to see the available commands. You should be able use the *dir*, *get*, and *put* commands.

Listing 2-14: The smbclient information and interactive prompt

```
Added interface ip=192.168.1.254 bcast=192.168.1.255 nmask=255.255.255.0
Unknown socket option TCP_NODELAY
Server time is Mon Dec 29 10:11:47 1997
Timezone is UTC-7.0
Password:
Domain=[WORKGROUP] OS=[Unix] Server=[Samba 1.9.17p4]
security=user
smb: \>
```

Two of the common errors are `invalid network name` and `bad password`. The first error probably means that the service for tmp is incorrectly set up in smb.conf. The latter error can have several meanings:

- ◆ You have shadow passwords without *smbd* support for them.

- ◆ You are using encrypted passwords without *smbd* support for them.

- ◆ Your *smb.conf* has misconfigured values for any of the following parameters:

  - ■ Valid users

  - ■ Password level

  - ■ Path

CHECKING SAMBA FROM YOUR WINDOWS 95 CLIENT

You conduct the last tests from your Windows 95 PC. Execute the following command from a DOS window:

```
NET USE G: \\BART\ROOT
```

Depending on the Windows 95 user name that you are using and the configuration of your Linux-Samba server, you may or may not be prompted for a password. If your Windows 95 user name matches a valid user name on the Linux server, you should be able to see the drive *g:* in your *My Computer* dialog box. If it doesn't appear, you'll be prompted for a password. If your Windows 95 user name and the password match one on the Linux box, you will see drive *g:* show up in *My Computer*. Otherwise, return to Chapter 1 and follow the instructions for creating the user Root on your Windows 95 box.

The final test is to browse the Samba server from your *Network Neighborhood* window. If you select the *Entire Network* icon, you should see your server. If you don't see your server, check your Windows 95 setup again.

TIP If you are a real Troubleshooter, the *tcpdump-smb* utility is for you. It gives you information about what's happening down at the packet level. It comes on the CD-ROM as an RPM package. Load it and read the documentation. But that goes way beyond the scope of this chapter.

Conclusion

You are now a troubleshooting expert, capable of commanding more than $100 per hour from your desperate customers. Okay, maybe not $100, but hopefully you have acquired the fundamentals of troubleshooting and a good measure of practical experience. I suggest that you view the simple system you have just set up as an invaluable laboratory. Before the arrival of Linux, it was rare that an individual had the opportunity to work on a UNIX system without fear of destroying valuable data and hardware. In this Catch-22 scenario, you needed access to a UNIX system that you could configure if you were to learn UNIX Administration, but you had to know UNIX Administration before you could gain access to a UNIX system. Fortunately, Linux is the perfect system for learning Linux!

Summary

This chapter covered the following topics:

♦ Troubleshooting your network. I introduce you to the concept of troubleshooting. You should try to identify the problem and then work your way to the solution by first eliminating the simple causes and then the harder ones.

♦ Using the Fault Tree concept. This concept helps you to view a problem and its solutions in a graphical way, using a rooted tree to represent the relationship between a problem and its root cause.

♦ Using the Microsoft Network Troubleshooter as an example Fault Tree. I convert the menu-based Troubleshooter into pseudocode, to show how it helps you solve simple networking problems.

♦ Using Paul's Troubleshooter. I use example problems resulting from setting up the client-server network in Chapter 1 to demonstrate real-world troubleshooting.

Part II

Background

IN THIS PART:

Part II introduces and describes the various resources, people, and fundamental systems that make Linux so useful. This part also reviews UNIX, Linux, and Internet history. You also learn how to make use of the enormous resources available via the Internet, magazines, books, and the companion CD-ROM.

Chapter 3

What's Under the Hood?

IN THIS CHAPTER

◆ Examining the Linux kernel's primary internal functions and its startup process

◆ Exploring the Linux file system

◆ Investigating the Linux File System Standard (FSSTND)

◆ Understanding the Red Hat configuration scripts

◆ Looking at networking protocols and the Open Systems Interconnect (OSI) model

◆ Discovering the Samba system's internal functions

◆ Looking at the Red Hat 5.0 CD-ROM

◆ Working with the X Window system

◆ Understanding the General Public License (GPL)

I PLOWED THROUGH my initial installations of Linux and Samba in an impatient quest to get it all running as soon as possible. I always take that approach and probably always will. I don't care what I have to do to get what I want! The elderly, children, friends, and relatives, I sweep them all out of my way in a hungry lust just to get that first prompt:

```
[root@bart /root]#
```

With this approach, I usually get to the prompt. But the dark side of this method – if I can even call it a method – is that I barely understand what I've done or how the system works after I get to the prompt. After I complete the installation, I painfully (and remorsefully) crawl my way toward competence. I have to take cold comfort in the prompt, because I no longer have any friends and my relatives won't speak to me.

I also find that I don't reach competence until I gain a fair understanding of the details – and if not the details then at least the general concepts – underlying the prompt and all that makes the prompt possible. Analogously, even though I don't want to know how to repair my car's transmission, I do like knowing how it works. (Come to think of it, I did take the transmission apart in my first car. I fixed fifth

gear but lived without third until the car finally rusted out. Do you think I over-
looked an important lesson in that experience?)

You don't need to know everything about Linux and Samba, but you should
understand a few essential points. In this chapter, I describe the fundamentals of
Linux and Samba. I also present the OSI networking model, which serves as the
basis for all networking applications and protocols. To manage your system effectively in the long term, you need to understand the basics of not only Linux and
Samba, but also internetworking. Without an understanding of these fundamentals, you are like a race car driver who doesn't know what a piston is. To get the
most out of your vehicle – be it a car or a computer – you need to know what happens underneath the hood.

Just What Is Linux Anyway?

The word *Linux* has several meanings. For example, it refers to the Linux kernel,
which is the program that controls the interaction between the hardware and the
application programs that you use and control. It also refers to everything that
comes packaged on the Red Hat (or other manufacturer's) distribution CD-ROM –
that is, all the software that works together as a Linux system. That includes the
Linux kernel, system programs, the X Window system, and GNU (which stands for
"GNU's not UNIX") programs. And, of course, the term *Linux* refers to all of us as
the Linux community or Linux users.

In other words, the meaning of the term *Linux* generally depends on the context
in which you use it. If I call up the Red Hat people and ask to purchase Linux, they
will happily send me their CD-ROM. But if I ask you to "start Linux," I want you to
start the Linux kernel. Or if you say, "bring me the Linux box," I know to bring you
the computer with a Linux distribution installed on it. After you digest the fundamentals of what makes up Linux, you should have no problem determining what
people mean when they refer to Linux.

This theme carries through to other subjects. The Linux file system, for example,
refers to information stored on a magnetic or optical disk that is organized in such
a way that Linux can make use of it. Don't worry, all the terms and concepts that I
introduce in this chapter make sense after some practice.

Exploring the Linux Kernel

The Linux kernel is a program that handles the following tasks:

◆ Determining when and how long programs get executed

◆ Determining when and where to store programs and data in memory

◆ Refereeing the interaction among the devices that your computer
   comprises

Basically, when a process — user and system — asks for resources (such as when opening a file), the kernel receives the request and doles out the resources. The kernel does not actually control the processes directly. Because they depend on the kernel to respond to their requests, however, it controls them indirectly.

When a program gets executed, it is referred to as a *process* or a *task*. A *user process* has limited access to system resources such as memory. A *system process* has fewer limitations. The kernel imposes these limitations on processes to prevent them from interfering with each other and possibly crashing the system.

What does this master of the Linux universe look like? Log onto your Linux box and enter the following command from your shell prompt:

```
ls -l /boot
```

You should see a list of files similar to the example in Listing 3-1.

Listing 3-1: A sample /boot directory listing

```
total 569
lrwxrwxrwx  1 root     root         17 Dec  8 13:55 System.map -> System.map-2.0.31
-rw-r--r--  1 root     root     104250 Nov  9 09:59 System.map-2.0.31
-rw-r--r--  1 root     root        512 Dec  8 14:01 boot.0300
-rw-r--r--  1 root     root       4536 Oct 19 12:08 boot.b
-rw-r--r--  1 root     root        300 Oct 19 12:08 chain.b
-rw-------  1 root     root       8192 Dec  8 14:01 map
lrwxrwxrwx  1 root     root         18 Dec  8 13:55 module-info -> module-info-2.0.31
-rw-r--r--  1 root     root      11773 Nov  9 09:59 module-info-2.0.31
-rw-r--r--  1 root     root        308 Oct 19 12:08 os2_d.b
lrwxrwxrwx  1 root     root         14 Dec  8 13:55 vmlinuz -> vmlinuz-2.0.31
-rw-r--r--  1 root     root     444595 Nov  9 09:59 vmlinuz-2.0.31
```

The file *vmlinuz-2.0.31* is the Linux kernel; the *2.0.31* refers to the version number. The file *vmlinuz* is a link, which is simply a pointer to *vmlinux-2.0.31*. When you upgrade your system, the kernel file sometimes changes — for instance, from *vmlinuz-2.0.31* to *vmlinuz-2.0.33* — and you delete that old link and create a new one pointing to *vmlinux-2.0.33*. Updating that link prevents the need to modify other programs that must access the kernel — they access the kernel by referencing the link. Everything else in this listing is just Linux housekeeping; I don't need to discuss it here. Overall, this list isn't too scary.

The kernel performs its magic by concentrating on a few things:

♦ **Multitasking:** Multiple programs can run at once.

♦ **Multiple users:** Multiple users can use the computer at one time.

♦ **Virtual memory:** Programs can use more memory than is available from just RAM.

♦ **The file system:** Your files are organized for you.

UNDERSTANDING MULTITASKING

A multitasking operating system allows more than one program to run at once. Actually, multiple processes – or *programs* – execute sequentially; the operating system schedules their execution and allocates resources to them. As long as the number of tasks is kept to a reasonable number and the computer is fast enough, all the programs appear to be running simultaneously.

Linux is a *preemptive multitasking* operating system. Each process is given a time slice – generally about 20 milliseconds ($20/_{1000}$ seconds) – to run within. Linux suspends the running process when its time slice expires and starts the next waiting process. This handling of time slices entails storing the environment – all the information that a process needs to run – of the current process in memory and loading the waiting process's environment from memory.

For comparison, MS-DOS is an operating system that allows only one program to run at once. MS-DOS has the Terminate and Stay Resident (TSR) feature, which gives the appearance of multitasking, but simply runs programs when you tell it to. Windows 3.*x* offers simple multitasking that doesn't always work. Windows 95 and Windows NT use preemptive multitasking that works.

For multitasking to work, the Linux kernel must coordinate the execution of all tasks. It also keeps track of all the details about each process that is running. However, the kernel does not start or stop any programs after it has been started at boot time. The *init* process and the programs themselves take care of that function. *Init* is the process that actually takes care of launching all system and application programs; I discuss *init* in the section, "Understanding the Linux Startup Process," later in this chapter.

A process table lists basic information about each process that is currently running. To see a typical process table (such as the example shown in Listing 3-2), enter the following command:

```
ps x
```

Listing 3-2: The Linux process table

```
PID TTY STAT   TIME COMMAND
   1 ?  S     0:02 init [3]
   2 ?  SW    0:00 (kflushd)
   3 ?  SW<   0:00 (kswapd)
  21 ?  S     0:00 /sbin/kerneld
 166 ?  S     0:00 syslogd
 175 ?  S     0:01 klogd
 197 ?  S     0:00 crond
 209 ?  S     0:00 inetd
 220 ?  S     0:00 lpd
 234 ?  S     0:00 sendmail: accepting connections on port 25
 246 ?  S     0:00 gpm -t ms
 257 ?  S     0:00 smbd -D
 266 ?  S     0:00 nmbd -D
 291 1  S     0:00 /bin/login -- root
 292 2  S     0:00 /sbin/mingetty tty2
 293 3  S     0:00 /sbin/mingetty tty3
 294 4  S     0:00 /sbin/mingetty tty4
 295 ?  S     0:00 update (bdflush)
 296 4  S     0:00 (mingetty)
 297 5  S     0:00 /sbin/mingetty tty5
 298 6  S     0:00 /sbin/mingetty tty6
 299 1  S     0:01 -bash
 328 ?  S     0:00 in.telnetd
5434 p0 S     0:00 su -
5435 p0 S     0:00 -bash
5450 p0 R     0:00 ps x
```

Linux uses a set formula to determine when each program is run, how long it runs, and which program takes precedence over the others. The formula tries to give each process its fair share of CPU time, based on a priority given to each process (you can manually change the priority with the *nice* command). The priority of a process is determined by a number of system parameters. The Linux kernel also transfers parts of or entire programs between disk and memory, keeping track of the details for each program. Thus, if you want to run a clock program and a nuclear reactor control program, the kernel should schedule the control program to run before the clock and for longer segments of time.

Note: You can tell a lot from the process table. For example, the process table in Listing 3-2 shows that I am logged on as *root* (Super User) from the console (PID 291). I have also logged on via Telnet (*in.telnetd*) and two bash shells are running to support the logins (bash stands for "Bourne Again Shell," which is used by a user to interactively run commands). I have used the *su* - command to change to *root* from the Telnet login. Also, several processes have process identifiers (PIDs) greater than 5000, which implies that the computer has been running for a while or is heavily used, because PIDs are assigned sequentially starting at 1.

UNDERSTANDING MULTIUSER SYSTEMS

Linux also allows more than one person to access the computer. By running programs (tasks or processes) that negotiate the logon process, more than one person can use the Linux box at once. In Listing 3-2, the process IDs (*PIDs*) 292, 293, 294, 297, and 298 are responsible for logging on users. The *mingetty* processes constantly monitor the virtual consoles waiting for you to log on (see the following Tip for further explanation). When you press a key on the console, the login program negotiates your authentication by prompting you for a user name and password. As you can see, I am logged on as *root*. (This generally isn't a good idea from a systems management perspective – see Chapter 10 for more on systems management.) From the console, I have also connected via the Telnet program, which enables you to use the network to connect from one computer to another without being physically present at the computer you're accessing. The *in.telnetd* process – PID 328 – is controlling my Telnet session. I have also changed to the *root* user via the *su* - command in my Telnet session. This change is made because the default Red Hat – and most Linux – distributions don't allow you to log on as *root* except from the console.

Each process that is associated with a user has file ownership and permissions associated with it. Any files that are created as a result of these processes will retain that file ownership and permissions. By those same permissions, the processes also will be limited in terms of which files they can access and use. Thus, Linux is a multiuser operating system.

By comparison, MS-DOS, Windows 3.*x*, and Windows 95 are all single-user operating systems. Windows NT is a multiuser operating system.

Linux uses the concept of a virtual console or terminal to make life easier for you. It simply maps two or more terminal sessions onto a single physical monitor. Any Linux distribution comes configured for between four and eight sessions. By pressing the *Alt* key in combination with the first four to eight function keys (*Alt+F1*, *Alt+F2*, and so on), you toggle between independent sessions. This technique is equivalent to running several shells as windows and switching between them via the mouse.

UNDERSTANDING VIRTUAL MEMORY

Linux is also a demand-paged, virtual-memory operating system. By transferring (mapping) parts of a program or a data structure from memory to disk, the system can work with a program or data structure that is larger than the available memory. If you have 8MB of memory and you want to load a 10MB spreadsheet, the virtual-memory system takes part of that 10MB spreadsheet file and loads it into memory. If you access the part that is still on disk, part of the file that is currently in memory is stored to disk and the new segment is loaded into the freed-up memory. Using virtual memory slows down the system, but it makes your computer appear to have much more memory than it actually has.

Do you remember the hoops you had to jump through back in the 1980s to get MS-DOS to access more than 640K of memory? Not only was it limited to 640K, but it also did not have virtual memory, so a program had to use less than that amount to work. Linux does have virtual memory, so if you have only 8MB, you can load and run stuff that uses more than that amount. As you may recall from Chapter 1, during the Linux installation you set aside some disk space for a swap partition. Linux uses that space to store the memory contents when it "swaps out."

The Linux "File"

In the Linux (and UNIX) world, a file is not just an entity used to store information. It is also used as an abstraction to connect the kernel to each device, as well as a view into the kernel. In this way, Linux simplifies the access of devices by treating them like any other file. The directory */dev* contains many files that are used as the common connection points between the kernel and device drivers. The drivers contain the internal specifics of a device, and the kernel knows about the drivers. The device file provides a convenient connection point that the administrator can easily view and modify.

For example, to use a mouse, it is not enough to have the device driver for the mouse installed (in the kernel itself); you also must have a device file associated with the mouse. I use a serial mouse connected to port cua0, so my system uses the file shown in Listing 3-3 to access the mouse.

Listing 3-3: The mouse device file

```
lrwxrwxrwx   1 root     root          4 Dec  8 14:00 /dev/mouse -> cua0
crw-rw----   1 root     uucp      5, 64 Dec  8 22:03 /dev/cua0
```

My kernel has the driver for a serial mouse and expects to find the device file as */dev/mouse*. As you can see in Listing 3-3, */dev/mouse* is a link, or pointer, to the first serial port device file – the device file to which my mouse is connected.

A device file is either a *character* or a *block* type, as specified by the first character on the listing (the *c* specifies that the mouse is a character device and a *b* specifies a block type such as a disk drive). A device also has major and minor numbers, which the kernel uses internally for its own bookkeeping. The major number, along with the device type, identifies the driver, while the minor number is passed to the driver to identify the device. The drivers themselves are contained either in Linux modules or compiled directly into the kernel.

You can create the */dev/cua0* device file by using the *mknod* command. For example, to create the mouse device file, log on as *root* and enter the following command:

```
/bin/mknod /dev/cua0 c 5 64
```

This command creates the file shown in Listing 3-3.

Linux has several file types:

◆ *Regular files* are the type you use all the time. In a long listing (which you produce by entering the command *ls -l*), a hyphen precedes the name of each regular file.

◆ *Directories* contain the names of files that are stored – or organized – as a group. The grouping is arbitrary; you can choose any combination you want. You also can change the grouping at any time. You create directories by entering the *mkdir* command. A lowercase *d* precedes the name of each directory in a long listing.

◆ *Character and Block device files* serve as the interface between the Linux operating system and the hardware devices. Character devices are accessed sequentially, a byte at a time; a serial port is a character device. Block devices – for example, disk drives – are accessed in chunks of bytes; you get a block (that is, 1,024 bytes) of data at one time. In a long listing, a lowercase *c* precedes the name of each Character device file, and a lowercase *b* precedes the name of each Block device file.

◆ The *named pipe* or FIFO (first-in-first-out) is a file that enables processes to communicate with each other. FIFOs are created with the *mknod* program and are designated by a *p* at the beginning of a long listing.

◆ The *pipe file* is an abstraction that enables processes to communicate with each other. Pipe files actually exist as sections of memory used to buffer the data going from one process to another. Pipe files are denoted as a vertical bar (|) and placed between two processes. For example, the command *ls -l / | more* lists the device directory one page at a time by piping the output of *ls* to the paging command *more*.

◆ *Sockets* facilitate communication between processes via the network.

◆ *Hard links* create additional names for a file. They are indistinguishable from the original file. The *ln* command creates hard links.

◆ *Symbolic or "soft" links* are files that contain the name of another file. They essentially point to that file. When a symbolic link is encountered by the kernel during the interpretation of a pathname, the pointer that the link contains is used as a new starting point. When you do a long listing – */bin/ls -l* – on a symbolic link you see it displayed with an arrow pointing to the target file, as follows:

```
mylink -> test.txt
```

For instance, if the file *test.txt* contains the characters *xyz* and if you enter the command **more mylink** you will see the string *xyz* displayed. This is because the symbolic link points to a text file *test.txt*.

For example, *gzip* is a GNU program used to compress data and files. If you want to decompress a file, you can use the command *gzip -d* or the command *gunzip*, which is a symbolic link to the command *gzip -d* (*gzip* looks at how it is called in order to determine its action).

Exploring the Linux File System

When I read technical discussions of Linux, I sometimes get confused about the meaning of the term *file system*. This is another one of those context-sensitive terms. It can refer to either how Linux organizes the raw bytes of data into files or how Linux organizes files and directories. The next two sections discuss these distinctions. The section after them explains how the Linux world is creating a standard for where to store standard and nonstandard Linux files.

UNDERSTANDING HOW LINUX ORGANIZES BYTES OF DATA INTO A FILE

The Linux file system organizes the raw bytes that are stored on a disk into files. Linux does not impose any structure on the bytes that make up files; it simply enables processes to access all the bytes that belong to any given file. The methods that it uses to do that are described in this section.

The *Extended File System 2* (*ext2*) is the *de facto* standard Linux file system. However, Linux is capable of using many other file systems, such as MS-DOS, Minix (the earliest Linux was based on it), the original Extended File System, and iso9660 (for CD-ROMs). When you create – or initialize – your disk partition, you have the choice of several different file systems. When you formatted your *root*, */home*, and */usr/local* partitions in Chapter 1, you used the *ext2* system.

When you create an *ext2* file system, a data structure called an *inode* (index node) is folded into the disk format. When you format the disk, *inodes* are periodically placed on the disk. Unlike MS-DOS, the number of *inodes* is fixed when you format the disk. (If you have a huge number of very small files, you can run out of *inodes*. That is unlikely in most circumstances, however.)

An *inode* is the essential element to a Linux file system. When you create a file an *inode* is allocated to it. It contains information on a file's ownership (*user* and *group*), access modes (*read*, *write*, and *execution*), time information (when a file was last accessed and modified, and when the *inode* itself was modified), the byte count, and the file's type (regular, special – that is, a device – or an abstract one such as those found in the */proc* directory). The *inode* contains the indexing information about the disk *blocks* where a file's data is located. However, an *inode* doesn't contain the name of the file; that information is stored in a directory file.

A *directory* is a *file* itself. It contains the name – or names – of the file(s) and its *inode(s)*.

Linux uses the information in *inodes* to access and work with files. For example, the file *chap_3.doc* – which contains the text for this chapter – is physically stored on a hard disk that my Linux box controls. When I open this file, Linux tells the disk controller to go to specific locations to retrieve the raw data off the disk platter. Linux determines where to go by checking the information stored in the *inode* associated with the file *chap_3.doc*. In other words, each file has an *inode* that points to data blocks scattered around on the disk platter. The kernel puts them all together into a human-useable form. To obtain the *inode* information, I enter the long listing command *ls* and include the *-i* option (you can also use the synonym *@2hinode*):

```
/bin/ls -il /home/book/chap_3.doc
```

This command returns the following information about the specified file (including the *inode* – 106499):

```
106499 -rwxr-xr-x   1 root     root       124928 Sep  2 19:10 chap_3.doc
```

Listing 3-4 shows the listing of the Red Hat */etc* directory and the *inodes* associated with each file and directory.

Listing 3-4: The Red Hat /etc directory and its inodes

```
total 612
  4081 -rw-r--r--  1 root     root         2045 Oct 22 19:52 DIR_COLORS
  4121 -rw-r--r--  1 root     root           17 Dec  8 14:01 HOSTNAME
 24385 drwxr-xr-x  3 root     root         1024 Dec  8 13:53 X11
  4089 -rw-r--r--  1 root     root           10 Nov  7 12:52 adjtime
  4108 -rw-r--r--  1 root     root          732 Oct 29 13:33 aliases
  4111 -rw-r--r--  1 root     mail        16384 Dec  8 13:59 aliases.db
  4087 -rw-------  1 root     root            1 Nov  9 17:10 at.deny
  4085 -rw-r--r--  1 root     root          302 Nov  7 12:13 bashrc
  4119 -rw-r--r--  1 root     root           17 Dec  8 14:01 conf.modules
105690 drwxr-xr-x  2 root     root         1024 Dec  8 13:59 cron.daily
 93505 drwxr-xr-x  2 root     root         1024 Aug 26 09:35 cron.hourly
 99605 drwxr-xr-x  2 root     root         1024 Jul 25 14:31 cron.monthly
105691 drwxr-xr-x  2 root     root         1024 Dec  8 13:56 cron.weekly
  4084 -rw-r--r--  1 root     root          248 Oct 24 15:07 crontab
  4067 -rw-r--r--  1 root     root          666 Oct 24  1996 csh.cshrc
119928 drwxr-xr-x  2 root     root         1024 Dec  8 13:53 default
  4068 -rw-r--r--  1 root     root            0 Jul  6  1995 exports
  4114 -rw-r--r--  1 root     root         1118 Oct 22 19:36 fdprm
  4118 -rw-r--r--  1 root     root          456 Dec  8 14:01 fstab
  4069 -rw-r--r--  1 root     root         2362 Oct 29 13:10 gettydefs
  4091 -rw-r--r--  1 root     root         1756 Nov  3 13:01 gpm-root.conf
  4128 -rw-r--r--  1 root     root          317 Dec  8 21:33 group
  4092 -rw-------  1 root     root          303 Dec  8 13:53 group-
  4070 -rw-r--r--  1 root     root           26 Jul 12  1994 host.conf
  4066 -rw-r--r--  1 root     root           79 Dec  8 21:02 hosts
  4071 -rw-r--r--  1 root     root          161 Jul 28  1995 hosts.allow
  4072 -rw-r--r--  1 root     root          347 Jul 28  1995 hosts.deny
  4103 -rw-r--r--  1 root     root         3327 Oct 30 08:43 inetd.conf
  4088 -rw-r--r--  1 root     root         5553 Dec  8 13:59 info-dir
  4113 lrwxrwxrwx  1 root     root           21 Dec  8 13:59 initrunlvl -> \
../var/run/initrunlvl
  4095 -rw-r--r--  1 root     root         1726 Nov  7 12:52 inittab
  4122 -rw-------  1 root     root           60 Dec  8 22:03 ioctl.save
  4124 -rw-r--r--  1 root     root           65 Dec  8 22:03 issue
  4074 -rw-r--r--  1 root     root           64 Dec  8 22:03 issue.net
  4115 -rw-r--r--  1 root     root         4442 Dec  8 14:00 ld.so.cache
  4096 -rw-r--r--  1 root     root           41 Dec  8 14:00 ld.so.conf
  4120 -rw-r--r--  1 root     root          134 Dec  8 14:01 lilo.conf
  4116 lrwxrwxrwx  1 root     root           33 Dec  8 14:00 localtime -> \
../usr/share/zoneinfo/US/Mountain
  4090 -rw-r--r--  1 root     root         1342 Nov  6 15:10 login.defs
  4097 -rw-r--r--  1 root     root          563 Oct 21 12:25 logrotate.conf
```

```
 81356 drwxr-xr-x  2 root     root       1024 Dec  8 21:17 logrotate.d
 95550 drwxr-xr-x  2 root     root       1024 Dec  8 13:59 mail
  4101 -rw-r--r--  1 root     root        107 Oct 21 11:29 mail.rc
  4098 -rw-r--r--  1 root     root       9344 Oct 21 11:28 mailcap
  4099 -rw-r--r--  1 root     root       9174 Oct 21 11:28 mailcap.vga
  4102 -rw-r--r--  1 root     root       2757 Oct 19 09:41 man.config
  4100 -rw-r--r--  1 root     root       1552 Oct 21 11:28 mime.types
  4073 -rw-r--r--  1 root     root          0 Jul  6  1995 motd
  4130 -rw-r--r--  1 root     root         52 Dec  8 15:03 mtab
  4082 -rw-r--r--  1 root     root       1208 Nov  8 21:46 nsswitch.conf
  6132 -rw-r--r--  1 root     root        127 Dec  8 13:56 pam.conf
103692 drwxr-xr-x  2 root     root       1024 Dec  8 21:17 pam.d
  4129 -rw-r--r--  1 root     root        575 Dec  8 21:34 passwd
  4117 -rw-r--r--  1 root     root        571 Dec  8 21:33 passwd-
107778 drwxr-xr-x  2 root     root       1024 Dec  8 13:56 pcmcia
107761 drwxr-xr-x  2 root     root       1024 Dec  8 13:55 ppp
  4075 -rw-r--r--  1 root     root        289 Jul 28  1995 printcap
  4076 -rw-r--r--  1 root     root        507 Aug 19  1996 profile
 16257 drwxr-xr-x  2 root     root       1024 Aug 19  1996 profile.d
  4077 -rw-r--r--  1 root     root        715 Dec 31  1979 protocols
  4123 -rw-rw-r--  1 root     root      12288 Dec  8 21:02 psdevtab
  4104 -rw-r--r--  1 root     root        134 Oct 24 13:00 pwdb.conf
 18304 drwxr-xr-x 10 root     root       1024 Dec  8 13:55 rc.d
  4105 -rw-rw-r--  1 root     root         24 Nov  9 15:16 redhat-release
  4094 -rw-r--r--  1 root     root         42 Dec  8 14:00 resolv.conf
  4083 -rw-r--r--  1 root     root       1577 Nov  8 21:45 rpc
  4078 -rw-------  1 root     root         40 Sep  4  1995 securetty
107772 drwxr-xr-x  2 root     root       1024 Dec  8 13:56 security
  4109 -rw-r--r--  1 root     root      30192 Oct 29 13:33 sendmail.cf
  4110 -rw-r--r--  1 root     root         59 Oct 29 13:33 sendmail.cw
  4079 -rw-r--r--  1 root     root       4491 Oct 24  1996 services
  4086 -rw-r--r--  1 root     root         55 Dec  8 13:59 shells
 28464 drwxr-xr-x  2 root     root       1024 Dec  8 13:54 skel
  4107 -rw-r--r--  1 root     root       6554 Oct 31 12:21 smb.conf
  4126 -rw-r--r--  1 root     root       5436 Oct 31 12:21 smb.conf.sampl
 85418 drwxr-xr-x  2 root     root       1024 Oct 29 13:33 smrsh
 42733 drwxr-xr-x  3 root     root       1024 Dec  8 14:00 sysconfig
  4112 -rw-r--r--  1 root     root        615 Oct 30 08:39 syslog.conf
  4080 -rw-r--r--  1 bin      bin      434729 Oct 23 13:44 termcap
  4125 -rw-r-----  1 root     root          0 Dec  8 21:08 wtmplock
```

A directory is itself a file whose data consists of filenames and *inode* pairs. The filename is a simple text string such as *HOSTNAME* in Listing 3-4; it has an *inode* associated with it — in this example, 4121. When you do something to HOSTNAME,

Linux looks at *inode* number 4121 to determine all the details about HOSTNAME, including where to access the data it contains.

The hierarchical directory structure is obtained by storing the names of other directories in a directory's *file/inode* list. Notice the directory *X11* (denoted by the *d* immediately after the *inode* number) in Listing 3-4. The *inode* 24385 points to a file that contains another list of file and *inode* pairs. And of course, any of those files can be directories that point to other files and directories.

 A file consists of an *inode*, the associated data blocks, and a filename stored in a directory file. Symbolic and hard links offer two different means for associating different names with a file.

The kernel knows where to look for *inodes* that make up any given file because it has a master table of file information called the *Superblock*. The Superblock contains the number of data blocks, the block size, the number of *inodes*, and the free and used *inodes* of the file system. The Superblock is loaded into memory at boot time. One of the reasons why you should perform a systematic shutdown (that is, *halt*) of your Linux computer is to write the updated Superblock to disk. (Linux generally is smart enough to reconfigure – that is, *fsck* – a Superblock after an unscheduled shutdown, but it is good administrative practice to avoid the risk of possible injury to your system.)

The Virtual File System (VFS) – I've also seen it called the Virtual File System Switch – sits in between the low-level file system where the software drivers directly control the hardware and the high-level file system that works with the various formats such as *ext2* and *msdos*. It provides a layer of abstraction so that the system programs that deal with features like opening and closing files don't have to deal directly with the device drivers themselves. VFS translates the high-level operations into the language that the device drivers understand.

When you specify a directory path – for example, in the command *ls -l /etc/X11* – the kernel first looks in the *root* (/) directory file for the string *etc*. If the kernel finds this string, it uses the *inode* to access the */etc* directory file. The kernel then looks for the string *X11* and if it finds this string, the kernel uses the *inode* to find the */etc/X11* directory and list its contents.

UNDERSTANDING HOW LINUX ORGANIZES FILES AND DIRECTORIES

The Linux file system also describes the structure that houses all the files that make up Linux. It is based on a *rooted-tree* model. The tree is made up of directories and files. Each directory can contain one or more subdirectories. Directories are used to organize files, and each directory or subdirectory can contain zero or more files. A file contains either information (data), an executable program or script, device information, or nothing.

As a system administrator, you need to be familiar with the file system organization, for troubleshooting as well as everyday management. The more you know it, the better. After you work with it for a while, you instinctively know the locations of the most important files and generally where you find most of the other files.

The *root* directory is the mother of all directories. Listing 3-5 shows a listing of the *root* directory as Red Hat configures it (other distributions such as Slackware have somewhat different setups, but are basically the same). Its structure is important because the *root* directory is your starting point for the rest of the Linux file system.

Listing 3-5: Root directory listing

```
total 48
drwxr-xr-x   2 root     root         2048 Dec  8 13:59 bin
drwxr-xr-x   2 root     root         1024 Dec  8 14:01 boot
drwxr-xr-x   2 root     root        20480 Dec  8 22:03 dev
drwxr-xr-x  19 root     root         2048 Dec  8 22:03 etc
drwxr-xr-x  16 root     root         1024 Dec  8 21:17 home
drwxr-xr-x   4 root     root         2048 Dec  8 13:58 lib
drwxr-xr-x   2 root     root        12288 Dec  8 13:51 lost+found
drwxr-xr-x   4 root     root         1024 Dec  8 14:01 mnt
dr-xr-xr-x   5 root     root            0 Dec  8 15:03 proc
drwxr-xr-x   3 root     root         1024 Dec  8 22:11 root
drwxr-xr-x   3 root     root         2048 Dec  8 13:59 sbin
drwxrwxrwt   2 root     root         1024 Dec  8 13:56 tmp
drwxr-xr-x  18 root     root         1024 Dec  8 13:55 usr
drwxr-xr-x  12 root     root         1024 Dec  8 13:56 var
```

Over the years, certain files have found homes in certain directories. For example, you can expect to find the password file, *passwd*, in the */etc* directory. Run the following command and take a look:

```
ls -l /etc
```

It should be there (if it isn't, you probably weren't able to log on). The file systems used by the various UNIX versions have evolved differently from one another. You can easily recognize a System V or BSD file system. They look similar in general, but on closer examination you see significant differences, such as the location of the startup rc scripts. (System V puts them in */etc/rc.d* while BSD leaves them in */etc*.) However, the Linux community is striving to avoid this situation.

TAKING A LOOK AT THE LINUX FILE SYSTEM STANDARD

The Linux community is working to standardize the Linux file system. Several Linux distributors – Red Hat and Caldera in particular – do a good job of following the Linux File System Standard (FSSTND). Because of evolving manufacturer standards and the whims of the marketplace, you can always find exceptions, but the

FSSTND actually takes that into account and is a work in progress itself. To find more information about the FSSTND, go to the following URL:

http://www.pathname.com/fhs/

One essential FSSTND requirement is that the */usr* directory must remain read-only. Thus, it can be mounted from a CD-ROM or a remote networked disk (for example, via NFS or Samba). This capability is important for both small and large organizations that want to minimize management costs. One server can share its */usr* directory with many clients, which in turn require smaller (or no) disks. A read-only */usr* directory also means lower administration costs, because you can't clutter up and rearrange things. If you follow the standard and mount your own */usr* directory as read-only, you have to put your own stuff in the places where it belongs. Thus, this standard has the added benefit of minimizing your own confusion – no small gain.

By following the FSSTND, Linux vendors do themselves a big favor. In its nascent state, Linux needs to be as uniform as possible to gain momentum and acceptance in the business community. The more established FSSTND becomes, the more everyone will benefit.

Under the FSSTND, some of the more important directories contain the following functions:

- ◆ The */etc* directory contains local configuration files. Files that describe the network, and other standard configurations, all go here. You should not place any binary or executable files in */etc*.

- ◆ The */etc/X11* directory contains the *X11* configuration file.

- ◆ The */etc/skel* directory contains the basic configuration files for new directories.

- ◆ The */lib* directory gets all the library files needed by the programs in */bin* and */sbin*. Library files contain common functions and data – such as fonts – that many programs use dynamically. When you run a program, the program dynamically links to the necessary libraries.

- ◆ The */sbin* directory contains the programs needed to boot the system in addition to those in */bin* and should only be executable by *root*.

- ◆ The */var* directory is for variable stuff. Because */usr* is supposed to be read-only, you use */var* for storing files that change constantly, such as printer spool and system logging files. It has numerous subdirectories that I don't describe in detail but list for reference:

  - ▪ */var/log:* log files

  - ▪ */var/catman:* manual pages

- *■ /var/lib:* library files

- *■ /var/local:* variable local files

- *■ /var/named:* name service files

- *■ /var/nis:* network information services (Sun)

- *■ /var/preserve*

- *■ /var/run*

- *■ /var/lock:* lock files used for process coordination

- *■ /var/tmp:* temporary files

- *■ /var/spool*: all spooling directories

- *■ /var/spool/at*: prescheduled commands

- *■ /var/spool/cron*: commands and scripts run automatically

- *■ /var/spool/lpd*: print queue files

- *■ /var/spool/mail*: mail files

- *■ /var/spool/mqueue*: mail queues

- *■ /var/spool/rwho*: rwho files

- *■ /var/spool/smail:* smail queue files

- *■ /var/spool/uucp*: UNIX to UNIX communication protocol

- *■ /var/spool/news*: news spools

◆ The */etc/sysconfig* directory contains the Red Hat startup scripts.

◆ The */usr/lib/rhs* directory contains the Red Hat control panel and other stuff.

◆ The */var/lib/rpm* directory has the Red Hat RPM files.

◆ The */usr* directory contains the files that can be sharable across an entire LAN. It should have its own partition. According to the FSSTND, */usr* should be read-only.

The */usr* directory contains the following directories:

◆ */usr/X11R6* contains most of *XFree86* (the X Window system). This directory has the following organization:

   - *■ /usr/X11R6/bin* contains the executable programs.

- */usr/X11R6/doc* contains the documentation that is not part of the standard *XFree86* manual system (*man pages*). (*Note:* XFree86 man pages have the same format as standard Linux man pages.)

- */usr/X11R6/include* houses the *include* files. These files contain constants and other stuff that you *include* into a source code file during compilation.

- */usr/X11R6/lib* contains the libraries specific to *XFree86*.

- */usr/X11R6/man* houses the manual pages for *XFree86*.

◆ */usr/bin*, along with */bin*, has most of the programs that are considered standard Linux — everything from *clear* to *gcc* to *zip*.

◆ */usr/dict* has the Linux dictionary.

◆ */usr/doc* contains many useful documents, FAQs, HOWTOs, and so on. More on that in Chapter 5.

◆ */usr/etc* is empty at this time. (*Note:* Slackware has a link to the *printcap* file, which configures the printers.)

◆ */usr/games* is where games are stored.

◆ */usr/ i486-linux-libc5* contains older libraries.

◆ */usr/include* has more include files.

◆ */usr/info* contains GNU info hypertext files on various topics. For more information on these files, see the man page on *info*.

◆ */usr/lib* contains more Linux libraries.

◆ */usr/man* houses most of the Linux man pages. It is divided into nine sections that reflect the Linux/UNIX convention. Table 3-1 details the organization of the Linux man pages.

◆ */usr/sbin* has system commands and daemons.

◆ */usr/share* is used to store general applications — *awk*, *ghostscript*, and so on — that are common to all users.

◆ */usr/src* is where you store the Linux or other important source codes.

◆ */usr/local* contains a hierarchy similar to */usr* and is used to store local programs and libraries. It is used to keep the */usr* as stable as possible. By following this convention, it is much easier to keep track of everything that you have installed on your system.

TABLE 3-1 LINUX MAN PAGE ORGANIZATION

Number	Contents
1	User commands and applications
2	System calls and kernel error codes
3	Library calls
4	Device drivers
5	File formats
6	The introductory man page
7	System and package descriptions
8	Network and system commands and utilities
9	Currently empty

Although System V and BSD generally have similar structures, they differ in many important details.

When you put all this together, you have an efficient, useful file system. As you use it over time, it will become a familiar, if somewhat dull, friend. I suspect that with time it will become the standard across the Linux world and you will know your way around a Linux system anywhere in the world.

Understanding the Linux Startup Process

The Linux startup process is fairly complicated. When the PC is turned on or restarted, a small bootstrap program located on the boot sector of the disk is executed automatically. The kernel is stored in a known location on disk, and the bootstrap program loads the kernel into memory and then starts it (you see a couple of lines of dots indicating the kernel is being loaded).

If you want to read about the details of this startup process, the *Linux Systems Administrator's Guide* discusses the topic at

http://www.redhat.com/linux-info/ldp/LDP/sag

After the kernel is started, it does an inventory of the computer's hardware configuration. As you watch the computer boot, you see information similar to the example shown in Listing 3-6. Notice how the kernel checks the memory, the floppy and hard disks, the CD-ROM, and the Ethernet adapters. It needs to know the parameters for these devices so it can manage their interaction with yours.

Listing 3-6: The kernel determines hardware configuration during the boot process

```
Console: 16 point font, 400 scans
Console: colour VGA+ 80x25, 1 virtual console (max 63)
pci_init: no BIOS32 detected
Calibrating delay loop.. ok - 33.18 BogoMIPS
Memory: 6848k/8448k available (736k kernel code, 384k reserved, 480k data)
This processor honours the WP bit even when in supervisor mode. Good.
Swansea University Computer Society NET3.035 for Linux 2.0
NET3: Unix domain sockets 0.13 for Linux NET3.035.
Swansea University Computer Society TCP/IP for NET3.034
IP Protocols: IGMP, ICMP, UDP, TCP
VFS: Diskquotas version dquot_5.6.0 initialized
Checking 386/387 coupling... Ok, fpu using exception 16 error reporting.
Checking 'hlt' instruction... Ok.
Linux version 2.0.31 (root@porky.redhat.com) (gcc version 2.7.2.3) #1 Sun Nov 9
 21:45:23 EST 1997
Starting kswapd v 1.4.2.2
Serial driver version 4.13 with no serial options enabled
tty00 at 0x03f8 (irq = 4) is a 16450
tty01 at 0x02f8 (irq = 3) is a 16450
Real Time Clock Driver v1.07
Ramdisk driver initialized : 16 ramdisks of 4096K size
hda: WDC AC21600H, 1549MB w/128kB Cache, CHS=3148/16/63
hdb: 20DY, ATAPI CDROM drive
ide0 at 0x1f0-0x1f7,0x3f6 on irq 14
Floppy drive(s): fd0 is 1.44M
FDC 0 is an 8272A
md driver 0.35 MAX_MD_DEV=4, MAX_REAL=8
scsi : 0 hosts.
scsi : detected total.
Partition check:
 hda: hda1 hda2 hda3 hda4
VFS: Mounted root (ext2 filesystem) readonly.
Adding Swap: 44348k swap-space (priority -1)
sysctl: ip forwarding off
Swansea University Computer Society IPX 0.34 for NET3.035
IPX Portions Copyright (c) 1995 Caldera, Inc.
Appletalk 0.17 for Linux NET3.035
```

```
eth0: 3c509 at 0x210 tag 1, BNC port, address  00 20 af 11 95 66, IRQ 11.
3c509.c:1.12 6/4/97 becker@cesdis.gsfc.nasa.gov
eth0: Setting Rx mode to 1 addresses.
```

After the kernel completes the inventory phase, it starts the independent *init* process, which manages the launching of all user and system processes. From that point on, the kernel only manages the computer resources that user and system processes request.

Log on as *root* and run the now-familiar command:

```
ps x | more
```

The process table shown in Listing 3-7 (which is a subset of Listing 3-2) shows these processes in parentheses. The *init* process has the PID of 1 because it is always the first process to start. The (*kflushd*) and (*kswapd*) are really part of the kernel but are shown as separate processes so that the kernel can schedule them. All the processes after them are separate from the kernel.

Listing 3-7: The system or kernel processes

```
PID TTY STAT TIME COMMAND
  1  ?  S     0:02 init [3]
    2  ?  SW   0:00 (kflushd)
    3  ?  SW<  0:00 (kswapd)
   21  ?  S    0:00 /sbin/kerneld
  166  ?  S    0:00 syslogd
  175  ?  S    0:01 klogd
  197  ?  S    0:00 crond
  209  ?  S    0:00 inetd
  220  ?  S    0:00 lpd
```

 You can see some of the internal details of these (or any) processes by looking in the */proc* directory. This special file system offers a window into the kernel. For example, if you display the contents of */proc/kcore*, you see the contents of all the memory in your system!

At startup, the *init* process first reads the */etc/inittab* file, shown in Listing 3-8. This file contains instructions for everything from staging the *run levels* of the kernel to starting the *getty* processes, which listen for terminal session logon attempts.

Listing 3-8: Run levels defined in /etc/inittab

```
#
# inittab        This file describes how the INIT process should set up
#                the system in a certain run-level.
#
# Author:        Miquel van Smoorenburg, <miquels@drinkel.nl.mugnet.org>
#                Modified for RHS Linux by Marc Ewing and Donnie Barnes
#

# Default runlevel. The runlevels used by RHS are:
#   0 - halt (Do NOT set initdefault to this)
#   1 - Single user mode
#   2 - Multiuser, without NFS (The same as 3, if you do not have networking)
#   3 - Full multiuser mode
#   4 - unused
#   5 - X11
#   6 - reboot (Do NOT set initdefault to this)
#
id:3:initdefault:

# System initialization.
si::sysinit:/etc/rc.d/rc.sysinit

l0:0:wait:/etc/rc.d/rc 0
l1:1:wait:/etc/rc.d/rc 1
l2:2:wait:/etc/rc.d/rc 2
l3:3:wait:/etc/rc.d/rc 3
l4:4:wait:/etc/rc.d/rc 4
l5:5:wait:/etc/rc.d/rc 5
l6:6:wait:/etc/rc.d/rc 6

# Things to run in every runlevel.
ud::once:/sbin/update

# Trap CTRL-ALT-DELETE
ca::ctrlaltdel:/sbin/shutdown -t3 -r now

# When our UPS tells us power has failed, assume we have a few minutes
# of power left.  Schedule a shutdown for 2 minutes from now.
# This does, of course, assume you have powerd installed and your
# UPS connected and working correctly.
pf::powerfail:/sbin/shutdown -f -h +2 "Power Failure; System Shutting Down"

# If power was restored before the shutdown kicked in, cancel it.
```

```
pr:12345:powerokwait:/sbin/shutdown -c "Power Restored; Shutdown Cancelled"

# Run gettys in standard runlevels
1:12345:respawn:/sbin/mingetty tty1
2:2345:respawn:/sbin/mingetty tty2
3:2345:respawn:/sbin/mingetty tty3
4:2345:respawn:/sbin/mingetty tty4
5:2345:respawn:/sbin/mingetty tty5
6:2345:respawn:/sbin/mingetty tty6

# Run xdm in runlevel 5
x:5:respawn:/usr/bin/X11/xdm -nodaemon
```

Eight run levels exist. A *run level* defines the types of processes that the system will execute. Run level S, for instance, is the single-user mode and is used to perform tasks that cannot be interfered with. Run level 3 is the normal operating mode. The *init* manual page describes run levels in detail.

As shown in Table 3-2, Red Hat Linux has seven execution levels. For the startup phase, after the boot phase in the startup process, the kernel runs at the Single User level (level 1) so it can complete all the necessary startup tasks before the system turns on multitasking. (For example, the kernel does an in-depth disk check during this part of the startup process.)

TABLE 3-2 RED HAT LINUX EXECUTION LEVELS

Level	Function
0	Low-level system initialization.
1	Single User or Administrative. Performs tasks that can't be done after multitasking is turned on — for example detailed disk checks.
2	Multiuser but without NFS (and, I suppose, SMB). In other words, no networking (similar to Windows 95 *Safe Mode*).
3	Full Multiuser. Networking, including NFS and SMB, turned on.
4	Not used.
5	X11. The X Window system that is run from system level. You log on and off from an X Window prompt rather than a shell prompt.
6	Reboot. First log off all users, stop all daemons, write all data waiting in memory to disk ("sync the disk"), and reboot the computer.

After the kernel hits level three (or five if you specify the system to run under X Window by default) where multieverything plus networking is enabled, it starts the general-purpose features such as the *getty* processes and the important *rc* scripts.

Red Hat Configuration Scripts (rc)

Configuration scripts are used to configure Linux systems when they are started. They perform tasks such as setting up routing tables as well as starting Samba. They are similar in function to the DOS AUTOEXEC.BAT file but much more flexible and powerful.

Red Hat — as well as other distributions such as Debian — keeps the traditional UNIX System V-like */etc/rc.d* directory, but this directory contains mostly links to the actual scripts in other directories. In this way, Red Hat can provide the type of added value that it thinks is best while still ostensibly maintaining compatibility with the rest of the Linux world and, to some extent, the UNIX world. Listing 3-9 shows the basic structure of this directory.

Listing 3-9: The Red Hat configuration script directory

```
total 17
drwxr-xr-x   2 root     root        1024 Dec  8 21:17 init.d
-rwxr-xr-x   1 root     root        1477 Nov  7 12:47 rc
-rwxr-xr-x   1 root     root         690 Nov  7 12:47 rc.local
-rwxr-xr-x   1 root     root        5470 Nov  7 12:47 rc.sysinit
drwxr-xr-x   2 root     root        1024 Dec  8 21:17 rc0.d
drwxr-xr-x   2 root     root        1024 Dec  8 21:17 rc1.d
drwxr-xr-x   2 root     root        1024 Dec  8 13:59 rc2.d
drwxr-xr-x   2 root     root        1024 Dec  8 21:17 rc3.d
drwxr-xr-x   2 root     root        1024 Dec  8 14:01 rc4.d
drwxr-xr-x   2 root     root        1024 Dec  8 21:17 rc5.d
drwxr-xr-x   2 root     root        1024 Dec  8 21:17 rc6.d
```

Here's a quick rundown on the contents of the Red Hat configuration script directory:

- The *init.d* directory contains many of the rc scripts for doing a basic system configuration. The *init.d* directory contains the rc scripts that handle such basic tasks as configuring the name of the computer, mounting the disks, and configuring the network interfaces. Table 3-3 lists the scripts and the functions they configure.

- The rc script is responsible for setting up the very basic stuff such as your hostname on startup. Then it takes care of starting and stopping services as run levels change.

◆ You can add your own functions to the rc.local script as you deem necessary.

◆ The directories *rc0.d* through *rc6.d* contain the links to the specific scripts to be executed when changing to each run level. These links are ordered by their names to start up their respective scripts in sequence.

◆ The *rc.sysinit* is run only once when the system is booted; it starts the general network script and turns on the swap partition.

◆ The network script in */etc/init.d/network* executes scripts found in the */etc/sysconfig/network-scripts* directory and shown in Listing 3-10.The scripts listed in Listing 3-10 perform the functions of rc.inet1 — that is, setting up the network adapters and basic routing.

TABLE 3-3 THE RC SCRIPT RESPONSIBILITIES

Script Name	Function
atd	Starts the *at* daemon, which schedules one-time execution of commands or scripts.
crond	Starts the *crontab* daemon, which schedules and executes periodic tasks.
functions	Contains functions used by other scripts.
gpm	Starts the *gpm* program, to enable mouse use from a text screen.
halt	Gracefully and safely stops the computer for reboot or shutdown.
inet	Starts TCP/IP networking. Configures Ethernet adapter interface, and sets routing and other services.
kerneld	Automatically loads kernel modules when needed.
keytable	Maps your keyboard.
killall	Stops unnecessary daemons.
lpd	Starts and stops the *lpd* printing daemon.
network	Starts and stops networking.
nfsfs	Mounts and unmounts remote NFS file systems.
pcmcia	Initializes PCMCIA adapters for laptops.
random	Initializes a random number generator.

continued

Script Name	Function
routed	Starts the *routed* daemon that uses the RIP protocol to automatically update the routing table.
rusersd	The *ruser* daemon helps locate users on remote machines. (It must be allowed as a service on the target machine.)
rwhod	The *rwhod* daemon lists the users logged into a remote machine. (It must be allowed as a service on the target machine.)
sendmail	Starts and stops the *sendmail* daemon, which transfers e-mail messages to their destination.
single	Sends computer into Single User (level 1) — also called Administrative state. It stops all daemons but retains all mounted partitions.
smb	Starts and stops Samba services (yeah!).
syslog	Starts system logging. This is very useful for security and other administrative functions.

Listing 3-10: Red Hat networking scripts — /etc/sysconfig/network-scripts

```
total 16
-rw-r--r--   1 root      root          110 Dec  8 14:00 ifcfg-eth0
-rwxr-xr-x   1 root      root          100 Nov  7 12:47 ifcfg-lo
-rwxr-xr-x   1 root      root          492 Nov  7 12:47 ifdhcpc-done
lrwxrwxrwx   1 root      root           20 Dec  8 13:55 ifdown -> ../../../sbin/n
-rwxr-xr-x   1 root      root          267 Nov  7 12:47 ifdown-post
-rwxr-xr-x   1 root      root         1191 Nov  7 12:47 ifdown-ppp
-rwxr-xr-x   1 root      root          672 Nov  7 12:47 ifdown-sl
lrwxrwxrwx   1 root      root           18 Dec  8 13:55 ifup -> ../../../sbin/ifp
-rwxr-xr-x   1 root      root          687 Nov  7 12:47 ifup-plip
-rwxr-xr-x   1 root      root          925 Nov  7 12:47 ifup-post
-rwxr-xr-x   1 root      root         2782 Nov  7 12:47 ifup-ppp
-rwxr-xr-x   1 root      root          346 Nov  7 12:47 ifup-routes
-rwxr-xr-x   1 root      root         1529 Nov  7 12:47 ifup-sl
-rw-r--r--   1 root      root          692 Nov  7 12:47 network-functions
```

As you can see in Listing 3-11, *ifcfg-eth0* is simple. It just configures the Ethernet network variables.

Listing 3-11: The ifcfg-eth0 script

```
DEVICE=eth0
IPADDR=192.168.1.254
NETMASK=255.255.255.0
NETWORK=192.168.1.0
BROADCAST=192.168.1.255
ONBOOT=yes
```

The *ifup* script makes use of that basic information to set up the kernel routing table so the system can communicate with the network adapter interface. Listing 3-12 shows the script.

Listing 3-12: The ifup script

```
#!/bin/bash
PATH=/sbin:/usr/sbin:/bin:/usr/bin

cd /etc/sysconfig/network-scripts

. network-functions

CONFIG=$1

[ -z "$CONFIG" ] && {
    echo "usage: ifup <device name>" >&2
    exit 1
}

[ -f "$CONFIG" ] || CONFIG=ifcfg-$CONFIG
[ -f "$CONFIG" ] || {
    echo "usage: ifup <device name>" >&2
    exit 1
}

if [ $UID != 0 ]; then
    if [ -x /usr/sbin/usernetctl ]; then
        exec /usr/sbin/usernetctl $CONFIG up
    fi
    echo "Users cannot control this device." >&2
    exit 1
fi

source_config
```

```
if [ "foo$2" = "fooboot" -a "${ONBOOT}" = "no" ]
then
    exit
fi


IPSETUP=no


DEVICETYPE='echo $DEVICE | sed "s/[0-9]*$//"'
REALDEVICE='echo $DEVICE | sed 's/:.*//g''
if echo $DEVICE | grep -q ':' ; then
    ISALIAS=yes
else
    ISALIAS=no
fi


# Old BOOTP variable
if [ "$BOOTP" = "yes" ]; then
    BOOTPROTO=bootp
fi


OTHERSCRIPT="/etc/sysconfig/network-scripts/ifup-${DEVICETYPE}"


if [ -x $OTHERSCRIPT ]; then
    exec $OTHERSCRIPT $CONFIG $2
fi


# is this device available? (this catches PCMCIA devices for us)
/sbin/ifconfig ${REALDEVICE} 2>&1 | grep -s "unknown interface" > /dev/null
if [ "$?" = "0" ]; then
    echo "Delaying ${DEVICE} initialization."
    exit 0
fi


if [ "$SLAVE" = yes -a "$ISALIAS" = no -a "$MASTER" != "" -a \
    -x /sbin/ifenslave ]; then
    RFLAG="" ; [ "$RECIEVE-ONLY" = yes ] && RFLAG="-r"

    ifconfig ${DEVICE} down
    echo "Enslaving $DEVICE to $MASTER"
    ifenslave $RFLAG "$DEVICE" "$MASTER"

    exit 0
fi
```

```
if [ "$BOOTPROTO" = bootp -a "$ISALIAS" = no ]; then
    ifconfig ${DEVICE} down
    ifconfig ${DEVICE} 0.0.0.0 broadcast 255.255.255.255 netmask 0.0.0.0
    route add default ${DEVICE}
    echo "Sending bootp request"
    TMPFILE='/bin/mktemp /tmp/bootp-${DEVICE}.XXXXXX'
    bootpc --returniffail --timeoutwait 6 --dev ${DEVICE} 2>/dev/null >
  ${TMPFILE}
    if [ "$?" = "0" ]; then
        . ${TMPFILE}
        BOOTPHOSTNAME="$HOSTNAME"
        echo "bootp response received -- using IP ${IPADDR}"
    elif [ -z "$IPADDR" ]; then
        echo "No bootp response recieved -- not configuring device ${DEVICE}."
        rm -f ${TMPFILE}
        exit 1
    else
        echo "No bootp response recieved -- using default configuration for
  device ${DEVICE}."
    fi

    rm -f ${TMPFILE}
elif [ "$BOOTPROTO" = dhcp -a "$ISALIAS" = no ]; then
    echo -n "Using DHCP for ${DEVICE}... "
    IFNAME=${DEVICE} \
        /sbin/dhcpcd -c /etc/sysconfig/network-scripts/ifdhcpc-done ${DEVICE}
    echo "echo \$$ > /var/run/dhcp-wait-${DEVICE}.pid; exec sleep 30" | sh

    if [ -f /var/run/dhcp-wait-${DEVICE}.pid ]; then
        echo "failed."
        exit 1
    else
        rm -f /var/run/dhcp-wait-${DEVICE}.pid
        echo "done."
        IPSETUP=yes
    fi
fi

if [ "$IPSETUP" != yes ]; then
    ifconfig ${DEVICE} ${MACADDR:+hw ether $MACADDR} ${IPADDR} \
        netmask ${NETMASK} broadcast ${BROADCAST}
    if [ "$ISALIAS" = no ] ; then
        route add -net ${NETWORK} netmask ${NETMASK} ${DEVICE}
    else
        route add -host ${IPADDR} ${DEVICE}
```

```
    fi

    # this is broken! it's only here for compatibility with old RH systems
    if [ "${GATEWAY}" != "" -a "${GATEWAY}" != "none" ]; then
        route add default gw ${GATEWAY} metric 1 ${DEVICE}
    fi


    . /etc/sysconfig/network

    if [ "${GATEWAY}" != "" ]; then
        if [ "${GATEWAYDEV}" = "" -o "${GATEWAYDEV}" = "${DEVICE}" ]; then
            # set up default gateway
            route add default gw ${GATEWAY} ${DEVICE}
            DEFGW=${GATEWAY}
        fi
    fi


    if [ "$BOOTPROTO" = bootp -a "$ISALIAS" = no ]; then
        if [ -n "$GATEWAYS" ]; then
            for gw in $GATEWAYS; do
                if [ $gw != "${DEFGW}" ]; then
                    route add default gw $gw ${DEVICE}
                fi
            done
        fi


        if [ -n "$DNSSRVS" -a -n "$SEARCH" ]; then
            echo "search $SEARCH" > /etc/resolv.conf
            for dns in $DNSSRVS; do
                    echo "nameserver $dns" > /etc/resolv.conf
            done
        fi


        if [ -n "$BOOTPHOSTNAME" -a "'hostname'" = "(none)" ]; then
            hostname $BOOTPHOSTNAME
        fi
    fi
fi

exec /etc/sysconfig/network-scripts/ifup-post $CONFIG
```

Note: As I mention in Chapter 1, Slackware has simpler scripts than Red Hat.
Red Hat wants to do more with the startup scripts because of its value-added
approach, but the scripts are not terribly difficult to understand. If you look in the
/etc/rc.d directory, you see a bunch of files that are called links. Links are simply

pointers to other files or directories. To maintain compatibility with other Linux and UNIX systems, Red Hat maintains the standard */etc/rc.d* structure, but it really stores the scripts in */etc/sysconf.*

Users and Groups

A *user* is an account owned by an individual. You log on to a Linux system as a user – *root* is an all-powerful user – and you have access to certain files, depending on the access privileges that the system administrator defines for your account. Each user gets a home directory and a password; this information is stored in the */etc/passwd* file. You can read, write, and execute files depending on your access privileges. If you own a file, you generally can do anything you want to it.

Files also have a group membership. Each user belongs to one or more groups. Inclusion in a group gives you access to files belonging to that group. The file */etc/group* governs group membership.

Every file has permissions assigned to it. Three classifications of permissions exist: *user*, *group*, and *other*. The user permissions apply to the owner of the file. Group permissions apply to the group that the file is a member of. Other includes every user that is not either the owner or a member of the group.

Red Hat uses a new convention in which each user belongs to a User Private Group (UPG). Each user belongs to a unique group. When individual users need to share work, a new group is assigned to that project and the users get membership in the new group. In this way, people get common access to similar work and yet maintain their own privacy.

Networking and the OSI Network Model

The International Standards Organization (ISO) has developed the Open Systems Interconnect (OSI) networking model. This model logically separates higher- and lower-level networking functions into seven layers. In Figure 3-1, I reduce the model to four layers, to make it easier to understand.

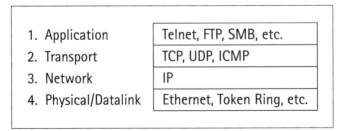

Figure 3-1: The seven-layer OSI networking model, reconfigured as four layers

My four-layer interpretation of the OSI networking model has the following layers:

◆ The Application layer deals with high-level protocols, including SMB, NFS, FTP, SNTP, DNS, SNMP, and Telnet. Application programs that rely on these protocols access them directly. For example, the ftp program speaks the FTP protocol. If you write one of these programs, you are concerned with this layer.

◆ The Transport layer includes the Transmission Control Protocol (TCP), the User Datagram Protocol (UDP), and the Internet Control Message Protocol (ICMP). The Application layer protocols depend on these protocols to ensure that the packets they produce reliably get to their destination. By "reliably," I mean that either sooner or later – depending on the protocol – each packet is acknowledged or not, and the Transport layer protocol informs the Application layer as to the status of each packet.

■ TCP is called a connection-oriented protocol because it makes sure that when each packet is received by the intended host, it is acknowledged immediately and in sequence. Telnet uses TCP for the obvious reason that when you enter a character sequence (for example, *abcd*), you want each character to arrive in sequence and be acknowledged in a timely fashion.

■ UDP is a connectionless protocol. It does not guarantee that a packet will reach its destination. The application is responsible for doing that. UDP is simpler than TCP, uses fewer resources, and is more efficient. Samba, for instance, uses UDP.

■ ICMP is an auxiliary protocol used for troubleshooting and maintenance. PING uses it.

TIP

The UNIX/Linux ports (sometimes referred to as Sockets) work at the Transport layer. You can connect to the TCP port 25 with Telnet, for example, and the *sendmail* daemon will talk to you. The Linux operating system provides this abstraction to ease the process of writing interprocess and inter-network communication.

◆ The Network layer contains the IP, or Internet Protocol, which deals with how to get each packet to its destination. It is responsible for encapsulating the higher-level packets (that is, a TCP packet) in an IP packet, which includes the destination and source addresses, the type of protocol, and several other chunks of information. If a packet is destined for a location outside of its LAN, routers down the line interpret this stuff and make their best guess on where and how to forward the packet.

◆ The Physical/Data Link layer deals with the physical media such as the cable and the electrical bits that come into and out of the network adapter. (*Note:* If your only network connection is a PPP or SLIP link, you can think of that link as your network adapter.) In an Ethernet adapter, the circuits on the adapter know how to interpret the electrical signals coming out of the demodulator – the actual wire conducts radio frequency (RF) signals – and then turn them into binary bits. From there, the bits are compared to the permanent Ethernet MAC (Medium-Access Control) address, and when they match, they are forwarded to the Network layer.

Note: Each network adapter has a unique binary address. Each manufacturer gets a range of addresses so that no two adapters in the world should ever get the same address (who knows about bootleggers). Looking back at Listing 3-6, one line shows my Ethernet adapter's address in hexadecimal:

```
eth0: 3c509 at 0x300 tag 1, BNC port, address  00 20 af 38 6a aa
```

To summarize, the OSI model logically breaks up the path that information – in the form of packets – takes in going from one computer to another as well as within the computer. The abstraction in this model enables you to ignore the messy details that need to occur for whatever process you need to create or use. Regardless of the level on which you are working, this model enables you to understand how your LAN – as well as the entire Internet – functions.

Samba

The existence of Samba is the primary reason why I am writing this book. It provides the straightforward and secure interface that NFS lacks, and it is considerably less expensive than Novell NetWare. Because Samba "speaks" the native Microsoft protocol, SMB, your Microsoft Windows PCs don't need any additional, expensive, or difficult-to-install software like they do with NFS. Samba turns your Linux PC into a powerful Microsoft Windows file and print server.

NFS is more complex to set up than Samba. It is not terribly difficult, but you need more patience. But the real problem is purchasing and configuring the software that makes your Windows client speak the NFS protocol. If you want to use Windows 3.*x* or MS-DOS as a client, you have to purchase software such as PC-NFS from SunSoft, Inc. (http://www.sunsoft.com); Windows 95 requires software such as DiskAccess from Intergraphics Corp. (http://www.intergraphics.com).

When you install Windows 95 out of the box, it comes equipped with Microsoft Client and Microsoft TCP/IP. You have to choose to install TCP/IP, but it is part of the Windows 95 package. Microsoft Client speaks the *Service Message Block (SMB)* protocol by default. That protocol is carried by the near-universal Internet Protocol (IP) or TCP/IP. TCP/IP is the default protocol for Linux, so Windows and Linux machines can converse. (Previously, with a UNIX/NFS server, you had to purchase additional software to install on the Microsoft Windows PC to make it speak NFS. This purchase was expensive because each PC client needed the software. Now, the single Linux PC already speaks the native Microsoft language.)

The Samba Protocol

The SMB protocol is responsible for negotiating the use of remote files and resources such as printers. Figure 3-2 shows the file *A*, which physically exists on the Linux server – in SMB terminology, it holds the *share*. When the Windows client wants to use this file, the client must tell the server to make *A* available to it and then to transfer the file's contents across the network. SMB is responsible for handling the details of the transaction negotiation.

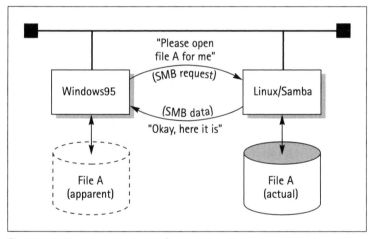

Figure 3-2: The server holds the file that the client needs.

For example, assume that I want to open the Microsoft Word file, A.DOC, which is physically stored on the hard drive of my Linux server. I have the Linux directory containing A.DOC mapped as the network *E:* drive. When I choose File→Open and then select E:\A.DOC in Word, Windows 95 sends an SMB request to the Linux box. Figure 3-3 shows a diagram of the process that occurs as the client asks for file access from the server.

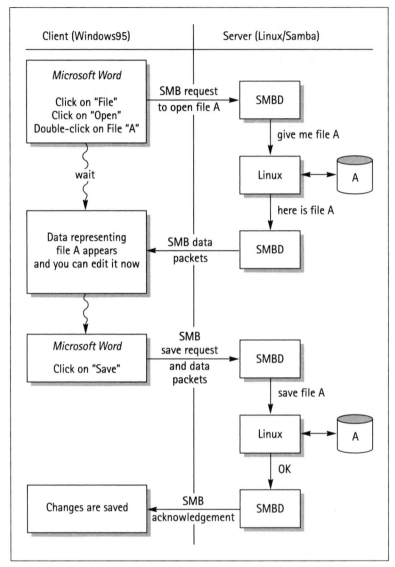

Figure 3-3: Client negotiates with the server for access to the file.

After the server receives a valid SMB request, it accesses its own file system to get the information. Samba acts as the interface between the SMB packets arriving on the network and the Linux operating system.

The Samba Daemons

The heart of Samba are the programs *smbd* and *nmbd*. They are usually run as daemons, which are processes that run all the time. Red Hat runs them as daemons by default. You have the option of launching them from *inetd* (a super daemon of sorts that looks for requests for any programs it has control of – as defined in *inetd.conf* – and launches them as needed). But that method slows down Samba, and the overhead of running *smbd* and *nmbd* as daemons is low, so the daemon method really does work best.

The *nmbd* process enables the Linux server to be browsed by other machines. The *smbd* daemon processes the SMB packets as they arrive on the network, and negotiates with the Linux kernel for access to its resources or shares. If a file is specified, the resource is a file; a printer request accesses a printer.

Actually, in the case of a printer, *smbd* stores the information to be printed in a print queue. For example, when I print CHAP_3.DOC to my network printer, Windows 95 sends the document data to the Linux server; *smbd* saves the data to */var/spool/lpd* and launches a print request on that file. The *lpd* daemon (enter *ps -x | grep lpd* to view it) is the process that handles the print request.

In the case of a file, *smbd* sends the data to the kernel, which ultimately saves it to disk.

The file *smb.conf* stores all the configuration information that *smbd* and *nmbd* use. Listing 3-13 shows part of the *smb.conf* file that Red Hat uses as a default. It should be on your system already, if you configured your system as I described in Chapter 1.

Listing 3-13: The Samba smb.conf file

```
; The global setting for a RedHat default install
; smbd re-reads this file regularly, but if in doubt stop and restart it:
; /etc/rc.d/init.d/smb stop
; /etc/rc.d/init.d/smb start
;======================= Global Setting ================================
[global]

; workgroup = NT-Domain-Name or Workgroup-Name, eg: REDHAT4
   workgroup = WORKGROUP

; comment is the equivalent of the NT Description field
   comment = RedHat Samba Server

; volume = used to emulate a CDRom label (can be set on a per share basis)
   volume = RedHat4

; printing = BSD or SYSV or AIX, etc.
   printing = bsd
```

```
    printcap name = /etc/printcap
    load printers = yes


; Uncomment this if you want a guest account
;   guest account = pcguest
    log file = /var/log/samba-log.%m
; Put a capping on the size of the log files (in Kb)
    max log size = 50


; Options for handling file name case sensitivity and / or preservation
; Case Sensitivity breaks many WfW and Win95 apps
;   case sensitive = yes
    short preserve case = yes
    preserve case = yes


; Security and file integrity related options
    lock directory = /var/lock/samba
    locking = yes
    strict locking = yes
;   fake oplocks = yes
    share modes = yes
; Security modes: USER uses Unix username/passwd, SHARE uses WfW type passwords
;       SERVER uses a Windows NT Server to provide authentication services
    security = user
; Use password server option only with security = server
;   password server = <NT-Server-Name>


; Configuration Options ***** Watch location in smb.conf for side-effects *****
; Where %m is any SMBName (machine name, or computer name) for which a custom
; configuration is desired
;   include = /etc/smb.conf.%m


; Performance Related Options
; Before setting socket options read the smb.conf man page!!
    socket options = TCP_NODELAY
; Socket Address is used to specify which socket Samba
; will listen on (good for aliased systems)
;   socket address = aaa.bbb.ccc.ddd
; Use keep alive only if really needed!!!!
;   keep alive = 60


; Domain Control Options
{ Deleted because we don't use Domain Controllers in this book. }
```

```
;============================ Share Declarations ======================
[homes]
   comment = Home Directories
   browseable = no
   read only = no
   preserve case = yes
   short preserve case = yes
   create mode = 0750

; NOTE: There is NO need to specifically define each individual printer
[printers]
   comment = All Printers
   path = /var/spool/samba
   browseable = no
   printable = yes
; Set public = yes to allow user 'guest account' to print
   public = no
   writable = no
   create mode = 0700

{Examples deleted. Please refer to /etc/smb.conf for more information. }
```

Unless you have configured your printer to work under this configuration, the only thing this sets you up to do is work in the *root* home directory. It's not terribly interesting except that it works! I find it fascinating that my keystrokes are being converted into electrical signals, which are then converted into electrical signals in binary form, shunted through a complex piece of silicon (a mere Intel 486), sent to other complex slabs of sand, converted into radio frequency energy to reappear in another room, converted back to bits and stored as magnetic domains on a mechanically spinning disk, and so on. Sure, it's only my ranting, but lots of things have to occur to save this ranting on a spinning disk.

The Samba Utilities

The utilities — *smbstatus, smbclient, nmbclient,* and so on — play an important role in configuring Samba. I show you how to use them to perform basic debugging in Chapter 2. As you build a more complex — production — system in Chapters 6 and 10, they become increasingly important. The more shares, clients, and users you build into your system, the more you need the utilities. Table 3-4 gives a synopsis of their uses.

TABLE 3-4 SAMBA UTILITIES

Name	Description
smbstatus	Displays the shares (resources) currently exported by Samba.
smbclient	Acts as a Linux-based Microsoft (smb) client. Useful for debugging.
nmbclient	Acts as a Linux-based browser client. Useful for debugging.
smbfs	A file system that works with the SMB protocol. With it you can mount SMB shares on Linux computers.
smbmount	Used to mount an *smbfs* on a Linux system.

The Red Hat 5.0 CD-ROM

The Red Hat CD-ROM itself is an invaluable resource. It contains not only the full Linux distribution, but also many other tools and documents. Table 3-5 lists the directories found on the CD-ROM.

TABLE 3-5 RED HAT CD-ROM CONTENTS

Directory	Contents
/RPMS/RedHat	The kernel and file system images installed directly onto hard disk.
doc	Red Hat and general documentation.
dosutils	MS-DOS programs and files used for creating Linux bootable floppy disks and creating or modifying hard disk partitions for installing Linux.
images	The kernel image that is copied directly to a floppy, which can then be used to boot Linux. This directory also contains supplemental floppy images used for PCMCIA disks.
live	The files, library, and programs as they exist on your disk after you install them. For example, you should be able to mount the *live/usr* directory from your CD-ROM and not need to have it on your hard disk. This is not a satisfactory way to work, because the CD-ROM is probably much slower than the hard disk, but it is possible.

continued

Directory	Contents
misc	The *autoboot* program and source code.
rr_moved	Empty.

 When you install the system for the first time, you use the MS-DOS program FIPS.EXE to repartition the hard drive in a nondestructive manner. You use the program RAWRITE.EXE to create a bootable Linux floppy disk; RAWRITE.EXE uses an image file from the \IMAGES directory.

When you install Linux for the first time (as I describe in Chapter 1), the installation program and the files it accesses are contained in the \DOSUTILS and \RPMS directories on this disk. If and when you upgrade or reinstall your system, you use the same programs.

The X Window System

Linux works just fine from a simple shell interface (that is, the *shell prompt*). An experienced administrator or user can do most things by entering commands at the prompts; this is analogous to working from the MS-DOS C: prompt. In fact, I believe that an administrator must perform a large percentage of tasks by entering explicit commands from the command line, to maintain an understanding of the underlying mechanics of the system. However, users of a Linux system – and administrators, to a lesser extent – greatly benefit by using a *Graphical User Interface (GUI)*. One reason is that you can do many things at once by separating tasks into different windows. Many tasks – for example, Web browsing – are best done graphically.

The X Window system is a GUI just like Windows 95 in that it insulates you from the underlying operating system. However, it operates "on top" of Linux, in much the same way as Windows 3.*x* uses MS-DOS as its base, while the Windows 95 GUI is tightly integrated with its operating system. The Linux version of the X Window system is called *XFree86*, reflecting its allegiance to the Free Software Foundation. It is produced by the XFREE86 Project, Inc. (I describe the Free Software Foundation in Chapter 4.)

XFree86 is stored primarily in the */usr/X11R6* directory. The executable programs and their libraries are stored in subdirectories. The configuration files are stored in the */var/X11R6* directory; however, the *XF86Config* main configuration file can be stored in */etc* if you wish. The *.xinitrc* file, which can configure the look and feel of your X Window main screen, is generally stored in your login directory.

If *XFree86* is anything, it is highly adaptable. You can configure it in so many ways that it is very confusing to the novice, and even to more experienced users. When I first installed it, I was lucky and actually got it working rather quickly with the help of the configuration program *Xconfig*. However, I quickly broke it, and I spent the next few days trying to recover the system. Red Hat obviously recognizes this problem as a major hurdle to mass acceptance, because the Red Hat distribution includes the commercial X Window system *Metro-X* by MetroLink, Inc. It works well. I have used it to configure several systems with different VGA cards, and each worked on the first try.

`/usr/bin/X11/configX`

Metro-X is a graphically based program that is readily used. To use it, you must know the manufacturer and the model number of your monitor and video card, as well as your mouse type and location. If you don't know about your monitor and video card, the program enables you to specify generic settings. I was surprised at how simple it was, considering the complexity of the task.

If you want to learn more about the workings of *XFree86*, you can use three other configuration programs from that organization: *Xconfigurator*, *XF86Setup*, and *xf86config*. All of these programs either narrow down the choices you need to make or attempt to probe for your settings, but they are not as simple or straightforward as *Metro-X*.

You can obtain more information about *XFree86* by visiting the following Web site: `http://www.xfree86.org`. For more information on *Metro-X*, check out `http://www.metrolink.com`.

The GNU General Public License

Linux uses the GNU General Public License (GPL). The Free Software Foundation developed the GPL as the key concept to its goal that software should be freely distributable. (For more information on the Free Software Foundation, see Chapter 4.) To that end, the GPL is designed to promote the freedom to distribute its software. The GPL does not necessarily mean that the software is free. Red Hat charges for the value it adds to Linux in the form of the CD-ROM and the configuration tools. But aside from the *Metro-X* software (and maybe some other packages that I am unaware of) you can distribute the software to others.

The GPL is printed in Appendix B, and I recommend that you read it. But here is a brief summary of its key points (I am not a lawyer; these are just my own opinions based on my reading of the GPL):

◆ Software published under the GPL is not in the public domain. It is not owned by the public but is copyrighted to the author(s) and protected by all international copyright laws. The author(s) choose(es) to allow you to use it in almost any way you want, but you do not own it.

◆ GPL published software is not shareware. Shareware authors own the copyright but ask you – without enforcement – to send them money after using their software.

◆ GPL software can be distributed for free or for a fee. When you get Linux off the Internet using anonymous ftp (see Chapter 5), the software is generally GPL and no charge is attached. When you buy a Linux distribution CD-ROM, you pay for the CD-ROM. Whatever GPL software comes on the CD-ROM, however, cannot be restricted. If I want to, I can give you the Linux source code, which I obtained on the Red Hat CD-ROM.

◆ GPL software can be modified and redistributed, but the new version must be covered by the GPL.

◆ GPL software must advertise that it is covered under the GPL.

This is an ingenious mechanism. First, it enables unhindered distribution of GPL software. Second, it enables money to be made by those who add value to the base software and thus propagate it further. Finally, it prevents someone or some organization from gaining a restrictive hold on GPL software in the future.

Conclusion

I could cover much more in this chapter, but my goal is to outline the most important fundamentals in the way that I would want to be taught. As you read further in this book and gain hands-on experience building and managing a Linux/Samba network, you will pick up more details. This chapter offers a framework from which you can proceed with confidence.

Summary

In this chapter, I discussed some of the internal workings of Linux:

♦ Rushing to get a system running in Chapter 1 precludes gaining much understanding of what's under the hood. Administering a network in the long term requires you to understand how it works.

♦ Understanding the meaning of the term *Linux* is important when discussing its internal workings. The meaning of Linux depends on the context in which it is used. It can refer to the entire system, or the kernel, or some combination of the two.

♦ The kernel is the heart of the Linux system. It controls when and how long processes are processed by the microprocessor (for example, the Pentium). It also controls access to the file system.

♦ The Linux *file system* translates the raw bytes that exist on disk drives into the files and directories that you use every day. It is important to understand how Linux works in order to manage a Linux system correctly.

♦ Understanding the Linux startup process is important to gaining an understanding of the total system. The kernel is loaded into memory and determines what devices it can use. It starts the *init* process, which starts the computer in a single-user mode for safety and guides it to whatever user state (multiple user, X Window, and so on) is defined in the *inittab* file. It also starts the *rc* scripts that configure everything from what disks are mounted to the network setup.

♦ Understanding the OSI network model helps you to conceptually understand how networks work. It is a logical protocol and separates the different types of processes that need to occur in order for networks to work. It would be much more difficult to modularize network communications without its discipline. Although the programs that it codifies don't make the distinctions it does (because they would be unwieldy), conceptually, it is useful.

♦ If Linux is the heart of the system, then Samba makes it practical. It replaces NFS as an economical way of connecting Microsoft Windows computers. It "speaks" the Windows native language, whereas NFS does not and requires expensive software to communicate.

♦ Originating as a Microsoft networking protocol, the Samba protocol, *smb*, provides a powerful method for connecting Microsoft Windows clients to Linux servers. Samba provides the interface between networked resource requests from Windows machines and the Linux kernel.

◆ Processing Samba network traffic is the job of the Samba daemons – *smbd* and *nmbd*. They run continuously in the background on the Linux server.

◆ Using the Samba utilities provides a useful, if not essential, set of tools for building and troubleshooting your client-server network.

◆ The Red Hat CD-ROM contains much more than just the Linux system. It also contains a wealth of documents, manual pages, HOWTOs, FAQs, and utilities.

◆ The X Window system is the graphical interface similar in some respects to the Windows 95 desktop. It provides the basis for many applications – including WordPerfect – and as a management tool. Without it, Linux would be a dull child.

◆ Linux and its GNU applications are copyrighted under the General Public License (GPL), which allows it to be distributed for free or for a fee but not restricted from being redistributed.

Chapter 4

Exploring the Origins of Linux

IN THIS CHAPTER

- ◆ The origins of UNIX

- ◆ Linus Torvalds – the inventor of Linux

- ◆ Andrew Tridgell and the development of Samba

- ◆ The history of the Free Software Foundation and GNU – "GNU's not UNIX"

- ◆ The conversion of the X Window system to Linux

- ◆ The Linux Journal

- ◆ The Internet, e-mail, SunSITEs, and the World Wide Web

ALTHOUGH I TAKE a hands-on approach throughout most of this book, knowing the history of the key subjects that make Linux possible is both interesting and useful. One person started the Linux project barely nine years ago, initiating a cascade of events that resulted in Linux's worldwide presence today. However, the foundation for Linux was laid more than 25 years ago (or even longer, depending on the perspective you take).

I can't possibly provide a complete history of everything that makes Linux, Samba, and all the rest possible. Just as historians will have a difficult time unearthing archeological e-mail remains in future centuries, I can only offer some background on the events (and the people) that make Linux possible.

To make a book such as this one necessary (well, I hope it is necessary), many events had to take place. The births of several key people were essential, but that's more detail than you really need. The following list summarizes – not necessarily in order of importance – the elements that I view as essential to the development and widespread deployment of Linux and Samba:

- ◆ The invention and propagation of UNIX

- ◆ The invention of Linux

- The invention of Samba

- The formation of the Free Software Foundation

- The GNU project

- The invention of the X Window system

- The Internet

- E-mail

- The World Wide Web

- Anonymous FTP

- The many people and publications that contribute insight and effort to support further development and deployment of Linux and Samba

I discuss these topics in the following sections. I leave it to you to decide whether you would be installing Linux and possibly using it to run your business if any particular element was missing.

UNIX

To trace the roots of Linux, I start with the invention of UNIX at the AT&T Bell Labs in 1969. The proprietary, mainframe-based operating systems did not meet the needs of some researchers. VMS, which would eventually serve the middle- and upper-middle range that science and researchers needed, had not yet been invented. Ken Thompson and others ended up writing their own, application-specific operating system for a spare Digital Equipment Corporation (DEC) PDP-7 minicomputer. Their development took on a life of its own and became UNIX.

 UNIX was originally written as Unics, which stands for Uniplexed Information and Computing System.

In 1976, Bell Labs released the Sixth Edition — commonly referred to as V6 — free of charge to universities. Bell Labs released V7 in 1979; it was widely distributed to universities and research labs, at a cost of $21,000 to commercial institutions and only $100 to universities. The inexpensive availability of UNIX made it very attractive to computer science departments all over the world, creating a huge base of users and developers. This distribution model would later be the driving force behind the development of Linux. Table 4-1 offers a timeline of the key events in the development and propagation of UNIX.

TABLE 4-1 UNIX TIMELINE

Year	Event
1969	Ken Thompson writes an experimental operating system on an unused DEC PDP-7. It becomes the UNIX operating system.
1970	Thompson and Dennis Ritchie port this operating system to a DEC PDP-11/20.
	Ritchie creates the C language, basing it on B. He writes it to be portable and incorporate modern programming techniques.
1971	Version 1 is released. It is written mostly in assembly language.
	Version 2 incorporates the pipe concept.
1973	Ritchie and Thompson write the first C compiler, designing it for UNIX.
	Version 4 is written mostly in C.
1974	AT&T permits UNIX source code to be distributed to universities.
1975	Version 6 is released. It is widely distributed to universities.
	University of California, Berkeley starts work on its own version (BSD).
1978	Version 7 is released as a portable operating system. It incorporates many of the features we now take for granted — for example, Bourne shell, Kernigan and Ritchie C, and uucp. Licensing fees are required.
1979	AT&T creates the commercial System III.
1983	AT&T releases its commercial UNIX System V.
	Berkeley releases BSD 4.2. (Sun Microsystems uses it for SunOS.)
1987	AT&T releases UNIX System V release 3. (Hewlett-Packard, Digital, and IBM base their versions on it.)
	BSD version 4.3 is released.
	Sun and AT&T agree to merge BSD and System V.
1990	AT&T releases System V release 4, which somewhat unifies BSD and System V.
	Digital, Hewlett-Packard, and IBM form the Open Software Foundation (OSF).
	Minix becomes available on the Internet.
1991	OSF-1 is released, to limited success.

continued

Table **4-1 UNIX TIMELINE** *(Continued)*

Year	Event
1992	Sun releases its Solaris OS, based on System V release 4.
	Linux 0.99pl5 is released.
1992/1993	Yggdrasil markets the first Linux distribution on a CD-ROM.
1994	Microsoft releases its Windows NT 3.5 server.
1996	Microsoft releases Windows NT 4.0 client and server.

Note: I obtained much of the preceding timeline information from the following Web sites:

```
http://www.cis.ohio-state.edu/hypertext/faq/usenet/unix-faq/faq/top.html
http://www.linux.ncsu.edu/LinuxDocProject/LDP/gs/node10.html
http://milieu.grads.vt.edu/unix_history.html
```

In 1975, researchers at the University of California at Berkeley began developing their own version of UNIX. The Computer Systems Research Group (CSRG) at Berkeley licensed V6 from AT&T and rereleased it as BSD (Berkeley Software Distribution), starting with 1BSD and evolving to 4.4BSD in the early 1990s. Although the CSRG developed much of the code, their version still included AT&T UNIX and so required the AT&T license. CSRG worked toward removing the AT&T code, but disbanded before completing that effort.

Thus, the two major flavors of UNIX are AT&T and Berkeley. With the arrival of the workstation class of computers in the 1980s, these forms of UNIX found their way into the commercial realm:

- Sun Microsystems's SunOS and Solaris

- IBM's AIX

- Digital's OSF/1 (now called Digital UNIX)

- Silicon Graphics's IRIX

- Hewlett-Packard's HP-UX

All of these versions are based on the AT&T or Berkeley versions, often with much cross-pollination and unique additions. Competing organizations have attempted to lay additional standards on top of the existing structures, resulting in a mish-mash of UNIX versions.

Note: The development of UNIX also heralded that of the C language. C evolved, logically, from the B language and introduced much of what we consider to be modern programming techniques: dynamic memory management, local variables, and so on. One of C's strong points is its portability. The fact that UNIX is written mostly in C (with the exception of some low-level device drivers) helped it spread quickly because if you had a C compiler, you could compile UNIX onto your architecture.

Out of this melee came the first freely distributable UNIX clones: NetBSD, 386BSD, FreeBSD, and of course Linux all arose from this primordial soup.

Linus Torvalds: Developing Linux

Several independent efforts to develop UNIX clones started in the late 1980s. Dr. Andrew Tanenbaum developed Minix as a teaching aid, basing this effort on the Intel 8086 microprocessor because it was universally available and inexpensive. Minix was useful for teaching operating system principles.

However, the 8086 has neither virtual- nor protected-memory capabilities, and it can address only 1MB at a time. That is nearly an absolute barrier to a modern operating system capable of running multiple tasks. So from its inception Minix was limited to its teaching role, though it did eventually move up to the 80386.

Linus Torvalds was a student at the University of Helsinki in the late 1980s. He realized that the Intel 80386 was the only widely available microprocessor that could run a fully functional UNIX clone. It was also, if not reasonably priced, the only one within reach. His choice of that platform was fortuitous because it guaranteed him the pool of willing hackers essential to perform the huge amount of programming needed to create a usable system.

 The terms *hacker* and *hacking* have negative connotations primarily because Hollywood uses them in that way and the mass media has picked up on this usage without doing much independent research. However, the term *hacker* really refers to someone who likes to experiment with and program computers and networks. For difficult programming tasks, you often have to make repeated, incremental changes on your way to making the code work. This is especially true when you are creating new and original work such as the Linux operating system; you have very few landmarks along the way and you end up hacking your way through the dense, dark jungle of programming code and networking protocols. So, at least in this book, *hacking* is a good thing.

Torvalds was determined to build a kernel featuring virtual memory, preemptive multitasking, and multiuser capability. (I think the current popularity and reliability of Linux obscures the fact that virtual memory was still relatively uncommon at that time. It was no small decision to include it.) This was a huge job and few people familiar with the complexities of operating systems would have given an individual a chance of creating a new one. For instance, a GNU project to create a UNIX clone called the *Hurd* had been in the works for several years and Torvalds was "just" a student.

In the spring of 1991, Torvalds started his project. By that time, Minix had started to support the advanced Intel processors. Linux version 0.01 appeared in September of 1991, followed by 0.02 in October, and 0.03 in November. During this period, other people became involved and the snowball started rolling downhill. Enhancements and bug fixes were daily occurrences via the Usenet (`comp.os.minix`) and e-mail. The kernel very quickly became UNIX-like.

Part of Torvalds' inspiration was getting other people involved in the project. Recognizing that one person is unable to develop a complete operating system, he used the Internet to get people involved. Here is an example of his sales strategy from `comp.os.minix`, as recounted by Matt Welsh (`www.linux.ncsu.edu/LinuxDocProject/LDP/gs/node10.html`):

> Do you pine for the nice days of Minix-1.1, when men were men and wrote their own device drivers? Are you without a nice project and just dying to cut your teeth on an OS you can try to modify for your needs? Are you finding it frustrating when everything works on Minix? No more all-nighters to get a nifty program working? Then this post might be just for you.

And:

> As I mentioned a month ago, I'm working on a free version of a Minix look-alike for AT-386 computers. It has finally reached the stage where it's even usable (though may not be depending on what you want), and I am willing to put out the sources for wider distribution. It is just version 0.02 . . . but I've successfully run *bash*, *gcc*, *gnu-make*, *gnu-sed*, *compress*, etc. under it.

You gotta love it!

Anyway, as the kernel took shape and news of it spread, other GNU functions were ported to it. Until the all-important compilers and shell — *gcc* and *bash* — became available at version 0.12, the compilations were done via Minix. Version 0.12 came online in January 1992.

GNU stuff had been around since 1983. In my own experience, it offers generally better quality than its commercial counterparts. When a bug is discovered or an essential enhancement is needed, the responsible people typically just do it. Personal pride and responsibility replace a formal, bureaucratic process. Anyway, the involvement and support of the GNU community was essential for the success of Linux. The *gcc* compiler was essential to the nuts-and-bolts development task, but all the other functions had to be done if Linux was to be more than a hacker's paradise.

Linux quickly approached the time to go public. Issues such as *how to continue the dispersed development while at the same time releasing updates* were addressed; even-numbered releases would remain stable or unchanged for relatively long periods, while the odd-numbered releases would be allowed to change quickly with enhancements and fixes. Release 1.0.0 quickly became 1.0.8, but then remained unchanged until midyear. The development class had many changes, however.

In early 1994, Torvalds determined that version 0.99pl14r would be his prerelease model. He worked on it and finally allowed 0.99pl15 to go out the Internet door. In true random propagation, news of it filtered out via the Internet and became available to the average computer user. I wasn't looking for it; I casually explored the various newsgroups for interesting software and stumbled on it. I don't remember seeing the first reference to Linux, but my subconscious somehow did, and here I am.

As development work increased, sundry issues such as coordination became important. One of the solutions was the implementation of the *distribution* concept. Rather than leave the novice to search for all the important pieces on the Internet, it was decided to organize those pieces into a central location that could be accessed via anonymous ftp. This decision led to putting it all on floppies. (Slackware is still organized on its CD-ROM in this way.) The ultimate solution arrived when Yggdrasil released the first CD-ROM distribution in late 1992. Putting the distribution on a CD-ROM was a pivotal development for Linux because it permits straightforward installation.

Development has proceeded fast and furious. Linus estimates that he has written, at most, 10 percent of the code that makes up Linux. This originality is a natural part of its success; Linux now has a life of its own. Linus continues to develop the heart of Linux, working on such things as symmetric multiprocessing and memory management. He has graduated from Helsinki University and has taken a job in California. To sum it all up, see the Linux timeline in Table 4-2.

TABLE 4–2 THE LINUX TIMELINE

Year	Event
1969	UNIX emerges at AT&T.
1974	UNIX is distributed to universities. The stage is set for a worldwide class of highly adept systems programmers. The dynamic of cross-pollination is started as programmers have access to a major operating system for the first time.
1983	Richard Stallman creates the Free Software Foundation (GNU project).
1984	X Window gets started at MIT.

continued

TABLE 4-2 THE LINUX TIMELINE *(Continued)*

Year	Event
1988	Minix emerges.
1990	Linus Torvalds takes his first C programming class.
1991	Linus Torvalds starts what will become Linux.
1992	Version 0.01 is discussed on the Internet.
	Version 0.95 is completed.
	Yggdrasil releases alpha Linux distribution in December.
1993	Yggdrasil releases production Linux distribution.
1994	Version 0.99pl14r is finalized.
	Version 0.99pl15 is released via the Internet.
	XFree86 is released via the Internet.
	(Spring) Yggdrasil releases the first CD-ROM containing a Linux distribution.
	Red Hat, Slackware, and others emerge on CD-ROM.
1995	The first modularized version emerges.
1996	Caldera releases v1.0 with Netscape included (WordPerfect for X shipped).

Note: You can read about the preceding events in more detail at the following locations:

```
http://www.linux.ncsu.edu/LinuxDocProject/LDP/gs/node10.html
http://www.linuxjournal.com/
```

Andrew Tridgell: Developing Samba

Andrew Tridgell is another person who saw a need and filled it – albeit in a round-about way. In 1991, he was a Ph.D. student in the Computer Sciences Laboratory at the Australian National University, in Canberra, Australia. He needed to beta test the Digital Equipment Corporation (DEC) product PC X server eXcursion on his MS-DOS PC.

Unfortunately, that product required the DEC proprietary network, Pathworks, to function. Andrew was no longer able to mount his Sun Microsystems file server's

NFS resources on his PC; he had used the SunSoft PC-NFS to make his PC speak the NFS protocol. He was unable to use both Pathworks and NFS at the same time.

Never having written a network program before and not knowing what a socket was, he decided to write a program to make his PC speak the NFS protocol. He had access to an old DecStation 3100 running Ultrix.

Note: A *socket* is a software abstraction used for interprocess and network communications in Linux and UNIX. The operating system translates low-level communications – for example, an arriving Ethernet packet – into a higher-level one, which an application can access with simple systems calls. For example, the Telnet server program listens to port 25 for incoming Telnet connections. The Linux operating system translates Ethernet packets into higher-level form, and they appear on port 25. Therefore, the Telnet server needs only to concern itself with handling Telnet sessions and not any of the lower-level networking issues.

What followed was a fascinating job of reverse engineering. First, he reasoned that he could determine the protocol by "spying" on the network traffic. So he looked at some of the Pathworks code used for socket communication and learned what was happening at that level. Then, he wrote a C program, *sockspy.c* (Tridgell's account of how he invented Samba is in the file /usr/doc/samba-1.9.16p11-3rh/history), to capture the network traffic that Pathworks exchanged with the Pathworks server.

With that information, he wrote some MS-DOS-based C programs to do simple file operations such as opening, reading, and writing to a remote file. By looking at the packets that the client and the server exchanged, he worked out the meaning of the bits and bytes in each packet. At that point, he started writing his own programs to perform the same functions on the Sun.

Very quickly – in a day or two – he managed to establish a connection to the Sun and read a file. Within a week, he was mounting directories from the Sun on his PC!

After consulting with the DEC representative who had given him the beta version of eXcursion about the legality of what he had done, he was pointed to the *NetBIOS* protocol. DEC had based their system on Microsoft's NetBIOS (specified in RFC1001 and RFC1002), which is public in the first place, so everything was perfectly legal. Andrew, in his own account, points this out a bit sheepishly; in some cases, great deeds are not arrived at directly! (Perhaps fate would have intervened somehow.)

Note: RFC stands for "Request For Comment." This is the method by which Internet standards are publicly displayed and sometimes developed. You can find RFC1001 and RFC1002 at the following Web sites:

```
http://www.cis.ohio-state.edu/htbin/rfc/rfc1001.html
http://www.cis.ohio-state.edu/htbin/rfc/rfc1002.html
```

In January 1992, he released his work, calling it Server 0.1. He received a good response from Pathworks users interested in running it with non-DEC UNIX computers. A month later, he released Server 0.5, which was quickly followed by Server 1.0.

But when he got an X-terminal, he no longer had any need for his work and let it go. Inquiries trickled in for a year, until one e-mail message caught his attention in November 1992. Dan Shearer, at the University of South Australia, had read Tridgell's news release from the previous year. He was interested in using Tridgell's software with Linux and wanted to know the status.

Andrew had not heard about Linux and was curious. Within months, he was a convert. Dan Shearer converted Andrew's software to Linux. By December 1993, discussion of the work appeared on `comp.protocols.tcp-ip.ibmpc`.

The next major step happened when Tridgell found out via the newsgroup that a Microsoft client worked with his server. It was available from Microsoft via anonymous ftp and worked the first time he tried it! It was only at this point that he learned about the SMB protocol. It too was available via ftp, and he jumped at it. He used it to remove the constants that he had independently determined; but those were the only changes he had to make.

In December 1993, he officially started NetBIOS for UNIX. Fortuitously, the working name – *smb-server* – was already trademarked and he changed it to *Samba*, to my eternal gratitude. From that point, Samba took on its own life and I, along with millions of others, have benefited from Andrew's curiosity, intelligence, and inspiration.

I love this story. Out of one person's need to use his computer with two pieces of incompatible software comes a new direction for the computer world. Am I exaggerating? Since late 1993, the use of his software has exploded. Linux distributions are reaching the mass market now, and soon millions will use his software. The whole point of this book is to show how to set up a professional network. Individuals and corporations in this country and the rest of the world can benefit immensely. You no longer need to spend a lot of money to set up a system.

Note: The history described here is available at the following Web site:

`http://www.ssc.com/lj/issue7/samba.html`

You can find discussions of the Samba protocols in the following newsgroups:

`comp.protocols.tcp-ip.ibmpc`
`comp.protocols.smb`

The Free Software Foundation and GNU

In 1983, Richard Stallman founded the Free Software Foundation (FSF) as a non-profit corporation. As he states, its purpose was to create a UNIX clone operating system, including the kernel and tools. The term *Free* in this group's name refers to the freedom to run, copy, distribute, study, and modify the software. This was the genesis of the GNU project, which stands for "GNU's Not UNIX." (It's a recursive pun.)

Most of the utilities that come with the various Linux distributions were created by the GNU project. The compilers (*gcc*, *gcc+*, and so on), the shells (for example, *bash*), and many other tools are all GNU programs. Without the FSF, Linux as we know it wouldn't exist. This has created some friction in the Linux community, because Linux gets all the publicity even though the various Linux distributions include numerous pieces of software other than just Linux itself.

For that reason, the Free Software Foundation has recently had a bit of a flap with the *Linux Journal*. Stallman wanted the *Linux Journal* to refer to Linux as GNU/Linux. *Linux Journal* replied that they simply reported what was being done in the Linux world and because only Debian (a nonprofit corporation that produces its own Linux distribution) was calling it GNU/Linux, the general term would remain *Linux*. Richard Stallman also wanted to call Linux "Lignux."

My perspective is as an end user. I use the software that others develop. Before writing this book, my view of GNU and the Free Software Foundation was very vague. I knew that the utilities I used – such as *bash*, *gcc*, and *gzip* – were from GNU. I had looked at the FSF license and that of Linux, but I did not have any appreciation for the subtleties that differentiate them. I bought the CD-ROM that contained all their software and was very happy that it had been developed and released to the public that way, but that's where my interest stopped.

Now I know more, but after I finish this book and go back to my consuming ways, it all will fade into the background. I'll be more aware, but that's all. From that perspective, I think it is ultimately silly and harmful for the infighting to continue. I can't help but recall the Monty Python movie, *The Life of Brian*, where the "Judean People's Front" brawls with the "People's Front of Judea" over their petty jealousies. Nothing gets accomplished under those types of circumstances.

In my opinion, the *Linux Journal* gives proper credit to the other groups that have made Linux possible. Linus Torvalds has explicitly acknowledged the debt Linux owes to the FSF.

Note: You can find a discussion of this topic at the following Web site:

```
http://www.kudonet.com/~markst/personal/gnu.html
```

Orest Zborowski: Translating X Window to Linux

The X Window system was developed at MIT Artificial Intelligence Labs in the 1980s. It was envisioned as a client-server, architecture-independent graphics platform. The idea is to run an X client on one computer and view graphically whatever you want on the server. For example, you run *xclock* on computer X and view it on computer Y. (You can also run *xclock* on X and view it on X.) Computer X can be a PC or a Mac or anything else, and so can Y. The concept is powerful and elegant.

Orest Zborowski experimented with Minix at home in the early 1990s. He realized that it did not have the possibility of running X. The BSD clones could conceivably support X, but needed a dedicated computer. When Zborowski saw that Linux supported multiple partitions and had memory management and other advanced features, he decided to attempt to port X to it.

He saw that it was an excellent platform and that the addition of X would enhance it even more. His first step was a strategic one. X required many System V system calls, so he decided to "make Linux fit X rather than X fit Linux." The first version of Linux he used was 0.12 in 1992. The kernel and C libraries were changing rapidly, so he was challenged just to keep up with coordinating with them. Thus, he wrote System V calls for Linux, which was based more on BSD at that time. Two things resulted: The X server for System V and Linux are nearly identical, and System V and BSD are now folded into Linux.

In its early stages, Linux had no graphics, so Zborowski had to develop very simple graphics just to do his work. His first major step was to use the dot character (.) to represent screen pixels. By using the familiar text screen of 80 characters by 24 lines, he was able to view part of his X display. That important step helped him to get true graphics working.

As his work progressed, the usual conglomeration of interested developers gathered. David Wexelblat, David Dawes, and others formed XFree86 to support X on 386 computers. They used the X11R5 version of X. XFree86 for Linux was born. XFree86 differs somewhat from Linux, however, in that submitted code must go through a peer process; Linux takes a more relaxed approach.

Work proceeded quickly and XFree86 was publicly released in 1993. ELF (Executable and Linking Format) support was publicly added in late 1995 or early 1996. Drivers and such are constantly being added. The end result is the quick, sophisticated windowing system that was optionally installed in Chapter 1 and is used throughout this book.

X Window is as big a piece of the Linux puzzle for users or clients of Linux as Samba is for Linux servers. Linux provides the basic platform and XFree86 provides the user interface. Without Microsoft Windows, your PC is useless. XFree86 provides the same function. Of course, general-purpose applications such as Word are not yet available (although Caldera has introduced WordPerfect for X) to turn your Linux box into a real consumer PC, but that will happen eventually. In any case, Orest Zborowski deserves credit for supplying this important system.

Note: You can find a discussion of this topic at the following Web site:

```
http://www.linuxjournal.com/
```

A Common Meeting Place: Linux Journal

One of the most endearing features of the Linux movement is the diverse and wide ranging nature of its development and use. In many ways, it mimics the Internet that cradles it – both have many independent but interconnected pieces. You can find out nearly anything about any feature just by searching the Internet.

However, users, developers, and programmers also need a common meeting place, and the *Linux Journal* fills that need. Phil Hughes envisioned, created, edited, and now publishes the journal. With the death of one founder, Gerry Hammons, it halted publication of the first issue. Robert Young and the ACC Corporation published the first two issues in January and March 1994. Phil Hughes became the editor.

In March 1994, Hughes decided to have Specialized Systems Consultants, Inc. (SSC) – the publishers of UNIX Pocket References – publish the journal. They produce an excellent publication. It is an essential tool for programmers, users, and administrators, with articles on everything from writing device drivers to managing firewalls. I can't live without it.

Note: You can find a discussion of this topic at the following Web site:

```
http://www.linuxjournal.com/
```

Recounting Yet Another History of the Internet

You may choke a bit if I say the Internet has been lost in all this discussion. (More than a few people have grown weary of hearing about the super-duper Information Superhighway.) Of course, I have mentioned it. But I find that I almost take it for granted – like electricity. Without the Internet, however, none of this great stuff could have occurred. The Internet provides the medium that makes possible the continued development and widespread deployment of Linux. And as Linux progresses toward maturity, the Internet continues to be essential for its further development.

I am fascinated by the whole process by which all those packets find their way to the right eyeballs. One idea can propagate around and around until it pings enough synapses to change the world. I am not being too enthusiastic. That is exactly what happens. The Internet is as important as any other development of the Post-Industrial age. It provides the basis for a truly collective effort that does not swallow up the individual.

Well, don't let that diatribe stop you from reading a little history about how it all came about.

It all started back in the 1950s and 1960s, because the United States Department of Defense (DOD) wanted to decentralize its communications. The Feds reasoned that a well-placed nuclear attack could target a few bottlenecks and kill its command-and-control capabilities. So the DOD formed the Defense Advanced Research Projects Agency (DARPA).

DARPA was given an unusual amount of freedom in those days. It was able to obtain the best hardware and some talented people. It sponsored an experimental project, which created the ARPANET. It experimented with the models and protocols that led to our current state. In 1969, the Interface Message Processor (IMP) – basically a router – was installed at the University of California, Los Angeles (UCLA). Soon, several other universities and defense research sites were connected to the ARPANET. In the following decade, the foundation of the internetworking protocols was developed.

As the protocols advanced toward the familiar TCP/IP Internet protocols (actually, I should probably say the TCP, UDP, ICMP/IP – but that would be a mouthful), interest in interconnecting networks grew. The National Science Foundation (NSF) adopted the Internet protocols to connect supercomputers. Using fast, leased telephone lines, the NSF set up the NSFNET, making it easy for universities and government laboratories and such to communicate over the continent. That proved to be the push that was needed, and soon businesses found that they could use the system. The Internet as we know it came into existence in the middle to late 1980s.

Until the middle 1990s, however, the Internet was available for the most part only to large institutions or organizations. Unless individuals had an account at a university, they were limited to commercial dial-ups, such as CompuServe, which provided their own network and services distinct from the Internet. Connecting your computer or LAN to the Internet (as opposed to just remotely logging into a connected computer as a terminal session) was very expensive. My company was interested in connecting as far back as 1988, but the costs were prohibitive – $10,000 to $20,000 per year (including a router). In 1990, we actually bought a little 386SX PC to put in a colleague's university office so we could connect via SLIP. We got as far as being able to establish a connection (unreliable, however), but were shot down by the administration.

Note: SLIP stands for Serial Line Internet Protocol; it was the first widely used system for connecting a computer to the Internet via the phone system. It is a very simple protocol that puts a control character at the beginning and end of each IP packet. It has been nearly replaced by the Point-to-Point Protocol (PPP). See Chapter 7 for more information on both protocols.

In 1994 Internet Service Providers (ISPs) started offering SLIP and PPP connections at consumer prices. I recall the first flyer I saw advertising PPP connections for only $30 per month! I couldn't believe it was true, but it was exactly what my company needed. That little ISP has been out of business for a while now, but enough of them survived that Internet access is a given in any major town or city.

That was the final key. The big providers such as CompuServe and America Online (AOL) started offering PPP connections and the smaller ISPs became very adept at providing sophisticated services such as frame relay connections (high-speed, permanent Internet connections). All of a sudden, after 20 years, almost everyone became connected – not with a simple terminal connection, but as part of the Internet.

Note: The Internet, as you recall, is the conglomeration of all the computers and networks in the world that can communicate with each other via the internet protocols. In other words, the Internet involves the interconnection of networks. Very few are connected directly, so it is the common set of rules, or protocols, they use that enables them to connect indirectly. When you connect your computer via the phone, you establish the same type of connection as if your computer were hooked into an Ethernet at a university. Your computer becomes part of the whole.

Your computer, connected via PPP, is on par with any computer on the Internet. All Internet services are available, and new ones are conceived continuously. You have access to the same functionality as the local university or corporation, if not at the same speed. However, that is going to change, too. Table 4-3 gives a synopsis of some important events in the development of the Internet. Stay tuned.

TABLE 4-3 THE INTERNET TIMELINE

Year	Event
1945	Vannevar Bush, President Roosevelt's science advisor, envisions a mechanical mechanism — Memex — that would store an individual's intellectual and personal database.
1957	In response to the Soviet Union's launch of Sputnik, Eisenhower establishes the Advanced Research Projects Agency (ARPA).
1965	ARPA sponsors the first computer network, with one machine at MIT's Lincoln Lab, in Massachusetts, and one at the System Development Corporation in California. The computers are linked directly.
1967	At the ACM Symposium on Operating System Principles, the packet switching concept is proposed. Lawrence G. Roberts proposes the ARPANET.
1969	The ARPANET comes online. Nodes are installed at UCLA, Stanford Research Institute (SRI), the University of Utah, and UC Santa Barbara.
1970	Norman Abrahamson, of the University of Hawaii, develops the ALOHAnet, which became the basis for the modern Ethernet.
1971	ARPANET grows to 15 nodes.
1972	Request For Comment (RFC) 318: Telnet is introduced.
1973	ARPANET connects to University College of London, UK, and Royal Radar Establishment, Norway. RFC 454: File Transfer Protocol (FTP) is introduced.

continued

TABLE 4-3 THE INTERNET TIMELINE *(Continued)*

Year	Event
1974	Vinton Cerf and Bob Kahn publish the design of TCP.
1976	Bell Labs develops UNIX-to-UNIX Copy (UUCP).
1979	Usenet connects University of North Carolina and Duke University.
1981	BITNET and CSNET are created with funding from NSF. Theodore Holm Nelson introduces the idea of *Xanadu* that connects documents in a way similar to the current Hypertext Transfer Protocol (HTTP) but with royalties paid to the original authors. Nelson also introduces the concept of *Transclusion*, which is similar to the Universal Resource Locator except it would enable addressing at the substring level.
1982	Transmission Control Protocol (TCP) and Internet Protocol (IP) are adopted by the Department of Defense. RFC 827: External Gateway Protocol is introduced.
1984	ARPANET consists of more than 1,000 nodes.
1986	NSFNET starts. Network News Transfer Protocol (NNTP) is created.
1987	ARPANET/NSFNET consists of more than 10,000 nodes.
1989	Tim Berners-Lee, of CERN, proposes a localized precursor to the World Wide Web (WWW).
1990	ARPANET is decommissioned and replaced by NFSNET. The World Wide Web project begins and later that year a simple browser is demonstrated.
1991	The NFSNET has traffic of 1GB per month. A WWW line-by-line browser is released for the DEC VAX, IBM RS/6000, and Sun 4 workstations. Later that year, the first U.S. Web server is started at Stanford Linear Accelerator Laboratory (SLAC).
1992	The first WWW software goes online at `alt.hypertext`.
1993	Mosaic for X is released. In the spring, the total http traffic on the Internet is 0.1 percent and 50 http servers are known to exist! By the fall, the figures are 1 percent and 200 servers.
1994	Marc Andreesen leaves NCSA to form, with Jim Clark, Mosaic Communication Corp., which becomes Netscape. NSFNET traffic is 10GB per month.
1995	NSFNET relinquishes its Internet backbone management role. Now, all Internet traffic flows through and between Internet service providers (ISPs) via the phone system.
1996	The Internet becomes widely accepted and used by the noncomputer professional public.
1997	ISPs are given the responsibility of distributing IP addresses.

Note: You can find the sources from which this timeline was derived at the following Web sites:

```
http://www.amdahl.com/internet/events/inet25.html
http://www.w3.org/pub/WWW/History.html
http://www.cis.ohio-state.edu/htbin/rfc/rfc318.html
http://www.cis.ohio-state.edu/htbin/rfc/rfc454.html
http://www.cis.ohio-state.edu/htbin/rfc/rfc827.html
```

E-Mail

Originally, UNIX e-mail was transported via UUCP (UNIX-to-UNIX Copy). When the Internet was simple, computers that needed to communicate could reasonably figure out where the other one was. So UUCP requires an explicit path to be defined. Ah, the good old days when I had to walk through three feet of snow to log on.

TIP If you want to use UUCP to mail a message to *Wishbone* on computer *Hambone*, which is connected to your computer via *Treat*, instead of the familiar mail address `someone@C.somelan`, you use the following address: `treat!hambone!wishbone`. UUCP is good for some situations. At my previous job, we had a private WAN and use UUCP because of security restrictions.

But modern e-mail enables you to send messages and files (attachments) to anyone in the world who has e-mail access. Thanks to the wonderful people who created TCP/IP, those protocols seamlessly send your e-mail packets merrily on their way to the recipient. Your message or file is broken into smaller chunks, or packets, and sent out onto the Internet. Each packet passes from network to network via any of several algorithms that make a best guess about the best direction. Those packets end up at their intended destination, unless the system is not configured or is not working.

The productivity enhancement that e-mail provides is immeasurable. Professionally, I use it as much if not more than the telephone, and I generally prefer it to the phone. It enables me to contact people quickly and reliably. Neither the recipient nor the sender is tied to a desk or even a building. As long as I check my e-mail, I am in touch. The other advantage is that it forces me to understand the problem that I am solving or the situation I am addressing. I have to be able to express the problem in words that both my contact and I can understand. Thus, I first must understand and be able to enunciate it to my contact. No more "um, well, ah, you know." Enunciate or die!

The World Wide Web

The World Wide Web (WWW) is the system that has truly popularized the Internet. It is the graphical tool for doing everything from viewing my dog's photographs to bargaining with an automobile dealership. Other than helping Linux distributors sell CD-ROMs, I don't believe it has helped Linux development directly. However, by popularizing the Internet so much, it has decreased connection costs and created new markets – in this way, the WWW has helped Linux indirectly. In sum, the WWW makes things better for Linux types like you and me.

The story behind the Web is a fascinating confluence of fanciful ideas, technology, and human ingenuity. Vannevar Bush, President Roosevelt's science advisor, envisioned a mechanical desk, named Memex, that would store a person's entire intellectual needs – books, records, and communication – way back in 1945. The need for combining randomly linked information, such as an address book and professional databases, was the genesis behind Tim Berners-Lee's idea for what would become the Web.

 In 1967, Dr. Andries van Dam of Brown University released the first *hypertext* system. IBM funded the research and the Apollo moon project used it on an IBM/360 mainframe for documentation.

In 1980, Berners-Lee was working at the European Laboratory for Particle Physics (CERN), using a number of different, incompatible systems to store his various databases. He pushed forward a project to store "random associations between arbitrary pieces of information" and called the resulting program *Enquire*.

 In 1987, Bill Atkinson of Apple Computers released the HyperCard, which uses hypertext concepts. It helped popularize the hypertext concept.

Berners-Lee left CERN in the middle 1980s, and the project lay fallow. When he returned in 1989, CERN had fully adopted the new TCP/IP standard and had evolved into a distributed computing and object-oriented environment. CERN's new direction suited his, and in 1989 he published the papers "Information Management: A Proposal" and "World-Wide Web: An Information Infrastructure for High-Energy Physics." In proposing the foundation for the modern Web, his motivation was to efficiently interconnect the high-energy physics world.

Berners-Lee's initial proposal called for two phases of three months each and included four software engineers and one programmer. In 1990, he started the project and based it on a NeXT workstation. By November, a WYSIWYG browser and server were running. In 1991, he and his team made their biggest contribution to the world of computing when they released the Hypertext Transfer Protocol (HTTP) and the Universal Resource Locator (URL) to the public.

The importance of this event can't be underestimated. Without the vast resources and publicity of the Internet, the World Wide Web would have remained a tool of particle physicists alone.

With the seed of the Web protocols drifting across the Internet, enter the graduate student Marc Andreesen at the National Center for Supercomputing Applications (NCSA). He and other graduate students developed a graphical browser called Mosaic for X. In February 1993, they released it for the Apple Macintosh and Microsoft Windows.

In 1993, Andreesen left NCSA and with its blessing formed a company that would become Netscape. Nearly all the original development team eventually joined. Netscape released their browser to the public, too. It was a great business decision. It was a great benefit to the world. Thank you, Mr. Andreesen. Thank you, Mr. Berners-Lee.

 James Gosling is the inventor of the Java language. He now works for Sun Microsystems. Bill Joy, one of the founders of Sun Microsystems, conceived the Java language as a tool to place computers into the consumer market. Reliability and simplicity are paramount if consumer products are to communicate, so different and better tools were required. Java failed in its first incarnation as the operating system of the *7 personal digital assistant (PDA), but in 1994, Java found its niche when Joy incorporated it into a Web browser and later when Netscape embraced it.

You can find further information on the history of the WWW at the following Web sites:

```
http://www.w3.org/pub/WWW/History.html
http://ei.cs.ut.edu/~wwwbtb/book/chapt1/web_hist.html#1.3.1
http://www.next.com/WebObjects/History.html
```

SunSITE and Anonymous FTP

The SunSITE (Software, Information, and Technology Exchange) was born at the University of North Carolina (UNC) at Chapel Hill in 1992. Sun Microsystems Computer Corp. offered a Request For Proposal (RFP) to establish an *anonymous FTP* (a system to which you can log on without an account and fetch files that are specifically made available to the public) archive on the Internet. They wanted to use information technology to expand information exchange between universities. UNC proposed to offer anonymous ftp plus new technologies such as Gopher and Wide Area Information Server (WAIS) – both used to search and retrieve documents off the Internet. The first anonymous ftp system went online in May 1992.

The UNC people quickly expanded the original intent to include information from nontechnical sources. They actively sought out the presidential campaigns to publish their stuff on the SunSITE. This effort was successful and the system now offers a wide range of subjects not limited to the nerd world. And you can get all the software you want off the system. Linux, GNU, X Window, and more are available on the SunSITE. Several Linux distributions – exactly what you get on CD-ROM – are available for the picking. The only trouble is that you may not want to download 600MB at 2.8Kbps (if a 28.8Kbps modem achieves 2.88 kilo-bytes-per-second, 600,000,000 bytes take 208,333 seconds or 3,472 minutes, or one heck of a lot of prime TV viewing time).

A single Sun SPARCstation 2 with 32MB of memory and 4GB of disk space served approximately 20,000 file transfers a month by October of 1992 (that was twice the original estimate). My, how times change! As of 1996, the SunSITE at UNC averaged 500,000 hits per day and held more than 47GB of data. A six-processor SPARCCenter 1000 with 1GB of memory and more than 50GB of disk space dishes out your file transfer requests.

The last time I actually tried to log on to the SunSITE at UNC, I was refused with the answer that it could not handle more than 50 requests at one time. That was about 1995, but it shows the limitation of one computer system. So it's not surprising that as the original SunSITE becomes more popular, the system has expanded to include more than one site. Dozens (by the time this book is published, hundreds) of SunSITE *mirrors* exist. They all keep up-to-date copies of the SunSITE information base. Generally, the data is updated daily.

Note: You can find more information about this topic at the following Web site:

```
http://sunsite.unc.edu/sun/inform/sunsites.html
```

And a Cast of Thousands

The success of the luminaries described in this chapter would not have been possible without the hundreds and thousands of people working on the smaller problems. I can't begin to list them, because it would take a whole book. But the spirit of doing it all for fun and pride is amazing. We should recognize the indispensable contributions that so many people have made.

Has there ever been another example of a product that is maintained and propagated by both volunteers and commercial interests? Will that dynamic continue or will it disintegrate? Assuming that it continues, what will it mean? I don't know, but stay tuned.

Looking to the Future

Oh, I don't know. Your guess is as good as mine.

Okay, this is my book, so I will pontificate. The future is bright! The glass is more than half full and it's going to get fuller. We now have an operating system that is easy to obtain, powerful, inexpensive, and moving forward. It has the tools to perform a set of functions that enable it to work as a server to other computers. Soon, desktop applications such as word processors will complete the picture for the average user. Linux is not only an alternative to Windows, but also to all the various UNIX versions.

Oh yes, my predictions. How about "Linux Inside" commercials?

Summary

In this chapter, I discussed the history of the important, if not essential, factors in the development of the Linux operating system and its important subsystems:

♦ UNIX is the invention of a few people who wanted an operating system based on their needs. Its development was an evolutionary process based on UNIX's availability to a large number of people.

♦ Linux is the invention of Linus Torvalds, who wanted a UNIX clone. He broke with convention and went against the common wisdom to push forward his idea of a UNIX clone.

♦ Andrew Tridgell created Samba because he saw a need and filled it. Working backward, he recreated a protocol he did not know existed. When he learned of its existence, he was able to push the last step and create a file and printer sharing system that was superior to the commercial NFS in both performance and security.

♦ Orest Zborowski ported the X Window system to Linux. It has been essential to the widespread use of Linux. Without it, you might still know and use Linux, but it would be far less popular. It also provides the basis to the future viability of Linux as a major operating system. Common desktop functions such as word processing require a graphical user interface, and X hits the spot.

♦ The growth and expansion of Linux has been greatly enhance by both the Free Software Foundation and GNU. Both have provided the tools and philosophy that Linux used to create itself and uses today to function as a general-purpose development platform. Some friction has resulted because of the popularity and attention given to Linux without recognizing the role of GNU.

◆ The Internet acts as the glue that held and holds all of this together. The Internet started as a U.S. DOD project – ARPANET – and evolved into the National Science Foundation's NFSNET, which became widespread in the university and government laboratory world. It provided the incubation funding and access to become the now universally used and accepted Internet.

◆ E-mail is the common communication method for both technical and social needs. It provides the efficient mechanism for concisely and quickly conveying ideas and is essential for technical progress.

◆ Usenet – news groups – has provided the common place for group discussions and dissemination of information. Linus Torvalds got the ball rolling by asking for help on the Minix group: `comp.os.minix`.

◆ The World Wide Web was born and grew exponentially from the start. Its creator, Tim Berners-Lee, has seen his invention create millionaires out of Marc Andreeson and seemingly everybody else who was initially involved, except himself. It created a market, which is similar to the one the original PC created in the early 1980s. Like the PC, it created a monster that generated a market many times larger than ever was imagined. The WWW indirectly helped us because by bringing more people and money in, more Linux installations will be ordered than would have been without it.

◆ The SunSITE, an anonymous ftp, helped spread Linux and GNU. SunSITE was originally the primary distribution method, and it remains the distribution point for ideas and software. It provides an efficient mechanism for a common archive of software. You can still get a full Linux distribution from dozens of SunSITEs or mirrors around the world by anonymously logging into one.

◆ The contributions of all the lesser known people and organizations have made everything that we know of as Linux possible. Currently, Linus Torvalds estimates that only 10 percent of the Linux kernel code is still his; that number was closer to 50 percent just over a year ago. The rest comes from people who will not get recognized but without whose efforts Linux would not be possible.

◆ In the future, Linux, Samba, and everything associated with them will only get better. The product is so good that the commercial efforts and word-of-mouth will increase their use.

Chapter 5

Finding and Using Resources

IN THIS CHAPTER

- ◆ Using the Internet as a technical resource
- ◆ Finding and requesting information in newsgroups
- ◆ Obtaining software from anonymous FTP sites
- ◆ Finding free software on vendors' Web sites
- ◆ Optimizing your searches on the Internet
- ◆ Acquiring commercial software
- ◆ Using the numerous resources on this book's CD-ROM
- ◆ Seeking out Linux-related magazines and books
- ◆ Attending a degreed Systems Administration program at a university

MY EARLY INVOLVEMENT with systems administration was spent groping around in the dark. Initially, my job was more as a programmer than as an administrator. As the job evolved, I tried to find resources to help me learn how to do it. However, I was somewhat isolated, because I did not work with other systems administrators. The few I knew were busy, and I was often too embarrassed to ask what I knew were very simple questions. The local university and community college did not offer any classes on the subject. I couldn't find many books on the subject, and those that I did find generally addressed an experienced audience. I faced the standard chicken-and-egg dilemma.

However, I did know about and started using the Usenet. The Usenet comprises newsgroups, each of which is dedicated to a single subject; hundreds of technically oriented ones exist. Accessing newsgroups enables me not only to find answers to my questions, but also to observe how the systems administration community interacts and works. Knowing the etiquette and the language of a profession goes a long way toward helping you successfully communicate and avoid feeling like an idiot. (If you don't feel like an idiot, does that mean you are not an idiot?) Anyway, being a professional and acting professionally require interaction with your peers.

In the absence of daily, person-to-person contact, the Internet provides a reasonable substitute.

I believe that I've learned something useful about the available resources and how to use them. In this chapter, I discuss the various resources available to you. Linux, Samba, and all the other subsystems you use to create client-server networks are available from different sources. Auxiliary and supplemental intellectual resources exist to complement them. As both an administrator and a user, you need these resources, because they enable you to troubleshoot and upgrade your system on-the-fly. The Internet and even the Red Hat CD-ROM (or other commercial Linux distributions) provide immediate access to help for any number of problems.

Knowing that such resources are available and accessing them are two different things. By sharing my experiences with using these resources, I can help you to find and use the resources that meet your needs. After you become familiar with the available resources, you can immediately use them. It's like learning to read a map; after you get oriented, you can find your way. Learn and discover.

Using the Internet as a Technical Resource

In some respects, the topics I discuss in this chapter fit in Chapter 2, which discusses troubleshooting. The Internet, the distribution CD-ROM, and good old-fashioned paper provide many tools that you can use for problem solving. Other useful troubleshooting tools include technical newsgroups, Web sites sponsored by manufacturers and interest groups, and e-mail. Maybe I can compile the information that I provide in this chapter as the Internet Troubleshooter.

But the Internet deserves special consideration because it is so much more than just a problem-solving aid; it is amorphous and vast. No one knows how many Web sites, networks, computers, or users are connected at one time or all together. No one knows how to find all the information that may be useful. In my opinion, very few people or organizations are ever sure that they can locate a significant subset of any given subject.

The Internet is also evolving into forms unforeseen. For example, the World Wide Web evolved from the need to link information arbitrarily and conveniently. Now, it is one of the most popular, and maybe even useful, inventions ever. Soon, developers will integrate Web technology into their operating systems so that you can't easily see where your personal computer ends and the Internet begins. Who knows what else may emerge from the swamp?

Back on the practical earth, I get a large quantity of software directly from the Internet (Net). Ignoring the human social component – that is, conversing with friends and colleagues, just for the heck of it – the Internet is a huge technical resource that is not easily measurable or quantifiable. Although I know that I can't necessarily find *all* the information I need, I usually get what I need and often more than I can handle.

When I use the Internet as a technical resource, I often start with the question, "How can I find something?" After a little searching, the question usually becomes, "How can I make sense of all the stuff I just found?" Philosophy isn't my bag, so this chapter focuses on problem solving and resource grabbing. In the following sections, I offer some examples from my own experiences, to show you how to find the information and the resources you need.

Using Newsgroups

In early 1995, I was loaned a Gateway 90MHz Pentium P5-90 with a huge – at the time – 700MB hard drive. It had an IDE/ATAPI (the CD-ROM drive uses the IDE interface) NEC 260CDR CD-ROM drive and 16MB of memory. I had just purchased a Slackware CD-ROM and was hot to try it.

The P5-90 came with MS-DOS/Windows 3.11 preinstalled. I used FIPS to repartition the disk, and installed Slackware Linux on the second partition. The CD-ROM booted fine under MS-DOS/Windows 3.11, but was not recognized by Linux. The IDE/ATAPI was new back then – at least in the Linux world. Linux had IDE/ATAPI drivers, but none seemed to work for the NEC.

I started browsing the `comp.os.linux.setup`, `comp.os.linux.hardware`, and `comp.os.linux.announce` newsgroups. I searched mostly on keywords such as `NEC`, `NEC260`, and `CD-ROM`. After a while, I found a couple of postings referring to the NEC drive.

I was lucky because Gateway 2000 PCs are popular machines, and other Linux users were having similar problems. After a little searching on the keywords `NEC`, `260`, and `NEC260` (see the following tip for more detailed instructions) I started seeing requests for help setting up machines similar to mine. I discovered that I needed a recently released driver for the NEC: *nec260.c*, which is a C program. I obtained this driver from the Net by using the anonymous FTP process, which I discuss later in this chapter. I recompiled my kernel to use the NEC driver, and my Linux system mounted the CD-ROM without a problem.

By accessing and searching newsgroups, you can tap into the large information base created by the technical people who read and respond to the newsgroups. Newsgroups are distributed worldwide, and you can probably find someone who has encountered and solved even the most obscure problem. By the way, it is really satisfying to be able to solve *someone else's* problem.

Using Text-based Linux News Readers

By using Web browsers such as Netscape and Internet Explorer, you can easily view newsgroups and post messages. If you do not have that capability for some reason (setting it up can be tricky), you can use the old shell-based news readers *rn* (read news), *trn* (threaded read news), and *xrn* (an X Window system, menu-based news reader).

Here's the procedure you follow to search for Linux-related information by using *rn*:

1. To start *rn*, enter **rn** at the prompt. To get help, press *h*. It's pretty simple after that; you can get by with just a few commands.

2. To access the `comp.os.linux.setup` newsgroup, enter the following command: **g comp.os.linux.setup**. If you are not already subscribing to this newsgroup, enter **y** to do so, when prompted. (To list the other Linux newsgroups, you should enter the command **l linux**. A list of unsubscribed groups is returned. At that point, you can enter the **g** command with the news group that you wish to go to — for example, **g comp.os.linux. networking**.) Here's a list of the current Linux newsgroups in the *comp.os* area:

```
comp.os.linux.advocacy
comp.os.linux.announce
comp.os.linux.development.apps
comp.os.linux.development.system
comp.os.linux.hardware
comp.os.linux.m68k
comp.os.linux.misc
comp.os.linux.networking
comp.os.linux.setup
comp.os.linux.x
```

3. To find the next subscribed newsgroup (which in this case is any Linux group), enter the following command: **/ linux**.

4. After you find the newsgroup you want, enter **y** to read the first article or enter **=** to see a list of articles.

5. From within a newsgroup, enter **h** to see the available commands.

6. From within a newsgroup, enter a search string to find articles related to the topic you want. For example, enter **/NEC** to find any articles with the string *NEC* in the title; enter **/NEC/h** to find the string *NEC* in the article header; enter **/NEC/a** to find the string *NEC* anywhere within the article (yes, this search takes longer than the others).

7. Press the – key to toggle between the last article you viewed and the current one.

8. After you read an article, *rn* marks the article as read, and the article doesn't show up again in your list. Press the *m* key to mark an article as unread.

9. You can hide stuff to avoid cluttering your screen. See the help window for instructions.

10. Enter **q** to quit from the newsgroup.

11. Enter **q** to quit from *rn*.

You can post articles to a newsgroup by responding to previously posted articles or by submitting new articles. After you read an article, you can post a response by pressing *r*. The news reader program guides you through each step in the response process. You can choose between writing the body of your response while you are still in the news reader or including an existing text file. In my opinion, you should take your time when preparing a response — with the possible exception of a one- or two-sentence reply. (It is embarrassing to have something you didn't really mean or think through clearly posted throughout the world and then have to endure the flames in response.) When I prepare a posting, I try to be precise, concise, and civil — just as I want to be treated in return.

If you want to post a new article, run *Pnews* from your shell. Again, you are guided through the article posting process.

The news article posting process asks you questions such as where to send your submission. The options range between your local area and the world. Because bandwidth is precious, please be judicious. If you want to ask a question such as when the next Linux user group meets in your town, don't ask to be posted to the world.

Using Anonymous FTP

When my last employer got its first full-blown Internet connection — a 56-Kbps (bit per second) leased line — I had to build a firewall. Firewalls were mysterious beasts, and I had only a general idea of what they did and how they did it. I didn't know where to start, so I went to my newsreader and listed all the unsubscribed groups related to security. I eventually found a reference to the *TIS (Trusted Information Systems)* corporation and went to the public (pub) section of their anonymous ftp site. After some searching using Archie, and an informal subscription process, I found their Firewall Toolkit (*fwtk*). I downloaded, untarred, and edited *Makefile*. With just a little work, I got it running. It worked well running our firewall until the company disbanded. (Currently I use the program *IP Firewall and Accounting Administration — ipfwadm —* at work and for my home network. I describe its use in Chapters 8 and 10.)

Configuring the firewall was difficult, even though it came with helpful manual pages and documentation. (The topic of firewalls is complex and has many nuances – it can fill books.) However, I was able to solve my basic problem with little work. Had I followed the normal – for me – path of randomly searching magazines, advertisements, and such, I might have eventually found one or more commercial packages – at least one of which would have been way out of my price range. After endless phone calls, I'd have made my best educated guess and made the purchase. I would have been either lucky or not, but I generally never felt comfortable until the hardware or software was working.

The end result of my search (and work) was that I got the raw material to work very quickly and at no cost other than my time. The educational process took much longer.

Finding Free Software from Other Sources

Not all freely distributable software comes from SunSITEs. Many commercial organizations use the Internet to distribute their software.

In early 1995, I was taking a course in systems administration at the University of New Mexico. For our class project, we each built a personal Web page. The hard part was to build a CGI-bin system (a secure, interactive Web page server). At the time, Mosaic was the dominant Web browser, and Netscape was just getting started. I started by looking at Mosaic and trying to figure out exactly how it was put together – I'm still not sure of anything except that you have to obtain a specific X Window library or something like that to make it run. Being a slacker in the classical sense, I didn't like the idea of spending money or doing a lot of work just to get started on my project.

But I had heard of Netscape, so I looked for their Web page. I used *Archie* – one of the original Internet search tools – to locate the anonymous ftp site that stored Netscape. I downloaded it and was surprised and pleased when it compiled and ran under Linux.

Right now, you can obtain almost anything – short of a full-blown word processor, spreadsheet, and some productivity tools – on the Internet for free. You just have to look and be willing to risk some time compiling and learning the stuff. However, if something is difficult, I may reach the point at which I have to open my checkbook.

Many companies, while not giving away their application software, often make updates and other information available at their Web sites. For example, in writing this book, I sometimes use an old PC that can't determine a disk drive's parameters from its BIOS at boot time; I must manually enter information such as the number of sectors. And, of course, I no longer have the spec sheet. I easily found the parameters by going to the manufacturer's Web page.

Searching the Internet

Yes, I use Netscape to search the Net. And no, I do not "surf the Internet, dude." I dislike that expression – don't ask why; I just do. (I'm not a purist like one friend who longs for the days when the Net was just for scientist nerds.) You can probably tell me how to do it better, because I just can't figure out why entering a key word such as *computer* gives you 24,000 hits on Tasmanian Wind Surfing. I'm just kidding of course, but sometimes the search engines (the software that tries to locate what you are looking for) are very difficult to use. The best advice that I can give is simply to start experimenting. The more experience you gain, the more easily you will be able to locate information on the Internet.

Web browsing is an important function. I have conducted most of my basic research for this book using a browser. I include numerous URL (Universal Resource Locator) links throughout the book, and I'm not going to ignore a multibillion dollar industry. I do feel somewhat ignorant because I don't know much more than the rudiments of how to conduct searches. Let me run down some of the simple stuff. It has worked pretty well for me, so it's worth something.

You should note that the distributed and independent nature of the Internet makes it difficult to search. The search algorithms (engines) basically go from one publicly available server to another and store information. This is a fairly haphazard method because so much changes so quickly. The algorithms themselves do a good job, but they are still limited by the sheer diversity of the Net.

Therefore, you need to think about your question before you start searching. You are smarter than the search engines in use today, and you need to help them. Also, remember that the Web is highly commercial now and sellers are constantly trying to outmaneuver the search engine people and vice-versa. A company selling surfboards may put the word "surfboard" in its Web page 100 times in an attempt to appear before its competitors when you search on the word "surfboard." The developers of search engines look for that trick and try to have their search engines ignore the resulting hits. Ugh! If all you are doing is looking for articles on surfing the Net, it's just going to clutter up your world. So consider exactly what you are looking for to start and then try to come up with a reasonable search phrase. In this case, using a string such as `"surfing the net"` is preferable to `surfing + net`.

So keep in mind the diverse and commercial aspect of the Net. To avoid getting too many hits, use precise keywords. However, if you use a phrase that's too specific, you may miss useable hits. I get the best results by using a short, two-, three-, or four-word phrase, enclosed in quotation marks. If you combine search words by using AND, search engines produce unsatisfactory answers. For example, rather than entering `UNIX + history`, I prefer to use `"UNIX history"`.

Acquiring Commercial Software

When you must acquire a commercial hardware or software package, the most difficult part of the process often involves asking the right questions. You compound the challenges of an already difficult task when you don't know the right questions. At the most basic level, you need to ask, "Can the product work with my machine?" Taking this question to the next level of detail: "Can this version of the product work with my machine, which already has the following features installed?" You must also consider whether the sales or technical person understands the question you are asking.

My recommendation: Carefully consider your requirements and how your system is constructed. Make diagrams; write out your questions beforehand; make lists – do anything that helps you clarify things in your mind.

Whenever possible, use e-mail for subsequent conversation after your initial call to a vendor. By doing so, you force yourself to think through your problem or question enough to convey it in writing. By calling first, you establish a human contact with your counterpart. But by using e-mail for subsequent contacts, both parties can carefully consider the written information and questions and thus reduce the possibilities for errors and misunderstandings. I find it far more efficient to answer e-mail at my keyboard than to talk on a phone. The side benefit is that I am not tied to my desk as much and do not have to worry about missing important phone calls. This hybrid approach works very well.

By conducting problem-solving sessions via e-mail, you also have a written record of the process. Do write notes, however. The combination of e-mail and written notes provides great records.

Never throw away notes. In writing this book, I am using notes from years ago. I never imagined that I'd ever have any use for these notes; fortunately, I was too lazy to clean up my mess. Okay, throw away some stuff. I don't want to encourage fire hazards, but think carefully before you discard something. The new tape technology and large disk drives lend themselves to conveniently archiving large amounts of old stuff. Pattern search programs such as *grep* or *egrep* enable keyword searches on the archives so you can actually find something. Consider saving your digital records, documents, and files for subsequent use. Paper is another matter, but you can scan those documents you consider somewhat important.

Using Your Linux CD-ROM

The Red Hat CD-ROM has a wealth of information (virtually all Linux distribution CD-ROMs have this documentation). It comes with online manuals (*man pages*), Frequently Asked Questions (FAQs) files, and HOWTO documents. You didn't install all the man pages during the installation process I describe in Chapter 1, but I show you how to install them in the following section, "Using Man Pages." They are well worth the few megabytes of disk space that they occupy.

Using Man Pages

The man pages are the most useful and most accessed documentation resource you have. Before installation, they are stored in RPM format on the CD-ROM. To install them, log on as *root* and, if you have an IDE CD-ROM drive, enter the following commands:

```
mount -r -t iso9660 /dev/hdb /mnt/cdrom
rpm -ivh man*
```

The first command mounts the CD-ROM — I give you more details about this command later in this section. If you have a CD-ROM drive with its own controller you should substitute its driver for the generic */dev/hdb*. For instance, with a Mitsubishi driver you should use */dev/mcd* instead of */dev/hdb*.

After you install the man pages, you access a specific man page by entering the following command:

```
man man
```

In place of *man*, you specify the subject you want to examine. (For example, *man* indicates that you want to find out about the *man* manual page itself.) Every Linux command, library, file format, and so on has a man page. They are generally located in the */usr/man* directory, though they can optionally be located in such places as */usr/local/man* and */usr/X11R6/man*.

If you have the Red Hat CD-ROM mounted, you can access the manual files even though you don't have them installed. To mount the CD-ROM, log on as *root* and enter the following command:

```
mount -r -t iso9660 /dev/hdb /mnt/cdrom
```

Where *iso9660* is the CD-ROM standard file format, *hdb* is the typical ATAPI device file (adjust accordingly for your system), and */mnt/cdrom* is the mount point. If */mnt/cdrom* does not exist, you can simply use the */mnt* directory alone as your mount point and adjust the preceding command accordingly, or you can create */mnt/cdrom* by entering the following command:

```
/bin/mkdir /mnt/cdrom
```

Now use the following command to access the man pages from the CD-ROM:

```
man -M /mnt/cdrom/live/usr/man ls
```

The *-M /mnt/cdrom/live/usr/man* parameter tells man to look in that directory for the man page file. This method is useful if you do not have enough disk space to load everything you want or if your environment is not set up to include the man page you want.

FAQs

The CD-ROM contains documents that describe how to do almost anything on your system. Before you install them to disk, they generally reside in the */live/usr/doc* directory on the CD-ROM. This directory contains the README files that describe how to use the HOWTOs, the HOWTOs themselves, and the Frequently Asked Questions (FAQs).

Mount the CD-ROM described in the preceding section, and look in the directories */mnt/cdrom/doc*, */mnt/cdrom/doc/FAQ*, and */mnt/cdrom/doc/HOWTO*. Use the following command to list the contents of the *doc* directory:

```
ls -l /mnt/cdrom/doc
```

Listing 5-1 shows the contents of the *doc* directory.

Listing 5-1: The CD-ROM doc directory

```
total 583
drwxr-xr-x   7 root      root         2048 Nov  6 23:48 FAQ
drwxr-xr-x   3 root      root        12288 Nov  6 23:49 HOWTO
-rw-r--r--   1 root      root        91842 Nov  7 04:55 LIN-XESS41.ps
-rw-r--r--   1 root      root         5870 Nov  7 04:55 LIN-XESS41.txt
-rw-r--r--   1 root      root       465575 Nov  7 04:56 MetroX41manual.ps
-rw-rw-r--   1 root      root        10531 Nov  7 03:41 README.ks
-r--r--r--   1 root      root          335 Nov 10 22:37 TRANS.TBL
drwxrwxr-x   4 root      root         2048 Nov 10 21:53 rhmanual
```

List the contents of the FAQ directory by entering the following command:

```
ls -l /mnt/cdrom/doc/FAQ
```

The files listed in Listing 5-2 contain information on both general and specific topics. For example, if you have problems with your ATAPI CD-ROM during the installation process (which I describe in Chapter 1), you can consult the ATAPI-FAQ. It has answers to the most commonly asked questions for that type of drive.

Listing 5-2: The CD-ROM Frequently Asked Questions directory

```
-rw-r--r--   1 root     root         10615 Feb  6  1996 ATAPI-FAQ
-rw-r--r--   1 root     root        124958 Oct 14 13:31 FAQ
-rw-r--r--   1 root     root         31539 Mar 29  1997 GCC-SIG11-FAQ
-rw-r--r--   1 root     root          2802 Jun 18 11:36 Joe-Command-Reference
drwxr-xr-x   2 root     root          2048 Nov  6 23:48 Linux-FAQ
drwxr-xr-x   2 root     root          2048 Nov  6 23:48 PPP-FAQ
-rw-r--r--   1 root     root            57 Sep  9 05:29 README
-r--r--r--   1 root     root           476 Nov 10 22:37 TRANS.TBL
drwxr-xr-x   3 root     root          2048 Nov  6 23:48 Threads-FAQ
drwxr-xr-x   2 root     root          2048 Nov  6 23:48 linux-faq
drwxr-xr-x   2 root     root          2048 Nov  6 23:48 security
```

The FAQ directory contains compiled lists of questions and answers. For example, if you have problems mounting your CD-ROM drive, you should consult the ATAPI-FAQ at the top of the directory by using the *more* command:

```
/bin/more /mnt/cdrom/doc/FAQ/ATAPI-FAQ
```

Listing 5-3 shows the first three questions answered in the FAQ, to give you an idea of its look and feel.

Listing 5-3: The first two pages of the ATAPI-FAQ

```
atapi.FAQ - Your most frequently asked questions about
            ATAPI/IDE CDROM drives.


        Author: Mathew E. Kirsch
                Systems Manager - Computing Graphics Engineering Technology
                SUNY at Alfred, Alfred NY 14802
                kirschm@snyalfva.cc.alfredtech.edu


Revisions:
1.0 - First public posting, 951010
1.1 - Added Q5 and Q6, 951011
1.2 - Added Q7, courtesy Steve Clarke; renamed the ATAPI CDROM FAQ
1.3 - Added Q8, due to number of people with this problem


Q1: Is the <Insert your brand/model here> IDE CDROM drive supported?


A1: Yes, of course it is. It is an ATAPI/IDE CDROM drive, meaning it utilizes
    the IDE hard drive interface that is present in most typical home PC's
    today. It has been like this since kernel version 1.1.85.
```

Q2: I already have two IDE hard drives. Will my ATAPI CDROM still work?

A2: Yes, but you need to have a second IDE interface card to make it work. Unfortunately, not just any IDE card will work. The secondary interface card that you choose must have jumper-selectable IRQs and base addresses, or, you need to purchase a card that is specifically manufactured for use as a secondary interface. One such card is the Data Technologies model 2183. It's typically only $15, so it's not a big expenditure on your part. If you bought a Mitsumi with an interface card, use that one. Another option is an EIDE card with dual IDE "ports", meaning it has two IDE/EIDE interfaces on the same card. I've been out of circulation for a while USENET-wise, but I heard that the 1.3.x kernels fully support EIDE interfaces.

Q3: I can't seem to find the driver for the FX400 in the kernel source, what should I be looking for?

A3: There isn't a SPECIFIC driver for the Mitsumi FX400 (or for any other ATAPI/IDE CDROM drive for that matter). What you need is the ATAPI CDROM driver that has been included in the kernel source officially since at least kernel version 1.1.85. It can be enabled just like any other driver when you "make config" and recompile the kernel. Recompiling the kernel is an entire FAQ in itself, so I won't cover it here.

(...)

If you page down, you see more detailed answers to specific problems – for example, the instructions for tuning a slow-working Mitsumi FX401 CD-ROM drive. You get the idea. If you don't find an answer to your question, post your question to the comp.os.linux.hardware or comp.os.linux.setup newsgroups. But check the FAQ first.

HOWTOs

The HOWTOs are similar to FAQs. They are written more as tutorials for configuring things than as troubleshooting guides. They include advice and instructions for setting up everything from your Ethernet to XFree86; they also include general instructions in several languages. List the contents of the HOWTO directory by entering the following command.

```
ls -l /mnt/cdrom/doc/HOWTO
```

The files listed in Listing 5-4 show a sampling of the numerous tutorials on most of the major subjects you encounter when setting up your Linux system. All of them are well written and understandable. They generally give numerous examples and are excellent tools.

Listing 5-4: The CD-ROM HOWTO directory sampling

```
ltotal 3432
-rw-r--r--   1 root    root      29852 Apr 16  1997 Bootdisk-HOWTO.gz
-rw-r--r--   1 root    root      13014 Aug 11 18:43 CD-Writing-HOWTO.gz
-rw-r--r--   1 root    root      22922 Aug  5 17:56 CDROM-HOWTO.gz
-rw-r--r--   1 root    root      16096 Apr 16  1997 Chinese-HOWTO.gz
-rw-r--r--   1 root    root      53170 Oct 12 16:44 Commercial-HOWTO.gz
-rw-r--r--   1 root    root      52432 Oct 12 16:44 Consultants-HOWTO.gz
-rw-r--r--   1 root    root      22553 Aug 17 17:09 Cyrillic-HOWTO.gz
-rw-r--r--   1 root    root      17842 Jun 18 16:10 DNS-HOWTO.gz
-rw-r--r--   1 root    root      16892 Mar 30  1997 DOS-to-Linux-HOWTO.gz
-rw-r--r--   1 root    root      11288 Oct  7 17:15 Danish-HOWTO.gz
-rw-r--r--   1 root    root      36304 Sep 14 17:40 Database-HOWTO.gz
-rw-r--r--   1 root    root      49134 Sep  2 17:25 Disk-HOWTO.gz
-rw-r--r--   1 root    root      16244 Aug  7 16:27 Distribution-HOWTO.gz
-rw-r--r--   1 root    root      77145 Feb  2  1997 Ethernet-HOWTO.gz
-rw-r--r--   1 root    root      10470 Mar 13  1996 Finnish-HOWTO.gz
-rw-r--r--   1 root    root      18815 Nov 13  1996 Firewall-HOWTO.gz
-rw-r--r--   1 root    root      22679 Oct  7 17:59 French-HOWTO.gz
-rw-r--r--   1 root    root      20455 Mar 29  1997 Ftape-HOWTO.gz
-rw-r--r--   1 root    root      23462 Mar 13  1996 GCC-HOWTO.gz
-rw-r--r--   1 root    root      21719 Mar 30  1997 German-HOWTO.gz
-rw-r--r--   1 root    root      20857 Sep 14 12:07 Hardware-HOWTO.gz
-rw-r--r--   1 root    root       8653 Mar 13  1996 Hebrew-HOWTO.gz
-rw-r--r--   1 root    root      12457 Sep 25 16:59 ISP-Hookup-HOWTO.gz
-rw-r--r--   1 root    root      19497 Sep 25 16:43 Installation-HOWTO.gz
-rw-r--r--   1 root    root      12629 Aug  7 15:36 Intranet-Server-HOWTO.gz
-rw-r--r--   1 root    root      33055 Aug 17 18:17 Italian-HOWTO.gz
-rw-r--r--   1 root    root       6820 Dec 15  1996 Java-CGI-HOWTO.gz
-rw-r--r--   1 root    root      21722 May 26  1997 Kernel-HOWTO.gz
-rw-r--r--   1 root    root    1682658 Oct 14 18:41 Linux-HOWTOs.tar.gz
-rw-r--r--   1 root    root      10752 Jun  1  1996 MGR-HOWTO.gz
-rw-r--r--   1 root    root      11500 Mar 13  1996 Mail-HOWTO.gz
-rw-r--r--   1 root    root      58625 Sep  2 16:58 NET-3-HOWTO.gz
-rw-r--r--   1 root    root      11218 Mar 30  1997 NFS-HOWTO.gz
-rw-r--r--   1 root    root       6557 Aug 11 18:50 Optical-Disk-HOWTO.gz
-rw-r--r--   1 root    root      37527 Mar 30  1997 PCI-HOWTO.gz
-rw-r--r--   1 root    root      48356 Apr 16  1997 PPP-HOWTO.gz
-rw-r--r--   1 root    root       7425 Jan 20  1997 Polish-HOWTO.gz
-rw-r--r--   1 root    root      18469 Sep 25 16:35 Printing-HOWTO.gz
-rw-r--r--   1 root    root       8156 Mar 30  1997 Printing-Usage-HOWTO.gz
-rw-r--r--   1 root    root      11774 Jul  6 16:27 RPM-HOWTO.gz
-rw-r--r--   1 root    root       7055 Aug 17 18:31 Reading-List-HOWTO.gz
-rw-r--r--   1 root    root      48000 Sep 25  1996 SCSI-HOWTO.gz
```

```
-rw-r--r--   1 root      root        25476 May 18  1996 SCSI-Programming-HOWTO.gz
-rw-r--r--   1 root      root         9585 Aug 18  1996 SMB-HOWTO.gz
-rw-r--r--   1 root      root         8691 Sep  2 17:18 SRM-HOWTO.gz
-rw-r--r--   1 root      root        22476 Jul  6 18:53 Serial-HOWTO.gz
-rw-r--r--   1 root      root         7968 Jul  6 18:53 Serial-Programming-HOWTOz
-rw-r--r--   1 root      root        21851 Jun  4  1996 Shadow-Password-HOWTO.gz
-rw-r--r--   1 root      root        12478 Nov  6  1996 Slovenian-HOWTO.gz
-rw-r--r--   1 root      root        26138 Aug  5 17:57 Sound-HOWTO.gz
-rw-r--r--   1 root      root        10877 May 26  1997 Sound-Playing-HOWTO.gz
-rw-r--r--   1 root      root        19622 Aug 25  1996 Spanish-HOWTO.gz
-r--r--r--   1 root      root         4500 Nov 10 22:37 TRANS.TBL
-rw-r--r--   1 root      root        11566 Jul 27 19:46 Thai-HOWTO.gz
-rw-r--r--   1 root      root        10996 Jan 20  1997 Tips-HOWTO.gz
-rw-r--r--   1 root      root        16308 Oct 12 16:22 User-Group-HOWTO.gz
-rw-r--r--   1 root      root         7841 Oct 12 16:44 VAR-HOWTO.gz
-rw-r--r--   1 root      root         9281 Oct  7 17:15 XFree86-HOWTO.gz
-rw-r--r--   1 root      root        22951 Aug 11 19:21 XFree86-Video-Timings-HOz
drwxr-xr-x   3 root      root        14336 Nov  6 23:48 mini
(...)
```

Many of these files are compressed using the GNU *gzip* format (look for the suffixes *gz*, *gzip*, and *tgz* – tar and gzip). If you want to unzip them permanently, you need to do so on a writable disk, and I recommend using RPM to do so. Otherwise, you can use the Linux piping capability to unfold them on-the-fly.

TIP The UNIX and Linux *pipe* function lets you transfer the output of one command, script, or program to the input of another. The vertical bar (|) is the symbol for the *pipe* command. A simple example is piping the output of the *ls* command to the *more* command, which stops your display at the end of every page. The following example shows how to do this using the long listing function:

```
ls -l  /mnt/cdrom/doc/HOWTO | more
```

This command displays the same directory information shown in Listing 5-4, but one page at a time. You control the output of the *more* command by pressing the spacebar to display the next page and the Return key to display the next line.

The *pg* command performs the same function as *more* but enables you to go back (up and down).

Most of the files are in gzip-compressed form on the CD-ROM. As the following example shows, you use the *gunzip* utility to decompress and view these files:

```
gunzip -c /mnt/cdrom/doc/HOWTO/Ethernet-HOWTO.gz | more
```

Listing 5-5 shows a portion of the contents of the Ethernet-HOWTO.

Listing 5-5: The first pages of the Ethernet-HOWTO

```
Linux Ethernet-Howto
  Paul Gortmaker, Editor.
  v2.62, 2 February 1997


  This is the Ethernet-Howto, which is a compilation of information
  about which ethernet devices can be used for Linux, and how to set
  them up. It hopefully answers all the frequently asked questions about
  using ethernet cards with Linux. Note that this Howto is focused on
  the hardware and low-level driver aspect of the ethernet cards, and
  does not cover the software end of things like ifconfig and route. See
  the NET2-Howto for that stuff.


1.  Introduction

  The Ethernet-Howto covers what cards you should and shouldn't buy; how
  to set them up, how to run more than one, and other common problems
  and questions. It contains detailed information on the current level
  of support for all of the most common ethernet cards available.

  It does not cover the software end of things, as that is covered in
  the NET-2 Howto. Also note that general non-Linux specific questions
  about Ethernet are not (or at least they should not be) answered here.
  For those types of questions, see the excellent amount of information
  in the comp.dcom.lans.ethernet FAQ. You can FTP it from rtfm.mit.edu
  just like all the other newsgroup FAQs.

  This present revision covers distribution kernels up to and including
  v2.0.28. Information pertaining to development kernels up to version
  2.1.24 is also documented.

  The Ethernet-Howto is edited and maintained by:

      Paul Gortmaker, Paul.Gortmaker@anu.edu.au

  The primary source of information for the initial ASCII version of the
  Ethernet-Howto was:
```

Donald J. Becker, becker@cesdis.gsfc.nasa.gov

who we should thank for writing the vast majority of ethernet card drivers that are presently available for Linux. He also is the original author of the NFS server too. Thanks Donald!

Net-surfers may wish to check out the following URL:

Donald Becker
<http://cesdis.gsfc.nasa.gov/pub/people/becker/whoiam.html>

Please see the Disclaimer and Copying information at the end of this document for information about redistribution of this document and the usual 'we are not responsible for what you do...' legal type mumblings.

1.1. New Versions of this Document

New versions of this document can be retrieved via anonymous FTP from:

Sunsite HOWTO Archive <ftp://sunsite.unc.edu/pub/Linux/docs/HOWTO/>

and various Linux ftp mirror sites. Updates will be made as new information and/or drivers become available. If this copy that you are reading is more than 6 months old, it is either out of date, or it means that I have been lazy and haven't updated it. This document was produced by using the SGML system that was specifically set up for the Linux Howto project, and there are various output formats available, including, postscript, dvi, ascii, html, and soon TeXinfo.

I would recommend viewing it in the html (via a **WWW** browser) or the Postscript/dvi format. Both of these contain cross-references that are lost in the ascii translation.

If you want to get the official copy off sunsite, here is URL.

Ethernet-HOWTO <http://sunsite.unc.edu/mdw/HOWTO/Ethernet-HOWTO.html>

1.2. Using the Ethernet-Howto

As this guide is getting bigger and bigger, you probably don't want to spend the rest of your afternoon reading the whole thing. And the good news is that you don't have to read it all.

Chances are you are reading this document because you can't get things
to work and you don't know what to do or check. The next section
("HELP - It doesn't work!") is aimed at newcomers to Linux and will
point you in the right direction.

Typically the same problems and questions are asked over and over
again by different people. Chances are your specific problem or
question is one of these frequently asked questions, and is answered
in the FAQ portion of this document. ("The FAQ section").
Everybody should have a look through this section before posting for
help.

If you haven't got an ethernet card, then you will want to start with
deciding on a card. ("What card should I buy...")

If you have already got an ethernet card, but are not sure if you can
use it with Linux, then you will want to read the section which
contains specific information on each manufacturer, and their cards.
("Vendor Specific...")

If you are interested in some of the technical aspects of the Linux
device drivers, then you can have a browse of the section with this
type of information. ("Technical Information")

You can find some of the most up-to-date FAQs and HOWTOs in the Linux
newsgroup, comp.os.linux.answers, found at any SunSITE.

Checking Out
Linux-Related Magazines

Magazines and newsletters fill a gap that the Internet can't fill. You can't lie down
on a couch with a monitor resting on your stomach. (At least, I've never tried. If you
have, I don't want to hear about it.) A magazine also creates a class of people –
journalists – who fill a gap between developers and consumers.

A magazine such as *Linux Journal* creates a focal point for the Linux universe. It
not only disseminates news and advice, but also organizes the Linux world in a
way that would not occur otherwise. By searching out news and information, publications such as the *Linux Journal* provide a service that is somewhat akin to a
school system for Linux users and developers.

Table 5-1 lists the Linux-related magazines and newsletters with which I am familiar.

TABLE 5-1 LINUX-RELATED MAGAZINES AND NEWSLETTERS

Publication	URL	E-mail/Phone
Linux Journal	`http://www.linuxjournal.com/`	`subs@ssc.com`
SysAdmin	`http://www.samag.com`	`sasub@mfi.com`
*UNIX Review**	`http://www.UNIXreview.com`	`webmaster@unixreview.com`
PC Magazine	`http://www.pcmag.com`	**303-665-8930**
Linux Gazette	`http://www.linuxgazette.com/`	`gazette@ssc.com`
GNU's Bulletins	`http://www.cs.pdx.edu:80/` `~trent/gnu/bull/index.html`	
Linux Doc Project	`http://www.nvg.unit.no/` `linux/lpd/linux.html`	
Linux Bible	`http://www.yggdrasil.com/bible`	
SunSITE	`ftp://sunsite.unc.edu/pub/Linux`	
SunSITE	`ftp://tsx-11.mit.edu/pub/linux/`	
SunSITE	`http://sunsite.unc.edu`	

*UNIX Review *has recently announced that they are becoming* Performance Computing *but as of this writing, their URL is still valid.*

Some of these publications, such as *PC Magazine*, rarely discuss Linux. That will change soon, but in the meantime these publications are still important for general news and product reviews. Besides, you gotta get out of the house occasionally.

Using Other Publications

Books and manuals provide the cornerstone of any person's education. They provide the comprehensive information source that you need to learn general concepts as well as specific information. You can find a useful reading list in this book's CD-ROM, in the file */usr/doc/faq/unix/[misc.books.technical]_A_Concise_Guide_to_UNIX_Books*.

To access this file, you must install the documentation RPM. Log on as *root* and enter the following commands.

```
mount -r -t iso9660 /dev/hdb /mnt/cdrom
rpm -ivh /mnt/cdrom/RedHat/RPMS/document*
```

Books

Here, in alphabetical order, are some books that I have found to be useful. (This list is independent of the one found on the CD-ROM.)

◆ *Data Communications, Computer Networks and Open Systems* (1992)
Fred Halsall
Addison-Wesley Publishing Company, Inc.
Reading, Massachusetts
ISBN 0-201-56506-4

This college textbook deals with network communication from a conceptual viewpoint and covers every protocol in detail. The book has three parts. The first part deals with the low-level protocol aspects. The second part addresses local and wide-area networks, including internetworking. The third part looks at open systems and concentrates on transport and application protocols. This book can give you a good underpinning, but you probably need a more example-oriented text to actually use networks.

◆ *Inside Linux: A Look at Operating System Development* (1996)
Randolph Bentson
Specialized System Consultants, Inc. (SSC)
Seattle, Washington
ISBN 0-916151-89-1

This book provides an informal introduction to a number of operating system issues by reviewing the history of operating systems, looking at how they are used, and by examining at the details of one operating system. The contents are a conscious effort to braid discussion of history, theory, and practice so the reader can see what goes on inside the system.

◆ *Linux Installation and Getting Started* (1994)
Matt Welsh
Specialized Systems Consultants, Inc. (SSC)
Seattle, Washington
ISBN 1-57831-001-6

This book was originally a HOWTO document only. It is so useful that I went to the trouble of printing it on a PostScript printer and had it bound by a local printer. SSC is now the official maintainer, and a printed edition is available from SSC (http://www.ssc.com). It is also stored in various formats (html, PostScript, and TXT) at the SunSITEs in the directory *linux/docs/linux-doc-project/install-guide*.

- ◆ *Linux Network Administrator's Guide* (1994)
  Olaf Kirch
  Specialized Systems Consultants, Inc. (SSC)
  Seattle, Washington
  ISBN 0-916151-75-1

This book is published under the GNU GPL. Olaf Kirch is well known within Linux circles. This book is a good tutorial for setting up a Linux network. It gives direct instructions for setting up the Linux environment, including SLIP and PPP. I used it extensively to set up my first Linux networks. It is written in clear and precise terms.

- ◆ *Linux SECRETS* (1996)
  Naba Barkakati
  IDG Books Worldwide, Inc.
  Foster City, California
  ISBN 1-56884-798-X

This book, from IDG's *Secrets* series, covers almost every aspect of using and setting up Linux. It covers, in detail, the setup and use of both hardware and software. It is a good reference book as well.

- ◆ *Samba: Integrating UNIX and Windows* (1997)
  John D. Blair
  Specialized System Consultants, Inc. (SSC)
  Seattle, Washington
  ISBN 1-57831-006-7

A combination of technical tutorial, reference guide, and how-to manual. This book contains the depth of knowledge experienced network administrators demand without skipping the information beginners need to get fast results. UNIX administrators new to Windows networking will find the information they need to become Windows networking experts. Those new to UNIX will find the details they need to install and configure Samba correctly and securely.

- ◆ *Tricks of the UNIX Masters* (1987)
  Russell G. Sage
  The Waite Group, Inc.
  Indianapolis, Indiana
  ISBN 0-672-22449-6

This comprehensive text deals with everything from UNIX basics to administration and security. It is a bit dated by now, but I find myself referring to it now and then. Like any book (except this one), it hits on subjects that others miss, and I find it quite useful to this day. It was my first UNIX book.

- *UNIX Power Tools* (1993)
  Jerry Peek, Tim O'Reilly, and Mike Loukides
  O'Reilly & Associates/Random House Book
  Sebastopol, California
  ISBN 0-679-79073-X

This reference book deals with UNIX, but much of it is useful for working with Linux.

- *UNIX System Administration Handbook, 2nd Edition* (1995)
  Evi Nemeth, Garth Snyder, Scott Seebas, and Trent R. Hein
  Prentice Hall PTR
  Englewood Cliffs, New Jersey
  ISBN 0-13-151051-7

This book is the compilation of about 100 years of collective experience by the authors. During my years in the wilderness, I wished for this book. I believe it was first published in 1989, but I purchased it for my Systems Administration class in 1995. It covers all aspects of administration. It comes with a CD-ROM full of useful tools; I find the collection of security tools (called COPS) to be great for checking my systems as well as understanding them. This book focuses on UNIX and only touches on Linux, which was relatively new at the time the book was written. But the philosophical advice is first-rate and universal. The details too can generally be applied to the Linux world if you are able to translate them (generally this just requires a change in syntax).

Manuals

At least two of the major Linux distributors produce very good manuals. Red Hat and Caldera both include 300 and 200-plus page manuals or books when you purchase their CD-ROMs. Both distributions provide excellent installation tutorials and short but significant administration guides. You will not become an expert with them, but they are good for getting started and as refresher material after you gain some experience. They are well worth the cost of purchasing each product. Red Hat costs only $50 and Caldera is in the same range – remember that one Caldera model comes with Netscape for the X Window system. For the record, here are listings for the Red Hat and Caldera manuals:

◆ *Red Hat Linux 5.0: The Official Red Hat Linux Installation Guide* (1997)
Red Hat Software, Inc.
Research Triangle Park, North Carolina
ISBN 1-888172-97-5

◆ *Getting Started Guide, Network Desktop 1.0* (1996)
Caldera, Inc.
Orem, Utah

Universities and Technical Schools

Attending a degreed Systems Administration program at a university is still just a dream. The immense popularity of computers has resulted in almost every organization requiring an administrator, and the time has come to treat the job as the profession that it is.

Where are the degreed programs in systems administration? Sure, you can take computer science classes in administration, but they are generally single courses and not comprehensive programs. Mainframes and minicomputers have been around for many decades now. UNIX has been used throughout the world for more than 20 years. Was I just living in the backwaters and the UNIX Systems Administration class I took in 1995 was more widespread than I realized? I don't think so.

I reiterate that computer systems and networks are everywhere. Serious networks exist in most midsized and larger businesses, and many small ones, too. Look in any newspaper, or search the Net, and you will find many jobs that fit the systems administrator profile. Microsoft and Novell offer certification programs in their products that are recognized and marketable in the workplace. But much, if not most, systems administration experience and expertise is learned ad hoc. The time has come for educational institutions to offer training and certification. A significant market exists that schools can tap.

Resources, Resources, Resources

By deciding to use Linux and its allies, you are foregoing the traditional commercial route. You must depend on your own intelligence and know-how to develop and administer your system. In my opinion, this is ultimately no sacrifice because you are your best resource. You must learn, however, what resources are available and where they are located.

More resources are available to you than you may realize. By keeping your eyes open and actively seeking out information sources, you can tap into a vast and useful reservoir of assistance. The more experienced you become in knowing the "lay of the land," the easier it is to find help and resources.

By having all the possible resources available to you, rather than selectively doled out by a vendor, you can govern your own system better than ever before.

Summary

In this chapter, I outlined several sources of help available to you. Keep the following points in mind when looking for help:

- ◆ The Internet has several different areas in which you can look for help:

  - Newsgroups, or Usenet, give you interactive access to technical people working in the same area as you. Often, people have the same or similar problems and ask for help in a newsgroup. The answers are often the ones you need. You can also ask the questions yourself. It is very gratifying to eventually lend assistance through this medium.

  - SunSITEs, or anonymous ftp, offer access to vast reservoirs of software and documentation. The complete Linux archive, including commercial distributions, is available for you to download (copy) to your own computer.

  - Other software is available from manufacturers themselves. Netscape is a prime example. It was good public relations and good business to flood the Net with their browser.

  - Many companies make updates and other information available on the Net for customers to use. It is a quick, efficient, and economical distribution system.

- ◆ Searching the Internet is still an art rather than a science. Part of the problem is the Internet's distributed and independent nature. That nature enables an incredible amount of information to be disseminated but creates problems finding it. The commercial search engines help, but you need to practice using them to be able to find what you are looking for.

- ◆ When you have to purchase commercial hardware or software, remember to ask the right questions. Think out your problem or need beforehand and summarize by making notes.

◆ The CD-ROM that carries your distribution is an important resource. The */usr/doc* directory is particularly important because it stores a great deal of documentation.

◆ The FAQs contain the answers to many common problems. They are particularly useful when you are first setting up your system because more people have similar problems at that time.

◆ The HOWTOs contain detailed instructions for doing many common (and uncommon) jobs.

◆ Man pages are useful for getting started with everything from application programs to entire systems.

◆ Magazines contain all sorts of useful information, commercial products, tutorials, and other technical discussions. They also serve as a common bond for inhabitants of the diverse and far-flung Linux world.

◆ Books provide a more stable and in-depth reference. They can cover a complex topic such as systems administration in a rational and comprehensive manner. They complete the information sphere for you as an administrator.

◆ Individual courses in system and network administration are available now. I highly recommend them as a way not only to learn new things but also to show you what you don't know. It is only a matter of time before universities and technical schools start offering complete systems administration curricula.

Part III

A Significant Client–Server Network

IN THIS PART:

Part III provides the tools to customize and expand the simple client-server network from Part I. Several detailed examples help you tap into the power of Samba. You are also shown how to further configure Linux by using the Red Hat Package Manager and other tools. Finally, you are shown how to safely connect your network directly to the Internet.

Chapter 6

Customizing Your Samba Server by Example

IN THIS CHAPTER

- ◆ Reconfiguring Samba

- ◆ Understanding the Samba daemons

- ◆ Understanding the Samba configuration file

- ◆ Modifying the Samba configuration file

- ◆ Modifying Linux

- ◆ Adding Samba printer shares

- ◆ Authenticating Samba service requests

IN CHAPTER 1, you learned how to set up a simple client-server network. This network has all the essential ingredients to work as the foundation for a practical, useful personal or business system:

- ◆ The multiuser, multitasking, virtual memory, and TCP/IP network-ready Linux operating system

- ◆ The resources exported to the network by the Microsoft network-compatible Samba server

- ◆ A Windows 95 client that can connect to and use the services provided by the Linux-Samba server

By adding some new parts to this foundation, you can create a powerful network. In this chapter, I show you how to expand your simple network to create a Linux-Samba server capable of running a small business or your home office. I describe the mechanics of that process and show you how to develop a workable system.

Starting with the basic recipe described in Chapter 1, you can add all the Windows 95 clients you want, until you overload the server. (Samba has no practical limits; the only limitation is that of your server or servers.) You add Windows clients by modifying the Samba configuration file */etc/smb.conf.* That file controls the following ingredients:

- ◆ Directories to be shared over the network. They are called *shares* or *services.*

- ◆ Printers to be shared over the network. These too are called *shares* or *services.*

- ◆ Who gets to use each directory. Access can be provided to an individual, specific individuals, groups, or everybody.

- ◆ Who gets to use each printer. Access can be provided to an individual, specific individuals, groups, or everybody.

- ◆ Miscellaneous parameters used for security, access, and tuning.

In this chapter, I focus on reconfiguring Samba. By modifying the Samba server, you can immediately transform what started as a simple example of Samba into a truly useable business or personal server. This chapter also describes how you can further expand your Samba system by adding some users and modifying permissions to the Linux system.

Customizing Samba

In principle, the process for adding Samba clients is simple. By editing the *smb.conf* file, you can add, delete, and modify *share*s. (I introduce the *smb.conf* file in Chapter 1; for a look at an excerpt from this file, see Listing 3-13 in Chapter 3.) A share is a resource – usually a directory or a printer – that the Samba server provides to the network. When viewed from the Samba configuration side – that is, in the *smb.conf* file – a share is known as a *service.* The *smb.conf* file is divided into sections that define the services.

You will modify the *smb.conf* file many times in this chapter, so make a backup copy of it before you begin the examples. At the beginning of every example, I ask you to restore *smb.conf* from the backup copy. Thus, you start each example with the original *smb.conf.* Enter the following command to create the backup copy:

```
cp /etc/smb.conf /etc/smb.conf.orig
```

Many parameters are available to configure Samba. Some are variations or synonyms of other parameters; others are used for fine-tuning the network. In this chapter, I concentrate on the most important and widely used parameters. Because you can combine even just a few parameters in many ways, configuring Samba can be a complicated task.

Before you get into the mechanics of reconfiguring Samba, however, you need to understand Samba daemons. The following section offers a quick review of the Samba daemons, which make use of the configuration parameters.

Understanding the Samba Daemons

Recall that at the heart of Samba are the two *daemons* — system processes that run continuously in the background — *smbd* and *nmbd*. The *smbd* daemon continuously monitors the network for share requests. When it detects a share request, *smbd* goes through Linux to get the resource that the share represents — that is, a directory or a printer — and makes this resource available to the Samba client(s) that requested it. The resource — a file, for example — stays on the Linux server, but the Samba client can make use of it just as if it were located on the client's disk.

The name server — *nmbd* — controls browsing done by Windows clients (such as when you open the *Network Neighborhood*), and responds to the Windows clients' requests to locate Samba servers. (A *name server* converts an IP name into its numeric IP address. Thus, *nmbd* converts *maggie.paunchy.com* into 192.168.1.2.) Both daemons read the *smb.conf* file when they start up, to discover exactly which services to export.

You ask for a share when you open a directory, a file, or a printer from your Windows environment. In Chapter 1, for example, you access a share when you open the *root* directory from the *Network Neighborhood*.

The *smbd* daemon creates a copy of itself whenever it answers a share request. Try opening the *root* share from the *Network Neighborhood* on your computer by double-clicking the computer icon; you should see a window open with the contents — if any — of the */root* directory. If you don't see anything, try copying a file into the */root* directory. Next, log on to your Linux server as *root* and enter the following command:

```
ps x | grep smbd
```

As shown in Listing 6-1, you should see two *smbd* daemons (unless you have already started to experiment and have mounted other shares). The process numbers you see will differ from those in the listing. Note that the *grep* command you entered is also shown, because it runs at the same time as the *ps* command. The question marks after the process IDs (PIDs) indicate that these processes are not associated with any I/O device, which makes sense because they are daemons.

Listing 6-1: An smbd daemon is created for each share exported

```
 183  ?   S    0:00 smbd -D
3664  ?   S    0:00 smbd -D
3693  p0  S    0:00 grep smbd
```

Recall from Chapter 1 that you can start the *smbd* and *nmbd* daemons by running the script */etc/rc.d/init.d/smb start*. (You can run the same script to stop the daemons, replacing the parameter *start* with *stop*.)

TIP

You can find complete descriptions of *smbd* and *nmbd* in their respective man pages. To view these man pages, log on to your Linux box and enter the following commands: **man smbd** or **man nmbd**.

Examining the Samba Configuration File: smb.conf

The Samba daemons get all their directions from the *smb.conf* file. The *smb.conf* file has a straightforward syntax and structure. The *smb.conf* file includes numerous – and in some cases, interdependent – commands. However, you can ignore most of these commands at first, because they deal with specialized functions.

EXAMINING THE SMB.CONF SYNTAX

The *smb.conf* file has a simple structure (it's similar to Microsoft's *WIN.INI* file), as listed here:

♦ The file is divided into sections. Each section contains parameters that define the shares Samba is to export and their operational details.

♦ A *global* section defines the parameters that control the general Samba characteristics.

♦ Other than the *global* section, each section defines a specific service. Each section begins with a name enclosed within square brackets – for example, *[home]* – and continues until the next section appears or the end of the *smb.conf* file occurs. Sections define *services*.

♦ You specify a parameter with the following syntax:

```
name = value
```

The *name* can be one or more words separated by spaces. The *value* can be Boolean (true or false; yes or no; 1 or 0), numeric, or a character string.

♦ Comments are preceded by a semicolon (;) and can appear either as a separate line or after a name-value pair.

◆ Lines may be continued from one to another by placing a backward slash (\) as the last character on the line to be continued.

◆ Section and parameter names are not case-sensitive. For example, the parameter *browseable = yes* works the same as *browseable = YeS*.

EXAMINING THE SMB.CONF FUNCTIONS

The *smbd* and *nmbd* daemons read the *smb.conf* configuration file when they are started (usually at boot time). The configuration file tells these daemons which shares to export, to whom the shares should be exported, and how to do so. The term *export* means to make available a service or share to one or more clients over the network. Because security is always a top priority, you must be specific about which computers can access a share. The *smb.conf* file offers tremendous flexibility for specifying precisely who has access to each service. As your Linux network grows, this control becomes increasingly important.

Note: You may already be familiar with Novell or NFS networks. They both share, or export, directory and print services to clients on the network. In this way, their function is the same as Samba's.

EXAMINING THE SMB.CONF STRUCTURE

The *smb.conf* file has three main parts:

◆ The *global* parameters

◆ The *directory shares* section – including the standard *[homes]* section

◆ The *printer shares* section

The *global* parameters, as you may guess, set the rules for the entire system. The *[homes]* and *[printer]* sections are special instances of services. The term *services* is the Samba terminology for the directories and printers to be shared or exported with the network clients. The services define who should be able to access them and how. Listing 6-2 shows a simple example of the *smb.conf* file.

Listing 6-2: The smb.conf structure

```
[global]
   printing = bsd
   printcap name = /etc/printcap
   load printers = yes
   log file = /var/log/samba
   lock directory = /var/lock/samba
   share modes = yes
   security = user
[homes]
   comment = Home Directories
```

```
    browseable = no
    read only = no
    create mode = 0750
[printers]
    comment = All Printers
    browseable = no
    printable = yes
    public = no
    writable = no
    create mode = 0700
```

In the *global* section of the example in Listing 6-2, the printers are the first shares to be described. This example specifies *BSD* – or *Berkeley* – style printing. (I have more to say about BSD style printing a bit later in this section.) The standard */etc/printcap* is the printer definition file, and the Boolean variable (it can only be yes or no – true or false) *load printers* says that all printers can be browsed on the network. These three lines in the *global* section set the printing for the entire Samba system.

The */etc/printcap* file contains the configuration information for the Linux printers. In Red Hat Linux, the *lpd* daemon reads the printcap file for its configuration information. Then it monitors the system for print requests and manages the printing process.

The *[global]* section also defines where the log and lock directories are located. The log files are useful for troubleshooting problems and for tuning your system. The lock files prevent multiple users from overwriting the same files.

The *[homes]* section defines the generic parameters for how an individual user's directories are exported. If your Windows 95 user name matches a Linux user name and you supply the correct password, you can double-click this icon in the *Network Neighborhood* and gain access to your home directory.

The *[printers]* section describes how printers are configured, of course.

You can expand on these special sections to create more specific services. They are useful in and of themselves, but you can also view them as templates.

The man page offers a complete description of *smb.conf.* To view it, enter the following command:

```
man smb.conf
```

Note: BSD printing is probably the most popular style of UNIX (and certainly Linux) printing. It uses the Berkeley model instead of System V. The daemon *lpd* and the program *lpr* both read the */etc/printcap* file to learn about the printer definitions. The daemon *lpd* is started at boot time – and can be restarted at any time by *root.* It prints any leftover print jobs and then runs continuously in the background, listening for print requests from *lpr.* The program *lpr* is used to initiate the printing of a file. It copies the file to a spool directory – a temporary place to hold the file – and then signals *lpd* that a file is ready to be printed. The spooled file is then converted by filter programs to a printable form and then sent to the printer by *lpd*.

EXAMINING THE RED HAT SMB.CONF FILE

As you may expect, Red Hat provides a nicely preconfigured *smb.conf* file. Listing 6-3 shows a copy of the file that you install in Chapter 1. This is the standard configuration file that comes with the Samba system.

Listing 6-3: The Samba smb.conf file

```
; The global setting for a RedHat default install
; smbd re-reads this file regularly, but if in doubt stop and restart it:
; /etc/rc.d/init.d/smb stop
; /etc/rc.d/init.d/smb start
;======================= Global Settings =======================================
[global]

; workgroup = NT-Domain-Name or Workgroup-Name, eg: REDHAT4
   workgroup = WORKGROUP

; comment is the equivalent of the NT Description field
   comment = RedHat Samba Server

; volume = used to emulate a CDRom label (can be set on a per share basis)
   volume = RedHat4

; printing = BSD or SYSV or AIX, etc.
   printing = bsd
   printcap name = /etc/printcap
   load printers = yes

; Uncomment this if you want a guest account
;  guest account = pcguest
   log file = /var/log/samba-log.%m
; Put a capping on the size of the log files (in Kb)
   max log size = 50

; Options for handling file name case sensitivity and / or preservation
; Case Sensitivity breaks many WfW and Win95 apps
;   case sensitive = yes
   short preserve case = yes
   preserve case = yes

; Security and file integrity related options
```

```
      lock directory = /var/lock/samba
      locking = yes
      strict locking = yes
;     fake oplocks = yes
      share modes = yes
; Security modes: USER uses Unix username/passwd, SHARE uses WfW type passwords
;         SERVER uses a Windows NT Server to provide authentication services
      security = user
; Use password server option only with security = server
;     password server = <NT-Server-Name>


; Configuration Options ***** Watch location in smb.conf for side-effects *****
; Where %m is any SMBName (machine name, or computer name) for which a custom
; configuration is desired
;     include = /etc/smb.conf.%m


; Performance Related Options
; Before setting socket options read the smb.conf man page!!
      socket options = TCP_NODELAY
; Socket Address is used to specify which socket Samba
; will listen on (good for aliased systems)
;     socket address = aaa.bbb.ccc.ddd
; Use keep alive only if really needed!!!!
;     keep alive = 60


; Domain Control Options
; OS Level gives Samba the power to rule the roost. Windows NT = 32
;     Any value < 32 means NT wins as Master Browser, > 32 Samba gets it
;     os level = 33
; specifies Samba to be the Domain Master Browser
;     domain master = yes
; Use with care only if you have an NT server on your network that has been
; configured at install time to be a primary domain controller.
;     domain controller = <NT-Domain-Controller-SMBName>
; Domain logon control can be a good thing! See [netlogon] share section below!
;     domain logons = yes
; run a specific logon batch file per workstation (machine)
;     logon script = %m.bat
; run a specific logon batch file per username
;     logon script = %u.bat
; Windows Internet Name Serving Support Section
; WINS Support - Tells the NMBD component of Samba to enable its WINS Server
;     the default is NO.
;     wins support = yes
```

```
; WINS Server - Tells the NMBD components of Samba to be a WINS Client
;   Note: Samba can be either a WINS Server, or a WINS Client, but NOT both
;   wins server = w.x.y.z
; WINS Proxy - Tells Samba to answer name resolution queries on behalf of a non
;   WINS Client capable client, for this to work there must be at least one
;   WINS Server on the network. The default is NO.
;   wins proxy = yes


;=========================== Share Declarations ===============================
[homes]
   comment = Home Directories
   browseable = no
   read only = no
   preserve case = yes
   short preserve case = yes
   create mode = 0750


; Un-comment the following and create the netlogon directory for Domain Logons
; [netlogon]
;   comment = Samba Network Logon Service
;   path = /home/netlogon
; Case sensitivity breaks logon script processing!!!
;   case sensitive = no
;   guest ok = yes
;   locking = no
;   read only = yes
;   browseable = yes   ; say NO if you want to hide the NETLOGON share
;   admin users = @wheel


; Note: There is NO need to specifically define each individual printer
[printers]
   comment = All Printers
   path = /var/spool/samba
   browseable = no
   printable = yes
; Set public = yes to allow user 'guest account' to print
   public = no
   writable = no
   create mode = 0700


;[tmp]
;   comment = Temporary file space
;   path = /tmp
;   read only = no
```

```
;    public = yes


; A publicly accessible directory, but read only, except for people in
; the staff group
;[public]
;    comment = Public Stuff
;    path = /home/samba
;    public = yes
;    writable = yes
;    printable = no
;    write list = @users


; Other examples.
;
; A private printer, usable only by fred. Spool data will be placed in fred's
; home directory. Note that fred must have write access to the spool directory,
; wherever it is.
;[fredsprn]
;    comment = Fred's Printer
;    valid users = fred
;    path = /homes/fred
;    printer = freds_printer
;    public = no
;    writable = no
;    printable = yes
;
; A private directory, usable only by fred. Note that fred requires write
; access to the directory.
;[fredsdir]
;    comment = Fred's Service
;    path = /usr/somewhere/private
;    valid users = fred
;    public = no
;    writable = yes
;    printable = no
;
; a service which has a different directory for each machine that connects
; this allows you to tailor configurations to incoming machines. You could
; also use the %u option to tailor it by user name.
; The %m gets replaced with the machine name that is connecting.
;[pchome]
;    comment = PC Directories
;    path = /usr/pc/%m
;    public = no
```

```
;   writeable = yes
;
;
; A publicly accessible directory, read/write to all users. Note that all files
; created in the directory by users will be owned by the default user, so
; any user with access can delete any other user's files. Obviously this
; directory must be writable by the default user. Another user could of course
; be specified, in which case all files would be owned by that user instead.
;[public]
;   path = /usr/somewhere/else/public
;   public = yes
;   only guest = yes
;   writable = yes
;   printable = no
;
;
; The following two entries demonstrate how to share a directory so that two
; users can place files there that will be owned by the specific users. In this
; setup, the directory should be writable by both users and should have the
; sticky bit set on it to prevent abuse. Obviously this could be extended to
; as many users as required.
;[myshare]
;   comment = Mary's and Fred's stuff
;   path = /usr/somewhere/shared
;   valid users = mary fred
;   public = no
;   writable = yes
;   printable = no
;   create mask = 0765
```

Recall from Chapter 1 that Red Hat preconfigures Samba to export the Linux user's home directories. Root is the only user that you have on your system so far. If you open the *Network Neighborhood* and open (double-click) your *Linux box* icon, you should see the *root* share displayed.

The Red Hat 5.0 Samba configuration file contains the basic three services from Listing 6-2, but the file adds several potential services that are commented out with the semicolon character (;). In the following examples, I uncomment several of these examples and modify them appropriately to show how Samba services work.

Explaining Bourne Again Shell Aliases

The Bourne Again Shell ("bash") that is standard to Linux and is automatically selected for you by Red Hat — and probably every other distribution — has the facility to associate a synonym, or *alias*, with a command or command string. Here's the form you use for setting an alias:

```
alias synonym=command
```

For example, to speed your ability to log out, you may set the following alias:

```
alias lo=exit
```

Or if you want to create an alias for a command and some accompanying parameters, enclose the command string in single quotes. For example, I like to use long listings but I don't like to type, so I like the following alias:

```
alias l='ls -l'
```

You can enter an alias from the *bash* command prompt, but it is more useful to have aliases set when you log on. The *.bashrc* file is executed every time you log on and can be found in your home directory (*~/.bashrc*). Some aliases are already defined in this file, but I like to have the same aliases on all my accounts so I define them in */etc/bashrc*, which *.bashrc* executes automatically. You can also define your own file (for example, *user_aliases*), place it anywhere, and then add a line to *.bashrc* to source your file. The file containing the alias definitions is not executed but is *sourced*. Therefore, you must remember to include a line such as this in your script:

```
source /etc/bashrc
```

Or, you can use this line in your script:

```
. /etc/bashrc
```

To remove an alias, use the *unalias* command. For example, to remove the *lo* alias, enter the following command:

```
unalias lo
```

You can list all aliases by using the *alias* command by itself.

Creating Samba Shares Without Modifying Linux

I believe in learning by example, so the following sections give you some examples to try. The first examples require only minimal modifications to the *smb.conf* file. Then, you need to add a printer and a user or two to your Linux system. Even so, you don't have to do very much to your system to get some work out of it.

Please be aware that the Red Hat Linux distribution that comes with this book supplies a Samba configuration and also starts Samba when you boot your system. (See Chapter 1 for Samba installation instructions.) The Samba configuration uses what is called *user level* security and is specified in the */etc/smb.conf* by the parameter security = user. Using this type of security requires that in order to open a Samba share, a Windows 95 login name and password must be supplied that matches an existing Linux user name and password.

However, I do not show you how to set up Linux user accounts until later in this chapter. For the time being, it is more instructive to show you Samba share examples that don't require modifying Linux. By limiting the examples in this way, I can show exactly what Samba is able to do within the confines of any given Linux configuration.

Making Your Entire Linux Disk Viewable to the Public

You can make use of some of the example shares that come in the Red Hat Samba configuration file. First, I want to make your entire Linux disk visible (but not writable) to your network.

Note: The names I use in this example for creating Linux user names and Samba shares are my own. Please feel free to use any names that you want to use.

1. Log on to your Windows computer as the user *root*. (Note that this user does not necessarily have any extra privileges as in Linux. I use it so the user name/password will match with the Linux server.)

2. Log on to your Linux-Samba server as *root*.

3. Restore your original *smb.conf* file from the backup copy (if you have not already done so – as advised earlier in this chapter – reverse the process and make a backup copy):

```
cp /etc/smb.conf.orig /etc/smb.conf
```

4. Edit the file any way you want (to see my quick guide to *vi*, turn to Appendix A), making the two changes I describe in the following steps.

5. Find the first instance of the *[public]* service section, as shown in Listing 6-4.

Listing 6-4: An excerpt from the Samba smb.conf file, showing the [public] section

```
;[public]
;    comment = Public Stuff
;    path = /home/samba
;    public = yes
;    writable = yes
;    printable = no
;    write list = @staff
```

6. Remove the comment designators (;), change the *writable* parameter to *no*, and change the path parameter to path = /, as shown in Listing 6-5. Leave write list = @staff commented out because you do not want to allow write permission to the entire disk.

Listing 6-5: The modified [public] service to export the entire Linux disk

```
[public]
    comment = Public Stuff
    path = /
    public = yes
    writable = no
    printable = no;
;    write list = @staff
```

7. Save the changes. (If you are using *vi*, press the *Escape* key to return to *command* mode. Then type **:wq** and press *Enter*. Alternatively, you can enter the two-character sequence ZZ after pressing the *Escape* key.)

Note: To manually force a process to reread its configuration file, send the *SIGHUP* signal to the process via the */bin/kill* command (*kill -SIGHUP* or *kill -1*). However, because Samba forks — that is, creates — a new *smbd* process for each new share, this is only necessary if you want to modify a current share. Each time a new *smbd* is created, it reads the *smb.conf* as it starts. Still, the process of signaling a process is important, so please review the following Tip, which shows how to do so.

TIP

As a system administrator, you should know how to send signals to processes. The Linux *kill* command is used to send signals to processes. The most widely used signals are *SIGHUP* (numeric value 1), which is generally used to signal a process to reread its configuration file, and *SIGKILL* (numeric value 9), which terminates a process.

The manual page on signals gives a complete list of Linux signals (as does the command *kill -l*). To access this man page, enter **man 7 signal**. (Note that nine divisions of man pages exist. That's why the */usr/man* directory has nine subdirectories — */usr/man/man1* through */usr/man/man9*. For example, you find the manual pages on user commands in */usr/man/man1*.

If you ask for a man page on a topic that exists in more than one area, the topic with the lowest number appears. That is why you need to specify the **7** in the preceding command — if you simply enter **man signal**, you get the same manual page as if you had entered **man 2 signal**.

8. Back on your Windows 95 box, double-click your Linux-Samba computer icon in your *Network Neighborhood*. Double-click the *public* icon and you should see the root level directory – / – on your disk, as shown in Figure 6-1.

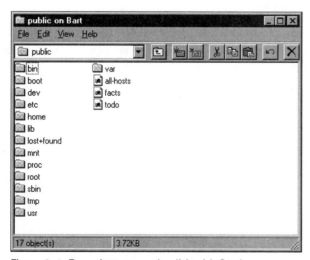

Figure 6-1: Exporting your entire disk with Samba

The end result is to make your entire disk visible to your network. (Actually, if you are connected to the Internet and don't have a firewall, it is possible to export your file system to the world, so be careful.)

9. You can examine the exported share from your Linux box as well. I discuss the */usr/bin/smbstatus* command in the section "Checking that Samba Is Running" in Chapter 1. Run this command, and you see the information shown in Listing 6-6.

Listing 6-6: Share information displayed from smbstatus

```
Samba version 1.9.17p4
Service      uid      gid      pid      machine
------------------------------------------------
public       root     root     716      maggie   (192.168.1.2) Thu Dec 11 21:27:7
root         root     root     716      maggie   (192.168.1.2) Thu Dec 11 21:28:7

No locked files
```

This output shows that one of the services is called *public*, which matches the service heading name that you just modified. The user and group ID is *root* in my case because that is the user name that I am logged in as on my Windows 95 box. (If I were to log on to my Windows 95 box as *maggie*, I show up as user and group ID *maggie*.) The process ID is the *smbd* process ID. The machine is my Windows 95 client, *maggie*, which has the IP address 192.168.1.2. The time shown in Listing 6-6 specifies when I opened this share. I have not opened any files yet, so the output doesn't show any locked files.

Because you are going to be editing the configuration file a lot, you may want to set some aliases to make your life easier. My aliases are as follows:

```
alias sm='/usr/bin/smbstatus'
alias sn='/usr/bin/nmblookup'
alias smbstop='/etc/rc.d/init.d/smb stop'
alias smbstart='/etc/rc.d/init.d/smb start'
alias st='/usr/bin/testparm'
alias se='vi /etc/smb.conf'
```

Add these aliases to */etc/bashrc*, or your own file, to retain them for successive logins. If you change them, you can make your system recognize the change by *sourcing* the file:

```
source /etc/bashrc
```

Note that */etc/aliases* and */etc/aliases.db* are not used for command aliases. They are, however, used by */usr/bin/sendmail* for its own purposes.

Starting and Stopping Samba

As you proceed to create more complex client-server networks, you must be more careful about making sure that you keep Samba up-to-date. In the preceding example, I leave it to the new *smbd* process to read the new configuration – that happens because each new share gets its own daemon. However, the original *smbd* does not know that *smb.conf* has changed. You have two Samba daemons running with two different configurations.

This situation can create difficulties as the number of *smbd* processes increases. Just imagine five or six *smbd* processes running at once as you experiment with new configurations. Trying to keep track of what's what becomes counter-productive – you can end up confused and traveling in circles very quickly. Of course, you can manually *HUP* all the Samba daemons – *kill -HUP* –, but that can be confusing and time-consuming, too.

Here's an easier way to stay current. Because Samba daemons are a dime a dozen, it's simpler just to terminate all *smbd* processes and then start them up again. Red Hat, being the value-added Linux hero, provides an easy way of doing just that. It runs an *rc* script – */etc/rc.d/init.d/smb* – at boot time to start the Samba daemons. You can also use this script anytime you want. Enter the following command (or the aliases, **smbstop** and **smbstart**, which I define in a Tip in the preceding section) to restart the daemon:

```
/usr/bin/killall HUP smbd nmbd
```

You may encounter irrecoverable errors if you stop and restart the Samba daemons while a share is being accessed. In my experience, if you restart Samba while you are reading or writing to a Samba share, you will lose your network connection. Most of the time, my Microsoft applications indicate that the connection was lost and prompt me either to *retry* to make the connection or *cancel* the attempt to reconnect. I generally click the *Retry* button and everything returns to normal; alternatively, if I click the *Cancel* button, my data may be saved on my local disk or lost entirely. However, on occasion, I've received an unrecoverable error message, which led to my application closing and me losing the data. The answer is to be careful when you reset the Samba daemons. If you are working with other people, make sure that you reset the daemons when you are sure nobody is working on the system.

Any services that you had open will not be active because they were tied to the daemon you just terminated. However, they return as soon as you access them again. For example, if I reopen the computer icon *Bart* from my *Network Neighborhood*, the same share becomes active again. Alternatively, if the window shown in Figure 6-1 is still open, simply choose the *Refresh* option from the *View* menu, and that same share becomes active again; the *smbd* daemon has a new PID, however, because it is a brand-new process.

Understanding Linux and Samba Permissions

Linux file permissions play a controlling role in how Samba shares behave. Linux permissions supersede Samba permissions. Therefore, even if Samba *says* that you can do something, if Linux does not permit it then you cannot do it.

What are file permissions? File permissions control who can read, write, and execute a file. Every file has file permissions for the user that it belongs to, the group that it belongs to, and everyone else. If you do a long format listing of a directory or a file, you get a listing that includes the file's permissions – among other information – in the order just listed. For example, you may enter this command:

```
ls -l /etc/rc.d/init.d/smb
```

Here's the information that this command displays:

```
-rwxr-xr-x   1 root     root          522 Apr  2 14:31 /etc/rc.d/init.d/smb
```

The characters `rwx` identify the permissions; as you probably have guessed, they stand for read, write, and execute – the hyphen (-) character means *no permission*. The order of their placement does not vary, so the hyphen in this example means *no write permission*.

These characters are grouped first as *owner permission*, then *group*, and finally *other permissions*. The owner is *root* in this case, as is the group (that information is, of course, shown to the right of the 1). The *other* group means any user who is not an owner or a member of the group – that is, other users.

UNDERSTANDING LINUX PERMISSIONS

Linux file permissions are important for Samba management because no matter what permission you set in the Samba configuration, it does not override the Linux file system permissions. For instance, if you set a share to be public but the directory that the share points to does not have the correct permissions set, that share will not be accessible to the public. The following example demonstrates this convention.

Note: The names I use in this example for creating Linux user names and Samba shares are my own. Please feel free to use any names that you want.

1. Log on to your Windows computer as the user *root.* (Note that this user does not necessarily have any extra privileges as in Linux. I use it so the user name/password will match with the Linux server.)

2. Log on to your Linux-Samba server as *root.*

3. Restore your original *smb.conf* file from the backup copy (if you have not already done so – as advised earlier in this chapter – reverse the process and make a backup copy):

   ```
   cp /etc/smb.conf.orig /etc/smb.conf
   ```

4. Edit the *smb.conf* file and change the *guest account* in the *[global]* section to *guest = nobody.* This entry matches the user *nobody* found in the */etc/passwd* file.

5. Edit the second *[public]* section, remove the comments, and change the path to */tmp*, as shown in Listing 6-7.

Listing 6-7: Exporting the /tmp directory

```
; A publicly accessible directory, read/write to all users. Note that all files
; created in the directory by users will be owned by the default user, so
; any user with access can delete any other user's files. Obviously this
; directory must be writable by the default user. Another user could of course
; be specified, in which case all files would be owned by that user instead.
[public]
    path = /tmp
    public = yes
    only guest = yes
    writable = yes
    printable = no
```

6. Save the changes, exit back to your shell prompt, and restart the Samba daemons with the following commands:

   ```
   /etc/rc.d/init.d/smb stop
   /etc/rc.d/init.d/smb start
   ```

7. Back on your Windows 95 box, double-click your Linux-Samba computer icon in your *Network Neighborhood.* Double-click the *public* icon and you should see the */tmp* directory, as shown in Figure 6-2.

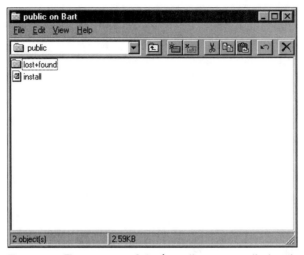

Figure 6-2: The contents of the /tmp directory are displayed.

8. Run the **smbstatus** command to show who Samba recognizes you as. The results should look like that in Listing 6-8.

Listing 6-8: The results of executing smbstatus

```
Samba version 1.9.17p4
Service     uid     gid     pid     machine
-------------------------------------------------
public      nobody  nobody  1142    maggie    (192.168.1.2) Fri Dec 12 19:57:7

No locked files
```

9. In my case, Samba sees me as the user – and group – *nobody* connecting from the machine *maggie*. I am using the *[public]* service, which points to the */tmp* directory (not shown in the *smbstatus* output).

10. The *install.log* file (which contains information on the Red Hat packages that you installed) is owned by *root*. If you do a long listing on the *install.log* file – **ls -l /tmp/install.log** – you'll see that only root has the *write* privilege:

```
-rw-r--r--    1 root      root        2662 Dec 10 13:23 install.log
```

11. You can open up the upgrade file from your Windows 95 box by double-clicking the *install.log* file icon. Unless you have already specified one, you are asked what application program you want to use to open it, as shown in Figure 6-3. If you choose an editor such as Microsoft WordPad, you can look at the contents of the file.

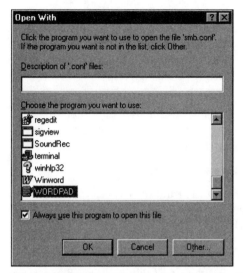

Figure 6-3: Windows 95 asks you what application
you want to use for smb.conf.

12. However, if you try to modify the file in any way, you get the response like the one shown in Figure 6-4. Even though you have marked the public Samba share pointing to */tmp* as writable, you do not have the permission from Linux to do so.

Figure 6-4: Windows 95 tells you that you do
not have the permissions to modify the share.

So remember that Linux permissions always supersede Samba's.

UNDERSTANDING SAMBA PERMISSIONS

In this next example, you export the */etc* directory to the *root* user. This is useful for viewing the various configuration files contained in that directory. This example once again makes use of the default *smb.conf* file. The following instructions show you how to export the */etc* directory as read-only.

The names I use in this example for creating Linux user names and Samba shares are my own. Please feel free to use any names that you want.

1. Log on to your Windows computer as the user *root*. (Note that this user does not necessarily have any extra privileges as in Linux. I use it so the user name/password will match with the Linux server.)

2. Log on to your Linux-Samba server as *root*.

3. Restore your original *smb.conf* file from the backup copy (if you have not already done so – as advised earlier in this chapter – reverse the process and make a backup copy):

```
cp /etc/smb.conf.orig /etc/smb.conf
```

4. Edit the *smb.conf* file and find the *[tmp]* share section. Remove the comments and then change the *[tmp]* share name to *[etc]* and the *path = /tmp* to *path = /etc*, as shown in Listing 6-9.

Listing 6-9: Modifying smb.conf to export the /etc directory (read-only)

```
[etc]
    comment = The /etc directory
    path = /etc
    read only = yes
    public = yes
```

5. Save the changes, exit back to your shell prompt, and restart the Samba daemons:

```
/etc/rc.d/init.d/smb stop
/etc/rc.d/init.d/smb start
```

6. Back on your Windows 95 box, double-click your Linux-Samba computer icon in your *Network Neighborhood*. You should see an icon labeled *etc* – in addition to the *root* icon. Double-click the *etc* icon and you should see the */etc* directory, as shown in Figure 6-5.

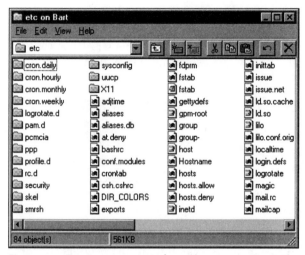

Figure 6-5: The contents of the /etc directory are displayed.

7. Run the **smbstatus** command to show who Samba recognizes you as. The results should look like those in Listing 6-10.

Listing 6-10: The results of executing smbstatus

```
Samba version 1.9.17p4
Service     uid     gid     pid     machine
-----------------------------------------------
etc         root    root    1226    maggie  (192.168.1.2) Fri Dec 12 20:22:7

No locked files
```

8. In my case, Samba sees me as the user – and group – *root* connecting from the machine *maggie*. I am using the *[etc]* service, which points to the */etc* directory (not shown in the *smbstatus* output).

9. The */etc* directory is owned by *root*, which has *write* privilege. If you do a long listing on the *smb.conf* file – *ls -l /smb.conf* – you'll see that root has the *write* privilege:

```
-rw-r--r--  1 root     root         6549 Dec 12 20:19 smb.conf
```

10. Open up the *smb.conf* file from your Windows 95 box by double-clicking the *smb.conf* file icon.

11. However, if you try to modify the file in any way, you get the response shown in Figure 6-6. Even though you are known by Samba as *root* and *root* owns the *smb.conf* file and has write permission, you cannot write to the file because – in this case – Samba has it marked as read-only.

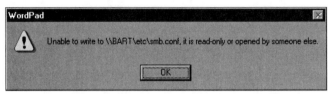

Figure 6-6: Windows 95 tells you that you do not have the permissions to modify the share.

12. If you wish to experiment, you can turn off the *read-only* option and change the *[etc]* share to *writable* and actually edit it. However, you generally should do systems configuration tasks like that from the Linux-Samba server itself.

This example shows how Samba can manipulate share privileges when the underlying Linux privileges exist.

Exporting the CD-ROM

I want to finish up this section by exporting the CD-ROM. By doing so, you can provide many useful functions to your network. For example, one very productive service is sharing software – say, your Linux distribution – or other material to your network. Exporting the CD-ROM cuts down on the number of CD-ROM drives you need (although CD-ROM drives are becoming ubiquitous, some of your older machines may not have them). Plus, it saves having to transport a CD-ROM disc from machine to machine.

The following example once again makes use of the default *smb.conf* file. The following instructions show you how to export the */mnt/cdrom* directory.

Note: The names I use in this example for creating Linux user names and Samba shares are my own. Please feel free to use any names that you want to use.

1. Log on to your Windows computer as the user *root*. (Note that this user does not necessarily have any extra privileges as in Linux. I use it so the user name/password will match with the Linux server.)

2. Log on to your Linux-Samba server as *root*.

3. Restore your original *smb.conf* file from the backup copy (if you have not already done so – as advised earlier in this chapter – reverse the process and make a backup copy):

```
cp /etc/smb.conf.orig /etc/smb.conf
```

4. Edit the *smb.conf* file and find the *[tmp]* share section. Remove the comments, and then change the *[tmp]* share name to *[cdrom]* and the *path = /tmp* to *path = /mnt/cdrom*, as shown in Listing 6-11.

Listing 6-11: Modifying smb.conf to export the /mnt/cdrom directory (read-only)

```
[cdrom]
   comment = Temporary file space
   path = /mnt/cdrom
   read only = yes
   public = yes
```

5. Save the changes, exit back to your shell prompt, and restart the Samba daemons:

```
/etc/rc.d/init.d/smb stop
/etc/rc.d/init.d/smb start
```

6. Mount the CD-ROM that came with this book by entering the following command:

```
mount -r -t iso9660 /dev/cdrom /mnt/cdrom
```

7. Double-click your Linux-Samba computer icon in your *Network Neighborhood*. Double-click the *cdrom* icon and you should see the */mnt/cdrom* directory, as shown in Figure 6-7.

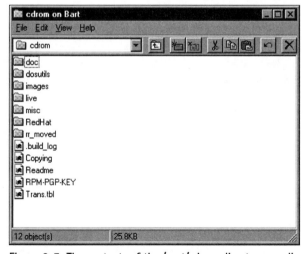

Figure 6-7: The contents of the /mnt/cdrom directory are displayed.

8. Run the **smbstatus** command to show who Samba recognizes you as. The results should look like those in Listing 6-12.

Listing 6-12: The results of executing smbstatus

```
Samba version 1.9.17p4
Service       uid       gid       pid       machine
-------------------------------------------------
cdrom         root      root      4234      maggie    (192.168.1.2) Sun Dec 14 14:24:7

No locked files
```

9. In my case, Samba sees me as the user – and group – *root* connecting from the machine *maggie*. I am using the *[cdrom]* service, which points to the */mnt/cdrom* directory (not shown in the *smbstatus* output).

 Mount points can be confusing. Mount points, such as /mnt/cdrom, are just simple directories. You can use them just like any other directory. However, after you use them to mount another device, their contents will not be visible again until you dismount the device.

Taking a Look at What You've Done

You've already done quite a lot of work. Here's a quick review of what you have accomplished. I start you off in this chapter at essentially the same place where you left off after Chapter 1. Red Hat configures a minimal Samba configuration that exports your Linux home directory – if your Windows 95 user name matches your Linux user name – when you open the *Network Neighborhood*. This minimal configuration lets you see Samba work from the start.

From there, I showed you how to extend your network by making incremental modifications to the Samba configuration file – *smb.conf*. The examples show how to make shares public; they also illustrate how the permissions of Linux supersede Samba permissions.

The next flurry of examples required the addition of users to the Linux system. They enable you to really configure your Linux-Samba server as a production file server.

The article, "Samba — Tuning the NT/UNIX Dance," in the May 1997 issue of *Sys Admin* magazine, offers a concise, informative tutorial on configuring Samba for use with Windows NT, and it appears to translate well for Windows 95. It has the interesting feature of including an *smb.conf* template in which you uncomment the services you desire. The author, Mark Nassal, also offers a menu-based *smb.conf* configuration system, which you can access at the following URL:

`http://www.tiac.net/users/nassalm/index.html`

I have just played around with it and created a couple of straightforward examples that worked well. Check it out.

Creating Samba Shares That Require Linux Modifications

The following Samba examples require the addition of user and printer shares. Adding user and printer shares requires that users and printers be known explicitly by Linux. Therefore, you need to know about some basic Linux administration tasks. This is a good time to address these tasks, because you have gone a long time without touching Linux.

Adding Users to Linux

To provide Samba shares, you must add one or more users to your Linux box. Users are defined in the */etc/passwd* and */etc/group* files.

Red Hat reasonably suggests that you use the *User Configuration* GUI from its *Control Panel* administrative tool, or command line programs */usr/sbin/useradd* and */usr/sbin/userdel*, to add, delete, and modify users. Both are good methods, but the *User Configuration* function runs under X, which I haven't introduced yet (see the section "Configuring the X Window system with the Xconfigurator" in Chapter 7 for more information on configuring X), and I would rather have you do it manually at least once to understand what needs to happen to add a user. So for now, I'll explain the password file, and give instructions for modifying the */etc/passwd* and */etc/group* files in order to add users.

All Linux distributions have the same */etc/passwd* file format, with fields separated by colons (:) in the order shown in Table 6-1. (The top item in this table corresponds to the left-most item and the bottom item to the right-most item.)

TABLE 6-1 THE /ETC /PASSWD FILE FORMAT

Field	Description
Login name	The name with which the user logs into the system.
Encrypted password	If the user has no password, this field is blank. An asterisk identifies a nonlogin account. Otherwise, this field shows an apparently random jumble of characters representing the encrypted password. (If you use shadow passwords, the encrypted password is moved to the file /etc/shadow, which is not readable by anyone except root and thus is more secure.)
User ID	The user identification number. The number corresponds to the login name after it is set in the passwd file. The numeric user ID can be shown by using the -n and -l options with the ls command (that is, ls -n -l, or, ls -nl).
Group ID	The default group identification number. The number identifies the default group to which the user belongs; you can belong to multiple groups, however. Red Hat uses the individual group convention in which each user belongs to a unique and exclusive group. In the past, a user would belong to one or more general-purpose groups, which created problems. The groups are defined in the /etc/group file.
Name and/or comment	This optional field should contain the user's full name and other pertinent information such as office location, phone number, and pager number (especially important for systems administrators). Commas separate these pieces of information.
Home directory	The user's default directory. This is where you go when you log in.
Shell	Your default login shell. All Linux distributions, including Red Hat, use bash, which is the most commonly used in the Linux world. You can change the shell to ksh, csh, sh, or whatever you want or whatever you desire and want to have access to.

Listing 6-13 shows the default /etc/passwd file that Red Hat provides. Most Linux distributions use the same login names, user IDs, and group IDs through the first ten or so users (but vary in some of the directories). From there, the distributions vary according to their own needs. Don't worry, the details may vary, but they are for the system to use and don't affect your setup.

Listing 6-13: The /etc/passwd file defining all users

```
root:yTSdWTprhi7u6:0:0:root:/root:/bin/bash
bin:*:1:1:bin:/bin:
daemon:*:2:2:daemon:/sbin:
adm:*:3:4:adm:/var/adm:
lp:*:4:7:lp:/var/spool/lpd:
sync:*:5:0:sync:/sbin:/bin/sync
shutdown:*:6:0:shutdown:/sbin:/sbin/shutdown
halt:*:7:0:halt:/sbin:/sbin/halt
mail:*:8:12:mail:/var/spool/mail:
news:*:9:13:news:/var/spool/news:
uucp:*:10:14:uucp:/var/spool/uucp:
operator:*:11:0:operator:/root:
games:*:12:100:games:/usr/games:
gopher:*:13:30:gopher:/usr/lib/gopher-data:
ftp:*:14:50:FTP User:/home/ftp:
nobody:*:99:99:Nobody:/:
```

Next are the steps for adding a user. Please note that the names I use in this example for creating Linux user names and Samba shares are my own. Please feel free to use any names that you want to use.

1. Log on to your Windows computer as the user *maggie*.

2. Log in to your Linux-Samba server as *root*.

3. Edit the */etc/passwd* file and add a user name such as the one in the following example:

```
maggie::500:500:Maggie Simpson, daughter of Homer:/home/maggie:/bin/bash
```

> The format is what is important, so you can use your own name and other details. To be compatible with Red Hat, however, I suggest you use their user and group ID convention and stick with 500 and 500 (unless you have already added one or more users, in which case, you don't really need to add a user here).

4. For now, leave the password field blank — you can set it later with the */usr/bin/passwd* command.

5. Save and exit the file.

> Now you must — well, should — create a personal group. You do this by editing the */etc/group* file shown in Listing 6-14.

Listing 6-14: The /etc/group file

```
root::0:root
bin::1:root,bin,daemon
daemon::2:root,bin,daemon
sys::3:root,bin,adm
adm::4:root,adm,daemon
tty::5:
disk::6:root
lp::7:daemon,lp
mem::8:
kmem::9:
wheel::10:root
mail::12:mail
news::13:news
uucp::14:uucp
man::15:
games::20:
gopher::30:
dip::40:
ftp::50:
nobody::99:
users::100:
```

6. First, add yourself to the users group (100) as shown in the following example (this is what Red Hat does when you use its *Control Panel User Configuration* process, and I want to stay consistent with it):

```
users::100:maggie
```

Notice the now-familiar *nobody* group that you have been using in the Samba configuration examples up to this point.

7. Next, add a line for your *personal group* at the bottom of the file, like the following example:

```
maggie::500:maggie
```

8. Save and exit the file.

9. The next step is to create a home directory for your new user. Red Hat likes its users to live in the */home* directory. I have no objection to this convention, so enter the *make directory* command, as in the following example:

```
/bin/mkdir /home/maggie
```

10. You need to copy some supporting files, such as the *bash* initialization script — *.bashrc* — to the new home directory. You can use a skeleton directory, */etc/skel*, from which to copy the new user's basic files. Enter the **copy** command, as in the following example:

```
cp /etc/skel/.*   /home/maggie
```

Don't worry about the messages omitting the directories. The directories "." and ".." are Linux's method of referring to the current and parent directories, respectively.

TIP   Linux uses the convention where support files, such as *.bashrc*, are hidden from normal directory listings such as *ls -l*. Linux does this because these files are generally of interest when you're configuring something. To show them, use the all (*-a*) parameter in the *list* command (for example, enter **/bin/ls -a**, or **/bin/ls -la**).

11. You need to change the owner and group for your new directory and configuration files. In the following two commands, I add my new user, *maggie*:

```
/bin/chown -R maggie /home/maggie
/bin/chgrp -R maggie /home/maggie
```

TIP   You can combine the *chown* and *chgrp* commands as follows:

```
chown -R maggie.maggie /home/maggie
```

The recursive flag (*-R*) saves you from having to execute commands several times to account for all the subdirectories and files that your directory contains. Many commands recognize the recursive flag; it tells a command to descend through all subdirectories and perform the same task. This flag is very useful.

12. You should change the permissions on */home/maggie*. The permissions you choose depend on the requirements of the account. That depends on more variables than I can describe here. However, you'll want to give the owner complete access to the home directory, which includes read, write, and execute. For this example, I give *read* access to Maggie's group and no privilege to everyone else (other). Enter the following command:

```
/bin/chmod 640 /home/maggie
```

13. Finally, you need to set your password (no password is set at this point). Root can do this via the *passwd* command. Enter the command **passwd maggie**. You are prompted for a new password. Enter a password and then the confirmation of that password. That's all you need to do. The user *maggie* has been added.

Getting Quick Help with GNU Commands

When you enter the **--h** or **--help** parameter with GNU commands, they print a short help menu. For example, entering **chown --help** displays the screen shown in Listing 6-15. This help tool is more convenient than running a man page because it is quicker and more to the point.

Listing 6-15: The chown --h short help menu

```
Usage: chown [OPTION]... OWNER[.[GROUP]] FILE...
  or:  chown [OPTION]... .[GROUP] FILE...
Change the owner and/or group of each FILE to OWNER and/or GROUP.
  -c, --changes          be verbose whenever change occurs
  -h, --no-dereference   affect symbolic links instead of any referenced file
                         (available only on systems with lchown system call)
  -f, --silent, --quiet  suppress most error messages
  -v, --verbose          explain what is being done
  -R, --recursive        change files and directories recursively
      --help             display this help and exit
      --version          output version information and exit
Owner is unchanged if missing.  Group is unchanged if missing, but changed
to login group if implied by a period.  A colon may replace the period.
```

Take a moment to examine the *.bashrc* file. It contains a line, *. /etc/bashrc*, that tells the shell to source – or put into effect – the generic *bashrc* script shown in Listing 6-16.

Listing 6-16: The .bashrc file

```
# /etc/bashrc

# System wide functions and aliases
# Environment stuff goes in /etc/profile

# For some unknown reason bash refuses to inherit
# PS1 in some circumstances that I can't figure out.
# Putting PS1 here ensures that it gets loaded every time.
PS1="[\u@\h \W]\\$ "

alias which="type -path"
```

The *bash* shell treats any text after a pound symbol (#) as a comment, except when the first line begins with the combination *#!*. In that case, the *bash* shell treats the following string as the command interpreter. For example, *#!/bin/bash* tells Linux to use the *bash* shell to interpret the script.

The first job the script does is to define your shell prompt, *[root@bart /etc]#*, and then the alias *which*. If you wish to customize the way your shell is configured you will want to modify this script.

Exporting an Individual User's Directory Using the [home] Service

Here's where things get interesting. In this section, I show you how to create a service out of the new user account, *maggie* (which I show you how to create in the preceding section of this chapter). After you create a new user account on the Linux-Samba server, you can automatically access its home directory from Samba. The default *smb.conf* file is preconfigured to export the home directory of Windows clients whose user names/passwords match the Linux user name/password. This is the same service that you use in Chapter 1, but the difference here is that a regular Linux user is created to make use of the service.

Note: The names I use in this example for creating Linux user names and Samba shares are my own. Please feel free to use any names that you want to use.

1. Log on to your Windows computer as the user *maggie.*

2. Log on to your Linux-Samba server as *root.*

3. Restore your original *smb.conf* file from the backup copy:

```
cp /etc/smb.conf.orig /etc/smb.conf
```

4. Restart the Samba daemons:

```
/etc/rc.d/init.d/smb stop
/etc/rc.d/init.d/smb start
```

5. Double-click your Linux-Samba computer icon in your *Network Neighborhood.* Double-click the *maggie* icon and you should see the */home/maggie* directory, as shown in Figure 6-8.

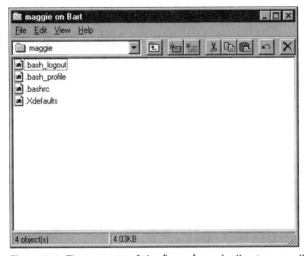

Figure 6-8: The contents of the /home/maggie directory are displayed.

6. Run the *smbstatus* command to show who Samba recognizes you as. The results should look like those in Listing 6-17.

Listing 6-17: The results of executing smbstatus

```
Samba version 1.9.17p4
Service   uid     gid     pid     machine
----------------------------------------
maggie    maggie  maggie  4434    maggie   (192.168.1.2) Sun Dec 14 17:41:25 1997

No locked files
```

7. In my case, Samba sees me as the user – and group – *maggie* connecting from the machine *maggie*. I am using the *[maggie]* service, which points to the */home/maggie* directory (not shown in the *smbstatus* output). The *[homes]* services have worked as advertised.

8. Unlike the previous examples in this chapter, you can read *and write* to this share. You can use it just like a local disk!

Exporting a Service to Two or More Users

In this section, I show you how to use the `valid users` parameter, which I introduce in the preceding example. You can use this variable to allow any number of users access to a particular service. This access is not the same as group access, but it works in a similar fashion.

Note: The names I use in this example for creating Linux user names and Samba shares are my own. Please feel free to use any names that you want to use.

1. Log on to your Windows computer as the user *maggie*.

2. Log on to your Linux-Samba server as *root*.

3. Restore your original *smb.conf* file from the backup copy:

   ```
   cp /etc/smb.conf.orig /etc/smb.conf
   ```

4. Edit the *smb.conf* file and find the *[myshare]* share section. Remove the comments, and then change the *[myshare]* share name to *[marge]* and the *path = /usr/somewhere/shared* to *path = /home/marge* and *valid users = mary fred* to *valid users = marge maggie*, as shown in Listing 6-18.

Listing 6-18: Adding multiple users to a Samba share

```
[marge]
comment = Marge's and Maggie's stuff
path = /home/marge
valid users = marge maggie
public = no
writable = yes
printable = no
create mask = 0765
```

5. Save the changes, exit back to your shell prompt, and restart the Samba daemons:

   ```
   /etc/rc.d/init.d/smb stop
   /etc/rc.d/init.d/smb start
   ```

6. Next, you need to add the new user *marge*. Follow the instructions in the section, "Adding Users to Linux," earlier in this chapter, or enter the following command:

```
useradd marge
```

7. Set the password for *marge* by entering the following command:

```
passwd marge
```

8. Add *marge* to the general purpose users group:

```
users::100:maggie,marge
```

9. Change the group ownership of the */home/marge* directory as follows:

```
chgrp users /home/marge
```

10. Change the permissions on */home/marge* to allow group access.

```
chmod 770 /home/marge
```

11. On your Windows 95 box, double-click your Linux-Samba computer icon in your *Network Neighborhood*. Double-click the *marge* icon and you should see the */home/marge* directory, as shown in Figure 6-9.

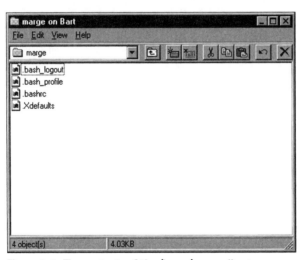

Figure 6-9: The contents of the /home/marge directory are accessed by maggie.

12. Run the *smbstatus* command to show who Samba recognizes you as. The results should look like those in Listing 6-19.

Listing 6-19: The results of executing smbstatus

```
Samba version 1.9.17p4
Service  uid     gid     pid     machine
----------------------------------------
marge    maggie  maggie  5005    maggie  (192.168.1.2) Tue Dec 16 21:12:17 1997

No locked files
```

13. In my case, Samba sees me as the user – and group – *maggie* connecting from the machine *maggie*. I am using the *[marge]* service, which points to the */home/marge* directory (not shown in the *smbstatus* output). The fact that my user ID is *maggie* is important because the service points to *marge's* directory, which is fully owned by the user *marge*. Thus, Samba has indeed allowed multiple users to access a single share.

    Note: If you had not set the others permission on *marge's* directory to read and execute, you would not be able to access *marge's* share. Remember, Linux supersedes Samba's permissions, and you are recognized as the user *maggie* and the group *maggie* here. So you will only gain access there from the other permissions.

    You can avoid this problem by changing the group of */home/marge* from *marge* to *users*. Both *maggie* and *marge* belong to that group, which has read, write, and execute permissions on */home/marge*.

14. Unlike the previous examples in this chapter, you can read *and write* to this share. You can use it just like a local disk!

Using Samba's Macro Capability

Samba can substitute macros for service parameters. Upon connection, it dynamically allocates its resources according to which machine, user, or other is asking for each resource.

You designate a macro by adding a percent (%) symbol as the first character of any of several predefined names. Table 6-2 shows the macros.

TABLE 6-2 SAMBA MACROS

Macro	Description
%S	Current service or share if it exists (if any exists)
%P	Root directory of the current service or share (if any exists)

continued

TABLE 6-2 SAMBA MACROS *(Continued)*

Macro	Description
%u	User name of the current service or share (if any exists)
%g	Primary group name of %u
%U	Session user name the client requested, but not necessarily the one received
%G	Primary group name of %U
%H	The home directory of the user given by %u
%v	Samba version number
%h	Host name of the Samba server
%m	NetBIOS name of the client computer
%L	NetBIOS name of the Samba server
%M	Internet name of the client computer
%d	Process ID of the current server process
%a	Architecture of the remote server
%I	IP address of the client computer
%T	Current date and time

Experiment with the %m macro in the following example.

Note: The names I use in this example for creating Linux user names and Samba shares are my own. Please feel free to use any names that you want to use.

1. Log on to your Windows computer as the user *maggie.*

2. Log on to your Linux-Samba server as *root.*

3. Restore your original *smb.conf* file from the backup copy:

```
cp /etc/smb.conf.orig /etc/smb.conf
```

4. Edit the *smb.conf* file and find the *[pchome]* share section. Remove the comments and then change the *path = /usr/pc/%m* to *path = /home/%m*, as shown in Listing 6-20. Notice that *smb.conf* uses the *%m* macro, which expands into the name (*netbios* name) of the Windows PC connecting to it.

Listing 6-20: Exporting a service pegged to the requesting machine name

```
; The %m gets replaced with the machine name that is connecting.
[pchome]
  comment = PC Directories
  path = /home/%m
  public = no
  writeable = yes
```

5. Save the changes, exit back to your shell prompt, and restart the Samba daemons:

```
/etc/rc.d/init.d/smb stop
/etc/rc.d/init.d/smb start
```

6. On your Windows 95 box, double-click your Linux-Samba computer icon in your *Network Neighborhood.* Double-click the *pchome* icon and you should see the */home/maggie* directory, as shown in Figure 6-10.

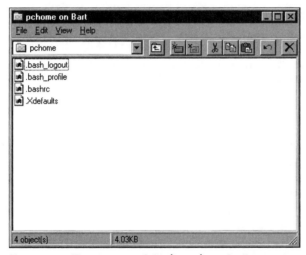

Figure 6-10: The contents of the /home/maggie directory are accessed by maggie.

7. Run the *smbstatus* command to show who Samba recognizes you as. The results should look like those in Listing 6-21.

Listing 6-21: The results of executing smbstatus

```
Samba version 1.9.17p4
Service   uid    gid    pid    machine
----------------------------------------
pchome    maggie maggie 5054   maggie  (192.168.1.2) Tue Dec 16 21:24:56 1997

No locked files
```

8. In my case, Samba sees me as the user – and group – *maggie* connected from the machine *maggie.* I am using the *[pchome]* service, which points to the */home/maggie* directory (not shown in the *smbstatus* output).

This Samba macro-based service attempts to connect every Windows client that comes down the pike. If a valid Linux user name exists, this service will connect a matching Windows client to it automatically. Using macros really simplifies the *smb.conf* file setup, because you can adapt one service section to numerous situations. If you have numerous shares to distribute (or are just plain lazy), this option is for you.

Adding Network Printers Using Linux and Samba

No client-server network is complete without a shared printer. Sharing printing gives you a lot of bang for your client-server buck. If you fold the services of just five $200 printers into one $1,000 printer, you come out ahead. You have less maintenance, lower overhead costs, maybe less initial cost, and probably better overall performance. It's a win-win situation.

Samba, of course, makes network printer sharing easy. You can use a printer that is already connected to your Linux box. All you have to do is configure Samba to use the Linux printer setup. The Linux setup is simple unless you have an unusual printer or some other irregularity. So give it a try. In the following section of this chapter, I use the existing Red Hat printer configuration and give you a quick tutorial on configuring Linux.

EXPORTING YOUR PRINTER

My last examples in this chapter show you how to use a printer over the network. It is perhaps superfluous to extol the virtues of using a printer over the network, but I want to do so anyway. This function alone makes the client-server network desirable, in my opinion. My old company wasted a great deal of time and money purchasing and sharing printers. Until we got our NFS network, we shared printers by means of switch boxes, long serial cables, physically moving printers, and with a floppy-disk/sneaker net. No method sufficed, and we basically ended up self-limiting our printing. This setup severely impaired our productivity, and we didn't realize the extent of the productivity drain until we could all access a common, fast, laser printer.

The following instructions show how to configure your Linux-Samba server to work as the printer server for your network.

Note: The default *smb.conf* file that comes on this book's CD-ROM does not require any editing to work. The following instructions that reference it are for instructional purposes only. I continue to use the names found on my system — such as the HP LaserJet 5L (PCL) — and you should make the appropriate substitutions for your system.

1. Log on to your Linux-Samba server as *root*.

2. Restore your original *smb.conf* file from the backup copy:

   ```
   cp /etc/smb.conf.orig /etc/smb.conf
   ```

   Do not restart the Samba daemons just yet, however.

3. Edit the *smb.conf* file and find the *[global]* share section, as shown in Listing 6-22.

Listing 6-22: The [global] section in the smb.conf file

```
[global]
   printing = bsd
   printcap name = /etc/printcap
   load printers = yes
```

This section tells Samba the following information:

- The `printing` entry specifies which printer daemon Linux uses. (BSD is the default, but Linux also uses *sysv*, *hpux*, *aix*, *qnx*, and *plp*. Linux works well with BSD; I mention the others for the sake of being complete.) It also tells Samba the default values for the *lpr* and *lpq* commands that Linux uses to perform the actual printing.

- The `printcap name` parameter defines where the Linux printer configuration file *printcap* is located.

- The `load printers` parameter indicates whether to load all the printers defined in the printcap for browsing.

4. Next, find the *[printers]* share section, shown in Listing 6-23.

Listing 6-23: Network printing

```
[printers]
   comment = All Printers
   browseable = no
   printable = yes
   public = no
```

```
writable = no
create mode = 0700
```

This section tells Samba the following information:

- A `comment` describing what it is set up for.

- If `browseable` is *yes,* you can browse all the printers defined in the *printcap* file from a Windows client.

- If `printable` is yes, it allows nonprinting access to the spool directories associated with the print service. If *printable* is set to no, it does not prevent you from printing, it simply denies you direct access to the printer spool directories – */var/spool/lpd/lp*, for instance.

- If `public` is set to no, those Windows clients that are not authenticated by a Linux user name (the guest account, for example) will not be able to use the Samba print services.

- If `writable` is set to *no,* you will not be able to write directly to the printer spool directory. You will still be able to print, however.

- The `create mode` determines which default permissions the printer spool files will have.

5. Exit from the *smb.conf* file and edit the */etc/printcap* file. It contains the Linux printer configuration information, and Samba reads this information when it starts. I have a Hewlett-Packard LaserJet 5L attached to my Linux box. Listing 6-24 shows the printcap file that I have created. (The comments are from the template printcap file that was installed automatically during the installation described in Chapter 1.)

Listing 6-24: My /etc/printcap file for connecting an HP LaserJet

```
# /etc/printcap
#
# Please don't edit this file directly unless you know what you are doing!
# Be warned that the control-panel printtool requires a very strict format!
# Look at the printcap(5) man page for more info.
#
# This file can be edited with the printtool in the control-panel.
lp:\
        :sd=/var/spool/lpd/lp:\
        :mx#0:\
        :sh:\
        :lp=/dev/lp1:\
        :if=/var/spool/lpd/lp/filter:
```

Here's an explanation of the file's contents:

- Anything after a pound sign (#) is treated as a comment.

- Colons (:) bound variables and their parameters.

- A back slash (\) specifies that the parameter continues on the next line.

- The first line after the comments defines the printer name and any aliases (not shell aliases) by which Linux knows the printer (it can have zero or more aliases). The printer name lp (line printer) is standard.

- The `sd=/var/spool/lpd/lpd` line identifies the location of the printer spool directory. Recall that the *lpd* daemon *spools* a print file to a temporary directory. The effect is to buffer the print file so the processor does not have to wait for the much slower printer.

- The `mx` variable specifies the largest file that can be printed. The pound-zero (#0) makes it unlimited.

- The `sh` variable is a flag that prevents the printing of a burst page (header page) before each print job. This feature is only useful if you have many users printing to a single printer.

- The `lp=/dev/lp1` line defines the device file (in this case, lp1 points to the first parallel port, which would be lpt1 in MS-DOS parlance).

- The `if=/var/spool/lpd/lp/filter` specifies my input filter. It is used to translate various file formats to a printer. It translates everything from straight text to PostScript into PCL, which is what the HP printer understands.

6. Save the changes, exit back to your shell prompt, and restart the Samba daemons:

```
/etc/rc.d/init.d/smb stop
/etc/rc.d/init.d/smb start
```

The preceding changes to your *smb.conf* file make all your printers available over your network, which in my case means that I can print to my LaserJet from any of my Windows clients. You can explicitly set parameters (such as where the spool directories are located), but I prefer to keep that information in the printcap file as much as possible.

Red Hat provides a *printtool* (via its *Control Panel*) that asks you most necessary questions and translates your responses to a printcap file. Because the *Control Panel* requires the X Window system, I defer further description until the section "Configuring the Print Server" in Chapter 10 where I show you how to configure the X Window system.

TIP

One very useful thing that the *Control Panel printtool* does is set up printer filters for you. A printer filter can enable you to do things such as print PostScript files to a non-PostScript printer by translating from one protocol to another.

7. Windows may not recognize the new printer when you try to mount it. If you have not configured the printer on your Windows PC, you have to do so. You get the message window shown in Figure 6-11. If you click the *Yes* button, the Windows Wizard guides you through the process with minimal confusion. You most likely need your Windows 95 or printer CD-ROM to get the print driver.

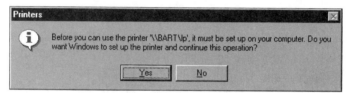

Figure 6-11: You have not set up Windows 95 for your Samba printer.

8. After you have Windows configured for your Samba printer, open the *Network Neighborhood* icon. You should see a Samba share *lp*, as shown in Figure 6-12.

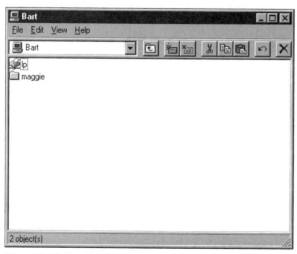

Figure 6-12: The Samba printer share

9. Double-click the *lp* icon and you get the *Windows 95 HP LaserJet 5L (PCL) queue* dialog box shown in Figure 6-13.

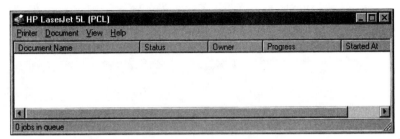

Figure 6-13: The Windows 95 printer queue dialog box

10. To test your Samba print service, click the *Printer* menu. Next, click the *Properties* menu item and you get the *Windows 95 HP LaserJet 5L (PCL) Properties* dialog box shown in Figure 6-14.

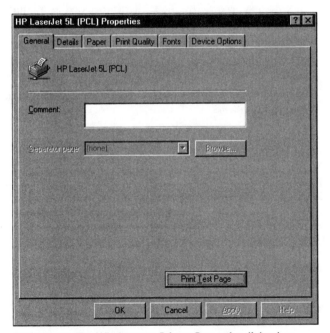

Figure 6-14: The Windows 95 Printer Properties dialog box

11. Click the *Print Test Page* button, and a test page is printed for you. In fact, if you keep an eye on the *HP LaserJet 5L (PCL) queue* dialog box (shown in Figure 6-13), you can see the progress of your print job. Figure 6-15 shows the first stage in which Windows 95 processes the job before sending it to the Linux-Samba server.

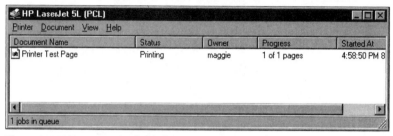

Figure 6-15: The test print job being processed by Windows 95

12. After the print job has been processed by Windows 95, it is copied as a file to the Linux-Samba server. The file is then processed as a Linux print job, as shown in Figure 6-16.

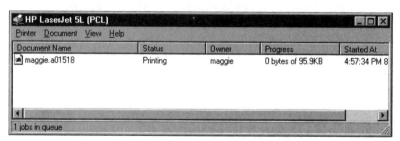

Figure 6-16: The test print job being processed by Linux-Samba

13. The test page is finally printed on your printer. It is a marvelous system.

TIP

You can print directly with Linux by redirecting output to the device driver of a printer. For example, if you have a printer connected to your parallel port — the common PC method — you can print the content of a file as follows:

```
/bin/cat /etc/smb.conf > /dev/lp1
```

This method is occasionally useful — usually for troubleshooting purposes — but unadvisable in general. Linux uses a spooling system to print. Recall from Chapter 3 how the daemon process, *lpd*, and the user program, *lpr*, work in tandem to send a print job to a spool directory and then to the printer. This method efficiently and safely shares a resource among many users and processes. The */etc/printcap* file contains the configuration information for each attached printer (both physically and via a network).

Summary

The examples in the previous sections give you an overview of Samba configuration. The variables you use to set the configuration are some of the most widely used ones. In Chapter 10, I give even more detailed examples. These examples cover – in essence – most of the situations you should encounter in setting up a business network. For instance, you can take the steps for allowing two users access to one service and easily expand to a dozen users by including their names in the `valid users` variable.

This chapter covered these topics:

◆ By working on the Samba configuration first, I show you how to expand the client-server network. This approach offers the most efficient method for obtaining a working system because modifying a simple text file is all that is required.

◆ I review the roles of the two Samba daemons: *smbd* and *nmbd*. Together they form the heart of Samba.

◆ I describe the process for restarting the Samba daemons. A new *smbd* process is started with every new share that is exported. Even so, it is advisable to restart these daemons when configuring Samba to make sure everything works the way you intend it to.

◆ I describe the *smb.conf* file: the *global* section, *directory*, and *printer shares*.

◆ The first set of examples concentrate on services that do not require any Linux modifications. Shares that are public or guest types are very easy to make and serve as good starting points. Some are useful in the real world.

◆ Making the entire Linux disk visible (but not writable) is the subject of the first example. This is a very simple way to demonstrate a working Samba share.

◆ Starting and stopping the Samba daemons with the */etc/rc.d/init.d/smb* script is the subject of the second example. This is an easier and safer method than doing it manually.

◆ Understanding how Linux permissions take precedence over those of Samba is the subject of the third example. This example demonstrates how even if you have Samba's permission to do something, you cannot do it if Linux does not let you.

◆ Understanding how Samba permissions work is the subject of the fourth example. If you have the necessary Linux permission, Samba can be used to modify who gets to do what.

◆ Exporting the CD-ROM is the subject of the final example that does not require modifying Linux. Because the CD-ROM is a read-only device, it can be made publicly available and provide a valuable network service.

◆ Using Samba services that require Linux modifications is the subject of the final set of examples. I use Samba user level security, which requires that in order to use a Samba share, the Windows user name must match a corresponding Linux user name. Thus the Linux modifications take the form of adding users.

◆ I describe the process for manually adding a user to Linux. This process entails adding a line to the */etc/passwd* and */etc/group* files and creating a home directory for each new user.

◆ Allowing multiple user access to a single share is the subject of the next example. The *allow users* parameter is used to provide that service.

◆ Using Samba's macro capability enables you to automate many services. Samba provides a set of macros that expand to match things such as the Windows machine name.

◆ Printing with Samba over the network is the final example. Samba is readily configured to allow access to common printers over the network.

Chapter 7

Configuring Linux

IN THIS CHAPTER

◆ Using the Red Hat Package Manager (RPM)

◆ Using the RPM query function

◆ Installing additional documentation and networking and compiler software with RPM

◆ Removing packages with RPM

◆ Upgrading packages with RPM

◆ Installing the X Window system with the help of RPM

◆ Understanding the basic parts of the X Window system

◆ Examining the commercial X Window configuration system Metro-X

◆ Configuring the Linux system by using the Red Hat *Control Panel*

◆ Exploring the concept of building a static or monolithic kernel

◆ Customizing your system by modifying the Red Hat startup scripts

THIS CHAPTER OFFERS in-depth coverage of the tools and techniques you use for configuring Linux. Of course, you have been configuring Linux all along as you have read the previous chapters in this book. However, those chapters keep the in-depth configuration information to a minimum – so far, I have presented only what you needed to know about configuration, in an *ad hoc* manner. In this chapter, I show you how to configure a Linux system in a systematic way.

I have deliberately minimized my discussion of Linux configuration in the previous chapters for two reasons. First, I wanted you to get a simple Linux server running as quickly as possible with a minimum of distraction. Second, I wanted you to complete the necessary configuration steps manually. Red Hat Linux provides powerful tools that tend to hide the underlying details, and as an administrator you need to learn and understand the fundamentals as much as possible. Throughout the rest of this book, I continue to show the manual methods as much as practical, but now I want to discuss Linux configuration, and the configuration tools are part of that discussion.

Red Hat provides three configuration systems that represent important evolutionary steps in the professionalization of Linux. Red Hat developed two of these systems, and the third is another proprietary system that Red Hat includes in its distribution. The first examples in this chapter discuss these systems and show you how to use them.

Another important aspect of Linux systems administration involves configuration of the kernel. The standard kernel that comes with Red Hat is a good base, but it doesn't include all the subsystems necessary for doing things such as establishing *Point-to-Point Protocol* (PPP) connections – that is, TCP/IP connectivity over a serial, or modem, line. One of the great features of Linux is that you can configure it *on-the-fly*. In other words, you can insert modules that include extra features such as PPP or other device drivers, while the kernel is running. You may use some of these extra features so often that you want to compile them permanently into the Linux kernel. You can easily recompile Linux, and I show you how to do so in this chapter.

RPM: The Red Hat Package Manager

One of the great frustrations of systems administration is managing software packages and systems. Adding, deleting, modifying, and just plain inventory are constant chores. I have several computers that I use on a daily basis. I have a good idea of what software I have and where to find the software that I use frequently, but my systems also have lots of software and configuration files that I have to rediscover when I find the need to use them. Add to that the necessity of changing a package, and I start getting really angry as I pick my way through endless directory trees and libraries. I'm not organized enough to make a formal database of the stuff – and doing so would take a lot of work. I just stumble along the best I can. There must be a better way.

The Red Hat Package Manager (RPM) goes a long way toward providing that *better way* for handling the complexities of systems administration. It automatically installs, uninstalls, and upgrades software. It operates like any other Linux command with the use of command-line options. RPM uses its database to keep track of what's what and where, and thus relieves you of that messy task.

RPM is a big improvement over distributions such as Slackware. In the past, I never hesitated to install a new package (how can you resist free software?), but I took deep breaths before upgrading those packages. Very often, I would completely delete stuff I knew I didn't have to delete, just to ensure that the upgrade would not stumble over its parents. Upgrading to significantly newer kernels entailed a number of disk formats! As you can imagine, I really appreciate the simplicity that RPM brings to the process of installing upgrades.

An RPM package consists of an archive of files and information describing its name, version, and contents. Packages are created to provide a particular Linux function. For instance, the Samba RPM package contains the Samba daemons, configuration files, manual pages, and other documentation.

RPM has 11 operational modes. (Red Hat says 10 but I include the upgrade as its own mode.) Five of these modes are most important to a systems administrator:

- **Install:** Install the package with the given options. Here's the syntax for this mode:

  ```
  rpm -i install-options package_file
  ```

- **Upgrade:** Install the upgrade package with the given options. You use the following syntax for this mode:

  ```
  rpm -U upgrade-options package_file
  ```

- **Erase (uninstall):** Erase or uninstall the package with the given options (removes all possible dependencies). This mode has the following syntax:

  ```
  rpm -e erase-options package_file
  ```

- **Query:** Find out if a package is already installed and where the package may be located. *Query* mode has the following syntax:

  ```
  rpm -q query-options
  ```

- **Verify:** Compare an installed package with the original, pristine package. The comparison includes size, a check sum, permissions, type, owner, and group of each file. Here's the syntax you use for *verify* mode:

  ```
  rpm -V|-y|--verify verify-options
  ```

The last six modes are for software distribution and are of less interest to a pure administrator, but I mention them for completeness:

- **Build:** Create the RPM packages themselves. (This mode is mostly for software developers.) Here's the syntax for *build* mode:

  ```
  rpm -bO build-options <package_spec>+ B
  ```

- **Rebuild database:** Rebuild the database with the package configuration information. You use the following syntax for this mode:

  ```
  rpm --rebuilddb
  ```

- **Fix permissions:** Reset the original file permissions to the files belonging to a package.

- **Signature check:** Verify that a package's integrity and origin are correct. This mode checks the digital signature of a package to make sure that it has not been tampered with.

◆ **Set owners and groups:** Resets the original owner and group to the files belonging to a package.

◆ **Show RC:** Displays the values of the *rpmrc* file. The *rpmrc* file is used to set various parameters used by RPM.

 You can find additional information on RPM in the manual page **man rpm**. You can find additional technical information — file formats and so on — in the text files in the */usr/doc/rpm-2.4.10* directory.

To make use of the RPM operating modes, you use various options or parameters. Some parameters are general purpose and work with any of the functions. Table 7-1 describes the general RPM parameters and their functions. You can use these parameters with any of the modes that I describe in the preceding lists.

TABLE 7-1 **RPM GENERAL PARAMETERS (CAN BE USED WITH ANY MODES)**

Parameter	Function
-vv	Print debugging information.
--keep-temps	Do not remove temporary files (/tmp/rpm-*). Useful primarily for debugging RPM.
--quiet	Print as little as possible — normally, only error messages are displayed.
--help	Print a longer usage message than normal.
--version	Print the version number of RPM.
--rcfile <file>	Specify a different personal setup file, rather than $HOME/rpmrc or /etc/rpmrc.
--root <dir>	Use dir as the top-level directory for all operations.

Some parameters are specific to one mode or another. You can customize the install and upgrade functions to suit your needs. Table 7-2 lists the parameters you use with install or upgrade.

TABLE 7-2 RPM INSTALL AND UPGRADE PARAMETERS

Parameter	Function
--force	Force the replacement of a package or file.
-h, --hash	Print 50 dots, or hash marks, as a package is installed.
--oldpackage	Replace a newer package with an older one. Normally, RPM balks if it is asked to write over a newer package.
--percent	Print percentage to completion during installation.
--replacefiles	Force previously installed files from other packages to be replaced.
--replacepkgs	Force previously installed packages to be replaced.
--root <dir>	Use another directory as a start point or root.
--nodeps	Skip the package dependency check before installing a package.
--noscripts	Skip to pre- and post-installation scripts.
--excludedocs	Skip installation of documentation.
--includedocs	Install documentation files. Used with excludedocs to be more specific.
--test	Perform the installation without installing anything. This function checks for problems.
-U, --upgrade	Install the new package over the old one. Remove the old package.

Note: With RPM, you can specify that the package file is a URL. In other words, you can install or upgrade a package directly from your Internet connection!

The *uninstall* option is a variation of the install function. Table 7-3 shows the options available for uninstalling RPM packages.

TABLE 7-3 RPM UNINSTALL PARAMETERS

Parameter	Function
--noscripts	Skip to the pre- and post-uninstall scripts.
--nodeps	Skip checking dependencies before uninstallation.
--test	Execute the uninstallation steps without deleting anything.
--nodeps	Remove the package even if broken dependencies exist.

You use the query parameters to determine which packages are installed on your present system, which packages are available on CD-ROM, which files belong to a particular package, and other information about a package. Tables 7-4 and 7-5 show the parameters you use with query.

TABLE 7-4 RPM QUERY PARAMETERS

Parameter	Function
-a	Find all installed packages.
--whatrequires capability	Locate packages that require a particular capability.
--whatprovides virtual	Locate packages that require a virtual capability.
-f file	Locate packages that own a file.
-p package_file	Query an uninstalled package. The *package_file* can be a URL.

TABLE 7-5 INFORMATION SELECTION OPTIONS

Parameter	Function
-i	Show various package information.
-R	List packages that this one depends on (same as *--requires*).
--provides	Show what a package does.
-l	List files in the package.
-s	Display the states of files in the package (implies *-l*). The state of each file is either normal, not installed, or replaced.
-d	List only documentation files (implies *-l*).
-c	List only configuration files (implies *-l*).
--scripts	List shell scripts used for installation and uninstallation.
--dump	List dump file information as follows: `path size mtime md5sum mode owner group isconfig isdoc rdev sym-link`. This parameter must be used with at least one of *-l*, *-c*, *-d*.

You use the verify parameters to determine which parts of a package differ from the original package. This option is useful for determining the state of your system. For example, if you are having problems with an application and need to determine whether the configuration files have been changed, you can use this function to find out what has changed. Table 7-6 shows the parameters you use with verify.

TABLE 7-6 RPM VERIFY PARAMETERS

Parameter	Function
--verify	Verify a package installation using the same package specification options as *-q*.
--dbpath <dir>	Use *<dir>* as the directory for the database.
--root <dir>	Use *<dir>* as the top-level directory.
--nodeps	Do not verify package dependencies.
--nomd5	Do not verify file *md5* checksums.
--nofiles	Do not verify file attributes.
--setperms	Set the file permissions to those in the package database using the same package.

I leave it to you to investigate the package building functions. As always, the man page for RPM provides excellent documentation.

Now that you have an overview of RPM, some examples are in order. The Red Hat installation process, which I introduce in Chapter 1, uses the RPM system to install the default packages plus the Samba package that I had you specify. Consequently, you have RPM packages available that you can use for practice. The beauty of the RPM system is that if something goes wrong during your experimentation, you can easily recover from the error. The RPM system takes care of the messy details.

Querying

Because you already have RPM packages installed, I start the examples with the Query function so you can see what's installed. I show you how to inventory the packages installed in Chapter 1 and then proceed to find details about the contents of an individual package.

FINDING ALL YOUR SYSTEM'S PACKAGES

Before you install any package, examine what the Red Hat installation process (which I describe in Chapter 1) has installed on your system. To display all installed packages, enter the following command with the -a option:

```
rpm -q -a
```

Listing 7-1 shows a sampling of the packages that you installed in Chapter 1. Recall that I had you choose only the default Red Hat packages plus Samba in the section on "Installing Red Hat Linux" in Chapter 1. The remaining software that you use in this book will be installed manually.

Listing 7-1: A sampling of the default Red Hat installation packages plus Samba

```
setup-1.9-2
filesystem-1.3.1-2
basesystem-4.9-1
ldconfig-1.9.5-2
termcap-9.12.6-7
libtermcap-2.0.8-6
grep-2.1-1
fileutils-3.16-6
bash-1.14.7-6
ash-0.2-10
chkconfig-0.9-2
at-3.1.7-2
ncurses-1.9.9e-6
info-3.9-7
bdflush-1.5-7
bind-utils-4.9.6-6
binutils-2.8.1.0.1-1
cracklib-dicts-2.5-4
crontabs-1.6-1
shadow-utils-970616-9
dev-2.5.4-1
diffutils-2.7-8
e2fsprogs-1.10-4
eject-1.5-1
etcskel-1.3-4
file-3.22-6
finger-0.10-2
ftp-0.10-1
gawk-3.0.2-2
gdbm-1.7.3-14
getty_ps-2.0.7j-2
```

```
groff-1.11a-3
gzip-1.2.4-9
hdparm-3.1-5
initscripts-3.25-1
kbd-0.94-5
kernel-2.0.31-7
kernel-modules-2.0.31-7
ld.so-1.9.5-3
libc-5.3.12-24
libg++-2.7.2.8-6
lilo-0.20-1
logrotate-2.5-2
lpr-0.21-2
MAKEDEV-2.3.1-1
man-1.4j-3
mingetty-0.9.4-5
mkinitrd-1.8-1
modutils-2.1.55-4
mount-2.7f-1
mouseconfig-2.21-1
mpage-2.4-3
mt-st-0.4-4
net-tools-1.33-4
netkit-base-0.10-5
pam-0.59-5
pamconfig-0.51-4
passwd-0.50-10
procmail-3.10-11
procps-1.2.4-1
pwdb-0.54-6
python-1.4-9
pythonlib-1.22-1
redhat-release-5.0-1
rhs-printfilters-1.44-1
rootfiles-1.5-3
routed-0.10-3
rpm-2.4.10-1glibc
samba-1.9.17p4-3
sendmail-8.8.7-12
setserial-2.12-3
setuptool-1.0-1
smbfs-2.0.1-1
stat-1.5-6
sysklogd-1.3-19
SysVinit-2.71-3
```

```
tar-1.12-1
tcp_wrappers-7.6-1
telnet-0.10-2
time-1.7-4
timeconfig-2.1-3
timed-0.10-2
traceroute-1.4a5-4
util-linux-2.7-11
which-1.0-7
words-2-6
```

This listing provides a good description of the Linux system. Every piece of software is treated as a package. This approach enables Red Hat to modularize its own installation process.

RETRIEVING INFORMATION ABOUT A PACKAGE

Examine the Samba package. Note that unlike the *install*, *uninstall*, and *upgrade* modes, the *query* mode does not require that you specify the full package name. Instead, you can use the generic name, as in the following example for Samba:

```
rpm -q -i samba
```

This command displays the general information about the Samba package, as shown in Listing 7-2.

Listing 7-2: The RPM Samba package information

```
[root@bart chap_7]# rpm -q -i samba
Name        : samba                    Distribution: Hurricane
Version     : 1.9.17p4                       Vendor: Red Hat Software
Release     : 3                          Build Date: Sat Nov  1 02:21:37 1997
Install date: Sun Dec 14 09:00:13 1997   Build Host: porky.redhat.com
Group       : Networking                Source RPM: samba-1.9.17p4-3.src.rpm
Size        : 1823600
Packager    : Red Hat Software <bugs@redhat.com>
Summary     : SMB client and server
Description :
Samba provides an SMB server which can be used to provide network
services to SMB (sometimes called "Lan Manager") clients, including
various versions of MS Windows, OS/2, and other Linux machines.
Samba also provides some SMB clients, which complement the built-in
SMB filesystem in Linux.

Samba uses NetBIOS over TCP/IP (NetBT) protocols and does NOT need
NetBEUI (Microsoft Raw NetBIOS frame) protocol.
```

As you can see in the sample listing, this command displays information about the version number, and the installation date and time. The type of package — Networking in this case — is shown, too. An abstract of the package function is also displayed. This listing provides quite a lot of useful information. If you compare the output from Red Hat's *query* mode to that of the traditional *tar* file, you can see that Red Hat is a superior system.

 A *tar* file is a good format for combining one or more files into one file or a pipe for storage or transport. You can use the *tar* command to copy files or directories from one place to another (including over a network), to a storage device such as a tape, or to a regular file.

LISTING A PACKAGE'S FILES

If you want to find out which files make up a package, you use the *-l* option. Enter the following command to examine Samba's files:

```
rpm -q -l samba
```

Listing 7-3 shows that Samba has quite a few files hiding in various places.

Listing 7-3: The files that compose the Samba system

```
/etc/logrotate.d/samba
/etc/pam.d/samba
/etc/rc.d/init.d/smb
/etc/rc.d/rc0.d/K35smb
/etc/rc.d/rc1.d/K35smb
/etc/rc.d/rc3.d/S91smb
/etc/rc.d/rc5.d/S91smb
/etc/rc.d/rc6.d/K35smb
/etc/smb.conf
/etc/smb.conf.sampl
/home/samba
/usr/bin/addtosmbpass
/usr/bin/mksmbpasswd.sh
/usr/bin/nmblookup
/usr/bin/smbclient
/usr/bin/smbpasswd
/usr/bin/smbrun
/usr/bin/smbstatus
/usr/bin/smbtar
```

```
/usr/bin/testparm
/usr/bin/testprns
/usr/doc/samba-1.9.17p4
/usr/doc/samba-1.9.17p4/Application_Serving.txt
/usr/doc/samba-1.9.17p4/BROWSING.txt
/usr/doc/samba-1.9.17p4/BUGS.txt
/usr/doc/samba-1.9.17p4/DIAGNOSIS.txt
/usr/doc/samba-1.9.17p4/DNIX.txt
/usr/doc/samba-1.9.17p4/DOMAIN.txt
/usr/doc/samba-1.9.17p4/DOMAIN_CONTROL.txt
/usr/doc/samba-1.9.17p4/ENCRYPTION.txt
/usr/doc/samba-1.9.17p4/Faxing.txt
/usr/doc/samba-1.9.17p4/GOTCHAS.txt
/usr/doc/samba-1.9.17p4/HINTS.txt
/usr/doc/samba-1.9.17p4/INSTALL.sambatar
/usr/doc/samba-1.9.17p4/MIRRORS.txt
/usr/doc/samba-1.9.17p4/NetBIOS.txt
/usr/doc/samba-1.9.17p4/OS2-Client-HOWTO.txt
/usr/doc/samba-1.9.17p4/PROJECTS
/usr/doc/samba-1.9.17p4/Passwords.txt
/usr/doc/samba-1.9.17p4/Printing.txt
/usr/doc/samba-1.9.17p4/README.DCEDFS
/usr/doc/samba-1.9.17p4/README.jis
/usr/doc/samba-1.9.17p4/README.sambatar
/usr/doc/samba-1.9.17p4/SCO.txt
/usr/doc/samba-1.9.17p4/SMBTAR.notes
/usr/doc/samba-1.9.17p4/Speed.txt
/usr/doc/samba-1.9.17p4/Support.txt
/usr/doc/samba-1.9.17p4/THANKS
/usr/doc/samba-1.9.17p4/Tracing.txt
/usr/doc/samba-1.9.17p4/UNIX-SMB.txt
/usr/doc/samba-1.9.17p4/UNIX_INSTALL.txt
/usr/doc/samba-1.9.17p4/Win95.txt
/usr/doc/samba-1.9.17p4/WinNT.txt
/usr/doc/samba-1.9.17p4/announce
/usr/doc/samba-1.9.17p4/examples
/usr/doc/samba-1.9.17p4/examples/README
/usr/doc/samba-1.9.17p4/examples/dce-dfs
/usr/doc/samba-1.9.17p4/examples/dce-dfs/README
/usr/doc/samba-1.9.17p4/examples/dce-dfs/smb.conf
/usr/doc/samba-1.9.17p4/examples/misc
/usr/doc/samba-1.9.17p4/examples/misc/extra_smbstatus
/usr/doc/samba-1.9.17p4/examples/misc/wall.perl
/usr/doc/samba-1.9.17p4/examples/printer-accounting
```

```
/usr/doc/samba-1.9.17p4/examples/printer-accounting/README
/usr/doc/samba-1.9.17p4/examples/printer-accounting/acct-all
/usr/doc/samba-1.9.17p4/examples/printer-accounting/acct-sum
/usr/doc/samba-1.9.17p4/examples/printer-accounting/hp5-redir
/usr/doc/samba-1.9.17p4/examples/printer-accounting/lp-acct
/usr/doc/samba-1.9.17p4/examples/printer-accounting/printcap
/usr/doc/samba-1.9.17p4/examples/printing
/usr/doc/samba-1.9.17p4/examples/printing/smbprint
/usr/doc/samba-1.9.17p4/examples/printing/smbprint.sysv
/usr/doc/samba-1.9.17p4/examples/redhat
/usr/doc/samba-1.9.17p4/examples/redhat/samba.log
/usr/doc/samba-1.9.17p4/examples/redhat/samba.log.newinit
/usr/doc/samba-1.9.17p4/examples/redhat/smb
/usr/doc/samba-1.9.17p4/examples/redhat/smb.conf
/usr/doc/samba-1.9.17p4/examples/redhat/smb.conf.newinit
/usr/doc/samba-1.9.17p4/examples/redhat/smb.newinit
/usr/doc/samba-1.9.17p4/examples/simple
/usr/doc/samba-1.9.17p4/examples/simple/README
/usr/doc/samba-1.9.17p4/examples/simple/smb.conf
/usr/doc/samba-1.9.17p4/examples/smb.conf.default
/usr/doc/samba-1.9.17p4/examples/svr4-startup
/usr/doc/samba-1.9.17p4/examples/svr4-startup/README
/usr/doc/samba-1.9.17p4/examples/svr4-startup/samba.server
/usr/doc/samba-1.9.17p4/examples/thoralf
/usr/doc/samba-1.9.17p4/examples/thoralf/smb.conf
/usr/doc/samba-1.9.17p4/examples/tridge
/usr/doc/samba-1.9.17p4/examples/tridge/README
/usr/doc/samba-1.9.17p4/examples/tridge/smb.conf
/usr/doc/samba-1.9.17p4/examples/tridge/smb.conf.WinNT
/usr/doc/samba-1.9.17p4/examples/tridge/smb.conf.fjall
/usr/doc/samba-1.9.17p4/examples/tridge/smb.conf.lapland
/usr/doc/samba-1.9.17p4/examples/tridge/smb.conf.vittjokk
/usr/doc/samba-1.9.17p4/examples/validchars
/usr/doc/samba-1.9.17p4/examples/validchars/msdos70.out
/usr/doc/samba-1.9.17p4/examples/validchars/nwdos70.out
/usr/doc/samba-1.9.17p4/examples/validchars/readme
/usr/doc/samba-1.9.17p4/examples/validchars/validchr.c
/usr/doc/samba-1.9.17p4/examples/validchars/validchr.com
/usr/doc/samba-1.9.17p4/faq
/usr/doc/samba-1.9.17p4/faq/Samba-Server-FAQ-1.html
/usr/doc/samba-1.9.17p4/faq/Samba-Server-FAQ-2.html
/usr/doc/samba-1.9.17p4/faq/Samba-Server-FAQ.html
/usr/doc/samba-1.9.17p4/faq/Samba-Server-FAQ.sgml
/usr/doc/samba-1.9.17p4/faq/Samba-meta-FAQ-1.html
```

```
/usr/doc/samba-1.9.17p4/faq/Samba-meta-FAQ-2.html
/usr/doc/samba-1.9.17p4/faq/Samba-meta-FAQ-3.html
/usr/doc/samba-1.9.17p4/faq/Samba-meta-FAQ-4.html
/usr/doc/samba-1.9.17p4/faq/Samba-meta-FAQ-5.html
/usr/doc/samba-1.9.17p4/faq/Samba-meta-FAQ-6.html
/usr/doc/samba-1.9.17p4/faq/Samba-meta-FAQ.html
/usr/doc/samba-1.9.17p4/faq/Samba-meta-FAQ.sgml
/usr/doc/samba-1.9.17p4/faq/Samba-meta-FAQ.txt
/usr/doc/samba-1.9.17p4/faq/sambafaq-1.html
/usr/doc/samba-1.9.17p4/faq/sambafaq-2.html
/usr/doc/samba-1.9.17p4/faq/sambafaq-3.html
/usr/doc/samba-1.9.17p4/faq/sambafaq-4.html
/usr/doc/samba-1.9.17p4/faq/sambafaq-5.html
/usr/doc/samba-1.9.17p4/faq/sambafaq.html
/usr/doc/samba-1.9.17p4/faq/sambafaq.sgml
/usr/doc/samba-1.9.17p4/faq/sambafaq.txt
/usr/doc/samba-1.9.17p4/history
/usr/doc/samba-1.9.17p4/samba.lsm
/usr/doc/samba-1.9.17p4/security_level.txt
/usr/doc/samba-1.9.17p4/wfw_slip.htm
/usr/man/man1/smbclient.1
/usr/man/man1/smbrun.1
/usr/man/man1/smbstatus.1
/usr/man/man1/smbtar.1
/usr/man/man1/testparm.1
/usr/man/man1/testprns.1
/usr/man/man5/smb.conf.5
/usr/man/man7/samba.7
/usr/man/man8/nmbd.8
/usr/man/man8/smbd.8
/usr/sbin/nmbd
/usr/sbin/smbd
/var/lock/samba
/var/log/samba
/var/spool/samba
```

Most of the files in this listing are document files, but just try keeping track of them without any help. By my count, the listing shows 26 directories with resident files. You eventually get to know the structure of a system such as Samba because it is integral to your client-server network. But without the help of Red Hat's *query* mode, you would never remember where everything is located.

LISTING A PACKAGE'S CONFIGURATION FILES

Another system administration job is to configure a software package. The *-c* parameter lists just the configuration files for a package. Using Samba as the example package again, enter the following command:

```
rpm -q -c samba
```

Listing 7-4 shows the configuration files that RPM finds for you. Note that these files are stored in nine separate directories. It would take a lot of work to trace these files down; you couldn't be completely certain that you had found all the files. RPM solves that dilemma.

Listing 7-4: The Samba configuration files found by RPM

```
/etc/logrotate.d/samba
/etc/pam.d/samba
/etc/rc.d/init.d/smb
/etc/rc.d/rc0.d/K35smb
/etc/rc.d/rc1.d/K35smb
/etc/rc.d/rc3.d/S91smb
/etc/rc.d/rc5.d/S91smb
/etc/rc.d/rc6.d/K35smb
/etc/smb.conf
/etc/smb.conf.sampl
```

The familiar smb.conf file is the main configuration file. The files in the *rc.d* directories are pointers to */etc/rc.d/init.d/smb*, which is the *start* and *stop* Samba script. This listing of configuration files tends to be useful information for a systems administrator.

FINDING THE PACKAGE THAT OWNS A FILE

As the final query example, use the *-f* parameter to locate the package that owns a particular file. Maybe you are having a good time one Friday night looking through the */etc/rc.d/rc3.d* directory, and you wonder what the *S99local* file is used for. You do a *man* on *S99local* and *rc.local* but don't find any entries. Hmmm, how do you find out what it is? No problem, enter the following command:

```
rpm -q -f S99local
```

It tells you that the file belongs to the *initscripts-3.25-1* package. So you do a *man* on *initscripts* and all the variations you can think of, and you don't find a man-page entry for it. You hope that *initscripts-3.25-1* is a simple program to startup scripts but you don't know for sure — UNIX and Linux can be deceptive sometimes. So you decide to use the RPM system again. Enter the following variation of the query:

```
rpm -q -i initscripts-3.25-1
```

You get the information shown in Listing 7-5.

Listing 7-5: RPM shows which package a file belongs to

```
Name        : initscripts              Distribution: Hurricane
Version     : 3.25                          Vendor: Red Hat Software
Release     : 1                         Build Date: Sat Nov  8 02:52:07 1997
Install date: Thu Dec 11 03:18:35 1997  Build Host: porky.redhat.com
Group       : Base                      Source RPM: initscripts-3.25-1.src.m
Size        : 63508
Packager    : Red Hat Software <bugs@redhat.com>
Summary     : inittab and /etc/rc.d scripts
Description :
This package contains the scripts used to boot a system, change run
levels, and shut the system down cleanly. It also contains the scripts
that activate and deactivate most network interfaces.
```

Now you have enough information to confirm that it is what you thought it is. It was installed by Red Hat default in Chapter 1. Good job.

Installing Packages

One of the most common systems administration functions is the addition of software packages to a network. In fact, I have you install the X Window system later in this chapter to start a Graphical User Interface (GUI) so that you can use the Red Hat *Control Panel* feature. You perform more installations in subsequent chapters of this book. It's an imprecise and often difficult administrative function, so get used to it. Fortunately, RPM makes this fact of systems administration life much easier.

There's not much to worry about with RPM. Just choose the package, enter the parameters, and hit the Return key. RPM tells you if any problems occur. Generally, RPM stops execution if it encounters problems, but in some cases it prompts you for additional information and continues. The following examples cover many possibilities.

First, however, you should get an overview of which packages are available. You need to mount the Red Hat CD-ROM, if it is not already mounted. To mount the CD-ROM, log in as *root* and enter the following command:

```
mount -r -t iso9660 /dev/cdrom /mnt/cdrom
```

If you used a CD-ROM drive to install Linux, Red Hat created an entry in your */etc/fstab* file — *fstab* stands for *filesystem table* and stores the mounting information for all drives on your system. You can save yourself some work when you mount disks by giving the *mount* command the name of the drive's mount point as a parameter. Therefore, you can mount the CD-ROM by entering the command: **mount /mnt/cdrom**.

Enter the following command to list the RPM packages on the CD-ROM:

```
ls -l /mnt/cdrom/RedHat/RPMS
```

Listing 7-6 shows the first few, and last, RPM packages.

Listing 7-6: A partial Red Hat RPM package list

```
AnotherLevel-0.5-2.noarch.rpm
BRU2000-15.0P-1.i386.rpm
BRU2000-X11-15.0P-1.i386.rpm
ElectricFence-2.0.5-5.i386.rpm
ImageMagick-3.9.1-1.i386.rpm
ImageMagick-devel-3.9.1-1.i386.rpm
MAKEDEV-2.3.1-1.noarch.rpm
SysVinit-2.71-3.i386.rpm
TRANS.TBL
X11R6-contrib-3.3.1-1.i386.rpm
XFree86-100dpi-fonts-3.3.1-14.i386.rpm
XFree86-3.3.1-14.i386.rpm
XFree86-75dpi-fonts-3.3.1-14.i386.rpm
XFree86-8514-3.3.1-14.i386.rpm
XFree86-AGX-3.3.1-14.i386.rpm
XFree86-I128-3.3.1-14.i386.rpm
XFree86-Mach32-3.3.1-14.i386.rpm
XFree86-Mach64-3.3.1-14.i386.rpm
XFree86-Mach8-3.3.1-14.i386.rpm
XFree86-Mono-3.3.1-14.i386.rpm
XFree86-P9000-3.3.1-14.i386.rpm
XFree86-S3-3.3.1-14.i386.rpm
XFree86-S3V-3.3.1-14.i386.rpm
XFree86-SVGA-3.3.1-14.i386.rpm
XFree86-VGA16-3.3.1-14.i386.rpm
XFree86-W32-3.3.1-14.i386.rpm
XFree86-devel-3.3.1-14.i386.rpm
```

```
XFree86-libs-3.3.1-14.i386.rpm
Xaw3d-1.3-13.i386.rpm
Xaw3d-devel-1.3-13.i386.rpm
Xconfigurator-3.25-1.i386.rpm
acm-4.7-6.i386.rpm
adjtimex-1.3-2.i386.rpm
amd-920824upl102-10.i386.rpm
anonftp-2.4-1.i386.rpm
aout-libs-1.4-8.i386.rpm


(...)


xwpe-1.4.2-12.i386.rpm
xwpe-X11-1.4.2-12.i386.rpm
xwpick-2.20-7.i386.rpm
xxgdb-1.12-3.i386.rpm
xzip-161-1.i386.rpm
yp-tools-1.2-3.i386.rpm
ypbind-3.0-3.i386.rpm
yppasswd-0.9-2.i386.rpm
ypserv-1.1.7-5.i386.rpm
ytalk-3.0.3-2.i386.rpm
zgv-2.8-1.i386.rpm
zip-2.1-2.i386.rpm
zlib-1.0.4-2.i386.rpm
zlib-devel-1.0.4-2.i386.rpm
zsh-3.0.5-1.i386.rpm
```

So far I have had you install only a minimal number of packages. The Red Hat distribution includes many additional packages that provide a great deal of functionality (see Appendix G for a list of packages organized by function). Throughout the rest of this book, I selectively pick packages to install that will enhance your system. Most packages are oriented to systems administrative functions.

INSTALLING THE HOWTO DOCUMENTS
As you know, Linux is not supported by any one organization. I discuss the various mechanisms available to you as a user and an administrator in Chapter 5. One important resource comes in the form of the tutorial documents describing how to use many different systems. They are called *Howto* documents and in my pursuit of the prompt, in Chapter 1, I skipped over their installation. Now is a good time to review them.

Again, log on as *root* and mount the CD-ROM drive as shown in the following command:

```
mount /mnt/cdrom
```

Enter the following command to list the RPMS directory, and you get the file listing shown in Listing 7-7.

```
ls /mnt/cdrom/RedHat/RPMS/howto*
```

Listing 7-7: The RPM Howto packages

```
/mnt/cdrom/RedHat/RPMS/howto-5.0-5.noarch.rpm
/mnt/cdrom/RedHat/RPMS/howto-dvi-5.0-5.noarch.rpm
/mnt/cdrom/RedHat/RPMS/howto-html-5.0-5.noarch.rpm
/mnt/cdrom/RedHat/RPMS/howto-ps-5.0-5.noarch.rpm
/mnt/cdrom/RedHat/RPMS/howto-sgml-5.0-5.noarch.rpm
/mnt/cdrom/RedHat/RPMS/howto-translations-5.0-5.noarch.rpm
```

If you do an RPM query on *howto-5.0-5*, you will find that it has not been installed, yet. Enter the following command to install it:

```
rpm -i -v -h /mnt/cdrom/RedHat/RPMS/howto-5.0-5.noarch.rpm
```

Red Hat gives you two simple methods for verifying the installation. One method uses the *query* and *inquiry* options, and the other method queries and lists the files. Either way is fine; I stick with the first one to keep the information to a manageable level. Enter the following command:

```
rpm -q -i howto-5.0-5
```

When you use the *hash* (-h) option, a sequential string of 50 pound characters (#) is displayed as a progress indicator. Because the number displayed is fixed, larger packages display them slower than smaller packages.

Listing 7-8 shows the basic information about this package. Note the location of the files because you will be spending some time in the library. Believe me, you will know many of these documents by heart in a short time.

Listing 7–8: The RPM Howto package information

```
Name        : howto                Distribution: Hurricane
Version     : 5.0                        Vendor: Red Hat Software
Release     : 5                      Build Date: Wed Oct 29 02:24:39 1997
Install date: Mon Dec 22 02:27:00 1997  Build Host: nimrod.redhat.com
Group       : Documentation          Source RPM: howto-5.0-5.src.rpm
Size        : 6274793
Summary     : Various HOWTOs from the Linux Documentation Project
Description :
This is the best collection of Linux documentation there is.  It
was put together on October 22, 1997.  If you want to find newer
versions of these documents, see http://sunsite.unc.edu/linux.
For the versions in this package, see /usr/doc/HOWTO.
```

INSTALLING THE GNU MAKE UTILITY AND C COMPILER

In this section I show you how to install some packages that you'll need in the near future – such as the GNU Make package and C compiler (*gcc*). The packages that you have used so far have come precompiled, but you often need to compile programs from their source. One huge advantage that Linux has over commercial UNIX is that it comes with source code without strings attached. While the RPM system is wonderful, it doesn't include everything you may need. Consequently, you will need to compile software directly into the kernel.

An essential utility to the compilers is the *make* facility. A *make* file is used to semiautomate the compilation – and often the installation – of a software package. It can be used not only to compile software but also to install it and keep bookkeeping up-to-date. In this way, it is similar to RPM.

Leave it at that for now, and install the RPM *make* package by logging on as *root* and entering the following commands:

```
cd /mnt/cdrom/RedHat/RPMS
rpm -i -v -h make-3.76.1-2.i386.rpm
```

Many files created by the Make utility in Linux use the GNU C compiler (*gcc*), so you need to install *gcc*. If you list the Red Hat CD-ROM RPMS directory and look for *gcc*, you can see that it is there (*/mnt/cdrom/RedHat/RPMS/ gcc-2.7.2.3-8.i386.rpm*). Go ahead and install it by entering the usual command (note that I have combined the *i*, *v*, and *h* parameters just to show that it can be done):

```
rpm -ivh gcc-2.7.2.3-8.i386.rpm
```

Most C programs need some additional libraries. Enter the following command to install the following library:

```
rpm -ivh glibc-devel-2.0.5c-10.i386.rpm
```

The *glibc-devel* package requires a library of common functions and gets the following message:

```
failed dependencies:
        kernel-headers is needed by glibc-devel-2.0.5c-10
```

You install that package first and then the *glibc-devel* package by entering the following commands:

```
rpm -ivh kernel-headers-2.0.31-7.i386.rpm
rpm -ivh glibc-devel-2.0.5c-10.i386.rpm
```

Many programs also make use of the Linux kernel header files.

Compiling many Linux software systems, especially the kernel source, requires that their include files be located in a standard place — either the */usr/include* or */usr/src/linux/include* directories. Symbolic links placed in the */usr/include* directory enable include files to be located in either location, so add them by entering the following commands:

```
cd /usr/include

/bin/ln -sf /usr/src/linux/include/asm-i386 asm

ln -sf /usr/src/linux/include/linux linux

ln -sf /usr/src/linux/include/scsi scsi
```

Now your Linux box can compile C programs using the *Make* utility.

Uninstalling

With 1GB disks now commonplace, the pressure has been relieved to constantly worry about running out of disk space. Although the pressure is still a concern, it is much less. I used to uninstall software all the time to free up disk space.

That said, you don't want to keep unneeded stuff around just because you have the disk space. You still can waste time figuring out what a particular package does, and if you never use a package, it is a drag on you and your system. You also may need to uninstall something because it is obsolete. In any case, uninstalling packages is very easy with RPM. I hesitate saying that any administration function is *easy* because so many little details can sneak up and bite you. But RPM keeps track and accounts for those little nasty details.

REMOVING A PACKAGE

Perhaps you've installed a package and experimented with it. But now you no longer need it and you want the disk space back.

I don't use the *nfs-server-clients* package that Red Hat installed by default, so I'll use it as an example of the *remove* command. Even if you find you want it in the future, you can always use RPM to install it. Enter the following command:

```
rpm -ev nfs-server-clients-2.2beta29-2
```

No message is returned; RPM just goes ahead and erases *nfs-server-clients*. Enter the following command:

```
rpm -q -i nfs-server-clients-2.2beta29-2
```

You get the following message:

```
package nfs-server-clients-2.2beta29-2 is not installed
```

This message verifies that the package was removed. That was simple as pie.

UNINSTALLING AND THEN REINSTALLING A PACKAGE

You can also use the erase (uninstall) function to fix a problem by reverting to the original package. For example, maybe your Samba configuration file has become hopelessly confused and you want to start from scratch. The Samba package contains a virgin copy of the *smb.conf* file. Enter the following command to do a query on the configuration files owned by Samba:

```
rpm -q -c samba
```

This command produces the list of files shown in Listing 7-9.

Listing 7-9: The files contained in the Samba package

```
/etc/logrotate.d/samba
/etc/pam.d/samba
/etc/rc.d/init.d/smb
/etc/rc.d/rc0.d/K35smb
/etc/rc.d/rc1.d/K35smb
/etc/rc.d/rc3.d/S91smb
/etc/rc.d/rc5.d/S91smb
/etc/rc.d/rc6.d/K35smb
/etc/smb.conf
/etc/smb.conf.sampl
```

If you proceed and follow the instructions given in this example, you will lose any Samba shares you have added to your system. I think experimenting with this package is reasonable while you are still learning how to configure your system. As long as you are not using your system for doing valuable work then the worst that can happen is you will need to install the entire Linux system again from scratch.

At this early stage in your system configuration you can probably erase the Samba package and reinstall it without losing lots of work. In fact, I advise that you do just that when you are ready to create a Linux/Samba server for your production or business environment. It is a good idea to start with a fresh configuration uncluttered by forgotten artifacts of your apprenticeship.

If you reinstall a package, it writes over all the existing files. This is a good deal if you think you have destroyed part of a package that was working.

Log in as *root* and enter the following command:

```
rpm -e samba
```

This command does not return any message if it is successful. If you want to verify that it worked, enter the following *query* command:

```
rpm -q -i samba
```

If the package was indeed removed, you get the following message:

```
package samba is not installed
```

Now reinstall the package by entering the following command:

```
rpm -i /mnt/cdrom/RedHat/RPMS/samba*
```

Edit */etc/smb.conf* file, and you find the configuration files set to their original state. Any shares that you added in Chapter 6 — or as part of experimenting with Samba on your own — are now lost! You can start from a clean slate.

TIP

Linux provides a simple, nongraphical utility for adding users. The */usr/sbin/useradd* command requires only that you provide the user name as a parameter and it adds the basic information to the */etc/passwd* and */etc/group* files. It assigns the next available user ID and group ID to the new user and creates a user directory in the */home* directory. It also copies some of the basic configuration files to the user's new home directory, including the bash shell and the X Window system setup files (*.bashrc*, *.Xclients*, *.bash_logout*, *.Xdefaults*, *.bash_profile*, and *.xsession*, which I discuss in the "Exploring the X Window System" section, later in this chapter). You must set the password by logging in to the new account and using the */usr/bin/passwd* command.

This is a surefire method for regaining a nominal Red Hat default setup. I mention it because it is a useful example and preferable to reinstalling the entire system. The user configuration can often get too confusing to continue without backing out to some known state. If possible, back out part of the way rather than all the way.

Verifying

The *verify* option takes the following form:

```
rpm -V|-y|--verify verify-options
```

RPM provides a way of checking, or verifying, the current contents of a package against the original *pristine* package as found on the CD-ROM or the Red Hat Web page. The *verify* option compares the size, MD5 sum (checksum), permissions, type, owner, and group of the current package files against the originals. That information can be used in a number of ways. It can provide simple information about what you have (similar to the query information), and it can help in debugging a problem by telling you which files have changed since the initial installation.

In the previous example, you simply removed the Samba package in order to completely restore its configuration information. This simple, brute-force method also removes a number of log files that you would not want to remove in a mature system. If you had used the RPM *verify* option as shown in the following command, RPM would tell you which files had been modified:

```
rpm -V samba
```

In my case, this command gives the following information:

```
S.5....T c /etc/smb.conf
```

The eight characters before the *c* — which means they are configuration files — identify each type, or attribute, of change that RPM recognizes. The *S* means the file size has changed, the *5* means the MD5 sum has changed, and the *T* means the modification time differs from the original. The dots (.) mean that a corresponding attribute has not changed (in this case, the L, D, U, G, and M attributes have not changed). Table 7-7 describes the meaning of each attribute.

TABLE 7-7 THE RPM VERIFY FORMAT

Character	Attribute	Description
5	MD5 sum	The file's checksum
S	File size	The file size in bytes
L	Symlink	The symbolic link
T	Mtime	The file's modification time
D	Device	Specifies that it is a device file
U	User	The file's user ID (the user ownership)
G	Group	The file's group ID (group ownership)
M	Mode	The file's permission and/or mode changed

To experiment, try changing the owner of */etc/smb* to say *bin*, as shown in the following command:

```
/bin/chown bin /etc/smb.conf
```

Run the following RPM command (*rpm -V samba*) and you get the following result:

```
S.5..U.T c /etc/smb.conf
```

The *U* specifies that the ownership of the */etc/smb.conf* file has changed. Don't forget to change it back to *root* again!

Upgrading

The upgrade function of RPM is useful in many ways. When the next version of Red Hat Linux comes along, you obviously will want to upgrade to some or all of the new packages. Linux is like any other operating system, and some packages will have bug fixes that need to be applied; most packages will be improved and updated over time and will need to be replaced.

Upgrading is very simple. Identify the package that you want to upgrade, and use the *-U* option instead of the *-i* option. RPM automatically uninstalls the old package and installs the new one; it will, however, save your old configuration files (with the suffix *.rpmsave*) that are not compatible with the new package. Otherwise, upgrading works the same way as installation.

For example, instead of explicitly erasing and reinstalling Samba (as I describe in the preceding section, "Uninstalling and Then Reinstalling a Package"), you could enter the following command:

```
rpm -Uvh --force /mnt/cdrom/RedHat/RPMS/samba*
```

The old files belonging to the Samba package will be deleted and the new ones installed. The old *smb.conf* file is saved as *smb.conf.rpmsave*.

Installing Linux Software the Old-Fashioned Way

Traditionally, software has been distributed and transferred to Linux systems with tape *ar*chive – *tar* – files. With a *tar* file, one or more files can be stored in a single file, saved to a storage device, or transferred through a Linux *pipe* with the */bin/tar* command. Anyway, the *tar* file offers a decent method for distributing software; this method is widely used throughout the Linux and UNIX world. (I have more to say about the *tar* command in Chapters 9.)

 Tarball is common UNIX/Linux slang for a *tar* file.

To install a software system that is stored and distributed in a *tar* file, you should use the following guidelines:

1. Un-*tar* the file (this generally means saving the individual files in one or more directories on your computer). If the *tar* file is compressed (it is compressed if it has one of the following suffices: *tgz*, *gz*, and *Z*), you can specify a *tar* option to uncompress it.

2. Most software systems come with a *makefile*, which contains rules for compiling and installing the software. Sometimes you need to explicitly modify the *makefile* or use it to create dependencies – in that case, enter the *make depend* command. See the manual page for *make* (*man make*) for more information.

3. The software is compiled. The syntax for doing this can be as simple as   · *make* or *make all*.

4. Optionally, the *makefile* installs the compiled software, configuration, and help files for you – typically by running a *make install* command.

That's it. If all goes well, you have your system installed. My experience is that most Linux *tar* systems compile and run with minimal problems.

 I didn't realize until I started writing this book that Red Hat does not include a single *tar* file on its CD-ROM distribution. That is quite a shift in philosophy from traditional Linux and especially the Slackware distribution. If the Red Hat philosophy becomes the de facto standard, a large division could result between the Internet community and the commercial side. I imagine that many in the Linux/GNU community will continue to use the *tar* method while the commercial side migrates quickly to RPM. Whether that means anything negative in terms of the so-far successful software development cycle is anyone's guess, but it could be quite a shift.   ·

You will have times when you can't use RPM. In Chapters 10 and 11 I use some security-oriented packages that are not available in the RPM format. They come in *tar* form and you will need to install and compile them manually.

Displaying Simple Help Messages

Most Linux commands and utilities provide a simple and quick help system. Enter the string --help or -h as the only parameter, and generally about one screen of options is displayed. For example, the following command displays the help information shown in Listing 7-10:

```
/bin/gzip --help
```

Listing 7-10: The command gzip --help displays a simple help screen

```
gzip 1.2.4 (18 Aug 93)
usage: gzip [-cdfhlLnNrtvV19] [-S suffix] [file ...]
 -c --stdout      write on standard output, keep original files unchanged
 -d --decompress  decompress
 -f --force       force overwrite of output file and compress links
 -h --help        give this help
 -l --list        list compressed file contents
 -L --license     display software license
 -n --no-name     do not save or restore the original name and time stamp
 -N --name        save or restore the original name and time stamp
 -q --quiet       suppress all warnings
 -r --recursive   operate recursively on directories
 -S .suf --suffix .suf    use suffix .suf on compressed files
 -t --test        test compressed file integrity
 -v --verbose     verbose mode
 -V --version     display version number
 -1 --fast        compress faster
 -9 --best        compress better
file...           files to (de)compress. If none given, use standard input.
```

Recall from Chapter 3 that the Linux File System Standard (*FSSTND*) specifies that the system administrator should use the */usr/local* directory for local software. It is a good idea to install new packages — especially when not supported by the distribution — in a well-known area separate from the standard system software. That keeps your *basic* system relatively clean and distinct. In the long run, keeping new software separate reduces confusion and the possibility of mistakenly erasing or corrupting software.

Exploring the X Window System

Note: It is important that you read this entire section carefully *before* working with the X Window system. (XFree86 is the Linux implementation of X Window.) You are manipulating physical monitor and video adapter settings which control high-voltage and high-frequency electricity. Some setting combinations are incompatible and can damage equipment and possibly you!

Note: XFree86 comes without any warranty of any kind. Anything that you damage even after reading these instructions is your own problem.

The X Window system was installed as part of the Red Hat installation system. This section is discusses a little about how the X Window system works.

 Much of Linux administration can be handled through the Red Hat *Control Panel* — a Graphical User Interface (GUI) front-end to several scripts that configure system functions such as network interfaces and user modification. The *Control Panel* requires the X Window system. Of course, the *Control Panel* is only one reason to install the X Window system. Dozens of other applications require X Window. Everything from Netscape to *Xclock* depends on it. It's hard to imagine a GUI-less world.

X Window system configuration has always been the touchiest system to configure under Linux. It requires many different, and sometimes competing, parameters to work together. It is not always obvious how one parameter affects another. However, with the addition of *Metro-X* — which is a commercial product and does not use the GNU General Public License — that chore has become much easier. Please keep in mind that three other configuration packages are available as well — I list them in Table 7-8. I leave it up to you to investigate these further.

TABLE 7-8 X WINDOW SYSTEM CONFIGURATION METHODS

Method	Description
Manual	You edit the various X Window system configuration files by hand.
Xconfigurator	A menu program that configures your X server. It is very competitive in terms of ease of use with Metro-X. In my experience, it can configure more monitors and video adapters than Metro-X.
XF86Setup	A graphical menu program that configures your X server.

continued

TABLE 7-8 X WINDOW SYSTEM CONFIGURATION METHODS *(Continued)*

Method	Description
xf86config	A question-and-answer program that configures your X server.
Metro-X	A commercial program, with a GUI front-end, that configures your X server. You get this package when you purchase the Red Hat 5.0 package (it is not included with the companion CD-ROM).

Whichever method you choose, they all end up modifying the same configuration files.

XFree86

XFree86 is the Linux version of the X Window system. It comes bundled with all Linux distributions. Its core is contained in the *XFree86-3.2-9* package. Note that it requires the same supporting packages as Metro-X, which I describe later in this chapter. If you want to use XFree86 instead of Metro-X, use the following instructions except leave out the *metroess* package.

You can access more information about XFree86 via the Web at `http://www.xfree86.org`.

The X Server

The X Server is the interface between Linux and your computer's video adapter. You can use a generic version – SVGA – that works with any system, or specialized ones that take advantage of one system or another – S3, for example. Several configuration packages come with Linux to assist you with configuring the X Window system on your computer.

Configuring the X Window System with the Xconfigurator

The Red Hat distribution now includes the *Xconfigurator* system. It simplifies the difficult task of configuring the X Window system. I have found that it works across my fairly heterogeneous systems.

I presented you with the option to skip the X Window system installation in Chapter 1. If you did so, either to save resources or time, you can configure it now.

The following packages make up the X Window system plus *Xconfigurator*.

```
XFree86-libs-3.3.1-14.i386.rpm
Xfree86-75dpi-fonts.3.3.1-14.rpm
XFree86-3.3.1-14.i386.rpm
XFree86-SVGA-3.3.1-14.i386.rpm
xinitrc-1.3-5.i386.rpm
xpm-3.4j-1.i386.rpm
xbanner-1.31-1.i386.rpm
```

The following packages provide the GUI layout. It mimics the look and feel of the ubiquitous Windows 95 interface:

```
m4-1.4-8.i386.rpm
fvwm-1.24r-13.i386.rpm
fvwm2-2.0.46-8.i386.rpm
fvwm2-icons-2.0.46-8.i386.rpm
AnotherLevel-0.5-2.noarch.rpm
```

The following instructions describe the configuration process for XFree86.

1. Start the process by entering the following command:

   ```
   /usr/bin/X11/Xconfigurator
   ```

   You get the *Xconfigurator* graphical setup window. Press *OK* to continue.

2. **Choose A Card.** The installation script runs the *Xconfigurator* program that lets you pick your video adapter and monitor from a large list of manufacturer's models as shown in Figure 7-1. Once you choose your card, the XFree86 server that works with that card is installed.

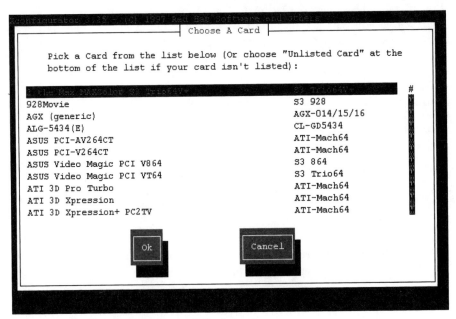

Figure 7-1: The Xconfigurator Choose A Card screen

3. **Monitor Setup.** The second screen, shown in Figure 7-2, shows the available monitors. If your monitor is on the list then you simply select it and go to the next step. If it is not on the list, then I generally choose the *Custom* option at the top of the screen and go to another window that explains the basics of choosing the monitor parameters.

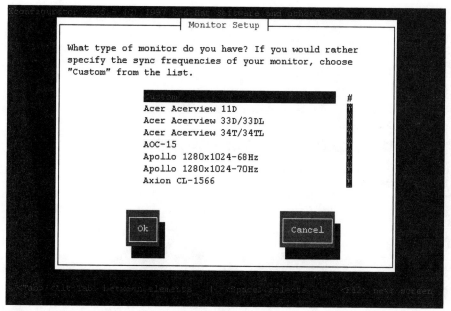

Figure 7-2: The Xconfigurator screen configurator window

4. **Monitor setup (Continued).** Figure 7-3 shows the second monitor setup
   screen, which lets you choose from ten generic monitor configurations.
   These include the horizontal and vertical resolutions as well as the
   horizontal sync rate. This information is contained in the manual that
   comes with your monitor. As the instructions point out, it is very
   important that you not pick a horizontal sync range that is greater than
   your monitor can handle. This is because a monitor can be damaged
   if you choose too high a value. If you are in doubt, then choose a
   conservative setting. The first choice, *Standard VGA, 640x480 @ 60 Hz,*
   is generally a safe one. My monitor can only handle *800x600 @ 60 Hz,*
   which is the lowest value that I find useful with the X Window system. I
   recommend that you be careful and search through that pile of papers in
   your office for your manual.

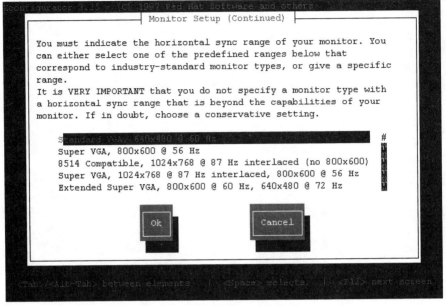

Figure 7-3: The Xconfigurator custom screen window

5. **Screen Configuration.** The next step is to probe or not probe your video card. If you successfully probe your video card, then it returns the exact values you can use. After those values are returned, you can let the system use them as the default or enter your own values. I generally use the return values as they are returned.

If you choose to probe, you are asked if it is okay to begin. Once it finishes, it displays the information that it acquires and either lets you select it as the defaults or enter them yourself. I select to use the defaults.

The following links are required for the X Window server to work.

```
ln -s /usr/X11R6/bin/XF86_SVGA /etc/X11/X
ln -s /etc/X11/X /usr/X11R6/bin/X
```

6. Start your X Window system by entering the following command:

```
/usr/X11R6/bin/startx
```

You will see a bunch of libraries load and then you should have the X Window system running!

You can find out more information about Metro-X at their Web site: http://www.metrolink.com.

The Red Hat Control Panel

The *Control Panel* gives you a common, graphical interface for performing basic system administration tasks. It handles package management, kernel daemon configuration, network configuration, printer configuration, user management, and many other tasks. In short, it handles everything you have done manually so far.

If you have followed my instructions up to this point, you still need to install the *Control Panel* package. Log on as *root* and mount the Red Hat CD-ROM. Enter the following commands to install the *Control Panel* and its dependent packages:

The following packages are required by the *control-panel*:

```
tclx-8.0.0.0-12.i386.rpm
tk-8.0.12.i386.rpm
glint-2.4-2.i386.rpm
control-panel-3.5-1.i386.rpm
```

The *Control Panel* is an X Window system application and can be accessed from several directions. You can start it from a command line, from the *fvwm2* desktop, or from a remote X Window system machine. I'll just mention that if you set the *DISPLAY* environment variable to point to your remote X Window system's display (that is, DISPLAY=*your_ip*:0.0), you can interact with it as if you were sitting at the Linux box's console.

To run the *Control Panel* from a command line, first start the X Window system and open a *shell* window. Enter the following command and use the *root* password when prompted for one:

```
su -c control-panel
```

Alternatively, you can open a *shell* window and enter the following command along with the root password when prompted for it:

```
su -
DISPLAY=:0 control-panel &
```

Finally, and most conveniently, you can simply position the mouse cursor on any part of the Desktop and click the left mouse button. You'll see a generic *fvwm95* menu, and if you click the *Utilities* submenu, you'll see the *Control Panel* option. Click it and you should get the main *Control Panel* window shown in Figure 7-4.

Figure 7–4: The Control Panel window

To select an option, click the module button that you wish to use. Note that if you position the mouse pointer over a button, a short description appears.

Package Management

Click the *Package Management* button and you get the window shown in Figure 7-5. It is a graphical method for doing the same package management that you have just done with RPM. I suggest you retry some of the same examples described earlier to get a feel for it. In some cases, such as dealing with a lot of similar packages, a graphical tool like this one is superior to a simple text-based one. It generally boils down to personal taste.

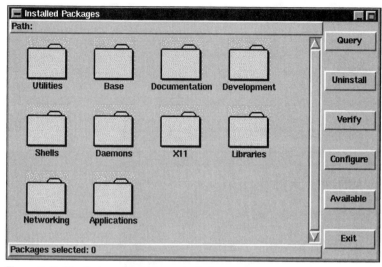

Figure 7-5: The Package Management window

Kernel Daemon Configuration

Red Hat includes a process called *kerneld* that dynamically loads kernel modules when application software calls for it. For example, when you fire up the *diald* program in Chapter 8 to establish an Internet connection, *kerneld* automatically loads the SLIP and PPP modules that *diald* depends on.

Some functions need to be explicitly specified to *kerneld* for it to work for them. Click the *Kernel Daemon Configuration* button in the *Control Panel* main window. The screen shown in Figure 7-6 shows that *kerneld* knows about my Ethernet adapter, which I configured during the initial installation. Had I not configured it then, or changed to another adapter, I could use *kerneld* to do so now.

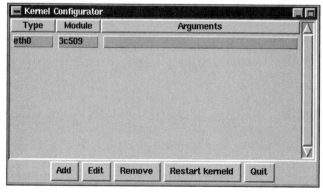

Figure 7-6: The Kernel Daemon Configuration window

The User Configurator

The *User Configurator* function handles user and group management in more detail than the simple *useradd* command. Click the *User and Group Configuration* button. Figure 7-7 shows the main *User Configurator* window showing the information for each user, which it gets from the */etc/passwd* file.

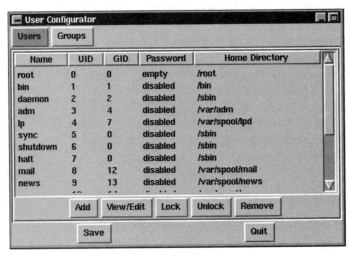

Figure 7-7: The User Configurator window

If you open a window for *Root*, you get the screen shown in Figure 7-8.

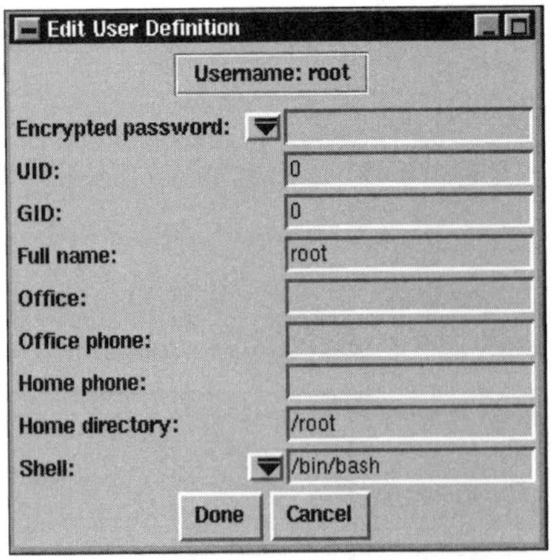

Figure 7-8: The Edit User Definition window

From here, you can edit any of the parameters shown. This method is nice because it does not let you do anything too foolish. Editing the */etc/passwd* and */etc/group* files by hand can wreak havoc but you can do little wrong here. This method also provides you with choices you may not know exist. For example, the Password field has five choices – *Original, Change, No Password, Lock,* and *Unlock.* It's a useful system.

With the *User Configurator,* you can add, delete, deactivate, and reactivate a user. You can also add, delete, and edit groups.

The RHS Linux Print System Manager

I haven't described editing the printer configuration very much yet. It is a good function to leave to the *Control Panel.* The */etc/printcap* file is not too difficult to master except when you have unusual printers or a complex network printer. Open the *Print System Manager* from the *Control Panel* and you get the window shown in Figure 7-9.

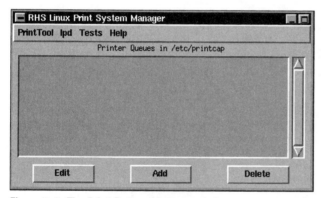

Figure 7-9: The Print System Manager window

Unless you have installed a printer already, choose *PrintTool* and then click the *Add* button. You get the three choices shown in Figure 7-10. Choose the *Local Printer* option if your printer is connected to your parallel port (this is the most common). Choose the *Remote Unix* option if you want to print to a printer connected to another Linux or UNIX computer over your network. Or choose the *Lan Manager Printer (SMB)* option if the printer is attached to a computer using the LAN Manager (SAMBA).

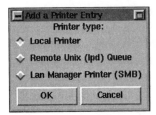

Figure 7-10: The Add a Printer Entry window

The last step is to fill the fields in the Edit Local/Network/Lan Manager Printer Entry where the *Local* option is shown in Figure 7-11. The details vary depending on the type of printer you choose, but the completed screen will look something like the example shown in Figure 7-11.

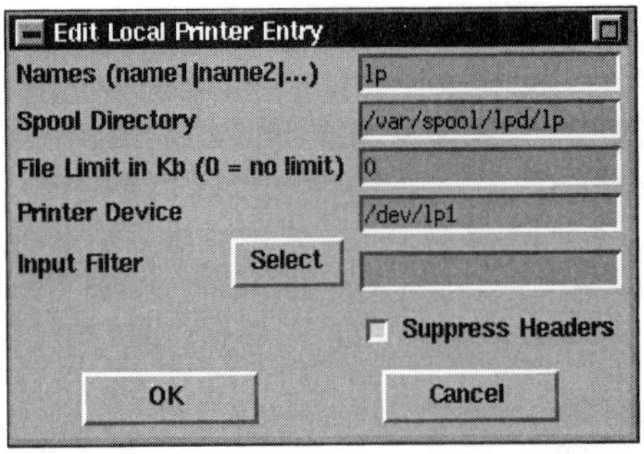

Figure 7-11: The Edit Local Printer Entry window

The fields are used to store the following information:

♦ Queue Name: The name by which your printer is known. Note that it can be a pipe.

♦ Spool Directory: The location where the intermediate file is stored while it is printed. It is a good idea to use the name of the printer.

♦ File Limit: The maximum file size – zero for no limit – to be printed. While it is important to avoid filling up your root file system where the spool directory is normally kept (*/var/spool*), until you are dealing with a production system you aren't likely to have these problems.

♦ Input File: You have the choice of printing Regular, PostScript, TeX, GIF, JPEG, TIFF, or even RPM file formats. You get another screen where you need to choose the printer manufacturer and type.

If you chose the *Network printer* option, you need to specify the *Remote Host* and *Remote Queue* for Linux network printers or *Printer Server Name, Printer Name,* and *Printer User* if it is a printer based on LAN Manager (SAMBA).

The Network Configurator

The *Control Panel* lets you configure most aspects of your network with the *Network Configurator.* From the *Control Panel,* click the *Modules* menu option and click the *Network Configuration* button and you get the screen shown in Figure 7-12. It displays the basic information about your current setup.

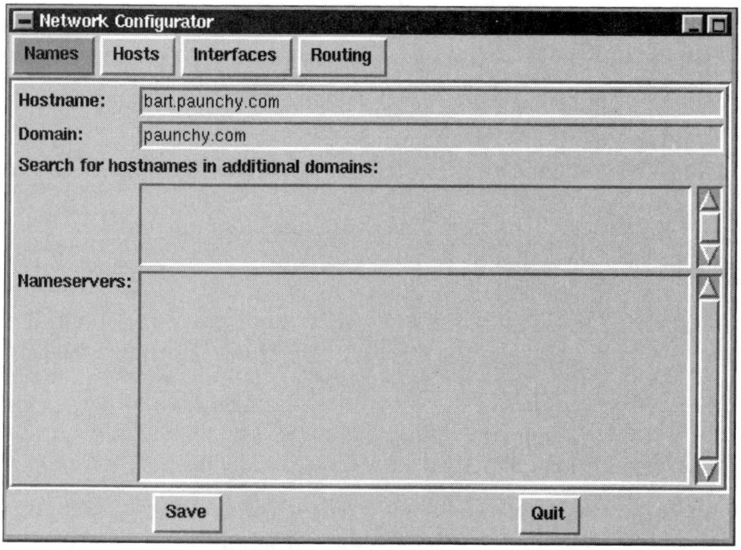

Figure 7-12: The Network Configurator window

In Chapter 8, I show you how to set up your Internet connection, and you use this function in more depth to counterbalance the manual changes that you make. In Chapter 10, I show you how to modify some of the LAN settings. I make use of the *Network Configurator* in both cases, so I do not want to go into any more depth here. However, here is a list of the network functions that the *Network Configurator* handles:

◆ Managing names. You can set the host and domain name of your Linux box. It also shows you which nameserver is used to look up other computers on a network.

It does not configure your machine as a name server. You must do that manually.

- Modifying the */etc/hosts* file, which explicitly assigns IP addresses to names and their aliases.

- Adding network interfaces. It can add hardware adapters such as Ethernet, Token Ring, Arcnet, and Pocket (ATP), as well as logical interfaces such as PPP, SLIP, and PLIP.

- Configuring logical interfaces with phone numbers, login names, and passwords

- Configuring hardware interfaces with the device name, IP address, Netmask, broadcast address, a boot activate flag, and a *BOOTP* option. The boot activate flag indicates that you want the device to turn on when the system boots, and the BOOTP indicates that your computer gets its IP address from another source.

- Adding, editing, or deleting static routes. A route is an IP address to which you can send all packets meeting a certain criteria. The criteria are generally an IP address itself. For example, when you run *diald* in the next chapter, it sets up a default route to the PPP connection and thus the modem. All packets that cannot be directed to another route go to this connection. In your case, that means the Internet.

Obviously, this is another powerful tool that I need to show you more about. The preceding list just gives you a taste of the *Network Configurator's* capabilities. In the following chapters, I show you how to put it to work.

Setting the Time and Date

Finally, you can set your system time and date from this window. The system time is not permanently set until you click the *Set System Clock* button.

The *Control Panel* is a dynamic system that shows only the options that are available to you. For example, the *Package Configurator* is actually a link to the GLINT system, which is an RPM package. If you remove that package and run the *Control Panel*, no *Package Configurator* option is displayed. Reinstall it, and the option returns. The options given depend on what packages were installed by the Red Hat installation process by default and what packages you have added yourself — whether by the initial installation process or individually since then. For that matter, so are the default menus you get by clicking the left mouse button against the window background. If you install a package such as XV, the next time you restart the X Window system and open the *Applications* menu you will see it there.

Building a Custom Kernel

The Linux kernel is a dynamic beast. It can be configured to recognize new devices or systems on-the-fly or by recompilation. The kernel accepts the executable device code as *modules*. The beauty of this approach is that you can experiment with new stuff without the time-consuming recompilation process. The kernel is also far more efficient in terms of space utilization because only the drivers that are needed are loaded at any one time; they can also be unloaded. You can still compile in drivers that are used all the time, but it is your option.

Modularized Kernels

Table 7-9 lists the Linux utilities that maintain and modify the kernel modules.

TABLE 7-9 LINUX KERNEL MODULE UTILITIES

Utility	Description
lsmod	Lists currently loaded modules
insmod	Inserts a module into the active kernel
modprobe	Loads a module or more than one module and their dependencies
depmod	Creates a dependencies file for a module (used by modprobe)
rmmod	Removes a currently loaded module

Note: Man pages are available for each module utility listed in Table 7-9.

Adding a Module to Provide SLIP Support

In anticipation of Chapter 8, where I describe how to set up a PPP connection to the Internet, this section shows you how to install the SLIP module. SLIP is short for Serial Line IP and is a simple method for establishing an IP connection over a serial (that is, telephone connection) line. It has been superseded by the Point-to-Point Protocol (PPP) but is still used by some good communications software to establish an IP connection.

Unfortunately, the base Red Hat kernel does not include SLIP support so you have to add it. That is not difficult with modular kernels. Log on as *root* and mount the Red Hat CD-ROM as usual. Install the package by entering the following command:

```
rpm -ivh /mnt/cdrom/RedHat/RPMS/slip*
```

You should have the SLIP system installed now.

Using the /proc File System to Display Linux System Internal Information

You can check to see if SLIP has already been installed. The */proc* file system is actually a view port into the kernel's internal tables. If you list the */proc* directory, the numbered directories correspond to the running process IDs and contain information about each process. The other directories and files deal with major kernel systems. The */proc/net* directory contains information about the network. If you list the contents of */proc/net/dev*, all the network devices are displayed. Enter the following command:

```
/bin/cat  /proc/net/dev
```

Listing 7-11, which follows this sidebar, shows the contents of */proc/net/dev*. You can see my Ethernet adapter — *eth0* — and the pseudo network lo device, but no SLIP devices. Alternatively, you can see if SLIP is installed with RPM. To do this, enter the following command:

```
rpm -q -l slip
```

RPM tells you that no SLIP package is installed.

There is no RPM SLIP package to install. Red Hat installs the kernel-modules package in its base configuration. Enter the following command to locate it:

```
rpm -q -l kernel-modules |grep -i slip
```

It returns the location as follows:

```
/lib/modules/2.0.31/net/slip.o
```

Listing 7-11: Displaying the installed network devices

```
Inter-|   Receive                     |  Transmit
 face |packets errs drop fifo frame|packets errs drop fifo colls carrier
   lo:    561    0    0    0    0      561    0    0    0    0    0
 eth0:  17684   12   12    0   12    13916    0    0    0    0    0
```

Go ahead and install the SLIP module with the following command:

```
/sbin/insmod  /lib/modules/2.0.31/net/slip.o
```

This command returns the message shown in Listing 7-12, indicating that you do not have all the necessary modules installed.

Listing 7-12: Insmod failed because slip.o is dependent on other modules

```
slip.o: unresolved symbol slhc_free_R3787e5b9
slip.o: unresolved symbol slhc_remember_Rbc0f8a5e
slip.o: unresolved symbol slhc_uncompress_Ra2ca7e04
slip.o: unresolved symbol slhc_compress_R5d6838a9
slip.o: unresolved symbol slhc_init_R20741a64
```

No problem. The *modprobe* utility looks at the module to be loaded and determines if it depends on any other modules. Any dependent modules are loaded first. Enter the following command:

```
/sbin/modprobe /lib/modules/2.0.31/net/slip.o
```

It does not return a message after it succeeds. Enter the *lsmod* command to make sure the modules were loaded:

```
/sbin/lsmod
```

This command returns the information shown in Listing 7-13.

Listing 7-13: The lsmod shows that the SLIP module was successfully loaded

```
Module:       #pages:  Used by:
slip            2             0
slhc            2      [slip]  0
3c509           2             1 (autoclean)
```

> **TIP** You can list all the available modules by using the *-l* option with *modprobe*. You can be more specific by using the *-t <module type>* option to list all modules of a given type. For example, to list all the network modules, enter the command as **modprobe -l -t net**.

Static Kernels

It is almost easy to recompile a kernel. The source code is stored in the */usr/src/linux* directory. The README file located in this directory provides a good description of the necessary steps (about halfway through, look for the lines that describe *make mrproper*, *make depend*, and so on).

To recompile a kernel, you must have several things in place:

◆ The GNU C compiler (*gcc*) must be ready. Recall from the section "Listing a Package's Files," earlier in this chapter, that you must have the following packages installed for gcc to work:

■ /mnt/cdrom/RedHat/RPMS/binutils-2.7.0.2-4.i386.rpm

■ /mnt/cdrom/RedHat/RPMS/gcc-2.7.2.1-2.i386.rpm

■ /mnt/cdrom/RedHat/RPMS/libc-devel-5.3.12-18.i386.rpm

◆ You also need the *Make* utility, which you find in the following location:

/mnt/cdrom/RedHat/RPM/make-3.75-1.i386.rpm

◆ The Linux kernel source code directory must be installed. Recall from "Listing a Package's Files," earlier in this chapter, that the following packages must be installed:

■ /mnt/cdrom/RedHat/RPMS/kernel-headers-2.0.30-2.i386.rpm

■ /mnt/cdrom/RedHat/RPMS/kernel-source-2.0.30-2.i386.rpm

◆ To avoid confusion, the Red Hat kernel source package creates a symbolic link to your current Linux source code directory. Thus, */usr/src/linux-2.0.31* has a link of */usr/src/linux* that is easy to remember and use. Keep in mind that if you manually upgrade your Linux version, you should delete and relink to the new directory. This relinking can be accomplished by entering the following commands:

```
cd /usr/src
rm /usr/src/linux
ln -s /usr/src/linux-2.0.31 linux
```

◆ Sophisticated source code tends to standardize the location of common functions. Include files store common variable and constant definitions and such in a file separate from the source code and therefore many different programs can use a common set of definitions. The Linux kernel source uses this method and looks in the */usr/include* directory for such definitions. Therefore, symbolic links are used to point to these places and you must define them as follows:

```
cd /usr/include
rm -rf asm linux scsi
ln -s /usr/src/linux/include/asm-i386 asm
ln -s /usr/src/linux/include/linux linux
ln -s /usr/src/linux/include/scsi scsi
```

◆ If you recompile your kernel more than once, make sure you start from a consistent point. The Linux kernel *makefile* provides a convenient mechanism for doing just that. The command *make mrproper* resets all configuration and definition files to a default state and deletes old compiled code. To perform this task, enter the following command:

```
cd /usr/src/linux
/usr/bin/make mrproper
```

◆ Next, you have to configure the kernel to be built. I still like to use the sequential, text-based yes/no system, but full-screen and the X Window system-based configuration systems are available for you to try – for example, *make menuconfig* and *make xconfig*. To use the sequential method, enter the following command:

```
make config
```

You get screen after screen (maybe I should learn the other systems) of yes-no questions. In most cases, you can simply press the *Enter* key to choose the default. Also, some questions have a third option – *M* – to choose a loadable module to be folded in at boot time. Listing 7-14 shows the section that deals with SLIP and PPP support. To use *diald*, you must have SLIP so enter **Yes (y)** to each.

By answering *yes* to the PPP module, the questions about SLIP are asked. Otherwise, it is assumed you will not use it.

◆ Next, you need to compile the new kernel. Modern Linux uses a compressed kernel, so use the *zImage* as follows:

```
make zImage
```

Listing 7-14: The Linux kernel configuration menu for SLIP and PPP

```
*
* Network device support
*
Network device support (CONFIG_NETDEVICES) [Y/n/?]
Dummy net driver support (CONFIG_DUMMY) [M/n/y/?]
EQL (serial line load balancing) support (CONFIG_EQUALIZER) [M/n/y/?]
PLIP (parallel port) support (CONFIG_PLIP) [M/n/y/?]
PPP (point-to-point) support (CONFIG_PPP) [M/n/y/?] y
*
* CCP compressors for PPP are only built as modules.
*
SLIP (serial line) support (CONFIG_SLIP) [M/n/y/?] y
CSLIP compressed headers (CONFIG_SLIP_COMPRESSED) [Y/n/?]
Keepalive and linefill (CONFIG_SLIP_SMART) [Y/n/?]
Six bit SLIP encapsulation (CONFIG_SLIP_MODE_SLIP6) [N/y/?]
```

 If you chose any functions as modules, you have to run *make* again to first compile the modules and then to make Linux aware of them. Enter the following commands:

/usr/bin/make modules

/usr/bin/make modules_install

Further instructions are included in the */usr/src/linux-2.0.30/Documentation/ modules.txt* file.

Depending on the speed of your system, it could take hours to compile and link or else just five to ten minutes. The new kernel is placed in the */usr/src/linux/arch//i386/boot* directory. You will need to make it bootable with the Linux Loader (LILO) system. I highly recommend you save your current kernel — which Red Hat places in */boot/vmlinuz* — so move the new *zImage* to that directory without renaming it (for now):

mv /usr/src/linux/i386/boot/zImage   /boot

LILO consults a configuration file, */etc/lilo.conf*, to get everything ready for booting. Listing 7-15 shows the default file, which still includes a reference to my original DOS partition.

Listing 7-15: The default /etc/lilo.conf file

```
boot=/dev/hda
map=/boot/map
install=/boot/boot.b
prompt
timeout=50
image=/boot/vmlinuz
        label=linux
        root=/dev/hda1
        read-only
```

I recommend that you copy the last four lines and edit them to point to the new kernel image as shown in Listing 7-16.

Listing 7-16: The new /etc/lilo.conf file

```
boot=/dev/hda
map=/boot/map
install=/boot/boot.b
prompt
timeout=50
image=/boot/vmlinuz
        label=linux
        root=/dev/hda1
        read-only
image=/boot/zImage
        label=new_linux
        root=/dev/hda1
        read-only
```

Enter the *LILO* command to make the changes stick:

```
/sbin/lilo
```

When you next reboot your Linux box, the LILO boot: prompt is displayed after the initial BIOS messages. The *timeout=50* gives you five seconds to choose the kernel to boot. If you press the *Shift* key and then the *Tab* key you get a list of the available kernels:

```
LILO boot:  dos vmlinuz new_linux
```

Type in **new_linux** to get your new kernel loaded. Otherwise, enter **vmlinuz**, or simply press the *Enter* key to get the old version. If you wait more than five seconds, the old kernel is booted automatically. You can change that time to any value you want.

This process took a lot of instruction but is really quite straightforward with a little practice. It is a process that is much less necessary with the advent of loadable modules but is useful after you arrive at a stable kernel-module setup. When your system is in a production mode, you probably want to recompile the common functions for simplicity sake.

Customizing the Red Hat Startup Process

I have already mentioned the *startup* process to some degree in Chapter 3. Recall that the *rc* scripts are used to start the various daemons and do other things. The */etc/rc.d/rc.local* script is intended for you to add instructions to start your own daemons. In the next chapter, I use it to launch a couple daemons, but I want to mention it here because it is an important feature.

This script is executed last after all the other startup scripts have been run. Therefore, your system should be fully functional by the time your scripts are started. For example, the network should be started and the disks mounted. Until you add your own functions, the *rc.local* script only sets the standard login screen that you see when you log on. Listing 7-17 shows this script.

Listing 7-17: The /etc/rc.d/rc.local file

```
#!/bin/sh

# This script will be executed *after* all the other init scripts.
# You can put your own initialization stuff in here if you don't
# want to do the full Sys V style init stuff.

if [ -f /etc/redhat-release ]; then
        R=$(cat /etc/redhat-release)
else
        R="release 3.0.3"
fi

arch=$(uname -m)
a="a"
case "_$arch" in
        _a*) a="an";;
        _i*) a="an";;
```

```
esac

# This will overwrite /etc/issue at every boot.  So, make any changes you
# want to make to /etc/issue here or you will lose them when you reboot.
echo "" > /etc/issue
echo "Red Hat Linux $R" > /etc/issue
echo "Kernel $(uname -r) on $a $(uname -m)" > /etc/issue

cp -f /etc/issue /etc/issue.net
echo > /etc/issue
```

You can modify other scripts if you need to, but it is a straightforward process to modify this one. You don't have to worry about ruining anything if you use it.

Summary

In this chapter, I describe how to configure Linux in a more systematic way. The Red Hat RPM system makes the task of adding, removing, and upgrading system functions, applications, and utilities very easy. The Linux system itself is modular and easy to modify. I cover the following topics in this chapter:

◆ I save the systematic configuration of Linux for this chapter. In previous chapters, you install only those subsystems that are absolutely necessary. This approach was used to quickly demonstrate Linux in action without cluttering up the landscape.

◆ The major installation and configuration topics this chapter covers include the RPM system, the X Window system, the Red Hat *Control Panel*, building a custom kernel, and the Linux startup scripts.

◆ The Red Hat Package Manager (RPM) provides a simple and sure method for installing, upgrading, uninstalling, querying, and verifying Linux packages. Linux packages are software stored in a format that works with RPM. They include the base Linux system, important Linux configuration files, and applications.

◆ Detailed descriptions of each of the RPM major functions (*install, upgrade, uninstall, query,* and *verify*) are given.

◆ I present several examples that demonstrate how to use the RPM query function to discover information about installed packages as well as ones available on the Red Hat distribution CD-ROM.

◆ The first RPM installation example is used to install some documentation. This is a simple and straightforward example that also provides useful information.

◆ The second RPM installation example is more complex because it requires two packages – one of which requires the other – so the installation order is important. It installs the basic networking support. The basic networking was not installed in Chapter 1 and is required if you are to remotely communicate with your Linux box.

◆ The last RPM installation example is quite complex. In anticipation of a number of systems that need to be installed and compiled in the future, I show you how to install the GNU C compiler (gcc) and the Make utility. The gcc compiler requires many libraries and the Linux kernel header files, so several other packages must be installed in the correct order.

◆ A *verify* example shows how to find out what package files have been changed. The information that is given is useful for debugging and as general information.

◆ Until the advent of RPM, most Linux subsystems were distributed through *tar* files. They were unpacked and semimanually installed. Installation often required compiling the source code. The Make facility helped the process by not only compiling the source code but also transferring it to its final destination.

◆ Red Hat does not include the important Internet access utility *diald*. IDG has included it on the CD-ROM that accompanies this book, however – it is also available via the SunSITE. It is stored in *tar* format, and you have to compile and install it yourself. I offer a tutorial on this process. It is useful not only to obtain *diald* but also as a template for other software that you may have to manually install in the future.

◆ The manual – non RPM – installation of *diald* is used to show you how things were done before RPM, and still are in many places. You use the *diald* system in Chapter 8.

◆ The installation of XFree86, via RPM and the commercial Metro-X configuration system, is described. In my opinion, this is the easiest method, but three other configuration systems are described.

◆ With the X Window system installed, the Red Hat *Control Panel* GUI is introduced. This method is convenient for performing many administrative functions. Some of the functions are package management, user and group management, and printers and network management.

◆ The concept of customizing the Linux kernel is introduced. You have the option of adding either modular functions or recompiling static functions indirectly. Modular functions, such as the SLIP module, can be added dynamically while your system is running. For example, when you want to establish an Internet connection with the PPP protocol (as I describe in Chapter 8) and you are using the base kernel from Chapter 1, you do not have to restart your system or even recompile the kernel; you simply have the SLIP module inserted.

◆ There is a brief description of the process for adding new functions to the Red Hat startup scripts. This is useful for customizing your system to meet your specific needs.

Chapter 8

Connecting to the Internet

IN THIS CHAPTER

- ◆ Connecting an entire network to the Internet

- ◆ Understanding SLIP and PPP

- ◆ Using a modem, frame relay via leased telephone lines, and ISDN

- ◆ Choosing an Internet Service Provider (ISP)

- ◆ Understanding the role of the Linux *pppd* daemon

- ◆ Connecting to your ISP with help from the *dip* and *chat* programs

- ◆ Using *dip* and *chat* for making dynamic and static connections

- ◆ Automating the PPP connection process with the *diald* daemon

- ◆ Using the Red Hat Network Configurator to make a PPP connection

- ◆ Monitoring PPP and SLIP connections

- ◆ Protecting your Linux computer with firewalls

- ◆ Exploring packet filtering and application-based (also called proxy) firewalls

- ◆ Constructing a simple, but effective, firewall

YOU PROBABLY ARE FAMILIAR with logging on to a remote computer via a modem. If you use a service provider such as America Online (AOL), CompuServe (now owned by AOL), AT&T, or a university account, you probably use a terminal emulator. However, if you use a protocol such as PPP (Point-to-Point Protocol) or SLIP (Serial Line Internet Protocol), you actually become a part of the Internet – you become a *node* or a LAN. I refer to this type of connection as a *node connection.*

An important difference exists between a terminal session and an Internet node connection. A terminal session is like riding on a bus – you control where you go by choosing the particular route, but then leave most of the control to the driver and the bus schedule. Using an Internet node connection is like using your own car – you have far more control over where, how, and when to go someplace, plus the responsibility for your decisions.

With a terminal session, you make a connection to a computer that is connected to the Internet. The session works the same as if you were physically sitting at that computer's monitor and keyboard, except it is slower. With a node connection, however, your computer becomes part of the Internet. It is the same as if your computer is physically connected to an *Internet Service Provider* (ISP) network, except the connection is slower. Figures 8-1 and 8-2 show diagrams of the two connection types.

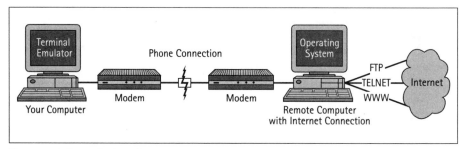

Figure 8-1: A terminal session

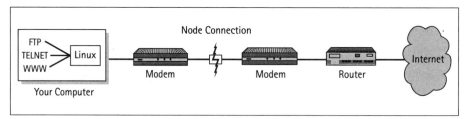

Figure 8-2: A node connection

At first glance, the node connection may not seem to offer a great advantage over a terminal connection. Companies such as CompuServe and AOL offer software that provides good Web browsing and file transfer capabilities. However, the capability of your computer or LAN to seamlessly become *part* of the Internet is a powerful one. It removes a layer of software to deal with. It removes your dependence on a particular service provider's proprietary software and service. It enables you to tap into a vast reservoir of software and gives you more control over your own destiny. Most important, you can run multiple applications over the serial connection at one time. For example, you can run a Web browser, a Telnet session or two, and an FTP job, all at once. The only limitation is the speed of your connection.

This chapter describes the mechanics of making node connections. To establish a foundation for managing your connection, I also describe the Internet and LAN protocols that are the basis of these types of connections. And to help you better manage your connections, I address management and security concerns.

Node Connections

Two protocols currently are used to make node connections. Both the Serial Line Internet Protocol (*SLIP*) and the Point-to-Point Protocol (*PPP*) provide a method for using the telephone network to speak IP to remote places. Both protocols encapsulate IP packets in order to deliver them over serial connections.

SLIP

SLIP is a simple method for delivering an IP packet over a phone line. It simply adds a control character to the beginning and end of every IP packet. The control characters are *SLIP-END* and *SLIP-ESC*. They are decimal values 192 and 219 in the ASCII 8-bit definition.

SLIP-END marks the end of an IP packet. *SLIP-ESC* marks *SLIP-ESC* and *SLIP-END* characters embedded in the IP packets. If data contained in an IP packet coincidentally matches the value of either of the control characters (192 or 219 decimal), the addition of a *SLIP-ESC* tells the other end of the connection not to treat it as a control character. Figure 8-3 shows a hypothetical SLIP packet encapsulating the message *hello world*.

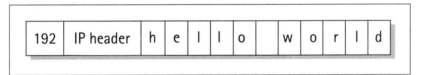

Figure 8-3: A SLIP-encapsulated message containing hello world

The *SLIP-END* is something of a misnomer because it starts as well as ends each packet. The *SLIP-START* character is not needed, because the *SLIP-END* acts to frame the IP packet.

TIP SLIP is defined in RFC 1055, "A Nonstandard for Transmission of IP Datagrams over Serial Lines: SLIP" (Ronkey, 1988). This is a de facto standard and not an official Internet protocol. (The term RFC stands for *Request For Comment* — this is the method by which Internet standards are introduced and discussed.) You can find RFC 1055 at http://www.landfield.com/rfcs.

I prefer simplicity whenever possible. Unfortunately, SLIP is just a bit too simple. It doesn't do anything other than signal the start and end of an IP packet. This limitation presents several problems:

◆ No IP address negotiation is possible. Each end of the connection must know the other end's IP address from the outset of the connection. The IP address can be determined outside of SLIP, but connections would be more efficient if SLIP could handle that task rather than relying on yet another protocol.

◆ Each IP packet must be the same size. If one packet is smaller, it must be padded with extra, meaningless characters to make up the size. If a packet is larger, it must be broken up (and maybe padded, too) to match the size that the other end of the connection expects.

◆ The underlying packet type (IP can handle several types) is invisible until the SLIP packet is unpacked, which makes connection less efficient.

My own experience with SLIP attests to these shortcomings. Several years ago, I wanted to connect my company to the Internet without paying the steep price of ISPs at the time. I placed an inexpensive MS-DOS 386SX PC in a colleague's office at the University of New Mexico and connected it to his LAN, which was routed to the Internet. At my office, I connected a Sun workstation to the 386SX via a modem. The PC ran under MS-DOS, the Sun ran with SunOS UNIX, and both had SLIP. I could establish a connection, and SLIP allowed IP connections to run, but only for a few minutes or seconds before SLIP would crash. Almost as soon as I got that far, the administration rejected – for several reasons that I had to agree with – my formal request for using that type of connection, and I ended that quest for the Holy Grail.

I am sure that with time it would have worked much more reliably. I have no doubt the problems were more my being low on the learning curve than the stated shortcomings with SLIP. However, PPP has established itself as the protocol of choice and SLIP is quickly fading. I don't have any hesitation in recommending the use of PPP for all your Internet needs.

TIP

CSLIP, which compresses the IP header but not the data, is defined in RFC 1144, "Compressing TCP/IP Headers for Low-Speed Serial Links" (Jacobson, 1990). You can find it at `http://www.landfield.com/rfcs`.

PPP

The PPP packet contains information that facilitates the establishment of not only the serial connection, but also the encapsulated packet type. Consequently, PPP is more complex than SLIP.

PPP uses the *Link Control Protocol* (LCP) to establish a connection, and to configure and test it. This is an increasingly important feature, as modems become faster and more complex. Other connection technologies, such as ISDN, further complicate your telecommunications landscape, and thus increase the importance of controlling things via your connection protocol.

PPP uses the internationally recognized *High-Level Data Link Control* (HDLC) protocol. It uses bit patterns as opposed to control characters to distinguish the start and end of packets. The receiving end looks at each bit coming in and if it recognizes a pattern, it starts passing the data to the next stage. (For more information on HDLC, see the discussion on page 216 in *Data Communications, Computer Networks and Open Systems*, by Fred Halsall; published by Addison-Wesley Publishing Company, Inc., Reading, MA, 1992.)

The *Network Control Protocol* (NCP) defines several network level packets that PPP can encapsulate. The most popular ones are IP, *IPX* (Novell's IP-like protocol), and Microsoft's *Network BIOS Extended User Interface* (NetBEUI). If your LAN speaks any or all of these protocols, they all get to go through your PPP connection to the outside world. Figure 8-4 shows a diagram of a PPP packet.

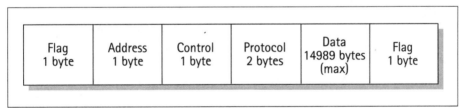

Flag 1 byte	Address 1 byte	Control 1 byte	Protocol 2 bytes	Data 14989 bytes (max)	Flag 1 byte

Figure 8-4: A PPP packet contents

The sequence for making a PPP connection is as follows:

1. You make the modem or other (for example, ISDN) connection.

2. The computer making the connection sends LCP packets to the receiving computer. These packets establish a data link, which exists at the Network level, according to the OSI network model that I describe in Chapter 3.

3. The sending computer sends NCP packets to tell the other end what type of protocols are to be carried by PPP.

4. You have a full-fledged Internet connection. Any protocols that are mentioned in Step 3 are now usable until another PPP connection is established.

PPP is defined in RFC 1661, "The Point-to-Point Protocol" (Simpson, 1994). You can find this official Internet standard at `http://www.landfield.com/rfcs`.

Making the Connection

Now comes the problem of making a PPP connection. I want to concentrate most of my attention on modem connections because they are the easiest, least expensive, and certainly the most popular method currently available.

However, I should mention a couple of the other widespread technologies. If you intend to run a business with any significant amount of Internet traffic, you are going to need more than a modem or two. (Linux does allow multiple modems to be used in parallel, however.) *Frame Relay* and *ISDN* are the most common high-speed methods widely available. Frame Relay is expensive but almost universally available, while ISDN is inexpensive, relatively fast, but less available; ISDN is much easier to get in metropolitan areas than outlying ones. The low-end Frame Relay connections run at only 56 kilobits per second (Kbps) – that is kilobits per second, not kilobytes per second (KBps) – and are only somewhat faster than today's high-end modems, cost several hundred dollars to establish and also per month to maintain. By spending roughly four times more per month, you can get a 1.5 megabit-per-second (Mbps) connection (called a T1 line), which is 28 times as fast, giving you a better price-performance ratio. ISDN is widely available in some locations but not in others, and still has the reputation for being difficult to set up.

Theoretically, you can lease a 45 Mbps connection called a T3. Unless you plan to be the next AOL, however, this is an expensive option.

LEASED LINES, FRAME RELAY, ISDN, AND OTHERS

If you need or want a continuous connection to your ISP, you literally need to lease a wire from the phone company. In most cases, you end up using a wire from your physical location to the nearest phone company switching station, and from there they send your packets to your ISP via their leased line. This system, called Frame Relay, is a very common system in the industry and is the one that I have used.

Frame Relay gives you a virtual circuit to your ISP that is also continuously connected so you have immediate access to the Internet. A device called a *Channel Service Unit/Data Service Unit* (CSU/DSU) converts the binary format of your network into that of the phone network; the phone company also uses the *CSU/DSU* to troubleshoot its network up to that unit. The packets or frames travel from your computer, through a router (a Linux computer can serve as one) to the *CSU/DSU* and into the phone company's cables. From there, the phone company switches your information stream through their system until it ends up at your service provider's *CSU/DSU*. The service provider converts it back into IP form and routes it to the Internet.

TIP If you are a real Troubleshooter, the tcpdump-smb utility is for you. It gives you information about what's happening down at the packet level. But that goes way beyond the scope of this chapter.

Most consumers' and many businesses' telephone connections start from the customer's premises as DS0 connections, which operate at 64 Kbps. A DS0 travels over a physical pair of wires (twisted-pair) to the nearest Telco switching station, where they enter a Channel Bank. Each Channel Bank can handle 24 DS0s and convert the analog signals to digital. The Channel Bank multiplexes all the DS0s into a DS1, which has a 1.45 Mbps capability; it is also known as a T1 circuit. All the DS1 circuits carry digital frames or packets. The DS1 circuits go to the local telephone company's main switching center, where each packet is routed to its final destination.

If you have the money, you can lease all or part of a DS1, or T1 (1.54 Mbps), circuit. As of early 1998, ISPs in my area charge $400 per month for a 56 Kbps circuit and a one-time setup fee of $500. They charge $850 per month for a 1/4 T1, $1,050 per month for a 1/2 T1, and $1,350 per month for the full T1 — each has a $1,000 one-time setup fee, and you can upgrade without additional setup fees. You can also purchase 128 Kbps and 256 Kbps circuits for $650 and $750 per month, but you are charged a setup fee to upgrade. In larger cities, where infrastructure is expensive, the costs probably are higher.

ISDN is generally available in most locations in the United States but it is more readily available in some places than in others. It is probably an acceptable alternative if it is actually marketed in your area. It is a fairly difficult service to set up, both from your point-of-view and the phone company's as well. I have not used ISDN; here in Albuquerque, it is officially not available, although it may be at a high cost. US West has resisted implementing it even though the state tariff commission ordered them to provide it almost a year ago. Even if it is available, I do not want a service that the provider does not want to support at any price.

ISDN can cost less than $100 per month and in many places less than $50. Linux is becoming more compatible with it as well. Linux kernel drivers are available to ISDN, and you can purchase ISDN PC adapters that plug directly into your PC. For more information about ISDN, consult the Howto file in */usr/doc* as well as the following ISDN-related URL:

```
http://www4.zdnet.com/wsources/content/current.featsub2.html
```

In some areas, cable TV companies are experimenting with cable modems. A cable modem works the same way as a normal modem except it converts your digital information into a form that the cable TV system can handle. If that service is available in your area, it is probably worth exploring.

I also like the idea of one-way satellite systems. I have read about a service called Direct-PC, which feeds you your data packets via a satellite while you send it your data over a traditional modem. Very often, you need high-bandwidth for receiving data but can get away with a lower rate going out. If you are working interactively, your outgoing data is limited to your keystrokes, while you may want to retrieve graphics or Linux distributions. A system such as Direct-PC – at least in theory – would be a cost-effective compromise. Again, I have not used it, but I want to give you a heads-up on it anyway.

I mention these connection methods for your information. For the purposes of this chapter, I stick with the ubiquitous analog phone system.

 A common acronym used in and out of the telephone industry for the analog phone system is *POTS,* which stands for "plain old telephone system" or "service."

MODEMS

A modem converts digital data to the analog form that your average telephone line carries. As of this writing, modems theoretically capable of return speeds of 56 Kbps are the current state of the art. However, several bottlenecks inhibit attainment of these speeds. First, two competing standards exist, and it will take some time for them to sort out. Second, ISPs are faced with which one (or both) to support. In any case, it will take some time to implement either standard in terms of actual modems. Third, the phone system itself has bottlenecks. If even one link in the chain can't handle the higher speed, the entire system is prevented from achieving it.

The 56 Kbps modems that recently began to appear are rated up to that speed only for data returning from the remote connection to your modem. Your outgoing data is limited to a lower rate. This limitation is okay because many functions require bringing back graphics or other data, which tends to be bigger than your outgoing keystrokes.

Those problems exist with any technology. It took a while for 1200 bps modems to be accepted. By the time you read this chapter, the whole issue probably will be settled. But I thought it worthwhile to mention.

Your problem – at any speed – is to use a modem to connect your network to the Internet. Linux provides both a manual and an automatic method for making connections.

If you want an Internet connection, you can't go wrong with a modem. Modems are the workhorses of the Net, and ISPs are configured to handle them.

The more recent Linux distributions and the GNU software that comes bundled with them have simplified the connection process. The programs for dialing an ISP and negotiating the PPP connection are included with Linux and have become progressively more sophisticated; the associated documentation also has improved. The explosion of demand for node connections and the desire of ISPs to meet the demand have further pushed the ease of connecting, as the necessary knowledge has permeated the market. Many ISPs use Linux, which further facilitates the ease of connecting.

OBTAINING AN ISP

Whichever method you choose for making the connection, you need to have an ISP to which you can connect. I use and recommend obtaining service from a local company. In my opinion, a local company will give you better service than a national one. If the ISP is properly managed, your service will come from a small number of technical people who know their system and will become familiar with you and your needs. This is a big "if" and you may need to try more than one ISP before you find the right one. Personal recommendations are very important; that's how I found my ISP.

Of course, nothing is wrong with a national or international ISP, but you will not get consistent personal attention. A central service group generally processes your questions. Even worse, the people who handle typical calls are accessing a question-answer database rather than relying on their own experience. Your call may eventually reach an engineer or technician who knows the system, but you have to thread your way through the system first. For this reason, I think the local ISP is the way to go.

Most ISPs give you the choice of several different kinds of accounts. The traditional login account is still one possibility, but as I mention earlier in this chapter, this type of account will not be part of this discussion.

CONFIGURING YOUR PPP ACCOUNT

Okay, one way or another you find a good ISP, so what's next? The ISP should supply you with the log-in information for your account. You need to pay attention to the PPP account information and the corresponding phone numbers. The PPP account will supply you with either a static or a dynamic IP address. A static address is one that is permanently assigned to you by your ISP; whenever you make a connection, you will be known as the same IP address. A dynamic address is one that your ISP picks out of a pool of addresses whenever you connect and thus will generally be different every time. Dynamic addresses are becoming more common, if not dominant, because they give ISPs more flexibility with their allocation of IP addresses.

You need several Linux utilities to establish the connection:

♦ The *pppd* daemon is a program that transfers IP packets across the PPP connection.

♦ You use the *pppd*, *chat*, or *dip* program to establish a PPP connection.

♦ The *chat* program helps you automate the negotiation of your PPP connection. Typically, you write a *chat* script that contains the username and password of your PPP account and supplies them as needed.

The following sections provide more details on using and installing these programs.

THE PPPD DAEMON

The *pppd* daemon converts your local network packets into PPP format and sends them out to the Internet via the PPP connection. The *pppd* is an RPM package and was installed as part of the default installation. Log on as *root* and enter the following command:

```
rpm -ivh /mnt/cdrom/RedHat/RPMS/ppp-2.2.0f-5.i386.rpm
```

You can manually start the *pppd* daemon and supply it with command-line parameters to show it how to make a connection. I prefer to use the *dip* application – which I describe in the following sections of this chapter – to make manual connections. Usually, I use the *diald* utility to connect automatically. (Subsequent sections of this chapter describe how to connect with *diald* and both dynamic and static addresses.)

Checking for SLIP Installation

Traditionally, you were able to check to see if SLIP was installed by looking at the contents of the */proc/net/dev* file. It would look like Listing 8-1 if SLIP were installed in the kernel.

If you recompile the kernel with SLIP support, it will indeed show up as in this listing. However, you also can add it dynamically as a loadable module. In that case, it doesn't show up here until you establish a PPP connection. Also, the SLIP and PPP modules will be loaded by the *kerneld* daemon if you are using it and *dip* or *diald* calls for them.

Listing 8-1: The /proc/net/dev file

```
Inter-|   Receive                   |  Transmit
face  |packets errs drop fifo frame|packets errs drop fifo colls carrier
  lo:    3610    0    0    0    0    3610    0    0    0    0    0
 eth0:  95247    7    7    0    7   90692    0    0    0  250    0
 ppp0:    921    0    0    0    0    1049    0    0    0    0    0
  sl0:      0    0    0    0    0      21    0    0    0    0    0
```

Consult the *pppd* manual page for more in-depth information.

DIP AND CHAT

The *Dial-up IP Protocol Driver – dip –* utility is a program that you can use interactively or automate with a script to dial the modem, authenticate your PPP or SLIP connection, and then fire up the *pppd* daemon. *Chat* is a script interpreter that the on-demand *diald* application uses.

You can use either of two primary *dip* command-line types. First, you can invoke *dip* in an interactive mode by including the *-t* option, as follows:

```
/usr/sbin/dip -t [-v]
```

And here's how you run from a script file:

```
dip [-v] [-m mtu] [-p proto]   scriptfile
```

I want to show how to use *dip* interactively only – the following two examples describe how to use *dip* with both static and dynamic IP addresses. I skip any script file examples because I show how to use *diald* via a script in the section "Finding the Package That Owns a File" in Chapter 7, and via the Red Hat *Control-Panel* in the section "Installing the Howto Documents," also in Chapter 7. The *diald* daemon is ultimately far more powerful than a manual *dip* script. However, the *dip* command examples are rather easily converted to scripts if you want to use *dip* that way.

CONNECTING WITH DIP AND STATIC ADDRESSES

If you contract with an ISP who still uses static IP addresses, use the following guidelines to connect to the ISP via PPP. Enter the following command to start *dip* in its interactive form:

```
dip -t
```

You get the *dip* prompt shown in Listing 8-2. Follow the sequence shown in this listing, substituting your ISP phone number, IP addresses, and port number. (*Note:* The ports *ttyS0* and *ttyS1* generally correspond to MS-DOS *com1* and *com2*.)

Listing 8-2: Establishing a PPP connection with dip

```
DIP: Dialup IP Protocol Driver version 3.3.7o-uri (8 Feb 96)
Written by Fred N. van Kempen, MicroWalt Corporation.

DIP>
DIP> port /dev/ttyS1
DIP> speed 38400
DIP> dial 555-5555
DIP> term
[ Entering TERMINAL mode.  Use CTRL-] to get back ]
Welcome to Myisp.  You're jacked in on pm2:S9.

myisp login: iwantppp
Password: bowowo
PPP session from (198.9.5.101) to 198.9.5.81 beginning . . .
   . . .
{enter Ctrl-] to return to command mode}
DIP> get $locip 198.9.5.81
DIP> get $rmtip 198.9.5.101
DIP> mode PPP
```

Note: The garbled looking text — after the word *beginning* — is the remote *pppd* attempting to negotiate the PPP connection with your local *pppd*.

Dip automatically exits after it completes the mode change to PPP. If you list the processes by entering the following command, you should see the *pppd* daemon and its child subprocess, as shown in Listing 8-3:

```
ps -x | grep ppp
```

Listing 8-3: The pppd daemons are running after exiting from dip

```
729  a0 S    0:00 pppd -detach defaultroute crtscts modem 198.9.5.81:198.9.5.101
733  p0 S    0:00 grep ppp
```

For your convenience, I summarize the *dip* parameters in Table 8-1. Those parameters for which I direct you to consult the man page are either too complex to describe briefly or are rarely used.

TABLE 8-1 THE DIP COMMANDS

Command	Purpose
beep *[times]*	Beeps.
bootp	Tells *dip* to use the bootp protocol. (*dip* gets its IP address via the *bootp* protocol.)
break	Sends a break signal.
chatkey *keyword*	Tells *dip* to accept the *keyword* from the modem.
config *[if][rout][pre|up|down|post] args*	Enables the interface (*if*) and route. Default = disabled.
databits *7|8*	Sets the number of bits to 7 or 8. You use 8 bits for binary data.
dec *$var (script variable)[num\|$var2]*	Decrements the *var* by one or the amount specified by *num* or *var2*.
default	Sets the default route to the remote system.
dial *number [num_secs]*	Dials the *number* and optionally waits the *num_secs*.
echo *on|off*	When *echo* is on, you see the modem's response. When *echo* is off, you don't.
exit *[status]*	Exits with the specified status (useful for debugging).
flush	Erases the most recent input from the modem.

continued

TABLE 8-1 THE DIP COMMANDS *(Continued)*

Command	Purpose
get *$var [num|ask|remote [timeout] | $var2] ask*	Obtains the value of *var*. Optionally, sets *var* to either *num*, interactively from you, or the remote system. Optionally sets amount of time to wait for the value. Can also get *var* from *var2*.
goto *label*	Go to the location of the label in the script.
help	Helps.
if *expression goto label*	If the *expression* is true (=1), go to the location of *label*.
inc *$var [num\|$var2]*	Increments *var* by one or the amount specified by *num* or *$var2*.
init *init_string*	Sends an initialization string to the modem before dialing.
mode *SLIP|CSLIP|PPP*	After the connection is established, sets the protocol to SLIP by default, or else CSLIP or PPP.
modem *modem_type*	Specifies the modem type. Hayes-compatible modem is the default.
netmask *X*	Sets the netmask on the established route to *X* (typically, 255.255.255.0).
parity *E|O|N*	Sets parity to even, odd, or none.
password	Specifies that you are to be prompted for the password.
proxyarp	Requests a proxy ARP (address resolution protocol) to be set.
print *X [$var]*	Prints the string *X* or *var*.
port *device*	Sets the communication port to device.
quit	Exits.
reset	Sends three consecutive plus characters (+++) and the string *ATZ* to the modem. The +++ string perks up the modem no matter what it's doing, and then the *ATZ* string resets it.

continued

Command	Purpose
securidf *fixed*	Stores the fixed part of the *SecureID*. (Normally, you get a *SecureID* device, and the first time you use it you are asked to enter a four-digit personal password. Every time after that, you enter your personal password followed by a comma and the number the device generates for you.)
securid	Asks you to enter the variable part (6-digit number) from your *SecureID* device.
send *text [$var]*	Sends the text string and optionally *var* to the modem.
skey *[timeout|$var]*	Allows *dip* to interactively negotiate an *S/Key*-based login. (*S/Key* is similar to *SecureID* in that it generates a one-time password that the remote system recognizes. If you are using plain-text passwords over the Internet that can be intercepted, a one-time password makes sense.)
sleep *X*	Waits *X* seconds.
speed *X*	Sets the serial port's speed in bits-per-second. Note that it does not set — at least directly — the speed of the modem.
stopbits *1|2*	Sets the number of stop bits to 1 or 2.
term	Switches *dip* to *terminal* mode. The combination *Ctrl-]* returns *dip* to *command* mode. (This command is useful for debugging a connection or learning how the connection is negotiated.)
timeout *X*	Specifies the number of seconds — *X* — for *dip* to wait for activity to occur.
wait *text [X|$var]*	Tells *dip* to wait for the string from the remote server to arrive. Optionally, the number of seconds to wait is either *X* or *$var* seconds.

Dip also recognizes several standard variables. Table 8-2 lists these variables.

TABLE 8-2 THE DIP STANDARD VARIABLES

Variable	Meaning
$errlvl	The result code of the last command. Zero means success; any other value means failure.
$local	Your computer's name.
$locip	Your computer's IP address.
$modem	Superfluous modem-type name. Hayes is the only one.
$mtu	The size of the largest packet in bytes.
$port	The serial port name.
$remote	The server computer's name.
$rmtip	The server computer's IP address.
$speed	The speed of your port in bits-per-second.

If all goes well, your *pppd* daemon is launched and you have a PPP route to the Internet. If you enter the following *netstat* command, the resulting information indicates that your default route is set to the *ppp0,* which in turn is connected to your modem and then your ISP:

```
netstat -r -n
```

This command produces the information shown in Listing 8-4.

Listing 8-4: The netstat command returns information about your PPP connection

```
Kernel IP routing table
Destination     Gateway         Genmask         Flags Metric Ref    Use Iface
198.9.5.101     0.0.0.0         255.255.255.255 UH    0      0        0 ppp0
192.168.1.0     0.0.0.0         255.255.255.0   U     0      0        9 eth0
127.0.0.0       0.0.0.0         255.0.0.0       U     0      0        1 lo
0.0.0.0         198.5.5.101     0.0.0.0         UG    0      0        0 ppp0
```

Try making a connection to someplace outside your own LAN — I sometimes try to Telnet to an account I have at the local university, as shown in the following example. (If you have not set up your *nameserver* yet, you need to use raw IP addresses. I discussed that in Chapter 1.)

```
telnet 192.168.111.84
```

Your ISP login computer is a good bet. You already know the IP of its PPP server and that may even double as the login device.

To disconnect the PPP connection, enter the following *dip kill* command:

```
dip -k /dev/modem
```

It may take a few seconds to disconnect and clean up its lock files. Ten years ago I would have killed for such convenience. But I'm spoiled now and still it gets better!

CONNECTING WITH DIP AND DYNAMIC ADDRESSES

Making a PPP connection with dynamic IP addresses is nearly the same as with static ones. Several parameters need to be changed, however.

Log on as *root*. Enter the following line again to start *dip* in its interactive form:

```
dip -t
```

You get the *dip* prompt, as shown in Listing 8-5. Follow the sequence shown in this listing, substituting your ISP phone number, IP addresses, and port number. (*Note:* The ports *cua0* and *cua1* generally correspond to MS-DOS *com1* and *com2*. If you have already linked the file */dev/modem* to your modem serial port, then you can use the command *port modem* in place of *port /dev/ttyS0*.)

Listing 8-5: Establishing a PPP connection with dip

```
DIP: Dialup IP Protocol Driver version 3.3.7o-uri (8 Feb 96)
Written by Fred N. van Kempen, MicroWalt Corporation.
DIP> port /dev/ttyS0
DIP> speed 38400
DIP> term
[ Entering TERMINAL mode.  Use CTRL-] to get back ]
atz
OK
atdt5555309
CONNECT 14000/ARQ/V34/LAPM

your_isp_login: iwantppp
Password: please
{garbled looking text -- this is the remote pppd attempting to query your local
  pppd}
{enter Ctrl-] to return to command mode}
DIP> get $local 0.0.0.0
DIP> mode PPP
```

Dip automatically exits after it completes the mode change to PPP. If all went well, you can start communicating with the outside world.

Installing the diald Communication System

Red Hat supplies a simple and effective way to connect to the Internet via its *Control-Panel,* which I describe in the section "Using the Network Interface Window to Establish a PPP Connection" later in this chapter. However, I highly prefer using the *diald* system, which automates the entire process. It monitors your computer for any communication going to the Internet. When it sees a packet destined for the outside world it dials your ISP and negotiates a PPP connection.

Red Hat does not include a *diald* RPM package on its CD-ROM. However, it does have an RPM *diald* package on its Web (and Anonymous FTP) server in the *contrib* directory. (You can also find it on the SunSITE in the *linux/distributions/redhat/contrib/i386* directory.) I have included a copy on the companion CD-ROM in the IDG directory.

1. Log on as *root.*

2. Mount the CD-ROM.

3. Install the *diald* package by entering the following command:

   ```
   rpm -ivh /mnt/cdrom/IDG/diald-0.16.4-1.i386.rpm
   ```

4. The *connect* script contains the information that *diald* needs to connect to your ISP. A generic copy comes in the *documents* directory. Enter the following command to copy it to its proper location:

   ```
   cp /usr/doc/diald -0.16.4-1/connect /etc/ppp
   ```

5. A generic configuration file also exists in the same directory. This file contains the rules about how *diald* will operate. The standard *diald* expects this file to be found in the */etc* directory, so enter the following command to copy it over:

   ```
   cp /usr/doc/diald -0.16.4-1/diald.conf /etc
   ```

6. *Diald* also likes to have a file — *diald.ctl* — that it uses for coordination in the */etc/diald* directory. Enter the following command to create that directory. *Diald* will create the *diald.ctl* file itself:

   ```
   mkdir /etc/diald
   ```

7. Create a link to your modem port. In my case, it is port */dev/ttyS1*.

```
ln -s /dev/ttyS1 /dev/modem
```

8. Finally, if you wish *diald* to start every time you reboot, you need to copy its startup script to the */etc/rc.d/init.d* directory and create a link to it in the startup run-level directories. (Otherwise, simply enter diald and you will start it manually.)

```
cp /usr/doc/diald-0.16.4-1/diald.init /etc/rc.d/init.d
ln -s /etc/rc.d/init.d/diald.init /etc/rc.d/rc3.d/S95diald
```

I usually only run in run-level 3, so I only make a link there. Your safest bet is to create a link in all the run-level directories. The links are numbered so they will be sorted from highest to lowest and thus execute in that order. I also choose the *S95* prefix because it is not used already and so that *diald* will be started toward the end of the boot process, after *Samba* but before *rc.local* script.

For *diald* to work, you still need to enter your own parameters into the */etc/diald.conf* and */etc/ppp/connect* scripts. I describe how to do that in the next section.

Connecting with diald and Dynamic Addresses

The *diald* program runs in the background as a daemon and appears as a SLIP device – *sl0* – to your network. The SLIP device is, in general, the default route to the external Internet. When packets appear on the SLIP device, destined for an outside network, *diald* starts up the *chat* script that dials the modem and negotiates the login process with the remote server. The *diald* daemon can set up either a SLIP or a PPP connection, but is most often used with PPP.

Diald gives your network a functional, effectively continuous Internet connection. Of course, you have a fairly long latency between the time the packets are generated and when they finally get delivered, but at least you do not have to deal with manually making the connection. It is a good compromise between a costly full-time connection and having to do it manually.

Until *diald* was put into RPM format I would enter its general parameters in a command line form as shown here:

```
/usr/sbin/diald [device1...] [options...] [-- [pppd options...]]
```

Note that you enter the *diald*-specific options as well as the parameters to pass to the *pppd* daemon. After *diald* establishes a connection to your ISP, it starts up *pppd* and passes that information to it.

However, *diald* now can be more easily configured by editing the */etc/ppp/connect* and */etc/diald.conf* scripts. Listing 8-6 shows the portion of the *connect* script that contains the ISP phone number and login information.

Listing 8-6: A sample diald connect script

```
#------------------------------------------------------------------
# For the RPM I've added a few lines to report the connect speed.
# See /usr/lib/diald for the original connect script. -- Dave Cook
#------------------------------------------------------------------


# Copyright (c) 1996, Eric Schenk.
#
# This script is intended to give an example of a connection script that
# uses the "message" facility of diald to communicate progress through
# the dialing process to a diald monitoring program such as dctrl or diald-top.
# It also reports progress to the system logs. This can be useful if you
# are seeing failed attempts to connect and you want to know when and why
# they are failing.
#
# This script requires the use of chat-1.9 or greater for full
# functionality. It should work with older versions of chat,
# but it will not be able to report the reason for a connection failure.


# Configuration parameters

# The initialization string for your modem

MODEM_INIT="ATZ&C1&D2%C0"


# The phone number to dial
PHONE_NUMBER="555-5309"


# The chat sequence to recognize that the remote system
# is asking for your user name.
###USER_CHAT_SEQ="ogin:--ogin:--ogin:--ogin:--ogin:--ogin:--ogin:"
USER_CHAT_SEQ="ogin:"


# The string to send in response to the request for your user name.
USER_NAME="mylogin"


# The chat sequence to recongnize that the remote system
# is asking for your password.
PASSWD_CHAT_SEQ="word:"


# The string to send in response to the request for your password.
PASSWORD="Iwantppp"
```

Diald makes use of the chat scripting utility to dial my ISP. *Chat* is used to respond to the login and password prompts. The string *ogin* refers to the Login prompt that I expect to get from my ISP – the "L" is left out to exclude any confusion about its case. It is considered good practice to leave out the first character in the strings *login* and *password*, to account for discrepancies in response time.

Listing 8-7 contains the *diald.conf* script that contains the information on how *diald* will act. A little later in this chapter, Tables 8-3, 8-4, and 8-5 give a synopsis of the *diald* configuration parameters.

Listing 8-7: My /etc/diald.conf file

```
fifo /etc/diald/diald.ctl
mode ppp
connect "sh /etc/ppp/connect"
device /dev/modem
speed 38400
modem
lock
crtscts
local 127.0.0.2
remote 127.0.0.3
dynamic
defaultroute
pppd-options asyncmap 0
include /usr/lib/diald/standard.filter
```

After you enter the previous command, you can verify that the *diald* daemon is indeed running the following command:

```
ps -x | grep diald
```

The resulting information shows that indeed you were successful and the *diald* daemon is running:

```
737  ?  S    0:00 /usr/sbin/diald /dev/ttyS1 -m ppp local 127.0.0.2 remote
  127.0.0.3
807  p0 S    0:00 grep ppp
```

The *diald* daemon is responsible for setting up your *default route* – the route that handles all packets that cannot be routed explicitly. Using the *defaultroute* option is a good idea if your LAN has no other Internet connections. (This is why I recommended that you leave the default route blank during the network configuration in Chapter 1.) Any packets not intended for your network you probably want going to the Internet. Many caveats exist, but this is a good rule of thumb. (If you have other Internet connections, you know what is what anyway.)

Nothing happens until a packet hits the default route. Try using a network program such as Telnet to access an outside machine – that is, one not on your LAN. Your ISP login computer is a safe bet. If you are in X Window, open another terminal window or go to an alternate screen and run the *ps/grep* command again. As shown in the resulting output, *diald* has spawned a *chat* script to *dial* the modem and log in to your ISP's PPP server:

```
1030  ?  S    0:00 diald
1045  ?  S    0:00 sh /etc/ppp/connect
1049  ?  S    0:00 chat -r /var/log/connect REPORT CONNECT TIMEOUT 45 ABORT NO
```

The modem fires up and dials your ISP. After it establishes a connection, it feeds your login name and password, and you're in! To see that the *pppd* daemon is running, run the following command:

```
ps -x | grep ppp
```

You see the *pppd* daemon as shown in the following line (note that the line is cut short):

```
1132  S0 S    0:00 /usr/sbin/pppd -detach modem crtscts mtu 1500 mru 1500 asyn
```

If you are fast enough (or just lucky), you can see the *kerneld* daemon load the *ppp.o* kernel module in anticipation of the *pppd* daemon. Here's what this information looks like:

```
1203  ?  R    0:00 modprobe -k -s ppp
```

Of course, it is a big potential problem leaving your PPP login name and password in plain text in your chat script file. There may be ways of encrypting it that I am unaware of, but at the very least you should only give root the permission to read the file.

That was relatively easy. There are many *diald* parameters, and I organize them into four tables in this section, to keep things as simple as possible. Tables 8-3 through 8-6 divide the parameters into general purpose, external device (modem), network interface, and time-out parameters. Because some parameters are either too complex or are rarely used, some entries in these tables simply specify that you should consult the man page (*man diald*).

Table 8-3 lists the general-purpose parameters. They include the parameters to read the configuration files and some pathnames.

TABLE 8-3 THE DIALD GENERAL-PURPOSE PARAMETERS

Parameter	Meaning
-f *\<f>*	Get commands from file *f.*
file *\<f>*	Synonym for the *-f* command.
include *\<f>*	Synonym for the *-f* command. Can be nested within a file.
mode *\<m>*	Specifies the protocol to use. The choices are: *SLIP, CSLIP, slip6, cslip6, aslip, PPP,* and *dev* (Ethernet device mode — used for ISDN adapters that look like Ethernet devices).
m *\<m>*	Synonym for the *mode* command.
keepalive *\<t>*	Keep the SLIP connection alive for *t* seconds.
outfill *\<t>*	SLIP outfill timer *t* seconds. (See man *diald* for more information.)
accounting-log *\<f>*	Stores information on connections in file *f.*
pidfile *\<f>*	Stores the *diald* process ID (PID) in file *f.*
fifo *\<f>*	Tells *diald* to read commands from the name pipe *f.*
debug *\<mask>*	Sets the debug mask. (See man *diald* for more information.)
daemon	Run *diald* as a process, not a daemon.
pppd-options *\<arg1>* ...	Pass *option(s) arg1,* and so on to the *pppd* daemon. Do NOT specify the following options: *crtscts, xonxoff, -crtscts, defaultroute, lock, netmask, -detach, modem, local, MTU,* and *proxyarp.* Instead, use the equivalent *diald* parameters.
lock-prefix *\<path>*	Use modem device lock files.
Pidstring	Name the lock files by the *diald* PID.
pidstring	Write lock files in binary format.
run-prefix *\<path>*	Write the PID file in *path* directory instead of */var/run.*
path-route *\<path>*	Tell *diald* where to find the *route* command. Its default is */sbin/route.*
path-ifconfig *\<path>*	Tell *diald* where to find the *ifconfig* command. Its default is */sbin/ifconfig.*

continued

TABLE 8-3 THE DIALD GENERAL-PURPOSE PARAMETERS *(Continued)*

Parameter	Meaning
path-pppd <path>	Tell *diald* where to find the *pppd* command. Its default is */usr/sbin/pppd*.
path-bootpc *<path>*	Tell *diald* where to find the *bootpc* command. Its default is */usr/sbin/bootpc*.
buffer-packets	Tells *diald* to buffer packets until the connection is established. This is the default.
buffer-packets	Tells *diald* NOT to buffer packets while the connection is established.
buffer_size *<n>*	Sets the size of the buffer. Default is 65,536 bytes.
buffer-fifo-dispose	Dispose of packets in *first-in-first-out* (FIFO) manner if it runs out of room while establishing the connection. This is the default.
buffer-fifo-dispose	Do NOT dispose of packets in first-in-first-out (FIFO) manner if it runs out of room while establishing the connection.
buffer-fifo-dispose	Do NOT dispose of old packets when buffer fills.
buffer-timeout *<n>*	Throw out packets in buffer after *n* seconds. The default is 600 seconds.

Table 8-4 shows the *diald* parameters used for configuring the external device used to establish the PPP connection. Note that this is usually a modem but could be a serial connection or ISDN.

TABLE 8-4 THE DIALD DEVICE CONFIGURATION PARAMETERS

Parameter	Meaning
device *<f>*	Add the device *<f>* to the list of devices that can be used for the outgoing connection. For *SLIP* and *PPP* modes, these should be serial devices. For the *dev* mode, this should be the name of an Ethernet device.

continued

Parameter	Meaning
rotate-devices	In normal operation, *diald* attempts to open each of the possible devices listed on its command line in the order they are given. If the first device in the list fails, it will be placed back in the list the next time *diald* is started.
connect *<p>*	Use the executable or shell script *<p>* to set up the serial line. This normally dials the modem and starts up the remote SLIP or PPP session. The script *<p>* is started with the standard output and input directed at the modem device.
disconnect *<p>*	Use the executable or shell script *<p>* to shut down the serial line. This could be used to hang up the modem on systems that don't do hardware hang-ups. As with the connect script, the script is run with the standard input and output redirected to the lock. This parameter performs UUCP-style locking of the serial line.
speed *<baud-rate>*	Set the baud rate to use on the serial line. The default value is 38400.
modem	Treat the serial device as a modem. This parameter will also be passed on to *pppd* in *PPP* mode.
crtscts	Use the hardware flow control lines (RTS and CTS) to control the serial line. This parameter will also be passed on to *pppd* in *PPP* mode. You almost certainly want to use this parameter.

Table 8-5 shows the parameters used for configuring the network interface that routes the packets meant for the PPP or SLIP connection.

TABLE 8-5 THE DIALD NETWORK CONFIGURATION PARAMETERS

Parameter	Meaning
local *<a>*	Specifies the local IP address. If you use a dynamic IP scheme, the actual address *a* is superfluous but must be specified (you could use a local loopback address such as 127.0.0.2). If you use a static IP address, this parameter must be the address your ISP has assigned to you.

continued

TABLE 8-5 THE DIALD NETWORK CONFIGURATION PARAMETERS *(Continued)*

Parameter	Meaning
remote *<a>*	Specifies the remote IP address. If you use a dynamic IP scheme, the actual address *a* is superfluous but must be specified (you could use a local loopback address such as 127.0.0.3). If you use a static IP address, this parameter must be the address of your ISP.
Dynamic	Tells *diald* to get the local and remote IP addresses from your ISP when the PPP or SLIP connection is established.
dslip-mode *<mode>*	See the man page for details.
netmask *<a>*	Sets the netmask for routing.
mtu *<m>*	Specifies the *Maximum Transmission Unit* (MTU) to *m*. This is the largest packet size allowed. The default is 1500.
mru *<m>*	Specifies the *Maximum Receive Unit* (mru) to *m*. In *PPP* mode, *pppd* tells the server to set its *MTU* to this number. Not applicable to SLIP.
window *<s>*	Sets the *TCP* window size. (See the man page for more information.)
Reroute	Change the route to point to the physical, rather than the proxy, interface. This is the default.
reroute	Change the route to point to the proxy, rather than the physical, interface. (See the man page for more information.)
Defaultroute	Specifies the system default route to point to the SLIP interface.
Proxyarp	Specifies an entry in the system *Address Resolution Protocol* (ARP) table with the IP address of the remote system and the local Ethernet adapter (unique in the world) address.
addroute *<script-name>*	Specifies a script to run when the proxy device is established. The script receives arguments containing the interface, netmask, metric (jumps to the remote address), and local and remote IP addresses.

continued

Parameter	Meaning
delroute <*script-name*>	Specifies a script to run just before the proxy device is deleted — just before *diald* exits. The script receives arguments containing the interface, netmask, metric (jumps to the remote address), and local and remote IP addresses.
ip-up <*script-name*>	Specifies a script to run when *diald* brings up the IP layer. The script gets the same information as *addroute*. *Diald* does NOT wait for the script to finish.
ip-down <*script-name*>	Specifies a script to run when *diald* brings down the IP layer. The script gets the same information as *addroute*. *Diald* does NOT wait for the script to finish.

Table 8-6 lists time-out parameters. These settings have various dependencies and factors. Some specify an action to be taken after the time-out occurs.

TABLE 8-6 THE DIALD TIME-OUT PARAMETERS

Parameter	Meaning
connect-timeout <*t*>	Wait *t* seconds for the connect-script (see Table 8-4) to complete. Default is 60 seconds.
disconnect-timeout <*t*>	Wait *t* seconds for the disconnect-script (see Table 8-4) to complete. Default is 60 seconds.
redial-timeout <*t*>	Wait *t* seconds between dial attempts. Default is 30 seconds.
nodev-retry-timeout <*t*>	Wait *t* seconds to attempt redial when no free modem device is available. Default is 1 second.
stop-dial-timeout <*t*>	Wait up to *t* seconds for a connect attempt to die after sending a SIGINT signal to *diald*. The default is 60 seconds.
kill-timeout <*t*>	Wait up to *t* seconds for a subprocess to die after sending a SIGKILL signal to *diald*. Default is 60 seconds. (See the man page for more information.)
start-pppd-timeout <*t*>	Wait up to *t* seconds for *pppd* to choose a PPP device. The default is 60 seconds.

continued

TABLE 8-6 THE DIALD TIME-OUT PARAMETERS *(Continued)*

Parameter	Meaning
stop-pppd-timeout *<t>*	Wait up to *t* seconds for *pppd* to die after sending a SIGINT signal to it. Default is 60 seconds.
first-packet-timeout *<t>*	Wait up to *t* seconds after the PPP connection is established for *pppd* to send the first packet and if exceeded shut down the connection. The default is 120 seconds.
retry-count *<n>*	Specify the maximum number of times *n* to attempt to make the initial connection before stopping and waiting for more network traffic. The default is 0.
died-retry-count *<n>*	Specify the maximum number of times *n* to try and restore a broken connection before stopping and waiting for more network traffic. The default is 1.
redial-backoff-start *<n>*	See the man page for a description.
redial-backoff-limit	See the man page for a description.
dial-fail-limit	Specifies the maximum number of consecutive failed connection attempts before *diald* blocks any further attempts. The default is 0. If set to 0, no limit is enforced.
route-wait	See the man page for a description.
two-way	If the PPP or SLIP server ends the connection and this parameter is set, *diald* does not attempt to reestablish the connection unless it receives outgoing packets.
give-way	See the man page for a description.

You can now do *everything* from your Linux box because your computer is connected directly to the Internet.

Connecting with diald and Static Addresses

Configuring *diald* for static addresses is similar to configuring it with dynamic ones. First, remove the *dynamic* parameter and then change the *local* and *remote* parameters to the static addresses. For example, if your ISP-supplied local and remote IP addresses are 192.168.1.45 and 192.168.1.249 respectively, then your *diald* command line looks like the one in Listing 8-8.

Listing 8-8: A diald.conf script configured for static IP addresses

```
fifo /etc/diald/diald.ctl
mode ppp
connect "sh /etc/ppp/connect"
device /dev/modem
speed 38400
modem
lock
crtscts
local 192.168.1.45
remote 192.168.1.249
defaultroute
pppd-options asyncmap 0
include /usr/lib/diald/standard.filter
```

Run the *diald* command in the same way as I describe in the preceding section entitled "Connecting with *diald* and Dynamic Addresses." When you run *netstat* or *route*, you will see the static IP addresses, however.

Using the Network Interface Window to Establish a PPP Connection

The Red Hat *Network Configurator* window simplifies the task of establishing a PPP connection. Log in as *root*, and start the X Window system (*startx*). Open the *Control Panel* and then open the *Network Configurator*, shown in Figure 8-5.

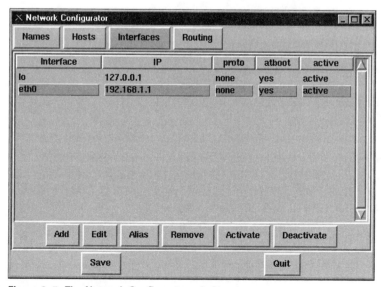

Figure 8-5: The Network Configurator window

Click the *Interfaces* menu button at the top middle of the *Network Configurator* window. The *Choose Interface* window activates, as shown in Figure 8-6.

Figure 8-6: The Choose Interface window

Click the *PPP* radio button, and the *Create PPP Interface* window appears. Enter your ISP account information, as shown in Figure 8-7.

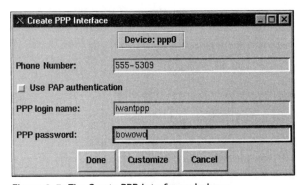

Figure 8-7: The Create PPP Interface window

If you need to tweak any of the hardware, communication interface (that is, serial port), or networking settings, click the *Customize* button, and you get the customization window (titled *Edit PPP Interface*) shown in Figure 8-8. Otherwise, click the *Done* button to finalize your PPP interface setup.

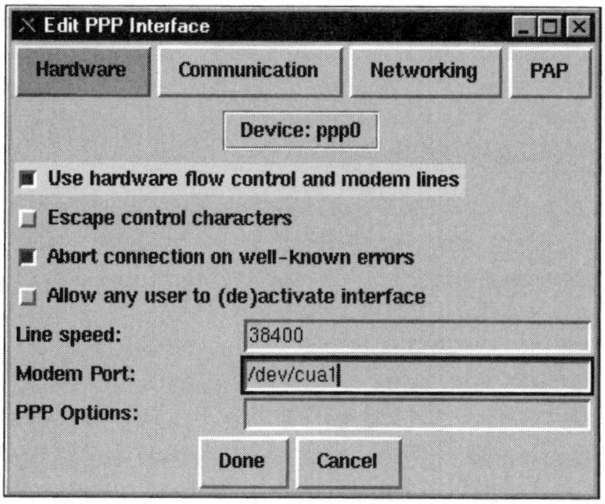

Figure 8-8: The customization window for the serial port

If you have not set the symbolic link from the serial device file to the modem file (either manually with the */bin/ln* command or via the *Modem Configurator* from the *Control Panel*), you should set the serial port in the *Customization* window. I have set the port to */dev/cua1* in Figure 8-8. This is the most likely setting if you have a mouse attached to */dev/cua0* (*Com1:* in MS-DOS), but your system may be different. You should not have any problems if you just experiment. You most likely want to keep the hardware handshaking, which is how the modem and the computer signal each other when one has filled its data buffer and needs time to process it.

Click the *Networking* button next, and the window shown in Figure 8-9 appears. This window is where you may have to change such things as your default route.

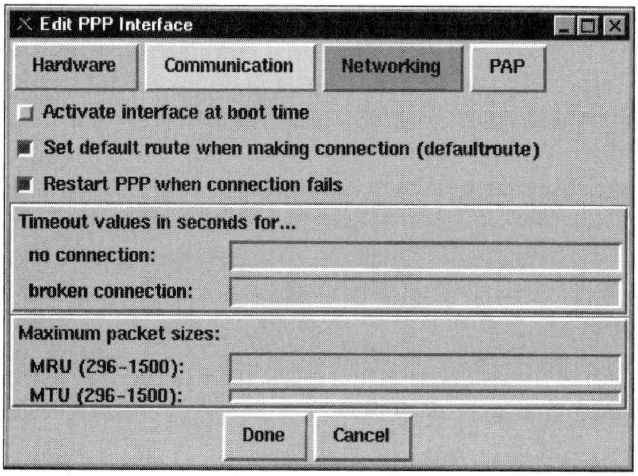

Figure 8-9: The customization window for the network settings

Finally, click the *Communication* button, and the window shown in Figure 8-10 appears.

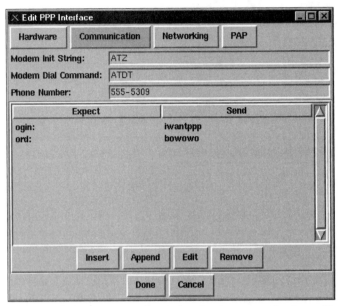

Figure 8-10: The customization window for the communication settings

Click the *Done* button and another window appears giving you the choice to *save* or *cancel* the edits that you just made. Click the *Save* button and you return to the *Network Configurator*. You have configured the PPP connection, and you can activate it by clicking the *Activate* button. If your modem is connected properly and turned on, the *pppd* daemon is started and a *chat* script is run.

The internal process is very similar to that of the *diald* example. Listing 8-9 shows that the shell script */etc/sysconfig/network-scripts/ifup-ppp* is run. It was created from the choices you just made in the Network Configurator.

Listing 8-9: The processes run by the customization window for the serial port

```
714   1 S    0:00 sh /etc/sysconfig/network-scripts/ifup-ppp daemon /etc/sysc
716   1 S    0:00 /usr/sbin/pppd -detach lock modem crtscts defaultroute /dev
718   ? D    0:00 modprobe -k -s ppp0
```

Notice that the *kerneld* daemon is inserting the *pppd* into the kernel with *modprobe*. The *chat* script to dial your ISP is run next, as shown in Listing 8-10.

Listing 8-10: The chat script spawns the pppd daemon

```
636  1 S   0:00 /usr/sbin/pppd -detach lock modem crtscts defaultroute /dev
641  1 S   0:00 /usr/sbin/chat -f /etc/sysconfig/network-scripts/chat-ppp0
```

Finally, the *chat* process finishes and the *pppd* daemon is left controlling the connection. Listing 8-11 shows the *pppd* daemon controlling the PPP connection.

Listing 8-11: The original pppd controlling the PPP connection

```
636  1 S   0:00 /usr/sbin/pppd -detach lock modem crtscts defaultroute /dev
```

You again have a full TCP/IP network connection. You are an Internet node. To disconnect, just click the *Deactivate* button in the *Network Configurator.*

Monitoring Your Connection

Three of the most useful network monitoring and configuration utilities are *ifconfig*, *route*, and *netstat*. You use *ifconfig* to configure the network interfaces – both physical and logical. *Route* adds, deletes, and edits static routes. *Netstat* displays network statistics.

If you enter **ifconfig** without any parameters, you get information about your interfaces, as shown in Listing 8-12:

```
ifconfig
```

Listing 8-12: The ifconfig displays interface information

```
lo        Link encap:Local Loopback
          inet addr:127.0.0.1  Bcast:127.255.255.255  Mask:255.0.0.0
          UP BROADCAST LOOPBACK RUNNING  MTU:3584  Metric:1
          RX packets:175 errors:0 dropped:0 overruns:0
          TX packets:175 errors:0 dropped:0 overruns:0

eth0      Link encap:10Mbps Ethernet  HWaddr 00:A0:24:2F:30:69
          inet addr:192.168.1.254  Bcast:192.168.1.255  Mask:255.255.255.0
          UP BROADCAST RUNNING MULTICAST  MTU:1500  Metric:1
          RX packets:8809 errors:0 dropped:0 overruns:0
          TX packets:6418 errors:0 dropped:0 overruns:0
          Interrupt:10 Base address:0x300

sl0       Link encap:Serial Line IP
          inet addr:127.0.0.2  P-t-P:127.0.0.3  Mask:255.0.0.0
          UP POINTOPOINT RUNNING  MTU:1500  Metric:1
          RX packets:0 errors:0 dropped:0 overruns:0
          TX packets:1 errors:0 dropped:0 overruns:0
```

To display the static routes available to your system, enter the *route* command with the *-n* parameter:

```
/sbin/route -n
```

This command displays the information shown in Listing 8-13. Note that you need to have your */etc/hosts* file configured to display the names of the interfaces. Otherwise, *route* takes a very long time to decide that it cannot resolve the IP addresses via a nameserver. If you have */etc/hosts* configured, you can remove the numeric option *-n* and have the IP addresses displayed with their mnemonics.

Listing 8-13: The route command displays the static routes

```
Kernel IP routing table
Destination     Gateway         Genmask         Flags Metric Ref    Use Iface
127.0.0.3       *               255.255.255.255 UH    1      0        0 sl0
192.168.1.0     *               255.255.255.0   U     0      0       46 eth0
127.0.0.0       *               255.0.0.0       U     0      0        8 lo
default         *               0.0.0.0         U     1      0        1 sl0
```

Enter the *netstat* command with the parameters as shown in the following line, to display the statistics on all network interfaces:

```
/bin/netstat -r -n
```

Listing 8-14 shows the information that this command displays. Again, if your */etc/hosts* file is configured, remove *-n* parameter to display IP names. You can also add the constant display option *-c* to continuously display the information – this option is useful for monitoring the status of a dynamic connection as it is negotiated or to check progress while you transfer a large file.

Listing 8-14: The route command displays the static routes

```
Kernel IP routing table
Destination     Gateway         Genmask         Flags  MSS Window  irtt Iface
127.0.0.3       0.0.0.0         255.255.255.255 UH    1500 0          0 sl0
192.168.1.0     0.0.0.0         255.255.255.0   U     1500 0          0 eth0
127.0.0.0       0.0.0.0         255.0.0.0       U     3584 0          0 lo
0.0.0.0         0.0.0.0         0.0.0.0         U     1500 0          0 sl0
```

An interesting new program is *statnet*. It shows a live display of network statistics, including various types of packets coming and going. This is a nifty process to watch and quite useful for monitoring traffic (something that can give you troubleshooting clues), so you should install *statnet*.

The *statnet* program is another RPM package that I obtained from the Red Hat *contrib* directory and have included on the companion CD-ROM. To install it, log on as *root*, mount the companion CD-ROM, and enter the following command:

```
rpm -ivh /mnt/cdrom/IDG/statnet-2.1-2.i386.rpm
```

After you install *statnet,* simply execute it from a shell as follows:

```
/usr/bin/statnet
```

It displays dynamic network information, as shown in Listing 8-15. Notice the PPP connection – which is inactive as shown – as well as the Ethernet connection.

Listing 8-15: The statnet information screen

```
STATISTICS OF NETWORKS
  GENERAL  Frame:   20/6  sec  ===== 802.2 SAP =====   ==== TCP/IP PORTS ====
           KB/s Frame/s AvLen                          fragment   17  85.0%
   all     0.19     3    58                            Telnet:     3  15.0%
   eth     0.14     2    62

  SLIP     0.00     0     0
  PPP      0.05     1    48
  loop     0.00     0     0


  Ethernet Load   0.01%
                              ===== PROTOCOLS =====   ==== UDP/IP PORTS ====
                              Ethernet   14  70.0%    NetB NS:    0   0.0%
  ==== IP PROTOCOLS ====                              RPC/NFS:    0   0.0%
                                                          962:    0   0.0%
    TCP:    20 100.0%
    UDP:     0   0.0%                  PPP    6  30.0%

                              Loop int    0   0.0%
                                  SLIP    0   0.0%


                              Other:      0   0.0%
```

This information is valuable for both troubleshooting and monitoring. For troubleshooting, it shows, at a glance, whether an interface exists and if any traffic is going over it. For monitoring purposes, you can see how much traffic is going through an interface.

Introducing Firewalls

Now that you are a full-fledged node on the Internet, you must start worrying about security. At this point, you do not have much to risk if all you have done is connect your basic Linux box to the Internet. However, if your LAN is connected to the Internet, you risk significant exposure. Either way, you need to start concerning yourself with the concept as well as the details of security.

 Network security is a complex and constantly evolving subject. There is always some weakness that has not been discovered yet, except maybe by someone with malicious intent. Unless you lock your system in the proverbial vault, you can never be completely protected. Constant education and vigilance is the requirement to sleep reasonably well at night. Of course, I can provide no assurance or guarantee that if you follow my advice here you will be safe. The administrator must beware.

I don't go into very much detail about security in this chapter. This section introduces you to firewalls and the *ipfw* package in particular. Chapters 9, 10, and 11 discuss firewalls and security in greater detail. However, whole books have been written on the subject, so my coverage is oriented to creating basic protection. Hopefully, this section and the following chapters will get you thinking in security terms as soon as possible. Security is as much an attitude as anything else.

With the advent of the Internet, firewalls are as important as passwords. At the least, they prevent casual break-ins; at the most, they put a significant barrier in the way of systematic threats.

Two types of firewalls exist: application-based firewalls and packet-oriented firewalls. The former typically replaces a network service with a proxy equivalent that adds another password barrier and/or has specific allow/disallow lists of users and/or computers. The latter is implemented on almost all commercial routers now, and it is available as software for Linux and UNIX systems. When implemented on routers, packet filtering is a reasonable first line of defense. For example, the practice of preventing IP *spoofing* – the filtering out of all packets that arrive at your external router interface (from the Internet) with either your internal network or the loopback address – is easily implemented. More significant filtering is implemented via the *ipfw* package that comes with the Red Hat distribution.

Application-Based Firewalls

An example of an application-based firewall is the TIS Firewall Toolkit, in which the *telnet* daemon is replaced by a proxy that checks its list of users/machines to allow or disallow connections. It also has the option of using one-time passwords to further enhance authentication.

I discuss application-level firewalls in the next two chapters of this book. The *ipfw* is an excellent package and quite capable of providing either a simple or full-fledged firewall. In this chapter, I describe the simple firewall that should be adequate for your current needs.

The best firewall is one that is dedicated to that purpose. It has two network interfaces: one for the LAN and the other for either the stand-alone router or the Internet interface such as the PPP connection. The firewall computer should allow the absolute minimum of access and run the fewest daemons and services.

Packet Filtering

If you do not allow any packets into your network from the Internet, you are not susceptible to any break-ins. Of course, you also cannot use the Internet. Obviously, some compromise must be achieved.

A good starting place is to deny all access and then start selectively allowing access. In this way, you start out safe and only incrementally reduce your safety. For example, if you deny all access and then allow only a *telnet* session from a trusted computer, any potential threat must have prior knowledge or get lucky to even start to break in.

The IPFW Firewall

The *ipfw* package provides the capability to set rules for what packets you let into and out of your network.

The *ipfw* system also provides for IP Masquerading, which lets you use a public IP address space on the Internet. Presently, only your Linux box with the PPP connection is visible and can use the Internet. I discuss the use of *ipfw* in the following chapters.

To install the *ipfw* package, log on as *root*, mount the Red Hat CD-ROM, and enter the following command (or use the *Package Configurator* – via the *Control Panel* – from X Window):

```
rpm -ivh /mnt/cdrom/RedHat/RPMS/ipfwadm-2.3.0-5.i386.rpm
```

The man page for *ipfw* makes the point that using it — especially at first — can put your computer in an unstable or unusable state. The man page recommends working from the console and not a Telnet session, especially while you are early in your learning curve. This advice makes sense because you can disallow the packets that your Telnet session uses. The man page also recommends that the *ipfw* flush command can fix any problems you create for yourself — it ends any rules that you implement.

After you install *ipfw*, you can interactively specify the *ipfwadm* filtering rules. The filtering rules check each incoming and outgoing IP packet to determine which packets are allowed to pass through the firewall. Here's the general syntax of an *ipfwadm* command:

```
/sbin/ipfwadm category commands parameters [options]
```

The following tables describe the categories, commands, parameters, and options available to you. As in previous tables, I distill the information given in the man page, FAQ, and Howto documents for the *ipfwadm* command. You should consult those documents for the definitive and detailed description.

Table 8-7 lists the fundamental filtering rules, or categories, of *ipfwadm*. The simple firewall example that I describe later in this chapter makes use of the *-I*, *-O*, and *-F* rules. I leave the Accounting and Masquerading rules for Chapter 10.

TABLE 8-7 THE IPFW CATEGORIES

Category	Description
A *[direction]*	The accounting rules that optionally can be directional (in, out, or both). Packets are counted. The default direction is both ways.
M	The rules that govern the masquerading of IP packets. Only valid when used with the list (*-l*) or set time-out values (*-s*) commands.

The following rules are known as firewall categories:

I	The rules governing incoming IP packets.
O	The rules governing outgoing IP packets.
F	The rules that govern the forwarding of IP packets.

Before describing the *ipfwadm* commands, I want to list the three policies that they all use. A policy is *accept, deny,* or *reject.* The *accept* policy means to allow a packet through the firewall. Both the *reject* and the *deny* policies prevent a packet from going through the firewall. If the *reject* policy is used, an ICMP "request for access denied" packet is returned to the sender; the *deny* policy packet simply dies and no response is provided. The *reject* policy potentially provides the malicious sender a clue that a possible point of attack exists to pursue.

Table 8-8 shows the commands that are used with the five categories from the previous table. Only one command can be used per instance of the *ipfwadm* command.

TABLE 8-8 THE IPFWADM COMMANDS

Command	Purpose
a *[policy]*	Append one or more rules to the existing set. Accounting does not use any. Firewall chains — incoming, outgoing, and forwarded packets — must have a defined policy.
i *[policy]*	Insert one or more rules at the beginning of a set. The order of rules is important. If a packet matches a rule, all successive ones are ignored. See the *-a* command for more details.
d *[policy]*	Delete one or more entries from the selected set. Only the first matching rule in the set is deleted.
l	List all the rules in a set. If the *-z* command is included, all counts are started at zero. The default is to use increments of kilobytes or megabytes, depending on the context.
z	Reset the counters of the selected rules. Useful when used with the *-l* command.
f	Flush or delete the selected list of rules.
p *[policy]*	Set or change the default policy for the given type of firewall. The default policy is generally the first one set in order to start from some uniform point. This command is only valid with the *-l, -O,* and *-F firewall categories.*
s *tcp tcpfin udp*	Used to set the time-out values for the masquerading rules.
c	Check if an IP packet would be accepted, denied, or rejected given a specific firewall. Only valid for the *-l, -O,* and *-F firewall categories.*
h	Display help screen (about a page and a half).

The parameters listed in the Table 8-9 are used with the *append, insert, delete,* and *check* commands.

TABLE 8-9 THE IPFWADM PARAMETERS

Parameter	Meaning
P *protocol*	Define the Internet protocol to which you want to apply the firewall rule. The protocols are *tcp, udp, icmp,* or *all* three. You can't use the *all* option with the *check* command. The default is *all*.
S *address[/mask] [port ...]*	Specify the source address to check IP packets against. The address format can be specified as a host name, a network name, or a numeric IP address. The mask is optional and can be in IP format (*x.x.x.x*) or a single number that translates to the IP format. A port number or range can be included. Please refer to the man page because it provides lots of additional details.
D *address[/mask] [port ...]*	Optionally specify the destination address to check IP packets against. As with the source -*S* parameter, a netmask and port can be specified. ICMP packets cannot be combined with this parameter. The man page offers lots of additional details about this parameter.
V *address*	Specify the interface at which you want to check incoming or outgoing IP packets. The address format can be specified as a host name, a network name, or a numeric IP address. If a host name is specified, it should resolve (via the */etc/hosts* or nameserver) to only one IP numeric address. When this parameter is omitted, the address 0.0.0.0 is assumed — this address matches any IP address. This parameter is required when the *check* command is used.
W *name*	Specify the name of the interface in which you want to check incoming or outgoing IP packets. When omitted, any interface is matched. This parameter is required when the *check* command is used.

Finally, Table 8-10 lists the options you can use with the commands and parameters that I describe in the preceding tables.

TABLE 8-10 THE IPFWADM OPTIONS

Option	Meaning
b	*Bidirectional* mode. The specified rule matches IP incoming and outgoing packets. Only valid with the *append, insert,* or *delete* commands.
e	Extended output. Forces the list command to display the interface address and rule options (if any). The packet and byte counters are also displayed for the *firewall categories.* If used in conjunction with the *-M* command, the delta sequence numbers are also listed. This option is only valid for *list* command.
k	Match *TCP* packets with their *ACK* bit set. The *ACK* bit is included in the TCP protocol header and specifies whether the *TCP* packet originated locally or remotely. This option is meaningless for any other protocol. It is also only valid in conjunction with the *append, insert,* and *delete* commands.
m	Masquerade packets that have been accepted for forwarding. This option specifies that the firewall IP address is substituted for the IP address of the originating node (computer or other device) on the local network before being sent out onto the Internet. With this option enabled, any local node appears to be the firewall to the outside world. Packets returned from the Internet are demasqueraded and the originating IP address is substituted for that of the firewall. This option allows any network to fully access the Internet without any formal registration. This option is only valid for the forwarding firewall rules.
n	Print the IP addresses and port numbers in numeric format (*x.x.x.x*). If you have a problem with your */etc/hosts* table or nameserver, this option bypasses using names and displays addresses as numbers. It lets you see what rules are set. By default, names are used.
o	Turn on kernel logging of packets that match a rule. This option is only usable if the kernel was compiled with the *CONFIG_IP_FIREWALL_VERBOSE* flag set. This option is only valid with the *firewall categories.*

continued

TABLE 8-10 THE IPFWADM OPTIONS *(Continued)*

Option	Meaning
r *[port]*	Redirect packets to a local socket. Packets that match this rule are redirected to a local socket regardless of their original destination. If the port is 0 (the default value), the destination port is used. This option is only valid with input firewall rules with the *accept* policy and if the kernel was compiled with the *CONFIG_IP_TRANSPARENT_PROXY* flag set.
t *andmask xormask*	See the man page for details.
v	Verbose output. Print detailed information about the *append, insert, delete,* or *check* command.
x	Expand numbers. Display the exact value of the packet or byte counter.
y	Only allow *TCP* packets with the SYN and ACK bits equal to zero. All other protocols are ignored. Only valid with the *append, insert,* or *delete* command.

I discuss the masquerading rules in subsequent chapters of this book. I also defer the accounting rules until later in the book.

Determining Firewall Policy

The most difficult aspect of designing firewall rules is balancing risk against benefits. The more services you allow for yourself and your network, the more risk you assume.

Because you are still early in the process of designing your Linux network, you have the luxury of having relatively little at risk. Any mistakes you make now with the firewall should have little impact on you. I don't want you to develop the bad habit of taking the topic of security cavalierly, but you should recognize that you have the opportunity to experiment and learn from your mistakes.

I also want to take advantage of the security offered – or that should be offered – by your ISP. At this point, I assume that you are not quite yet a budding America Online and have limited needs. If you determine that you will let your ISP provide many external services to your colleagues, clients, or friends, you will reduce your exposure by an order of magnitude. That is the model that I use to serve my professional needs. *Pay someone else to take the capital equipment and security risk whenever possible.*

If you have been following along with the installation and configuration instructions that I provide in this book, you have not done anything that you cannot reinstall in less than an hour or so. In fact, I encourage you to consider reinstalling your entire system or parts of it at this point or in the near future. If you are like me, the extra practice will cement your education up to this point. Being familiar with Linux, Samba, and the Red Hat administrative tools should make the entire process go very quickly. In the future, when you are administering a real network, you will not be intimidated by the need to recreate a system if necessary.

So for this example I am going to pay my ISP to provide my WWW server, anonymous FTP, e-mail server, nameserver, and IP interface. My network and firewall only need to forward my internal Internet service requests to the proper location and allow the return packets back in. This procedure lets me concentrate on making my firewall as secure as possible.

My critical data storage needs still measure less than 10MB, so I also keep my emergency backups on my personal account at my ISP. I either FTP files individually or via *tar* files, which is not particularly elegant but effective and reasonably fast. (I usually bootstrap on a connection I already have going — for instance, while I am looking at a Web page but not transferring data to it — so it is relatively convenient, too.) The added benefit is that my data is stored *off-site*.

Now my firewall can be simpler and thus more secure.

Configuring a Simple Firewall

The following instructions show how to configure a simple but effective firewall for your Linux computer. I use a simple philosophy of allowing you to go out onto the Internet but not permitting any traffic — initiated externally — to come back in. This is a reasonable strategy for now because your system is a simple one. With your current configuration, you should have little need to allow anyone to access it externally.

The first step in designing a firewall is to *DENY* everything and everybody. Sound extreme? Yes, it is. But by starting at that point, you put a solid wall between yourself and all the bad guys. Every rule you use from now on should allow only specific and well-defined activities. Thus, there should not be any — or at least an absolute minimum of — holes or back doors that you are not aware of or specifically allow. By the way, I do not think it is poor form to have a PPP connection active right now. If you do, you will see the effects of your moves immediately for good or bad. The caveat is, of course, that you do not have anything you do NOT want to lose or corrupt and that your ISP does NOT have some policy against such activity. Enter the *ipfwadm* commands as shown in the following paragraphs. I assume that you are using the public network address 192.168.1.0 and that your firewall machine is address 192.168.1.1 and has a PPP connection to your ISP and thus the Internet.

You need to log on as *root* at the Linux server console. This is because I have you set up the firewall in such a way that it will temporarily shut down your network interfaces (see the *deny everything* policy in the preceding paragraph). If you are using a dynamic PPP connection, you need to find out the IP address that your ISP has supplied to you. Enter the following command:

```
ifconfig ppp0
```

You should get a display like that shown in Listing 8-16 (I have changed my real IP addresses, of course).

Listing 8-16: Your dynamic IP address

```
ppp0      Link encap:Point-Point Protocol
inet addr:192.168.15.10  P-t-P:192.168.15.101  Mask:255.255.255.0
UP POINTOPOINT RUNNING  MTU:1500  Metric:1
RX packets:1757 errors:0 dropped:0 overruns:0
TX packets:2080 errors:0 dropped:0 overruns:0
```

You want to use the *inet* address and not the *P-t-P* address. This is the address that the outside world sees you as, so make note of it. Enter the initial blanket denial commands:

```
/sbin/ipfwadm -I -p deny
/sbin/ipfwadm -O -p deny
/sbin/ipfwadm -F -p deny
```

It is good practice to clean out any rules that may be left over from the last setup. Even though this is the first time setting up firewall rules, go ahead and flush all three rules by entering the following commands:

```
ipfwadm -I -f
ipfwadm -O -f
ipfwadm -F -f
```

Next, you need to add the rules to prevent IP *spoofing*. This is the practice in which someone tries to gain access to your system by massaging their IP packets to contain your network address (or the default address). Early on, routers did not consider this possibility and were easily fooled into thinking such packets were part of their network. That was a big security hole and allowed access to the supposedly protected network. Enter the following commands (note that the 192.168.1.0/24 syntax is shorthand for 192.168.1.0/255.255.255.0):

```
ipfwadm -I -a deny -V 192.168.15.10   -S 192.168.1.0/24 -D 0.0.0.0/0
ipfwadm -I -a deny -V 192.168.15.10   -S 192.168.15.10 -D 0.0.0.0/0
```

These commands specify that any IP packets showing up on the external PPP interface with either your local network address or the universal anywhere address (0.0.0.0) should be rejected outright. Note that if the *reject* rule were used here, the adversary would receive an ICPM rejection packet informing that person that something interesting has been encountered.

Now, set up rules that allow unlimited, internal usage of your local network:

```
ipfwadm -I -a accept -V 192.168.1.1   -S 0.0.0.0/0   -D 0.0.0.0/0
ipfwadm -O -a accept -V 192.168.1.1   -S 0.0.0.0/0   -D 0.0.0.0/0
```

Next set up your firewall to allow your local network to access the Internet:

```
ipfwadm -O -a accept -P tcp -S 192.168.15.10 -D 0.0.0.0/0 smtp pop-3 telnet www
 ftp
ipfwadm -I -a accept -P tcp -k -S 0.0.0.0/0 smtp pop-3 telnet www ftp -D
 192.168.15.10
ipfwadm -O -a accept -P tcp -S 192.168.15.10 -D 0.0.0.0/0 ftp-data
ipfwadm -I -a accept -P tcp -S 0.0.0.0/0 ftp-data -D 192.168.15.10
ipfwadm -O -a accept -P udp -S 192.168.15.10 -D 0.0.0.0/0 domain
ipfwadm -I -a accept -P udp -S 0.0.0.0/0 domain -D 192.168.15.10/24
```

The first two commands set up outgoing *TCP* packets for the *smtp* (e-mail), *telnet*, *FTP*, and the WWW. The following four commands are used for outgoing *TCP* and *udp* IP packets. The first two allow your outgoing and return *TCP* packets for *smtp*, *pop3* (e-mail), *telnet*, *FTP*, and the *WWW*. The next two are for the second channel (data) that *FTP* sets up for itself. The last two configure outgoing and return *udp* packets for *domain name* service lookups (DNS). Other services such as gopher can be included – see the man page and HOWTO documents and the */etc/services* file for more information about them.

Note that the incoming (*-I*) rule for TCP connection has the *-k* flag set. This option allows only *TCP* packets with their *ACK* bit set through. Basically, it allows only *TCP* packets that you initiated back in. For example, when your start a Telnet session, the first packet you send out has the *SYN* bit set, and the Telnet server sets the *ACK* bit in response.

Well, that's it. You have a firewall! Your system is reasonably safe and you have quite a bit of Internet access. In the following two chapters, I show you how to build on this model. The Linux-Samba server you built serves as the basis for the more complex and powerful system you now have, and this firewall will work in the same way.

Take a look at the rules you just set with the listing function of *ipfwadm*. Enter the following commands:

```
/sbin/ipfwadm -0 -l
/sbin/ipfwadm -I -l
/sbin/ipfwadm -F -l
```

These commands list the rules you just set for outgoing, incoming, and forwarded packets. Listing 8-17 shows the results.

Listing 8-17: All the firewall rules that you just set are listed

```
IP firewall output rules, default policy: deny
type  prot source               destination          ports
acc   all  anywhere             anywhere             n/a
acc   tcp  198.59.115.81        anywhere             any -> smtp,pop-3,telnet,hp
acc   tcp  198.59.115.81        anywhere             any -> ftp-data
acc   udp  198.59.115.81        anywhere             any -> domain
IP firewall input rules, default policy: deny
type  prot source               destination          ports
deny  all  192.168.1.0/24       anywhere             n/a
deny  all  198.59.115.81        anywhere             n/a
acc   all  anywhere             anywhere             n/a
acc   tcp  anywhere             198.59.115.81        smtp,pop-3,telnet,http,ftpy
acc   tcp  anywhere             198.59.115.81        ftp-data -> any
acc   udp  anywhere             198.59.115.81        domain -> any
IP firewall forward rules, default policy: deny
```

 I like to define some aliases for simplifying the firewall definition process. You may find the following list helpful (I'm sure you'll find more):

```
alias ip='ipfwadm'
alias ipi='ipfwadm -I'
alias ipo='ipfwadm -0'
alias ipf='ipfwadm -F'
alias ipl='ipfwadm -l'
alias ipp='ipfwadm -h |more'
```

To finalize this process, go ahead and enter all the commands you interactively executed into a script file. Call it something like *fire.rules* and make sure you change the *mode* to executable by *root* only, because you want to keep tight control over such a critical system. If you have a frame relay or static route PPP network connection, you can set the firewall rules at boot time. In that case, enter the following lines in the */etc/rc.d/rc.local* script file so that the rules will be executed every time you boot up:

```
if [ -f /etc/rc.d/init.d/fire.rules ] ; then
/etc/rc.d/init.d/fire.rules
fi
```

If you have dynamic PPP connection, run it manually after establishing a connection. It is possible to have *diald* start the script, but I describe that in Chapter 10.

The *rc.local* script is the last of the *rc* startup scripts to be executed. When you next boot your system, your firewall will come up after the rest of your network. This procedure is not a good idea in the long term, because your network interfaces will be active before your firewall. (Plus, if the script fails, you may not be aware and leave your network open to the world.)

Summary

This chapter describes how to connect your network to the Internet, which is the last important step to completing your client-server network. After this chapter, you have all the parts necessary to run your internal and external network.

I cover the following topics in this chapter:

◆ Understanding the difference between a terminal and a node connection to the Internet is important to understanding the power that is available to you and your network. A node connection offers comprehensive Internet access, giving your network the functionality that a terminal session cannot provide.

◆ It is important to have a basic understanding of the PPP and SLIP protocols. PPP is the de facto standard, providing the stability and flexibility required for consistently using phone connections for Internet access.

◆ The type of connection you use to carry your PPP or SLIP packets to the Internet depends on your needs and budget. If you have high-bandwidth requirements, you need a Frame Relay or ISDN connection. Otherwise, the traditional modem offers the best compromise. Note that Linux can combine multiple modems in parallel – load balancing – to increase bandwidth.

◆ Frame Relay offers medium- to high-bandwidth connection to the Internet but is expensive. It is generally carried, in part, over a leased telephone wire and provides continuous service. Although specialized equipment is required, it is reasonably priced.

◆ ISDN is an intermediate alternative to modems and Frame Relay. It is reasonably priced and gives several times the bandwidth of a modem. However, it is not universally available.

◆ You must obtain an Internet Service Provider (ISP) to serve as your gateway to the Internet. Your PPP or SLIP packets ultimately get routed through your ISP.

◆ Your ISP provides you with the information you need to connect your system. Most often, it is just a phone number, account name, and password if dynamic IP addresses are used. Otherwise, ISPs give you your IP address and theirs.

◆ The Linux *pppd* daemon is used to encapsulate your network's IP packets and send them across the serial connection to your ISP, where they are decoded.

◆ Several methods are used to establish a PPP connection via the *pppd* daemon. *Dip*, *chat*, *diald*, the *Control Panel*, and even *pppd* can be used to dial up your ISP, negotiate the PPP connection, and set your local routing tables.

◆ *Dip* is a utility that you can run interactively or from a script to establish PPP and SLIP connections.

◆ To show you in detail how a PPP connection is established, I provide several examples using interactive *dip*. Both static and dynamic IP addressing are used.

◆ The *diald* daemon, which you install in this chapter, monitors your network traffic and automatically establishes a PPP connection when necessary. It makes your network look like it is continuously connected to the Internet. It does take a few seconds, however, to make the connection after outgoing packets are detected.

◆ Examples are given to show how to make *diald* connections using both static and dynamic IP addresses. I show you how to enter the *diald* commands interactively, and how to put them into a script file, which you can add to the *rc.local* script. This script is run at boot time so *diald* is loaded at that time.

◆ The Red Hat *Network Configurator* is used to establish a PPP connection. It is a GUI and simplifies making a connection by using point-and-click methods. It is a good one-time connection alternative to both *dip* and *pppd*.

◆ Several methods (programs) exist to help you monitor your PPP and entire network connection. The programs *ifconfig, route,* and *netstat* are used to configure and monitor your network. The *statnet* program provides a concise method for continuously monitoring your important network statistics.

◆ The concept of firewalls is introduced. After password protection, firewalls are the most important component in your security system. They allow and prevent access to your LAN from the Internet.

◆ Two types of firewalls exist: application-based and packet filtering. Both provide security from different viewpoints. Application-based firewalls generally substitute one server program – with added security features – for another. Packet-filtering firewalls check each packet passing through the Internet interface and either stop or allow them through based on information contained in the packet checked against rules you set up.

◆ The IP firewall comes as a package with the Red Hat distribution. It is a packet-filtering firewall. It provides for the accounting of packets and masquerading of IP addresses in addition to the filtering functions. Masquerading is an important tool for getting your LAN on the Internet if you use public IP addresses (see Chapter 1). I discuss Masquerading in more detail in Chapter 10.

◆ The policy you set for your firewall is as important as the software itself. Obviously, the best firewall in the world is useless if you set up poor policy. Because the firewall topic is introductory at this point, it is briefly discussed.

◆ A relatively simple firewall is configured to get you started. Limited use of the Internet from the outside in is assumed to keep things simple. The example allows you to use the Internet in the most common ways. Directions are given on how to automate its start at boot time.

◆ The assumptions made in constructing the firewall are used to introduce the concept of paying your ISP to provide a certain amount of security. They are a firewall themselves because packets have to travel through them and get explicitly routed to you. If you have them provide your WWW or anonymous FTP, or e-mail services then not only do you not have to use the bandwidth of your PPP connection for it but the resulting activity takes place on their computers and network. The added bonus is that you do not have to administer the daemons and stuff.

Part IV

Running a Real-World Business

IN THIS PART:

Part IV discusses the real-world issues you must deal with when administering a network. These chapters describe how to set up many of the components necessary for a safe, efficient, well-run network. Configuring a firewall is discussed in some detail.

Chapter 9

Network and Computer Administration

IN THIS CHAPTER

- ◆ Creating and interpreting administration policy
- ◆ Creating and maintaining backups
- ◆ Creating and maintaining security
- ◆ Creating Internet firewalls
- ◆ Using *cron* to automate repetitive jobs
- ◆ Using shell scripts
- ◆ Starting and stopping a Linux system
- ◆ Maintaining your computer network system
- ◆ Recovering from disaster

As you know, much of this book focuses on systems administration. In previous chapters, I give you the basics for constructing a network and configuring both your clients and servers. Along the way, I touch on the subject of systems administration – you can apply many of my examples and descriptions to that job.

Because an entire book is required to discuss administration in any detail, this chapter is intended only as an introduction to the subject. I give you enough information to get started, and I discuss some of the more important aspects of systems administration in greater depth, to ensure that you have a good starting point for handling your systems administration responsibilities.

The job of an administrator is to serve the needs of the computer user. To this end, an administrator must address human as well as technical concerns. From my experience, the technical side of systems administration is the simpler of the two. In other words, systems administration is as much an art as a science.

Every administration job is completely different in its details. I can't possibly quantify the sum of the tasks, equipment, and people involved. However, most organizations – from a home office to a Fortune 500 corporation – share essentially the same set of core functions. My intention in this chapter is to describe the major

functions that you have to do anywhere. The human factor is, of course, more difficult to quantify and describe, but I offer comments and advice wherever I can.

Systems administration is a complex, amorphous subject. No two administrative
jobs are the same because the sum of all the parts is always unique. Throughout
this chapter, and the rest of the book, I try to provide you with the tools you need
for devising solutions to the unique problems that you will encounter in your role
as a systems administrator.

Administration Essentials

In some cases, systems administration is a purely part-time job; in other cases, you
may inherit (or create) the administrator's job as a system grows, or it may be a
specific, full-time job to begin with. In any case, the essential functions are the
same, but they vary in terms of size, interaction, and complexity. The following list
summarizes those functions:

◆ **Creating, modifying, interpreting, and enforcing policy.** This is the most
   important philosophical aspect of any administrator's job. All the other
   functional duties stem from it. The administrative policies you create and
   inherit will rule your life. They can be in the form of company law or they
   may be completely verbal. Even if you do not set the rules, your
   interpretation of them will be the effective law. Because the nature of
   administration is managing chaos, your policy road map is essential for
   keeping everything under control.

◆ **Creating and maintaining backups.** This is the most important single
   function of a systems administrator. You need secure, reliable backups of
   your servers and possibly the client computers.

◆ **Creating and maintaining an effective security system.** Security is both
   a technical and a human concern. Technically, it spans everything from
   individual computer configurations to your firewall design. The human
   side encompasses everything from how you set up and enforce password
   policy to people's feelings.

◆ **Managing users.** It is your responsibility to add, remove, and modify user
   accounts.

◆ **Maintaining file systems.** It is your responsibility to add, remove, and
   modify the various file systems on your servers. (I introduce the topic of
   file systems in Chapter 3.)

◆ **Modifying and maintaining hardware.** Unless you work for a large
   company (and even if you do not, in some cases), you are responsible for
   the installation and maintenance of computers and peripherals.

- ◆ **Modifying and maintaining software.** The need here is obvious. Computers must have their operating systems installed and upgraded. Applications such as databases, word processors, and spreadsheets need to be installed and maintained, too.

- ◆ **Troubleshooting.** This is an everyday task. When something goes wrong — big or small, real or imagined — you get called. This responsibility generally requires that you carry a pager.

- ◆ **Reliability.** This is your ultimate goal. Ensuring reliability is both a specific job and a general goal. It is achieved by properly doing your job as outlined in the preceding items as well as planning and designing for the unforeseen problems as best you can.

- ◆ **Crawling under floors and through ceilings, carrying a pager, answering the phone, and taking out the trash.**

As you can see, the administrator's responsibilities are wide-ranging and complex. The following sections describe these responsibilities in more detail.

Creating and Interpreting Policy

Any computer system and network needs a road map to operate reliably and efficiently. This book aims at giving you the tools for operating a network. I introduce those tools in a systematic way, to bring you to the point where you have an overall understanding of a complete, albeit simple, system. Now that you know where the roads and the towns are, you need to connect them together so you can use them effectively.

The policy that you set and the policy that you enforce often are two different things. You may determine certain things yourself — for example, the backup policy that I discuss a bit later in this chapter. Outside of your own business or home office, many administration and security issues generally cross into policy areas that management determines. You may collaborate in the establishment of these policies, or they may be completely out of your hands. It's up to you to implement such policies as best you can and be willing to draw a line if a policy becomes impossible to enforce.

If you have a personal home network, you need to know which tasks you need to perform to keep your system up and running. You do not need to write a manual of rules you want to follow, but you do need to perform certain tasks at specific times. You certainly need to back up your valuable data regularly and in a way that you know how to recover lost files. It is okay to keep such tasks on an informal level; however, you may find it helpful to write down the instructions for performing more complex processes. You may need only to write down the exact instruction that you use to create a backup, but that can be invaluable information and it doesn't take much effort to write it down on a slip of paper and stick it in the cassette case.

If you manage a small to medium network for someone else, you must systematically write things down. At this level, the line between policy and pure instructions begins to blur. A page or two of backup instructions can serve as both the policy and the instructions. The instructions may say first do step A, then B, and finally C, three times a week. That is your company's policy.

For larger operations, you most likely inherit policy. The exception is when a takeover or a major reorganization occurs. In most cases, you still have a great deal of power in the way you interpret and implement the rules given to you. Once again, I measure the importance of the job by the number of people that ultimately depend on you.

Another purpose of writing policy down is to make yourself dispensable. Your goal should be to enable someone else – with some computer experience – to come in cold and perform the basic system administration. The more functions I systematize, the better I am doing my job.

Part of your general policy should be to document both your everyday tasks and your occasional ones. The more you write down and diagram procedures, the easier your job will be and the easier it will be for your successor. Also, documenting a process can lead to that process becoming policy. If you do a job a certain way and you can document it in a reasonable way, it's likely to become the way it is done all the time. By writing it down, you can make it the official method by default.

 Web browsers can make the job of documentation easier. By placing all or most of your documents on an internal (intranet) Web page, you make them easy to find and view. If you make part of the documentation into an FAQ, you may even reduce your workload after you educate your users to access it for everyday problems. If you possess an artistic streak, you can actually relieve the drudgery of documentation by using HTML as your brush and palate.

The rest of this chapter discusses the distinct functions of systems administration. Each function is governed by a policy, written or not. My discussion is as much a matter of policy as a description of how to perform the administrative functions.

Creating and Maintaining Backups

Your backup policy determines your single most important job as an administrator. With backups, you can recover from any catastrophe. At one end of a catastrophe (even if all your computers burn to the ground or a virus destroys your data), if you have reliable, complete backups, you can recreate your system. At the other, less ominous, end of a catastrophe, backups enable you to recover individual files or groups of files that have been accidentally erased. Therefore, you must have a system to make backups and follow it religiously.

You need secure, reliable, *multiple* backups of your servers. Do not trust just one or even two backups. Whatever your method, make multiple, overlapping backups, and keep at least one, but preferably two, backups offsite. By *offsite*, I mean in another building separate from your normal working location. At one job, I took backups home because we only had one office. In another job, I took the backups to another company building. Having offsite backups helps you to sleep well at night.

You should periodically test your backup system. By practicing restoring data, you keep yourself confident and also test for data integrity. Periodic testing should be an essential part of your backup policy.

You can use various utilities to create backups. The standard Linux (and UNIX) methods are the *tar, cpio* – and now – *dump* utilities:

◆ The *tar* utility creates an archive file and has the advantage of being nearly universal. The GNU *tar* now enables you to specify compression as an option. It also provides for making incremental backups (an incremental backup includes whatever files have been created or modified since a full backup was last made; a full backup includes every file in the directory or file system that is specified to be backed up). In my opinion, *tar* is the easiest system to use.

◆ The *cpio* utility also creates an archive file, with fewer restrictions in terms of the depth of a directory structure that it can traverse and also the length of a filename it can handle. It also handles localized tape errors by skipping over them.

◆ The *dump* program is oriented toward backing up entire file systems and then keeping track of changes in order to provide incremental backups. It also provides a hierarchy of incremental backup levels (ten levels) that gives you a convenient system to use on weekly and monthly intervals.

USING THE TAR UTILITY

The *tar* utility archives directories and files to a *tar file*. A *tar* file can be a tape, a pipe, or a normal file. The first parameter specifies one of the primary functions – such as *create, list,* or *extract* – for *tar* to perform. The next parameters are optional modifications to the primary function. The last parameters are files or directories to archive (note that when a directory is given, it and all its subdirectories will be archived).

It is a simple program to use. For example, to create a *tar* file of the example user *maggie* that you created in Chapter 6, enter the following command:

```
/bin/tar cf maggie.tar /home/maggie
```

TIP

You can also use a *hyphen* (-) to specify command-line parameters. For example, you would run the previous command as follows:

```
tar -cf maggie.tar /home/tar.
```

All the files in the */home/maggie* directory are stored in the *tar* file *maggie.tar*. The *f* parameter specifies that the next argument will be the *tar* file. The following command lists the contents of *maggie.tar*:

```
tar tf maggie.tar
```

Listing 9-1 shows the listing of *maggie.tar*.

Listing 9-1: The tar-formatted file maggie.tar

```
./
.Xclients
.Xdefaults
.bash_logout
.bash_profile
.bashrc
.xsession
.bash_history
```

TIP

You can get more information displayed by using the verbose — *v* — parameter. If you use it while creating or extracting an archive, each file is displayed as it is copied or extracted. Using it with the listing option *t* produces a listing like the one you would get with the long format of the *ls* command (*ls -l*).

To restore those files, use the extract option as shown in the following command:

```
tar xf maggie.tar
```

The extracted files are placed in your current directory unless you specify that *tar* use the absolute path – *P* – option, in which case *tar* attempts to restore the files to their original location at */home/maggie*.

The *tar* version that comes on your CD-ROM (Red Hat 5.0) is smart enough not to include the archive in itself. That is, if you are copying to a *tar* file that happens to be in the directory from which you are saving, the *tar* file that you are creating will not be included in the *tar* file. However, older versions will happily include themselves in the *tar* file they create.

The more recent versions of GNU *tar*, such as the one that comes on this book's CD-ROM, now have *gzip* compression included as an option. The previous examples for creating and extracting *tar* files can include compression by using the *gzip − z −* option, as shown in the following commands:

```
tar czf maggie.tgz /home/maggie
tar xzf maggie.tgz /home/maggie
```

Note that I use the *tgz* filename suffix to indicate that the file is a *gzipped tar* file.

Table 9-1 lists the primary *tar* function parameters: *A, c, d, r, t, u,* and *x*. In addition to creating, listing, and extracting to/from *tar* file archives as demonstrated in the previous examples, they also enable you to modify and delete files from *tar* files. Note that you generally have several different ways to specify the same function. For instance, to create a *tar* archive, you can use either the -*c* or --*create* parameter.

Note: Tar cannot archive special files such as those found in the */dev* directory.

TABLE 9-1 **THE TAR UTILITY PRIMARY FUNCTION PARAMETERS**

Parameter	Description
-A, --catenate, --concatenate	Append a *tar* archive file to the end of another *tar* archive.
-c, --create	Create a new *tar* archive.
-d, --diff, --compare	Determine the differences between a *tar* archive and a file system. This parameter makes the verification of a *tar* archive possible.
--delete	Delete files from an archive. Do not use with magnetic tapes!
-r, --append	Append files to the end of a *tar* archive.

continued

TABLE **9-1** **THE TAR UTILITY PRIMARY FUNCTION PARAMETERS** *(Continued)*

Parameter	Description
-t, --list	List a *tar* archive. You can list an archive while it is created or you can list one that already exists.
-u, --update	Append files to a *tar* archive that are newer than the ones it already contains.
-x, --extract, --get	Extract (restore) files from a *tar* archive.

Table 9-2 lists the parameters that modify the actions of the *tar* commands. If you have used *tar* in the past, note that this version can perform incremental backups as well as compress the data. Note that you generally have several different ways to specify the same function. For instance, to specify the filename of a *tar* archive, you can use either the *-f* or *--file* parameter.

TABLE **9-2** **THE TAR UTILITY OPTIONAL PARAMETERS**

Parameter	Description
--atime-preserve	Retain the access times of the *tar* files.
-b, --block-size *N*	Set the block size to *N* times 512 bytes. This setting is important for *tar* archives stored to tapes, which sometimes require nondefault values. The default is 20.
-B, --read-full-blocks	Reset the blocks size during *tar* reads. This is for reading BSD 4.2 UNIX pipes.
-C, --directory *DIR*	Change the *tar* default directory to *DIR*. This is useful for controlling what directories *tar* copies or extracts to. For instance, you may want to archive only two directories in a highly complex, multibranched structure, so you would have *tar* change to those two directories by specifying the *-C* parameter.

continued

Parameter	Description
`--checkpoint`	Display the directory names during an archive read. This is good for a progress monitor or verifying that your *tar* command is doing what you intend it to do.
`-f, --file [HOSTNAME:]F`	Specify a file, device, or pipe to send output to. The default is */dev/rmt0*, which is usually a tape drive.
`--force-local`	The *tar* archive file is local.
`-F, --info-script F, --new-volume-script F`	Run the script F at the end of each tape. Implies the *-M* parameter.
`-G, --incremental`	Create, list, or extract an old GNU format incremental archive.
`-g, --listed-incremental F`	Create, list, or extract a new GNU format incremental archive.
`-h, --dereference`	Use the actual files that symbolic links point to instead of the links themselves in the *tar* archive.
`-i, --ignore-zeros`	Ignore blocks of zeros, which usually mean an EOF mark, in an archive.
`--ignore-failed-read`	Do not indicate an error (a nonzero exit status) when unreadable files are encountered.
`-k, --keep-old-files`	Do not overwrite existing files in an archive.
`-K, --starting-file F`	Begin with file *F* when encountered in an archive.
`-l, --one-file-system`	Stay within the local file system when creating an archive. Use this parameter when you do not want to include a mounted file system in your archive. For instance, if your CD-ROM drive is mounted as */mnt*, this parameter prevents its contents from being archived — a good idea because they are read-only.

continued

TABLE 9-2 THE TAR UTILITY OPTIONAL PARAMETERS *(Continued)*

Parameter	Description
-L, --tape-length *N*	Specify the length of a tape in kilobytes. You are prompted to insert another tape when *tar* fills up the current one.
-m, --modification-time	Do not restore the file modification time when extracted.
-M, --multi-volume	Specify a multivolume (that is, tapes) archive for *create*, *list*, and *extract* commands.
-N, --after-date *DATE*, --newer *DATE*	Store files newer than *DATE*. Used for incremental backups.
-o, --old-archive, --portability	Use the old V7 *tar* format archive instead of the current ANSI format.
-O, --to-stdout	Send extracted files to the standard output.
-p, --same-permissions, --preserve-permissions	Restore extracted file protection bits.
-P, --absolute-paths	Use absolute file path names — save the leading / in the path name.
--preserve	Equivalent to combining the *-p* and *-s* parameters.
-R, --record-number	Display the record number — the *tar* internal format — for each message displayed.
--remove-files	Delete the original files after adding them to a *tar* archive.
-s, --same-order, --preserve-order	List of names to extract is sorted to match archive.
--same-owner	Save the file ownership during extraction.
-S, --sparse	Save space in the *tar* archive.
-T, --files-from *F*	Contain filenames to be extracted in the file *F*.

continued

Parameter	Description
`--null`	Used in conjunction with -T to read null-terminated names from file *F.* Also disable the -*C* option.
`--totals`	Display the number of bytes written to a newly created archive.
`-v, --verbose`	Display what's happening.
`-V, --label` *NAME*	Create an archive with volume name *NAME.*
`--version`	Display the GNU *tar* version number.
`-w, --interactive,` `--confirmation`	You are prompted for each *tar* action.
`-W, --verify`	Go back and verify the actual file against what was just written to an archive for the file.
`--exclude` *FILE*	Do not include the *FILE* in an archive.
`-X, --exclude-from` *FILE*	Do not include the files contained in the file *FILE* in an archive.
`-Z, --compress, --uncompress`	Use the older, non-GNU compression or decompression utilities — *compress* and *uncompress* — to create or extract an archive. This is equivalent to the piped commands: `tar cf - filenames | compress > archive.`
`-z, --gzip, --ungzip`	Use the GNU file compression or decompression utilities — *gzip* and *ungzip* — to create or extract an archive. This is equivalent to the piped commands: `tar cf - files | gzip > archive.`
`--use-compress-program` *PROG*	Use another compression program *PROG* (this program must accept the -*d* parameter).
`--block-compress`	Do not allow the output of compression for tapes.
`-[0-7][lmh]`	Specify drive and density.

Throughout this book, I use the *gzip* program to compress a file or files and pipe its output to *tar*. This is the traditional combination, but is no longer necessary with the modern *tar* with the *gzip* and *ungzip* options. In some circumstances, I have continued to use the old combination because it shows the use and operation of pipes as well as the *gzip* and *tar* programs.

USING THE CPIO UTILITY

The GNU *cpio* utility creates *cpio* archives to store files in. It is more complex to use than *tar* because you must feed it the files that you want it to process. That extra step, however, makes it extremely flexible for picking files and directories to archive. Because it archives whatever filenames you pass to it, you can archive complex directory trees.

Creating a *cpio* archive is referred to as *copy-out* mode and is specified by using the *-o* parameter. Here's a simple *cpio* process to archive the files in the */home/maggie* directory to a *cpio* archive called *maggie.cpio*:

```
find /home/maggie | cpio -o > maggie.cpio
```

Here, the *find* command simply sends the name and path of each file in the */home/maggie* directory. (In this case, */home/maggie* does not have any subdirectories so you could simply use the *ls* command to send the filenames to *cpio* and it would work the same as it does in this example.) *Cpio* converts the contents of each file into its own format. If you do not redirect it to a file or device, the contents of each file are sent to standard output and you'll see them flash by.

Extracting files from a *cpio* archive is referred to as *copy-in* mode and is specified by using the *-i* parameter. If you want to extract the files, omit the *t* option and *cpio* attempts to recreate the files in the current directory. Enter the following command to recreate the files relative to the current directory:

```
cat maggie.cpio | cpio -i
```

You can take advantage of bash's capability to redirect standard input and output by substituting the following single command, which is more elegant and efficient than the previous example:

```
cpio -i < maggie.cpio
```

In this case, *cpio* balks because the files it has archived already exist in the current directory. If you redirect its output to another directory, it will happily create them at that location. The following command redirects them to the */tmp* directory (Red Hat removes all files from */tmp* that are older than ten days):

```
cat maggie.cpio | (cd /tmp ; cpio -i )
```

You can list the files in a *cpio* archive by using the following command:

```
cat maggie.cpio | cpio -it
```

Unlike the *tar* utility, *cpio* requires that you prefix all option parameters with a hyphen (-). For example, the previous command does not work if you enter it as **cpio it**.

Cpio also has the capability to copy files from one directory tree to another. This capability – called *copy-pass* – combines the function of copy-in and copy-out but does not create a *cpio* archive. The following command copies the files in */home/maggie* to */tmp*:

```
find /home/maggie -print | cpio -p /tmp
```

The *cpio* operating modes are *copy-in*, *copy-out*, and *copy-pass*. They enable you to *create*, *delete*, *list*, or *modify cpio* archives. The archives can be stored to a file, a pipe, or a device (such as a tape). Please refer to the *cpio* man page for more details.

USING THE TAR UTILITY FOR LOW-VOLUME BACKUPS

If you have a simple network – such as a home office or small business – then you may not even need a dedicated backup system. In my own home network, I simply do not have much data to back up. I have several megabytes of word processing files, some spreadsheets, a few HTML files, and my Linux configuration files. Because I store all my data files on my Linux server, my Microsoft Windows workstations have zero data – aside from their own configuration files and application software – stored on them. I keep a backup of some of their configuration files and application software on the Linux server. I use the *tar* application to back up the critical directories, and the *gzip* application to compress the *tar* file and then back up the resulting file to floppies and also my ISP account. This system is neither elegant nor sophisticated, but it is – most importantly – effective and cheap.

The following example illustrates the simple command I use to make my personal backups:

```
/bin/tar cvf - /etc /home | gzip > /tmp/backup.tar
copy to floppy
copy to ISP
```

> **TIP** The Linux *tar* command has the option to compress the data without piping it explicitly to the *gzip* or compress utilities. The *-z* or *-gzip* parameters invoke the *gzip* utility; the *-gunzip* calls the *gunzip*; and the *-Z* or *-compress* invokes the *compress* command, while *-uncompress* calls for the uncompress option.

Making backups this way is simple and effective. To save time and limited bandwidth, I also make incremental backups. During critical periods such as while writing this book, I make frequent full backups to a floppy disk during the day and then an incremental backup to my ISP account at the end of the day. Here's the command I use for the incremental backup that uses the newer − *-N date* − feature of *tar* where the date is a simple four-digit month–day format. Note that in this case I use the compression − *z* − feature of *tar* in place of placing *gzip* in the pipeline:

```
tar -czvf /tmp/incr.tgz -N 0128 /etc /home
```

For my personal network, I use this simple system, which simply does not require a log. At this level, the work involved in keeping a log would probably reduce the number of times a day I back up my work. Now if I was administering a small system for someone else, I would certainly keep a log. When you do work for someone else, you need to be as systematic as possible so that more records exist about the system than just what is in your own memory.

> **TIP** Actually, I do keep a minimal log. On a slip of paper that I keep with the floppy disk, I write a quick date and time at the end of the day when I copy my files to it. Of course, I have been making copies to it all day but the end of day notation helps me to remember when my last backup was if I leave my work for a day or two.

PERFORMING INTERMEDIATE-VOLUME BACKUPS

For larger networks – including most small- to medium-sized businesses, or a home office where you happen to use lots of data – a more substantial backup system is necessary. If you need to store several gigabytes (GB) of data then you need some sort of backup mechanism. You can choose from several technologies: PC tape drives, Digital Audio Tape (DAT), Digital Linear Tape (DLT), writeable CD-ROMs, and additional, removable hard disks. Tapes are preferred because of their durability, compact size, and ubiquitous nature. I recommend making several overlapping full backups every month. I also recommend that you create long-term archive tapes of particularly important information. You could use a portable hard disk, but it would be too expensive and cumbersome to carry around. Tapes are the way to go.

Although I think PC tape drives and DAT drives are the best general choices, the others can fit specialized needs. For instance, a writeable CD-ROM is reliable, reasonably inexpensive, but fairly slow, and only has about 650MB of storage. I recommend that you invest in an SCSI interface and a 4mm DAT drive. They are fast and reliable, they can store between 2 and 4GB of data, and the tapes are inexpensive. In my opinion, it is important to keep at least a dozen tapes in order to maintain multiple overlapping backups, spread wear and tear, and keep several tapes offsite. Note that it is also important to follow the manufacturer's tape cleaning guidelines, because DAT drive mechanisms are complex and more prone to failure if not cleaned properly.

It is also possible to use the inexpensive PC Travan tape drives. Drivers are available for drives such as Iomega Ditto Tape Insider 3200 or the Colorado drives. They use either inexpensive proprietary interfaces or the parallel port. The high-end drives can back up gigabytes of data at reasonable speeds. However, the tapes themselves are expensive at around $35 apiece. At that price, they have never been attractive to me because of my desire to keep a dozen or more tapes.

It is also important to keep detailed and accurate logs. Figure 9-1 outlines the format for such a log.

If you have large backups, you should consider making incremental backups at frequent intervals. Remember that if you need to restore a file or files from an incremental backup, you will need to start the restoration from the most recent full backup and supply the incremental backup or backups in chronological order.

```
Date __ / __ / __

Computer name _____     IP address ___ . ___ . ___ . ___
Location _____

Backup device _____     Capacity

Date      Directories          Command                              Notes
  /  /  _____  _____          _____
  /  /  _____  _____          _____
  /  /  _____  _____          _____
  /  /  _____  _____          _____
  /  /  _____  _____          _____
  /  /  _____  _____          _____
  /  /  _____  _____          _____
  /  /  _____  _____          _____
  /  /  _____  _____          _____
  /  /  _____  _____          _____
  /  /  _____  _____          _____
  /  /  _____  _____          _____
  /  /  _____  _____          _____
  /  /  _____  _____          _____
  /  /  _____  _____          _____
  /  /  _____  _____          _____
  /  /  _____  _____          _____
  /  /  _____  _____          _____
  /  /  _____  _____          _____
  /  /  _____  _____          _____
```

Figure 9-1: Your tape backup log

HANDLING HIGH-VOLUME BACKUPS

When you get to the point of backing up many gigabytes of data, you need to con-sult the big-time vendors or consultants. You can expect that your organizational problems will skyrocket. Just consider the difficulty of keeping track of numerous 4mm DAT tapes and you will realize that the possibility for making errors is signif-icant. Keeping the tape sequence in order while doing the backups, correctly label-ing the tapes, and storing them over time all require unerring consistency. Making just one mistake at the wrong time could jeopardize your entire operation.

What is the solution? The solution is a tape or optical disk *juke box*. They are expensive and difficult to set up, but in the long-term they pay for themselves. Add commercial software that further automates the process and you end up needing to do nothing other than monitor the process and occasionally add and remove tapes.

If you must use many tapes, your top priorities are systematically labeling your tapes and keeping precise logbooks. Your job is further complicated if others per-form the backups. In either case, but especially the latter, you should systematically conduct your own data integrity tests. This testing involves choosing some data to restore, finding the appropriate tape, and checking to see if the data is really there. The last thing you want to have happen is to need to restore some data and find out that it was never saved in the first place due to some foul up.

With version 5.0, Red Hat has included the BRU2000 (backup and restore) backup utility. It was created by Enhanced Software Technologies, Inc., and provides device-independent operation as well as verified backup and restore operations. I used *bru* with a Silicon Graphics workstation years ago and found it superior to *tar*. However, it is new to Linux and I have not had the time yet to investigate it.

Creating and Maintaining Security

The problem with any rating system is that you have to come up with a methodology and adhere to it. As much as I would like to have two most-important items, I can't honestly do that. Therefore, I have decided to put the subject of security second, after backups. It is a very close second. My reasoning is as follows: Security is much more complex than the issue of maintaining proper backups and therefore more prone to imperfections and breakdown over time. It is also highly dependent on the participation in and the belief of other people (it is very easy to become complacent if you do not see a direct threat and especially if you do not understand the underlying issues). As an administrator, you are at the mercy of variables over which you have less than perfect control. Therefore, any system you design will be less than perfect. Ultimately, if you have a reliable backup, you can recover from most security failures.

The caveat to that reasoning is that if your security is broken in a subtle manner, the breach may go undetected and propagate over time. If your system has been broken into by a malicious person who subtly changes or destroys your system over time, your backups may become worthless because they will eventually contain the corrupted software. If your work is compromised over time, your efforts may become worthless or worse – you may become liable in other ways. In that case, my ranking system breaks down. Perhaps it would be better not to rate things like this, so that you don't get a false sense of security. In any case, I want to at least make you aware of the potential problems and let you decide for yourself.

The difficult nature of security makes it as much a function of vigilance as of the policy itself. Security is a day-in, day-out grind that you simply have to do. An effective system makes itself appear to be unnecessary. If you lock your house every time you leave it and you never have been robbed, it may appear to be an unnecessary task. But if you start leaving your house unlocked, the one time you are broken into will focus the necessity of having to do it without fail.

Security is also part of every task you do. For instance, while I have listed backups separately, backups are actually the last bastion of your security policy because they enable you to recover from malicious activities. Security should be viewed as integral to every aspect of systems administration.

You should concentrate on several security areas:

◆ **Human Factors.** All security starts with the people who use the system. Unless you are the only user of your system, you must depend on other people to adhere to your security policy. Your users have the ability to make your system safe or not. Unfortunately, dealing with people is a lot messier than dealing with computers because people have lives and stuff like that. We all tend to lose enthusiasm for what seems like unnecessary work with time. Therefore, you must be oriented toward that messy fact. Education is an important factor in this equation. Your own attitude will affect how seriously others view the issue.

◆ **Passwords.** Your passwords are your first line of defense. They are the locks on your doors. If you do not demand good passwords and their consistent use, all your other security measures will be compromised.

◆ **Firewalls.** They are your primary defense from unauthorized Internet connections. A firewall must be transparent enough to allow effective and efficient use of the Internet but, at the same time, prevent unwanted outside access. The type and level of effectiveness depends on what you use the Internet for.

◆ **Internal Network Security.** Your network configuration and layout determine much of your security structure. If you have varying security requirements within your own organization, you can, and probably should, arrange your network topology to reflect those realities. This arrangement can divide your network into subnets to isolate the functional areas of your network, and it can specify file permissions to further divide your network.

◆ **External Network Security.** This area basically boils down to not advertising how your network is configured and what security measures you use.

◆ **Layered Security.** All the previous items should be constructed to work together. One layer should back up another and vice versa. If your firewall is breached, you should still have all your user accounts protected with effective passwords. Even if you are not sure about all your passwords, you still have your firewall. If a burglar is attempting to break in and a user happens to notice something amiss, that person recalls the security education enough to inform you about the suspicious activity. When you put all this together, it works well enough to strengthen each individual measure.

◆ **Vigilance.** You should regularly test your system. You can do this with a number of helpful software systems, such as *Satan* and *COPS*. Testing should be done regularly and with the attitude that prevention is the best policy.

ADDRESSING HUMAN FACTORS

If you have more than one person involved in your system, you have to concern yourself with managing people. Systems administrators must walk the fine line between requiring too much and too little security. If you are too harsh, your users will actively and passively find ways around your measures. On the other hand, if you are too lax, the users will not respect your system and you leave yourself open to external threats.

What is the fine line? I'll take the easy way – actually, the reasonable way – out. It depends on your situation. If you are the systems administrator for a bank, you must take more precautions than if you run a hobby shop. However, any operation must take a core group of measures, and I concentrate on those core measures here.

The most important measure you should strive for is the respect and education of your system's users. The average person respects the need for basic security measures. If the users know the basics of how passwords are used and why they are important, you can count on a higher level of consistency in their use. Otherwise, if someone doesn't understand the philosophy and implementation of their use, you can expect far more problems.

An important aspect of education should be a simple, straightforward usage policy that everyone signs in order to obtain access. You should emphasize the essential rules that are most important to your organization. Include other policy statements, but restrain yourself from cluttering this essential document. If you end up with more than one page and can't reduce it, I suggest dividing it up into two documents: one essential and the other important items.

Individual or group classes should also be considered. They are unpleasant but can greatly help in the long run. For instance, even though a new user signs the usage policy, you still do not know whether it has been fully read and understood. Even if the policy has been read and understood, a short tutorial will reinforce it and hopefully emphasize that you take security seriously. If the person has not understood it fully, such a lesson will clear things up. In the long term, an occasional refresher class or meeting can redirect people in the right direction.

The occasional person who refuses or is incapable of taking security seriously presents a difficult issue. I can't offer much advice other than to suggest that a patient, consistent, and firm direction from you may help over time. The difficult people I have run into in my career were relatively benign in that they generally refused to follow policies such as logging off when leaving the small building where we worked. It was frustrating because I didn't have the horsepower to force adherence but I accomplished it by default when I installed automatic computer locks (Linux and Windows screen locks) during operating system upgrades. Dealing with people who actively eschew security measures is a difficult issue. The best advice I can offer is to have management draw a line over which someone will actually be fired if crossed. What constitutes the line is for each organization to determine. A reasonable starting point is the malicious use of the organization's computer resources such as sending threatening e-mail. I have never had to go close to such measures, but I would be willing to do so if pushed far enough.

DEVISING A PASSWORD POLICY

A good password is a difficult animal to define. On one hand, a good password should not be crackable with a standard cracking program, which compares passwords against dictionaries and also uses heuristics to guess at them. However, if a password is too complex, it will either not be used or it will be written down and become almost as dangerous as not having a password at all.

Cracking programs work like this: The Linux password-encrypting algorithm is publicly known. So a cracker starts with an already encrypted password and works backward by encrypting words and making a comparison. If your password is *apple* and its encrypted form is *al2sdjf*, the cracking program goes to a dictionary and encrypts each word in order until it comes to *apple* and finds that its encrypted form matches the string found in the password file. At that point it has broken your password.

The idea is to find a compromise between too much simplicity and too much complexity. It should work over the long term, too. The method I prefer is to choose two short names or things and concatenate them. The idea is to design a password that is easy to remember, does not have an entry in any dictionary in the world, and is not connected to you directly. A password should adhere to the following points:

◆ It should not exist in any dictionary found in the world. An apparently obscure word is only obscure to you because you are not a computer. However, a computer essentially has instant access to — and knowledge of — any word that is in a database to which the computer has access. The same goes with any place or proper name because they may be in an encyclopedia somewhere. You should assume that if you can locate it, anyone else can, too.

Note: The use of trivial passwords is a moot point on new systems. For instance, the */usr/bin/passwd* program shipped with Red Hat uses the *Pluggable Authentication Modules* (PAM) and does not allow you to use words that can be found in a dictionary anymore. It also prevents you from using slight variations on dictionary words. Older versions do not make such checks, so beware.

◆ It should not have any direct connection to you. For obvious reasons, you should not use numbers or words that are related to your personal situation such as a date of birth or an address. Conversely, avoid using things that could be reversed – if guessed – and used against you, such as PIN numbers.

- Simple variations of the preceding items should be avoided, too. Computers – especially supercomputers – are capable of a huge number of operations per second. Therefore, programs using heuristics – rules that define methods for guessing – can perform enough permutations of things such as existing words so that variations can be discovered. For instance, if your name is Big Blue and you choose a password such as "BiBlue," a burglar knowing you can readily program a crack to start with Big Blue and variations thereof until the correct one is discovered. The lesson is do not depend on changing a word or a personal number slightly because it can be cracked. Again, the password may seem obscure to you but to a mindless computer it is no problem at all.

- On the other side of the spectrum, random strings generated by password-generating programs are difficult to remember. People tend to write down things that are difficult to remember. Things that are written down can be left laying around. Passwords that are left laying around are of no protection to you. Even if you do not leave them laying around, the fact that your shop generates random passwords is a hook for a determined burglar. If I wanted to break into a computer system and I knew that it used such passwords, I would plan on looking for such a list. A determined burglar could probably find the list one way or another. Is this a little paranoid? Yes, unless your system is valuable enough to somebody. That depends on your situation.

The solution I like avoids those pitfalls. First I'll describe the algorithm and then I'll explain it.

I choose two simple words and concatenate them. The words should be short enough so that together they do not add up to much more than eight characters. The words should not be normally used together. I use a nonalphanumeric concatenation character such as the tilde (~) character. Here's an example of such a password:

radio~road

Why did I make such a choice? I just looked out my window and saw the road in front of my place. I am also listening to the radio. Put together, they are not in any dictionary. Any cracking program will have to check nearly as many combinations as if the password was a completely random string of characters.

Note: Because only the first eight characters are significant, the effective password is as follows:

radio~ro

This password is actually better because ~*road* becomes ~*ro*, which is essentially random. Nobody knows that your concatenation character is ~, which is also good. It is not truly a random string, but a cracker program will have to attempt a large number of permutations of all the words in a dictionary. It is not perfect, but even though it is a compromise, it is a good one in my opinion.

An alternative to the preceding method is to use one of the random or pseudo-random password generators and keep generating passwords until one appears that you like. If you like it, then that implies you can remember it, too. I used this method to get such classics as *gglujoy* and *shoeboe*.

After you choose a password, you must decide how long to keep it. The extremes are changing too often or never at all. If you change it too often, your password will be difficult to remember. If you never change it, you run the risk of having your password become common knowledge. Personally, I think changing every six months to a year is best. Keeping a password longer than a year is dangerous, in my opinion, but I cannot quantify a precise time-frame other than to say that a year seems like a long time to keep the same password.

SHADOW PASSWORDS

Even with correctly conceived passwords, you are still vulnerable to attack. The fact that the encrypted (technically they are referred to as *encoded*) passwords are contained in the */etc/passwd* file makes them vulnerable to attack. That file must be world readable (recall that three sets of permissions exist for a file: *owner*, *group*, and *world*) because many application programs need to check it. If a burglar gains access to your system, files can be retrieved to another machine and cracked at leisure.

The way around this problem is to use *shadow passwords*. When used, shadow passwords store the encrypted passwords in another file – */etc/shadow* – that only the system can read. Therefore, a burglar must gain root access to your machine to access the shadow password file, which would be a superfluous act at that point. Shadow passwords add another layer of security for the burglar to break through.

You can use the RPM to install shadow passwords under Red Hat. The default *pam_pwdb.so* module can support shadow passwords. To convert your system to shadow passwords, follow these steps:

1. Log on as *root*.

2. Enter the following command to change to the */etc* directory:

   ```
   cd /etc
   ```

3. Enter the following command to convert your */etc/passwd* file to use shadow passwords:

   ```
   pwconv5
   ```

4. The encrypted passwords are now contained in the */etc/shadow* file. The original */etc/passwd* file is renamed to */etc/passwd-* and also contains the encrypted passwords. These files are only accessible by *root* and thus nobody else can attempt to crack your passwords.

The *pam_pwdb.so* module will automatically detect that you are using shadow passwords and will make all necessary changes to your system to use shadow passwords.

CHOOSING A FIREWALL

The job of a firewall is to filter communications from the Internet into and out of your internal network. Firewalls are divided into two types: filtering and proxying. I describe each type in the following sections.

FILTERING FIREWALLS

Filtering firewalls allow or deny network traffic from the Internet into a private network and vice-versa. Access is determined based on IP addresses and ports.

Filters are very effective if they do not allow much, if any, access into your internal network. This is a problem of determining whether the glass is half-full or half-empty. If you deny all incoming and outgoing packets, then of course you have a safe firewall. However, that approach defeats the purpose of a firewall so the answer lives somewhere between all and no access.

Filters are rather rigid. If you want to allow some users to externally log in to your network, for instance, then you must provide explicit rules for each user. In my opinion, this is not a bad thing. It may be somewhat inconvenient, but I believe that is a reasonable price to pay.

Conceptually, filtering firewalls are simple to configure. Rules are set for the Linux kernel itself to follow, and to allow or disallow IP packets to pass into and out of a network interface as well as from one network interface to another. This is simplicity in essence, which is good for a firewall. The fewer components, the fewer possible loopholes can exist.

In practice, however, it can become difficult to configure a filtering firewall. As your network (or networks) increase in size and become more complex, the filtering rules will necessarily grow more complicated. The filtering rules introduced in Chapter 8 were straightforward and simple because they protected only one computer. The more complete and complex network described in Chapter 10 requires more filtering rules and is considerably more convoluted. If you keep the fundamental simplicity and if you systematically add the filtering rules, you can construct very good filtering firewalls.

The underlying simplicity makes it easy to adapt to a changing security landscape. New avenues of attack occur frequently. Recently, a new type of attack has focused not on getting into private networks but on flooding their servers with so much network traffic that they are effectively halted. Without going into the details, this particular type of attack takes advantage of the fact that nobody ever considered that possibility. (This is similar to the "spoofing" attacks in which incoming packets mimic your internal addresses and are allowed in because your router is fooled into thinking they are from a trusted host. See the simple firewall in Chapter 8 for the simple rules to prevent this from occurring.) Filtering firewalls are very good at adapting to things that nobody ever thought of before because you can immediately add rules to account for the new threat or at least immediately disallow incoming traffic until the threat has been considered.

The firewall that I introduce in Chapter 8 is a filtering type. The *ipfwadm* firewall is designed to filter IP packets. It looks at the IP address and port number of each IP packet entering or leaving your connection to the Internet. The rules that you entered determine which packets are allowed to pass and which ones are not.

PROXYING FIREWALLS

A proxying firewall substitutes – that is, proxies – one network application for another. By substituting one for another, authentication and logging can be performed.

Red Hat Linux comes with a package called *tcp_wrappers*. It is a proxying firewall. This package replaces the standard network applications such as Telnet and FTP with its own. It "wraps" the request for a service in an application of its own. For instance, if you telnet from your home computer to one at work, the proxying firewall intercepts your request and substitutes its own, which might require you to pass through a random password program such as *S/Key* before allowing you in.

Proxy firewalls can be secure but you have to configure them correctly. Because they generally require several services to be accounted for they require more knowledge and practice to get right. This is not necessarily a problem but does require more care.

I personally believe that proxy firewalls offer more potential security holes because of the "we never considered that" effect. The fact that several proxy applications are used means that several points of attack exist. Proxies may not have any holes, but having more proxies means having more places to attack.

An excellent proxy firewall comes from Trusted Information Systems (TIS). They produce an application-proxying firewall called the Firewall Toolkit (*fwtk*). It can be obtained from TIS's Web page (www.tis.com) or their anonymous FTP site (ftp.tis.com) but you have to register with them first; after registering, they e-mail you the exact location from which you can download *fwtk*.

A HYBRID FIREWALL

If you just need to go out to the Internet, the firewall I describe in Chapter 8 is very good. You may want to add or modify the rules, but the basic configuration is complete. However, if you want to go both ways, it becomes more difficult. You can make rules to allow incoming traffic, but that offers a potential security hole if someone knows or obtains the addresses you allow in.

You can use a proxy firewall to allow incoming traffic. As you know, I'm not quite comfortable with that approach — please note that many reasonable administrators and security consultants disagree with me. You could combine a proxy and a filtering firewall, too. That is another reasonable configuration, in my opinion. However, that means you must learn two systems. That is entirely reasonable, too, but it takes time and means that it will be a while before you fully understand your system. It also means more work.

If your incoming connections do not require high bandwidth, I offer the alternative of a hybrid system of a filtering firewall for your outgoing network traffic and a telephone-based, dial-up system, protected by a random-generated password system, for incoming traffic. Anyone wanting to use your internal network dials into a modem or modem bank and authenticates the connection using a password-generating program or device such as *S/Key* or *SecureID*.

This method has several advantages. First, you immediately reduce the number of people who are possible intruders because your doorway is not on the Internet but via the semiprivate telephone network. One must know a phone number rather than an IP address; it is certainly possible to obtain the phone number either by random dialing or other means, but more work is certainly involved. Second, the Secure ID, and to a lesser extent *S/Key*, presents a nearly impossible hurdle for intruders. The Secure ID is a physical device that you must be in possession of to use. When you attempt to log on to a system using *SecureID*, you first enter a unique numeric ID and then the 6-digit number that the *SecureID* device regenerates every minute or so. *S/Key* is not as safe because it is a publicly available software program; so if someone knows your personal ID, it can be used against you.

Regardless of whether you use *SecureID* or *S/Key*, the idea is to separate your incoming and outgoing Internet traffic. It is perhaps a little less convenient but it is far less convenient to have your network breached. I highly recommend this method.

FIREWALL TOPOLOGY

Several firewall configurations exist. It is beyond the scope of this book to describe all the firewall topologies. The simple firewall I describe in Chapter 8 is expanded into a dedicated one in Chapter 10. That firewall includes two network adapters, stands between two separate Ethernets, and is called a *dual-homed* firewall. That configuration physically separates your Internet connection from your internal network and forces anyone wishing to break into your system to break through several layers of security before gaining access to your system.

A dedicated, dual-homed firewall is the only method I recommend if you are protecting a network of any size. (If all you have is a simple home network, the firewall I describe in Chapter 8 is adequate.) This may sound expensive but really is not. A 386 or 486 PC running Linux – with at least 8MB but preferably 16MB – is plenty fast enough to serve this purpose and only costs approximately $200. You can even purchase a video/keyboard switch so that you do not need a separate monitor or keyboard for your system. It is also quite possible to create a single Linux boot/root floppy disk with the firewall software so that you do not need a hard disk.

The one thing that you want a dedicated firewall to do is provide the maximum protection for your network. Before I approach the active filtering involved, it is important to close all the possible loopholes that you can think of. To that end, you want to eliminate all the extraneous daemons and application programs that the firewall does not need. The fewer pieces of software you have, the fewer the possible security holes you will have. You want to start with a "clean" machine.

If you can afford to do so, purchase an old PC and install Linux as I describe in previous chapters of this book. The minimum configuration I use in Chapter 1 is a good one for this purpose. (However, if you are redoing it from scratch, leave out the Samba package.) As you may recall, I recommend purchasing – or reusing – an inexpensive, older 200MB to 400MB hard disk. This, again, is a good platform for a firewall (although you should run the standard disk-checking programs to eliminate any obviously shaky disks) as you do not need a lot of space. If you want to use a more powerful machine, don't let me stop you, but the bottleneck on a firewall is going to be the Internet connection, which is generally going to be slow compared to even a 386 CPU.

INTERNAL NETWORK SECURITY

Unless you are the only user of your system, you need to consider internal security. People who work together expect fellow workers to respect their privacy, but sometimes that doesn't happen and extra measures are needed. For instance, locking a file cabinet with sensitive financial information is considered to be standard and acceptable policy. Although I discuss passwords in terms of external security, they also are a form of internal security. Passwords offer a form of internal security by protecting valid users from each other as well as nonusers. No one feels slighted by such measures because they are expected.

To provide further internal security, you may want to divide your network into subnetworks and set different file protections on different user groups to prevent casual snooping.

If you split your LAN into two or more subnets, you keep the subnets from interacting directly with each other. You may put the accounting people on one subnet and the development people on another. Each subnet can be on the same physical network or on separate ones. The idea is to place client computers along strategic divisions of your network in order to enhance security.

Using Subnetworks

Briefly, subnetworks (subnets) divide IP network address spaces into smaller groups. The smaller groups can only communicate directly with other group members. Otherwise, for one subnet to communicate with another, it must be explicitly routed.

This is accomplished via the subnet mask that you may recall configuring at the end of Chapter 1. The 32-bit IP address is split into a network address and the host address. The class C address uses the first 24-bits for the network address and the last 8 for the host address. Recall that you have used the public class C addresses 192.168.1.1–3 throughout this book. The network address is 192.168.1, and the host address has been 1, 2, and 3 (out of a total possibility of 254).

The subnet mask for a class C address is 255.255.255.0. When packets from a particular host first arrive at your network interface, their IP address is masked by the subnet mask and compared with your own network address. (The masking process is carried out by the mathematical AND process, which means that if one bit is 1 and the other bit is also a 1, the result is a 1. Otherwise, for a 1 and a 0, a 0 and a 1, or a 0 and a 0, the result is 0. You may want to think of a 1 as true and a 0 as false.) So if you have an IP address of 192.168.1.3, your network address is 192.168.1. Combine the network address with the subnet mask of 255.255.255.0 and the resulting masked network address is still 192.168.1, and any packets with a network address of 192.168.1 are accepted.

However, if you divide your LAN into two subnets, your subnet mask becomes 255.255.255.128. Only IP packets with addresses of 192.168.1.129–254 will be accepted.

Splitting your network into subnetworks can also improve performance. The network packets of one subnetwork stay on that subnetwork unless they are routed to another subnetwork. In other words, packets stay within their own segment and don't clog up other segments unnecessarily.

You can also accomplish separating client computers along natural divisions by making use of Linux groups and file permission. The division will not be as clear cut as with subnets because the client computers will be able to communicate, but the idea is the same.

Red Hat Linux creates individual groups for each user. But you can also create groups of your own determination. By editing the */etc/group* file as root, you can create any groups that you want. Individual users are provided access to a group by adding their name after the group. The */etc/group* file shown in Listing 9-2 was created after you added the user *maggie* back in Chapter 6.

Listing 9-2: The /etc/group file after the user maggie was added

```
root::0:root
bin::1:root,bin,daemon
daemon::2:root,bin,daemon
sys::3:root,bin,adm
adm::4:root,adm,daemon
tty::5:
disk::6:root
lp::7:daemon,lp
mem::8:
kmem::9:
wheel::10:root
mail::12:mail
news::13:news
uucp::14:uucp
man::15:
games::20:
gopher::30:
dip::40:
ftp::50:
nobody::99:
users::100:
floppy:x:19:
maggie:x:500:maggie
```

To add a group for the accounting department, edit the */etc/group* file. Enter the following line to give the accounting group the arbitrary group number 200:

```
account::200:maggie
```

You now have a group called *accounting* and only *maggie* has access. To add users to a group, append each user name separated by a comma. A program called *useradd* automatically performs this operation. The Control Panel also provides a *User and Group Configuration* GUI.

You can instruct Samba to limit access to shares by including the group parameter in the share. Recall from Listing 6-5 in Chapter 6 that writing to a share could be limited with the *write list* parameter. You can go further and limit all access to users in a group by devising a share as shown in Listing 9-3.

Listing 9-3: The public service from the smb.conf file

```
; A publicly accessible directory, but read only, except for people in
; the staff group
[public]
    comment = Public Stuff
    path = /home/samba
    public = yes
    writable = yes
    printable = no
    force group = accounting
;    write list = @staff
```

I replaced the `write list` with `force group`, which only allows access by users in that group — as determined by the Linux user and group information. It's that simple.

EXTERNAL SECURITY

The only advice that I can give here is to keep your doors locked and be careful about discussing details of your network to people outside your organization. Don't be paranoid (for example, "If I tell you about our firewall, I'll have to kill you"), but keep in mind that the more someone knows about the construction of your network and security, the more that information can be used against you. If someone is out to compromise your security, and you have done a good technical job of security, then the obvious way to attack is to look for ways around your system.

One job that I worked on involved work on a sensitive environmental waste site. It was informal company policy not to casually discuss our work with people unfamiliar with it. There were no explicit restrictions, but we reasonably believed that there were people who would "monkey wrench" us if they could. We simply did not want to make targets of ourselves and thus did not advertise what we were doing. I certainly did not want to make more work for myself by giving anyone a hook into our system.

LAYERING SECURITY

After you put all the separate items together to form your security system, you should view them as a whole as well as separately. You should not depend on your firewall alone, just as you should not depend on your passwords alone. One system depends on the other and vice-versa.

To this end, some useful utilities can assist you in looking for security loopholes in one system or another:

♦ **Systems Administrator's Tool for Analyzing Networks (SATAN).** This suite of programs searches the computers on your network for known security holes and misconfigured files. It is built on a Web browser platform (although it can be run as a command-line program) so you can graphically configure the way it runs and graphically view the results.

♦ **Computer Oracle and Password System (COPS).** You can find COPS on the Internet and download it to your system. This suite of individual programs systematically checks for known security holes as well as other possible problems such as the wrong file permissions on strategic files and directories.

♦ **Tripwire.** This suite of programs monitors your computer network and computers for possible intrusions by checking such things as file size and date against known good values.

In the following sections, I provide brief descriptions of these programs. I use SATAN and Tripwire in the network example in Chapter 11.

SATAN

SATAN got a lot of hype when it was first introduced several years ago. This was more from its name than anything else, of course. The media at first presented it as the silver bullet of network security; this was understandable in view of the hype about viruses and spoofing-spies. Later, when the first version of SATAN had a security hole of its own, it got a lot of negative hype.

Well, the hole was plugged a long time ago and the hype has passed, too. What is left is a good tool for the cautious administrator. SATAN is a suite of programs that check mundane things such as file permissions and user accounts without passwords. Systems such as COPS have done that same task in much the same way. But SATAN uses your Internet browser as its GUI, and it also can be configured to check an entire network.

SATAN is a good tool for systematically checking your network. Instead of manually performing many tasks on many machines, I can tell it to do so automatically.

COPS

COPS is an older system than SATAN. It is also based on the idea of searching for known problems and security holes. It also runs the password cracker program. It does not have the nice bells and whistles that SATAN has. In addition, it cannot be run to check entire networks, which is the real disadvantage in today's world.

I do not use it much any more because it does not have network capability and SATAN performs the same job as COPS. It is still useful, however, to provide a slightly different check from that of SATAN. Because it is different, COPS may find a problem that SATAN does not.

TRIPWIRE

Tripwire is a system that detects changes in files. The changes can be in the form of an added virus or a "back door." A clever vandal can easily hide such changes from casual checks such as file size and creation time.

Tripwire is much more difficult to fool. If you run Tripwire on your important system files when you first install them, you can periodically check your current files against the originals. Not only can you detect maliciously changed files but, if you wish, you also can substitute your own Trojan Horses and monitor the vandals.

Tripwire monitors the changes made to file permissions, modification times, and their inodes. It works on directories as well as individual files.

Maintaining Your System

The more you plan ahead and maintain your system, the fewer problems you'll have in the long term. Maintenance requires you to look at both hardware and software. It requires you to know what is on your system and where it is located. This may sound trivial, but over time a computer network is like any living thing and changes in both subtle and not so subtle ways. Especially as a network grows, it is very easy to forget where software applications and equipment are located. You can also easily forget when it is time to do such tasks as clean tape drives.

The solution is to divide your system into functional areas such as hardware and software. Within these divisions you can keep lists and logs that will help you keep your computer network running smoothly and reliably. The following list shows how I like to divide a system:

- ◆ **Vigilance.** You must perform boring tasks reliably and consistently.

- ◆ **Network.** You should view your network separately from the individual machines. Computers and devices will be added to and deleted from your network, and you need to know what and where they are.

- ◆ **User accounts.** Users will be added to and deleted from both your server(s) and the client machines. You need to know who is on your system.

- ◆ **Hardware.** Computers and other devices will be added to and deleted from your system. Subcomponents will be added to and deleted from individual computers and devices. You must know what you have and where everything is.

- ◆ **Software.** System and application software will be added to and deleted from your system. You need to know what you have and where it is located. This is especially important for keeping track of software licenses because the lack of a license can have severe legal ramifications.

MAINTAINING VIGILANCE
(PERFORMING MUNDANE TASKS RELIABLY)

Part of your job as an administrator is to do boring jobs consistently and reliably. This means checking such things as the log of Super User (su) logins – users changing into root – and your firewall logs on a daily basis, including weekends. Backups also come under this heading.

The hardest part of doing something for what seems like the millionth time is when nothing ever happens. But something may happen on the one-million-and-first time, and you want to know when it does.

The best advice I can give is to just do it. It becomes habit after a time and is worth it in the long run. Plus, when something does happen, it can become very interesting and challenging.

It also helps to have a small notebook with lists of tasks and logs of those tasks. Lists of daily, weekly, and monthly tasks should be included.

The following list offers examples of tasks that recur on a daily basis, showing the time, the job, and a description of each task:

- **08:00.** `tail -100 /usr/adm/sulog`. Check root logins for possible security violations.

- **08:00.** `tail -100 /usr/adm/syslog |more`. Check system log for problems.

- **08:00.** `tail -100 /usr/adm/messages |more`. Check system messages for problems.

- **08:00.** `mail root`. Check root's mail for Tripwire (file integrity) early morning check.

- **04:00.** `mail root`. Check root's mail for general messages.

It is impossible to account for every, or even most, of the tasks that occur on a daily basis but the idea is to account for as many as you can.

The following list shows sample tasks that may occur on a weekly basis:

- **Monday:** *mail root.* Check root mail for status of full system backup (Monday, 4 am).

- **Monday:** *offsite backup.* Take last week's system backups to another location for safety.

- **Tuesday:** *job 1.* Do company's job number 1 (that is, pull point-of-sales data from remote stores).

- **Friday:** *Tripwire check.* Check Tripwire's database against original stored on floppy.

Notice how tasks are listed in a more general fashion – no explicit command to run. This layout is because not every recurrent job is exactly defined; many are amorphous in nature.

Finally, the following list shows examples of jobs that occur on a monthly basis:

◆ **1st of the month:** *Tripwire.* Manually check Tripwire database against read-only, offsite copy.

◆ **1st of the month:** *offsite backups.* Take older tapes to offsite storage location and return current offsite backups for recycling.

◆ **15th of the month:** *offsite backups.* Take older tapes to offsite storage location and return current offsite backups for recycling.

If you keep accurate logs of all such tasks, you will have little doubt about whether you're doing your job right.

MAINTAINING YOUR NETWORK

Maintaining the network is another amorphous job. You need to know both the physical and logical configuration of the network topology. You need to fix and replace broken cables, network adapters, and computers. Maintaining the network also involves adding and deleting computers and other devices – such as network printers – from the network.

It is a good idea, if not essential, to keep both a tabular list and a representative graphical diagram of your network. If you have that information, you do not have to guess at what devices are where in the network. A simple diagram showing the layout of the network can also be helpful in understanding how your system is constructed, and the tabular list provides a good equipment and user reference.

A list of network devices is also useful. If your network has more than two or three devices, such an inventory system will help you in the long run. Table 9-3 shows the layout for a simple inventory system. I recommend that you keep the number of fields to a minimum so that each device needs only one line. You can use the computer name or IP address to peg each device to a more complete inventory (see the example given in Figure 9-3, in the "Maintaining Hardware" section later in this chapter).

TABLE 9-3 THE NETWORK INVENTORY

Number	Computer Name	IP Address	User Name	Description
1	Bart	192.168.1.254	System	Linux server
2	Maggie	192.168.1.2	Maggie	Windows 95 client

The idea is to have a complete overview of your network. As time passes and your system changes, the network inventory will help you remember how your system is constructed. Having that information will save you time in the long run.

MAINTAINING USER ACCOUNTS

The mechanics of maintaining user accounts are straightforward, especially if you use the *useradd* script or the Control Panel GUI, which I describe in previous chapters. However, other concerns exist that you should carefully consider.

First, if you have more than a few users, you need a system for keeping track of them. My personal preference is a simple paper and spreadsheet system. You give a new user, or one asking for modification, a simple application form such as the example in Figure 9-2. You then enter that information in a spreadsheet or a database. This simple system should keep confusion to a minimum while not presenting any big hurdles to obtaining an account. You may even add a disclaimer or policy statement on the application.

Dog House Computers, Inc.
34 Barkers Lane,
Albuquerque, NM 87110

Last name _____ First name _____ M.I. __
Location _____
City _____ State _____ Zip _____
Office phone ____-____X_____ Pager (optional) ___-___-____ Home phone ___-___-____

Policy: By signing this form, you agree to adhere to the corporation's computer usage policy on the opposite side of this application form.
Signature _____ Date _____

Figure 9-2: A sample user account application form

The computer usage policy statement should be a legal document and clearly describe your company's expectations and requirements. I am no fan of paperwork, but this is one place where it is appropriate and useful. Knowing what is expected of you up front is very important, and where the line(s) are drawn is even more important.

MAINTAINING HARDWARE

The process of maintaining hardware spans new systems and old. For new systems, you can go in two general directions: purchasing turnkey, retail systems or creating your own by purchasing a component system. With the former approach, you simply purchase the computer from a mail-order or local company (generally at retail prices). In the latter approach, you purchase one or more components – case, power-supplies, system boards, disks, and so on – and slap them together yourself. Unless you need more than a dozen or so all at once, this method gives you more control over your destiny, at a lower price than purchasing a turnkey system. The added benefit is the familiarity you obtain, which helps with your troubleshooting skills down the line. I prefer this method.

Modifying existing systems is an ongoing job, too. Disks need to be replaced or upgraded, memory added, power supplies replaced, and so on. Get used to it.

Your choice of peripherals is important, too. Spending money up front on a network laser printer instead of a less expensive desktop one will ultimately save you money both in terms of maintenance as well as productivity if you have more than a handful of users.

Finally, you should keep track of all your equipment. It is one of those boring, thankless jobs that only pays off occasionally. But knowing what you have is important. If you can consult a simple paper folder or a spreadsheet or a simple database to see what equipment user XYZ has, then your day-to-day management will be easier. For instance, if you want to install Linux on a client computer and also know what kind of video and Ethernet adapters it has, you look like you know what you're doing when you immediately install the system. The value of such a database really is apparent when you need to troubleshoot a problem. The information is helpful especially if the problem system is remote.

Figure 9-3 shows a sample form that you can use for both your paper file as well as a spreadsheet. I maintain both types. As much as I like and use computers, I still like being able to open a file cabinet and putting my hands on a piece of paper. (Especially if my computer is giving me problems and I need to find out what hardware it contains!) The spreadsheet or database, however, has the advantage of taking less physical space – important for large systems with many users – and being able to summarize data for you. Obviously, you will want to customize your own. The point is to maintain a systematic inventory.

Computer name ____________ Domain name ____________ IP address __.__.__.__

Location ______________________ User phone # ____________________

Manufacturer ____________ Brand name ______________ Type __________

Video adapter ____________ Monitor ________________

Network adapter __________________

CD-ROM drive ____

Hard disk make/model __________________ Capacity ______________________

Floppy ________

Memory ____

Notes ____

____

Figure 9-3: A sample hardware equipment inventory form

MAINTAINING SYSTEM AND APPLICATION SOFTWARE

Software installation and maintenance is generally more difficult than maintaining hardware. Almost no limit exists to the amount of software you can have on a computer. Installing software can be a challenge at best. The Microsoft world is getting a little better with system registries and such, but the onus is still on you to figure things out when problems occur. With the RPM system, the Linux world is definitely getting better.

Keeping track of software is a more involved job than keeping track of hardware. You can only have a few adapter cards in a computer, but the only real limit on software is determined by the available disk space – which is constantly and quickly growing larger – you can have almost limitless software installed. This presents both maintenance and legal problems.

Maintenance is difficult for several reasons. First, everyone has their own preferences, which could involve lots of different packages and variations thereof. You also face the problem of software creep, in which some workstations get updated and others do not. The result is a plethora of different versions of the same package. Last, you must face the problem of obtaining proper licenses. The advent of CD-ROM distribution makes it easy to make illegal copies of software, and it is your job to prevent such acts.

You need to create and maintain a software inventory. Doing so requires lots of work but ultimately minimizes your trouble. I suggest that you maintain both a paper and an electronic inventory. Figure 9-4 shows a sample organizer at the computer workstation level to give an overview of all the packages on one machine.

Computer name _____	Domain name _____	IP address __.__.__.__
Location _____		
User name _____	User phone # __-__-__ ext ____	
Primary OS _____	License # _____	Date installed __-__-__
Secondary OS _____	License # _____	Date installed __-__-__
Software package _____	License # _____	Date installed __-__-__
Software package _____	License # _____	Date installed __-__-__
Software package _____	License # _____	Date installed __-__-__
Software package _____	License # _____	Date installed __-__-__
Software package _____	License # _____	Date installed __-__-__
Software package _____	License # _____	Date installed __-__-__
Software package _____	License # _____	Date installed __-__-__
Software package _____	License # _____	Date installed __-__-__

Figure 9-4: A sample computer software inventory form

You can't keep all the important information on each individual package on one form, so use the sample form shown in Figure 9-5 for each package.

```
Computer name _____   Domain name _____   IP address __.__.__.__
Location _____   User name _____
_____   Phone #   ___ - ___ - ____

Primary OS _____   License # _____   Date installed __-__-__
Secondary OS _____   License # _____   Date installed __-__-__
Software package _____
License # _____   Date Registered _____
Manufacturer _____
Address _____
Phone ___-___-____ ext _____  Contact _____
Notes _____
_____
_____
```

Figure 9-5: A sample individual software package inventory form

You should keep one folder per computer with one of the general inventory forms and as many of the individual forms as necessary. I also recommend that you make a copy of the registration form, note the date you submitted the form, and keep the copy in this folder. (Yes, I really do send in the registration form.)

People will believe that you are organized when they come to you for information and you whip out the appropriate folder. It really does help to minimize confusion, too.

Ensuring Reliability

All the preceding topics are really aimed at making your system reliable. The dream of any administrator is a completely reliable system. Of course we'd all like to win the lottery and be skinny. The reality of life has never prevented me from dreaming the impossible dream. However, you can do some things to make the world safer for your system.

The first thing you can do is think in terms of reliability. The attitude you take has a lot to do with how things work. If you have the luxury of designing your system from the ground up, you can do many things to fold reliability into its core. If you inherit a system, you can still do many things – from your system management policies to the replacement components you purchase. By thinking in terms of reliability, you are more likely to make big and small choices that point in that direction.

Your policy decisions can have a significant effect on reliability. If you give users too much privilege, they can – and will – delete files that they should not. If you do not schedule regular maintenance down-time, your system will gradually degrade and eventually fail altogether. If you do not protect your network with a firewall, your system will fail when a malicious person breaks in to it and wrecks havoc. These are somewhat extreme examples, but they illustrate the fundamental role that your policy decisions play in terms of reliability.

Whether you design your own system or simply maintain an older one, your component selection plays an important role in the system's overall reliability. For example, purchasing computer power supplies with ball-bearing based fans, for a few dollars more, can have a significant long-term impact on your system up-time. If you have 100 workstations, and two power supplies per year fail, you may have two users down for a half day each while you identify and fix the problem. Add to that the extra trouble if remote troubleshooting and travel are involved. By spending a few dollars more initially, you very likely will get zero to one failure per year, and end up saving as much as a full user-day of work and frustration.

Following that line of reasoning, think about the cost of network wiring connectors. The individual component cost is a few cents for BNC (10base2) connectors. But if one fails, the whole network goes down. The costs can be huge even for small operations. The cost to you as an administrator is large: your time taken away from the fun tasks and your reputation, for instance. If you are a part-time administrator, your problems are only amplified, as any problems probably will take you away from your *real* job.

RAID SYSTEMS

Redundant Arrays of Inexpensive Disks – RAID – is coming to Linux. RAID is used to write data onto multiple disks, to increase data integrity and availability. It can also act to improve disk input/output (I/O) performance by using multiple disk controllers simultaneously to store and retrieve data.

TIP Disk striping is increasingly used by UNIX systems and is just beginning to appear in Linux. It is used to combine one or more disks into a single partition. It is used to increase I/O performance and increase the size of a file system. Striping splits data transfers across multiple disk controllers and is less limited by the bandwidth of the individual controllers (this is akin to having multiple toll booths at the entrance of a bridge). Combining multiple disks into one partition also increases the available storage space.

Of the six standard RAID levels, only four are commonly used today:

◆ Level 0 – *Disk striping only.* This increases I/O bandwidth and storage capacity.

◆ Level 1 – *Disk mirroring only.* The same data exists on two or more disks. Disk failures do not result in lost data.

◆ Level 2 – *Rarely used in practice.*

- ◆ Level 3 — *Disk striping with parity.* Data is split across multiple disks on a byte-to-byte basis. An additional, dedicated disk is used to store parity information which enables all data to be *reconstructed* if a disk fails.

- ◆ Level 4 — *Rarely in practice.*

- ◆ Level 5 — *The same as level 3 but the parity information is split across multiple disks.* This is done to increase I/O performance by splitting the parity information storage across multiple controllers.

Linux 2.0 supports RAID Level 0. Linux kernel *patches* are available for levels RAID-1, RAID-4, and RAID-5 at `http://ftp.kernel.org/pub/linux/daemons /raid`. (A patch contains additional code that can be added to the Linux kernel source. When the modified kernel is compiled, it gains the added capability from the patch.)

UPS SYSTEMS

One of the simplest things you can do to increase reliability is to use an uninterruptible power supply (UPS) for your server(s). They vary in price from around $100 to many thousands of dollars for commercial systems. They provide your computers and other equipment with several minutes to more than an hour of power after a blackout. The advantage is that at least part of your operation can continue at all times.

A UPS offers other advantages, too. For example, it acts as a great filter. Your equipment is isolated from not only blackouts, but also brownouts (reduction of voltage) and lightning strikes. If you live in a place with marginal or "dirty" power, they will smooth it out for you. In the long run, they can save you money on component replacements because of the isolation from the vagaries of your electrical supply, which may otherwise find their way into your PC bus.

READY DISKS

In my last job, our Sun server failed one Saturday afternoon. I had been planning on shifting from the old Sun server to a Pentium PC running Linux for some time. However, at the time the Sun failed, its capacity had exceeded that of the PC's disk. I had held off asking my boss for more money for my experiment when I thought the Sun still had more life in it. So when it did fail, I did not have the spare disk ready at the time and had to run out to the nearest chain electronics store and purchase a new IDE disk. It actually only took me an hour and a half to go to the store, find and purchase the disk, and get back to the office. Then it took another two hours to install Slackware Linux and set up the Samba file server and copy over the old file systems (the Sun did not completely fail but instead would run for between one and several hours before rebooting itself). I was lucky that no one was busy on a project at that time, so the pain was minimal and not having a ready disk turned out to be okay. But I could have saved myself the worry of having a downed system during that interval if I had a spare disk. (Over the next couple of days, I purchased an SCSI controller for the PC and got the old Sun SCSI disk running on it.)

So, you can see that if you can afford it, you should keep one or more disks on your premises. The number of disks, of course, depends on your situation. If you are a large operation, you need more disks. Even the smallest operation, however, benefits from keeping one handy. The idea is to be able to replace a disk when it fails in the minimum amount of time. It is more important to have a spare disk if you have a SCSI system than if you have an IDE. This is simply because they are less immediately available – you cannot simply go to any store and purchase one.

READY SERVER

The need for a ready server is more problematic than that of a ready disk. The ease of Linux installation makes it quick and simple to reconfigure the operating system. It is also quite easy to replace any PC subsystem. If your PC-based server stops functioning, in all likelihood, you need only replace a power supply, a controller, or even the system board. Because none of the hardware components except the system disk affect the server's function, the problem is a matter of identifying the malfunctioning component and then finding a replacement.

This solution breaks down if you can't find the culprit or if you are using proprietary hardware. The reason I replaced the Sun with the PC (in the example I describe in the preceding section) was because it was proprietary and expensive to maintain. I knew how to work with each component on a PC but only a few on a Sun. I did not need a maintenance contract for a PC but I did for a Sun. With the advent of Linux and Samba (or NFS under Linux), I was sure I could duplicate the function of the Sun server.

Some operations could benefit from keeping a spare server. If your server is based on a proprietary system or if you cannot afford any down-time, you should carefully consider this option. The spare can be in the form of a computer normally used for another function that will substitute for your primary server when necessary or a computer that is specifically set aside for that purpose.

You need to know how to substitute your ready server. Without going into the details, you need a plan for implementing your spare. The main problem is how to synchronize your file system. In some cases you should be able to place your old disk in the ready server. If that is not possible, you either have to use your backups or transfer the file system directly – that is, over the network with *tar*, *cpio*, or another program. The idea is to make the change to the new system as transparent to the user as possible.

After you decide how to make the switch, it is best to practice for it. The amount of practice you need depends on the complexity of your entire network. When I practiced to switch the PC for the Sun, I started by constructing an experimental file system that mimicked the Sun's file system. Later, I switched a couple of our noncritical word processing directories from the Sun to the Linux PC and found that it did not create any problems when used by their owners. I left the file services split between the Sun and the PC until the Sun failed and switched over to the PC with little trouble. (I had not used the network printer via Samba, so that actually caused me some worry but it worked with fewer problems than the Sun had in the end. I should have tested it first, of course.)

Using cron

Cron is a system for scheduling and executing systematic Linux system and user tasks. When you start your system, the *crond* daemon is started and reads the system and user configuration files in the */etc/crontab* and */var/spool/cron* directories. The */etc/crontab* configuration file contains the system *cron* jobs reconfigured by Red Hat and can only be edited by a privileged user (generally root). The user *crontabs* are limited to things the users can normally do – for instance, a normal user cannot schedule *cron* to erase another user's files.

This system is useful for doing system maintenance as well as anything that you want to have done regularly. For instance, Red Hat configures the default *crontab* to rotate the log files found in the */var/log* directory on a daily basis.

Listing 9-4: The Red Hat default crontab /etc/crontab for cleaning up the /tmp directory

```
SHELL=/bin/bash
PATH=/sbin:/bin:/usr/sbin:/usr/bin
MAILTO=root

# run-parts
01 * * * * root run-parts /etc/cron.hourly
02 1 * * * root run-parts /etc/cron.daily
02 2 * * 0 root run-parts /etc/cron.weekly
02 3 1 * * root run-parts /etc/cron.monthly
```

To create/edit, list, or remove a user *crontab*, you simply run the *crontab* command with the appropriate option. Whoever you are logged in as determines what user *crontab* is accessed. A privileged user (generally root) can use the -*u* option to edit other users' *crontabs*. Table 9-4 lists the user *crontab* editing options.

TABLE 9-4 THE USER CRONTAB EDITING OPTIONS

Option	Description
crontab -e	Edits your *crontab* (uses your default editor)
crontab -l	Lists your *crontab* entries
crontab -r	Removes (deletes) your *crontab*
crontab - u *username*	Edits, lists, or removes another user's *crontab*

The *crontab* utility uses the *vi* editor (you can specify another editor by setting the VISUAL or EDITOR environmental variables) to edit the *crontab* file (see my instructions in Chapter 1 for the basic *vi* commands). For example, to edit your *crontab* – the first time you do so you create it – enter the following command:

```
/usr/bin/crontab -e
```

Note: You are put into *command* mode immediately upon execution of this command, and you must enter the *i*, *a*, or *o* command to start editing. After you finish editing, you need to press the *Escape* key and enter the character sequence :**wq** to save and then quit from the editor.

To send yourself the message "Hello from Cron" simply add the following line:

```
* * * * *   echo "Hello from Cron"
```

The message will be mailed to you every minute. To examine the *crontab* file, enter the command **crontab -l** and you'll see the listing of your *crontab* as shown in Listing 9-5.

Listing 9-5: Your crontab file listing

```
# DO NOT EDIT THIS FILE - edit the master and reinstall.
# (/tmp/crontab.1018 installed on Sat Jul 19 14:36:03 1997)
# (Cron version — $Id: crontab.c,v 2.13 1994/01/17 03:20:37 vixie Exp $)
* * * * *       echo "Hello from Cron"
```

I doubt that you'll want to have such a trivial message mailed to you every minute. To delete that example *cron* entry, enter the following command:

```
crontab -r
```

The formats of the */etc/crontab* and the user *crontabs* differ somewhat. The two formats use the same time format as well as the file or program to execute. However, the */etc/crontab* file includes the user name (as found in */etc/passwd*) and first describes the time and day to run the job, then the user name to execute as, and finally the file name, including the directory, to execute. Table 9-5 shows the details of each field.

TABLE 9-5 THE CRONTAB FORMAT FIELDS

Field Number	Function	Range	Notes
1	minute	0–59	The asterisk (*) means every minute, hour, day, and so on
2	hour	0–23	
3	day-of-month	0–31	
4	month	0–12	Or names such as *jan*
5	day-of-week	0–7	0 or 7 is Sun, or use names
6	user name and then command or file to execute		Only for the */etc/crontab* file
6	command or file to execute		

The tasks that can be accomplished via *cron* extend far beyond simply cleaning up your */tmp* directory. Any job that you want to be run regularly without having to manually run yourself you can have *cron* run for you. For instance, if you want to have some or all of your backups run at a time of day when the system is not being used or is used only lightly, execute the backup via *cron*. For example, if you have a 4mm DAT drive attached to a SCSI interface at */dev/rmt0* and you want to run a full backup of your system at 4:00 a.m. every Monday (Sunday = 0, Monday =1, and so on), log in as *root* and add the following *crontab* job (*crontab -e*):

```
0 4 * * 1 /bin/tar czvf /dev/rmt0 /
```

At 4:00 a.m. on Monday, *tar* will copy all files from the Root (/) directory to the device attached to */dev/rmt0*. It will compress each file using *gzip* and produce a listing as it works. The listing will be mailed to root, giving you the opportunity to examine the backup on Monday morning. Of course, you could use *cpio* or dump to do the same job.

Cron has at least one alternative. The commercial product, *Autosys*, from Platinum Technologies (`www.platinum.com/products/sysman/asys_ps.htm`), gives you more control than *cron* does. It also can control jobs on other UNIX/Linux computers and thus consolidate all your *cron* jobs into a more manageable system. Such a system is useful if you have many different servers doing many different jobs.

Using Shell Scripts

Shell scripts are generally simple text files that contain shell commands, variables, and conditional statements. They provide programming capability to the system without the complexity of compilers. However, even while lacking the sophistication of programming languages such as C, they are powerful enough to do much, if not most, of your systematic, day-to-day chores.

One of the most common uses of shell scripts is to have *cron* run them. If you have a job that requires more than a one-line command but is not complex enough to require subroutines, a shell script is the way to go. For instance, if you need to compress and then transfer files from one machine to another, it is better to create a script than to force a single command to do too much.

I summarize some of the more important *bash* functions and conditional statements in Chapter 1. In Chapter 11, I describe the script that comes configured with Tripwire to check your file system integrity on a nightly basis — *cron* is used to start it every morning. It is a simple script but descriptive of the type of job that can be readily automated with a little knowledge of shell scripting.

Shutting Down and Starting Linux

Linux keeps a dynamic file system. If you turn off the power without having it shut down gracefully, then parts of the file system will need to be reconfigured when you start it up again. Generally, this simply increases the time it takes to boot, but why risk possible problems? The file system is also *buffered* — that is, data to be written to disk are first stored in memory before actually being written to the disk. You may lose that data if you simply power the computer off.

The preferred method for shutting down a Linux system is to use either the halt/reboot or shutdown commands. The */sbin/shutdown* command performs a systematic termination of user and system processes, writes the buffers to disk (*syncs*), and informs the */sbin/init* process to put the system into runlevel 0, 1, or 6. Runlevel 0 is a complete halt; runlevel 1 is a single user administrative state; and 6 reboots the system. Logged-on users are given a specified amount of time to log off (default of 1 minute). Here's the syntax for the */sbin/shutdown* command:

```
/sbin/shutdown [-t sec] [-rkhncf] time [warning-message]
```

Table 9-6 shows the options to the shutdown command. Note that you can also reboot your Linux computer by entering the **reboot** command as *root* or simply pressing the *Ctrl+Alt+Del* key sequence long familiar to DOS users.

TABLE 9-6 THE /SBIN/SHUTDOWN COMMAND OPTIONS

Option	Description
-t *S*	Wait *S* seconds before changing the run level.
-k	Execute the other shutdown options without actually shutting down the system.
-r	Reboot the system after shutting down.
-h	Halt the system after shutting down.
-n	Do the shutdown yourself (don't use *init*). Use of this option is discouraged because it can have unpredictable results.
-f	Do a fast reboot. The normal startup process skips such time-consuming tasks as disk checks (*fsck*).
-c	Cancel a shutdown already in progress.

Minimizing Wear and Tear

You can do a couple of things to reduce the wear and tear on your system. The following information is based on common sense:

♦ **Keep your systems powered on.** The thermal expansion and contraction of turning your systems off at night wears them out faster than leaving them on. Also, most nonportable hard disks have heads that "land" on the disk platter. This is worse than the wear and tear on the bearings.

♦ **Minimize shaking and bumping.** The most delicate system is your hard disk. It spins at several thousand rpm with a delicate head floating on a cushion of air. If it is bumped too hard, it can physically impact the disk platter and fail. Even if it is not bumped hard enough for immediate failure, the ill-effects simply add up over time.

Disaster Recovery

Disaster comes in many forms – for example, a fire, an earthquake, or a flood. But anything that catastrophically destroys or renders your operation unusable is a disaster. It is essential that you make recovery plans commensurate with the value and the importance of your operation.

Your plan can be as complex and expensive as contracting with a company that specializes in such things. You can pay someone to maintain a computer or computers compatible with your own system. They should be in another geographical location, to remove the possibility of a local event rendering them inoperable. However, you should consider the likely travel time and means of travel, too. If you choose a location on the other side of the continent, you eliminate the possibility of a common natural disaster but you may not be able to get there in a reasonable amount of time. However, if they are too close, a common event may affect everybody. A location reached by an airline shuttle may be a good benchmark. A few hundred to a thousand miles seems reasonable to me.

On the other end of the spectrum – a small business or home office – you probably do not need a formal contract. You should have a simple plan of action, however. First, the offsite backups are obviously essential. If your shop burns down, you are going to live off your backups. Having stored them in another location, your plan will go something like this:

1. Assess your physical damage.

2. Restore the minimal network necessary to run your operation.

   - Use computers and equipment that were not damaged significantly.

   - Borrow or purchase the additional equipment necessary.

   - Set up your network in the most convenient location.

   - Restore your file systems.

   - Restore your Internet connections.

3. Systematically restore customer or your own services as quickly as safety allows.

Obviously, the specifics of your situation will determine the details of these steps, but the process of acting instead of reacting is the essential factor. Even if you end up doing everything completely different from what you planned, the fact that you planned at all will probably save you.

I should state that training is also essential. In my present job, we do at least two practice recoveries a year, including the travel and complete restorations of our essential services. However, I realize that it may not be possible for you. In that case, I recommend that you do as many of the subsets of disaster recovery as possible. Even "paper runs" are helpful – go through the plan by talking it through with your peers and management. Any practice is better than no practice.

> A small operation that handles life-and-death matters or has people depend on it for their livelihood is another matter. If you run an organ donor database or an ambulance service, a formal contract as well as a plan is essential even though you may have only one or two computers.

Summary

In this chapter, I describe the basic elements of systems administration. Systems administration is a large topic that would take an entire book to cover in any detail. As a result, I can only cover the essential aspects in this chapter. It is to your advantage, though, to investigate the subject in more detail.

This chapter covers the following topics:

♦ **Setting policy.** This is the road map that is essential to navigate in your system. If you have the luxury of setting it, you are a step ahead. If the policy is set for you, your interpretation still gives you considerable power.

♦ **Reliably making backups.** Backups are used for recovering misplaced or accidentally deleted files as well as recovering from disaster. You should devise a system that accounts for both possibilities. To that end, you need to decide on what method to use to make backups and how often to make them. This generally depends on the size of your operation. I divide backups into three camps: small, medium, and large. Each has its own requirements and limitations:

  ▪ Small backups can be performed using media as ubiquitous as floppy disks. You can also make use of the Internet as a storage media. Your records can be minimal.

  ▪ Medium-sized backups generally require specialized media such as 4mm DAT tapes. They also require that you use formal, regimented scheduling and record keeping.

  ▪ Large backups are a world apart from smaller ones. If you are backing up more than a gigabyte a day, then highly-specialized media such as juke-boxes are often required.

◆ **Ensuring security.** This responsibility is next in importance to your backups. It is a very large field and no one book, much less a single chapter, can cover it in detail. You can do several specific things from the start, however, that will greatly improve your network's security. If you learn the basics, you can learn about security as an ongoing task. Those basic tasks were outlined.

◆ **Administering users.** You are generally responsible for adding, deleting, and modifying user accounts.

◆ **Administering file systems.** Adding, deleting, and modifying them is an everyday job.

◆ **Administering software.** This is generally one of the more difficult administrative tasks. So many combinations of operating system and application programs are possible that installing, maintaining, and upgrading software is an art in itself. This is one of those areas where you have to experiment.

◆ **Maintenance.** This is a constant and ongoing job. The more you can anticipate both hardware and software problems, the less trouble you have. I outline some areas that you look at in order to do just that:

   ■ Keeping some spare equipment in a ready state can minimize downtime due to equipment failure.

   ■ RAID systems enable you to build redundancy into your disk drives. It is just starting to find its way into the Linux world. RAID level 0 is now available for Linux.

◆ **Troubleshooting.** This is another constant of the systems administrator's job. This area is an art and must be learned well. Experience and logical thought are the keys.

The systems administrator must learn to wear many hats. I have done everything from answering phones to wiggling through crawl spaces in the line of duty. I do, however, draw the line at woodwork (one of the people I worked with wanted me to fix his chair once).

Chapter 10

Setting Up a Real-World Network

IN THIS CHAPTER

◆ Building an example office network

◆ Configuring Windows 95 clients

◆ Configuring the Linux-Samba server for the office network

◆ Configuring a separate Firewall Network

YOU SHOULD NOW have a good grasp of the various tools needed to run a Linux-based network system. In Chapter 1, you get a simple Linux-Samba server running. In subsequent chapters, you quickly move on to expand that system into a more powerful one. Along the way, you learn a bit about the history and the underpinnings of Linux, UNIX, and the Internet – all the stuff that when put together makes it all possible. Throughout the previous chapters, I provide additional details about Linux configuration, Samba, and the Internet. I also introduce the essential elements of systems administration.

In the previous chapters of this book, I present a fairly comprehensive overview of how to build and then manage a Linux-based network. What remains is to give you an example of how all this works together in the real world.

This chapter provides a detailed office-environment network example. It is representative of many networks in use today. Although this type of network has infinite variations, it provides the basis for many networks. The example concentrates on a single office with people using Windows client workstations, a Linux-Samba server, and a Linux firewall.

Building an Office Network

This example builds a 10-node LAN for an office environment. The network consists primarily of Windows 95 client computers that connect to a Linux-Samba file and print server. (From here on, I refer to the Linux-Samba file and print server as the *File Server*. Later, when I have the file act as a router to the Firewall Server, I refer to it as the *File Server/Router*.) I add a 486-based Linux firewall to provide

403

access to and protection from the Internet. (I refer to the Linux firewall as the *Firewall Server*.)

The Office Network is built in two parts, as follows:

1. Construct and configure the Windows-based network based around the File Server. This is where most of the work gets done. People access the resources of the File Server from their Windows clients. The network is self-contained and totally secure. I refer to it as the *Private Network*.

2. Construct and configure a separate network for the Internet connection. I call it the *Firewall Network*. The File Server is modified to act as a router between the two networks, and a separate Linux computer is added to work exclusively as the firewall. Security, both active and passive, is added to both machines to provide protection from Internet intrusion.

Ready to get started?

Constructing the Private Network

In anticipation of connecting the office network to the Internet, I refer to it as the *Private Network*. This name implies that the network will be secured from unauthorized access from the Internet. A second network will be constructed connecting a Firewall Server and the File Server to provide isolation. The diagram in Figure 10-1 shows the layout of the Private Network.

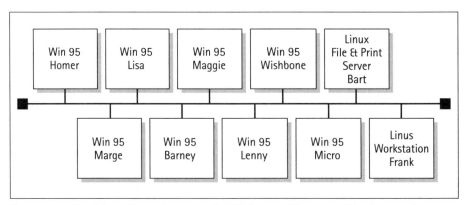

Figure 10-1: The Private Network, a 10-node LAN for an office or small business environment

To construct this network, follow these steps:

1. Wire the Private Network together. If you are using a Thinnet (10base2), connect each Ethernet card on each computer using BNC T connectors and RG58 coaxial cables – each end of the cable must be terminated with a 50-ohm BNC terminator (described in Chapter 1).

2. Configure each Windows 95 computer's *Network Configuration* to use *Client for Microsoft Networks*, your Ethernet adapter, and the *TCP/IP* protocol; the TCP/IP protocol should specify a unique IP address and the File Server as the gateway (192.168.1.254). You should give each computer a unique name in the *Identification* menu and set the workgroup name to *WORKGROUP*. I describe the details of these settings in Chapter 1; I suggest the addresses and other macro details in subsequent sections of this chapter.

3. Configure the File Server to accept each Windows client. This step entails editing the */etc/hosts* file to show the name and IP address for each client and the Samba shares found in */etc/smb.conf*. You can gain more control over which computer/user can use each Samba share by adding extra groups to the */etc/group* file and then modifying the Samba share to give access to that group.

In the following sections, I describe these steps in more detail.

Wiring the Private Network

I describe the basics of wiring a network in Chapter 1. Now, you need only to duplicate that process for each computer in the Private Network. If, for instance, you have one room with all the computers in it, then all you need is a Thinnet cable with connectors on each end for each computer. Add a 50-ohm terminator to each end, and you have constructed a 10-node network.

More commonly, your computers are located in different rooms so you must decide how best to locate your cables. I have teetered on more than one ladder and twisted and contorted to pull cable through a ceiling, and I have struggled through a crawl space to reach a cable, so I know that every situation is unique. If you build such a network, you should consider using Twisted-Pair (10baseT) Ethernet if your building has extra telephone wiring that you can use.

Configuring the Windows 95 Clients

I describe the details for configuring Windows 95 networks in Chapter 1. In this section, I describe the network settings, such as IP addresses for each of the eight Windows clients for this network. Because this is a simple network, configuring the Windows 95 clients is a simple process. The key is to keep the names and addresses unique.

The names and addresses are arbitrary, and you can make up anything you want. Of course, if you have an official, InterNIC-registered IP network address (the first three decimal numbers if you are using a class C network), then you must use that address.

In this example, I continue to use the public IP network address of 192.168.1.0 and use IP masquerading to access the Internet. Recall from Chapter 8 that IP masquerading substitutes a single, Internet-legal IP address – obtained from your ISP via your PPP connection – for any IP address on your network so that your network packets can legally travel on the Internet. Table 10-1 shows the names and addresses that I have conjured up.

TABLE 10-1 THE INVENTORY OF YOUR PRIVATE NETWORK

Number	Computer-Name	IP Address	User-Name	Description
1	Bart	192.168.1.254	Admin	File Server
2	Maggie	192.168.1.2	User 1	Windows 95 client
3	Wishbone	192.168.1.3	User 2	Windows 95 client
4	Brancusi	192.168.1.4	User 3	Windows 95 client
5	Homer	192.168.1.5	User 4	Windows 95 client
6	Marge	192.168.1.6	User 5	Windows 95 client
7	Barney	192.168.1.7	User 6	Windows 95 client
8	Osomaloso	192.168.1.8	User 7	Windows 95 client
9	Micro	192.168.1.9	User 8	Windows 95 client
10	Frank	192.168.1.10	User 9	Linux workstation

Configuring each computer is a tedious yet straightforward job. As you configure each computer, make sure that it is properly connected to the network by using the MS-DOS *ping* command (described in Chapter 2) to verify TCP/IP connectivity. The details of doing this depend on which machines are connected at any given time. If you already have the File Server configured, you would execute the following command from any Linux or Windows computer:

```
ping 192.168.1.254
```

If you get a response like that shown in Listing 10-1, you are properly connected. If you don't get any response or it is intermittent, consult the troubleshooting tips and information that I offer in Chapter 2.

Listing 10-1: The proper response from the ping command

```
bart:~$ ping 192.168.1.254
PING 192.168.1.254 (192.168.1.254): 56 data bytes
64 bytes from 192.168.1.254: icmp_seq=0 ttl=64 time=1.4 ms
64 bytes from 192.168.1.254: icmp_seq=1 ttl=64 time=1.2 ms
64 bytes from 192.168.1.254: icmp_seq=2 ttl=64 time=1.1 ms

--- 192.168.1.254 ping statistics ---
3 packets transmitted, 3 packets received, 0% packet loss
round-trip min/avg/max = 1.1/1.2/1.4 ms
```

You can further test your new connection by mounting the public share from your File Server, as I describe in Chapter 6. Recall that you do this by double-clicking the *Network Neighborhood* and then double-clicking your server share. That process results in a dialog box on your Windows 95 machine.

Finally, double-click the public share and you should get a dialog box that shows the contents of the directory that the share points to (Red Hat sets it to the */home/samba* directory when first installed). If you get no response, try using the Microsoft Explorer, as I describe in Chapter 2. If you still cannot access the File Server, follow the troubleshooting methods I describe in Chapter 2.

After you verify that the new Windows client is communicating on the network, you need to configure the File Server to give access to the appropriate shares. I introduce that process in Chapter 1 and go into more detail in Chapter 6.

Configuring a Linux/X Window Client (Optional)

I have been using Linux exclusively in the role of a server, and Windows 95 computers as clients of the Linux server. However, it is entirely possible to use a Linux box as a client workstation. I have configured many Linux boxes as engineering workstations, making use of X Window to provide the GUI and the many GNU compilers as the applications.

Corel WordPerfect 7 is now available for Linux. For more information, see the Corel Web page at www.sdcorp.com/wplinux. You can download a demo version or place an order for a complete version (first-time purchase price is $199, and the upgrade/trade-up price is $149). I mention this product because a full-fledged, commercial word processor was one of the last elements left in the Linux-as-a-workstation puzzle. With WordPerfect available, even less need exists to depend on commercial operating systems. (Because I have just started to experiment with it, I have not formed an opinion about its quality, but my experiences with WordPerfect in the Windows world have been positive.)

I leave it up to you to configure a Linux box as a client. It is quite simple to configure the network parameters. You will see no difference from the method you have already used to configure the File Server.

It is also quite simple to use a Linux box as a Samba client. From a command shell, simply enter the following command:

```
/usr/sbin/smbmount //bart/pchome /mnt
```

You are prompted for the password to that share unless you've declared it a public share. The directory */mnt* is a convenient mount point to test the Samba share. If you create a directory called */home/pchome*, you can just as readily use that as a mount point. That's all it takes! If you want to automate the mount, simply include the command in the */etc/rc.d/rc.local* script.

Configuring the File Server

I describe the configuration of a File Server in Chapters 1, 6, and 8. You must repeat that process for each of the new clients. The process involves the following steps:

1. Log on to the File Server as *root*.

2. Modify the */etc/hosts* file to add the name of each new host on the network. To add the computer *maggie*, edit the file so that it looks like the example in Listing 10-2.

Listing 10-2: Adding the computer maggie to the /etc/hosts file

```
127.0.0.1          localhost.localdomain
192.168.1.2        maggie.paunchy.com maggie
192.168.1.254      bart.paunchy.com bart
```

3. Use the *useradd* utility to add a user login name to the File Server. This utility modifies the */etc/passwd* and */etc/group* files. To add the user *maggie*, enter the following command.

```
useradd maggie
```

4. Edit the */etc/passwd* file and remove the asterisk (*) from *maggie*'s login — when present, it disables logins for the account. It is found after the first colon (:) immediately after the login name (*maggie*).

5. Log on as *Maggie* from the console or from a new *Telnet* session, but not via the *su* command, and set the password by running the */usr/bin/passwd* program.

6. Modify the */etc/smb.conf* file to add Samba shares for those new hosts. When you set the Samba parameter *security=username*, Samba will use the Linux user name to access shares. The simplest method is to add the generic *pchome* share that tries to match each computer name to a user name using the *%m* macro. As shown in Listing 10-3, the computer name must match the user name added in Step 2 to match the computer name entered into */etc/hosts*.

Listing 10-3: Uncomment the Samba machine macro definition pchome

```
; a service which has a different directory for each machine that connects
; this allows you to tailor configurations to incoming machines. You could
; also use the %u option to tailor it by user name.
; The %m gets replaced with the machine name that is connecting.
[pchome]
  comment = PC Directories
  path = /usr/pc/%m
  public = no
  writeable = yes
```

7. From your Windows client, *maggie*, double-click the *Network Neighborhood* and then double-click the *File Server* icon.

8. Double-click the share *pchome*.

9. If your Windows 95 login name and password match those of the user login, you gain access to that share. Otherwise, you are prompted for the password that you just entered in Step 5. After you enter the correct password, you gain access to the share.

TIP You may notice that logging onto your File Server via *Telnet* can take several minutes. There could be several reasons for this, but the most likely is that you do not have the nameserver or */etc/hosts* configured properly or you do not have access to a nameserver. If you do not have a nameserver running — it converts a name such as *maggie.paunchy.com* into an IP address such as 192.168.1.2 — and do not have an explicit entry in the hosts table, the *Telnet* daemon may take several minutes to finish completing the session while it waits for the name resolution to time-out. To eliminate the delay, either configure/install the nameserver or enter the IP address of the host you use to *Telnet* from into the */etc/hosts* file.

CONFIGURING SAMBA FOR DIFFERENT GROUPS

Next, you need to configure several Linux user-groups to separate the work done on the File Server. For this example, you will have an accounting/financial group and a general group. The accounting group will be responsible for – you guessed it – accounting and financial work. After that, create an administration, or secretarial group, for the general business of the company. The last, or users, group will be responsible for the work that the company does.

To keep things straight, add a *group* field to the information in Table 10-1. This field, of course, will help you know who is in what group. Table 10-2 shows the new inventory of your Private Network.

TABLE 10-2 THE MODIFIED INVENTORY OF YOUR PRIVATE NETWORK

Number	Computer-Name	IP Address	User–Name	Group	Description
1	Bart	192.168.1.254	Root	Admin	File Server
2	Maggie	192.168.1.2	User_1	Users	Windows 95 client
3	Wishbone	192.168.1.3	User_2	Accounting	Windows 95 client
4	Brancusi	192.168.1.4	User_3	Accounting	Windows 95 client
5	Homer	192.168.1.5	User_4	Accounting	Windows 95 client
6	Marge	192.168.1.6	User_5	Users	Windows 95 client
7	Barney	192.168.1.7	User_6	Secretarial	Windows 95 client
8	Osomaloso	192.168.1.8	User_7	Users	Windows 95 client
9	Joe	192.168.1.9	User_8	Users	Windows 95 client
10	Frank	192.168.1.10	User_9	Users	Windows 95 client

CONFIGURING THE USERS (GENERAL) GROUP

Recall, from Chapter 7, that when you add a user (via *useradd*), a personal group is created for that user. If you examine the */etc/passwd* and */etc/group* files, you'll see that the user ID (for example, 500 for *maggie*) matches the group ID found in */etc/group*. But note that a group called *users* also exists that includes all the users added by the *useradd* (or Control Panel) utility. It has a group ID of 100. This is a good place to leave all your general-purpose users. If you choose that convention, all your users are configured for that group. However, if you do not want your specialized users (say from the accounting group) to have access to that group, you can simply remove their names from that group.

CONFIGURING THE ACCOUNTING GROUP

Create the accounting group and corresponding directory by completing the following steps:

1. Log on as *root*.

2. Edit the */etc/group* file and add the following line. (I like to put it immediately after the users group.) Include the users that you want to belong to this group by adding their names separated by commas as shown here:

   ```
   account::200:bart,maggie
   ```

3. Create the accounting directory, which will be used to store common information for users in that group, by entering the following command.

   ```
   mkdir /home/account
   ```

4. Change the group ownership to *accounting* by entering the following command (the *-R* parameter tells the *chgrp* program to change the group of all the files and subdirectories within the */home/account* directory). You could optionally assign ownership of this directory to any other valid user if you wish.

   ```
   chgrp -R account /home/account
   ```

5. Configure Samba to restrict access to the accounting share of the accounting group. One way to do that is to use the *valid user = @agroup* parameter. Listing 10-4 shows a share that makes use of that parameter.

Listing 10-4: Specifying group access to a Samba share

```
[accounting]
   comment = Accounting group
   path = /home/account
   valid users = @account
   public = no
   writable = yes
   printable = no
   create mask = 0770
```

6. Double-click the File Server's *Network Neighborhood* icon. You see the accounting group share.

At this point, the */home/accounting* directory is owned by root but its group ownership is accounting (200). Depending on how you connect to Samba on the File Server, you may or may not have to enter a password.

CONFIGURING THE SECRETARIAL GROUP

To configure the secretarial group, follow the same steps as in the preceding section, but change the parameters to reflect the new group. Add the following line to the */etc/group* file:

```
secty:300:krusty,barney,bart
```

The *smb.conf* share could look like the example in Listing 10-5.

Listing 10-5: Specifying group access to the Samba Secretarial share

```
[secretarial]
    comment = Secretarial group
    path = /home/secty
    allow users = @secty
    public = no
    writable = yes
    printable = no
    create mask = 0760
```

You now have Samba shares for each user and two separate groups. If you run an accounting package, its data can be stored in */home/accounting* or a subdirectory. Only those users who belong to the accounting group will have access to it. The same goes for the secretarial group. Only those users who need access to sensitive company memos and such will have access to that data. Likewise, only those users who are working on whatever your product is will have access to that work.

As you can see, it is quite easy to create a custom system to suit your specific File Server needs. As your company grows, you can become more sophisticated, perhaps adding additional servers or networks as needed.

Configuring the Print Server

Red Hat's *Configurator* simplifies the process of setting up the print server. I leave it to you to use the *Printer* GUI option because it is straightforward. Instead, I describe how to manually configure a standard HP Laser Jet 5-L printer. I use the Linux-Samba server as the print server, but I refer to it as the Print Server when discussing its use with the printer.

1. Connect the printer to the computer with a printer cable.

2. Log on to the Print Server as *root*.

3. If you did not configure a printer during the initial Red Hat installation, the */etc/printcap* file is installed without any configuration information. You need to edit it and add the information shown in Listing 10-6.

Listing 10-6: The /etc/printcap file configured for an HP Laser Jet 4/5/6 series printer

```
# /etc/printcap
#
# Please don't edit this file directly unless you know what you are doing!
# Be warned that the control-panel printtool requires a very strict format!
# Look at the printcap(5) man page for more info.
#
# This file can be edited with the printtool in the control-panel.

##PRINTTOOL3## LOCAL ljet4 600x600 letter {} LaserJet4 Default {}
lp:\
        :sd=/var/spool/lpd/lp:\
        :mx#0:\
        :sh:\
        :lp=/dev/lp1:\
        :if=/var/spool/lpd/lp/filter:
```

4. You need to inform the *lp* printer daemon of the new printer. You can accomplish this by sending the HUP signal to the *lp* daemon or by rebooting the Print Server. To send the HUP signal, you first need to find out the process ID (PID) of the *lp* daemon. Enter the following command:

   ```
   ps -x |grep lp
   ```

5. Enter the following command with the PID as the final argument:

   ```
   kill -HUP pid
   ```

6. You should be able to print directly from your Print Server by entering the following command:

   ```
   lpr /etc/printcap
   ```

   You also should be able to print from any application that is aware of the Linux *lpr* command. For instance, Web browsers such as RedBaron and Netscape use the *lpr* command when you press their *Print* buttons.

The rest of your network will be able to access this printer with the help of Samba. Chapters 6 and 7 have detailed instructions on connecting to remote printers via the Samba print shares.

Constructing the Firewall Network

Constructing the Firewall Network is the most difficult part of the system-building process. It involves constructing numerous components that must work together. You can construct such a system in any number of ways. For instance, I have mentioned (but do not use) Proxy Server software. You can also forgo the construction of a separate Firewall Network and move the Firewall Server onto your main network, if you wish to forgo some security. However, the benefits of building a separate Firewall Network are considerable enough to justify the extra work, in my opinion; depending on how nervous you are about security, it can translate into sleeping better. Anyway, I leave it up to you to decide.

TIP If you choose not to implement the Firewall Network, simply connect the Firewall Server to the Private Network but do not add the second Network adapter to the File Server and the corresponding routes. You also do not have to recompile the kernel for IP Forwarding on the File Server. You do not have to add the entries for the Firewall Network (192.168.32.x), either — all the computers should be on the 192.168.1.x network. Everything else should be done as I specify.

Complete the following steps:

1. Configure the File Server to route all outgoing Internet traffic through the firewall. This requires recompiling the kernel to allow IP packets to be forwarded from the Private Network's interface to the Firewall Network interface.

2. Configure the Firewall Server to dial up the ISP and filter the Internet traffic.

3. Configure the Firewall Server to accept external connections via a dial-up telephone connection.

To connect your Private Network to the Internet in a secure fashion, you need to create a firewall. I introduce firewalls in Chapter 8. The firewall I describe in that chapter serves the single computer home office very well. But if you have a larger network, it is better to use a dedicated firewall, which I call a *Firewall Server*.

I introduce you to a simple but effective firewall in the preceding chapter. The *ipfwadm* is a packet-oriented firewall. It looks at the address and port number of each packet entering or leaving the firewall. You also can use application-oriented firewalls, which base their security on substituting security-tuned network programs for the default network programs. For this example, however, I prefer to use the packet-oriented firewall. It is simpler to configure, offers very good security but, in some ways, is not as flexible as an application-based or proxy-based firewall. Please refer to my discussion in Chapter 9 for further details.

You place the Firewall Server between your LAN and your Internet connection. Figure 10-2 shows this *dual-homed* configuration. The advantage of this type of system is that no IP packet can pass to or from the Internet and your LAN without passing through the firewall. Your Private Network is isolated from direct contact with the Internet.

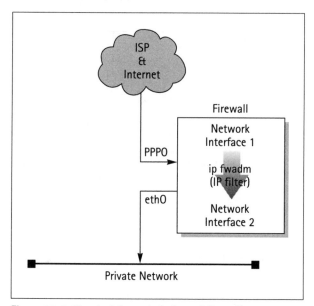

Figure 10-2: The dual-homed, dedicated firewall

When you add the dual-homed firewall to your network, your network diagram (shown previously in Figure 10-1) changes to that shown in Figure 10-3.

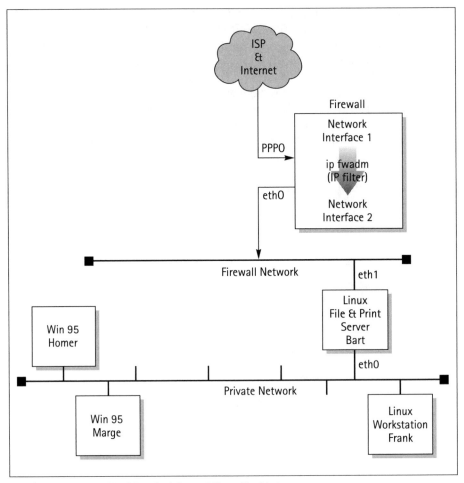

Figure 10-3: Your LAN with a dual-homed firewall added

For this example, call the Firewall Server *Burns* and add it to your network inventory as shown in Table 10-3.

TABLE 10-3 THE NEW NETWORK INVENTORY

Number	Computer-Name	IP Address	User-Name	Group	Description
1	Bart	192.168.1.254	Root	Admin	File Server/Router
	bart_firwall	192.168.32.254	Root	Admin	File Server/Router
2	Maggie	192.168.1.2	User_1	Users	Windows 95
3	Wishbone	192.168.1.3	User_2	Accounting	Windows 95
4	Brancusi	192.168.1.4	User_3	Accounting	Windows 95
5	Homer	192.168.1.5	User_4	Accounting	Windows 95
6	Marge	192.168.1.6	User_5	Users	Windows 95
7	Barney	192.168.1.7	User_6	Secretarial	Windows 95
8	Osomaloso	192.168.1.8	User_7	Users	Windows 95
9	Joe	192.168.1.9	User_8	Users	Windows 95
10	Frank	192.168.1.10	User_9	Users	Windows 95
11	Burns	192.168.32.1	Root	Admin	Linux firewall

You need to perform two main steps to add the Firewall Server to your network:

1. Modify the File Server to work with the Firewall Server — I call the *File Server* the *File Server/Router* from here on. The *File Server/Router* requires the following modifications:

   - Modify the Linux Kernel to allow forwarding IP packets between the Private and Firewall Networks. To allow the Private Network to communicate with the Internet, you must route the Private Network Internet-bound packets to the Firewall Server through the File Server/Router.

   - Modify the Linux Kernel to allow IP masquerading. Private Network packets are routed to the Firewall Network in order to get out to the Internet. If you have the File Server/Router masquerade those packets, the Firewall Server will not need to know anything about the Private

Network. All the IP packets that show up on the File Server/Router's Private Network's Ethernet interface, and are destined for the Internet, will be masqueraded and have an IP source address of the File Server/Router (192.168.32.254). The Firewall will simply route all the returning packets back to the File Server/Router, where they will be demasqueraded and sent on to their final destination on the Private Network. If you do not masquerade them, you need to add a route back to the Private Network on the Firewall Server, which is not only clumsy but also conceivably dangerous because anyone gaining access to the Firewall Server will know the address of the protected network.

■ Modify the Linux kernel to accept the second network adapter. The second adapter connects the File Server/Router to the Firewall Network.

■ Add the additional interface and routing commands to the *boot* process. The commands to activate and configure the second Ethernet adapter and the Firewall Network route must be added to the system.

■ Test the new connections.

2. Configure the Firewall Server to connect the Firewall Network to your ISP. This requires the following modifications:

■ Add the IP filtering rules to your Firewall Server. It will protect your network from unauthorized external connections while at the same time allow your Private Network to connect to the resources that it needs.

■ Add a dial-up connection, with one-time passwords, to provide you and your users the capability of connecting to your Private Network from the outside.

■ Add active security tools that you, as the administrator, use to check the system for breaches and potential problems. I discuss this process in Chapter 11.

■ Add passive security tools to minimize unforeseen security holes. This basically means removing all unnecessary software from your Firewall Server. I describe this process in Chapter 11.

I explain most of these steps in the following sections of this chapter.

Modifying the File Server/Router to Work with the Firewall Server

As shown previously in Figure 10-3, you need to create a second LAN, called the *Firewall Network*, to create the physical isolation between the Internet and your Private Network. To construct this network, you should use a dedicated computer as a router. If you do not have an extra computer, however, you must add a second network interface to your File Server/Router and then configure it as a router in addition to its File Server role. I use this approach.

For the File Server/Router to act as the router, it must be able to forward IP packets between the interfaces. Until recently, you had to compile IP forwarding and several other security features into the kernel itself. Now, both IP forwarding and IP masquerading can be loaded as modules.

MODIFYING THE KERNEL FOR MASQUERADING AND A SECOND NETWORK ADAPTER (OPTIONAL)

Before we begin, please note that recent advancements have allowed IP masquerading and IP forwarding to be added to the kernel as loadable modules. Multiple network adapters can now be reliably (at least for me) probed as well. This obviates the need to compile those capabilities directly into the kernel. I started this book with those old requirements and I leave the instructions for doing so just in case you run into problems with your hardware. It is also instructive if you wish to see how a kernel is compiled.

For your Linux file server to work as a router between your private and firewall networks it must be capable of recognizing two network adapters, forwarding packets between devices, and providing IP masquerading. When I started this book all three parts had to be compiled directly into the kernel. Now, Red Hat 5.0 automatically recognizes multiple network devices and supports masquerading. Just in case your particular setup proves to be the exception to the rule I will leave the instructions in for compiling the services into the kernel.

1. Log in as *root*, mount your CD-ROM if necessary, and use RPM to load the kernel source code as I describe in the next two steps.

2. Install the kernel headers and source code:

```
rpm -ivh /mnt/cdrom/RedHat/RPMS/kernel-headers-2.0.31-7.i386.rpm
rpm -ivh /mnt/cdrom/RedHat/RPMS/kernel-source-2.0.31-7.i386.rpm
```

3. To compile the code, the compiler must know where to find certain support (header) files to create links for them:

```
cd /usr/include
rm -rf asm linux scsi
ln -s /usr/src/linux/include/asm-i386 asm
ln -s /usr/src/linux/include/linux linux
ln -s /usr/src/linux/include/scsi scsi
```

Note: The following instruction is no longer necessary. When Red Hat upgraded from 4.2 to 5.0 they enhanced the hardware-probing capability of modules such as *3c509.o.* When my Ethernet adapter is probed during my system boot both devices are recognized. The possibility always exists that it will not work on your hardware, so I am leaving the instruction for hardwiring the kernel to a specific device.

4. (Optional.) In my case, I use 3Com 3c509 Ethernet adapters. I need to edit the */usr/src/linux/drivers/net/Space.c* file and replace the default I/O address setting of eth1 from *0xffe0* to *0*. This forces the kernel to probe for the second 3c509 card. Listing 10-7 shows the modified *Space.c* file. You may or may not need to do this depending on your hardware. I recommend skipping this step unless your new kernel does not recognize your adapter, then revisit this step.

Listing 10-7: The /usr/src/linux/drivers/net/Space.c file modified for a 3c509

```
/* "eth0" defaults to autoprobe (== 0), other use a base of 0xffe0 (== -0x20),
   which means "don't probe".  These entries exist only to provide empty slots
   which may be enabled at boot-time. */

static struct device eth7_dev = {
"eth7", 0,0,0,0,0xffe0 /* I/O base*/, 0,0,0,0, NEXT_DEV, ethif_probe };

{ The code for eth6 through eth2 is omitted. }

static struct device eth1_dev = {
    "eth1", 0,0,0,0,0 /* I/O base*/, 0,0,0,0, &eth2_dev, ethif_probe };

static struct device eth0_dev = {
    "eth0", 0, 0, 0, 0, ETH0_ADDR, ETH0_IRQ, 0, 0, 0, &eth1_dev, ethif_probe };
```

5. Enter the following command to ensure that your source code is in the correct state to be recompiled:

```
make mrproper
```

6. Enter the following command to configure the new kernel:

```
make config
```

 You can run the *make menuconfig* tool from a login shell to configure the kernel. *Menuconfig* is a very nice system. I use the text-based system here because I prefer that you get accustomed to all the potential configuration options the first few times you compile the kernel. You have many options and I believe that you will understand them better if you do it manually here.

7. Keep pressing the *Enter* key (accepting the default for each prompt) until you come to the part that prompts you about your network options. Make sure that the answer is *yes* (Y) to the questions about *IP Forwarding, firewalling, masquerading,* and *defragmenting,* as shown in Listing 10-8.

Listing 10-8: Kernel configuration IP Forwarding

```
*
* Networking options
*
Network firewalls (CONFIG_FIREWALL) [Y/n/?]
Network aliasing (CONFIG_NET_ALIAS) [Y/n/?]
TCP/IP networking (CONFIG_INET) [Y/n/?]
IP: forwarding/gatewaying (CONFIG_IP_FORWARD) [Y/n/?] Y
IP: multicasting (CONFIG_IP_MULTICAST) [N/y/?]
IP: syn cookies (CONFIG_SYN_COOKIES) [Y/n/?]
IP: rst cookies (CONFIG_RST_COOKIES) [N/y/?]
IP: firewalling (CONFIG_IP_FIREWALL) [Y/n/?]
IP: firewall packet logging (CONFIG_IP_FIREWALL_VERBOSE) [N/y/?]
IP: masquerading (CONFIG_IP_MASQUERADE) [N/y/?] Y
*
* Protocol-specific masquerading support will be built as modules.
*
IP: ipautofw masq support (CONFIG_IP_MASQUERADE_IPAUTOFW) [N/y/?]
IP: ICMP masquerading (CONFIG_IP_MASQUERADE_ICMP) [N/y/?]
IP: transparent proxy support (EXPERIMENTAL)(CONFIG_IP_TRANSPARENT_PROXY)[N/y/?]
IP: always defragment (CONFIG_IP_ALWAYS_DEFRAG) [N/y/?] Y
IP: accounting (CONFIG_IP_ACCT) [Y/n/?]
IP: optimize as router not host (CONFIG_IP_ROUTER) [N/y/?]
IP: tunneling (CONFIG_NET_IPIP) [M/n/y/?]
IP: aliasing support (CONFIG_IP_ALIAS) [M/n/y/?]
```

TIP Do not be afraid to break out of the configuration process at any time (press *Ctrl+C*). The process simply writes your choices to a configuration file when it finishes. You can always do it again.

8. Continue choosing the defaults until you arrive at the "Network Device Support" section. Enter *y* for your particular adapter. I use 3Com 3c509 adapters, so I answer yes to that device, as shown in Listing 10-9.

Listing 10-9: Kernel configuration for 3Com 3c509 adapters

```
*
* Network device support
*
Network device support (CONFIG_NETDEVICES) [Y/n/?] Dummy net driver support (CO
PLIP (parallel port) support (CONFIG_PLIP) [M/n/y/?] n
PPP (point-to-point) support (CONFIG_PPP) [M/n/y/?] n
*
* CCP compressors for PPP are only built as modules.
*
SLIP (serial line) support (CONFIG_SLIP) [M/n/y/?] n
 CSLIP compressed headers (CONFIG_SLIP_COMPRESSED) [Y/n/?] n
 Keepalive and linefill (CONFIG_SLIP_SMART) [Y/n/?] n
 Six bit SLIP encapsulation (CONFIG_SLIP_MODE_SLIP6) [N/y/?] n
Radio network interfaces (CONFIG_NET_RADIO) [N/y/?] n
Ethernet (10 or 100Mbit) (CONFIG_NET_ETHERNET) [Y/n/?]
3COM cards (CONFIG_NET_VENDOR_3COM) [Y/n/?]
3c501 support (CONFIG_EL1) [M/n/y/?] n
3c503 support (CONFIG_EL2) [M/n/y/?] n
3c505 support (CONFIG_ELPLUS) [N/y/m/?] n
3c507 support (CONFIG_EL16) [N/y/m/?] n
3c509/3c579 support (CONFIG_EL3) [M/n/y/?] y
```

Note that I have answered *no* to most of these questions because my File Server/Router will never use any of them. My choices reflect the components that I use, and you should answer them according to your configuration.

9. Continue pressing the *Enter* key until the configuration is finished.

10. To create the dependencies and compile the source code to create your new kernel, enter the following commands:

```
make dep
make zImage
```

11. After the new kernel is created, you need to move the file into the */boot* directory and tell LILO where it is located. The make zImage creates a file called zImage in the */usr/src/linux/arch/i386/boot* directory. To move it to the */boot* directory, enter the following command:

```
mv /usr/src/linux/arch/i386/boot/zImage /boot
```

12. Edit */etc/lilo.conf* to include the new kernel. Listing 10-10 shows my *lilo.conf.*

Listing 10–10: My /etc/lilo.conf edited to include the new kernel

```
boot=/dev/hda
map=/boot/map
install=/boot/boot.b
prompt
timeout=50
#append="ether=0,0,eth0 ether=0,0,eth1"
image=/boot/zImage
        label=newlinux
        root=/dev/hda1
        read-only
image=/boot/vmlinuz
        label=linux
        root=/dev/hda1
        read-only
```

I have labeled the new kernel *zImage* file as *newlinux*. This is what you would type in at the LILO prompt to explicitly have it run. However, I have made the new kernel the default kernel by placing it first in the configuration. If you want to boot the old kernel, *vmlinuz*, you need to enter the label, *linux*, at the LILO prompt at boot time.

13. Make all this permanent by telling LILO to reconfigure itself by entering the following command.

```
lilo
```

14. Gracefully shut down your File Server/Router by entering the following command (the *-h* option tells the system to halt instead of rebooting):

```
/bin/shutdown -h now
```

15. When the computer has shut down, turn off the power.

16. Disconnect the power cable.

17. Open up the case and install the second network adapter. It is best to physically separate the two adapters because it can be difficult to connect two Thinnet T-adapters if they are right next to each other.

18. Close the case and insert the power cable.

19. Turn on the power. The new kernel is automatically booted. You should see references to both network adapters as the *boot* process information is displayed on the system console. Listing 10-11 shows my adapters.

Listing 10-11: My 3c509 Ethernet adapters are recognized by the new kernel at boot time

```
scsi : 0 hosts.
scsi : detected total.
eth0: 3c509 at 0x210 tag 1, BNC port, address  00 20 af 11 95 66, IRQ 11.
3c509.c:1.07 6/15/95 becker@cesdis.gsfc.nasa.gov
eth1: 3c509 at 0x300 tag 2, BNC port, address  00 a0 24 2f 30 69, IRQ 10.
3c509.c:1.07 6/15/95 becker@cesdis.gsfc.nasa.gov
Partition check:
 hda: hda1 hda2 hda3 hda4
```

Note that the I/O addresses and interrupt information are displayed.

CONFIGURING THE NETWORK ADAPTER PARAMETERS AND ROUTES

Although I continue with my practice of manually configuring your system, you can use the *Control Panel's Network* and *Kernel configurators* if you wish. These GUIs modify the files that I show you how to modify directly.

I use my original network adapter for my Private Network. Linux knows it as *eth0*. The Firewall Network attaches to the new adapter and is *eth1*. You might have to reverse the ordering of these devices depending on how your system is configured.

The following instructions describe how to edit the network scripts directly:

1. Log on to your File Server/Router as *root*.

2. Go to the */etc/sysconfig/network-scripts* directory by entering **cd /etc/sysconfig/network-scripts**. There should already be a file *ifcfg-eth0*, which contains the information for the *eth0* interface. Listing 10-12 shows this file, which you should not need to change.

Listing 10-12: The /etc/sysconfig/network-scripts/ifcfg-eth0 file

```
DEVICE=eth0
IPADDR=192.168.1.254
NETMASK=255.255.255.0
NETWORK=192.168.1.0
```

```
BROADCAST=192.168.1.255
ONBOOT=yes
BOOTPROTO=none
```

3. Copy *ifcfg-eth0* to *ifcfg-eth1*:

```
cp ifcfg-eth0 ifcfg-eth1
```

4. Edit *ifcfg-eth1* to look like what is shown in Listing 10-13. I use the *vi* editor.

Listing 10-13: The /etc/sysconfig/network-scripts/ifcfg-eth1 file

```
DEVICE=eth1
IPADDR=192.168.32.254
NETWORK=192.168.32.0
NETMASK=255.255.255.0
BROADCAST=192.168.32.255
ONBOOT=yes
BOOTPROTO=none
```

TIP Please take note that I allocate the *public network* address of 192.168.32.0 to the Firewall Network. This is an arbitrary decision on my part. I chose the number 192.168.32 because it is easier to distinguish from the *Private Network* address of 192.168.1 than, say, 192.168.2.

5. Press the *Escape* key to exit from *insert* mode.

6. Save your new file by entering :wq (the commands to save and quit) and the file will be saved as you exit from *vi*.

7. Go up one directory by using the change directory command:

```
cd ..
```

8. Edit the file */etc/sysconfig/network*. You need to set the *FORWARD_IPV4* flag to true so that IP packets can be transferred by the kernel from the Private Network to the Firewall Network and the Firewall Server (which acts as a gateway to the Internet). That provides the path for Internet-bound packets to find their way to the PPP connection. You also need to set the GATEWAY and GATEWAYDEV variables to specify how packets from your private network can find their way out to the Internet via the Firewall Server. Use *vi* to edit the file to look like what is shown in Listing 10-14.

Listing 10-14: The /etc/sysconfig/network file

```
NETWORKING=yes
FORWARD_IPV4=true
HOSTNAME=bart.paunchy.com
DOMAINNAME=paunchy.com
GATEWAY=192.168.32.1
GATEWAYDEV=eth1
```

9. Go to directory */etc/rc.d* by using the change directory command:

   ```
   cd /etc/rc.d
   ```

10. Edit the file */etc/rc.d/rc.local*. You need to start masquerading at boot time. With masquerading turned on, IP addresses from the Private Network are changed to those of the Firewall Network. That means that they automatically get transferred from one network adapter to another on the File Server/Router without needing to specify an explicit route. Once on the Firewall Server they are routed out to the Internet. The return packets find their way back to the File Server/Router and are changed back to their original IP address. At that point, they are transferred back to the Private Network and finally back to their origin. By using this method you do not need to add any explicit routes to either the File Server/Router or the Firewall Server. I believe it makes for a safer network because no direct path leads back to your private network. Anyone breaking into your Firewall Server will not be able to directly see the Private Network.

    Add the *ipfwadm* command as the last line in *rc.local* as shown in Listing 10-15. Use *vi* to edit the file, add the second line, and then save and quit.

Listing 10-15: The /etc/rc.d/rc.local file

```
{ Only the last three lines are displayed. }
cp -f /etc/issue /etc/issue.net
echo > /etc/issue

echo "Masquerade priv net packets as firewall net ones."
echo "This precludes the need to add an explicit route"
echo "  back to your private network on the firewall"
echo "    server."
ipfwadm -F -a masquerade -S 192.168.1.0/24 -D 0.0.0.0/0
```

11. You need to make the system recognize all this new information. Use the */etc/rc.d/init.d/network* script to stop the network and restart it again as shown in the following commands:

```
/etc/rc.d/init.d/network stop
/etc/rc.d/init.d/network start
```

Your File Server/Router is now configured as a router between your Private and Firewall Networks.

CHECKING YOUR NETWORK CONNECTIONS

If everything went well, the second network interface should be activated. Unfortunately, unless you've skipped ahead and configured the Firewall Sever (which is fine by me) you cannot try to directly communicate with it, yet. (If it is configured and connected, try pinging it – **ping 192.168.32.1.**)

1. Enter the following command from a shell window to see if both network adapters are activated:

```
ifconfig
```

2. You should see entries for the two network adapters and the local loopback interface (lo) as shown in Listing 10-16.

Listing 10-16: The ifconfig listing

```
lo        Link encap:Local Loopback
          inet addr:127.0.0.1  Bcast:127.255.255.255  Mask:255.0.0.0
          UP BROADCAST LOOPBACK RUNNING  MTU:3584  Metric:1
          RX packets:307 errors:0 dropped:0 overruns:0
          TX packets:307 errors:0 dropped:0 overruns:0

eth0      Link encap:Ethernet  HWaddr 00:20:AF:11:95:66
          inet addr:192.168.1.254  Bcast:192.168.1.255  Mask:255.255.255.0
          UP BROADCAST RUNNING MULTICAST  MTU:1500  Metric:1
          RX packets:1645 errors:0 dropped:0 overruns:0
          TX packets:1366 errors:0 dropped:0 overruns:0
          Interrupt:11 Base address:0x210

eth1      Link encap:Ethernet  HWaddr 00:A0:24:2F:30:69
          inet addr:192.168.32.254  Bcast:192.168.32.255  Mask:255.255.255.0
          UP BROADCAST RUNNING MULTICAST  MTU:1500  Metric:1
          RX packets:799 errors:0 dropped:0 overruns:0
          TX packets:905 errors:0 dropped:0 overruns:0
          Interrupt:10 Base address:0x330
```

3. If you do not see the second interface, *eth1*, try to configure it manually as follows:

```
ifconfig eth1 192.168.32.254
```

4. If it could not configure the interface, it returns a message such as the following:

```
SIOCSIFADDR: No such device
```

5. In this case, the second interface has not been recognized. The *kerneld* daemon, most likely, did not install the network adapter module (unfortunately, the *Kerneld Configurator* does not return error messages). Try to load the module yourself. In my case, I enter the following command to load the *3c509.o* module found in the */lib/modules/2.0.31/net* directory:

```
/sbin/modprobe 3c509
```

6. If it works, you see information displayed about your second interface. If not, try reloading the module and specify the I/O address and Interrupt number (*irq*) as shown in the following example:

```
modprobe 3c509 io=0x330, irq = 10
```

Of course, you first need to find out these numbers. One way you might do that is to reboot your computer with MS-DOS and use the network adapter configuration software that came bundled with it, to view its parameters. (Normally, you would find such information by viewing the */proc/ioaddress*, */proc/interrupts*, and */proc/net/dev* files, but because that information has not been loaded — because the module did not load — it cannot be found there.)

7. If this does not work, you still have the option of compiling the kernel to include static network interfaces. Follow the instructions I offer in this chapter that describe the process. You need to answer *Yes* when prompted for your particular network adapter.

Configuring the Firewall Server

To complete the protection of your Private Network, you need to create and configure a Firewall Server. The Firewall Server needs to perform the following functions:

◆ Providing as few (potential) entrance points for burglars and thieves. This means removing all but the essential daemons and applications from the Firewall Server.

◆ Masquerading IP packets to and from your ISP — it needs to provide masquerading if you do not possess a registered IP network address.

◆ Providing a connection to your ISP and the Internet. I use the *diald* and *pppd* daemons for that purpose.

 TIP If you can afford to do so, pick up a used PC and install Linux as described previously. The minimum configuration used in Chapter 1 is a good one for this purpose. (However, if you are redoing it from scratch, leave out the Samba package.) As you may recall, I recommend purchasing — or reusing — an inexpensive, older 200MB to 400MB hard disk. Again, this is a good platform for a firewall (although you should run the standard disk-checking programs to eliminate any obviously shaky disks) because you do not need much space. If you want to use a more powerful machine, don't let me stop you, but the bottleneck on a firewall is going to be the Internet connection, which is generally going to be slow, even compared to a 386 CPU. Minimalism is one of the driving ideas behind firewalls because you want to leave as few opportunities for people to break in. So you don't need gigabytes of space for software.

I recommend that you use the instructions in Chapter 1 to create a new Linux computer. After doing so, use the following instructions in this chapter and Chapter 11 to configure it as a Firewall Server.

CONFIGURING FIREWALL FILTERING AND MASQUERADING RULES

In Chapter 8, you created a bare-bones Linux system to act as your firewall. It was simple but effective for your simple network. That system can readily be enhanced to work as a firewall for your about-to-be substantial network. The next step is to add the IP packet filtering rules that turn your Linux box into your Firewall Server. The remainder of this chapter and Chapter 11 are dedicated to enhancing the Firewall Server even further.

In Chapter 8, I introduced the *diald* daemon, which automatically senses network traffic going to the Internet and establishes a PPP connection to your Internet service provider (ISP). If you are connecting to the Internet from just one machine, as described in Chapter 8, the filtering rules described in the "Configuring a Simple Firewall" section in that chapter are all you need. However, if you want to allow any computer on your Private Network to make external connections, you must do one of two things:

◆ Obtain a class C IP network address from your ISP and use those addresses on your Private Network. (This is getting more difficult because you must prove that you have – or demonstrate that you will have very shortly – at least 128 network devices.

◆ Masquerade your Private Network on the Internet.

If you are in the first category, you may want to obtain your own addresses. However, masquerading works very well in either case. All you need is a PPP connection and you can immediately use masquerading and get on the Net.

Masquerading maps an outgoing IP address to a valid IP address. It also remaps the returning packet(s) back to their original IP address. It also changes the originating port number to another port number and then back again. This enables you to use nonregistered IP addresses for your internal network. Your ISP provides you with a registered (valid) IP address for your PPP connection, and that is what the rest of the world sees you as. This has two benefits:

◆ You do not need to register with anyone. You can connect your Private Network right out of the box.

◆ Your IP packets are partially hidden. Anyone sniffing your traffic sees you as an address on your ISP's network. (Sniffing is the process of monitoring network traffic. A sniffer collects IP packets on a network and is used for debugging network problems but also can be used to gain information about your network that can be used against you). If your ISP uses dynamic addressing for your PPP connection, your IP address will change frequently as you make new connections.

When computer *A* sends a packet to the Internet, the masquerading firewall converts machine *A*'s IP address to another IP address that is registered with the InterNIC. It also converts the port number to an arbitrary port number – in the numbers for unregistered ports above 1024. The return packets are converted back so that they match what the originating network device expects. In this way, any network computer or device can use the Internet.

For example, assume that your ISP uses an IP network address of 192.168.142.0 and a registered InterNIC network name is acme.com. After you establish a PPP connection, you are assigned an address of 192.168.142.23. If a computer *bart* has an address of 192.168.1.3 and it tries to *Telnet* to a computer on the Internet, the IP address and port number of the packets that it sends get changed from 192.168.1.3 and 23 to 192.168.142.23 and 2094 (the second port number is arbitrary). The destination host sees packets arriving from what it thinks is acme.com and sends its response packets back to that address. These packets show up on the PPP interface, and the firewall recognizes them as masqueraded packets. It converts their address back to 192.168.1.3 and 23 and forwards them to its Private Network interface. Computer *bart* sees packets with its address and the *Telnet* port number and sends them back to the originating *Telnet* session.

I have included two scripts, *firewall.rules* and *firewall.reset*, on the companion CD-ROM. I recommend copying them to the */usr/local/etc* directory in order to follow the FSTND. Listing 10-17 shows the script. It is basically a compilation of the individual rules that I introduce in command form in Chapter 8. I have added the capability to automatically determine the IP address of your PPP connection on the first line. I have also added a masquerading rule to the end of the script.

Listing 10-17: The firewall.rules script for creating a firewall with masquerading

```
# This script is called by diald after it has established a PPP connection
# is established. There, the dynamic PPP IP address can readily be obtained.
# That is done by piping the output of ifconfig to grep which strips out all the
# lines except the one containing the address and pipes it to awk which strips
# out the 2nd field containing the IP address. In the final step, sed eliminates
# the text string "addr:" leaving just the numeric IP address.
   ISP_IP='ifconfig ppp0 |grep 'inet addr'| awk '{print $2}'|sed -e "s/addr\://"'

# Display the PPP IP address.
   echo $ISP_IP

# Define the known, fixed addresses
   ME="192.168.32.1"
   FIRE_NET="192.168.32.0/24"
   PRIV_NET="192.168.1.0/24"
   ALLIP="0.0.0.0/0"
   HIPORTS="1024:65535"

# Clear out whatever rules are still set.
ipfwadm -I -f
ipfwadm -O -f
ipfwadm -F -f

# Start by completely denying any network access.
ipfwadm -I -p deny
ipfwadm -O -p deny
ipfwadm -F -p deny

# Deny spoofed packets. Those are packets which show up on your external
# (PPP) interface with the source address of your PPP connection and/or
# your internet network. My ISP automatically filters out such addresses
# but it's still better to be safe.
ipfwadm -I -a deny -V $ISP_IP \
                   -S $FIRE_NET \
                   -D $ALLIP
ipfwadm -I -a deny -V $ISP_IP \
                   -S $PRIV_NET \
                   -D $ALLIP
ipfwadm -I -a deny -V $ISP_IP \
                   -S $ISP_IP \
                   -D $ALLIP
```

```
# Allow unlimited traffic within the local network
# (All traffic on the ethernet interface - attached to the
# Linux file/print server. This does not affect the behavior of
# the PPP/Internet connection.)
#
ipfwadm -I -a accept -V $ME \
                     -S $ALLIP \
                     -D $ALLIP
ipfwadm -O -a accept -V $ME \
                     -S $ALLIP \
                     -D $ALLIP


# Allow outgoing TCP packets for the specified protocols
# I use duplicate rules for both the specific PPP IP address (obtained
# from the first command line in this script) as well as the firewall
# subnet. The first rule allows you to access the Internet from the firewall
# network since outgoing packets use the PPP connection IP as their source
# address (Note that this is superfluous if you follow the instructions
# in Chapter 11 that remove most network applications from the firewall to
# increase security.) The second rule permits computers on the Firewall Network
# and the Private Network to reach the Internet since they arrive at the
# PPP interface with the source address of the Linux file/print server which
# routes packets from the Private Network to the Firewall Network and
# masquerades them.
ipfwadm -O -a accept -P tcp \
                     -S $FIRE_NET $HIPORTS \
                     -D $ALLIP pop-3 smtp ftp ftp-data www telnet domain
ipfwadm -O -a accept -P tcp \
                     -S $ISP_IP $HIPORTS \
                     -D $ALLIP pop-3 smtp ftp ftp-data www telnet domain


# Allow outgoing UDP packets for the specified protocols
ipfwadm -O -a accept -P udp \
                     -S $FIRE_NET $HIPORTS \
                     -D $ALLIP domain
ipfwadm -O -a accept -P udp \
                     -S $ISP_IP $HIPORTS \
                     -D $ALLIP domain


# Allow the return packets of sessions originating internally for the specified
# protocols. The -k option allows only those packets with their SYN bit set.
# When the SYN bit is set, it means that the packet is being returned by a
# remote process after having originated locally.
ipfwadm -I -a accept -k -P tcp \
```

```
                       -S $ALLIP pop-3 smtp ftp www telnet domain \
                       -D $FIRE_NET $HIPORTS
ipfwadm -I -a accept -k -P tcp \
                       -S $ALLIP pop-3 smtp ftp www telnet domain \
                       -D $ISP_IP $HIPORTS

# Allow the remote ftp server to initiate a connection back to you. This happens
# when you issue an ftp command like "dir" or "get" or "put", etc. Note that
# this is not necessary if you use the ftp passive mode.
ipfwadm -I -a accept -P tcp \
                       -S $ALLIP ftp-data \
                       -D $FIRE_NET $HIPORTS
ipfwadm -I -a accept -P tcp \
                       -S $ALLIP ftp-data \
                       -D $ISP_IP $HIPORTS
#
ipfwadm -I -a accept -P udp \
                       -S $ALLIP domain \
                       -D $FIRE_NET $HIPORTS
ipfwadm -I -a accept -P udp \
                       -S $ALLIP domain \
                       -D $ISP_IP $HIPORTS

#
# Set masquerading rules. (The second rule is necessary if you do not
# set up masquerading on the Linux File Server/Router between the
# Private and Firewall Networks. If that is the case, you also have
# to add an explicit route on the firewall server to point back to
# the Private Network. For example:
# route add -net 192.168.1.0 gw 192.168.32.254
#
   ipfwadm -F -a masquerade  -S $FIRE_NET -D 0.0.0.0/0
#   ipfwadm -F -a masquerade  -S $ISP_IP   -D 0.0.0.0/0
```

TIP

I derived these rules from an excellent paper written by Jos Vos and Willy Konijnenberg of *X/OS Experts in Open Systems BV*, which you can find on their Web site at `www.xos.nl`.

Finally, set *FORWARD_IPV4* to *true* in the */etc/sysconfig/network* file.

CONNECTING THE FIREWALL SERVER TO YOUR ISP

I introduced the *diald* utility in Chapter 8. It automatically establishes a PPP connection to your ISP when IP packets destined for the Internet are generated. This is the method I'll use to connect the Firewall Server to the Internet.

Most ISPs use dynamic IP address allocation for dial-up PPP connections. You can have *diald* run the *firewall.rules* script whenever it negotiates a PPP connection – you use the *ip-up* and *ip-down* options to run the specified scripts when *diald* establishes and stops a connection. Edit the *connect* script from Chapter 8 (Listing 8-7) and add the *ip-up* and *ip-down* options as shown in Listing 10-19.

Listing 10-19: The /etc/ppp/connect script that sets and resets the ipfwadm rules

```
fifo /etc/diald/diald.ctl
mode ppp
connect "sh /etc/ppp/connect"
device /dev/modem
speed 38400
modem
lock
crtscts
local 127.0.0.2
remote 127.0.0.3
dynamic
defaultroute
pppd-options asyncmap 0
include /usr/lib/diald/standard.filter
ip-up /usr/local/etc/firewall.rules
ip-down /usr/local/etc/firewall.reset
```

To ensure that the firewall filters don't interfere with the operation of the firewall computer when the PPP connection is off, I also include the script, *firewall.reset*, shown in Listing 10-20, which clears all the rules. It is also useful to have such a utility for debugging purposes so that you can easily restart from a known state.

Listing 10-20: The script firewall.reset that clears all firewall packet filtering rules

```
/sbin/ipfwadm -I -f
/sbin/ipfwadm -O -f
/sbin/ipfwadm -F -f
/sbin/ipfwadm -I -p accept
/sbin/ipfwadm -O -p accept
/sbin/ipfwadm -F -p accept
```

When the *firewall.rules* script is run, your Linux box filters out all incoming IP packets that did not originate from your Private Network. For instance, if you start a *Telnet* session with a remote computer, the packets that are sent back to you in response to your actions are allowed to pass through your firewall. You will not be able to start a *Telnet* session from outside your Private Network that makes a connection into your network.

You can list the input, output, and forwarding filtering rules by entering the following commands (include the -*e* option to display the extended information, including the interfaces, protocols, and various other information):

```
ipfwadm -I -1
ipfwadm -O -1
ipfwadm -F -1
```

Listing 10-21 shows the results of listing the filtering rules.

Listing 10-21: Displaying the filtering rules set up by the firewall.rules script

```
IP firewall output rules, default policy: deny
type  prot source           destination        ports
acc   all  0.0.0.0/0        0.0.0.0/0          n/a
acc   tcp  192.168.32.0/24  0.0.0.0/0          1024:65535 -> 110,25,21,203
acc   tcp  204.134.5.6      0.0.0.0/0          1024:65535 -> 110,25,21,203
acc   udp  192.168.32.0/24  0.0.0.0/0          1024:65535 -> 53
acc   udp  204.134.5.6      0.0.0.0/0          1024:65535 -> 53

IP firewall input rules, default policy: deny
type  prot source           destination        ports
deny  all  192.168.32.0/24  0.0.0.0/0          n/a
deny  all  204.134.5.6      0.0.0.0/0          n/a
acc   all  0.0.0.0/0        0.0.0.0/0          n/a
acc   tcp  0.0.0.0/0        192.168.32.0/24    110,25,21,80,23,53 -> 10245
acc   tcp  0.0.0.0/0        204.134.5.6        110,25,21,80,23,53 -> 10245
acc   tcp  0.0.0.0/0        192.168.32.0/24    20 -> 1024:65535
acc   tcp  0.0.0.0/0        204.134.5.6        20 -> 1024:65535
acc   udp  0.0.0.0/0        192.168.32.0/24    53 -> 1024:65535
acc   udp  0.0.0.0/0        204.134.5.6        53 -> 1024:65535

IP firewall forward rules, default policy: deny
type    prot source           destination        ports
acc/m all  192.168.32.0/24    0.0.0.0/0          n/a
```

If you want to access your Private Network from outside your building, you could reconfigure your firewall rules to allow access. Otherwise, follow the guidelines in the next section on establishing an external phone dial-in.

TESTING YOUR IP FILTERING SETUP

It is informative to see how your new firewall works. To accomplish this, establish an Internet connection via your ISP. After your filtering rules are activated (whether by the startup script, the *diald ip-up* option, or manually) *Telnet* to your ISP account. Enter the following command from your Firewall Server:

```
ifconfig ppp0
```

Ifconfig should return information like that shown in Listing 10-22.

Listing 10-22: Your PPP connection parameters

```
ppp0     Link encap:Point-Point Protocol
inet addr:192.168.115.151  P-t-P:192.168.115.101  Mask:255.255.255.0
         UP POINTOPOINT RUNNING  MTU:1500  Metric:1
         RX packets:16 errors:0 dropped:0 overruns:0
         TX packets:17 errors:0 dropped:0 overruns:0
```

The *inet addr* (I have changed the actual address to protect the innocent) is what you're interested in. This is the IP address that my ISP has dynamically assigned to me. Without IP filtering, or network application proxies, anyone can attempt to log in to your system. Try doing just that yourself. First log in to your *Telnet* account on your ISP's network. Then try to *Telnet* back into your system as follows:

```
telnet 192.168.115.151
```

If your filters are working, you get no response. However, if you turn the rules off, you should be able to log in to your system.

The filtering rules I have used prevent all communication originating from the Internet into your network. You can set up rules to allow a limited amount of incoming connections. You can find a good description of such rules at http://simba.xos.nl/linux/ipfwadm. I prefer to avoid allowing such connections and use a dial-in method, as I describe in the next section.

The filtering rules, as I have set them up, only allow IP packets that originate from within your Private Network to pass back through the firewall. (Actually, packets from your network application find their way to a server at another IP address, and that server sends back packets with its own IP address in addition to the information derived from your packets.)

The problem with configuring your IP filter to allow connections from the outside is that it introduces far more problems than simply allowing the return packets from your own applications back in. In the following sections, you follow the packets originating from within your Private Network and then those that originate from the outside.

FOLLOWING AN IP PACKET ORIGINATING FROM WITHIN YOUR PRIVATE NETWORK

Here's the simplest example: You have a Firewall Server connected to the Internet with an IP packet filter set to allow only *Telnet* sessions originating from your network. Everything else is denied. Start a *Telnet* session on your Firewall Server to a computer on the Internet, which has the fictitious IP address: 192.168.114.1. The *Telnet* program sends out TCP packets with the source address and port number set to 192.168.32.1/{*any port above 1024*} and the destination address and port number set to 192.168.114.1/23. The *Telnet* server daemon at 192.168.114.1 responds by reversing the IP address and port numbers and also – very important – setting the ACK bit.

Suppose that someone is monitoring your *Telnet* session (sniffing) and derives a complete portrait of your firewall configuration. That person could try to either piggyback onto an active *Telnet* session of yours or wait until it ends and try to start another – invalid – session. But two problems must be overcome:

♦ If the usurper tries to piggyback on an active session, the illegal piggyback packets can only find their way to your *Telnet* program – remember that the IP filter will only allow packets back into your network that have the IP address and port number of *your Telnet* session. You may see spurious characters but unless a bug or a trapdoor exists within your *Telnet* program that can be exploited, that is all that will happen.

♦ If the person tries to start a new *Telnet* session, those packets will be rejected outright by the IP filter because it is configured only to accept packets with the SYN bit set. If, on the other hand, the burglar sets the ACK bit, then no server will act on the packets. The *Telnet* daemon will only respond to "fresh" packets. (Just in case, I have you remove all the network daemons such as *Telnet* in the section "Eliminating All Unnecessary System Daemons and Applications from the Firewall Server," in Chapter 11.

So, the IP packet filter that allows you to use the Internet from your Private Network is a reasonably safe system. The only way I can conceive of a breach occurring is if a bug or a trapdoor exists in the filtering software or in a network application server (that is, the *Telnet* daemon). And if you follow my advice and eliminate those daemons from your Firewall Server, you are that much safer.

FOLLOWING AN IP PACKET ORIGINATING
FROM OUTSIDE YOUR PRIVATE NETWORK

On the other hand, if you allow connections from the outside, you have more potential problems to deal with. You have to set up rules like that shown in Listing 10-23, to allow anyone to connect to one of your computers. (In the example shown, I imply the use of the Firewall Server as the *Telnet* server but that is only for illustration. In Chapter 11, the section "Eliminating All Unnecessary System Daemons and Applications from the Firewall Server" discusses the removal of all such capability, so this is a moot point.)

Listing 10-23: IP filter rules for external Telnet access to the Firewall Server

```
ipfwadm -I -a accept -P tcp -S 0.0.0.0/0 -D 192.168.32.254 telnet
ipfwadm -O -a accept -P tcp -S 192.168.32.254 telnet -D 0.0.0.0/0
```

Now you can take some comfort that in order to log in to your File Server/Router, someone must know about your network and ISP. You also gain some additional safety by masquerading your network because your original IP and port address get replaced, but the fact remains that if a potential intruder gets the IP/port address combination right, your system *can* be attacked.

That may be an acceptable risk for you. Proxy firewalls work better in this situation because you can require all attempted logins to pass through extra hoops. You can even continue to use your filtering firewall and add *S/Key* or *SecureID* to your login for additional security. However, I sleep better by separating incoming and outgoing communication. I discuss that in the next section.

CONFIGURING YOUR FIREWALL SERVER FOR DIAL-IN

I recommend that you keep your IP filtering rules as they are. This section deals with setting up external connection capability.

However, it is often very desirable, if not essential, to gain access to your Private Network from outside that network. You can do that by manipulating the filtering rules to allow limited traffic in from the Internet on a limited basis. You can also use proxies for that purpose – the Firewall Toolkit from Trusted Information Systems provides such software. But that presents additional security hole possibilities. I think it's better to provide a different pathway for incoming traffic. By providing an alternative pathway, you can concentrate on keeping it as secure as possible.

You need a separate telephone line and modem, of course. After you have both, you need to configure your Firewall Server and modem to work together, by completing the following steps:

1. If you need to install an internal modem, log on to your Firewall Server as *root*, shut down Linux, turn the power off, and disconnect the power cable. Here's the shutdown command:

   ```
   shutdown -h now
   ```

2. You need to choose the serial port to use for incoming calls. The choice depends on if you are using internal or external modems. If you are using external modems, you have fewer choices. PCs can have as many as four serial ports without adding additional adapters. However, the four ports share only two interrupts (IRQ), so you can run only two devices, such as external modems, attached to the serial ports at the same time. If you are using internal modems, you can force them to use different interrupts.

I use a combination of both: an internal modem to make my PPP connections to the Internet and an external modem for my dial-in connections; I like the external modem for dial-in because I can simply turn the power off when I don't want to allow connections. I have my primary – PPP – modem configured for serial port 3 (COM4 in DOS terminology) and my secondary – Dial-In – on port 0 (COM1). Table 10-4 lists the serial ports that Linux recognizes.

If you have not already added a link to your modem's serial port then do so now:

```
ln -s /dev/ttyS0 /dev/modem
```

TABLE 10-4 LINUX SERIAL PORTS

Number	Device–Outgoing	Device–Incoming
1	/dev/ttyS0	/dev/cua0 Dial-in, external modem
2	/dev/ttyS1	/dev/cua1 Direct serial connection to File Server/Router – see Chapter 11
3	/dev/ttyS2	/dev/cua2 Unused
4	/dev/ttyS3	/dev/cua3 Dial-out/PPP internal modem (IRQ 5)

3. Connect your external modem to the serial port or insert your internal modem into an empty slot, turn on the power, and log in as *root*.

4. The *setserial* is a program that configures the serial ports. I use a relatively high-speed 34.4 Kbps modem, and the *spd_vi* parameter sets the port to function up to 115,200 baud:

```
/bin/setserial /dev/modem spd_vhi
```

5. Check to see if you can connect to the modem. I use the *dip* program in *terminal* mode. Here's the sequence of *dip* commands you enter to connect to the modem (you do not enter the string *DIP>*, which is the prompt that *dip* gives you after you start it):

```
dip -t
DIP> port modem
DIP> term
at
```

The modem should return the two-character response: *OK*.

6. Configure your modem to work with Linux (as described in the following steps). Enter the following modem commands:

```
AT&V
ATS0=0
ATE1
ATQ0
ATV1
AT&C1
AT&S0
AT&W
```

The commands do the following:

- &V simply displays the modem's current configuration.

- S0=0 turns off *auto answer* mode because the Linux *uugetty* program will perform that function.

- E1 turns on the *command echo*.

- Q0 means result codes are reported.

- V1 turns on *verbose* mode.

- &C1 sets the modem to control the carrier-detect (CD) line.

- &S0 turns on the Data Set Ready (DSR) permanently.

- &W saves these settings as the default setting.

7. When you log on to a Linux box, a *getty* daemon that is continually monitoring its input ports (that is, the console) detects your keystroke(s) and starts the */bin/login* program. The *login* program negotiates the rest of the process, including authentication (validating your password). I use the *uugetty* configuration file that comes with the Red Hat distribution and

works well with modems. If you are missing the *getty_ps* RPM package, which contains the *uugetty* daemon, then install it now:

```
rpm -ivh /mnt/cdrom/RedHat/RPMS/getty_ps-2.0.7j-2.i386.rpm
```

8. Listing 10-24 shows the sample *uugetty* configuration file designed for Hayes compatible modems with their *auto answer* mode turned off. I derived this from the example *uugetty* configuration file found on Red Hat's Web page: `www.redhat.com/support/docs/Dialup-Tips/Dialup-Tips.5.html`.

Listing 10-24: The /etc/conf.uugetty.modem file

```
# /etc/conf.uugetty.modem

# Define some system parameters
SYSTEM=burns
VERSION='/bin/uname -s -r'
# Use the standard login
LOGIN=/bin/login
ISSUE=/etc/issue
# Define the serial port to monitor
INITLINE=cua1
TIMEOUT=30
HANGUP=YES
# Send the initialization string to the modem.
#
# The three pluses (+++) interrupts the modem even if it is connected.
# The ATHO forces the modem to hang up.
# The AT..Z resets the modem
INIT="" \d+++\dAT\r OK\r\n ATHO\r OK\r\n AT\sZ\r OK\r\n
# Waitfor string... A call is occurring when the string RING is detected.
WAITFOR=RING
# Once the WAITFOR=RING occurs the A\ sequence sets the baudrate
# automatically.
#
CONNECT="" ATA\r CONNECT\s
# Delay for 2 seconds
DELAY=2
# Uncomment to use debug option
#DEBUG=010        # uncomment this for debug output
#
# END /etc/conf.uugetty.modem
```

9. You may or may not need to modify the default *gettydefs* file. (Just to be safe, make a backup copy */etc/gettydefs.orig*.) *Gettydefs* should contain the line that tells *uugetty* about the modem that it connects to. The one I use and which should work for all modern modems is as follows:

```
# 38400 Fixed Baud Modem entry with hardware control (it should be only one
  line)
F38400# B38400 CS8 CRTSCTS # B38400 SANE -ISTRIP HUPCL CRTSCTS #@s \
  login: #F38400
```

10. The */etc/inittab* file is used by *init* to configure the system – generally at boot time or when you change run levels. It also contains information about the serial port configurations and needs to be modified to make all this work automatically. Make a backup copy to */etc/inittab.orig* to be safe. Next, add a line that contains the information about your dial-in port – in my case *S0*. Listing 10-25 shows the lines that I added to my system.

Listing 10-25: The /etc/inittab modified to set up the dial-in port

```
# Dial in lines enabled in standard runlevels

S0:23456:respawn:/sbin/uugetty ttyS0 F38400 vt100
```

Table 10-5 explains the meanings of the fields.

TABLE 10-5 THE INITTAB SERIAL PORT FIELDS

Field Number	Field	Explanation
1	S0	Serial port
2	234	The run levels where this line can be activated
3	respawn	Restart the process defined in field number 4 if it dies
4	/sbin/uugetty	Specifies that *uugetty* is to monitor the serial port for logins
5	ttyS0	The device associated with this port
6	F38400	The maximum allowed speed for this port
7	vt100	The default terminal type for this port

11. To force Linux to recognize all these changes, you must tell it to reread its configuration file. Enter the following command as *root*:

```
telinit q
```

If you look at the end of the message log */var/log/messages* (*tail /var/log/messages*), you should see an indication that Linux did the job. It also lists any errors that occurred.

12. Test your setup by dialing in to your new port. If you have two telephone lines and modems, the process is easy. I use *dip* to dial out on my one modem (the one I normally use for PPP connections) and back into my second modem.

Your Firewall Server can now be accessed from outside. At this point, you can still communicate with the rest of your network because *Telnet* is still installed. However, in Chapter 11, you remove that service (as well as many others) from the Firewall Server in order to minimize potential security holes. With those changes, you can only gain access to the Firewall Server from the outside.

You can fix this shortcoming in two ways:

♦ Configure another machine as the dial-in server and leave the *Telnet* service installed. You may either dedicate an old computer for this purpose or piggyback the function onto an existing computer such as the File Server/Router.

♦ Add a serial connection between the Firewall Server and a computer on the Private Network. You can dial-in to the firewall and then use a terminal emulator to connect to the *File Server/Router* on the Private Network. From there, you can *Telnet* to any machine you want.

The drawback of the former approach is that you now have two points of access to your Private Network rather than one and have to maintain two machines rather than one. The advantage is that you only need to log on to one machine. The latter, of course, is inconvenient to use because you must log on to the Firewall Server, start the terminal emulator, and then log on to a second machine. However, it is more secure.

I prefer the latter approach because it enhances security and makes for better sleeping patterns. In Chapter 11, I describe the installation process in the section "Adding a Serial Connection to Your Firewall Server."

> For more information about setting up modems, see the Linux Serial Interface HOWTO at */usr/doc/HOWTO/Serial-HOWTO*. Also, you can find a good troubleshooting reference at `www.redhat.com/linux-info /lpd/HOWTO/Serial-HOWTO-13.html`.

ADDING A ONE-TIME PASSWORD GENERATOR – S/KEY – TO YOUR SYSTEM

A dial-in modem with a one-time password entry system enables you to make your Private Network as safe as possible while remaining accessible from the outside world and without spending additional money. A system that generates passwords that are only valid once is an excellent way to keep burglars and vandals out of your system.

First, even though you send the passwords as plain text, if they are intercepted somehow, they are useless after you have logged in yourself. Second, you and your associates are prevented from getting lazy and giving away your passwords or using trivial ones (although you must exercise caution to keep your private keys secret).

Commercial and freeware products provide varying levels of authentication. Having a separate phone line for entry removes many potential break-ins because an intruder must use the phone system as opposed to the Internet as the medium. It is simply more difficult to program a device or program to make phone calls as opposed to sending out packets. It is also more traceable.

I am familiar with two products that provide one-time passwords: *SecureID* and *S/Key* by Bellcore. *SecureID* uses a small, credit card–like device to generate the password key. That device continuously generates one-time numeric keys (six digits) that change every minute or so. When you want to log in to a computer or network guarded by *SecureID*, you first enter your own individual and private four-digit number and then the key that it generates. If it is correct, you are allowed entry.

S/Key uses a software-based system in which you enter your private password into a program and it generates a password that is six words long. You then enter that password onto the *S/Key* compatible *login* program, on the remote system, to gain entry. This process seems complicated, but if you are using a Microsoft Windows computer, you can cut and paste the password between windows and it is a reasonably easy process to perform.

I use *S/Key* for this example because it is free and available from the Internet. You can use anonymous FTP to obtain it. I divide installation and configuration instructions into two parts: one for installing the *S/Key* on your Firewall Server and the other for installing an *S/Key* client (also called a password calculator) onto your Windows computer.

INSTALLING AND CONFIGURING S/KEY ON YOUR LINUX FIREWALL SERVER

You must install and compile the *S/Key* programs that initialize the one-time password database. You also must install and compile the *S/Key login* program that accepts *S/Key* passwords (it replaces your current */bin/login* program). You can find the *S/Key tar* file at any SunSITE mirror in the */pub/linux/system/security* directory. The following instructions describe obtaining the software, installing, and then using it.

Note that when you initialize the *S/Key* system starting in Step 13, you need to run two programs — *keyinit* and *key* — at the same time. I suggest that you log on to two virtual consoles; I described virtual terminals in Chapter 1. One program generates input for the other, which in turn uses it to generate further input, which it feeds back to the first program. It is a little confusing at first, but it will become clear as you do it.

1. Log on to your Firewall Server as *root*.

2. Enter the following command to move to the directory where it is best to store unique software:

   ```
   cd /usr/local/src
   ```

3. I have included the *S/Key tar* file on the companion CD-ROM. Enter the following command to log on to the site:

   ```
   cp /mnt/cdrom/IDG/skey-2.2.tar.gz
   ```

   (You can also find *skey-2.2.tar.gz* at any SunSITE in the */pub/linux/system/security* directory.)

4. The *S/Key login* program does not compile correctly with the current version of the C-libraries that come with Red Hat 5.0. I have not found the correction to the problem so I have included the C-libraries from Red Hat 4.2 that do work. I have included them in the IDG directory on the companion CD-ROM. Listing 10-26 describes how to temporarily update current software:

Listing 10-26: Updating the C-libraries for S/Key

```
rpm -e glibc-devel
cd /mnt/cdrom/IDG
rpm -Uvh --force libc-static-5.3.12-18.i386.rpm
rpm -Uvh --force libc-devel-5.3.12-18.i386.rpm
```

5. Next, unpackage the *tar* file:

```
tar xzf skey-2.2.tar.gz
```

6. The directory *skey-2.2* is created in */usr/local/src* when you unpack the *tar* file. Change to that directory:

```
cd skey-2.2
```

7. Examine the README file. It tells you how to prepare the *skey* package for compilation.

8. Edit the *Makefile* and change the *LDFLAGS* = line to the following:

```
LDFLAGS = -static
```

This means that the actual code contained in the C-libraries that you just installed will be directly compiled into the *S/Key* programs. I want to do this because I will reinstall the current (Red Hat 5.0) libraries after the *S/Key* programs have been installed. The standard C-libraries are normally dynamically linked into the compiled code and are accessed whenever the compiled program is executed. That could present problems because we are going back to older libraries to make this code work. The statically compiled programs are self-contained and do not present this problem.

9. Compile the programs:

```
make
```

The *make* program proceeds to descend into and compile the programs in each directory. Part of the process is shown in Listing 10-27.

Listing 10-27: The make program compiles each of the S/Key programs in sequence

```
for i in libskey libmd keyinit key keyinfo login; do (cd $i && make \
        CC="gcc" CFLAGS="-O2" LDFLAGS="-static" \
        prefix="/usr" all); done
make[1]: Entering directory '/usr/local/skey-2.2/libskey'
gcc   -O2 -DPERMIT_CONSOLE -I. -I../libmd -c skeyaccess.c
gcc   -O2 -DPERMIT_CONSOLE -I. -I../libmd -c put.c
gcc   -O2 -DPERMIT_CONSOLE -I. -I../libmd -c skey_crypt.c
gcc   -O2 -DPERMIT_CONSOLE -I. -I../libmd -c skey_getpass.c
gcc   -O2 -DPERMIT_CONSOLE -I. -I../libmd -c skeylogin.c
gcc   -O2 -DPERMIT_CONSOLE -I. -I../libmd -c skeysubr.c
ar crs libskey.a skeyaccess.o put.o skey_crypt.o skey_getpass.o skeylogin.o skeo
make[1]: Leaving directory '/usr/local/skey-2.2/libskey'
make[1]: Entering directory '/usr/local/skey-2.2/libmd'
gcc   -O2 -I. -c md2c.c
gcc   -O2 -I. -c md4c.c
```

```
gcc  -O2 -I. -c md5c.c
sed -e 's/mdX/md2/g' -e 's/MDX/MD2/g' mdXhl.c > md2hl.c
gcc  -O2 -I. -c md2hl.c
```

```
{the rest of the display is omitted}
```

10. Install all the programs and man-pages to their respective system directories, as shown in the following command:

```
make install
```

The *S/Key login* program replaces the original Linux *login* program. It is incompatible with shadow passwords, but you haven't installed shadow passwords on the Firewall Server. Because this machine is highly restricted, it is relatively safe from unauthorized access to the */etc/passwd* file, so this will work. In the future, I hope to be able to use *S/Key* with shadow passwords. (Because the Firewall Server is to be a very limited-access machine, I have removed *group* and other *read* privileges. This accomplishes the same security as shadow passwords in that no one but *root* can access the passwords. When you log in as a non-*root* user, you get the message "I have no name." This does not appear to affect me too adversely because I can always become *root*, which does have access to *passwd*. The server appears to work as it should in terms of its Internet service functions.)

The file */etc/skey.access* controls if and how the *S/Key* system is used. If it is omitted, no user needs to use the *S/Key* password. If the file exists, the rules are either *permit* or *deny*. Each rule may have zero or more parameters. Only one rule per line can be specified. Rules go in order so that when one is activated, *S/Key* does not search for any more. Comments begin with the pound (#) character. The skey-access man-page describes the details of the rules.

11. Edit the */etc/skey.access* file to include a test user. I add the test user, *micro*, with the *useradd* command first described in Chapter 7. Use the command *passwd micro* to give *micro* a password. Listing 10-28 shows my modified */etc/skey.access* file.

Listing 10-28: The S/Key configuration file /etc/skey.access

```
deny user micro
permit user root
permit user maggie
```

S/Key will challenge the user *micro* to enter the correct one-time password. The last line — permit user maggie — states that the user *maggie* will be allowed normal access. I have it like that so that I can easily access the Firewall Server while I configure it. You can remove that line, later, so everyone will get challenged.

12. Restore the original C-libraries after removing the old ones as follows:

```
rpm -e libc-devel
rpm -e libc-static
rpm -ivh /mnt/cdrom/RedHat/RPMS/glibc-devel-2.0.5c-10.i386.rpm
```

13. You must initialize the *S/Key* database so it can accept the one-time passwords that you generate. Enter the following commands to first change to user micro and then initialize the key:

```
su - micro
keyinit -s
```

You get the response shown in Listing 10-29.

Listing 10-29: The S/Key system is initialized

```
Adding micro:
Reminder you need the 6 English words from the skey command.
Enter sequence count from 1 to 9999:
```

14. Enter any number, but make sure you remember it until the initialization is finished. I enter the number *99*.

15. You are prompted to enter a key:

```
Enter new key [default ba79529]:
```

I use the default and therefore just press the *Enter* key at the prompt.

16. Now *keyinit* wants an access password generated by the *key* program:

```
s/key 99 ba79529
s/key access password:
```

It has not been generated yet, so you need to obtain it.

17. From another virtual console or window, run the *key* program. I use the sequence number of *99* and the key *ba79529* from the previous steps:

```
key 99 ba79529
```

18. You are given the response shown in Listing 10-30. At this point, you must enter a secret password of your own. You need to be just as careful with this password as you would be with a normal one. I recommend that you use the method I describe in Chapter 9. I enter the password *radi~otalk*.

Listing 10-30: Enter your own password to the key program

```
Reminder - Do not use this program while logged in via telnet or rlogin.
Enter secret password:radi~otalk
```

19. The *key* program responds with a six-word password, as in the following example:

```
KUDO GELD AVE TINA MEN APS
```

You need to enter it as the response to the *keyinit* prompt back in Step 16.

20. You now proceed from where you left off in Step 18. Enter the six-word password (case is important) generated in Step 19 at the prompt of *keyinit* and you get the response as follows:

```
s/key access password: KUDO GELD AVE TINA MEN APS
```

21. The *S/Key* system is initialized. Every time you run the *key* program, it will generate a one-time password for you to use.

22. Try to log on to the Linux firewall, *burns*, as *micro* and you should be presented with the *S/Key* challenge, as shown in Listing 10-31.

Listing 10-31: Enter your own password to the key program

```
burns.firenet.com login: micro
s/key 98 ba79529
Password:
```

23. To generate the *S/Key* password, run the *key* program from another virtual terminal or window and use the sequence number and key shown in Listing 10-31, as shown in the following example:

```
key 98 ba79529
```

24. The *key* program responds by requesting your secret password – *radi~otalk* – and when it is correctly entered, it gives you the password that you need:

```
Reminder - Do not use this program while logged in via telnet or
  rlogin.
Enter secret password:
WALT TRAY MITE FIG AIRY FOIL
```

25. Use the one-time password *WALT TRAY MITE FIG AIRY FOIL* at the password prompt and you can log on as the user *micro*.

The process of generating the *S/Key* password is made simpler by *S/Key calculators* that greatly facilitate the *logon* process. I describe a Windows-based calculator in the following section.

USING AN S/KEY PASSWORD CALCULATOR FOR MICROSOFT WINDOWS

The task of logging in to an *S/Key* protected system is made much easier if you use a password calculator GUI program. You can run the calculator GUI in one window on your Windows computer while you log on to the protected machine from another – for instance, Telnet – window. After you generate a one-time password, you can cut and paste it to the *S/Key* login challenge in the other window. The calculator program is called *KEYAPP.EXE* and is located at another anonymous FTP site. The following instructions detail the process of obtaining and installing *KEYAPP.EXE*:

1. Log on to your Firewall Server as *root.*

2. Enter the following command to move to the directory where it is best to store unique software:

   ```
   cd /usr/local/src
   ```

3. You need to obtain the *S/Key* calculator software from an anonymous FTP site. Enter the following command to log on to the site:

   ```
   ftp ftp.yak.net
   ```

4. Log on as *anonymous.* (Listing 10-32 shows my connection via anonymous FTP.)

Listing 10-32: Logging on as anonymous FTP at ftp.yak.net

```
ftp ftp.yak.net
Connected to ftp.yak.net.
220 nando FTP server (SunOS 4.1) ready.
Name (ftp.yak.net:skeyer): anonymous
331 Guest login ok, send ident as password.
Password:
230 Guest login ok, access restrictions apply.
ftp>
```

5. Change to the directory where the software is stored:

   ```
   cd /pub/skey/for-mswindows
   ```

6. You will be downloading a binary (nontext) file, so change to *binary transfer* mode:

   ```
   bin
   ```

7. Start transferring the file:

```
get keyapp.exe
```

8. Exit from FTP:

```
quit
```

9. From your Windows computer, FTP to your Firewall Server and log on as a regular user (Red Hat Linux default configuration does not allow you to log on as *root*).

10. Transfer *keyapp.exe* to your Windows machine.

11. Click the *Start* button.

12. Click the *Run* option.

13. From the *Run* dialog box, enter the *KEYAPP.EXE* program preceded by its directory (for example, **c:\keyapp.exe**).

14. You get the *S/Key* window, as shown in Figure 10-4.

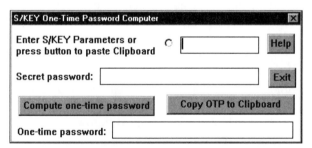

Figure 10-4: The Windows S/Key program KEYAPP.EXE

15. Use *Telnet* to connect to your Firewall Server. As shown in Listing 10-33, the new *S/Key login* program should prompt you.

Listing 10-33: The S/Key challenge from your Firewall Server

```
Red Hat Linux release 5.02 (Hurricane)
Kernel 2.0.31 on an i486

burns.firenet.com login: maggie
s/key 95 ba795200
Password:
```

16. Use your mouse to cut the *S/Key* sequence and key number from your Firewall Server login prompt (for example, *95 ba795200*).

17. The *S/Key* calculator offers a button that copies the text string that you just cut into its *S/Key* parameter slot. Click the button next to the sentence that says *Enter S/KEY Parameters or press button to paste Clipboard*, and the string you just copied will be copied there. Alternatively, you could type it in yourself.

18. Enter your "secret" password in the dialog box that says *Secret password:*. The calculator substitutes asterisks (*) for your entries.

19. Click the *Compute one-time password* button. The six-word one-time password is generated and displayed in the box below the button.

20. You can optionally click the *Copy OTP to Clipboard* button. Then you can use the mouse to paste the one-time password onto the *S/Key* prompt on the Firewall Server. Otherwise, you have to copy by hand. Whatever method you use, when you press the *Enter* key after entering the one-time password, you should gain access to the Firewall Server.

Using the *S/Key* calculator makes the entire system much more reasonable to use. Without it, you and your users could easily get frustrated and pull the system. This tool should prevent that and provide an excellent security tool.

Summary

In this chapter, I describe how to configure a "real" Linux client-server network. The example system is constructed with eight Microsoft Windows 95 clients, a Linux-based File and Printer server, and a Linux-based firewall.

I cover the following topics in this chapter:

♦ Adding several Windows 95 clients to create a "real-world" example network. The clients represent a small- to medium-sized office example.

♦ Configuring the Linux/Samba file and print server. The server introduced in Chapter 1 is expanded to include additional Windows 95 clients. The process is a simple one in which a user is added to the Linux *passwd* and *group* files. The new user matches the name of a Windows 95 client. Red Hat configures Samba to the user security authentication method and so you must match user names on the Linux file-print server to the name of the Windows client. This is preferable to the share security method, which is very confusing to learn.

♦ Subdividing Samba users into Linux groups to provide separation of work and extra security. Linux groups are created to match the type of work being performed on the network. Next, Samba shares are created to match the Linux groups. Two or more client computers can then access the work common to those groups. People can then work together with ease.

♦ Configuring a separate Firewall Network to connect the file-print server and the Firewall Server. This separates the Private Network from the Internet.

♦ Configuring the Linux IP filtering Firewall Server. The Firewall Server transfers IP packets between the Private Network and the Internet. Therefore, anyone attempting to break into your Private Network must first break through the Firewall Server. To make your network as difficult as possible for anyone to break into, you can remove all but the most essential software from the Firewall Server.

Chapter 11

Adding Security Measures to Your Real-World Network

IN THIS CHAPTER

◆ Adding active security measures to your network

◆ Detecting security problems before they occur with SATAN, Crack and Tripwire

◆ Adding passive security measures to your network

◆ Increasing security and reducing the load on your Internet connection

◆ Removing all unnecessary daemons and applications from your firewall server

YOU CAN NEVER "FINISH" UP your security. As you grow as a systems administrator/security monitor, you can add to the picture as you see fit. In this chapter, I guide you through the process of adding both active and passive security measures to the "real-world" network that you set up in Chapter 10.

Adding Active Security Measures to Your Private and Firewall Networks

The Tripwire and SATAN systems, introduced in Chapter 9, are two useful programs to build security into your network. Recall that Tripwire uses the MD5 (message digest algorithm) to calculate a checksum on important system files (any file you wish to check, actually). These checksums can periodically be compared to the current files to see if any files have been changed to possibly hide a Trojan Horse. SATAN uses a Web browser to graphically configure and display the results of various security checks that it performs. In the following sections, I show you how to install and get started with these two systems.

In addition to presenting Tripwire and SATAN, I also introduce the Crack system here. It checks your existing passwords against words that can be found in dictionaries. By using Crack, you can proactively protect your system from trivial or easily guessed passwords.

It is a good time to point out that I install these systems on the File Server/Router. I do this because SATAN can use a great deal of resources and I use an older PC as the Firewall Server. I also have you remove all compilers and development libraries from the Firewall Server, and SATAN needs to be compiled. Optionally, you can install SATAN and Tripwire on another Linux box if you wish, but in my example, I have only one such machine.

Installing and Configuring Tripwire

Tripwire is available as an RPM package on this book's CD-ROM. It is generally not considered good security practice to install a binary (especially of a code that is used for security itself) rather than to compile source code. The worry is that the binary can more readily hide viruses and back doors (fixed passwords or other entrances known only to the designer of the executable code) than source code can. However, I consider Red Hat to be a reliable source and trust them to have made every reasonable precaution. Therefore, I have installed it on my system but leave it up to you to decide for yourself whether you accept my reasoning. If you wish to obtain the source code, it is available from a SunSITE.

I use Tripwire on my File Server/Router. In my network, this is the most important computer, so I want to keep it as secure as possible. Tripwire can also be configured to check other computers on the network (for example, the Firewall Server), so as long as it has access to the Firewall Network, it can be placed anywhere. The following instructions detail the installation of Tripwire:

1. Log on to your Linux file server/router as *root*.

2. Mount your CD-ROM, if it is not already mounted, by entering the following command:

   ```
   mount /mnt/cdrom
   ```

3. Install Tripwire by entering the following command:

   ```
   rpm -ivh /mnt/cdrom/IDG/tripwire-1.2-1.i386.rpm
   ```

   Tripwire is installed into the directories shown in Listing 11-1.

Listing 11-1: The Tripwire distribution

```
/etc/cron.daily/tripwire.verify
/etc/tw.config
/usr/doc/tripwire-1.2-1
/usr/doc/tripwire-1.2-1/Changelog
/usr/doc/tripwire-1.2-1/FAQ
/usr/doc/tripwire-1.2-1/INTERNALS
```

```
/usr/doc/tripwire-1.2-1/README
/usr/doc/tripwire-1.2-1/README.FIRST
/usr/doc/tripwire-1.2-1/Readme
/usr/doc/tripwire-1.2-1/TODO
/usr/doc/tripwire-1.2-1/WHATSNEW
/usr/doc/tripwire-1.2-1/docs
/usr/doc/tripwire-1.2-1/docs/README
/usr/doc/tripwire-1.2-1/docs/appdev.txt
/usr/doc/tripwire-1.2-1/docs/designdoc.ps
/usr/doc/tripwire-1.2-1/docs/sans.txt
/usr/man/man5/tw.config.5
/usr/man/man8/siggen.8
/usr/man/man8/tripwire.8
/usr/sbin/siggen
/usr/sbin/tripwire
/var/spool/tripwire
```

4. View the Tripwire configuration file, */etc/tw.config*, shown in Listing 11-2.

Listing 11-2: The Tripwire configuration file /etc/tw.config

```
# $Id: tw.config,v 1.4 1993/11/22 06:38:06 genek Exp $
#
# tw.config
#
# This file contains a list of files and directories that System
# Preener will scan. Information collected from these files will be
# stored in the tw.database file.
#
# Format:     [!|=] entry [ignore-flags]
#
# where:      '!' signifies the entry is to be pruned (inclusive) from
#                 the list of files to be scanned.
#             '=' signifies the entry is to be added, but if it is
#                     a directory, then all its contents are pruned
#                     (useful for /tmp).
#
# where:    entry is the absolute pathname of a file or a directory
#
# where ignore-flags are in the format:
#           [template][ [+|-][pinugsam12] ... ]
#
#     - :  ignore the following atributes
#     + :  do not ignore the following attributes
```

```
#
#     p :  permission and file mode bits   a: access timestamp
#     i :  inode number                    m: modification timestamp
#     n :  number of links (ref count)     c: inode creation timestamp
#     u :  user id of owner                1: signature 1
#     g :  group id of owner               2: signature 2
#     s :  size of file
# Modes we want:

# Log file
@@define LOGFILEM E+pugn

# Config file
@@define CONFM E+pinugc

# Binary
@@define BINM E+pnugscil2

# Directory
@@define DIRM E+pnug

# Data file (same as BIN_M currently)
@@define DATAM E+pnugscil2

# Device files
@@define DEVM E+pnugsci

#
#
# Ex: The following entry will scan all the files in /etc, and report
#     any changes in mode bits, inode number, reference count, uid,
#     gid, modification and creation timestamp, and the signatures.
#     However, it will ignore any changes in the access timestamp.
#
#     /etc   +pinugsm12-a
#
# The following templates have been pre-defined to make these long ignore
# mask descriptions unnecessary.
#
# Templates:     (default)  R :  [R]ead-only (+pinugsm12-a)
#                           L :  [L]og file (+pinug-sam12)
#                           N :  ignore [N]othing (+pinusgsamc12)
#                           E :  ignore [E]verything (-pinusgsamc12)
#                           > :  like [L], but ignore growing files
```

```
#
# By default, Tripwire uses the R template -- it ignores
# only the access timestamp.
#
# You can use templates with modifiers, like:
#     Ex:   /etc/lp       E+ug
#
#     Example configuration file:
#             /etc        R       # all system files
#             !/etc/lp    R       # ...but not those logs
#             =/tmp       N       # just the directory, not its files
#
# ====
#
# Preprocessor directives:
#
#     The following directives provide C-preprocessor and m4 like
#     functionality:
#
#             @@ifhost hostname :    included if (hostname) matches
#             @@ifhost hostname :    included if (hostname) doesn't
#                                    match.
#                                    (both need matching @@endif)
#
#             @@define x      :      defines (x)
#             @@undef x       :      undefines (x)
#
#             @@ifdef x       :      included if (x) is defined.
#             @@ifndef x      :      included if (x) is not defined.
#                                    (both need matching @@endif)
#
#             @@endif         :      closes up @@ifhost, @@ifdef,
#                                    and @@ifndef.
#
#     Example:
#     host-dependent inclusion can be specified many ways so tw.config
#     files can be shared among multiple machines.  So, if the machine
#     "mentor.cc.purdue.edu" is the only machine that has a certain file,
#     you could use:
#
#             @@ifhost mentor.cc.purdue.edu
#             /etc/tw.log.mentor       R
#             @@endif
#
```

```
# exclude all of /proc
=/proc E

#=/dev @@DIRM
/dev @@DEVM

#=/etc @@DIRM
/etc @@CONFM

# Binary directories
#=/usr/sbin @@DIRM
/usr/sbin @@BINM

#=/usr/bin @@DIRM
/usr/bin @@BINM

#=/sbin @@DIRM
/sbin @@BINM

#=/bin @@DIRM
/bin @@BINM

#=/lib @@DIRM
/lib @@BINM

#=/usr/lib @@DIRM
/usr/lib @@BINM

=/usr/src E

=/tmp @@DIRM
```

The configuration file tells Tripwire to check each of the standard system directories: */dev*, */etc*, */usr/sbin*, */sbin*, */bin*, */lib*, and */usr/lib*. Each of these directories has various attributes checked dependent on the macro defined for it. For instance, the macro for */usr/lib* is @@BINM, which is specified at the top of the file. Its attributes are *E+pnugsci12*, which means that Tripwire checks every possible change (please see the list of attributes in the beginning of the file).

You can tell Tripwire to check on the directories of other machines on the network by defining the *IFHOST* macro.

A template also exists for a shell script that can be run daily by *cron* to check your system's integrity. The next several files are all documents describing Tripwire. I recommend you read the *FAQ* and the *README* files; *README.FIRST* deals more with compilation issues so you can skip it. There are three man-page files. The *siggen* file is a program that lets you generate Tripwire signatures without running Tripwire itself. And Tripwire is the heart of Tripwire.

For now, leave Tripwire as is. I leave it to you to experiment with it as you gain experience with your system.

5. Next, you need to have Tripwire initialize its database. Tripwire can take a long time to run depending on the complexity of your system and its speed, so give yourself some time to run it.

   Tripwire has four operational modes:

   - **Database generation.** Tripwire needs a database of initial file integrity checksums to check current files against. It uses the configuration file */etc/tw.config* to determine which files to generate checksums. This mode creates such a database.

   - **Database update.** This mode updates the database to account for files that have legitimately been changed.

   - **Interactive update.** This mode performs the same task as the previous one but prompts the user for which files to check.

   - **Integrity checking.** This mode has Tripwire check current files against their known, good values stored in the database.

   Enter the following command to initialize the database:

   ```
   /usr/sbin/tripwire -init
   ```

   Tripwire chugs away. If it finishes without problems, it looks like Listing 11-3.

Listing 11-3: The Tripwire database generation

```
### Warning:    creating ./databases directory!
###
### Phase 1:    Reading configuration file
### Phase 2:    Generating file list
### Phase 3:    Creating file information database
###
### Warning:    Database file placed in ./databases/tw.db_bart.tulane.com.
###
```

```
###      Make sure to move this file and the configuration
###          to secure media!
###
###          (Tripwire expects to find it in '/var/spool/tripwire'.)
```

6. Next, test your new system by making a trivial change to a system file. I recommend that you change a file that is changed often so that you don't have to recompile the Tripwire database again. The */etc/passwd* file is changed whenever you add or delete a user, so it is a good choice. (Otherwise, if you change a file like /bin/login, you could confuse yourself later on if you ever check it against the original distribution.) The *touch* program will modify the file time stamp without doing anything else (note that Tripwire will not show that a file has been changed if you change the modification date and do not specify the modification timestamp – *m* – in the *tw.config* file). Enter the following command:

```
touch /etc/passwd
```

7. Now run the Tripwire integrity check by entering the following command:

```
tripwire -interactive
```

8. Tripwire shows that */etc/passwd* has been modified, as shown in Listing 11-4.

Listing 11-4: Tripwire detects a change in the /etc/passwd file

```
changed: crw-------  maggie           0 Oct 26 02:09:34 1997 /dev/ttyp2
changed: drwxr-xr-x root          2048 Oct 26 02:10:22 1997 /etc
changed: -rw-r--r-- root           589 Oct 26 02:09:53 1997 /etc/passwd
```

Tripwire prompts you to update its database with the changed file. You have the option to enter Y or n to update the database for that file or not. You also have the option to update all the files in which changes have been detected by entering Y, but unless you are sure that you are the only person to have changed anything I advise against doing so. It may be a lot of work to check each file, but that is an important process so you should just resign yourself to the work.

9. Because your goal is to reliably check your current files for compromise, you must keep your database safe and pristine. You should not leave it on the machine that Tripwire is to protect. The best way to store it is to copy it to a CD-ROM. But that isn't practical for most people, so a reasonable alternative is to copy it to a floppy, and flip the disk's write-protect tab. Doing so enables you to automatically run Tripwire from *cron*. (If you require a more secure installation you could store the disk in a safe place. That prevents you from automatically running Tripwire from *cron* but removes the possibility of the disk being physically modified.)

A compromise is to keep the Tripwire database on the File Server/Router and create a separate checksum on it alone. You can take the simple precaution of marking it as readable by root alone to prevent anyone without root access from modifying it. Of course, if someone has modified a system file such as the *login* command to allow secret access as *root*, they can still modify the database. To minimize that possibility, you can then use your databases stored on floppy to check both the system database and the database checksum on a weekly or semiweekly basis. That way, if someone does compromise your system database you'll at least know it eventually and at the same time you can automate the daily checks.

10. The Red Hat RPM Tripwire package places the file *tripwire.verify* in the */etc/cron.daily* directory. It is run automatically by cron every night in the early morning. The results are e-mailed to root. If nothing has been changed, the results appear as shown in Listing 11-5. This is another good function that comes ready to run out of the box. Log in as *root* and check your Tripwire mail daily. Periodically compare the stored database to the one you saved on floppy disk.

Listing 11-5: The tripwire.verify file results as e-mailed to root

```
Received: (from root@localhost)
        by wishbone.paunchy.com (8.8.5/8.8.5) id BAA01746
        for root; Wed, 30 Jul 1997 01:14:07 -0600
Date: Wed, 30 Jul 1997 01:14:07 -0600
From: root <root@wishbone.paunchy.com>
Message-Id: <199707300714.BAA01746@bart.tulane.com>
To: root@wishbone.paunchy.com
Subject: File integrity report
Status: R


This is an automated report of possible file integrity changes, generated by
the Tripwire integrity checker. To tell Tripwire that a file or entire
directory tree is valid, as root run:

/usr/sbin/tripwire -update [pathname|entry]

If you wish to enter an interactive integrity checking and verification
session, as root run:

/usr/sbin/tripwire -interactive

Changed files/directories include:
```

Installing and Configuring Crack

Your passwords are your first — and often last — line of defense. Linux makes it difficult to choose trivial or easily guessed passwords, but it is still important to check them anyway. The Cracker library makes the checking process a simple task to do.

The *Cracker* program checks a file — either your /etc/passwd or /etc/shadow file — against dictionaries of common words and phrases. It looks at each word in the dictionary and encrypts it using the same algorithm that the Linux *passwd* program uses to generate the encrypted word that it generates after you enter your plain-text password. If the encrypted word matches one found in a passwd file, then it has found a match.

The Crack RPM package is included on your CD-ROM as */mnt/cdrom/IDG/ crack-4.1f-1.i386.rpm*. Install it (rpm -ivh /mnt/cdrom/IDG/crack*) onto your File Server/Router. It installs itself into the */root/crack-4.1f* directory because *root* should be the only user with access to it. To run a check on the */etc/passwd* file (*/etc/shadow* if you have installed shadow passwords), enter the following command:

```
/root/crack-4.1f/Crack /etc/passwd
```

It shows some information on the screen and then announces that it is running as a background task. After it is finished, it writes the results of its search to a file with the process ID as its suffix, such as *out.1978*. For demonstration purposes, I removed the password completely for maggie and ran a test. Listing 11-6 shows the results.

Listing 11-6: The results of running Crack on my /etc/passwd file

```
join: Oct 26 02:41:18 User uucp (in /etc/passwd) has a locked password:- *
join: Oct 26 02:41:18 User operator (in /etc/passwd) has a locked password:- *
join: Oct 26 02:41:18 User games (in /etc/passwd) has a locked password:- *
join: Oct 26 02:41:18 User gopher (in /etc/passwd) has a locked password:- *
join: Oct 26 02:41:18 User ftp (in /etc/passwd) has a locked password:- *
join: Oct 26 02:41:18 User bin (in /etc/passwd) has a locked password:- *
join: Oct 26 02:41:18 User daemon (in /etc/passwd) has a locked password:- *
join: Oct 26 02:41:18 User adm (in /etc/passwd) has a locked password:- *
join: Oct 26 02:41:18 User lp (in /etc/passwd) has a locked password:- *
join: Oct 26 02:41:18 User sync (in /etc/passwd) has a locked password:- *
join: Oct 26 02:41:18 User shutdown (in /etc/passwd) has a locked password:- *
join: Oct 26 02:41:18 User halt (in /etc/passwd) has a locked password:- *
join: Oct 26 02:41:18 User mail (in /etc/passwd) has a locked password:- *
join: Oct 26 02:41:18 User nobody (in /etc/passwd) has a locked password:- *
join: Oct 26 02:41:18 User news (in /etc/passwd) has a locked password:- *
join: Oct 26 02:41:18 Warning! maggie (/home/maggie in /etc/passwd) has a NULL
    password!
```

As you can see, it found that the user *maggie* has no password. (The standard Linux users have locked passwords, which means they can never be used as regular users.) That is unacceptable, and I will add a password to it immediately.

I want to add a not too difficult password to the user *maggie* before I put my original, rather difficult one back in place. I run the *passwd* program and enter the string *mybook* as the new password. The *passwd* program objects to that choice by telling me that *mybook* is based on a dictionary word. Obviously, *my* and *book* are two real words that are simply concatenated. I want to test *Crack*, however, so I go ahead and confirm *mybook* and run *Crack* again. It does not find the password even though passwd objected — but did not reject it. Combining two words was obviously enough to foil this attempt at breaking into my own system.

Installing and Configuring SATAN

You need to obtain the SATAN distribution of 1.1.1 or later that is configured for Linux (other versions will work but require a lot of work to get going). This suite of programs can be obtained, in *tar* format, from a SunSITE anonymous FTP site. The following steps describe its installation and configuration:

1. Log on to your Linux file server/router as *root*.

2. If you have not installed both the GNU C compiler and the Perl 5.0.1 (or greater) interpreter, you need to install them. A sample RPM instruction is shown for installing Perl:

   ```
   rpm -ivh /mnt/cdrom/RedHat/RPMS/perl*
   ```

3. I prefer to install all new system source code in */usr/local/src*, so go to that directory:

   ```
   cd /usr/local/src
   ```

4. Next, log in to the SunSITE. I happened to use the Georgia Tech mirror:

   ```
   ftp ftp.cc.gatech.edu
   ```

5. Log in as the user *ftp* and enter your e-mail address as the password, as shown in Listing 11-7. The text after the password line is typical of the greeting you get when logging into anonymous FTP sites.

Listing 11-7: Obtaining satan–1.1.1.linux.fixed2.tgz from a SunSITE mirror

```
Connected to santanni.cc.gatech.edu.
220 santanni.cc.gatech.edu FTP server (Version wu-2.4.2-academ[BETA-13](1) Thu
  Apr 24 17:28:04 EDT 1997) ready.
Name (ftp.cc.gatech.edu:me): anonymous
331 Guest login ok, send your complete e-mail address as password.
Password:
```

```
230--------------------------------------------------------------------------
230-    Welcome to the Georgia Tech College of Computing FTP service.
230-
230-    Access from gauss.math.unm.edu is being logged.
230-    There are currently 67 users on this system, out of a possible 150.
230-
230-    IMPORTANT NOTICE:
230-    We are moving this server from SunOS 5.5.1 to IRIX 6.2, so please
230-    let us know if you have any problems.
230-
230-    This server is set up to automatically compress, gzip, and/or tar
230-    files or directories which you request - simply add the appropriate
230-    suffix to the requested file.
230-
230-            Example: Retrieve a directory named graduate_info,
230-                     as a gtar'd, gzip'd file:
230-
230-            ftp> cd coc
230-            ftp> get graduate_info.tar.gz
230-
230-    Some ftp clients may have problems with these messages.  Prompting
230-    and verbose messages can be shut off by entering a "-" at the
230-    beginning of your password.
Connected to santanni.cc.gatech.edu.
220 santanni.cc.gatech.edu FTP server (Version wu-2.4.2-academ[BETA-13](1) Thu A
ftp>
```

6. You need to go to the directory where the SATAN distribution is stored:

```
cd /pub/linux/system/network/admin
```

7. Set FTP for binary — as opposed to ASCII — transfers. At the *ftp>* prompt, enter the command to change to binary:

```
bin
```

8. Start transferring the SATAN distribution to your computer by entering the following command at the *ftp>* prompt:

```
get satan-1.1.1.linux.fixed2.tgz
```

9. Exit from your FTP session by entering the following command at the *ftp>* prompt:

```
quit
```

Listing 11-8 shows the sequence from Step 6 through Step 9.

Listing 11-8: Downloading SATAN from the anonymous FTP site

```
ftp> cd /pub/linux/security/network/system
ftp> bin
200 Type set to I.
ftp> get satan-1.1.1.linux.fixed2.tgz
200 PORT command successful.
150 Opening BINARY mode data connection for satan-1.1.1.linux.fixed2.tgz (306360
  bytes).
226 Transfer complete.
local: satan-1.1.1.linux.fixed2.tgz remote: satan-1.1.1.linux.fixed2.tgz
306360 bytes received in 122 secs (2.5 Kbytes/sec)
ftp>
```

10. You need to extract the files from the *tar* distribution:

```
tar xzvf satan-1.1.1.linux.fixed2.tgz
```

11. A Perl script – reconfig – searches your system for all the parameters and programs that SATAN needs. (Perl is a language that provides many of the best features of shell scripts such as Bash and compiled languages such as C.) One thing that it does, for instance, is locate your Web browser so that SATAN can automatically use it. Enter the following command to run this script:

```
perl reconfig
```

The script reports on what it finds, as shown in Listing 11-9.

Listing 11-9: The perl reconfig script output

```
checking to make sure all the target(s) are here...
Ok, trying to find perl5 now... hang on a bit...
Perl5 is in /usr/bin/perl5.003

changing the source in: bin/get_targets bin/faux_fping satan bin/boot.satan bin/
dns.satan bin/finger.satan bin/ftp.satan bin/nfs-chk.satan bin/rex.satan bin/rpc
.satan bin/rpcgen.satan bin/rsh.satan bin/rusers.satan bin/showmount.satan bin/t
cpscan.satan bin/tftp.satan bin/udpscan.satan bin/xhost.satan bin/yp-chk.satan b
in/ypbind.satan perl/html.pl

HTML/WWW Browser is /usr/bin/lynx

So far so good...
Looking for all the commands now...

AEEEIIII...!!! can't find uudecode
```

```
Ok, now doing substitutions on the shell scripts...
Changing paths in config/paths.pl...
Changing paths in config/paths.sh...
```

The files that it didn't find are not essential to the operation of SATAN, so don't worry about them.

12. In my case, I have not configured a Web browser on my File Server/Router because I do not intend to run X Window on it. Without a graphical browser, SATAN defaults to *Lynx*, which is a text-based Web browser. This is actually a good choice at this point because it will work whether or not you are using X Window and a Web browser. You can always go back and install a browser like Netscape if you wish (Netscape version 4 is currently available for Linux.)

13. Compile SATAN by running the *make* command with the *linux* parameter:

```
make linux
```

The make utility chugs along – I am using an old 486 with only 8MB of RAM – until it compiles all the codes in the SATAN directory.

14. Run SATAN:

```
./satan
```

It automatically starts your Web browser as shown in Figure 11-1.

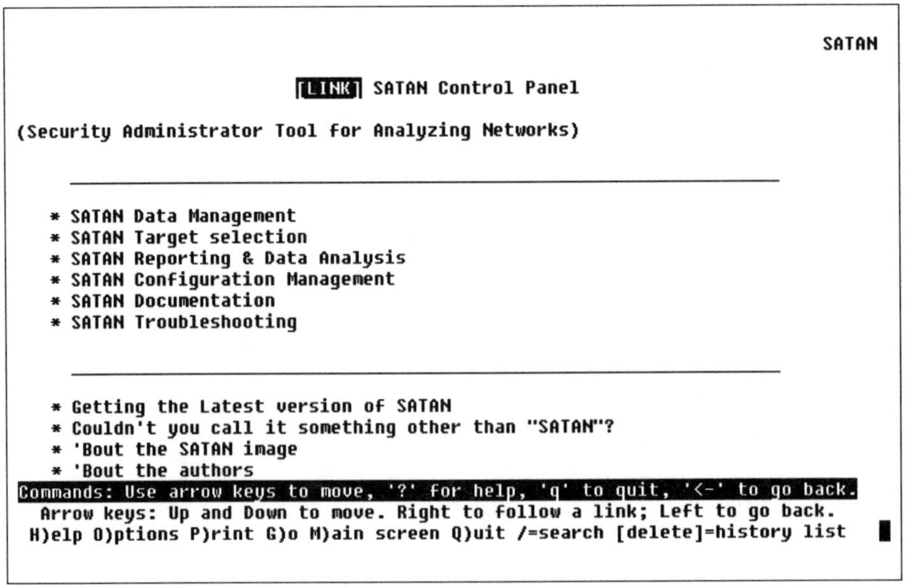

```
                                                                      SATAN

                     [LINK] SATAN Control Panel

      (Security Administrator Tool for Analyzing Networks)
      _____


         * SATAN Data Management
         * SATAN Target selection
         * SATAN Reporting & Data Analysis
         * SATAN Configuration Management
         * SATAN Documentation
         * SATAN Troubleshooting

      _____


         * Getting the Latest version of SATAN
         * Couldn't you call it something other than "SATAN"?
         * 'Bout the SATAN image
         * 'Bout the authors
      Commands: Use arrow keys to move, '?' for help, 'q' to quit, '<-' to go back.
        Arrow keys: Up and Down to move. Right to follow a link; Left to go back.
        H)elp O)ptions P)rint G)o M)ain screen Q)uit /=search [delete]=history list  ▮
```

Figure 11-1: SATAN running under the Lynx Web browser

15. Use your down-arrow key to move the cursor to the *SATAN target selection* option. Press *Enter* and you go to that window, as shown in Figure 11-2.

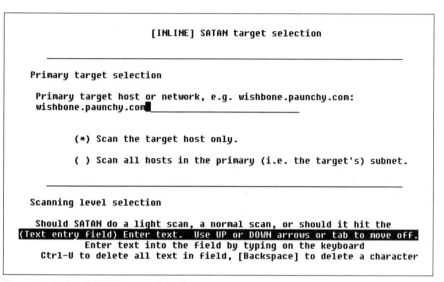

```
                    [INLINE] SATAN target selection
    ─────────────────────────────────────────────────────────────

    Primary target selection

      Primary target host or network, e.g. wishbone.paunchy.com:
      wishbone.paunchy.com█_____

            (*) Scan the target host only.

            ( ) Scan all hosts in the primary (i.e. the target's) subnet.

    ─────────────────────────────────────────────────────────────

    Scanning level selection

      Should SATAN do a light scan, a normal scan, or should it hit the
    (Text entry field) Enter text.  Use UP or DOWN arrows or tab to move off.
             Enter text into the field by typing on the keyboard
       Ctrl-U to delete all text in field, [Backspace] to delete a character
```

Figure 11-2: The SATAN Target Selection menu

16. I have my computer configured for my network and SATAN knows that it is currently running on *wishbone*, which is my File Server/Router. For now, limit the scope of SATAN to the Primary target host, which is of course *wishbone*. This is the default as indicated by the *Scan the target host only* button. Press the *down-arrow* key three times and then press the *Enter* key and you go to the next window, shown in Figure 11-3.

17. For now stick with a Light scan. Press the *down-arrow* key three times and then press the *Enter* key to start the scan. Every time that you start up SATAN and then start a scan, you get the SATAN tutorial displayed. I recommend that you read through it. However, to proceed with the scan, press the *Ctrl+R* key combination and you get the screen shown in Figure 11-4.

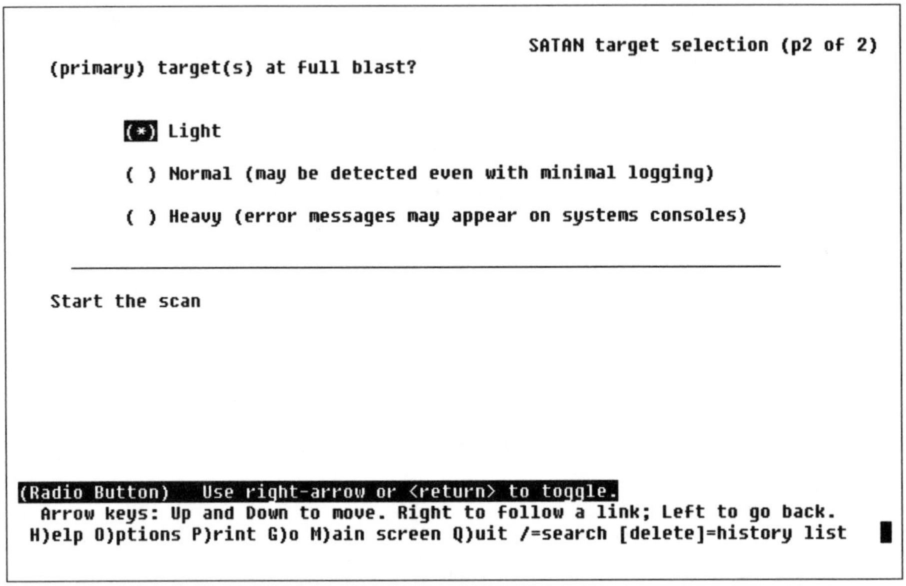

```
                                            SATAN target selection (p2 of 2)
     (primary) target(s) at full blast?


          [(*)] Light

          ( ) Normal (may be detected even with minimal logging)

          ( ) Heavy (error messages may appear on systems consoles)
     _____


     Start the scan







 (Radio Button)    Use right-arrow or <return> to toggle.
   Arrow keys: Up and Down to move. Right to follow a link; Left to go back.
   H)elp O)ptions P)rint G)o M)ain screen Q)uit /=search [delete]=history list    ▮
```

Figure 11-3: Running SATAN in a light search mode

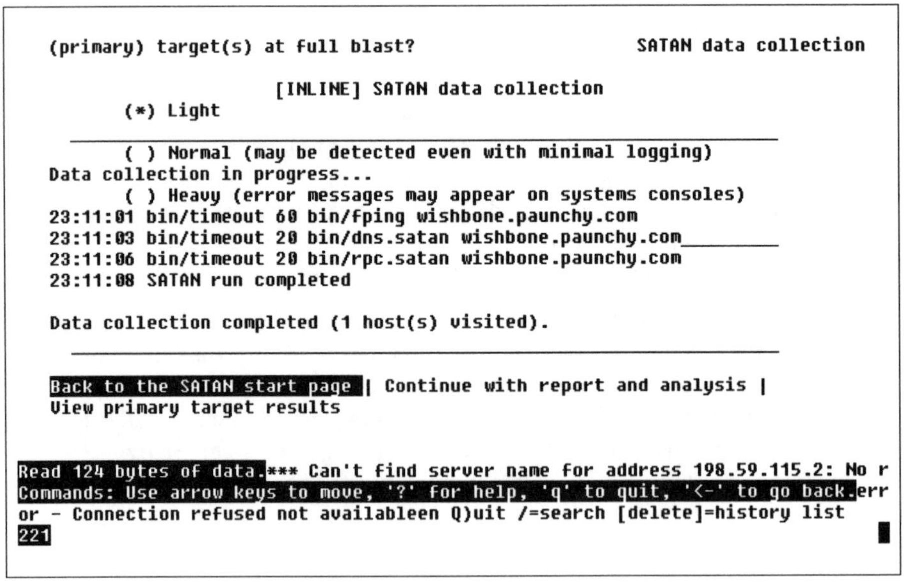

```
     (primary) target(s) at full blast?            SATAN data collection

                     [INLINE] SATAN data collection
          (*) Light
     _____
               ( ) Normal (may be detected even with minimal logging)
     Data collection in progress...
               ( ) Heavy (error messages may appear on systems consoles)
     23:11:01 bin/timeout 60 bin/fping wishbone.paunchy.com
     23:11:03 bin/timeout 20 bin/dns.satan wishbone.paunchy.com_____
     23:11:06 bin/timeout 20 bin/rpc.satan wishbone.paunchy.com
     23:11:08 SATAN run completed

     Data collection completed (1 host(s) visited).
     _____

      Back to the SATAN start page | Continue with report and analysis |
     View primary target results


     Read 124 bytes of data.*** Can't find server name for address 198.59.115.2: No r
     Commands: Use arrow keys to move, '?' for help, 'q' to quit, '<-' to go back.err
     or - Connection refused not availableen Q)uit /=search [delete]=history list    ▮
      221
```

Figure 11-4: The results of a "light" SATAN scan

18. To view the results in more detail, press the *down-arrow* key and you get the screen shown in Figure 11-5. You can choose any number of ways to view the results.

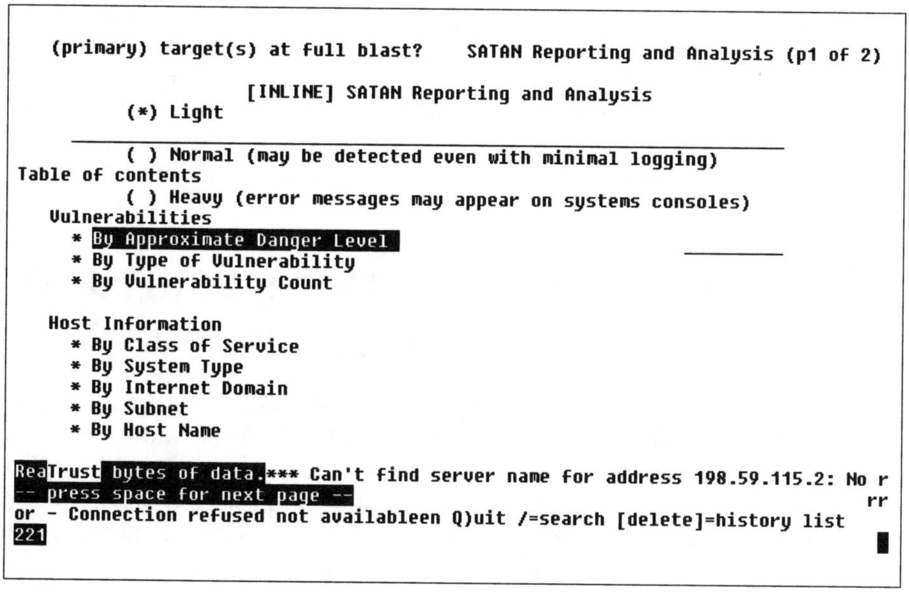

```
   (primary) target(s) at full blast?     SATAN Reporting and Analysis (p1 of 2)

                        [INLINE] SATAN Reporting and Analysis
            (*) Light

            ( ) Normal (may be detected even with minimal logging)
Table of contents
            ( ) Heavy (error messages may appear on systems consoles)
   Vulnerabilities
      * By Approximate Danger Level
      * By Type of Vulnerability
      * By Vulnerability Count

   Host Information
      * By Class of Service
      * By System Type
      * By Internet Domain
      * By Subnet
      * By Host Name

ReaTrust bytes of data.*** Can't find server name for address 198.59.115.2: No r
-- press space for next page --                                               rr
or - Connection refused not availableen Q)uit /=search [delete]=history list
221
```

Figure 11-5: The SATAN Reporting and Analysis screen

19. Use the down-arrow key to go to the *Vulnerabilities - By Approximate
    Danger Level* option and press the *Enter* key. The final results of the scan
    are shown in Figure 11-6.

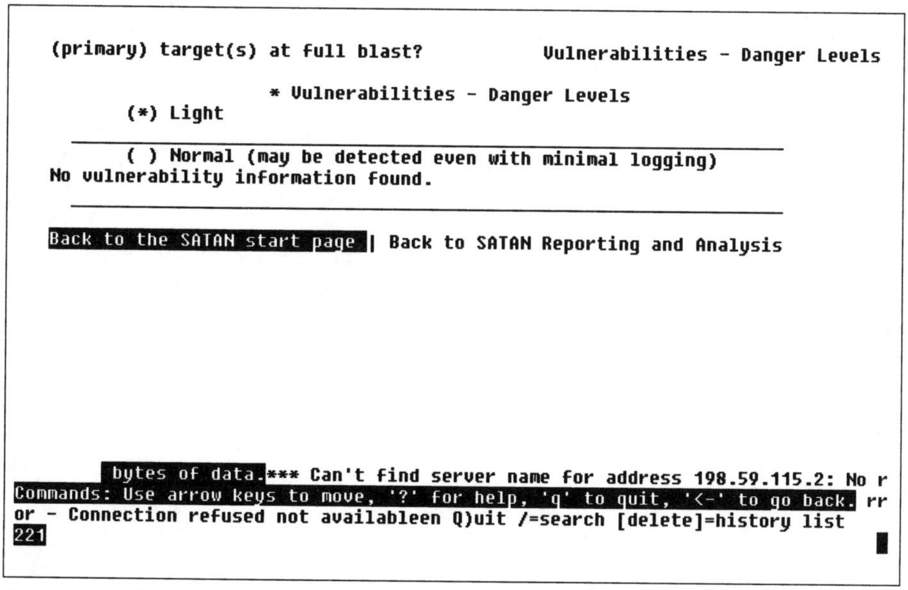

```
   (primary) target(s) at full blast?          Vulnerabilities - Danger Levels

                        * Vulnerabilities - Danger Levels
            (*) Light

            ( ) Normal (may be detected even with minimal logging)
No vulnerability information found.


   Back to the SATAN start page | Back to SATAN Reporting and Analysis










             bytes of data.*** Can't find server name for address 198.59.115.2: No r
Commands: Use arrow keys to move, '?' for help, 'q' to quit, '<-' to go back. rr
or - Connection refused not availableen Q)uit /=search [delete]=history list
221
```

Figure 11-6: The vulnerabilities of the scan are displayed.

As you can see, the Red Hat installation is a pretty good one for security. You get the same results if you use the *Heavy scan* option. You can also view the results by looking at the files in the *satan-1.1.1/results/satan-data* directory.

I encourage you to experiment with SATAN over your entire network. It can detect numerous potential and actual security problems. It will also teach you about the type of problems to look for, such as the wrong file permissions.

Adding Passive Security Measures to Your Private and Firewall Networks

Now that you have installed and configured your active security measures – the IP filtering rules, the dial-up connection, Tripwire, SATAN, Crack, and so on – it is important to address the passive side of security. It is necessary to close all the possible entrances that you can think of. To that end, I want you to eliminate all the Linux daemons, application programs, and programming libraries that the firewall absolutely does not need. The idea is that the fewer pieces of software exist, the fewer the possible security holes you have. I have you remove stuff in the following sections, not because I know of any particular security hole, but because one may be lurking out there (or could be in the future). The idea is to start configuring your firewall on a "clean" machine.

Configuring Your Firewall Server for E-Mail

E-mail is always a tricky problem. Add a firewall, with an on-demand Internet connection, to the equation and it becomes even trickier. I know of no system that meets all the needs of such a system completely.

I use a very simple system, however, which works well on the type of network you've configured. Its simplicity minimizes the configuration and security problems associated with this difficult subject. The fat book sitting next to me devoted entirely to *sendmail* graphically illustrates the difficulty of this subject!

My system uses the e-mail queuing system that many ISPs provide. It is called "Post Office Protocol version 3" (POP3). My ISP receives e-mail addressed to me and holds it. When I connect to my ISP from my Netscape browser via my PPP connection, my ISP's POP server prompts me for my user name and password. My mail is then downloaded to my computer. Figure 11-7 shows my Netscape e-mail configuration screen.

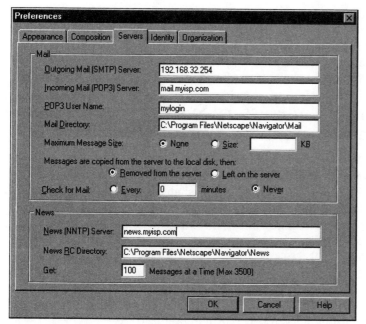

Figure 11–7: Configuring Netscape to use my ISP's POP3 e-mail service

Alternatively, you could configure your Mail Server (any computer that you designate to provide that function — the File Server/Router could also act as a Mail Server) to regularly connect to your ISP and download all your system's and user's e-mail. If you run *sendmail* or any of the new substitutes and distribute it locally, your local e-mail would get delivered immediately, but you would have to wait for external mail delivery and retrieval according to the times you set. For instance, if you configure *cron* to check for external mail every 15 minutes, your Mail Server would have to fire up a PPP connection that often, if one did not already exist.

You need to set up an e-mail account for each of your network's users. Most ISPs will set up individual accounts for a small fee. When you start your Web browser's mail window, you are prompted for your password. Your password, along with your account name, is sent to your ISP's POP server. When you are authenticated, your mail is downloaded to your computer. You have the choice of either leaving it on your ISP's POP server or erasing it after it's downloaded.

This is not a particularly elegant solution. Although it works well for e-mail going to the Internet, it is inefficient for internal e-mail, as those messages must travel to your ISP to be routed right back. It works, however. And it is indeed simple to set up. I am not aware of any elegant solution for a network like the one you've constructed in this book.

Eliminating All Unnecessary System Daemons and Applications from the Firewall Server

This section deals with eliminating unnecessary processes, daemons, and applications in order to increase the security of your firewall. With fewer processes (daemons) and software on the firewall, you simply have fewer potential — undiscovered — security holes available to be exploited.

I assume that you are starting with the base Red Hat Linux installed and running. To find the unnecessary processes, look at the process table by entering the following command:

```
ps x
```

You should see a list of processes, as shown in Listing 11-10.

Listing 11-10: The initial Linux process table

```
PID TTY STAT  TIME COMMAND
  1 ?   S     0:01 init
  2 ?   SW    0:00 (kflushd)
  3 ?   SW<   0:00 (kswapd)
 19 ?   S     0:00 /sbin/kerneld
143 ?   S     0:00 syslogd
152 ?   S     0:00 klogd
163 ?   S     0:00 crond
175 ?   S     0:00 inetd
181 ?   S     0:00 named
189 ?   S     0:00 lpd
204 ?   S     0:00 sendmail: accepting connections on port 25
209 ?   S     0:00 smbd -D
211 ?   S     0:00 nmbd -D
216 ?   S     0:00 gpm -t ms
288 1   S     0:00 /bin/login -- root
289 2   S     0:00 /sbin/mingetty tty2
290 3   S     0:00 /sbin/mingetty tty3
291 4   S     0:00 /sbin/mingetty tty4
293 ?   S     0:00 update (bdflush)
```

```
294   5 S    0:00 /sbin/mingetty tty5
295   6 S    0:00 /sbin/mingetty tty6
296   1 S    0:00 -bash
308   ? S    0:00 in.telnetd
323  p0 S    0:00 su -
324  p0 S    0:00 -bash
336  p0 R    0:00 ps -x
```

You have several ways to eliminate the various daemons from running. You can delete the programs themselves, delete the links in the */etc/rc.d* run-level directories, or modify the startup scripts. I prefer to modify the scripts that start up the various daemons because I can document what I have done — and why — by adding comments to the scripts. This leaves the computer in its near original state, which helps you or whoever is working on the system in the future. (If you simply eliminate the links, for instance, it is far more difficult to document what you've done and why.)

The following steps aim to eliminate each of the unnecessary daemons listed in Listing 11-10. I start from the top and work my way down. The first three processes are all part of the Linux kernel (see Chapter 3). The *kerneld* daemon is the first process we deal with in the next section. The *klogd* is part of the Linux logging process and we want to keep it. *Crond* executes periodic processes and we want to keep it as well. The *inetd*, *named* (if you installed the optional Red Hat service in Chapter 1), *lpd*, *sendmail*, *smbd*, and *nmbd* daemons are all unnecessary for a firewall server in my opinion. The remaining processes in Listing 11-10 all relate to my own logins except for the *update* process, which is part of the kernel. The *mingetty* processes all process logins from the console and should not present any security problems. The *login* process and the *bash* shell (288 and 296) is me logged in as *root* from the console and running the *bash* shell. You can also ignore the last several processes (308, 323, 324, and 336) because they are the processes that I used to log in remotely via Telnet (*in.telnetd*), then changed to *root* (*su*), the shell for *root* (*bash*), and the command to show all the processes (*ps -x*). I will, however, eliminate the capability to log in via Telnet in the section "Stopping the *inetd* Startup Script" later in this chapter, but for now it is okay because I am still configuring the Firewall Server.

The following sections describe how I configure my minimalist Firewall Server.

Red Hat 5.0 lets you to specify which system daemons are started at boot time. See Step 12, "Configure Services," in the section "Configuring Linux for General Operation" in Chapter 1, for more information.

STOPPING THE KERNELD STARTUP SCRIPT (OPTIONAL)

A firewall should be the most stable system in your network because it has just one job to do. If you decide to compile in IP masquerading support, then I think it wise to use a monolithic kernel and not use loadable modules. Once again, my reasoning is to leave as little room as possible for potential intruders. It makes sense that you can decide what devices you need from the beginning and compile them directly into the kernel. Let me emphasize that I know of no known, or potential, security problem with loadable modules or *kerneld*, but I am following my minimalist philosophy. Therefore, remove the *kerneld* (process number 19) capability:

1. Log on to your Linux Firewall Server as *root*.

2. Edit the */etc/rc.d/init.d/rc.sysinit* file, shown in Listing 11-11.

Listing 11-11: The /etc/rc.d/rc.sysinit file segment that starts the kerneld daemon

```
#! /bin/sh
#
# /etc/rc.d/rc.sysinit - run once at boot time
#
# Taken in part from Miquel van Smoorenburg's bcheckrc.
#

# Set the path
PATH=/bin:/sbin:/usr/bin:/usr/sbin
export PATH

# Read in config data.
if [ -f /etc/sysconfig/network ]; then
    . /etc/sysconfig/network
else
    NETWORKING=no
    HOSTNAME=localhost
fi

# Start up swapping.
echo "Activating swap partitions"
swapon -a

# Set the hostname.
hostname ${HOSTNAME}
echo hostname: 'hostname'
```

```
# Set the NIS domain name
if [ -n "$NISDOMAIN" ]; then
    domainname $NISDOMAIN
fi


(... several lines of script not shown ...)


if [ -x /sbin/kerneld -a -n "$USEMODULES" ]; then
    /sbin/kerneld
    KERNELD=yse
fi


(... the remainder of the script not shown ...)
```

3. Simply comment out the line that starts the *kerneld* daemon, as shown in
   Listing 11-12.

Listing 11-12: Preventing the kerneld daemon from starting

```
if [ -x /sbin/kerneld -a -n "$USEMODULES" ]; then
### Prevent kerneld from starting because this is a firewall.
### 6/21/97 -- PS
###     /sbin/kerneld
###     KERNELD=yse
fi
```

4. You need to recompile your Linux kernel. Consult the section "Building a
   Custom Kernel" in Chapter 7 for instructions. Note that at a minimum you
   must choose the network adapter, SLIP, and PPP options when choosing
   your kernel configuration with *make config.* You also must turn *off* the IP
   forwarding and turn *on* the IP firewall options.

5. Take note from the process table shown in Listing 11-10 that the *nfsiod*
   processes (process numbers 4–7) give your system Network File System
   (NFS) capability. NFS is similar to Samba but is less secure. It comes
   compiled into the Red Hat base system. Because you are recompiling
   your kernel now, it is a good idea to remove NFS. You can do this by
   answering *no* to the NFS options in the file system section.

6. After you reconfigure (*make config*) and recompile the kernel (*make
   zImage*), remember to make LILO recognize it. Edit the */etc/lilo.conf* file
   and run the *LILO* command:

   ```
   lilo
   ```

TIP If you want remote access to the Firewall Server (other than from the physical system console), you should connect a serial cable between a trusted computer and the firewall. You can telnet to the trusted computer and then use a terminal emulation program such as *dip* or *cu* to connect to the firewall without having to sit in front of the firewall console. This is more than just a convenience because you want to monitor the firewall closely. For details about adding the serial connection, see the section "Adding a Serial Connection to Your Firewall Server," later in this chapter.

STOPPING THE INETD STARTUP SCRIPT

The idea is to eliminate as many possible security breaches as you can think of. To do this, you want to have as few daemons running as possible and still run the firewall function. Many processes are started by the *inetd* daemon. The *inetd* is a general-purpose daemon that spawns off all sorts of processes when they are demanded and reduces the number of specific daemons that need to run separately. You can either not run it at all or else edit its configuration file. In my opinion, it is best not to run *inetd* at all because there will be no doubt about what is and what is not running.

1. Log on to your Linux Firewall Server as *root*.

2. You have numerous ways to not run *inetd*. First, you could remove the execution privilege by logging on as *root* and entering the following command:

   ```
   chmod -x /etc/rc.d/init.d/inet
   ```

   You could also simply eliminate the link in the run-level startup directories. For instance, you could remove the */etc/rc.d/rc3.d/S50inet* file, which is a link to the */etc/rc.d/init.d/inet* script. Without the link, the *inetd* script will never be executed when you boot your computer.

   A better alternative, in my opinion, is to edit the *inetd* script shown in Listing 11-13 and somehow prevent it from running.

Listing 11-13: Edit the /etc/rc.d/init.d/inet file to stop inetd from running

```
#! /bin/sh
#
# inet          Start TCP/IP networking services. This script
#               sets the hostname, creates the routes and
#               starts the Internet Network Daemon & RPC portmapper.
#
# Author:       Miquel van Smoorenburg, <miquels@drinkel.nl.mugnet.org>
```

```
#                Various folks at Red Hat
#
# chkconfig: 345 50 50
# description: The internet superserver daemon (commonly called inetd) \
#              starts a variety of other internet services as needed. It \
#              is responsible for starting many services, including telnet, \
#              ftp, rsh, and rlogin. Disabling inetd disables all of the \
#              services it is responsible for.

# Source function library.
. /etc/rc.d/init.d/functions

# Get config.
. /etc/sysconfig/network

# Check that networking is up.
if [ ${NETWORKING} = "no" ]
then
        exit 0
fi


[ -f /usr/sbin/inetd ] || exit 0

# See how we were called.
case "$1" in
  start)
        echo -n "Starting INET services: "
        daemon inetd

        echo
        touch /var/lock/subsys/inet
        ;;
  stop)
        # bringing down NFS filesystems isn't inet's problem I don't know
        # why this script used to do that  -- ewt

echo -n "Stopping INET services: "
        killproc inetd

        echo
        rm -f /var/lock/subsys/inet
        ;;
  status)
        status inetd
```

```
      ;;
  restart)
      killall -HUP inetd
      ;;
  *)
      echo "Usage: inet {start|stop}"
      exit 1
esac

exit 0
```

3. To prevent the script from running, put an *exit* statement at the beginning of the file, as shown in Listing 11-14. I also include a comment line with the date and my initials and an echo statement so that information about why the script is not executed is displayed every time the script is executed – this information is displayed during the startup process. The reasoning behind my edit is now documented and should be obvious the next time it is inspected – months or years later by myself or the next administrator.

Listing 11-14: The first part of the edited /etc/rc.d/init.d/inet file

```
#! /bin/sh
#
# inet          Start TCP/IP networking services. This script
#               sets the hostname, creates the routes and
#               starts the Internet Network Daemon & RPC portmapper.
#
# Author:       Miquel van Smoorenburg, <miquels@drinkel.nl.mugnet.org>
#               Various folks at Red Hat
#
# chkconfig: 345 50 50
# description: The internet superserver daemon (commonly called inetd) \
#              starts a variety of other internet services as needed. It \
#              is responsible for starting many services, including telnet, \
#              ftp, rsh, and rlogin. Disabling inetd disables all of the \
#              services it is responsible for.

# Source function library.
. /etc/rc.d/init.d/functions

# Exit without starting inetd because this machine is a firewall.
# 6/21/97 - PS.
echo "To enhance network security do not start inetd"
```

```
exit 0

# Source function library.
. /etc/rc.d/init.d/functions
```

4. If, however, you want to retain the convenience that the *inetd* daemon provides – and sacrifice some potential safety – you should edit the *inetd* configuration file */etc/inetd.conf*, which is shown in Listing 11-15. Otherwise, stop the *inetd* process (PID = 175) by entering the following command:

```
kill -9 175
```

Listing 11-15: The /etc/inetd.conf configuration file for the inetd daemon

```
#
# inetd.conf    This file describes the services that will be available
#               through the INETD TCP/IP super server.  To re-configure
#               the running INETD process, edit this file, then send the
#               INETD process a SIGHUP signal.
#
# Version:      @(#)/etc/inetd.conf  3.10  05/27/93
#
# Authors:      Original taken from BSD UNIX 4.3/TAHOE.
#               Fred N. van Kempen, <waltje@uwalt.nl.mugnet.org>
#
# Modified for Debian Linux by Ian A. Murdock <imurdock@shell.portal.com>
#
# Modified for RHS Linux by Marc Ewing <marc@redhat.com>
#
# <service_name> <sock_type> <proto> <flags> <user> <server_path> <args>
#
# Echo, discard, daytime, and chargen are used primarily for testing.
#
# To re-read this file after changes, just do a 'killall -HUP inetd'
#
#echo      stream  tcp  nowait  root    internal
#echo      dgram   udp  wait    root    internal
#discard   stream  tcp  nowait  root    internal
#discard   dgram   udp  wait    root    internal
#daytime   stream  tcp  nowait  root    internal
#daytime   dgram   udp  wait    root    internal
#chargen   stream  tcp  nowait  root    internal
#chargen   dgram   udp  wait    root    internal
#
# These are standard services.
```

```
#
ftp      stream  tcp      nowait  root    /usr/sbin/tcpd   in.ftpd -l -a
telnet   stream  tcp      nowait  root    /usr/sbin/tcpd   in.telnetd
gopher   stream  tcp      nowait  root    /usr/sbin/tcpd   gn

# do not uncomment smtp unless you *really* know what you are doing.
# smtp is handled by the sendmail daemon now, not smtpd.  It does NOT
# run from here, it is started at boot time from /etc/rc.d/rc#.d.
#smtp    stream  tcp      nowait  root    /usr/bin/smtpd    smtpd
#nntp    stream  tcp      nowait  root    /usr/sbin/tcpd    in.nntpd
#
# Shell, login, exec and talk are BSD protocols.
#
shell    stream  tcp      nowait  root    /usr/sbin/tcpd    in.rshd
login    stream  tcp      nowait  root    /usr/sbin/tcpd    in.rlogind
#exec    stream  tcp      nowait  root    /usr/sbin/tcpd    in.rexecd
talk     dgram   udp      wait    root    /usr/sbin/tcpd    in.talkd
ntalk    dgram   udp      wait    root    /usr/sbin/tcpd    in.ntalkd
#dtalk   stream  tcp      wait    nobody  /usr/sbin/tcpd    in.dtalkd
#
# Pop and imap mail services et al
#
pop-2    stream  tcp      nowait  root    /usr/sbin/tcpd    ipop2d
pop-3    stream  tcp      nowait  root    /usr/sbin/tcpd    ipop3d
imap     stream  tcp      nowait  root    /usr/sbin/tcpd    imapd
#
# The Internet UUCP service.
#
#uucp    stream  tcp    .nowait   uucp    /usr/sbin/tcpd    /usr/lib/uucp/uucico -l
#
# Tftp service is provided primarily for booting.  Most sites
# run this only on machines acting as "boot servers." Do not uncomment
# this unless you *need* it.
#
#tftp    dgram   udp      wait    root    /usr/sbin/tcpd    in.tftpd
#bootps  dgram   udp      wait    root    /usr/sbin/tcpd    bootpd
#
# Finger, systat and netstat give out user information which may be
# valuable to potential "system crackers." Many sites choose to disable
# some or all of these services to improve security.
#
# cfinger is for GNU finger, which is currently not in use in RHS Linux
#
finger   stream  tcp      nowait  root    /usr/sbin/tcpd    in.fingerd
```

```
#cfinger stream  tcp     nowait  root    /usr/sbin/tcpd  in.cfingerd
#systat  stream  tcp     nowait  guest   /usr/sbin/tcpd  /bin/ps -auwwx
#netstat stream  tcp     nowait  guest   /usr/sbin/tcpd  /bin/netstat -f inet
#
# Time service is used for clock syncronization.
#
time     stream  tcp     nowait  nobody  /usr/sbin/tcpd  in.timed
time     dgram   udp     wait    nobody  /usr/sbin/tcpd  in.timed
#
# Authentication
#
auth    stream  tcp     nowait    nobody    /usr/sbin/in.identd in.identd -l -e -
  o
#
# End of inetd.conf
```

5. Comment out all the functions by inserting a pound sign (#) at the beginning of each line. Definitely eliminate *rlogin, finger, tftp, bootps, gopher,* and *ftp. Telnet* is a great convenience, but consider the following alternative: Connect a serial (RS 232) cable between a trusted computer on your network and your firewall computer. *Telnet* to that trusted computer and then use a terminal emulation program such as *cu* or *dip* to login to the firewall. That isolates your firewall from outside Telnet sessions but gives you the convenience of remote access from within your own network.

STOPPING THE NAMED (NAME SERVER) STARTUP SCRIPT (OPTIONAL)

If you installed the *Domain Name Service* (DNS) in Chapter 1 as I have, then you should eliminate the *named* (it is part of the RPM *bind-4.9.6* package). The File Server/Router can handle this function and you do not want the Firewall Server to be able to provide any extra information. Any information about the computers on your network can potentially help an intruder.

1. Log on to your Linux Firewall Server as *root*.

2. Edit the */etc/rc.d/init.d/named.init* file, shown in Listing 11-16. Note that the initial comments mistakenly refer to the *lpd* daemon rather than the *named*.

Listing 11-16: The /etc/rc.d/init.d/named file

```
#!/bin/sh
#
# named           This shell script takes care of starting and stopping
#                 named (BIND DNS server).
```

```
#
# chkconfig: 345 55 10
# description: named (BIND) is a Domain Name Server (DNS) \
# that is used to resolve host names to IP addresses.

# Source function library.
. /etc/rc.d/init.d/functions

# Source networking configuration.
. /etc/sysconfig/network

# Check that networking is up.
[ ${NETWORKING} = "no" ] && exit 0

[ -f /usr/sbin/named ] || exit 0

[ -f /etc/named.boot ] || exit 0

# See how we were called.
case "$1" in
  start)
        # Start daemons.
        echo -n "Starting named: "
        daemon named
        echo
        touch /var/lock/subsys/named
        ;;
  stop)
        # Stop daemons.
        echo -n "Shutting down named: "
        killproc named
        echo "done"
        rm -f /var/lock/subsys/named
        ;;
  status)
  status named
  exit $?
  ;;
  restart)
  named.restart
  exit $?
  ;;
  *)
        echo "Usage: named {start|stop|status|restart}"
```

```
      exit 1
esac


exit 0
```

3. Add the *exit* command again, as shown in Listing 11-17, to prevent its startup at the next boot.

Listing 11-17: Eliminating named from your firewall

```
#!/bin/sh
#
# named          This shell script takes care of starting and stopping
#                named (BIND DNS server).
#
# chkconfig: 345 55 10
# description: named (BIND) is a Domain Name Server (DNS) \
# that is used to resolve host names to IP addresses.


### Exit without starting named because this machine is a firewall.
### 6/21/97 - PS.
echo "To enhance network security do not start named"
exit 0

# Source function library.
. /etc/rc.d/init.d/functions
```

If you want the name service — *named* — running on your network, you should make sure that it is running on your File Server/Router. The name service converts computer names, such as *bart.paunchy.com*, into their IP addresses. If you do not run *named* somewhere on your network, you will need "host" table files defined on each computer if they are to access all computers on the network. This may or may not be necessary or even desirable, depending on your needs.

STOPPING THE LPD (PRINT SPOOLER) STARTUP SCRIPT

You may want to keep the printing daemon *lpd* (process number 189) because it is desirable in some circumstances to continually print out your system logs. One security trick is to print out all logins – especially that of the *Super User* – to have a record in case an intruder erases or modifies the logs to hide the illegal entry. It is also handy to have a printout with that information to look over during your first cup of coffee in the morning (or whenever you have your first cup of Java). In my case, I prefer to have the *syslog* daemon automatically e-mail all such messages to my workstation – which minimizes the number of places that I have to track physically.

1. Log on to your Linux Firewall Server as *root*.

2. Edit the */etc/rc.d/init.d/lpd.init* file, shown in Listing 11-18.

Listing 11-18: The /etc/rc.d/init.d/lpd file

```
#!/bin/sh
#
# lpd           This shell script takes care of starting and stopping
#               lpd (printer daemon).
#
# chkconfig: 2345 60 60
# description: lpd is the print daemon required for lpr to work properly. \
# It is basically a server that arbitrates print jobs to printer(s).

# Source function library.
. /etc/rc.d/init.d/functions

# Source networking configuration.
. /etc/sysconfig/network

# Check that networking is up.
[ ${NETWORKING} = "no" ] && exit 0

[ -f /usr/sbin/lpd ] || exit 0

[ -f /etc/printcap ] || exit 0

# See how we were called.
case "$1" in
  start)
        # Start daemons.
        echo -n "Starting lpd: "
        daemon lpd
        echo
        touch /var/lock/subsys/lpd
        ;;
  stop)
        # Stop daemons.
        echo -n "Shutting down lpd: "
```

```
killproc lpd
      echo
      rm -f /var/lock/subsys/lpd
      ;;
status)
status lpd
;;
restart)
$0 stop
$0 start
;;
*)
      echo "Usage: lpd {start|stop|restart|status}"
      exit 1
esac

exit 0
```

3. Add the *exit* command again, as shown in Listing 11-19, to prevent its startup at the next boot.

Listing 11-19: Eliminating lpd from the firewall

```
#!/bin/sh
#
# lpd           This shell script takes care of starting and stopping
#               lpd (printer daemon).
#
# chkconfig: 2345 60 60
# description: lpd is the print daemon required for lpr to work properly. \
# It is basically a server that arbitrates print jobs to printer(s).

### Exit without starting lpd because this machine is a firewall.
### 6/21/97 - PS.
echo "To enhance network security do not start lpd"
exit 0

# Source function library.
. /etc/rc.d/init.d/functions
```

STOPPING THE SENDMAIL STARTUP SCRIPT

If you run a proxy-based (application) firewall, you will want it to handle e-mail. Because that is a rather involved process, you need to consult the instructions for your system. For an IP filtering firewall, however, that function will be handled elsewhere and you need to turn off *sendmail* (process number 204).

Sendmail has traditionally been a source of many network security problems. Those problems have been greatly reduced in recent years and it is a reasonable system now. But it is also a very complex piece of software and it makes sense to simply eliminate it from our network.

1. Log on to your Linux Firewall Server as *root*.

2. Edit the */etc/rc.d/init.d/sendmail* file, shown in Listing 11-20.

Listing 11-20: The /etc/rc.d/init.d/sendmail.init script file

```
#!/bin/sh
#
# sendmail       This shell script takes care of starting and stopping
#                sendmail.
#
# chkconfig: 2345 80 30
# description: Sendmail is a Mail Transport Agent, which is the program \
# that moves mail from one machine to another.

# Source function library.
. /etc/rc.d/init.d/functions

# Source networking configuration.
. /etc/sysconfig/network

# Check that networking is up.
[ ${NETWORKING} = "no" ] && exit 0

[ -f /usr/sbin/sendmail ] || exit 0

# See how we were called.
case "$1" in
  start)
     # Start daemons.
     echo -n "Starting sendmail: "
     daemon /usr/sbin/sendmail -bd -q1h
     echo
     touch /var/lock/subsys/sendmail
     ;;
  stop)
     # Stop daemons.
     echo -n "Shutting down sendmail: "
     killproc sendmail
     echo
```

```
    rm -f /var/lock/subsys/sendmail
    ;;
  restart)
    $0 stop
    $0 start
    ;;
  status)
    status sendmail
    ;;
  *)
  echo "Usage: sendmail {start|stop|restart|status}"
  exit 1
esac

exit 0
```

3. Add the *exit* command to the sendmail scripts, as shown in Listing 11-21, to prevent its startup at the next boot.

Listing 11-21: Eliminating sendmail from the firewall

```
#!/bin/sh
#
# sendmail      This shell script takes care of starting and stopping
#               sendmail.
#
# chkconfig: 2345 80 30
# description: Sendmail is a Mail Transport Agent, which is the program \
# that moves mail from one machine to another.

### Exit without starting sendmail because this machine is a firewall.
### 6/21/97 - PS.
echo "To enhance network security do not start sendmail"
exit 0

# Source function library.
. /etc/rc.d/init.d/functions
```

STOPPING THE SAMBA STARTUP SCRIPT

A firewall should definitely not run any file or printer sharing utilities. If you do not set up your IP filter rules properly, your Samba shares can potentially be shared with the Internet!

1. Log on to your Linux Firewall Server as *root*.

2. First, stop Samba by entering the following command as *root*:

   ```
   /etc/rc.d/init.d/smb stop
   ```

3. To stop it from being started at the next system boot, log on as *root* and
   edit the */etc/rc.d/init.d/smb* file, shown in Listing 11-22.

Listing 11-22: The /etc/rc.d/init.d/smb file

```
#!/bin/sh
#
# chkconfig: 345 91 35
# description: Starts and stops the Samba smbd and nmbd daemons \
#        used to provide SMB network services.

# Source function library.
. /etc/rc.d/init.d/functions

# Source networking configuration.
. /etc/sysconfig/network

# Check that networking is up.
[ ${NETWORKING} = "no" ] && exit 0

# See how we were called.
case "$1" in
  start)
     echo -n "Starting SMB services: "
     daemon smbd -D
     daemon nmbd -D
     echo
     touch /var/lock/subsys/smb
     ;;
  stop)
     echo -n "Shutting down SMB services: "
     killproc smbd
     killproc nmbd
     rm -f /var/lock/subsys/smb
     echo ""
     ;;
  status)
     status smbd
     status nmbd
     ;;
  restart)
     echo -n "Restarting SMB services: "
```

```
    echo -n "smbd "
    kill -HUP 'pidof -s smbd'
    echo -n "nmbd "
    kill -HUP 'pidof -s nmbd'
    echo "done."
    ;;
  *)
  echo "Usage: smb {start|stop|restart|status}"
  exit 1
esac
```

4. Once again, I prefer to add an *exit* command at the beginning of the script. Look at Listing 11-23 to see the exit statement and comment.

Listing 11–23: Eliminating Samba from the firewall

```
#!/bin/sh

### Exit without starting Samba because this machine is a firewall.
### 6/21/97 - PS.
echo "To enhance network security do not start smbd or nmbd"
exit 0

# chkconfig: 345 91 35
# description: Starts and stops the Samba smbd and nmbd daemons \
#       used to provide SMB network services.

# Source function library.
. /etc/rc.d/init.d/functions
```

TIP

I like to make a distinction between my code and script modifications and the original or that of other people. My method is to use three consecutive comments. In the previous shell script, that means three pound characters (###). That makes it obvious — to me — that I have modified something. It also makes it easy to use a utility such as *grep* to search for all of my modifications. This capability becomes increasingly important as time rusts your memory away.

5. Stop the *daemon* process by using the *kill -9 209 211* command, or reboot the computer.

Note: The *login* process (number 288) and the *bash* process (number 296) are from my login on the firewall's console, so they're okay. The kernel, for its own internal organization, uses the *update* process (number 293), so it's okay, too. The *mingetty* processes manage your login process from the console (although you may want to reduce the number of logins you allow at one time by limiting the number of *mingettys*).

STOPPING THE GPM STARTUP SCRIPT

Next, what do you want to do about the harmless *gpm* process? It is used to interface the mouse to your console. What could be wrong with that? Well nothing probably, except if someone was really clever, they could write their own Trojan-horse program to look – and possibly act – like it. It's not likely, but the whole purpose of this exercise is to eliminate as many threats as possible. And because I do not make much use of that program, I choose to eliminate it.

1. Log on to your Linux Firewall Server as *root*.

2. Edit the */etc/rc.d/init.d/gpm* startup script, shown in Listing 11-24.

Listing 11-24: The /etc/rc.d/init.d/gpm startup script

```
#!/bin/bash

# source function library
. /etc/rc.d/init.d/functions

MOUSECFG=/etc/sysconfig/mouse

case "$1" in
  start)
     echo -n "Starting gpm mouse services: "
     if [ -f "$MOUSECFG" ]; then
         . "$MOUSECFG"
     else
         echo "(no mouse is configured)"
         exit 0
     fi

     if [ "$MOUSETYPE" = "Microsoft" ]; then
         MOUSETYPE=ms
     fi

     if [ -n "$MOUSETYPE" ]; then
         daemon gpm -t $MOUSETYPE
     else
```

```
        daemon gpm
    fi
    echo
    touch /var/lock/subsys/gpm
    ;;
  stop)
    echo -n "Shutting down gpm mouse services: "
    killproc gpm
    rm -f /var/lock/subsys/gpm
    echo
    ;;
  *)
    echo "Usage: gpm {start|stop}"
    exit 1
esac

exit 0
```

3. Add the *exit* command again, as shown in Listing 11-25, to prevent its
    startup at the next boot.

Listing 11-25: Eliminating the gpm from the firewall

```
#!/bin/bash

### Exit without starting GPM because this machine is a firewall.
### 6/21/97 - PS.
echo "To enhance network security do not start gpm"
exit 0

# source function library
. /etc/rc.d/init.d/functions

MOUSECFG=/etc/sysconfig/mouse
```

4. Stop the *daemon* process by using the *kill -9 216* command, or reboot the
    computer.

STOPPING THE NFSFS, ROUTED, RUSERSD, AND RWHOD STARTUP SCRIPTS

Continuing with our minimalist theme, eliminate the *nfsfs*, *routed*, *rusersd*, and *rwhod*
daemons. (These are not shown in the process table if you have not either manually
started them or did not specify their startup during the installation process. I mention
them because if they are running, then you should stop them.) These systems allow
other users to query who is logged onto machines on a network. The *nfsfs* daemon

provides *nfs* mount capability, *routed* sets up dynamic routes, and *rusersd/rwhod* provides information about your users to remote machines. These are unnecessary for your Firewall Network and could potentially give a burglar access or useful information to your network.

1. Log on to your Linux file server/router as *root.*

2. Edit the */etc/rc.d/init.d/nfsfs* script file, shown in Listing 11-26.

Listing 11-26: The /etc/rc.d/init.d/nfsfs file

```
#!/bin/sh
#
# nfsfs          Mount NFS filesystems.
#
# Version:       @(#) /etc/init.d/skeleton 1.01 26-Oct-1993
#
# Author:        Miquel van Smoorenburg, <miquels@drinkel.nl.mugnet.org>
#
# chkconfig: 345 15 95
# description: Mounts and unmounts all Network File System (NFS) \
#              mount points.

# Source networking configuration.
if [ ! -f /etc/sysconfig/network ]; then
    exit 0
fi

. /etc/sysconfig/network

# Check that networking is up.
[ ${NETWORKING} = "no" ] && exit 0

# See how we were called.
case "$1" in
  start)
    echo -n "Mounting remote filesystems."
    mount -a -t nfs
    touch /var/lock/subsys/nfsfs
    echo
    ;;
  stop)
    echo -n "Unmounting remote filesystems."
    umount -a -t nfs
    rm -f /var/lock/subsys/nfsfs
```

```
      echo
      ;;
  status)
      status nfsfs
      ;;
  restart)
      $0 stop
      $0 start
      ;;
  *)
  echo "Usage: nfsfs {start|stop|restart|status}"
  exit 1
esac

exit 0
```

   3. Add the *exit* command again, as shown in Listing 11-27, to prevent its
      startup at the next boot.

Listing 11-27: Eliminating nfsfs from the firewall

```
#!/bin/sh
#
# nfsfs         Mount NFS filesystems.
#
# Version:      @(#) /etc/init.d/skeleton 1.01 26-Oct-1993
#
# Author:       Miquel van Smoorenburg, <miquels@drinkel.nl.mugnet.org>
#
# chkconfig: 345 15 95
# description: Mounts and unmounts all Network File System (NFS) \
#              mount points.

### Exit without starting nfsfsd because this machine is a firewall.
### 6/21/97 - PS.
echo "To enhance network security do not start nfsfsd"
exit 0

# Source networking configuration.
if [ ! -f /etc/sysconfig/network ]; then
    exit 0
fi
```

   4. Repeat the process for the */etc/rc.d/init.d/routed, rusersd,* and *rwhod*
      script files.

REMOVING ALL UNNECESSARY COMPILERS

Finally, remove any, and all, of the compilers from your firewall computer. Without a compiler, an intruder will have far fewer tools with which to work. On a Red Hat Linux firewall, use the RPM to find out which compilers you have installed:

1. Log on to your Linux file server/router as *root.*

2. Enter the following command to find installed compilers:

   ```
   rpm -q -a | more
   ```

3. Look for *gcc, libc, libg, python, perl,* and so on. Remove those packages by entering the RPM *erase* command (*rpm -e xyz*) like that shown for the GNU C-compiler:

   ```
   rpm -e gcc
   ```

4. You can certainly make other changes to eliminate loopholes. I am learning all the time. Continue to eliminate unneeded applications and packages.

There you have it. You've got yourself a minimalist Firewall Server. It has just enough resources to perform its function. As a result, it has fewer temptations for burglars, too.

Note: I chose not to run X Window on the Firewall Server. If you have installed it on your Firewall Server, remove it with the RPM package. It takes away resources such as memory and disk space and is not needed. Remember that this is a simple machine and I like to run everything on it from a command line. You also save a valuable serial port by not having a mouse – that becomes important if you use a separate phone line for incoming communications and need the second serial port for that modem. Use the RPM *query* command to see how many X-related packages are installed and then remove them with the RPM *delete* command.

Adding a Serial Connection to Your Firewall Server (Optional)

You may want to add a serial line connection from your File Server/Router to your Firewall Server. Because you removed *Telnet* and *Rlogin* from the Firewall Server, the only way you can work on your Firewall Server is to log in from its console (that is, sit next to it). Adding a serial connection enables you to work on your Firewall Server from anywhere on your Private Network. The way this works is to *telnet* into the machine with the serial connection. From there, you run a terminal emulation program – *dip* has that capability – and connect to the Firewall Server via the serial connection.

Unfortunately, it is a great convenience to remotely work on the Firewall Server. (I dare say that it enhances security, in the long term, because as time rolls on it becomes tempting to add Telnet back on to save the time and hassle of walking to the console every time you want to check the logs or change something.) The answer is to add a serial cable from a trusted computer to the Firewall Server. You then can use a serial communication program such as */bin/cu* or */bin/dip* to log on remotely.

The simplest method is to buy a preconfigured cable with the *transmit* (#2) and *receive* (#3) wires crossed-over. This is called a *Null Modem.* Your remote computer sends outgoing data on line 2 and that data needs to be *received* on line 3 and vice versa.

You also may need to add a third serial interface if you use external modems and choose to have a separate phone line for incoming communication. You can purchase inexpensive serial interfaces to add another couple of interfaces.

You need to modify both computers to recognize the serial connection. This process is similar to configuring the dial-up connection, which I describe in Chapter 10. Complete the following steps:

1. Purchase or make a *null modem cable.* This is a serial cable with the send and receive lines crossed. Pin 2 on one connector becomes pin 3 on the other side.

2. Connect the two computers with a serial cable. PC serial ports are electrically buffered so you do not have to turn off the power to the computers to insert the cables, but be careful not to move them too much or you may damage the hard disks. *Note:* If you are already using two external modems, you must install another serial port.

3. You need to modify the *inittab* file on the Firewall Server to enable logins via a serial port.

4. Log on to the Firewall Server as *root.*

5. If you have not already installed the RPM package *getty_ps*, which contains the *uugetty* that I use, then do so now:

   ```
   rpm -ivh /mnt/cdrom/RedHat/RPMS/getty_ps-2.0.7j-2.i386.rpm
   ```

6. Make a backup copy of */etc/inittab*:

   ```
   cp /etc/inittab /etc/inittab.orig
   ```

   You can skip this step if you have already made a backup copy of *inittab*, described in Chapter 10, in the section "Configuring Your Firewall Server for Dial-In." You may, however, want to make a copy of your dial-in modified inittab.

7. Edit the */etc/inittab* file and modify the entry for the serial port that you want to enable. In Listing 11-28, I have added the entry for uugetty to monitor a serial device (*/dev/ttyS0*) for logins after the standard *mingettys* that monitor the console.

Listing 11-28: The /etc/inittab file modified for logins on serial port 0 (ttyS0)

```
# Run gettys in standard runlevels
1:12345:respawn:/sbin/mingetty tty1
2:2345:respawn:/sbin/mingetty tty2
3:2345:respawn:/sbin/mingetty tty3
4:2345:respawn:/sbin/mingetty tty4
5:2345:respawn:/sbin/mingetty tty5
6:2345:respawn:/sbin/mingetty tty6


s0:3456:respawn:/sbin/uugetty ttyS0 38400 vt100
```

8. To force *init* to recognize all these changes, you must tell it to reread its configuration file. Enter the following command as *root*:

   ```
   telinit q
   ```

   If you look at the end of the message log */var/log/messages* (*tail /var/log/messages*), you should see an indication that *init* did the job. It will also list any errors that occurred.

9. Test the new connection from the File Server/Router by using a serial-line communication program such as *dip* (you must be logged on as *root*):

   ```
   dip -t
   ```

10. Set the port to the appropriate serial device and the speed to match the Firewall Server. I connect to */dev/modem*:

    ```
    dip> port modem
    dip> speed 38400
    ```

11. Change to *terminal* mode:

    ```
    dip> term
    ```

12. You should get a login prompt from the Firewall Server. You can log on to it now. (If you get garbled text, you most likely have a speed mismatch.)

If you installed a dial-in modem connection (discussed in Chapter 10, in the section "Configuring Your Firewall Server for Dial-In") and have removed the network clients such as Telnet from the Firewall Server, you will want to configure the File Server/Router for direct serial connect as well. Without *Telnet* or *Rlogin*, you will not be able to communicate with the Private Network without a serial connection capability. To communicate with the Private Network, you must be able to log on to the File Server/Router in the same way as you can log on to the Firewall Server.

To install *uugetty* on the File Server/Router, repeat Steps 4 through 8. You can then dial up and log on to the Firewall Server. At that point, you can use *dip* or another program to log on to the File Server/Router. From there, you can make use of the network application programs to access other machines on the Private Network.

 I use two modems and a serial connection on my Firewall Server. The four potential serial ports, by default, share only two interrupts (IRQs 3 and 4), but you can manually reconfigure them if necessary. To avoid conflicts, I set my internal modem to use interrupt 5, which is unused on my system. If you have only external modems that must be connected to the standard serial ports, you must purchase a multiple serial port adapter. Otherwise, you must plan not to use one of the modems that shares the interrupt (either 3 or 4) with the serial port that is used for the serial connection to the File Server/Router.

Providing Web Services

If you want to provide a Web Server to your system, I advise that you pay someone else to provide the actual server capabilities. I have two reasons for this:

◆ You do not want to sacrifice your scarce Internet connection bandwidth to this purpose. If you have a puny PPP/modem connection, you'll immediately clog it up if you allow *http* packets down your pipe. Even with higher speed connections, why sacrifice your own speed?

◆ You have extra security concerns when you allow *http* packets into your network. Security measures are built into the protocol. CGI-bin is designed to isolate interactive services from passive ones (that is, straight browsing versus interactive browsing). But you still have to add IP filtering rules and configure your own *http* system. Therefore, in my opinion, it is easier in most cases if you have your ISP run your Web server.

The solution is to have your ISP act as your Web server. Most ISPs are set up to do just that and would love to do it. You never clog your Internet connection with that traffic and don't have to worry about configuring extra security.

Listing the Functions of the File Server/Router and Firewall

Table 11-1 lists the functions that the two servers (Firewall and File Server/Router) should perform.

TABLE 11-1 THE FUNCTIONS OF THE SERVERS

Function	Computer
File Server	Bart
Print Server	Bart
Network Router	Bart
SATAN	Bart
Tripwire	Bart
IP masquerading	Bart, Burns
PPP/Diald	Burns
IP Filtering	Burns
S/Key	Burns
Dial-Up	Burns

Where to Go Next

That's it! You are now on your way to being a full-fledged systems administrator ready to design, build, and run client-server networks. Linux and Samba are the reasons for your newfound profession. They provide the fundamental tools for building and managing commercial-quality client-server networks. Just as important, these tools are available to *everybody*.

UNIX in the form of Linux is no longer available to a select few. The open nature of Linux has created a huge base of developers who aspire to create the highest quality and functional software. The flux of ideas and tools has created an immensely creative environment. Thus, Linux – and its associated applications and utilities – is as high a quality and useful a product as anything else out there. No other operating system available is as easily obtained and used and yet very powerful. The fact that it is essentially free makes it that much better.

Everyone and every organization can now afford to have modern and productive networks. That means there is, and will be, that much more need for people with the skills and knowledge to manage these systems. Systems administrators need more systematic education.

With time, I hope and expect that more college-level Systems and Network Administration/Engineering courses will appear. There will be a point where the discipline is recognized as an important and distinct field of study and degreed programs will be offered. This is necessary because the demand for systems people is expanding fast and this discipline needs to be taught in a systematic manner.

The time for ad hoc education is ending. My own education is as an electrical engineer. I share with my colleagues a common background. That educational background gave me a solid foundation with which to start my career. When I graduated, I knew the basics of my profession and more importantly how to learn the tasks presented to me. I also recognized what I didn't know and could better judge how to avoid potential hazards and thus grow professionally.

We all will benefit when our profession is acknowledged and treated like any other engineering or technical specialty.

Red Hat has recently proposed a certification program for training consultants and organizations in Linux, the Internet, and PC hardware. You can find out more about it at `http://www.interweft.com.au/redhat/`.

Summary

In this chapter, I describe how to add both active and passive security measures for the "real-world" Linux client-server network that I first introduce in Chapter 10. I cover the following topics in this chapter:

◆ Adding security monitoring systems to the Linux file and print server.

  ■ Tripwire is a system that enables you to detect changes to important systems files that might mean an attempt to compromise your security.

  ■ Crack is a system that checks passwords for vulnerabilities.

  ■ SATAN is a system that actively checks for security holes on individual machines or over your entire network. It uses your Web browser as its GUI to make configuration and execution of your checks easy and straightforward.

♦ Adding a separate phone connection to your Firewall Server to allow incoming communication. You explicitly do not allow communication originating on the Internet because it presents too large a security problem. Therefore, by using a phone connection to call in, you allow yourself a relatively obscure entrance.

♦ Using the S/Key system to make your incoming communication even more secure. S/Key uses a one-time password system that prevents you or anyone else from using easily breakable passwords. Without it, someone can locate your call-in phone number and potentially break into your system if a user account password is guessed at or nonexistent. S/Key prevents that from happening.

♦ Adding a serial cable between your File Server/Router and Firewall Server to provide a safe, reasonably easy way to remotely communicate with your Firewall Server from your Private Network. Your Firewall Server does not run *Telnet* or *Rlogin* for security reasons, so without the serial connection, you otherwise would have to work from the console.

♦ Creating a simple and effective e-mail system by using your Web browser to access a POP account on your ISP. It is very simple to configure and is a reasonably secure system. E-mail is a difficult and complex subject. The standard Linux mail router daemon *sendmail* has entire books devoted to it. A simple alternative is to use a Post Office Protocol version 3 (POP3) client to read e-mail that is stored by your ISP. This approach lets you use e-mail on the Internet and avoids the difficult security issues involved with *sendmail.*

Appendix A

Quick Guide to vi

IF YOU ARE NEW to UNIX, the most universal screen editor is the Visual Editor, or *vi* (which is really a front-end to the *ed* line editor). This appendix outlines the basic */bin/vi* commands that let you perform simple edits in any text file.

You can operate vi in either *command* or *input* mode. If you start vi and specify a file – *vi filename* – you will see the contents of the file displayed on the screen. This is called the *buffer*. Any changes you make to the buffer will not be reflected in the file until you explicitly save it.

Command Mode

When you start vi you are placed in the *command* mode. You can enter all sorts of commands when in this mode, but I only cover the essentials. To read more about the commands, use the manual page for vi by entering the **man vi** command.

Tables A-1, A-2, and A3 describe some of the most commonly used commands.

TABLE A-1 FILE COMMANDS

Command	Description
:q	Quit from vi
:q!	Ignore all changes and quit from vi
:w	Write your file to disk
:wq	Write your file to disk and quit from vi

The commands listed in Table A-2 switch vi into input mode, so your keystrokes are interpreted as text, rather than commands.

TABLE A-2 INPUT MODE COMMANDS

Command	Description
a	Append characters from the current cursor position
A	Append characters to the end of the line of text where the cursor is positioned
i	Insert characters from the current cursor position
o	Open a line below the cursor for insertion

To perform editing operations, press the characters or keys listed in Table A-3, enter your edits, and then press *Esc*.

TABLE A-3 EDITING AND SEARCH COMMANDS

Command	Description
x	Delete the character at the current cursor position
3x	Delete the next three characters, starting at the current cursor position
dd	Delete the current line
3dd	Delete three lines from the current one
Ctrl+f	Page down
Ctrl+b	Page up
Up-arrow key	Move up one line
Down-arrow key	Move down one line
/xyz	Search forward for the string *xyz*
?xyz	Search backward for the string *xyz*

Input Mode

This mode is used to enter text into the buffer. You can get to the *input* mode with any of several commands, of which *insert* is one of the most common. To do this, press the *i* key. After you do so, anything you type will be entered on the screen but not saved until you tell vi to do so.

To return to *command* mode from *insert* mode, press the *Esc* key.

To save and exit from a file without first returning to *command* mode, press the capital *Z* twice in a row – ZZ.

Appendix B

GNU General Public License

Version 2, June 1991
Copyright © 1989, 1991 Free Software Foundation, Inc.
675 Mass Ave., Cambridge, MA 02139, USA

Preamble

The licenses for most software are designed to take away your freedom to share and change it. By contrast, the GNU General Public License is intended to guarantee your freedom to share and change free software – to make sure the software is free for all its users. This General Public License applies to most of the Free Software Foundation's software and to any other program whose authors commit to using it. (Some other Free Software Foundation software is covered by the GNU Library General Public License instead.) You can apply it to your programs, too.

When we speak of *free software*, we are referring to freedom, not price. Our General Public Licenses are designed to make sure that you have the freedom to distribute copies of free software (and charge for this service if you wish), that you receive source code or can get it if you want it, that you can change the software or use pieces of it in new free programs; and that you know you can do these things.

To protect your rights, we need to make restrictions that forbid anyone to deny you these rights or to ask you to surrender the rights. These restrictions translate to certain responsibilities for you if you distribute copies of the software, or if you modify it.

For example, if you distribute copies of such a program, whether gratis or for a fee, you must give the recipients all the rights that you have. You must make sure that they, too, receive or can get the source code. And you must show them these terms so they know their rights.

We protect your rights with two steps: (1) copyright the software, and (2) offer you this license, which gives you legal permission to copy, distribute, and/or modify the software.

Also, for each author's protection and ours, we want to make certain that everyone understands that there is no warranty for this free software. If the software is modified by someone else and passed on, we want its recipients to know that what they have is not the original, so that any problems introduced by others will not reflect on the original authors' reputations.

Finally, any free program is threatened constantly by software patents. We wish to avoid the danger that redistributors of a free program will individually obtain patent licenses, in effect making the program proprietary. To prevent this, we have made it clear that any patent must be licensed for everyone's free use or not licensed at all.

The precise terms and conditions for copying, distribution and modification follow.

Terms and Conditions for Copying, Distribution, and Modification

0. This License applies to any program or other work which contains a notice placed by the copyright holder saying it may be distributed under the terms of this General Public License. The "Program," below, refers to any such program or work, and a "work based on the Program" means either the Program or any derivative work under copyright law: that is to say, a work containing the Program or a portion of it, either verbatim or with modifications and/or translated into another language. (Hereinafter, translation is included without limitation in the term "modification.") Each licensee is addressed as "you."

   Activities other than copying, distribution, and modification are not covered by this License; they are outside its scope. The act of running the Program is not restricted, and the output from the Program is covered only if its contents constitute a work based on the Program (independent of having been made by running the Program). Whether that is true depends on what the Program does.

1. You may copy and distribute verbatim copies of the Program's source code as you receive it, in any medium, provided that you conspicuously and appropriately publish on each copy an appropriate copyright notice and disclaimer of warranty; keep intact all the notices that refer to this License and to the absence of any warranty; and give any other recipients of the Program a copy of this License along with the Program.

   You may charge a fee for the physical act of transferring a copy, and you may at your option offer warranty protection in exchange for a fee.

2. You may modify your copy or copies of the Program or any portion of it, thus forming a work based on the Program, and copy and distribute such modifications or work under the terms of Section 1 above, provided that you also meet all of these conditions:

   a) You must cause the modified files to carry prominent notices stating that you changed the files and the date of any change.

   b) You must cause any work that you distribute or publish, that in whole or in part contains or is derived from the Program or any part thereof, to be licensed as a whole at no charge to all third parties under the terms of this License.

   c) If the modified program normally reads commands interactively when run, you must cause it, when started running for such interactive use in the most ordinary way, to print or display an announcement including an appropriate copyright notice and a notice that there is no warranty (or else, saying that you provide a warranty) and that users may redistribute the program under these conditions, and telling the user how to view a copy of this License. (Exception: If the Program itself is interactive but does not normally print such an announcement, your work based on the Program is not required to print an announcement.)

   These requirements apply to the modified work as a whole. If identifiable sections of that work are not derived from the Program, and can be reasonably considered independent and separate works in themselves, then this License, and its terms, do not apply to those sections when you distribute them as separate works. But when you distribute the same sections as part of a whole which is a work based on the Program, the distribution of the whole must be on the terms of this License, whose permissions for other licensees extend to the entire whole, and thus to each and every part regardless of who wrote it.

   Thus, it is not the intent of this section to claim rights or contest your rights to work written entirely by you; rather, the intent is to exercise the right to control the distribution of derivative or collective works based on the Program.

   In addition, mere aggregation of another work not based on the Program with the Program (or with a work based on the Program) on a volume of a storage or distribution medium does not bring the other work under the scope of this License.

3. You may copy and distribute the Program (or a work based on it, under Section 2) in object code or executable form under the terms of Sections 1 and 2 above provided that you also do one of the following:

a) Accompany it with the complete corresponding machine-readable source code, which must be distributed under the terms of Sections 1 and 2 above on a medium customarily used for software interchange; or,

b) Accompany it with a written offer, valid for at least three years, to give any third party, for a charge no more than your cost of physically performing source distribution, a complete, machine-readable copy of the corresponding source code, to be distributed under the terms of Sections 1 and 2 above on a medium customarily used for software interchange; or,

c) Accompany it with the information you received as to the offer to distribute corresponding source code. (This alternative is allowed only for noncommercial distribution and only if you received the program in object code or executable form with such an offer, in accord with Subsection b above.)

The source code for a work means the preferred form of the work for making modifications to it. For an executable work, complete source code means all the source code for all modules it contains, plus any associated interface definition files, plus the scripts used to control compilation and installation of the executable. However, as a special exception, the source code distributed need not include anything that is normally distributed (in either source or binary form) with the major components (compiler, kernel, and so on) of the operating system on which the executable runs, unless that component itself accompanies the executable.

If distribution of executable or object code is made by offering access to copy from a designated place, then offering equivalent access to copy the source code from the same place counts as distribution of the source code, even though third parties are not compelled to copy the source along with the object code.

4. You may not copy, modify, sublicense, or distribute the Program except as expressly provided under this License. Any attempt otherwise to copy, modify, sublicense, or distribute the Program is void, and will automatically terminate your rights under this License.

However, parties who have received copies, or rights, from you under this License will not have their licenses terminated so long as such parties remain in full compliance.

5. You are not required to accept this License, since you have not signed it. However, nothing else grants you permission to modify or distribute the Program or its derivative works. These actions are prohibited by law if you do not accept this License. Therefore, by modifying or distributing the Program (or any work based on the Program), you indicate your acceptance of this License to do so, and all its terms and conditions for copying, distributing or modifying the Program or works based on it.

6. Each time you redistribute the Program (or any work based on the Program), the recipient automatically receives a license from the original licensor to copy, distribute, or modify the Program subject to these terms and conditions. You may not impose any further restrictions on the recipients' exercise of the rights granted herein. You are not responsible for enforcing compliance by third parties to this License.

7. If, as a consequence of a court judgment or allegation of patent infringement or for any other reason (not limited to patent issues), conditions are imposed on you (whether by court order, agreement or otherwise) that contradict the conditions of this License, they do not excuse you from the conditions of this License. If you cannot distribute so as to satisfy simultaneously your obligations under this License and any other pertinent obligations, then as a consequence you may not distribute the Program at all. For example, if a patent license would not permit royalty-free redistribution of the Program by all those who receive copies directly or indirectly through you, then the only way you could satisfy both it and this License would be to refrain entirely from distribution of the Program.

   If any portion of this section is held invalid or unenforceable under any particular circumstance, the balance of the section is intended to apply and the section as a whole is intended to apply in other circumstances.

   It is not the purpose of this section to induce you to infringe any patents or other property right claims or to contest validity of any such claims; this section has the sole purpose of protecting the integrity of the free software distribution system, which is implemented by public license practices. Many people have made generous contributions to the wide range of software distributed through that system in reliance on consistent application of that system; it is up to the author/donor to decide if he or she is willing to distribute software through any other system and a licensee cannot impose that choice.

   This section is intended to make thoroughly clear what is believed to be a consequence of the rest of this License.

8. If the distribution and/or use of the Program is restricted in certain countries either by patents or by copyrighted interfaces, the original copyright holder who places the Program under this License may add an explicit geographical distribution limitation excluding those countries, so that distribution is permitted only in or among countries not thus excluded. In such case, this License incorporates the limitation as if written in the body of this License.

9. The Free Software Foundation may publish revised and/or new versions of the General Public License from time to time. Such new versions will be similar in spirit to the present version, but may differ in detail to address new problems or concerns.

   Each version is given a distinguishing version number. If the Program specifies a version number of this License which applies to it and "any later version," you have the option of following the terms and conditions either of that version or of any later version published by the Free Software Foundation. If the Program does not specify a version number of this License, you may choose any version ever published by the Free Software Foundation.

10. If you wish to incorporate parts of the Program into other free programs whose distribution conditions are different, write to the author to ask for permission. For software which is copyrighted by the Free Software Foundation, write to the Free Software Foundation; we sometimes make exceptions for this. Our decision will be guided by the two goals of preserving the free status of all derivatives of our free software and of promoting the sharing and reuse of software generally.

No Warranty

11. BECAUSE THE PROGRAM IS LICENSED FREE OF CHARGE, THERE IS NO WARRANTY FOR THE PROGRAM, TO THE EXTENT PERMITTED BY APPLICABLE LAW. EXCEPT WHEN OTHERWISE STATED IN WRITING, THE COPYRIGHT HOLDERS AND/OR OTHER PARTIES PROVIDE THE PROGRAM "AS IS" WITHOUT WARRANTY OF ANY KIND, EITHER EXPRESSED OR IMPLIED, INCLUDING, BUT NOT LIMITED TO, THE IMPLIED WARRANTIES OF MERCHANTABILITY AND FITNESS FOR A PARTICULAR PURPOSE. THE ENTIRE RISK AS TO THE QUALITY AND PERFORMANCE OF THE PROGRAM IS WITH YOU. SHOULD THE PROGRAM PROVE DEFECTIVE, YOU ASSUME THE COST OF ALL NECESSARY SERVICING, REPAIR, OR CORRECTION.

12. IN NO EVENT UNLESS REQUIRED BY APPLICABLE LAW OR AGREED TO IN WRITING WILL ANY COPYRIGHT HOLDER, OR ANY OTHER PARTY WHO MAY MODIFY AND/OR REDISTRIBUTE THE PROGRAM AS PERMITTED ABOVE, BE LIABLE TO YOU FOR DAMAGES, INCLUDING ANY GENERAL, SPECIAL, INCIDENTAL, OR CONSEQUENTIAL DAMAGES ARISING OUT OF THE USE OR INABILITY TO USE THE PROGRAM (INCLUDING BUT NOT LIMITED TO LOSS OF DATA OR DATA BEING RENDERED INACCURATE OR LOSSES SUSTAINED BY YOU OR THIRD PARTIES OR A FAILURE OF THE PROGRAM TO OPERATE WITH ANY OTHER PROGRAMS), EVEN IF SUCH HOLDER OR OTHER PARTY HAS BEEN ADVISED OF THE POSSIBILITY OF SUCH DAMAGES.

End of Terms and Conditions

How to Apply These Terms to Your New Programs

If you develop a new program, and you want it to be of the greatest possible use to the public, the best way to achieve this is to make it free software that everyone can redistribute and change under these terms.

To do so, attach the following notices to the program. It is safest to attach them to the start of each source file to most effectively convey the exclusion of warranty; and each file should have at least the "copyright" line and a pointer to where the full notice is found:

<One line to give the program's name and a brief idea of what it does.>
Copyright (c)19yy (name of author)

This program is free software; you can redistribute it and/or modify it under the terms of the GNU General Public License as published by the Free Software Foundation; either version 2 of the License, or (at your option) any later version.

This program is distributed in the hope that it will be useful, but WITHOUT ANY WARRANTY; without even the implied warranty of MERCHANTABILITY or FITNESS FOR A PARTICULAR PURPOSE. See the GNU General Public License for more details.

You should have received a copy of the GNU General Public License along with this program; if not, write to the Free Software Foundation, Inc., 675 Mass Ave., Cambridge, MA 02139, USA.

Also add information on how to contact you by electronic and paper mail.

If the program is interactive, make it output a short notice like this when it starts in an interactive mode:

```
Gnomovision version 69, Copyright (c) 19yy name of author
Gnomovision comes with ABSOLUTELY NO WARRANTY; for details type 'show w'
This is free software, and you are welcome to redistribute it under certain
 conditions; type 'show c' for details.
```

The hypothetical commands show w and show c should show the appropriate parts of the General Public License. Of course, the commands you use may be called something other than show w and show c; they could even be mouse-clicks or menu items – whatever suits your program.

You should also get your employer (if you work as a programmer) or your school, if any, to sign a "copyright disclaimer" for the program, if necessary. Here is a sample; alter the names:

Yoyodyne, Inc., hereby disclaims all copyright interest in the program "Gnomovision" (which makes passes at compilers) written by James Hacker.

(signature of Ty Coon), 1 April 1989

Ty Coon, President of Vice

This General Public License does not permit incorporating your program into proprietary programs. If your program is a subroutine library, you may consider it more useful to permit linking proprietary applications with the library. If this is what you want to do, use the GNU Library General Public License instead of this License.

Appendix C

X Copyright

Appendix D

The BSD Copyright

Appendix E

Request For Comments (RFC) 768: The User Datagram Protocol

THE REQUEST FOR COMMENT (RFC) system helped form the basis for the modern Internet. It is the vehicle for arriving at the protocols that are used to connect networks and computers together to form the Internet. I include the User Datagram Protocol (UDP) – RFC 768 – here because it is quite readable and one of the cornerstones of much of the world's communications.

Introduction

This User Datagram Protocol (UDP) is defined to make available a datagram mode of packet-switched computer communication in the environment of an interconnected set of computer networks. This protocol assumes that the Internet Protocol (IP)[1] is used as the underlying protocol.

This protocol provides a procedure for application programs to send messages to other programs with a minimum of protocol mechanism. The protocol is transaction oriented, and delivery and duplicate protection are not guaranteed. Applications requiring ordered reliable delivery of streams of data should use the Transmission Control Protocol (TCP).[2]

Format

```
 0      7 8     15 16    23 24    31
+--------+--------+--------+--------+
|      Source     |   Destination   |
|      Port       |      Port       |
+--------+--------+--------+--------+
|                 |                 |
|     Length      |    Checksum     |
+--------+--------+--------+--------+
```

```
|
|              data octets ...
+---------------- ...
```

User Datagram Header Format

FIELDS

Source Port is an optional field; when meaningful, it indicates the port of the sending process, and may be assumed to be the port to which a reply should be addressed in the absence of any other information. If not used, a value of zero is inserted.

Destination Port has a meaning within the context of a particular Internet destination address.

Length is the length in octets of this user datagram including this header and the data. (This means the minimum value of the length is eight.)

Checksum is the 16-bit one's complement of the one's complement sum of a pseudo header of information from the IP header, the UDP header, and the data, padded with zero octets at the end (if necessary) to make a multiple of two octets.

The pseudo header conceptually prefixed to the UDP header contains the source address, the destination address, the protocol, and the UDP length. This information gives protection against misrouted datagrams.

This checksum procedure is the same as is used in TCP.

```
 0       7 8      15 16    23 24    31
+--------+--------+--------+--------+
|            source address         |
+--------+--------+--------+--------+
|          destination address      |
+--------+--------+--------+--------+
|  zero  |protocol|   UDP length    |
+--------+--------+--------+--------+
```

If the computed checksum is zero, it is transmitted as all ones (the equivalent in one's complement arithmetic). An all zero transmitted checksum value means that the transmitter generated no checksum (for debugging or for higher level protocols that don't care).

User Interface

A user interface should allow the creation of new receive ports, receive operations on the receive ports that return the data octets and an indication of source port and source address, and an operation that allows a datagram to be sent, specifying the data, source and destination ports, and addresses to be sent.

IP Interface

The UDP module must be able to determine the source and destination Internet addresses and the protocol field from the Internet header. One possible UDP/IP interface would return the whole Internet datagram including all of the Internet header in response to a receive operation.

Such an interface would also allow the UDP to pass a full Internet datagram complete with header to the IP to send. The IP would verify certain fields for consistency and compute the Internet header checksum.

Protocol Application

The major uses of this protocol are the Internet Name Server,[3] and the Trivial File Transfer.[4]

Protocol Number

This is protocol 17 (21 octal) when used in the Internet Protocol. Other protocol numbers are listed in RFC 762.[5]

References

[1] Postel, J., "Internet Protocol," RFC 760, USC/Information Sciences Institute, January 1980.

[2] Postel, J., "Transmission Control Protocol," RFC 761, USC/Information Sciences Institute, January 1980.

[3] Postel, J., "Internet Name Server," USC/Information Sciences Institute, IEN 116, August 1979.

[4] Sollins, K., "The TFTP Protocol," Massachusetts Institute of Technology, IEN 133, January 1980.

[5] Postel, J., "Assigned Numbers," USC/Information Sciences Institute, RFC 762, January 1980.

Appendix F

SunSITE Mirrors

THIS APPENDIX LISTS all the known SunSITE mirrors and was obtained from a SunSITE mirror itself. The list is organized by continent, with the SunSITEs listed by country. For each site, the list shows the city, the named IP address, and the directory where the SunSITE mirror is located.

Africa

South Africa

- ◆ **Johannesburg:** ftp.is.co.za. /linux/sunsite/
- ◆ **Stellenbosch:** ftp.sun.ac.za. /pub/linux/sunsite/

Asia

Hong Kong

- ◆ **Hong Kong:** ftp.cs.cuhk.hk. /pub/Linux/
- ◆ **Hong Kong:** sunsite.ust.hk. /pub/Linux/

Japan

- ◆ **Tokyo:** ftp.spin.ad.jp. /pub/linux/sunsite.unc.edu/

Korea

- ◆ **Seoul:** ftp.nuri.net. /pub/Linux/

Malaysia

- ◆ **Unknown:** ftp.jaring.my. /pub/Linux/

Republic of Singapore

◆ Singapore: ftp.nus.sg. /pub/unix/Linux/

Thailand

◆ Bangkok: ftp.nectec.or.th. /pub/mirrors/linux/

Australia

◆ Brisbane: ftp.dstc.edu.au. /pub/linux/

◆ Canberra: sunsite.anu.edu.au. /pub/linux/

◆ Melbourne: ftp.monash.edu.au. /pub/linux/

◆ Sydney: ftp.sydutech.usyd.edu.au. /pub/linux/

Europe

Austria

◆ Vienna: ftp.univie.ac.at. /systems/linux/sunsite/

Czech Republic

◆ Brno: ftp.fi.muni.cz. /pub/UNIX/linux/

Finland

◆ Espo: ftp.funet.fi. /pub/Linux/sunsite/

France

◆ Angers: ftp.univ-angers.fr. /pub/Linux/

◆ Belfort: ftp.iut-bm.univ-fcomte.fr/pub/linux

◆ Nancy: ftp.loria.fr. /pub/linux/sunsite/

◆ Paris: ftp.ibp.fr. /pub/linux/sunsite/

Germany

- **Aachen:** ftp.dfv.rwth-aachen.de. /pub/linux/sunsite/
- **Dortmund:** ftp.germany.eu.net. /pub/os/Linux/Mirror.SunSITE/
- **Dresden:** ftp.tu-dresden.de. /pub/Linux/sunsite/
- **Erlangen:** ftp.uni-erlangen.de. /pub/Linux/MIRROR.sunsite/
- **Göttingen:** ftp.gwdg.de. /pub/linux/mirrors/sunsite/
- **Karlsruhe:** ftp.rz.uni-karlsruhe.de. /pub/linux/mirror.sunsite/
- **Mannheim:** ftp.ba-mannheim.de. /pub/linux/mirror.sunsite/
- **Paderborn:** ftp.uni-paderborn.de. /pub/Mirrors/sunsite.unc.edu/
- **Rostock:** ftp.uni-rostock.de. /Linux/sunsite/
- **Stuttgart:** ftp.rus.uni-stuttgart.de. /pub/unix/systems/linux/MIRROR.sunsite/
- **Tübingen:** ftp.uni-tuebingen.de. /pub/linux/Mirror.sunsite/
- **Ulm:** ftp.rz.uni-ulm.de. /pub/mirrors/linux/sunsite/

Hungary

- **Budapest:** ftp.kfki.hu. /pub/linux/

Italy

- **Casale Monferrato:** linux.italnet.it. /pub/Linux/
- **Naples:** ftp.unina.it. /pub/linux/sunsite/
- **Padova:** giotto.unipd.it. /pub/unix/Linux/
- **Pisa:** cnuce-arch.cnr.it. /pub/Linux/
- **Rome:** ftp.flashnet.it. /mirror2/sunsite.unc.edu/

Netherlands

- **Amsterdam:** ftp.nijenrode.nl. /pub/linux/sunsite.unc-mirror/
- **Leiden:** ftp.LeidenUniv.nl. /pub/linux/sunsite/

Norway

◆ Trondheim: ftp.nvg.unit.no. /pub/linux/sunsite/

Poland

◆ Warsaw: sunsite.icm.edu.pl. /pub/Linux/sunsite.unc.edu/

Spain

◆ Barcelona: ftp.upc.es. /pub/sistemes/linux/

◆ Madrid: ftp.rediris.es. /software/os/linux/sunsite/

◆ Madrid: sunsite.rediris.es. /software/linux/

◆ Oviedo: ftp.etsimo.uniovi.es. /pub/linux/

◆ Seville: ftp.cs.us.es. /pub/Linux/sunsite-mirror/

◆ Tarragone: ftp.etse.urv.es. /pub/mirror/linux/

◆ Valladolid: ftp.luna.gui.es. /pub/linux.new/

Switzerland

◆ Zurich: ftp.switch.ch. /mirror/linux/

Turkey

◆ Ankara: ftp.metu.edu.tr. /pub/linux/sunsite/

United Kingdom

◆ Canterbury: unix.hensa.ac.uk. /mirrors/sunsite/pub/Linux/

◆ Coventry: ftp.maths.warwick.ac.uk. /mirrors/linux/sunsite.unc-mirror/

◆ Greenwich: ftp.idiscover.co.uk. /pub/Linux/sunsite.unc-mirror/

◆ London: sunsite.doc.ic.ac.uk. /packages/linux/sunsite.unc-mirror/

◆ Mildenhall: ftp.dungeon.com. /pub/linux/sunsite-mirror/

North America

Canada

- Toronto, Ontario: ftp.io.org. /pub/mirrors/linux/sunsite/

United States

- Atlanta, Georgia: ftp.cc.gatech.edu. /pub/linux/
- Chapel Hill, North Carolina: sunsite.unc.edu. /pub/Linux/
- Concord, California: ftp.cdrom.com. /pub/linux/sunsite/
- Dallas, Texas: ftp.siriuscc.com. /pub/Linux/Sunsite/
- Fayetteville, Arkansas: ftp.engr.uark.edu. /pub/linux/sunsite/
- Flagstaff, Arizona: ftp.infomagic.com. /pub/mirrors/linux/sunsite/
- Laurel, Maryland: ftp.linux.org. /pub/mirrors/sunsite/
- Minneapolis, Minnesota: ftp.cs.umn.edu. /pub/Linux/sunsite/
- Norman, Oklahoma: ftp.uoknor.edu. /linux/sunsite/
- Pasadena, California: ftp.fuller.edu. /mirror/sunsite/
- Raleigh, North Carolina: ftp.redhat.com. /pub/mirrors/sunsite.unc.edu/
- Rochester, New York: ftp.rge.com. /pub/systems/linux/sunsite/
- Salt Lake City, Utah: ftp.pht.com. /mirrors/linux/sunsite/
- San Jose, California: ftp.yggdrasil.com. mirrors/sunsite/
- Sunnyvale, California: ftp.drcdrom.com. /pub/linux/sunsite/
- Urbana, Illinois: uiarchive.cso.uiuc.edu. /pub/systems/linux/sunsite/
- Waukesha, Wisconsin: ftp.wit.com. /unix/linux/

South America

Brazil

- ◆ Campinas: ftp.fee.unicamp.br. /pub/Linux/mirrors/sunsite.unc.edu/
- ◆ Rio de Janeiro: ftp.iis.com.br. /pub/Linux/
- ◆ Sao Paulo: linux.if.usp.br. /pub/mirror/sunsite.unc.edu/pub/Linux/
- ◆ Unknown: farofa.ime.usp.br. /pub/linux/

Chile

- ◆ Unknown: sunsite.dcc.uchile.cl/pub/OS/linux

Note: If you know the location (including city) of any sites listed as "Unknown" in the preceding list, please mail ewt@sunsite.unc.edu.

Appendix G

RPM Packages on the CD-ROM

THE FOLLOWING LIST was compiled and edited from all the RPM packages contained on the companion CD-ROM. Each entry contains the name of the package, the full RPM package name (which includes the version and release numbers), and a short description of the package's purpose. (Nearly all the packages are from Red Hat.) The packages are divided into the groups and subgroups that they belong to. I used the following command to extract the information contained in this appendix:

```
rpm -q -p -i /mnt/cdrom/RedHat/RPMS/*
```

You may list the complete information on any package by using the following command (refer to Chapter 7 for a discussion of the RPM query function):

```
rpm -q -p -i /mnt/cdrom/RedHat/RPMS/anypackage*
```

Note: The groups and subgroups correspond to the groups and the subgroups that the Red Hat installation presents to you (as I detail in the section "Installing Red Hat Linux," in Chapter 1).

Applications

The application group encompasses programs that you — the user — execute and use.

Applications/Communications

- ◆ **efax:** This program sends and receives faxes over class 1 or class 2 fax modems. Its interface facilitates faxing.

- ◆ **ircii:** This popular Internet Relay Chat (IRC) client program is used to connect to IRC servers around the globe so you can chat with other users.

- ◆ **ircii-help:** This package contains the help files and other documentation for the ircii client package.

- lrzsz: This collection of commands can be used to download and upload files using the Z, X, and Y protocols. Many terminal programs (like minicom) make use of these programs to transfer files.

- minicom: This communications program resembles the MS-DOS Telix program. It has a dialing directory, color, full ANSI and VT100 emulation, an (external) scripting language, and more.

Applications/Databases

- mb: MetalBase is a relational database system. It is a client-server system to allow for all database needs.

Applications/Editors

- ed: This is the GNU line editor. It is an implementation of one of the first editors under *nix. Some programs rely on it, but in general you probably don't need it.

- jed: Jed is a fast, compact editor based on the slang screen library. It has special editing modes for C, C++, and other languages. It can emulate emacs, WordStar, and other editors, and can be customized with slang macros, colors, keybindings, and so on.

- jed-xjed: Xjed is the same editor as jed; it just runs in its own X Window.

- joe: Joe is a friendly and easy to use editor. It has a nice interface and would be a good choice for a novice who needs a text editor. It uses the same WordStar keybindings as those used by Borland's development environment.

- vim: The VIsual editor iMproved is an updated and feature-added clone of the vi editor that comes with almost all UNIX systems. It adds multiple windows, multi-level undo, block highlighting, and many other features to the standard vi program.

- vim-X11: This package is a version of VIM with the X Window libraries linked in, allowing you to run VIM as an X Window application with a full GUI interface and mouse support. To enable GUI usage, you must start vimx with the -g command line option.

Applications/Editors/Emacs

◆ **emacs:** Emacs is the extensible, customizable, self-documenting, real-time display editor. Emacs has special code editing modes, a scripting language (elisp), and comes with many packages for doing mail, news, and more, all in your editor.

This package includes the libraries necessary to run the emacs editor – the actual program can be found in either the emacs-nox or emacs-X11 packages, depending on whether you use X Window.

◆ **emacs-el:** This package contains the emacs-lisp sources for many of the elisp programs included with the main emacs package. You do not need this package unless you want to modify these packages, or see some elisp examples.

◆ **emacs-nox:** This package contains an emacs binary built without support for X Window. Although the emacs binary in the main emacs package works fine outside of X Window (on the console, for instance), the one in this package has a smaller memory image.

◆ **emacs-X11:** This package contains an emacs binary built with support for X Window. It works fine outside of X Window (on the console, for instance) but supports the mouse and GUI elements when used inside X Window.

Application/Emulators

◆ **dosemu:** This package enables you to run numerous DOS programs under Linux. You must have DOS available because this package only emulates the system-level interface; it does not provide a replacement for command.com. To try it, put a DOS boot disk in your first floppy drive, log in as root, and type **dos**.

Applications/Engineering

◆ **spice:** SPICE is a general-purpose circuit simulation program for nonlinear dc, nonlinear transient, and linear ac analyses. Circuits may contain resistors, capacitors, inductors, mutual inductors, independent voltage and current sources, four types of dependent sources, transmission lines, and the four most common semiconductor devices: diodes, BJTs, JFETs, and MOSFETs.

◆ **units:** The units program converts quantities expressed in various scales to their equivalents in other scales. The units program can only handle multiplicative scale changes.

Application/Graphics

◆ **ghostscript:** Ghostscript is a PostScript interpreter. It can render both PostScript and PDF compliant files to devices that include an X window, many printer formats (including support for color printers), and popular graphics file formats.

◆ **ghostscript-fonts:** These fonts can be used by the GhostScript interpreter during text rendering.

◆ **giftrans:** This program can convert and manipulate GIF images from the command line. It is most useful for making a color transparent for Web sites.

◆ **libgr-progs:** This package includes various utility programs for manipulating JPEG files for use by libgr programs.

◆ **netpbm:** This is the netpbm set of image conversion and manipulation tools. They are all command line tools for playing with images. (Because of a very restrictive redistribution clause, hpcd support is missing.)

Applications/Mail

◆ **elm:** ELM is one of the most popular terminal mode mail handling programs. It is powerful, easy to use, and easy to find help on. It has all the mail handling features you would expect, including MIME support (via metamail).

◆ **exmh:** exmh is a graphical interface to the MH mail system. It includes MIME support, faces, glimpse indexing, color highlighting, PGP interface, and more.

◆ **fetchmail:** fetchmail is a program that you use to retrieve mail from a remote mail server. It can use the Post Office Protocol (POP) or IMAP (Internet Mail Access Protocol) for this, and delivers the mail through the local SMTP server (normally sendmail).

◆ **mailx:** The /bin/mail program can be used to send quick mail messages, and is often used in shell scripts.

◆ **metamail:** Metamail is an implementation of MIME, the Multipurpose Internet Mail Extensions, a proposed standard for multimedia mail on the Internet. Metamail implements MIME, and also implements extensibility and configuration via the mailcap mechanism described in an informational RFC that is a companion to the MIME document.

◆ **mh:** MH (with POP support) is a popular mail handling system but includes only a command line interface. It is an important base, however, for programs like xmh and exmh.

◆ **pine:** Pine is a full-featured, text-based mail and news client, aimed at both novice and expert users. It includes an easy to use editor – pico – for composing messages. Pico has gained popularity as a standalone text editor in its own right. It features MIME support, address books, and support for IMAP, mail, and MH style folders.

Applications/Math

◆ **bc:** bc is a text mode calculator of sorts. It has many extended features such as base translation. It can also accept input from stdin and return output.

◆ **gnuplot:** This is the GNU plotting package. It can be used to graph data in an X window or to a file.

Applications/Networking

◆ **lynx:** This a terminal-based Web browser. Although it does not make any attempt at displaying graphics, it has good support for HTML text formatting, forms, and tables.

◆ **ncftp:** Ncftp is an ftp client with many advantages over the standard one. It includes command line editing, command histories, support for recursive gets, automatic logins, and much more.

◆ **tcpdump:** Tcpdump prints out the headers of packets on a network interface. It is very useful for debugging network problems and security operations.

Applications/News

◆ **slrn:** Slrn is an easy to use but powerful full-screen, NNTP-based newsreader. It relies extensively on the S-Lang programmer's library for many of its features. Slrn works particularly well over slow network connections.

◆ **tin:** Tin is a full-screen, easy to use Netnews reader. It can read news locally (that is, /usr/spool/news) or remotely (rtin or tin -r option) via an NNTP (Network News Transport Protocol) server.

◆ **trn:** trn is one of the original threaded news readers. This version is configured to read news from an NNTP news server.

Applications/Productivity

◆ **ical:** ical is a popular X-based calendar/scheduler application that can help you keep track of single events and recurring events (daily, weekly, monthly, or yearly), and sets off alarms to warn you of appointments.

Applications/Publishing

◆ **bm2font:** This package converts bitmaps to LaTeX fonts. It is useful for LaTeX users who need to create their own fonts, and it also can be used to embed graphics in documents.

◆ **groff:** The groff text formatting system can be used to create professional-looking documents on both paper and a computer screen. All the man pages are processed with groff, so you need this package to read man pages.

◆ **groff-gxditview:** This package contains the gxditview program, which can be used to format and view groff documents in X Window. For example, man pages can be read using gxditview.

◆ **linuxdoc-sgml:** Linuxdoc-SGML is an SGML-based text formatter that allows you to produce various output formats. You can create PostScript and dvi (with LaTeX), plain text (with groff), HTML, and texinfo files from a single SGML source file.

◆ **lout:** The Lout system reads a high-level description of a document, similar in style to LaTeX, and produces a PostScript file that can be printed on many laser printers and graphic display devices. Plain text output is also available.

   Lout offers an unprecedented range of advanced features, including optimal paragraph and page breaking, automatic hyphenation, PostScript EPS file inclusion and generation, equation formatting, tables, diagrams, rotation and scaling, sorted indexes, bibliographic databases, running headers and odd-even pages, automatic cross-referencing, multilingual documents including hyphenation (most European languages are supported, including Russian), formatting of C/C++ programs, and much more, all ready to use. Furthermore, Lout is easily extended with definitions that are much easier to write than troff of TeX macros because Lout is a high-level language, the outcome of an eight-year research project that went back to the beginning.

◆ **lout-doc:** This package includes the complete Lout documentation, including the user and expert manuals, written in Lout and with PostScript output. The documentation offers useful examples of writing large docs with Lout.

◆ **texinfo:** The GNU project uses the texinfo file format for much of its documentation. This package includes the tools necessary to create .info files from .texinfo source files, as well as an emacs interface to all these tools.

Applications/Publishing/TeX

◆ **tetex:** TeX formats a file of interspersed text and commands and outputs a typesetter independent file (called DVI, which is short for DeVice Independent). TeX capabilities and language are described in The TeXbook, by Knuth.

◆ **tetex-afm:** PostScript fonts are (or should be) accompanied by font metric files such as Times-Roman.afm, which describes the characteristics of the font called Times-Roman. To use such fonts with TeX, you need TFM files that contain similar information. afm2tfm does that conversion.

◆ **tetex-dvilj:** Dvilj and siblings convert TeX-output .dvi files into HP PCL (that is, HP Printer Control Language) commands suitable for printing on an HP LaserJet+, HP LaserJet IIP (using dvilj2p), HP LaserJet 4 (using dvilj4), and fully compatible printers.

◆ **tetex-dvips:** The program dvips takes a DVI file produced by TeX (or by some other processor such as GFtoDVI) and converts it to PostScript, normally sending the result directly to the laserprinter.

◆ **tetex-latex:** LaTeX is a TeX macro package. The LaTeX macros encourage writers to think about the content of their documents, rather than the form. The ideal, very difficult to realize, is to have no formatting commands (like `switch to italic` or `skip 2 picas`) in the document at all; instead, everything is done by specific markup instructions – for example, `emphasize`, `start a section`.

◆ **tetex-texmf-src:** This package contains the source for the documents and TeX components in the teTeX distribution. This package IS NOT REQUIRED to use teTeX, but is useful for those who need to customize it. The documented source files (*.dtx) are examples of what this package contains.

◆ **tetex-xdvi:** xdvi is a program that runs under the X Window system. It is used to preview dvi files, such as are produced by tex and latex.

Applications/Sound

◆ **aumix:** This program provides a tty-based, interactive method of controlling a sound card's mixer. It lets you adjust the input levels from the CD, microphone, and on-board synthesizers as well as the output volume.

◆ **cdp:** This program allows you to play audio CDs on your computer's CD-ROM drive. It provides a version with a full screen interface as well as a command line version.

◆ **maplay:** This program plays MPEG 2 format audio files through your PC's sound card. MPEG audio files are popular for sending high-fidelity music over the Internet, and `http://www.iuma.com` contains a large archive of MPEG 2 sound files.

◆ **playmidi:** Plays MIDI sound files through a sound card synthesizer. It includes basic drum samples for use with simple FM synthesizers.

◆ **playmidi-X11:** This X program for playing MIDI sound files through a sound card synthesizer includes basic drum samples for use with simple FM synthesizers.

◆ **sox:** The self-described "swiss army knife of sound tools," sox can convert between many different digitized sound formats and perform simple sound manipulation functions.

◆ **tracker:** Amiga MOD files are a very popular format for distributing sound files and the digital samples that are required to play them. Tracker can play a wide range of .mod files through any sound card supported by Linux.

Base

◆ **crontabs:** The root crontab file is used to schedule execution of various programs.

◆ **dev:** UNIX and UNIX-like systems (including Linux) use file system entries to represent devices attached to the machine. All these entries are in the /dev tree (though they don't have to be), and this package contains the most commonly used /dev entries. These files are essential for a system to function properly.

◆ **etcskel:** This is part of the Base Red Hat system. It contains the files that go in /etc/skel, which are in turn placed in every new user's home directory when new accounts are created.

◆ **filesystem:** This package contains the basic directory layout for a Linux system, including the proper permissions for the directories. This layout conforms to the Linux Filesystem Standard (FSSTND) 1.3.

◆ **initscripts:** This package contains the scripts you use to boot a system, change run levels, and shut the system down cleanly. It also contains the scripts that activate and deactivate most network interfaces.

◆ **inn:** INN is a news server, which can be set up to handle USENET news, as well as private newsfeeds. You can find lots of information about setting up INN in /usr/doc – read it.

◆ **mailcap:** This is the Red Hat Mailcap package. Installing it enables programs like lynx to automatically use zgv to display pictures (provided zgv is installed).

◆ **pam:** PAM (Pluggable Authentication Modules) is a powerful, flexible, extensible authentication system that allows the system administrator to configure authentication services individually for every pam-compliant application without recompiling any of the applications.

◆ **pamconfig:** This package has been made obsolete by pam-0.56, and is provided for compatibility purposes only. To determine whether you have any packages that require this package, enter the following command:

```
rpm -q --whatrequires pamconfig
```

If this command returns no package names, you may remove this package with the following command:

```
rpm -e pamconfig
```

◆ **passwd:** This password-changing program uses PAM (Pluggable Authentication Modules) to set or change a password. Like all PAM-capable applications, it can be configured using a file in the /etc/pam.d/ directory.

◆ **pwdb:** pwdb (Password Database Library) allows configurable access to and management of /etc/passwd, /etc/shadow, and network authentication systems including NIS and Radius.

◆ **redhat-release:** This is the Red Hat Linux release file.

◆ **rootfiles:** This package contains all the startup files for the root user. These are basically the same files that the etcskel package contains.

◆ **setup:** This package contains numerous very important configuration and setup files, including the passwd, group, and profile files.

♦ **termcap:** The /etc/termcap file is a database defining the capabilities of various terminals and terminal emulators. Programs use /etc/termcap to gain access to various features of terminals such as the bell, color, and graphics.

Base/Kernel

♦ **iBCS:** This package allows you to run programs in the iBCS2 (Intel Binary Compatibility Standard, version 2) and related executable formats.

♦ **kernel:** This package contains the Linux kernel that is used to boot and run your system. It contains few device drivers for specific hardware. Most hardware is instead supported by modules loaded after booting.

♦ **kernel-headers:** These are the C header files for the Linux kernel, which define structures and constants that are needed when building most standard programs under Linux, as well as to rebuild the kernel.

♦ **kernel-modules:** This package includes the modules that provide the support for most supported hardware devices. The modules are loaded into the running kernel after it is booted.

♦ **kernel-source:** This is the source code for the Linux kernel. It is required to build most C programs as they depend on constants defined in here. You can also build a custom kernel that is better tuned to your particular hardware.

✦ **umsdos_progs:** These are the utilities for doing UMSDOS file system operations. You can use these programs to have long filenames on a DOS partition under Linux and still have those files available under DOS (with mangled filenames).

Daemons

♦ **SysVinit:** Part of the Red Hat Linux Vanderbilt distribution, SysVinit is the first program started by the Linux kernel when the system boots, controlling the startup, running, and shutdown of all other programs.

♦ **at:** at and batch read commands from standard input or a specified file, which are to be executed at a later time, using /bin/sh.

♦ **bdflush:** This program flushes the disk buffers the kernel keeps to prevent them from growing too stale.

♦ **gpm:** GPM adds mouse support to text-based Linux applications such as emacs and Midnight Commander. It also provides console cut-and-paste operations using the mouse. This package includes a program to allow pop-up menus to appear at the click of a mouse button.

◆ **pcmcia-cs:** Many laptop machines (and some others) support PCMCIA cards for expansion. Also known as "credit card adapters," PCMCIA cards are small cards for everything from SCSI support to modems. They are hot swappable (meaning they can be exchanged without rebooting the system) and quite convenient. This package contains support for numerous PCMCIA cards and supplies a daemon that allows them to be hot swapped.

◆ **procmail:** Red Hat Linux uses procmail for all local mail delivery. In addition to regular mail delivery duties, procmail can be used to do many automatic filtering, presorting, and mail handling jobs. It is the basis for the SmartList mailing list processor.

◆ **sendmail:** Sendmail is a Mail Transport Agent, which is the program that moves mail from one machine to another. Sendmail implements a general internetwork mail routing facility, featuring aliasing and forwarding, automatic routing to network gateways, and flexible configuration. If you need the capability to send and receive mail via the Internet, you need sendmail.

◆ **sendmail-cf:** This package contains all the configuration files used to generate the sendmail.cf file distributed with the base sendmail package. You'll want this package if you need to reconfigure and rebuild your sendmail.cf file. For example, the default sendmail.cf is not configured for UUCP. If you need to send and receive mail over UUCP, you may need this package to help you reconfigure sendmail.

◆ **sendmail-doc:** This package includes release notes, the sendmail FAQ, and a few papers written about sendmail. The papers are available in PostScript and troff.

◆ **sysklogd:** This is the Linux system and kernel logging program. It is run as a daemon (background process) to log messages to different places. These are usually things like sendmail logs, security logs, and errors from other daemons.

◆ **uucp:** UUCP is a UNIX-to-UNIX transfer mechanism. It is used primarily for remote sites to download and upload e-mail and news files to local machines. If you didn't already know that, you probably don't need this package installed.

◆ **vixie-cron:** cron is a standard UNIX program that runs user-specified programs at periodic scheduled times. vixie cron adds a number of features to the basic UNIX cron, including better security and more powerful configuration options.

Development

Development/Building

♦ **autoconf:** GNU's autoconf is a tool for source and Makefile configuration. It assists the programmer in creating portable and configurable packages, by allowing the person building the package to specify various configuration options. autoconf is not required for the end user – it is needed only to generate the configuration scripts.

♦ **automake:** automake is an experimental Makefile generator. It was inspired by the 4.4BSD make and include files, but aims to be portable and to conform to the GNU standards for Makefile variables and targets.

♦ **make:** The program make is used to coordinate the compilation and linking of a set of sources into a program, recompiling only what is necessary, thus saving a developer lots of time. In fact, make can do a lot more – read the info docs.

♦ **pmake:** pmake is a particular version of make that supports some additional syntax not in the standard make program. Some Berkeley programs have Makefiles written for pmake.

Development/Debuggers

♦ **gdb:** This is a full-featured, command driven debugger. It allows you to trace the execution of programs and examine their internal state at any time. It works for C and C++ programs compiled with the GNU C compiler gcc.

♦ **strace:** Strace prints a record of each system call another program makes, including all the arguments passed to it and the system call's return value.

Development/Languages

♦ **basic:** This is a BASIC language interpreter. You can use it to run programs written in BASIC.

♦ **bin86:** This package provides an assembler and linker for real mode 80x86 instructions. Programs that run in real mode, including LILO and the kernel's bootstrapping code, need to have this package installed to be built from the sources.

♦ **ElectricFence:** ElectricFence is a library that can be used for C programming and debugging. You link it in at compile time and it will warn you of possible problems such as freeing memory that doesn't exist.

◆ **gcc:** The GNU C compiler – a full-featured ANSI C compiler, with support for K&R C as well. GCC provides many levels of source code error checking traditionally provided by other tools (such as lint), produces debugging information, and can perform many different optimizations to the resulting object code. This package contains the back end for C++ and Objective C compilers as well.

◆ **gcc-c++:** This package adds C++ support to the GNU C compiler. It includes support for most of the current C++ specification, including templates and exception handling. It does not include a standard C++ library, which is available separately.

◆ **gcc-objc:** This package adds Objective C support to the GNU C compiler. Objective C is an object-oriented derivative of the C language, mainly used on systems running NeXTSTEP. This package does not include the standard objective C object library.

◆ **guavac:** Guavac is a standalone compiler for the Java programming language. It was written entirely in C++, and should be portable to any platform supporting Gnu's C++ compiler or a similarly powered system.

◆ **kaffe:** This is Kaffe, a virtual machine designed to execute Java bytecode. This machine can be configured in two modes. In one mode, it operates as a pure bytecode interpreter (not unlike Javasoft's machine); in the second mode, it performs "just-in-time" code conversion from the abstract code to the host machine's native code. This conversion will ultimately allow execution of Java code at the same speed as standard compiled code but while maintaining the advantages and flexibility of code independence.

◆ **kaffe-bissawt:** Biss-AWT is an AWT-like windowing toolkit integrated into the kaffe Java virtual machine. It supports a full widget set and allows Java applications to take advantage of the X Window system.

◆ **python:** Python is an interpreted, object-oriented scripting language. It contains support for dynamic loading of objects, classes, modules, and exceptions. Adding interfaces to new system libraries through C code is straightforward, making Python easy to use in custom settings.

This Python package includes most of the standard Python modules, along with modules for interfacing to the Tix widget set for Tk and RPM.

◆ **python-devel:** The Python interpreter is relatively easy to extend with dynamically loaded extensions and to embed in other programs. This package contains the header files and libraries needed to do both of these tasks.

◆ **python-docs:** This package contains documentation on the Python language and interpreter as a mix of plain ASCII files and LaTeX sources.

◆ **umb-scheme:** UMB Scheme is an implementation of the language described in the IEEE Standard for the Scheme Programming Language (December, 1990).

◆ **p2c-devel:** This is the development kit for the Pascal to C translator. It contains the header files and some other programs that may be useful to someone using the translator.

Development/Languages/Tcl

◆ **blt:** BLT is an extension to the Tcl/Tk toolset. It provides more widgets for Tk. It is useful for folks writing programs that make use of the Tk widget set and need more widgets.

◆ **blt-devel:** This is the development environment for BLT. It provides the headers and static libraries for doing BLT development.

◆ **ctags:** A better ctags that generates tags for all possible tag types: macro definitions, enumerated values (values inside enum{...}), function and method definitions, enum/struct/union tags, external function prototypes (optional), typedefs, and variable declarations. It is far less easily fooled by code containing #if preprocessor conditional constructs, using a conditional path selection algorithm to resolve complicated choices, and a fall-back algorithm when this one fails. It can also be used to print out a list of selected objects found in source files.

◆ **expect:** Expect is a tool for automating interactive applications such as telnet, ftp, passwd, fsck, rlogin, and tip. Expect makes it easy for a script to control another program and interact with it.

◆ **tcl:** TCL is a simple scripting language that is designed to be embedded in other applications. This package includes tclsh, a simple example of a tcl application. TCL is very popular for writing small graphical applications because of the TK widget set that is closely tied to it.

◆ **tclx:** TclX is a set of extensions to make TCL more suitable for common UNIX programming tasks. It adds or enhances support for files, network access, debugging, math, lists, and message catalogs. It can be used with both tcl and tcl/tk applications.

◆ **tix:** Tix is an add-on for the tk widget set that adds many complex widgets built from tk building blocks. The extra widgets include combo boxes, file selection, notebooks, paned windows, spin controls, and hierarchical list boxes.

◆ **tk:** Tk is an X Window widget set designed to work closely with the tcl scripting language. It allows you to write simple programs with full-featured GUIs in only a little more time than it takes to write a text-based interface. Tcl/Tk applications can also be run on Windows and Macintosh platforms.

Development/Languages/Fortran

◆ **f2c:** f2c is a Fortran to C translation and building program. It can take Fortran source code, convert it to C, and then use gcc to compile it into an executable.

◆ **fort77:** This is the driver for f2c, a Fortran to C translator.

Development/Libraries

◆ **cracklib:** This package checks passwords for security – length, uniqueness, and so on.

◆ **e2fsprogs-devel:** This package contains libraries and header files needed to develop ext2 filesystem-specific programs.

◆ **gpm-devel:** This package allows you to develop your own text-mode programs that take advantage of the mouse.

◆ **inn-devel:** This library is needed by several programs that interface to INN, such as newsgate or tin.

◆ **libg++-devel:** This is the GNU implementation of the standard C++ libraries, along with additional GNU tools. The GNU C++ library, libg++ is an attempt to provide a variety of C++ programming tools and other support to GNU C++ programmers. This package includes the header files and libraries needed for C++ development.

◆ **libgr-devel:** This package is all you need to develop programs that handle the various graphics file formats supported by libgr.

◆ **linuxthreads-devel:** This package contains the header files and libraries needed to develop programs that use the linuxthreads library.

◆ **ncurses-devel:** This package includes the header files and libraries necessary to develop applications that use ncurses.

◆ **pythonlib:** This package contains code used by various Red Hat programs. It includes code for multifield listboxes and entry widgets with nonstandard keybindings, among others.

◆ **rpm-devel:** The RPM packaging system includes a C library that makes it easy to manipulate RPM packages and databases. It is intended to ease the creation of graphical package managers and other tools that need intimate knowledge of RPM packages.

◆ **slang-devel:** This package contains the slang static libraries and header files required to develop slang-based applications. It also includes documentation to help you write slang-based apps.

◆ **typhoon:** Typhoon is a relational database management system. It is shipped as a C library with headers and man pages.

Development/Libraries/Libc

◆ **libc-debug:** These libraries have the debugging information that debuggers use for tracing the execution of programs. These are only needed when the shared libraries themselves are being debugged – they are not needed to debug programs that use them.

◆ **libc-devel:** To develop programs that use the standard C libraries (which nearly all programs do), the system needs to have these standard header files and object files available for creating the executables.

◆ **libc-profile:** When programs are being profiled used gprof, they must use these libraries instead of the standard C libraries for gprof to be able to profile them correctly.

◆ **libc-static:** Although most programs are distributed dynamically linked, and therefore need access to the standard shared libraries, some developers prefer to ship programs statically linked, which includes all the standard library code in the executable. Although this method results in significantly larger programs and increases their memory usage, it does increase the portability of programs between Linux systems.

Development/Tools

◆ **binutils:** binutils is a collection of utilities necessary for compiling programs. It includes the assembler and linker, as well as a number of other miscellaneous programs for dealing with executable formats.

◆ **bison:** This is the GNU parser generator, which is mostly compatible with yacc. Many programs use this as part of their build process. Bison is only needed on systems that are used for development.

◆ **byacc:** This is a public domain yacc parser. It is used by many programs during their build process. You probably want this package if you do development.

◆ **cdecl:** This is a package to translate English to C/C++ function declarations and vice versa. It is useful for programmers.

◆ **cproto:** Cproto generates function prototypes for functions defined in the specified C source files to the standard output. The function definitions may be in the old style or ANSI C style. Optionally, cproto also outputs declarations for variables defined in the files. If no file argument is given, cproto reads its input from the standard input.

◆ **flex:** This is the GNU fast lexical analyzer generator. It generates lexical tokenizing code based on a lexical (regular expression based) description of the input. It is designed to work with both yacc and bison, and is used by many programs as part of their build process.

◆ **gencat:** This is the gencat message catalog program. The sources were taken from NetBSD.

◆ **gettext:** The gettext library provides an easy to use library and tools for creating, using, and modifying natural language catalogs. It is a powerful and simple method for internationalizing programs.

◆ **indent:** This is the GNU indenting program. It is used to beautify C program source files.

Development/Version Control

◆ **cvs:** CVS is a front end to the rcs(1) revision control system that extends the notion of revision control from a collection of files in a single directory to a hierarchical collection of directories consisting of revision controlled files. These directories and files can be combined to form a software release. CVS provides the functions necessary to manage these software releases and to control the concurrent editing of source files among multiple software developers.

◆ **rcs:** The Revision Control System (RCS) manages multiple revisions of files. RCS automates the storing, retrieval, logging, identification, and merging of revisions. RCS is useful for text that is revised frequently – for example, programs, documentation, graphics, papers, and form letters.

Documentation

◆ **faq:** This is a package of the Frequently Asked Questions (FAQs) about Linux from sunsite.unc.edu. It is one of the best sources of information about Linux.

- **howto:** This is the best collection of Linux documentation. It was put together on April 18, 1996. If you want to find newer versions of these documents, see `http://sunsite.unc.edu/linux`. For the versions in this package, see /usr/doc/HOWTO.

- **howto-dvi:** These are the dvi versions of the HOWTOs. They are probably useful only to TeX hackers.

- **howto-html:** These are the html versions of the HOWTOs. You can view them with your favorite Web browser.

- **howto-ps:** These are the PostScript versions of the HOWTOs. You can view them with ghostview or print them on PostScript printers.

- **howto-sgml:** These are the SGML versions of the HOWTOs. They are the source files that the HOWTOs are built from (using linuxdoc-sgml).

- **howto-translations:** These are translations of the HOWTOs into foreign languages. Currently the only language supported is German, and it is only for part of the HOWTOs.

- **indexhtml:** This is the Red Hat html index page.

- **ldp:** This is the contents of the Linux Documentation Project in exploded HTML format. It is most useful for the HOWTOs.

- **man-pages:** A large collection of man pages covering programming APIs, file formats, protocols, and so on:

  - Section 1 = user commands (intro only)

  - Section 2 = system calls

  - Section 3 = libc calls

  - Section 4 = devices (for example, hd, sd)

  - Section 5 = file formats and protocols (for example, wtmp, /etc/passwd, nfs)

  - Section 6 = games (intro only)

  - Section 7 = conventions, macro packages, and so on (for example, nroff, ascii)

  - Section 8 = system administration (intro only)

Extensions/Japanese

- **kterm:** kterm is the Kanji Terminal Emulator. It uses the kanji character set instead of the English set for those who prefer kanji.

Games

◆ **bsd-games:** This package contains a bunch of games. Highlights include backgammon, cribbage, hangman, monop, primes, trek, and battlestar.

◆ **christminster:** This is a text adventure game for use with xzip.

◆ **colour-yahtzee:** This is a terminal mode version of the popular dice game, Yahtzee.

◆ **doom:** DOOM is the original awesome game from ID software. It is a first person graphical (and very graphic!) game that runs under SVGA lib or X Window. It is also networkable.

◆ **fortune-mod:** This is the ever popular fortune program. It will gladly print a random fortune when run. This can be fun to put in the .login for your users on a system so they see something new every time they log in.

◆ **gnuchess:** This is the famous GNU chess program. It is text based, but can be used in conjunction with xboard to play X based chess.

◆ **koules:** This arcade-style game is novel in conception and excellent in execution. No shooting, no blood, no guts, no gore. The play is simple, but you still must develop skill to play. This version uses SVGAlib to run on a graphics console.

◆ **koules-sound:** These sound files enhance game play when playing koules.

◆ **mysterious:** Brian Howarth's Mysterious Adventure game series is a text-based adventure game.

◆ **pinfocom:** pinfocom is an interpreter for those old Infocom-compatible text adventure games (remember those?).

◆ **scottfree:** scottfree is an interpreter for Scott-Adams-format text adventure games (remember those?).

◆ **trojka:** The aim of this game is to control and to place the falling blocks, so that at least three blocks horizontally or diagonally, or both, have matching patterns. This sequence is then removed, and the above blocks will coll you reach the top of the screen, the game is finished.

◆ **vga_cardgames:** This package contains various card games for the Linux console, including Klondike, Oh Hell, Solitaire, and Spider, as well as some other popular time-wasters.

◆ **vga_gamespack:** This package has various mind games for the Linux console using SVGAlib. The selection includes such favorites as Othello, Minesweeper, and Connect 4.

◆ **vga_tetris:** The amazingly fun game of Tetris comes to the Linux console with this package. Twist falling blocks to make them fit in the holes and create a solid row. Addictive!

Libraries

◆ **aout-libs:** Old Linux systems used a format for programs and shared libraries called a.out, while newer ones use the ELF format. To run old a.out format programs, you need the a.out format libraries that this package provides. With it, you can run most a.out format packages for text, X, and SVGAlib modes.

◆ **db:** DB provides routines for creating simple database indexes. It is used by many applications, including Python and Perl, so this should be installed on all systems.

◆ **db-devel:** DB provides routines for creating simple database indexes. It allows you to create hash, record number, or BTree indexes whose elements have arbitrary sizes. This package contains the header files, libraries, and documentation for building programs that use DB.

◆ **f2c-libs:** These are the shared libs for f2c. They are required if you want to build dynamic Fortran executables.

◆ **faces-devel:** This is the xface development environment. It contains the static libraries and header files for doing xface development.

◆ **gdbm:** This is a database indexing library. It is useful for those who need to write C applications and need access to a simple and efficient database or build C applications that use it.

◆ **gdbm-devel:** These are the development libraries and header files for gdbm, the GNU database system. These are required if you plan to do development using the gdbm database.

◆ **jdk:** This is the Linux port of the Sun Java Development Kit 1.0.2. It includes an interpreted JVM with Motif support statically linked.

THESE FILES HAVE BEEN MODIFIED FROM THEIR ORIGINAL SUN VERSIONS AND SUN MICROSYSTEMS CANNOT BE HELD LIABLE FOR ANY PROBLEMS.

◆ **ld.so:** This package contains the dynamic loader for shared libraries. It is required for all dynamically linked packages.

◆ **libc:** This package contains the standard libraries that are used by multiple programs on the system. To save disk space and memory, as well as to ease upgrades, common system code is kept in one place and shared between programs. This package contains the most important sets of shared libraries, the standard C library, and the standard math library. Without these, a Linux system will not function.

◆ **libelf:** This library gives you access to the internals of the ELF object file format. It lets you poke around in the various sections of an ELF file, check out the symbols, and so on.

◆ **libg++:** This is the GNU implementation of the standard C++ libraries, along with additional GNU tools. This package includes the shared libraries necessary to run C++ applications.

◆ **libgr:** This package is a library for handling various graphics file formats, including FBM, JPEG, PBM, PGM, PNM, PPM, REL, and TIFF.

◆ **libpng:** The PNG library is a collection of routines used to create and manipulate PNG format graphics files. The PNG format was designed as a replacement for GIF, with many improvements and extensions.

◆ **libpng-devel:** The header files and static libraries are only needed for development of programs using the PNG library.

◆ **libtermcap:** This is the library for accessing the termcap database. It must be installed for a system to be able to do much of anything.

◆ **libtermcap-devel:** This is the package containing the development libraries and header files for writing programs that access the termcap database. It may be necessary to build some other packages as well.

◆ **linuxthreads:** This library provides a POSIX compatible interface for threads in user programs.

◆ **ncurses:** The curses library routines give the user a terminal-independent method for updating character screens with reasonable optimization. This implementation is new curses (ncurses) – the approved replacement for 4.4BSD classic curses, which is being discontinued.

◆ **newt:** Newt is a windowing toolkit for text mode built from the slang library. It allows color text mode applications to easily use stackable windows, push buttons, check boxes, radio buttons, lists, entry fields, labels, and displayable text. Scrollbars are supported, and forms may be nested to provide extra functionality. This package contains the shared library for programs that have been built with newt as well as a /usr/bin/dialog replacement called whiptail.

◆ **newt-devel:** These are the header files and libraries for developing applications that use newt. Newt is a windowing toolkit for text mode, which provides many widgets and stackable windows.

◆ **p2c:** p2c is the Pascal to C translation system. It is used to convert Pascal source code into C source code so that it can be compiled using a standard C compiler (such as gcc).

◆ **readline:** The readline library reads a line from the terminal and returns it, allowing the user to edit the line with the standard emacs editing keys. It allows the programmer to give the user an easier-to-use and more intuitive interface.

◆ **readline-devel:** The readline library will read a line from the terminal and return it, using prompt as a prompt. If prompt is null, no prompt is issued. The line returned is allocated with malloc(3), so the caller must free it when finished. The line returned has the final newline removed, so only the text of the line remains.

◆ **slang:** Slang (pronounced "sssslang") is a powerful, stack-based interpreter that supports a C-like syntax. It has been designed from the beginning to be easily embedded into a program to make it extensible. Slang also provides a way to quickly develop and debug the application embedding it in a safe and efficient manner. Because slang resembles C, it is easy to recode slang procedures in C if the need arises.

◆ **svgalib:** SVGAlib is a library that allows applications to use full screen graphics on various hardware platforms. Many games and utilities are available that take advantage of SVGAlib for graphics access, as for machines with little memory, it is more suitable than X Windows is.

◆ **svgalib-devel:** These are the libraries and header files that are needed to build programs that use SVGAlib. SVGAlib allows programs to use full screen graphics on various hardware platforms and without the overhead that X requires.

Networking

◆ **NetKit-B:** NetKit-B provides the clients and servers for many standard UNIX network services. Network logins, ftp, and talk (among others) are provided here.

◆ **pidentd:** pidentd is a program that implements the RFC1413 identification server. identd operates by looking up specific TCP/IP connections and returning the user name of the process owning the connection.

◆ **samba:** Samba provides an SMB server that can be used to provide network services to SMB (sometimes called Lan Manager) clients, including various versions of MS Windows, OS/2, and other Linux machines. Samba also provides some SMB clients, which complement the built-in SMB filesystem in Linux.

Networking/Admin

◆ **anonftp:** This package contains the files needed for allowing anonymous ftp access to your machine. This lets any user get files from your machine without having an account, which is a popular way of making programs available on the Internet.

◆ **net-tools:** This is a collection of the basic tools necessary for setting up networking on a Linux machine. It includes ifconfig, route, netstat, rarp, and some other minor tools.

◆ **nfs-server-clients:** This package contains client programs that interact with NFS servers. It is not needed to mount NFS volumes. The only program in this package is showmount, which can be used to show exported and mounted filesystems.

Samba uses NetBIOS over TCP/IP (NetBT) protocols and does *not* need NetBEUI (Microsoft Raw NetBIOS frame) protocol.

◆ **tcp_wrappers:** With this package, you can monitor and filter incoming requests for the SYSTAT, FINGER, FTP, TELNET, RLOGIN, RSH, EXEC, TFTP, TALK, and other network services.

Networking/Daemons

◆ **amd:** amd is the Berkeley automount daemon. It has the capability to automatically mount filesystems of all types, including NFS filesystems, CD-ROMs, and local drives, and unmount them when they are not being used any more.

The default setup allows you to enter **cd /net/hostname** and get a list of directories exported from that host.

◆ **apache:** The Apache Web server is the best free Web server available in the UNIX world. It uses HTTP (HyperText Transfer Protocol) to enable Web browsers to view documents and submit data remotely. It performs numerous functions, including proxying and caching, and offers features such as a status monitor and dynamic type conversion.

◆ **bind:** This package includes the named name server, which is used to define host name to IP address translations (and vice versa). It can be used on workstations as a caching name server, but is generally only needed on one machine for an entire network.

◆ **bootp:** This server can handle both bootp and DHCP requests. It is intended for the network administrator who wants to be able to set up networking information for clients via an /etc/bootptab on a server so that the clients can automatically get their networking information.

◆ **cmu-snmp:** This is a derivative of the original Carnegie Mellon University Simple Network Management Protocol. It is useful for managing networks and doing accounting.

◆ **gn:** This is a gopher server. Gopher is an information sharing system designed shortly before the Web. It is now getting superseded by the Web because it doesn't support graphics and text-based Web browsers are available.

◆ **imap:** IMAP is a server for the POP (Post Office Protocol) and IMAP mail protocols. The POP protocol allows a "post office" machine to collect mail for users and have that mail downloaded to the user's local machine for reading. The IMAP protocol provides the functionality of POP and allows users to read mail on a remote machine without moving it to their local mailboxes.

◆ **intimed:** intimed is a server that will tell networked machines what time it currently has. It is useful for keeping networks of machines in sync with the proper time.

◆ **mars-nwe:** MARS is a NetWare compatible file and printer server. It lets you use a Linux machine as a file and print server for NetWare-based clients using NetWare's native IPX protocol suite.

◆ **nfs-server:** The NFS and mount daemons are used to create an NFS server that can export filesystems to other machines. This package is not needed to mount NFS filesystems – that functionality is already in the Linux kernel.

◆ **portmap:** The portmapper manages RPC connections, including NFS. This portmapper can use hosts.{allow,deny} type access control.

◆ **ppp:** This is the daemon and documentation for PPP support. It requires a kernel greater than 2.0 built with PPP support. The default Red Hat kernels include PPP support as a module.

◆ **wu-ftpd:** wu-ftpd is the daemon (background) program that serves FTP files to ftp clients. It is useful if you wish to exchange programs between computers without running a network filesystem such as NFS, or if you want to run an anonymous FTP site (in which case, you will want to install the anonftp package).

Networking/News

◆ **inews:** The inews program is used by some news readers to post news. It does some consistency checking and header reformatting, and forwards the article to the news server specified in inn.conf.

Networking/Utilities

◆ **bind-utils:** This is a collection of utilities for querying name servers and looking up hosts. These tools let you determine the IP addresses for given host names, and find information about registered domains and network addresses.

◆ **bootpc:** bootpc is the bootp client for Linux that will allow a Linux machine to retrieve its networking information from a server via the network. It sends out a general broadcast asking for the information, which is returned.

◆ **cmu-snmp-devel:** These are the development libraries and header files for CMU SNMP. This package allows the network administrator to write programs for use with network management.

◆ **cmu-snmp-utils:** These are the various utilities for use with CMU SNMP, including utilities such as snmpwalk and snmptest.

◆ **dip:** dip is a program to allow for automatic scripting of modem dialing. It's useful for setting up PPP and SLIP connections, but isn't required for either. It is used by netcfg for setting up SLIP connections.

◆ **fwhois:** This is the whois program. It enables you to find out information on people stored in the whois databases around the world.

◆ **ipxutils:** This package includes utilities necessary for configuring and debugging IPX interfaces and networks under Linux. IPX is the low-level protocol used by NetWare to transfer data.

◆ **mgetty:** This package contains an intelligent getty for allowing logins over a serial line (such as through a modem). It allows automatic callback and includes fax support (though mgetty-sendfax needs to be installed to make full use of its fax support).

◆ **mgetty-sendfax:** This package includes support for FAX Class 2 modems to send and receive faxes. It also includes simple FAX queuing support.

- **mgetty-voice:** This package includes support for some modems that have voice mail extensions.

- **ncpfs:** This package contains tools to help configure and use the ncpfs filesysten, which is a Linux filesystem that understands the NCP protocol. This protocol is used by Novell NetWare clients to talk to NetWare servers.

- **rdate:** rdate is a program that can retrieve the time from another machine on your network. If run as root, it also sets your local time to that of the machine you queried. It is not super accurate; get xntpd if you are really worried about milliseconds.

- **rdist:** Rdist is a program to maintain identical copies of files over multiple hosts. It preserves the owner, group, mode, and mtime of files if possible and can update programs that are executing.

- **statnet:** statnet is a full terminal network traffic monitor. It can tell you things like the number of TCP or UDP packages over an interface. It can also give you total numbers of packets over PPP or SLIP lines.

- **traceroute:** Traceroute prints the route packets take across a TCP/IP. The names (or IP numbers if names are not available) of the machines that are routing packets from the machine traceroute is running on to the destination machine are printed, along with the time taken to receive a packet acknowledgement from that machine. This tool can be very helpful in diagnosing networking problems.

Shells

- **ash:** ash is a Bourne shell clone from Berkeley. It supports all the standard Bourne shell commands and has the advantage of supporting them while remaining considerably smaller than bash.

- **bash:** Bash is an sh-compatible command language interpreter that executes commands read from the standard input or from a file. Bash also incorporates useful features from the Korn and C shells (ksh and csh).

  Bash is ultimately intended to be a conformant implementation of the IEEE Posix Shell and Tools specification (IEEE Working Group 1003.2).

- **csh:** C-Shell from Berkeley is an implementation of the csh that is faithful to the original BSD implementation. It is smaller than the enhanced tcsh, but contains fewer features as well.

- **mc:** Midnight Commanders is a visual shell much like a file manager, only with many more features. It is a text mode program, but includes mouse support if you are running GPM or in an xterm window. Its coolest feature is the capability to poke into RPMs for specific files.

- **pdksh:** pdksh, a reimplementation of ksh, is a command interpreter that is intended for both interactive and shell script use. Its command language is a superset of the sh(1) shell language.

- **tcsh:** tcsh is an enhanced version of csh (the C shell), with additional features such as command history, filename completion, and fancier prompts.

Utilities

The utility packages provide administrative functions such as archival programs and programs to adjust your system clock.

- **rgrep:** This is a recursive grep utility that can highlight the matching expression, by the author of Jed.

Utilities/Archiving

- **cpio:** cpio copies files into or out of a cpio or tar archive, which is a file that contains other files plus information about them, such as their file name, owner, timestamps, and access permissions. The archive can be another file on the disk, a magnetic tape, or a pipe. cpio has three operating modes.

- **dhcpcd:** dhcpcd is an implementation of the DHCP client specified in draft-ietf-dhc-dhcp-09 (when the -r option is not specified) and RFC1541 (when the -r option is specified). It gets the host information (IP address, netmask, broadcast address, and so on) from a DHCP server and configures the network interface of the machine on which it is running. It also tries to renew the lease time according to RFC1541 or draft-ietf-dhc-dhcp-09.

- **gzip:** This is the popular GNU file compression and decompression program, gzip.

- **lha:** This is an archiving and compression utility. It is mostly used in the DOS world, but can be used under Linux to extract DOS files from LHA archives.

◆ **ncompress:** ncompress is a utility that does fast compression and decompression compatible with the original *nix compress utility (.Z extensions). It cannot handle gzipped (.gz) images (although gzip can handle compress images).

◆ **tar:** GNU tar saves many files together into a single tape or disk archive, and can restore individual files from the archive. It includes multivolume support, the capability to archive sparse files, automatic archive compression/decompression, remote archives, and special features that allow tar to be used for incremental and full backups. If you want to do remote backups with tar, you need to install the rmt package as well.

◆ **unarj:** The unarj program is used to uncompress .arj format archives, which were somewhat popular on DOS-based machines.

◆ **unzip:** unzip will list, test, or extract files from a ZIP archive, commonly found on MS-DOS systems. A companion program, zip, creates ZIP archives; both programs are compatible with archives created by PKWARE's PKZIP and PKUNZIP for MS-DOS, but in many cases the program options or default behaviors differ.

Utilities/Console

◆ **open:** This program runs a command on any given virtual console number. It can also run the program on the first virtual console that isn't already in use.

◆ **vlock:** vlock either locks the current terminal (which may be any kind of terminal, local or remote), or locks the entire virtual console system, completely disabling all console access. vlock gives up these locks when either the password of the user who started vlock or the root password is typed.

Utilities/File

◆ **file:** This package is useful for finding out what type of file you are looking at on your system. For example, if an fsck results in a file being stored in lost+found, you can run file on it to find out if it's safe to *move* it or if it's a binary. It recognizes many file types, including ELF binaries, system libraries, RPM packages, and many graphics formats.

◆ **fileutils:** These are the GNU file management utilities. This package includes programs to copy, move, list, etc., files. The ls program in this package now incorporates color ls.

◆ **findutils:** This package contains programs to help you locate files on your system. The find program can search through a hierarchy of directories looking for files matching a certain set of criteria (such as a filename pattern). The locate program searches a database (created by updatedb) to quickly find a file matching a given pattern.

◆ **git:** GIT is a file system browser for UNIX systems. An interactive process viewer/killer, a hex/ascii file viewer, an auto-mount shell script, and a per file type action script are also available. The standard ANSI color sequences are used where available. Manual pages and info documentation are also provided.

◆ **macutils:** This is a set of utilities for manipulating files from the Macintosh. Popular utilities like macunpack, hexbin, and binhex are included.

◆ **mtools:** Mtools is a collection of utilities to access MS-DOS disks from UNIX without mounting them. It supports Win95 style long filenames, OS/2 Xdf disks, ZIP/JAZ disks, and 2m disks (store up to 1,992k on a high-density 3¹/₂ inch disk).

◆ **sharutils:** The shar utilities can be used to encode and package a number of files, binary, and/or text, in a special plain text format. This format can safely be sent through e-mail or other means where sending binary files is difficult.

◆ **smbfs:** This package includes the tools necessary to mount filesystems from SMB servers.

◆ **stat:** The stat program prints out filesystem level information about a file, including permissions, link count, and inode.

◆ **symlinks:** This program checks for numerous problems with symlinks on a system, including symlinks that point to nonexistent files (dangling symlinks). It can also automatically convert absolute symlinks to relative symlinks.

◆ **tree:** This program is basically a UNIX port of the very useful DOS utility *tree*, which prints out a view of the specified directory tree, along with the files it owns. This package includes support for color ls-style listings.

◆ **which:** Give it a program name, and it tells you if it is on your PATH. For example, **which ls** would print `/bin/ls`, because the ls program, which is in one of the directories listed in your PATH environment variable, is located in the /bin directory.

Utilities/Printing

◆ **mpage:** mpage formats multiple pages of ASCII text onto a single page of PostScript. It supports many different layouts for the final pages.

Utilities/System

◆ **MAKEDEV:** The /dev tree holds special files, each of which corresponds to a type of hardware device that Linux supports. This package contains a script that makes it easier to create and maintain the files that fill the /dev tree.

◆ **adduser:** The adduser program creates a new username on your system by adding the name to the username and group databases and (optionally) creating and populating a home directory for the user.

◆ **adjtimex:** adjtimex is a kernel clock management system. It is useful in adjusting the system clock for accuracy.

◆ **caching-nameserver:** This package includes configuration files for bind (the DNS nameserver) that make it behave as a simple caching nameserver. Many users on dial-up connections use this package (along with bind) and make its own nameserver to speed up name resolutions.

◆ **control-panel:** The Red Hat Control Panel is an X program launcher for various configuration tools. Other packages provide information that allows them to show up on the Control Panel's menu of available tools.

◆ **cracklib-dicts:** This package includes the cracklib dictionaries for the standard /usr/dict/words, as well as utilities needed to create new dictionaries.

◆ **dump:** dump and restore can be used to back up extended 2 (ext2) partitions in a variety of ways.

◆ **eject:** This program allows the user to eject media that is autoejecting, such as CD-ROMs, Jaz, and Zip drives, and floppy drives on SPARC machines.

◆ **ext2ed:** This is a package to allow for hacking of your extended two file systems. It is for hackers only and should only be used by experienced personnel. If you aren't sure whether this package is for you, it isn't. Also, do not smoke near this software. You have been warned. This is not a recording.

◆ **e2fsprogs:** This package includes various utilities for creating, checking, and repairing ext2 filesystems.

◆ **fstool:** The fstool is an X program for manipulating /etc/fstab. It enables you to add, delete, and modify amount points. It also lets you mount and unmount partitions through its graphical interface.

◆ **gcal:** gcal is an extended calendar program. It is terminal mode, but does highlighting of holidays and offers other fancy features.

◆ **getty_ps:** getty and uugetty are used to accept logins on the console or a terminal. They can handle answering a modem for dial-up connections (although mgetty is recommended for that purpose).

◆ **glint:** Glint is a graphical interface to the RPM package management tool. It enables you to browse packages installed on your system and verify and query those package. It also enables you to update packages with new versions and install new packages.

◆ **hdparm:** This is a utility for setting hard drive parameters. It is useful for tweaking performance and for doing things like spinning down hard drives to conserve power.

◆ **helptool:** The help tool provides a unified graphical interface for searching through many of the help sources available, including man pages and GNU texinfo documents.

◆ **info:** The GNU project uses the texinfo file format for much of its documentation. This package includes a standalone browser program to view these files.

◆ **ipfwadm:** This is the IP firewall and accounting administration tool. It is useful if you need to run a firewall (a machine that acts as a secure gateway to the Internet).

◆ **kbd:** This package contains utilities to load console fonts and keyboard maps. It also includes numerous fonts and keyboard maps.

◆ **kbdconfig:** This is a terminal mode program for setting the keyboard map for your system. Keyboard maps are necessary for using non-U.S. default keyboards. Kbdconfig loads the selected keymap before exiting and configures your machine to use that keymap automatically after rebooting.

◆ **kernelcfg:** Red Hat Linux kernelcfg provides a GUI interface that allows you to easily administer your kerneld configuration.

◆ **lilo:** Lilo is responsible for loading your Linux kernel from either a floppy or a hard drive and giving it control of the system. It can also be used to boot many other operating systems, including the BSD variants, DOS, and OS/2.

◆ **logrotate:** Logrotate is designed to ease administration of systems that generate large numbers of log files. It allows automatic rotation, compression, removal, and mailing of log files. Each log file may be handled daily, weekly, monthly, or when it grows too large.

◆ **losetup:** Linux supports a special block device called the loopback device, which maps a normal file onto a virtual block device. This package contains programs for setting up and removing the mapping between files and loopback devices.

Block loopback devices should not be confused with the networking loopback device, which is configured with the normal ifconfig command.

◆ **lpr:** This package manages printing services. It manages print queues, sends jobs to local printers and remote printers, and accepts jobs from remote clients.

◆ **man:** The man page suite, including man, apropos, and whatis. These programs are used to read most of the documentation available on a Linux system. The whatis and apropos programs can be used to find documentation related to a particular subject.

◆ **mingetty:** mingetty, by Florian La Roche, is a lightweight, minimalist getty for use on virtual consoles only. mingetty is not suitable for serial lines (the author recommends using mgetty for that purpose).

◆ **mkdosfs-ygg:** This is the mkdosfs package. You can use this tool under Linux to create MS-DOS FAT file systems.

◆ **mkinitrd:** Generic kernels can be built without drivers for any SCSI adapters that load the SCSI driver as a module. To solve the problem of allowing the kernel to read the module without being able to address the SCSI adapter, an initial ramdisk is used. That ramdisk is loaded by the operating system loader (such as lilo) and is available to the kernel as soon as it is loaded. That image is responsible for loading the proper SCSI adapter and allowing the kernel to mount the root filesystem. This program creates such a ramdisk image using information found in /etc/conf.modules.

◆ **mkisofs:** This is the mkisofs package. It is used to create ISO 9660 file system images for creating CD-ROMs. It now includes support for making bootable "El Torito" CD-ROMs.

◆ **modemtool:** The modem tool is a simple, graphical configuration tool for selecting which of your serial ports is connected to a modem.

◆ **modules:** The Linux kernel allows new kernel pieces to be loaded and old ones to be unloaded while the kernel continues to run. These loadable pieces are called modules, and can include device drivers and filesystems among other things. This package includes programs to load and unload programs both automatically and manually.

◆ **mount:** Mount is used for adding new filesystems, both local and networked, to your current directory structure. The filesystems must already exist for this to work. It can also be used to change the access types the kernel uses for already-mounted filesystems.

This package is critical for the functionality of your system.

◆ **mouseconfig:** This is a text-based mouse configuration tool. You can use it to set the proper mouse type for programs like gpm. It also can be used in conjunction with the Red Hat Xconfigurator to set up the mouse for the X Window System.

◆ **mt–st:** The mt program can be used to perform many operations on tapes, including rewind, eject, and skipping files and blocks.

◆ **netcfg:** Red Hat Linux netcfg provides a GUI interface that allows you to easily administer your network setup.

◆ **printtool:** The printtool provides a graphical interface for setting up the printer queue. It manages both local printers and remote printers. Windows (SMB) printers can also be configured.

◆ **procinfo:** procinfo is a package that enables you to get useful information from /proc, the kernel filesystem. This is a place you can go to acquire information from your running kernel.

◆ **procps:** This is a package of utilities that report on the state of the system. Particular emphasis is placed on inspecting the states of running processes, the amount of memory available, and currently logged-in users.

◆ **psacct:** The tools necessary for accounting the activities of processes are included here.

◆ **psmisc:** This package contains programs to display a tree of processes, find out what users have a file open, and send signals to processes by name.

◆ **quota:** Quotas allow the system administrator to limit disk usage by a user and/or group per filesystem. This package contains the tools that are needed to enable, modify, and update quotas.

◆ **rhmask:** rhmaskR is intended to allow the distribution of files as masks against other files. This lets new versions of software be freely distributed on public Internet servers but limits their usefulness to those who already have a copy of the package. It uses a simple XOR scheme for creating the file mask and uses file size and md5 sums to ensure the integrity of the result.

◆ **rhs-printfilters:** The Red Hat print filter system provides an easy way to handle the printing of numerous file formats. It is meant primarily to be used in conjunction with the Red Hat printtool.

◆ **rmt:** rmt provides remote access to tape devices for programs like dump, restore, and tar.

◆ **rpm:** RPM is a powerful package manager that can be used to build, install, query, verify, update, and uninstall individual software packages. A package consists of an archive of files, and package information, including name, version, and description.

◆ **setconsole:** setconsole sets up /etc/inittab, /dev/systty, and /dev/console for a new console. The console may be either the local terminal (directly attached to the system via a video card) or a serial console.

◆ **sh-utils:** The GNU shell utilities provide many of the basic common commands used (among other things) for shell programming, hence the name. Nearly all shell scripts use at least one of these programs.

◆ **shadow-utils:** This package includes the programs necessary to convert standard UNIX password files to the shadow password format:

- pwconv5 converts everything to the shadow password format.

- pwunconv unconverts from shadow passwords, generating a file in the current directory called npasswd that is a standard UNIX password file.

- pwck checks the integrity of the password and shadow files.

- lastlog prints out the last login times of all users.

  A number of man pages are also included that relate to these utilities, and shadow passwords in general.

◆ **sliplogin:** This utility attaches a SLIP interface to standard input. This is often used to allow dial-in SLIP connections.

◆ **statserial:** Statserial displays a table of the signals on a standard 9-pin or 25-pin serial port and indicates the status of the handshaking lines. It can be useful for debugging problems with serial ports or modems.

◆ **swatch:** Swatch is used to monitor log files. When it sees a line matching a pattern you specify, it can highlight it and print it out, or run external programs to notify you through mail or some other means.

◆ **taper:** This is a tape backup and restore program that provides a friendly user interface to allow backing up and restoring files to a tape drive. Alternatively, files can be backed up to hard disk files. Selecting files for backup and restore is very similar to the Midnight Commander interface and allows easy traversal of directories. Recursively selected directories are supported. Incremental backup and automatic most recent restore are default settings. SCSI, ftape, zftape, and removable drives are supported.

◆ **time:** The time utility is used as a sort of stopwatch to time the execution of a specified command. It can aid in the optimization of programs for maximum speed, as well as other uses.

◆ **timeconfig:** This is a simple tool for setting both the timezone and the way your system clock stores the time. It runs in text mode using a simple windowing system.

◆ **timetool:** Timetool is a graphical interface for setting the current date and time for your system.

◆ **tksysv:** This is a graphical tool for manipulating run levels. It allows you to control what services get started and stopped for every run level.

◆ **tmpwatch:** This package provides a program that can be used to clean out directories. It recursively searches the directory (ignoring symlinks) and removes files that haven't been accessed in a user-specified amount of time.

◆ **tunelp:** tunelp aids in configuring the kernel parallel port driver.

◆ **usercfg:** The User and Group Configurator Tool provides a graphical user interface that allows you to add users to your system, remove them, edit their characteristics, and manage groups of users.

◆ **util-linux:** util-linux contains a wide variety of low-level system utilities necessary for a functional Linux system, including configuration tools such as fdisk and system programs such as login.

Utilities/Terminal

◆ **dialog:** Dialog is a utility that allows you to build user interfaces in a TTY (text mode only). You can call dialog from within a shell script to ask the user questions or present choices in a more user-friendly manner. See /usr/doc/dialog-*/samples for some examples.

◆ **screen:** Screen is a program that allows you to have multiple logins on one terminal. It is useful in situations where you are telnetted into a machine or connected via a dumb terminal and want more than just one login.

Utilities/Text

◆ **diffstat:** diffstat provides numerous statistics on a patch generated by diff, including number of additions, number of removals, and total number of changes. It can be useful, for example, to find out what changes have been made to a program, just by feeding the update patch to diffstat.

◆ **diffutils:** The diff utilities can be used to compare files and generate a record of the differences between files. This record can be used by the patch program to bring one file up to date with the other. All these utilities (except cmp) work only on text files.

◆ **faces:** The faces package is for use mainly with exmh. You can take a photo of something and turn it into a face that can be transmitted in all e-mail and will show up in exmh and other mailers.

◆ **faces-xface:** These are the utilities to handle X-Face mail headers. They are called by mail readers to display a face from a message.

◆ **gawk:** This is GNU awk. It should be upwardly compatible with the Bell Labs research version of awk. It is almost completely compliant with the 1993 POSIX 1003.2 standard for awk.

  Gawk can be used to process text files and is considered a standard Linux tool.

◆ **grep:** This is the GNU implementation of the popular grep *nix utility. It allows for the fast locating of strings in text files.

◆ **ispell:** This is the GNU interactive spelling checker. You can run it on text files and it will interactively spell check. This means it will tell you about words it doesn't know and will suggest alternatives when it can.

◆ **less:** less is a text file viewer much like more, only better.

◆ **locale:** This package includes the tools necessary to generate and manipulate the locale definition files that libc uses to provide multilingual support.

◆ **mawk:** Mawk is a version of awk, which is a powerful text processing program. In some areas mawk can outperform gawk, which is the standard awk program on Linux.

◆ **m4:** This is the GNU Macro processing language. It is useful for writing text files that can be parsed logically. Many programs use it as part of their build process.

◆ **nenscript:** nenscript is a print filter. It can take ASCII input and format it into PostScript output and at the same time can do useful transformations like putting two ASCII pages on one physical page (side by side).

◆ **patch:** Patch is a program to aid in patching programs. You can use it to apply diffs. Basically, you can use diff to note the changes in a file, send the changes to someone who has the original file, and they can use patch to combine your changes to their original.

◆ **perl:** Perl is an interpreted language optimized for scanning arbitrary text files, extracting information from those text files, and printing reports based on that information. It's also a useful language for many system management tasks. The language is intended to be practical (easy to use, efficient, complete) rather than beautiful (tiny, elegant, minimal).

◆ **sed:** Sed copies the named files (standard input default) to the standard output, edited according to a script of commands.

◆ **textutils:** These are the GNU text file (actually, file contents) processing utilities. They include programs to split, join, compare, and modify files.

◆ **words:** This package contains the English dictionary in /usr/dict. It is used by programs such as ispell as a database of words to check for spelling and so forth.

X11

All the programs and libraries for the X Window system are contained in these packages.

X11/Amusements

◆ **multimedia:** This package contains XPlaycd, XMixer, and XGetfile. XPlaycd is a program to play audio CDs using a CD-ROM drive. XMixer is used to control the mixer on a sound card. XGetfile is a versatile file browser, made for use in shell-scripts.

◆ **xbanner:** XBanner displays text, patterns, and images on the root window. This allows users to customize both their normal X background and the background used on xdm style login screens.

X11/Applications

- ◆ **seyon:** Seyon is a complete, full-featured telecommunications package for the X Window System. Its features include a dialing directory that supports an unlimited number of entries; terminal emulation window supporting DEC VT02, Tektronix 4014, and ANSI; script language to automate tedious tasks such as logging into remote hosts; unlimited number of slots for external file transfer protocols; and support for Zmodem auto-download.

X11/Applications/Graphics

- ◆ **ghostview:** This is an X front end to the GhostScript PostScript renderer. It allows you to switch pages in a PostScript document, magnify it, and print selected pages. It requires GhostScript to be installed.

- ◆ **gv:** gv enables you to view and navigate through PostScript and PDF documents on an X display by providing a user interface for the ghostscript interpreter. gv is based on an earlier program known as ghostview.

- ◆ **ImageMagick:** ImageMagick is an image display, conversion, and manipulation tool. It runs under X Window. It is very powerful in terms of its capability to allow the user to edit images. It can handle many different formats as well.

- ◆ **mxp:** This is a very fast Mandelbrot set generator for X Window. It lets you select regions to zoom in on and allows you to control other aspects of fractal generation.

- ◆ **transfig:** TransFig is a set of tools for creating TeX documents with graphics that are portable, in the sense that they can be printed in a wide variety of environments.

- ◆ **xanim:** This is a viewer for various animated graphic formats, including QuickTime and FLiC.

X11/Applications/Networking

- ◆ **arena:** Arena is a simple HTML 3 Web browser for X Window. It is incomplete and buggy, but has the big advantage that it is freely redistributable under an MIT style license.

- ◆ **grail:** Grail is a full-featured Web browser written in Python by the folks at CNRI. In many respects, Grail is better than arena, so if you aren't running Red Baron, Netscape, or Mosaic, you should try Grail.

◆ **redbaron:** Red Baron is a full-featured Web browser with SSL and SET security features. It includes support for forms, interlaced GIFs, incremental loading of pages, tables, and most other recent HTML enhancements.

◆ **x3270:** This program emulates an IBM 3270 terminal, commonly used with mainframe applications, in an X window.

X11/Games

◆ **acm:** ACM is an X-based flight simulator. It also has network capabilities for multiple player games.

X11/Games/Video

◆ **cxhextris:** cxhextrix is a color version of the popular hextris game. Both are close cousins of the popular Tetris video game, a game in which you try to stack odd-shaped blocks together perfectly. This game requires X Window to work properly.

◆ **flying:** This is a package of games that run under X Window. It contains pool, snooker, air hockey, and other table games. WARNING: This software could become addictive and could cause serious levels of sleep deprivation or loss of mobility in the legs if used at extreme levels.

◆ **paradise:** Netrek is a very popular Internet-based arcade game. You fly around with a team of players shooting at and capturing planets from the enemy (another team). A good way to drop out of college.

◆ **xbill:** This package has seen increased popularity with the dawn of the Linux age. Very popular at Red Hat. The object of the game? To seek out and destroy all forms of Bill, to disestablish new and alien operating systems, and to boldly go where no geek has gone before.

◆ **xbl:** A three-dimensional version of the popular arcade game Tetris (see the xtetris and vga_tetris packages).

◆ **xboing:** xboing is an X Window game in the tradition of the classic Breakout arcade game. The object is to keep a ball bouncing on the bricks until they break down. Even more fun comes in later levels when you have to handle multiple balls and ball traps.

◆ **xchomp:** The classic arcade action game comes to your screen with xchomp, the PacMan-like game. Not as extensive as the original game, but still lots of fun!

X11/Games/Strategy

- **spider:** spider is a particularly challenging double-deck solitaire. Unlike most solitaires, it provides extraordinary opportunities for the skillful player to overcome bad luck in the deal by means of careful analysis and complex manipulations.

- **xboard:** xboard gives you an easy-to-use, graphical interface to the GNU chess program, allowing you to enjoy hours of mind-boggling chess action without having to learn complicated commands.

- **xdemineur:** This is a game of intense concentration, where you must successfully determine the locations of mines through logic and deduction.

X11/Libraries

- **ImageMagick-devel:** This is the ImageMagick development package. It includes the static libraries and header files for use in developing your own applications that make use of the ImageMagick code and APIs.

- **nls:** This is a package of files used by some older X11R5 binaries such at Netscape. It isn't required by versions of Netscape greater than 3.0, however.

- **Xaw3d:** Xaw3d is an enhanced version of the MIT Athena Widget set for X Window that adds a three-dimensional look to the applications with minimal or no source code changes.

- **Xaw3d-devel:** Xaw3d is an enhanced version of the MIT Athena Widget set for X Window that adds a three-dimensional look to the applications with minimal or no source code changes. This package includes the header files and static libraries for developing programs that take full advantage of Xaw3d's features.

X11/MetroX

- **metroess:** This is the Metro-X X11R6 Enhanced Server Set (not part of the Red Hat Linux distribution).

X11/Utilities

- **mkxauth:** mkxauth aids in the creation and maintenance of X authentication databases (.Xauthority files). Use it to create a ~/.Xauthority file or merge keys from another local or remote .Xauthority file. Remote .Xauthority files can be retrieved via ftp (using ncftp) or via rsh. For security, mkxauth does not create any temporary files containing authentication keys.

- **moonclock:** This utility displays the time of day and the current moon phase. Colors change depending on time of day (day/night), and the moon is displayed in a neat little wedge with a star field.

- **procps-X11:** This is a package of X-based utilities that report on the state of the system. These utilities generally provide graphical presentations of information available from tools in the procps suite.

- **rxvt:** Rxvt is a VT100 terminal emulator for X. It is intended as a replacement for xterm(1) for users who do not require the more esoteric features of xterm. Specifically rxvt does not implement the Tektronix 4014 emulation, session logging and toolkit style configurability. As a result, rxvt uses much less swap space than xterm – a significant advantage on a machine serving many X sessions.

- **Xconfigurator:** This is the Red Hat X Configuration tool. It is based on the sources for xf86config, a utility from XFree86. It has an improved user interface added to make it easier for the end user.

- **xdaliclock:** The xdaliclock program displays a digital clock; when a digit changes, it melts into its new shape. It can display in 12- or 24-hour modes, and displays the date when a mouse button is held down. It has two large fonts built into it, but it can animate other fonts.

X11/Window Managers

- **fvwm:** fvwm is a small, fast, and very flexible window manager. It can be configured to look like Motif, and has a useful button bar.

- **fvwm95:** fvwm95 is a version of the popular Feeble Virtual Window Manager that emulates the look and feel of Windows 95. Now you can have the look and feel of the Windows world with the power and convenience of Linux.

- **fvwm95-icons:** This package contains icons, bitmaps, and pixmaps for fvwm95 and fvwm.

- **TheNextLevel:** The Next Level desktop was created by Greg J. Badros and was the winning entry in the 1996 Red Hat Desktop Contest. It features a powerful and attractive fvwm configuration that works with both fvwm95 and fvwm2. Lots of documentation is available in /usr/doc/TheNextLevel in html format.

  This desktop is defined to be easily reconfigured. Most attributes may be redefined by copying /etc/X11/TheNextLevel/.fvwm2rc.defines to a user's home directory and modifying the copied file appropriately.

X11/XFree86

◆ **X11R6-contrib:** This is a collection of X programs from X11R6's contrib tape, which contains programs contributed by various users. It includes listres, xbiff, xedit, xeyes, xcalcm, xload, and xman.

◆ **XFree86:** X Window is a full-featured graphical user interface featuring multiple windows, multiple clients, and different window styles. It is used on most UNIX platforms, and the clients can also be run under other popular windowing systems. The X protocol allows applications to be run on either the local machine or across a network, providing flexibility in client-server implementations.

This package contains the basic fonts, programs, and documentation for an X workstation. It does not provide the X server that drives your video hardware – those are available in other packages.

◆ **XFree86-100dpi-fonts:** These are the 100dpi fonts used on most Linux systems. Users with high-resolution displays may prefer the 100dpi fonts available in a separate package.

◆ **XFree86-75dpi-fonts:** The 75dpi fonts used on most Linux systems. Users with high-resolution displays may prefer the 100dpi fonts available in a separate package.

◆ **XFree86-devel:** This package contains libraries, header files, and documentation for developing programs that run as X clients. It includes the base Xlib library as well as the Xt and Xaw widget sets. For information on programming with these libraries, Red Hat recommends the series of books on X Programming produced by O'Reilly and Associates.

This package contains the shared libraries most X programs need to run properly. They are in a separate package to reduce the disk space needed to run X applications on a machine without an X server (over a network).

◆ **XFree86-XF86Setup:** XF86Setup is a graphical configuration tool for the XFree86 family of servers. It allows you to configure video settings, keyboard layouts, mouse type, and other miscellaneous options. It is slow, however, and requires the generic VGA 16-color server be available.

X11/XFree86/Servers

◆ **XFree86-8514:** This is the X server for older IBM 8514 cards and compatibles from companies such as ATI.

◆ **XFree86-AGX:** This is the X server for AGX-based cards such as the Boca Vortex, Orchid Celsius, Spider Black Widow, and Hercules Graphite.

♦ **XFree86-I128:** This is the X server for the #9 Imagine 128 board.

♦ **XFree86-Mach32:** This is the X server for cards built around ATI's Mach32 chip, including the ATI Graphics Ultra Pro and Ultra Plus.

♦ **XFree86-Mach64:** This is the X server for ATI Mach64-based cards such as the Graphics Xpression, GUP Turbo, and WinTurbo cards. This server is known to have problems with some Mach64 cards, which newer versions of XFree86 (which were only available as beta releases at the time of this release) may fix. Look at `http://www.xfree86.org` for information on updating this server.

♦ **XFree86-Mach8:** This is the X server for cards built around ATI's Mach8 chip, including the ATI 8514 Ultra and Graphics Ultra.

♦ **XFree86-Mono:** This is the generic monochrome (two-color) server for VGA cards, which works on nearly all VGA style boards with limited resolutions.

♦ **XFree86-P9000:** This is the X server for cards built around the Weitek P9000 chips such as most Diamond Viper cards and the Orchid P9000 card.

♦ **XFree86-S3:** This is the X server for cards built around chips from S3, including most #9 cards, many Diamond Stealth cards, Orchid Farenheits, Mirco Crystal 8S, most STB cards, and some motherboards with built-in graphics accelerators (such as the IBM ValuePoint line).

♦ **XFree86-S3V:** This is the X server for cards built around the S3 Virge chipset.

♦ **XFree86-SVGA:** This is the X server for most simple framebuffer SVGA devices, including cards built from ET4000 chips, Cirrus Logic chips, Chips and Technologies laptop chips, and Trident 8900 and 9000 chips. It works for Diamond Speedstar, Orchid Kelvins, STB Nitros and Horizons, Genoa 8500VL, most Actix boards, and the Spider VLB Plus. It also works for many other chips and cards, so try this server if you are having problems.

♦ **XFree86-VGA16:** This is the generic 16-color server for VGA boards. This server works on nearly all VGA style graphics boards, but only in low resolution with few colors.

♦ **XFree86-W32:** This is the X server for cards built around the ET4000/W32 chips, including the Genoa 8900 Phantom 32i, Hercules Dynamite cards, LeadTek WinFast S200, Sigma Concorde, STB LightSpeed, TechWorks Thunderbolt, and ViewTop PCI.

Appendix H

What's on the CD-ROM

THIS APPENDIX LISTS the contents of the Linux Network Toolkit companion Red Hat 5.0 CD-ROM. In this listing, I designate directories by appending a slash (/) to the end of the directory name. I use an arrow (->) to designate links, and file names are simply listed as is.

Red Hat Linux 5.0

The following listing shows the directory structure and contents of the Red Hat Linux 5.0 distribution, as well as the files added for this book. For the sake of brevity, I do not list the individual files in some directories. For instance, Appendix G lists the RPM packages you can find in the */RedHat/RPMS* directory, so I don't duplicate the more than 400 file names from that directory here.

```
COPYING
README
RPM-PGP-KEY
IDG/
    connect
    crack-4.1f-1.i386.rpm
    diald-0.16.4-1.i386.rpm
    diald-config-0.1-1.i386.rpm
    diald.conf
    firewall.reset
    firewall.rules
    gcc-2.7.2.1-2.i386.rpm
    libc-devel-5.3.12-18.i386.rpm
    skey-2.2.tar.gz
    tripwire-1.2-1.i386.rpm
    user_aliases
RedHat/
    RPMS/
        {the RPM packages listed in Appendix G.}
    TRANS.TBL
    base/
        TRANS.TBL
        comps
```

```
        comps.new
        comps.orig
        fsstnd.cgz
        hdlist
        rpmconvert
        skeleton.cgz
        uglist
        version
    i386
    instimage/
        TRANS.TBL
        lib/
            TRANS.TBL
            ld-linux.so.1 -> ld-linux.so.1.7.14
            ld-linux.so.1.7.14
            libc.so.5 -> libc.so.5.3.12
            libc.so.5.3.12
            libcom_err.so.2 -> libcom_err.so.2.0
            libcom_err.so.2.0
            libe2p.so.2 -> libe2p.so.2.3
            libe2p.so.2.3
            libext2fs.so.2 -> libext2fs.so.2.3
            libext2fs.so.2.3
            libm.so.5 -> libm.so.5.0.6
            libm.so.5.0.6
            libtermcap.so.2 -> libtermcap.so.2.0.5
            libtermcap.so.2.0.5
            libuuid.so.1 -> libuuid.so.1.1
            libuuid.so.1.1
        usr/
            bin/
                TRANS.TBL         ash
                badblocks         bash
                cat               chmod
                cp                cpio
                df                fdisk
                gdb               grep
                gunzip            gzip
                install2          ldd
                ln                ls
                lsmod             mkdir
                mke2fs            mknod
                mount             open
                ping              ps
```

```
        rm                       route
        rpm                      runinstall2
        sh                       strace
        umoun                    vi
        wc

    lib/
rpmcontents.gz


cdrom/
doc/
    FAQ/
        ATAPI-FAQ                Cryptographic-File-System
        FAQ                      GCC-FAQ
        GCC-FAQ.html             GCC-SIG11-FAQ
        INDEX                    INDEX.html
        NFS-FAQ                  PPP-FAQ.txt
        README                   TRANS.TBL
        Wine.FAQ                 ext2fs-FAQ
        linux-faq.README         linux-faq.ascii
        linux-faq.ps.gz


    HOWTO/
        AX25-HOWTO.gz            Access-HOWTO.gz
        Assembly-HOWTO.gz        BootPrompt-HOWTO.gz
        Bootdisk-HOWTO.gz        Busmouse-HOWTO.gz
        CDROM-HOWTO.gz           COPYRIGHT
        Chinese-HOWTO.gz         Commercial-HOWTO.gz
        Consultants-HOWTO.gz     Cyrillic-HOWTO.gz
        DNS-HOWTO.gz             DOS-to-Linux-HOWTO.gz
        DOSEMU-HOWTO.gz          Danish-HOWTO.gz
        Distribution-HOWTO.gz ELF-HOWTO.gz
        Emacspeak-HOWTO.gz       Ethernet-HOWTO.gz
        Finnish-HOWTO.gz         Firewall-HOWTO.gz
        Ftape-HOWTO.gz           GCC-HOWTO.gz
        German-HOWTO.gz          HAM-HOWTO.gz
        HOWTO-INDEX              Hardware-HOWTO.gz
        Hebrew-HOWTO.gz          INDEX
        INDEX.html               INFO-SHEET
        IPX-HOWTO.gz             ISP-Hookup-HOWTO.gz
        Installation-HOWTO.gz Italian-HOWTO.gz
        Java-CGI-HOWTO.gz        Kernel-HOWTO.gz
        Keyboard-and-Console-HOWTO.gz
        Linux-HOWTOs.tar.gz
```

```
    META-FAQ                MGR-HOWTO.gz
    Mail-HOWTO.gz           Module-HOWTO.gz
    NET-3-HOWTO.gz          NFS-HOWTO.gz
    NIS-HOWTO.gz            News-HOWTO.gz
    PCI-HOWTO.gz            PCMCIA-HOWTO.gz
    PPP-HOWTO.gz            Polish-HOWTO.gz
    Portuguese-HOWTO.gz     Printing-HOWTO.gz
    Printing-Usage-HOWTO.gz  README
    SCSI-HOWTO.gz           SCSI-Programming-HOWTO.gz
    SMB-HOWTO.gz            Serial-HOWTO.gz
    Shadow-Password-HOWTO.gz  Slovenian-HOWTO.gz
    Sound-HOWTO.gz          Sound-Playing-HOWTO.gz
    Spanish-HOWTO.gz        TRANS.TBL
    TeTeX-HOWTO.gz          Tips-HOWTO.gz
    UMSDOS-HOWTO.gz         UPS-HOWTO.gz
    UUCP-HOWTO.gz           VAR-HOWTO.gz
    VMS-to-Linux-HOWTO.gz WWW-HOWTO.gz
    XFree86-HOWTO.gz
    mini/
        3-Button-Mouse      ADSM-Backup
        AI-Alife            Advocacy
        Backup-With-MSDOS   Boca
        BogoMips            Bridge
        Bridge+Firewall     CD-Writing
        Clock               Colour-ls
        DHCPd               Diald
        Dip+SLiRP+CSLIP
        Diskless            Dynamic-IP-Hacks
        Ext2fs-Undeletion   GTEK-BBS-550
        GUI-Development     Graphics-Tools
        Gravis-UltraSound   HTML-Validation
        HTTP+Netware
        INDEX               INDEX.html
        IO-Port-Programming
        IP-Alias            IP-Masquerade
        IP-Subnetworking    JE
        Jaz-Drive           Kerneld
        Key-Setup           LBX
        LF1000              LILO
        Large-Disk          Linux+DOS+Win95
        Linux+DOS+Win95+OS2
        Linux+OS2+DOS       Linux+Win95
        Linux+WinNT         Linux+WinNT++
        Linux-mini-HOWTOs.tar.gz
```

```
        Locales              MIDI+SB
        Mail-Queue           Mail2News
        Man-Page             Modeline
        Multiple-Disks-Layout
        Multiple-Ethernet    NFS-Root
        NFS-Root-Client      Netscape+Proxy
        Online-Support       PLIP
        PPP-over-ISDN        PPP-over-minicom
        Pager                Partition
        Print2Win            Process-Accounting
        Proxy-ARP            Public-Web-Browser
        Qmail+MH             Quota
        README               Reading-List
        Remote-Boot          SLIP+proxyARP
        Sendmail+UUCP        Serial-Port-Programming
        Soundblaster-16      Swap-Space
        TIA                  TRANS.TBL
        Term-Firewall        Tiny-News
        Token-Ring           Upgrade
        Virtual-Web          Virtual-wu-ftpd
        Visual-Bell          Win95+Win+Linux
        WordPerfect          X-Big-Cursor
        X-Notebook           XFree86-XInside
        Xterm-Title          Xterminal
        ZIP-Drive            ZIP-Install

  TRANS.TBL
  rhmanual/
     { HTML and GIF files for the Red Hat manual.}

dosutils/
  README
  TRANS.TBL
  autoboot/
     TRANS.TBL
     initrd.img
     vmlinuz
  autoboot.bat
  copying
  fips.exe
  fips15.zip
  fipsdocs/
     TRANS.TBL      errors.txt
     fips.doc       fips.faq
```

```
            history.txt readme.1st
            special.doc    techinfo.txt
        gzip.exe
        loadlin.exe
        lodlin16.tgz
        rawrite.exe
        rawrite3.doc
        rdev.exe
        restorrb.exe

images/
    TRANS.TBL
    boot.img
    other/
        README.FlashPoint    TRANS.TBL
        bootFlashPoint.img
    supp.img
live/
    {a copy of a complete Linux file system}
misc/
    TRANS.TBL
    boot/
        TRANS.TBL      autoboot.img  boot.cat
    src/
        TRANS.TBL
         init/
            Makefile    RCS
            TRANS.TBL  init
            init.c     init.o
         install/
            {miscellaneous source and object code}
         trees/
            {Red Hat system creation files}
         upgrade/
            {Red Hat upgrade files}
    rr_moved/
```

Scripts, Utilities, and Other Files

The */IDG* directory in the preceding listing contains the files that I have added to the CD-ROM – that is, files in addition to those you find in the standard Red Hat distribution. Here's a quick run-down:

◆ user_aliases

This file is described in Chapter 6, in the sidebar "Explaining Bourne Again Shell Aliases." I personally find the aliases useful. To set these aliases enter the command:

```
source user_aliases
```

◆ diald-0.16.4-1.i386.rpm
  diald-config-0.1-1.i386.rpm
  connect
  diald.conf

These files are described in Chapter 8, in the section "Installing the Diald Communication System." Note that `diald-config-0.1-1.i386.rpm` is a useful utility for *diald* that I do not discuss in the book but include for you to explore. Also note that the `connect` and `diald.conf` files are also found in the `diald-0.16.4-1.i386.rpm` package, but have been customized slightly here to better describe how you should modify them for your own use.

◆ firewall.reset
  firewall.rules

These files are used in Chapter 10, in the section "Configuring Firewall Filtering and Masquerading Rules."

◆ skey-2.2.tar.gz
  gcc-2.7.2.1-2.i386.rpm
  libc-devel-5.3.12-18.i386.rpm

These files are used in Chapter 10, in the section "Installing and Configuring S/Key on Your Linux Firewall Server."

◆ crack-4.1f-1.i386.rpm

This file is used in Chapter 11, in the section "Installing and Configuring Crack."

◆ tripwire-1.2-1.i386.rpm

This file is used in Chapter 11, in the section "Installing and Configuring Tripwire."

Index

(continued)

Linux Journal Free Issue Offer!

Mail in this offer and receive a free issue of *Linux Journal* compliments of IDG Books Worldwide and *Linux Network Toolkit*.

Every month *Linux Journal* brings you the most in-depth information on what the powerful Linux operating system can do for you.

- **Stay informed about current trends in Linux**
- **Interviews with Linux developers and other personalities**
- **Avoid common mistakes by reading our tutorials**
- **Reviews of Linux-related books and products**
- **Articles on Linux business solutions**

Contact *Linux Journal* for your free issue today!
Toll-free 1-888-66-LINUX

- **Phone: 1-206-782-7733**
- **FAX: 1-206-782-7191**
- **E-Mail: subs@ssc.com**
- **URL: www.linuxjournal.com**

☐ **YES!** Please send me my free issue
☐ **YES!** I also want to subscribe

2 YEARS
☐ $39 US
☐ $49(USD) Canada/Mexico
☐ $64(USD) International

1 YEAR
☐ $22 US
☐ $27(USD) Canada/Mexico
☐ $37(USD) International

NAME _____

COMPANY _____

ADDRESS _____

CITY _____ STATE _____ POSTAL CODE _____

COUNTRY _____ TELEPHONE _____

FAX _____ E-MAIL _____

☐ Visa   ☐ MasterCard   ☐ American Express   ☐ Check Enclosed

CREDIT CARD # _____ EXPIRATION DATE _____

SIGNATURE _____

Checks and money orders must be drawn in US dollars. Please allow 4-8 weeks for delivery of your first issue.
Your free magazine will be an upcoming issue shipped in the next available mailing.

IDG Books Worldwide, Inc.
End–User License Agreement

<u>READ THIS.</u> You should carefully read these terms and conditions before opening the software packet(s) included with this book ("Book"). This is a license agreement ("Agreement") between you and IDG Books Worldwide, Inc. ("IDGB"). By opening the accompanying software packet(s), you acknowledge that you have read and accept the following terms and conditions. If you do not agree and do not want to be bound by such terms and conditions, promptly return the Book and the unopened software packet(s) to the place you obtained them for a full refund.

1. <u>License Grant.</u> IDGB grants to you (either an individual or entity) a nonexclusive license to use one copy of the enclosed software program(s) (collectively, the "Software") solely for your own personal or business purposes on a single computer (whether a standard computer or a workstation component of a multiuser network). The Software is in use on a computer when it is loaded into temporary memory (RAM) or installed into permanent memory (hard disk, CD-ROM, or other storage device). IDGB reserves all rights not expressly granted herein.

2. <u>Ownership.</u> IDGB is the owner of all right, title, and interest, including copyright, in and to the compilation of the Software recorded on the disk(s) or CD-ROM ("Software Media"). Copyright to the individual programs recorded on the Software Media is owned by the author or other authorized copyright owner of each program. Ownership of the Software and all proprietary rights relating thereto remain with IDGB and its licensers.

3. <u>Restrictions On Use and Transfer.</u>

    (a) You may only (i) make one copy of the Software for backup or archival purposes, or (ii) transfer the Software to a single hard disk, provided that you keep the original for backup or archival purposes. You may not (i) rent or lease the Software, (ii) copy or reproduce the Software through a LAN or other network system or through any computer subscriber system or bulletin-board system, or (iii) modify, adapt, or create derivative works based on the Software.

    (b) You may not reverse engineer, decompile, or disassemble the Software. You may transfer the Software and user documentation on a permanent basis, provided that the transferee agrees to accept the terms and conditions of this Agreement and you retain no copies. If the Software is an update or has been updated, any transfer must include the most recent update and all prior versions.

4. **Restrictions On Use of Individual Programs.** You must follow the individual requirements and restrictions detailed for each individual program in Appendixes A, B, C, and G of this Book. These limitations are also contained in the individual license agreements recorded on the Software Media. These limitations may include a requirement that after using the program for a specified period of time, the user must pay a registration fee or discontinue use. By opening the Software packet(s), you will be agreeing to abide by the licenses and restrictions for these individual programs that are detailed in Appendixes A, B, C, and G and on the Software Media. None of the material on this Software Media or listed in this Book may ever be redistributed, in original or modified form, for commercial purposes.

5. **Limited Warranty.**

   (a) IDGB warrants that the Software and Software Media are free from defects in materials and workmanship under normal use for a period of sixty (60) days from the date of purchase of this Book. If IDGB receives notification within the warranty period of defects in materials or workmanship, IDGB will replace the defective Software Media.

   (b) IDGB AND THE AUTHOR OF THE BOOK DISCLAIM ALL OTHER WARRANTIES, EXPRESS OR IMPLIED, INCLUDING WITHOUT LIMITATION IMPLIED WARRANTIES OF MERCHANTABILITY AND FITNESS FOR A PARTICULAR PURPOSE, WITH RESPECT TO THE SOFTWARE, THE PROGRAMS, THE SOURCE CODE CONTAINED THEREIN, AND/OR THE TECHNIQUES DESCRIBED IN THIS BOOK. IDGB DOES NOT WARRANT THAT THE FUNCTIONS CONTAINED IN THE SOFTWARE WILL MEET YOUR REQUIREMENTS OR THAT THE OPERATION OF THE SOFTWARE WILL BE ERROR FREE.

   (c) This limited warranty gives you specific legal rights, and you may have other rights that vary from jurisdiction to jurisdiction.

6. **Remedies.**

   (a) IDGB's entire liability and your exclusive remedy for defects in materials and workmanship shall be limited to replacement of the Software Media, which may be returned to IDGB with a copy of your receipt at the following address: Software Media Fulfillment Department, Attn.: *LINUX Network Toolkit*, IDG Books Worldwide, Inc., 7260 Shadeland Station, Ste. 100, Indianapolis, IN 46256, or call 1-800-762-2974. Please allow three to four weeks for delivery. This Limited Warranty is void if failure of the Software Media has resulted from accident, abuse, or misapplication. Any replacement Software Media will be warranted for the remainder of the original warranty period or thirty (30) days, whichever is longer.

(b) In no event shall IDGB or the author be liable for any damages whatsoever (including without limitation damages for loss of business profits, business interruption, loss of business information, or any other pecuniary loss) arising from the use of or inability to use the Book or the Software, even if IDGB has been advised of the possibility of such damages.

(c) Because some jurisdictions do not allow the exclusion or limitation of liability for consequential or incidental damages, the above limitation or exclusion may not apply to you.

7. <u>U.S. Government Restricted Rights.</u> Use, duplication, or disclosure of the Software by the U.S. Government is subject to restrictions stated in paragraph (c)(1)(ii) of the Rights in Technical Data and Computer Software clause of DFARS 252.227-7013, and in subparagraphs (a) through (d) of the Commercial Computer – Restricted Rights clause at FAR 52.227-19, and in similar clauses in the NASA FAR supplement, when applicable.

8. <u>General.</u> This Agreement constitutes the entire understanding of the parties and revokes and supersedes all prior agreements, oral or written, between them and may not be modified or amended except in a writing signed by both parties hereto that specifically refers to this Agreement. This Agreement shall take precedence over any other documents that may be in conflict herewith. If any one or more provisions contained in this Agreement are held by any court or tribunal to be invalid, illegal, or otherwise unenforceable, each and every other provision shall remain in full force and effect.

my2cents.idgbooks.com

CD-ROM Installation Instructions

THE CD-ROM THAT ACCOMPANIES this book contains a complete distribution of Red Hat Linux 5.0 from Red Hat Software, as well as custom scripts from the author. For details on the contents of the CD-ROM and how to install the software and scripts, see Chapter 1, and Appendixes G and H.